# THE COLONIAL PERIOD OF AMERICAN HISTORY

*ENGLAND'S
COMMERCIAL AND COLONIAL
POLICY*
IV

# THE COLONIAL PERIOD

OF

# AMERICAN HISTORY

BY

CHARLES M. ANDREWS

*With a New Foreword by Leonard W. Labaree*

ENGLAND'S
COMMERCIAL AND COLONIAL
POLICY

IV

NEW HAVEN AND LONDON · YALE UNIVERSITY PRESS

Printed in the United States of America by
Alpine Press, South Braintree, Massachusetts.

Published in Great Britain, Europe, Africa, and
Asia (except Japan) by Yale University Press,
Ltd., London. Distributed in Latin America by
Kaiman & Polon, Inc., New York City; in
Australia and New Zealand by Book & Film
Services, Artarmon, N.S.W., Australia; and in
Japan by Harper & Row, Publishers, Tokyo
Office.

# CONTENTS

# FOREWORD

THE four volumes of *The Colonial Period of American History* which Charles McLean Andrews published between 1934 and 1938 were the culmination of a lifetime of thought and study by the man who was generally recognized as the outstanding American colonial historian of his generation. He had produced his first work in the field in 1889, and as his books and articles continued to appear during the years that followed, the special features of his approach and interpretation became increasingly evident. They found their fullest expression in these four volumes, his last major contributions to our understanding of the Colonial Period.

A combination of three characteristics sets this work apart from all other general histories of the American colonies which had gone before or have appeared since Andrews wrote: First, the volumes give strong emphasis to the English background. He viewed the colonies as what they were at the time—parts of the expanding English world—and not as what some of them later became—units of a transatlantic republic. They were the products of a great movement in the British Isles for the occupation and settlement of fruitful areas across the ocean. The men, the circumstances, and the institutions in England responsible for that movement and later the policies developed in Great Britain for the exploitation and development of these "plantations" all receive major attention. Second, Andrews wrote not only of the colonies which declared their independence in 1776, but also of those which did not: Bermuda, the West Indies, Nova Scotia, and Newfoundland. In the seventeenth century and most of the eighteenth the English colonial world was a single indivisible whole; to understand that world as it actually was, it became necessary in Andrews' judgment to understand all its interrelated parts. No other work on a comparable scale has treated all these seventeenth-century settlements as equally significant parts of the general history of English colonization in the New World. Third, in common with many scholars of his generation, Andrews adopted a largely institutional approach. While earlier writers usually followed a narrative "political" thread for the most part, and many more recent scholars have been chiefly interested in social, economic, or intellectual developments, Andrews believed that a people's institutions—chiefly though by no means exclusively their political institutions—offered the best clues to that people's character and development.

The first three volumes, subtitled *The Settlements,* deal with the English background of the colonizing movement and with the establishment of communities of Englishmen along the Atlantic coast of North America and on nearby islands. Each such community is treated separately. The first two volumes are concerned with those projected before 1650, the third with those settled in the second half of the seventeenth century. In each instance the author carries the narrative down to the date (which differs from one colony to another) at which it can be said to be firmly established, when its institutions are well rooted and the direction of its further development can be clearly discerned. The fourth volume, called *England's Commercial and Colonial Policy,* describes the gradual development in the mother country of a program through which these overseas possessions could be brought into an effective and profitable relationship to Britain herself. As the subtitle suggests, this program and the laws and regulations adopted to carry it out were largely economic in emphasis. In the minds of Englishmen of the seventeenth and eighteenth centuries colonies were worth having and worth protecting against foreign enemies only if their trade and commerce could be so channeled and controlled and their economic life so developed that they would benefit the homeland as well as themselves. This volume is still the most thorough and complete treatment in print of the evolution of British colonial policy and of the means adopted to carry out that policy, its successes, and its failures, in the years before 1763.

One day early in December 1937, Andrews said to the writer of this foreword: "This morning I took the finished manuscript of my fourth volume to the Press. I have now done the job I promised the Press and myself that I would do. If I live and am able to complete the other volumes I planned, well and good. But if not, I am satisfied. These four volumes are the ones I just *had* to write." He had indeed planned three more parts of this work, but serious illness intervened while the fourth volume was in page proofs (he had just celebrated his seventy-fifth birthday), and though he lived until September 1943, he never regained sufficient physical strength to resume the heavy burden that writing on this extensive scale required.

The fact that he never completed the other volumes called for by his original plan has led some critics to accuse him of having only a limited and partial approach to the general subject of his *magnum opus*. Recognizing that this might be so, he wrote an extended paper, probably sometime in 1938 or 1939, in which he explained his scheme for the whole work, which he said had been "clearly in mind from the beginning," and his specific intent for the volumes which he never wrote. In accordance with his wishes, this paper remained unpublished until after his death.[1]

Upon the broad base of the first three volumes on colonial settlement, he explained, stood the fourth volume representing the British side of the developing Anglo-American structure. The fifth projected volume was to present the other side; in it "we would take our stand on colonial soil and see what was happening there during the first sixty years of the eighteenth century." Instead of dealing with institutional aspects of colonial history, it would be concerned with the "social, economic, educational, domestic, and religious, and in some respects political," evolution of American life and would reveal "trends and divergencies [from British patterns] indicating a progressive movement and indicative of what may be called an Americanizing process." These developments, as Andrews saw them, fostered change and growth in the political and institutional aspects of colonial society. Volume 6 would therefore be a political, and especially a constitutional, history of eighteenth-century America, which would give particular emphasis to the evolution of the colonial assembly and its slow winning "of a place in each colony analagous to that of the House of Commons in England at the same time." The seventh and last volume would deal with the years after 1763, when the colonies, with "practical self-government" achieved, came into conflict with the British government, which still adhered to its policy of holding the colonies in strict subjection and was even introducing new forms of enforcement. "Thus the colonial situation which was hardly American at all in the seventeenth century, takes on an Anglo-American coloring during the first sixty years of the eighteenth, owing to the formulation for the first time by the mother country of a clear-cut colonial policy, and becomes discordantly Anglo-American during the years 1763-1776, when the issue takes

1. "On the Writing of Colonial History," *William and Mary Quarterly*, 3d Series, I (1944), 27–48.

the form of an open conflict between self-government on one side and centralization on the other."

This was the plan on which Andrews would have carried through his project had he been able. We must regret that the final three volumes had to be left unwritten. Yet we can only be grateful for the four he did write during the five years after his retirement from more than four decades as a college and university professor. In this reissue of *The Colonial Period of American History* a new generation of readers will still find not only a great narrative of American beginnings, skillfully told, but a broad view of the characteristics and attitudes of the men and women on both sides of the Atlantic whose faith and optimism made those beginnings possible.

*New Haven, Connecticut*
*February 1964*
                                        LEONARD W. LABAREE

# A FEW WORDS TO THE READER

IN continuing our exposition of the essentials necessary to an understanding of what our colonial history is all about, let us keep in mind certain fundamental conditions that have emerged in the course of our study thus far.

To recapitulate. The English colonies, whether on mainland or island, in proprietary hands or under corporate charters, were not independent, self-sufficient communities, maintaining a separate existence and free from all outside control. Though at the beginning of their careers they were settled under private auspices, without the interfering hand of king or statesman or military head, and so were compelled to live largely by their own efforts and of their own resources, they were still outlying parts of the mother state and, indirectly at least, subordinate both as a matter of law and as a matter of policy, to the higher sovereign power across the sea at Whitehall and Westminster. As private colonies, far away beyond the horizon, they lay at first outside any immediate concern of king and ministers; but eventually they were recognized as assets of importance to the realm itself, legally the king's colonies and subject to his will and pleasure. As far as they could contribute to England's national stock of wealth and add to her strength and prosperity they were required to do so; and whether that contribution were important or otherwise, they were expected to conform to the principle, laid down at the very dawn of their history, that whatever of value a colony might furnish was to redound to the advantage of the state under whose aegis it had been established. This principle was never lost sight of as long as the colonies remained colonies, and it governed England's policy to the end of our colonial period.

Again, in furtherance of this policy England was not alone, for the maritime and colonizing states of Europe were shaping their colonial programmes along similar lines. In the Middle Ages men's lives and ambitions had been largely bounded by the geographical limits of their feudal lordships, city-states, municipalities, communes, manors, and other local institutions and their activities had been mainly restricted to the affairs of groups and neighborhoods. But later, during the sixteenth and seventeenth centuries, all the states along the western seaboard of the European continent gradually became centralized and monarchical in form, ready to compete on a larger scale in a race for wealth and power, each with the others. Men were crossing local boundaries, seeking broader fields of enterprise, and facing new rivalries, which in their turn were creating heavier responsibilities and demanding greater uniformity of plan and unity of effort. In government, administration, and justice, in commerce, the navy, the mercantile marine, and finance, these maritime states of Europe were coördinating systems, consolidating energies, and equipping themselves both for offense and defense. They were becoming more mature and self-conscious; their outlook was widening; their necessities and demands were increasing; and their knowledge and experience were expanding with every decade that passed. The states of western Europe were attaining their majority and, cutting loose from the political and religious dominance of empire and church, were becoming contentious and even aggressive in the exercise of their newly developed attributes of statehood.

As regards colonization the position of these states is not difficult to understand. While no one today would doubt that the problem of the government of remote communities is best solved if these communities can be made able and willing to govern themselves, to the men of that day such a proposal would have seemed not only unnatural but destructive of the best interests of the states of their origin. Whether the colonial and commercial policies of the seventeenth and eighteenth century statesmen and capitalists were politically or economically sound or unsound is not the question; nor is it necessary at this point to determine the effects of these policies upon the colonists themselves or to compare them with present-day ideas. All I am attempting to do in the following chapters is to make clear as best I may the essential features of these policies as England shaped them and to trace their history from the beginning of England's experience with colonies down to the eve of the American Revolution. In so doing I am inspired by the famous dictum of Bishop Stubbs that "the history of institutions cannot be mastered—can scarcely be approached—without an effort, but it has a deep value and an abiding interest to those who have the courage to work upon it." The story of England's outlook on the colonies would seem to have few alluring or dramatic qualities, yet, institutional as it is in many of its features, it possesses for me a fascination of its own, in that it deals with some of the least known and most vital among the activities of human existence—activities which lie within the restricted fields of marine law and the customs service and the broader fields of ships, commerce, and the sea. Furthermore, the subject forms an integral part of that most fundamental of colonial questions, the relationship which existed for more than one hundred and fifty years between England and her colonies overseas.

I am greatly indebted to my friend, associate, and former student, Mr. Stanley M. Pargellis, himself an authority on eighteenth century English history, for reading and commenting upon the last two chapters of this volume; and to Mr. Lawrence A. Harper, of the University of California, whose knowledge of the antecedents, content, and operation of the navigation acts is unrivalled, for reading in proof my volume and for allowing me to see the proof of as much as has appeared to date, and will appear during the spring, of his own work on the *English Navigation Acts*. If I do not always follow the advice of these generous collaborators it is my own fault, and such mistakes as I may have made must not be imputed to either of them for historical unrighteousness.

C. M. A.

*Jupiter Inlet,*
  *February 1, 1938.*

## POSTSCRIPTUM

On February 1, 1938—as the Preface above records—the manuscript of this volume was finished and sent to the printer, that it might be issued, as promised, in September of this year.

Unhappily, when the time came for correcting the final proofs in May, I was prevented by a sudden illness from doing work of any kind; but happily, both for the book and for me, my loyal friend and able colleague, Leonard W. Labaree, came to the rescue. Not only did he perform the labor of checking and rechecking references, titles, dates, etc., but he incorporated into the text certain emendations which I had planned to include in my final revision. Assisted by Miss Lois L. Comings, the indexer of this volume, and Mr. A. H. Stevens, Jr., the head of the proofroom of the Yale University Press, Mr. Labaree has been able to render the text available for immediate publication.

For this labor of love and friendship I want here to express my warmest appreciation and thanks.

C. M. A.

*New Haven, Connecticut,*
  *August 24, 1938.*

# THE COLONIAL PERIOD OF AMERICAN HISTORY

## CHAPTER I

## THE BEGINNINGS OF ENGLAND'S COMMERCIAL POLICY

DURING the Elizabethan era England, hitherto an agricultural country, emerged from the shadow of her previous isolation and inferiority and took her stand as an equal and rival among the older Continental powers. Barred for the moment from the Portuguese route to the Indies and from the Spanish route to the Antilles and beyond, she realized that her future upon the seas lay in entering the field of competition and contesting the claims of others. As early as the days of Henry VII and Henry VIII she had begun to prepare for her great destiny. A revival of interest took place in the navy. John Cabot, bearing letters of discovery, was instructed to find islands and continents then unknown. The powers of the admirals at sea were considerably extended and their jurisdiction placed on a definite statutory basis. Trinity House, a company of seamen authorized to look after sailors, pilots, and navigation, was incorporated in 1514, with a house at Deptford. At about the same time the Ordnance Office was remodeled and the dockyards at Deptford and Woolwich were constructed. The records of the High Court of Admiralty begin in 1524 and those of the Navy Board in 1526, both institutions having been revived and strengthened and placed on a permanent footing by Henry VIII. During the remaining years of the century a powerful merchant marine and an efficient war fleet were brought into being. Trade followed the flag, and the shipbuilding activities of the outports, accompanying the growing commercial connections with the Continent, culminated in the ambitious designs of the Merchant Adventurers of London and their monopoly of the woolen export business. The publicity efforts of Richard Eden (1555) and of Richard Hakluyt (1582), whose collections of travels disclosed alluring vistas of profit and glory, stimulated English merchants and capitalists to undertake new and larger enterprises and to open up routes to the East, partly by way of the northeastern and northwestern seas, and partly by way of the Baltic through Russia and so on to the Caspian and Persia. Later they sought the Levant, and in time began to encroach upon the possessions which Spain and Portugal were claiming for themselves in the New World. England was seeking new opportunities, by means of exploration, discovery, and trade, for the benefit of the state and the good of her people. She was stirred by the first impulses of a pride in national achievement; by a determination to share in those products of the soil which her own lands did not furnish or her own people supply and which could be obtained only from distant and tropical countries; and by a deep-seated enmity for the Spanish power, which in the days of the Counter Reformation and of the religious wars that followed had been one of the leading motives inspiring the voyages of Hawkins and Drake.

The state thus in process of formation was not the national state of today, with its freedom of trade under certain protective conditions, its world area of supply, and its more highly developed sense of mutual responsibility leading to coöperation and the dependency of nation upon nation. The state of the seventeenth century was in a sense an enlarged municipality, self-sufficing and exclusive, protecting itself against the outer world, conserving all its resources for its own advantage, and as jealous of other states as the old municipalities were jealous of each other. It was passing through a stage of transition, during which it was influenced less by those in official authority than by private individuals engaged in colonial and commercial enterprise, whose experience and advice, whether made known verbally or in printed form, often guided the government in its effort to chart the policy of the administration. England's commercial policy was slow in the making; it never reached the stage of exact definition, even in the days of its greatest influence; and it can be understood only by a study of its principles in actual operation over a period of one hundred and fifty years. In its relation to the colonies in America, it was never an exact system, except in a few fundamental particulars. Rather was it a *modus operandi* for the purpose of meeting the needs of a growing and expanding state. It followed rather than directed commercial enterprise, and as the nation grew in stature it adapted itself to that nation's changing needs. Mercantilism, as this commercial policy came to be called, was not a theory but a condition, an expression in practical form of the experience of those concerned directly with trade and commerce, and indirectly with coinage, credit, interest, and exchange, with banks, customs, and excise, with the naturalization of aliens and the treatment of the poor, the vagrant, and the criminal, that is, with all that had to do with the agricultural, commercial, financial, and social life of the realm. It was the inevitable accompaniment of a state of society in which foreign trade and commerce were rapidly attaining an ascendancy and were determining the attitude of statesman and merchant alike toward the other material interests of the nation.

The first settlement of America, as we have already seen in a previous volume, was but the culminating phase of those great voyages of discovery which had engaged the attention of at least six of the maritime powers of northern and western Europe. This transit of peoples across the Atlantic was a very remarkable movement in the way of social transplantation, for it meant the grouping of peoples of the old world in a new and hitherto untested frontier environment. What the future might have in store for these emigrants was not a matter of importance to those who were influential in promoting their exodus. The chief concern of these promoters was the immediate relation of these plantations to the states of their origin, and the measure of advantage and disadvantage that might accrue to themselves from the possession of distant settlements many miles away from the land whence they had gone forth. Were they likely to be useful or otherwise? Were the gains from such an exodus destined to be greater than the losses, the good greater than the evil? During the whole period of mercantile ascendancy men differed about these things, their differences growing less as time went on and the value of the colonies to the mother country became evident to all. Though these men were never wholly in accord as to certain features and details, they were in entire agreement on one point, that plantations were of value only as far as they aided the mother state to become strong, prosperous, and independent; and only as far as they recognized their obligation to subserve the general good of the kingdom were they worth keeping at all.

Though England was one of the earliest of the European states to enjoy a considerable measure of administrative unity, she was late in entering the field of colonization. Despite the activities of the Elizabethan forerunners, she was unable to gain a permanent foot-

ing upon the soil of America until 1607, when Jamestown was settled. With the founding of that colony, through private enterprise
sanctioned and legalized by the government at home, England entered upon a new experience. She had never before possessed a
colony, and neither the private company that settled Virginia nor
the king's advisers who took it over after the fall of the company in
1624 knew how to govern a group of men, English born and bred,
living three thousand miles away from the centers of English life.
One experiment followed another, until in Virginia a form of organization was finally contrived—the result of adjustment rather
than design—which combined royal control with popular representation. The movement thus begun went forward with accelerated pace
for three-quarters of a century, promoted in part by members of the
nobility who were seeking landed estates in the unoccupied spaces
of the West; in part by enterprising capitalists pursuing commercial
opportunities for the profitable investment of money; and in part
by adventurous sea-captains and men of action with an eye to booty
and prizes. It was promoted, even more conspicuously, by those of
strong religious convictions, who saw in the New World a retreat
and a refuge, where, as Roman Catholics or Quakers, they might establish proprietary settlements of their own religious coloring or, as
Puritans, they might set up little religious commonwealths, isolated
from the world and patterned after their own ideas as to how men
should live in the service of God. Before seventy-five years had
passed, under circumstances representative of the many vicissitudes
of that turbulent seventeenth century in English history, there had
come into being more than twenty plantations, stretching from New
England to Barbados. Some of these, as we know, were royal colonies, in the king's hand; others were proprietary, in the hands of
single men or groups of men to whom the king had granted rights
of ownership in the soil and powers of government over those who
dwelt thereon; and still others, in New England only, were self-
governing Puritan communities, having their own way in matters
of government and religion and free, for the time being at least,
from the interference of the crown. All these settlements presented
a great variety of political practice and religious thought and polity,
due in part to their origin and to the plans and experiences of those
who founded them, and in part to the peculiarities of soil, topography, and climate of the temperate, semi-tropical, and tropical

regions in which they had been planted. For as the years wore on and the colonists settled more and more into the mold of their environment; as their numbers increased by birth and accretion; and as expansion took place by sea in the search for markets and by land in the search for homes, these distinctions became increasingly marked, and New England, the Middle Colonies, the South, and the West Indies began to assume the character of separate sections, each with definite traits and habits of its own.

England's interest in these colonies was not political but commercial, owing to the determination of her merchants to share in the new discoveries and to profit from the new lands which these discoveries had brought to light. Stirred by the national enthusiasm which the Elizabethan adventurers had aroused, Englishmen entered the lists to dispute with the Portuguese the control of the spice trade and with the Spaniards the monopoly of the precious metals of Peru. England was as yet, comparatively speaking, a poor country and she needed to increase the sum of her public and private wealth by booty, by gold and silver obtained in normal trade, and by such exchange of commodities as would be advantageous to her merchants as creditors in the world market. In all these respects commerce was the instrument of prosperity.

During our colonial period England's rivals and competitors were successively four in number, Portugal, Spain, Holland, and France. Portugal had been annexed by Spain in 1582 and did not win its independence from the personal domination of the Spanish king until in 1641–1642 the Duke of Braganza, afterward John IV, led the revolt against the declining Spanish monarchy. Freed from subordination to the house of Castile, Portugal, whose king during the Interregnum had been on the wrong side in protecting the Stuart princes, Rupert and Maurice, was compelled by Cromwell to sign a disadvantageous and humiliating treaty, that of July 10, 1654, and afterward to coöperate with Cromwell against Spain. Charles II restored the friendly relations of earlier days, that is, of 1642,[1] and in 1661 entered into new diplomatic arrangements with Portugal, largely on colonial and commercial grounds. He took in marriage Catherine of Braganza, daughter of John IV and a not particularly attractive lady, who brought two million cruzadoes (Portuguese

---

1. *Articles of Peace and Commerce between Charles I and John IV and their subjects, concluded at London* (London, 1642). This treaty was signed January 29, 1642.

crowns) to his treasury and Tangier in Morocco, Bombay in India, and Galle in Ceylon to his royal domain, all of which were welcomed in England as assets in the expansion of English trade. In return he bound himself to defend Portugal, as he would England herself, against her enemies, chief among whom was Spain.[1] In 1703, by the Methuen treaties of that year (May 16), England entered into such commercial relations with Portugal as to render her, commercially speaking, England's vassal, for henceforth British merchants residing in Lisbon monopolized entirely her foreign trade.[2] Portugal had suffered heavily during her subordination to the Spanish crown, for the Dutch had seized much of her territory and many of her stations in the Far East and had occupied parts of Brazil, so that despite the expense at which the alliance was bought, it proved advantageous in the long run, bringing to Portugal's defense the aid of a growing maritime power and opening, on very favorable terms, a rich market for Portuguese wines. From this time forward port (Oporto) and sherry (Jerez) took their place on English tables beside Burgundy and Madeira, the latter of which had entered England by way of the colonies; and in 1808 Portugal reaped her greatest reward when Wellington came to her aid against Napoleon.

Spain controlled the precious metal output of that part of America which had been assigned to her by the papal line of demarcation of 1494, and she gained her wealth so easily that she was never called upon to establish strong colonies or to arouse among her merchants a desire to undertake industrial or commercial enterprises in the New World.[3] When, therefore, her monopolistic and restrictive policy aroused other nations to encroach upon her sphere of control, and the plundering of her ships and cities became the favorite game of the freebooting sailors of Holland, England, and France, she gave way under the strain. With her possessions widely scattered and her

1. Prestage, *The Diplomatic Relations of Portugal with France, England and Holland from 1640 to 1668*, pp. 98–104, 142–149; Davenport, *European Treaties bearing on the History of the United States and its Dependencies*, II, 57–62.

2. Lodge, "The English Factory at Lisbon," *Transactions*, Royal Historical Society, 4th series, XVI, 211–247; *The Privileges of an Englishman in the Kingdom and Dominions of Portugal* (London, 1736); Andrews, *Journal of a Lady of Quality*, p. 244, note.

3. Joshua Gee said of Spain in 1721, "The Spaniards have very great quantities of extraordinary oak and vast quantities of fine large pine trees fit for masts within themselves; but their indolent temper is such that if they can purchase what they want with money, they don't care to stretch out a hand to help themselves." Memorial presented to the Board of Trade, C. O. 323:22.

navy in decay, because of corruption and bad management, she gradually passed off the stage as the colossus of the central Atlantic, the menace of the ocean. Holland and England were left to struggle alone, not so much for the possession of the precious metals as for the control of the carrying trade, until by a series of parliamentary statutes, the use of force in war, and the weakening of Holland's strength, England was able to drive the Dutch from their monopoly and to make the carrying trade her own. Then followed the long-drawn-out rivalry between England and France, not for the precious metals or for the carrying trade but for supremacy in the whole colonial and commercial sphere. Beginning with the last quarter of the seventeenth century the struggle lasted, with varying vicissitudes, for a hundred and fifty years.

In this rivalry of states the colonies became fundamentally important factors, giving shape to certain governmental policies that were everywhere accepted as self-evident truths. Among these, four hold prominent place. First, that colonial interests and advantages were to be subordinated to those of the mother state. Secondly, that every state had a right to restrict the trade of its colony to its own subjects. Thirdly, that the surplus commodities of a colony should be sent, as a rule, to the mother country only. And, lastly, that the entire trade and resources of a colony should be kept out of the hands of a competing rival. Colonies were not looked upon as the stuff out of which an empire was to be made,[1] but rather as the source of raw materials that could not be obtained in England and were needed there either for consumption or for manufacturing purposes. No one at this time took any other view. To allow the benefits which colonies might confer upon the mother country to pass, by means of a free and open trade, into the hands of competing rivals, however advantageous such freedom of trade might be to the colonies themselves, was construed in the light of petty treason, in the same class as trade with the enemy. In that day, if it could help it, no government would

1. The words "empire," "imperial," and "imperialism" should be used very cautiously, if used at all, to define England's relations with her colonies before the year 1763. "Empire" is permissible, and was used contemporaneously in the sense of power and authority, but "imperial" and "imperialism" are not, if by the latter word is to be understood (as defined by a recent authority) "the rule or control, political or economic, direct or indirect, of one State, nation, or people over other similar groups, or perhaps one might better say the disposition, urge, or striving to establish such rule or control." In this sense "imperial" and "imperialism" have no place in the vocabulary of our early colonial history.

allow another state to profit at the expense of its own. Altruism and cosmopolitanism were no part of the existing state doctrine of the seventeenth and eighteenth centuries.

In international relations states were construed as in a condition of perpetual conflict with each other, each endeavoring to gain all it could at the expense of the rest. Whether the contest were for territory, or for markets, trade routes, staple products, negroes, gold, silver or other metals, or for such commercial advantages as would enrich one state at the expense of the others, the situation was the same—what one state gained another state lost. Within the boundaries of the state itself the same principle applied, the outlying parts had to give way before the welfare and prosperity of the central and leading member. This meant, in the case of England, that Scotland (till 1707), Ireland, the Channel Islands, the Isle of Man, and the plantations were all expected to subordinate their interests to those of the realm—England, Wales, and the town of Berwick-upon-Tweed. Even within the realm a struggle had been going on for many years to bring the boroughs and municipalities into line, to break the power of the gilds, to establish the supremacy of the common law, and to regulate manufactures and exports as a matter of state rather than of local concern.

As England emerged from the long period of Elizabeth's reign and entered definitely and for the first time upon a career of commercial and colonizing activity, she began to apply similar principles to her commercial relations with the outside world. What these principles were can be determined from the executive orders of government and more or less speculatively from the writings of the early mercantilists of the seventeenth century. They may be defined as follows.

First of all, England desired to increase the strength of the state by means of a favorable balance of trade with the other countries of Europe, that is, to export more than she imported, to sell more than she bought, to see that the income was greater than the outgo, in order that the money drift should always be in her direction and that there should be plenty of wealth within the realm.[1] The same result might be attained by the discovery somewhere within the kingdom or any of its subordinate parts of mines of gold and silver,

1. "As for commerce, the duke stated that when everything is cheap there is scarcity of money, and when everything is dear, there is plenty of money. It might therefore be deduced that it is good policy to keep prices, and therefore rents, high. The kingdom was full of money if exports exceeded imports. No attempt was made to adjust

by the capture of Spanish plate fleets, or by the recovery of ships or wrecks containing bullion or coin—all of which aided the accumulation of metal reserves. The balance of trade was unfavorable when such wealth left England, as would happen when foreign goods were obtained by purchase instead of exchange—such as naval stores from the Baltic lands, wines from France and Spain, calicoes from India, spices and tropical products from the Far East by way of Portuguese and Dutch ports, and fish from Holland. The carrying of money out of the kingdom by individuals, such as those migrating to the colonies, was frowned upon, though in later years the question of the export of money roused great differences of opinion among statesmen and merchants alike and was frequently allowed and defended.

In the second place, England sought to build up a carrying trade of her own. Until nearly the end of the sixteenth century, she had depended on the Hanseatic League and the Venetians, to a lesser extent on the Portuguese, who eventually ousted the Venetians from the Spice Islands, and in some measure on the Dutch, who during the first half of the seventeenth century controlled the carrying trade of the colonial world. The Dutch were the great middlemen of that time and, as distributors of all sorts of needed commodities, were the foster fathers of the early colonies, some of which could hardly have grown to maturity without them. To secure the carrying trade meant an enormous increase of England's wealth, but to do so required an enlargement of the number and tonnage of the English ships employed in it, the doubling and tripling of the seamen necessary to man those ships, and the addition of new vessels to the royal navy, in the hands of which lay the supplying of convoys and the guarding of the coasts.

In the third place, England found it necessary to adopt a highly protective tariff policy against the world, partly to safeguard her own industries against the competition of foreigners and partly to increase her revenue from customs dues. Such a policy was conceived solely in the interest of the realm. Scotland, Ireland, the Isle of Man, the Channel Islands, and all the plantations lay outside the fiscal boundaries and so were obliged to pay customs duties on all commodities imported into English ports. Such a policy called for heavy

or reconcile these economic axioms. The study of trade was, he thought, an essential part of politics, and he cited 'old Burley' to demonstrate that a man cannot be a statesman unless he understands commerce." Advice of William Cavendish, Earl of Newcastle. Quoted by Ogg, *Charles II*, I, 144–145, from Clarendon Manuscripts, 109.

tariff duties, both export and import, which tended to increase as time went on. Under the early Stuarts these duties were controlled by the crown, but during the Long Parliament they were brought under the administration of the legislative body. The amounts to be paid were entered in books of rates drawn up by parliament and given validity by statute. With the rates went an elaborate system of net duties, drawbacks, bounties, and the like, often of a very intricate character.[1] There was nothing simple in the plan and operation of the English customs service. It played an important part in the affairs of the colonies, the inhabitants of which registered many protests against its burdensome character; and it led to frequent controversies over the relative merits of customs, excise, and land taxes and to many disagreements as to where the incidence of taxation should fall. It required frequent adjustment by means of additional parliamentary legislation, for the purpose of encouraging trade and the fishery, of aiding manufacturing in England and preventing it in Ireland and the colonies, of checking smuggling, and in general of strengthening the revenue and so helping the exchequer.

As the area of discovery widened and knowledge of the remoter parts of the world increased, expectations of what these tropical and semi-tropical regions might contribute to England's advantage increased enormously. The range and variety of food and household comforts enjoyed at this time by even the most prosperous of English people were very limited. The clothes that men and women wore were rough and heavy, their victuals coarse and monotonous, and their medicines impure, crude, and very inadequate to meet the purposes intended. People generally had little fruit and that probably small and sour; no tea, coffee, or chocolate; and they had no spices except at very high cost.[2] In these respects the seventeenth century marks a revolution in social habits and customs, in domestic economy, and in the practice of medicine. Men wanted what the newly discovered countries could furnish, partly as assets in trade and partly to meet the demand for novelties in dress, food, house-furnishings, adornment, decoration, and other things that went to the making of a more comfortable and agreeable life. From trading connections with the old world and the new, they hoped to obtain nearly everything they needed; and as the colonies came to be settled and their products known, there was scarcely a single tropical or

1. Such as are to be found in 1 Elizabeth, c. 20; 12 Charles II, c. 4; 11 George I, c. 7.
2. Gillespie, *Influence of Overseas Expansion*, chs. II, IX.

semi-tropical commodity that Englishmen craved but was thought capable of production there on a marketable scale.

From the forests of the New World they expected to get lumber, pitch, tar, turpentine, and rosin; potash for the making of glass and soap and for use in the woolen industry; dyes, such as were obtained from braziletto, a brick red, fustic, a yellow, and logwood or block-wood, variously reddish brown to purplish blue, supplemented by the orange reds from madder, the blues from indigo, and the reds from cochineal. From gum-bearing trees they sought products for per-fumery and scents, of which the Elizabethans were already becom-ing fond, and which were as pleasing to them as were the old-time frankincense and myrrh. From certain animals—musk deer, civet cat, and whale—they sought musk and civet and especially amber-gris,[1] already known and used in considerable quantities. From flora of every variety they thought to obtain pomegranates, figs, ginger, oranges, lemons, pepper, nutmegs, cinnamon, cloves, and other spices and fruits, jalap, castor oil, licorice, anotto, and senna. Throughout the seventeenth century Englishmen were greatly interested in the possibilities of tropical production, and occasional individuals—Lord Clarendon, Samuel Hartlib, Dr. Benjamin Worsley, John Evelyn, Sir Hans Sloane, and many a wealthy peer and country gentleman—sought by one means or another to encourage the cultivation in the colonies of some of these things—cacao, senna, and ginseng, for ex-ample—or to experiment with such exotic fruits as pineapples in their own gardens at home. On a larger scale, the government, colo-nizing companies, and proprietors, particularly in the early years of settlement before 1700, tried by every means in their power, by com-mands, recommendations, and the expenditure of money, to per-suade the colonists to turn their attention to the raising of the staples that England needed at home. To obtain such materials from Eng-land's own possessions, either for use or consumption or for shipment abroad in order to help the balance of trade, was a cardinal principle of all the mercantilists. Even as late as 1670–1674 the special councils of trade and plantations were urging the cultivation in America of a wide variety of agricultural products for export to the mother country.[2] But nothing of real importance ever came of these efforts.

1. Vol. I, 216, note 3.
2. On this general subject see *Records of the Virginia Company*, I, 266–267; II, 36; *Records of the Massachusetts Bay Company*, I, 388, 403; *Calendar State Papers, Colo-nial*, 1660–1668, §84; Andrews, *British Committees*, pp. 119–120, 124, 125, 128, 129.

The only colonial staples of value to the mother country that contributed in any marked degree to her financial prosperity were tobacco, sugar including rum and molasses, dye-woods, rice, and indigo. To a limited extent the colonies furnished chocolate, lime juice, lemons, salt, cotton, ginger, and pepper; New England and North Carolina supplied naval stores; and nearly all of the continental plantations shipped, in vast quantities, furs, pelts, and skins, obtained in largest part by traffic with the Indians. On the agricultural side, New England and the Middle Colonies produced staples similar to those that were raised in England and Ireland, and in the seventeenth century these colonies were viewed rather as competitors than partners, hindering and not aiding England's advancement.

The earliest of all colonial products to become a staple for export was tobacco, raised in Virginia as early as 1612 and available as a surplus for marketing abroad two or three years later. Tobacco was comparatively easy to raise and for the trouble taken paid its cultivators well. It required neither capital nor skilled labor, and for years was the only article that could be handled for the home market at a reasonable profit. Its cultivation was opposed, partly because it was a single staple where the promoting companies in England wanted diversified staples, and partly because it was a luxury-breeding weed, held in low esteem by many contemporary Englishmen, including James I and Charles I.[1] Nevertheless it won its way. However much the Virginia and Bermuda companies might urge, as they did over and over again,[2] that other staple commodities be produced; however often the Privy Council might order the colonists to "use their best endeavors to bring all other commodities to perfection"; and however firmly the Providence Company might threaten to prohibit entirely the export of tobacco, if the colonists continued to raise it to excess, and offered liberal rewards to those who would produce something else, they could make no headway against the influence of a favoring climate and soil and the demands of the tobacco users at home and on the Continent.[3] The ease with which tobacco could

1. The antipathy of James I to tobacco is well known. That of Charles I is indicated in the account of his trial in 1649. "His Majesty being taken away by the Guard, as he passed down the Stairs, the Soldiers scoffed at him, casting the smoke of their Tobacco (a thing very distasteful unto him) and throwing their Pipes in his way." Rushworth, *Historical Collections*, VII, 1425.

2. *Virginia Company Records*, I, 413, 499; II, 35.

3. *Acts Privy Council, Colonial*, I, §§154, 320; *Calendar State Papers, Colonial, 1574–1660*, pp. 126, 295, 296, 297; Brigham, *Royal Proclamations*, pp. 13, 18; Beer,

be raised, the wide stretches of virgin land, and the use of slave labor led to the neglect in these colonies of nearly every other form of agricultural and industrial activity; while the demand in England, where tobacco was sold in every tavern and ale-house, and in so many other places also that London in 1614 contained (according to one estimate) seven thousand shops where it could be obtained and Englishmen spent £200,000 a year for it, overwhelmed opposition based on moral, sanitary, and economic grounds. When in the years from 1614 to 1620 the tobacco surplus in Virginia and Bermuda steadily increased and all efforts to divert attention from its production proved of no avail, the Virginia and Bermuda companies, though never relaxing entirely their attempts to broaden the staple base of their respective colonies, yielded to the inevitable, and tried to make the best terms they could with the king in order to import their tobacco with profit. Their colonial tobacco had to compete not only with that raised at home but also with that which Spain was producing in her colonies, chiefly of northern South America, a tobacco of particularly fine grade.

As a result of the prolonged and often heated debates which, beginning as early as 1619, arose over the Virginia Company's tobacco contract with the crown,[1] certain specific statements of policy were laid down by the English authorities. These statements, based to some extent on older precedents, may be taken as the beginnings of a colonial programme on the commercial side, a programme that was adopted even before a decision was reached by England as to what should be her policy toward Virginia in matters of local government and administration.

There were five parts to this commercial scheme, as finally agreed to after many experiences during these early years. These parts may be stated as follows. First, the colonies were to be given a monopoly of the English market; secondly, England was to have a monopoly of the colonial output; thirdly, England was to obtain, as essential to her commercial independence, entire control of the carrying trade; fourthly, the colonies were to be reckoned outside the fiscal realm and therefore under obligations to pay the regular customs duties;

---

*Origins of the British Colonial System*, p. 78. In 1661 a committee of the Privy Council took a favorable view of tobacco, because "it smells well" and paid four times the customs that the imports of the East India Company did. *Acts Privy Council, Colonial*, I, p. 320.

1. Vol. I, ch. VII.

and fifthly, in order to enforce these regulations, England was to enlarge her navy and her mercantile marine, increasing by every means in her power the number of her ships, their tonnage, men, and equipment. Let us examine these in turn.

1. The colonies were to be given a monopoly of the home market. This was to be done in the first place by the complete exclusion of all foreign tobacco, notably that of the Portuguese and Spanish colonies. Such a policy of exclusion was designed to relieve the colonies of competition and to improve the balance of trade where it was unfavorable, as was particularly the case with Spain. Later, under pressure from the demand in England of those who preferred foreign tobacco, imports of Brazilian and Venezuelan tobacco were allowed, but only on the payment of a much higher rate of duty than that assessed on tobacco from the colonies.[1] Next, all raising of tobacco in England was strictly forbidden, probably, in part at least, because, being a home product, it brought in no customs revenue. The domestic cultivation of the plant had been inconsiderable during Elizabeth's reign, but within the first fifteen years of the new century, confidence in the virtues of the herb increased greatly and, in 1615, "C. T." issued his pamphlet, *An Advice how to plant Tobacco in England and How to bring it to Colour and Perfection*. From this date, which coincides almost exactly with the arrival of the first shipload of tobacco from Virginia, the growing of tobacco at home went on rapidly, despite every effort made to prevent it. Proclamations, orders in council, statutes, sheriffs, posse comitatus, and soldiers were massed against it.[2] Over and over again local crops, chiefly in the western counties, were destroyed and heavy penalties imposed,

1. Stock, *Debates*, I, 30–35; *Proclamations*, April 9, 1625, February 17, August 9, 1627, January 6, 1631; *Acts Privy Council, Colonial*, I, §§139, 142, 148; Baldwin, *British Customs*, Part I, p. 63 (10 shillings as against 1 shilling, 8 pence).

2. *Proclamations*, December 30, 1619, September 29, 1624, February 17, August 9, 1627, March 14, 1638; *Acts Privy Council, Colonial*, I, 27, 592, §§197, 198, 278; *Calendar State Papers, Colonial*, 1574–1660, p. 423; Firth and Rait, *Acts and Ordinances*, II, 870 (act of April 1, 1652, and ordinance of April 11, 1654); *Statutes*, 12 Charles II, c. 34, §i; 15 Charles II, c. 7, §xviii; 22–23 Charles II, c. 26, §ix; 1 James II, c. 17, §xiii; C. T., *An Advice how to plant Tobacco in England and How to bring it to Colour and Perfection, to whom it may be profitable, and to whom harmfull. The Vertues of the Hearbe in generall, as well in the outward application as taken in Fume. With the Danger of the Spanish Tobacco* (London, 1615). There are copies of this rare pamphlet in the British Museum, the Huntington Library, and the George Arents collection. C.T. estimates the loss of gold to England in the purchase of tobacco from Trinidad and Orinoco at £200,000, a great prejudice, he says, to the state. He speaks also of tobacco from Santo Domingo, Guiana, St. Lucia, Dominica, etc., bought

but in vain.[1] Tobacco planting continued in England, until it gradually declined of its own accord and finally ceased altogether toward the end of the century. After 1700 we hear no more of efforts to suppress it, and from that time forward colonial tobacco, in fact as well as in law, had preferential treatment in the English market.[2]

2. England was to have a monopoly of the colonial output. In giving the colonies a monopoly of the English market, England claimed in her turn the right to monopolize the entire colonial output. As an expression of a general principle this claim involved nothing new, for in all grants to explorers and trading companies and to proprietors and companies holding patents under the great seal, the crown reserved to itself, in return for a monopoly of trade, the right to enjoy whatever advantages might accrue from the concession, and to demand that the products of newly discovered and occupied lands should be sent to England and to England only.[3] The first order of the kind issued to the Virginia Company, October 24, 1621, reads as follows: "Whereas the Kinges most excellent Majestie duely waighing in his princely judgement the great advantages both of honor and profitt which this Crowne and state might receiue from a setled and well ordered plantation in Virginia was graciously pleased for the better encouragement and furtherance

of the natives by returning vessels; urges the planting of tobacco in England to offset the heavy exportation of gold, and mentions tobacco from Bermuda, but does not seem to be aware of any from Virginia. Carew Reynel, writing in 1674, said that to forbid the planting of tobacco in England was a mistake; that in his day there were 6000 plantations of it in Gloucestershire, Devonshire, Somersetshire, and Oxfordshire, and that "all the objections against it connot vye with the advantages it produces" (*The True English Benefit*, London, 1674, p. 33). The subject is well discussed at considerable length in MacInnes, *The Early English Tobacco Trade*, chs. III, IV, V. Additional information can be obtained from *Calendar Treasury Books*, IX, 733, 1223, 1435, 1566–1567, and succeeding volumes.

1. *Acts Privy Council, Colonial*, I, §§361, 433, 563, 564, 602, 616, 623, 682, etc. Many of the entries in the Privy Council Register relating to this subject have not been calendared in the Colonial Series, because apparently having nothing to do with the colonies. See also, *Virginia Magazine*, IX, 34, 35; XVII, 357, 358; Stock, *Debates*, I, 215, 228 note; II, 364; Beer, *Origins*, pp. 403–408. The Rump Parliament passed acts against tobacco planting in 1650 and 1652.

2. MacInnes, *Early English Tobacco Trade*, pp. 123–124.

3. England's policy in this respect was merely an elaboration of that which had already been adopted toward all the great commercial companies. The order of October 24, 1621 (*Acts Privy Council, Colonial*, I, §77), was repeated in 1623 (§96), in 1625 (§148), in 1626 (§165), in 1628 (p. 129), and many times thereafter. See also *Virginia Company Records*, I, 527–529, 530; II, 298, 305, 315–316, 317, 322, 323, 325–326; *Virginia Magazine*, VII, 267; IX, 41; Historical Manuscripts Commission, *Report*, VIII, appendix 2, §§293, 325; *Acts Privy Council, Colonial*, I, §332.

of the vndertakers therein to grant vnto them sundrie verie large immunities and priviledges, as not doubting but that they would apply themselues vnto such courses as might most firmely incorporate that plantation vnto this Commonwealth and be most beneficiall to the same, which will best be done if the Commodities *brought from thence were appropriated vnto his Majesties subiectes, and not communicated to forraine countries, but by way of Trade and commerce from hence onely.* fforasmuch as their lordshipps having beene informed that the said Vndertakers haue for private respectes setled their Magazin of Commodities to be brought from Virginia in a *forraine Countrie* which course in noe wise is to be suffered, *neither in policie nor for the honor of the state* (*that being but a Colonie derived from hence*) as also for that it may be a losse vnto his Majestie in his Customes, if not the hazarding of the Trade, which in future times is well hoped may be of much profitt vse and importance to this Commonwealth. Their Lordshipps for these and sundry other reasons of state, and vpon full hearing of the foresaid vndertakers now the second time called to the Board, thought fitt and accordingly ordered that from *henceforth all Tobacco and other commodities whatsoeur to be brought and traded from the foresaid plantation shall not be carried into any forraine partes vntil the same haue beene first landed here and his Majesties Customes paid therefore.*"[1]

Two chief objectives determined this decision: that commerce must be under the control of the state and regulated in its interest; and that colonies, existing as they did for the benefit of the mother country, must send their surplus staples, not to Holland or any other foreign country, but to certain designated English ports, such as London or Bristol. As the Privy Council expressed it in 1628, when instructing Harvey as governor of Virginia, "Whereas many Shipps

---

1. *Acts Privy Council, Colonial*, I, §77. Italics are the writer's. Nearly a century later, Dr. Nehemiah Grew, an ardent mercantilist but one who opposed monopolies, wrote, "And it is necessary, so far as it may promote the Interest, not of any Company but of England, that every English merchant should be free, so is it that all the English plantations should be bound; bound I mean to trade with England alone. The Danes keep the trade of Izland to themselves, the Dutch of Surinham and the Spice Islands, the Portuguese of Brazil, the Spaniards of all the plantations they have in the West Indies; and so we the trade of all those belonging to your Majesty." "The Meanes of a Most Ample Encrease of the Wealth and Strength of England" (manuscript), p. 126. Copies of this treatise are in the British Museum and the Huntington Library. The same view of the case is presented in section v of the act of 1663, "it being the Usage of other Nations to keep their Plantation Trade to themselves."

laden with Tobacco and other marchandize from thence, carry the same ymediately into forraigne Countries, whereby his majestie looseth the Custome and duties thereupon due," therefore no ship was to sail from England without giving bond to go directly to the plantations and no ship was to return thence without bringing "a Bill of Lading from thence [the port of Jamestown], that the Staple of those Commodities may be made here."[1] In this paragraph we have in anticipation two of the leading features of the later navigation acts—the enumeration and the bond—both appearing in the government's regulation of the early Virginia tobacco industry; and there is also implied, in the same paragraph, the idea of the staple, which is so conspicuous a part of the acts of 1660 and 1663.

We know that these early orders in council were very loosely obeyed. The Virginia planters continued for many years to send their tobacco to Holland, in both English and Dutch ships that went directly from the colony to Amsterdam, Middleburg, or Flushing, where resided agents or factors who handled the cargoes. It is very likely that the Courteens were engaged in this business, for Sir William was in London and Peter in Middleburg and they probably used English as well as Dutch vessels in their carrying trade.[2] Governor Yeardley of Virginia was accustomed to send all his tobacco to Holland and others did the same.[3] Probably no tobacco was shipped in colonial vessels, for the colony of Virginia had not yet begun to build ships that could take a cargo across the ocean.

The use of Dutch ships was undoubtedly very common. Such ships were in all parts of the world and naturally found their way to the continental plantations and to those of the West Indies.[4] They trafficked in manufactured goods and took on colonial cargoes in return, whenever they had an opportunity, stopping at any colonial port or river, either buying colonial commodities for cash or with goods or taking freight on consignment to some merchant at a Dutch port. The Providence Company reported in 1636 that the Dutch ships had carried away the entire crop of the island, even when the company's own vessel was in the harbor, the settlers preferring to

1. *Acts Privy Council, Colonial*, I, p. 129; *Virginia Magazine*, VII, 267.
2. *Acts Privy Council, Colonial*, I, §§332, 334; see Vol. II, 245, and note 2.
3. C. O. 1:4, no. 22, incompletely calendared in *Calendar State Papers, Colonial*, 1574–1660, p. 84 (22). Yeardley had a factor, Rosingham, in Holland and was accustomed, in the years from 1621 to 1624, to ship his tobacco there. Bancroft Transcripts, New York Public Library, I, 11; III, 491–492, 576.
4. *New York Colonial Documents*, I, 436–437.

trade with the Dutch who gave better prices.[1] In Barbados, we are told, during the years before and at the time of the civil wars in England, the Dutch traders were the planters' only hope; and such was their monopoly that even when charging high prices, they could still undersell the English supercargoes.[2] The Dutch traded with Virginia, Bermuda, Maryland, and Rhode Island,[3] and in the French West Indies they seem to have controlled the trade before 1648, going to the islands in ever-increasing numbers and building up a lucrative commerce.[4]

3. England was to control the carrying trade. The continuance of Dutch success led to a renewed and explicit declaration of policy on England's part against the foreign carrying trade. This declaration stated that England must control the trade of her own colonies and that strangers must be excluded entirely from the colonial market, on the ground that if Dutch, French, Hamburgers, and Jews were allowed to carry manufactured goods to the colonies, they would certainly take away colonial raw materials and so injure England's resources. Such statement of policy covered not only the island and continental colonies, but the Newfoundland fishery also.[5] In a letter to the governor and council of Virginia, dated August 16, 1633, the Privy Council informed them that under no circumstances were they to allow strangers to trade there, and strictly enjoined the governor to take bond of all the king's subjects that they land their goods in England only. This injunction was repeated with added emphasis the next year, when in a letter to Harvey himself the Privy Council expressed its surprise at his neglect of the royal command and bade him execute carefully and fully the orders sent him.[6] Though the

1. Newton, *Colonial Activities of the English Puritans*, p. 21, ch. IX.

2. Harlow, *Barbados*, p. 38, and index under "Holland." In his answers to queries in 1671, Governor Modyford wrote, "The Dutch, Hamburghers and Jewes were our chief supply in Barbados and would sell very cheape and would give us and not seldome two years day of pay, by which creditt the poorer sort of Planters did wonderfully improve their plantations." C. O. 138:1, pp. 102–103 (omitted in *Calendar State Papers, Colonial*, 1669–1674, p. 304).

3. *Calendar State Papers, Colonial*, 1574–1660, pp. 171, 216, 250, 251, 285, 370, 378, 390 (Virginia, Bermuda, and Rhode Island); Steiner, "Maryland during the Civil Wars," *Johns Hopkins University Studies*, 1907, pp. 155–156; 1911, p. 23; *Virginia Magazine*, VIII, 149; IX, 35, 177; X, 424; XVII, 116–117.

4. Mims, *Colbert's West India Policy*, pp. 20–23, 40, 45–51. On the whole subject, see Beer, *Origins*, ch. VIII.

5. *Acts Privy Council, Colonial*, I, §282.

6. *Ibid.*, §§321, 334. As a result of this letter, based on the king's proclamation of 1631, the governor and council of Virginia issued an order allowing a certain vessel to go by way of New England, but requiring that its captain give security not to

charge was renewed in the instructions to Berkeley in 1641 and the requirement was extended from Virginia to Bermuda and St. Christopher, it is doubtful if it had any effect or that the government in England, during the troubled times that followed, was in any position to enforce this restriction upon the trade of the colonies.[1]

4. The colonies were to be construed as outside the fiscal boundaries of the realm. The reason most frequently assigned for the adoption of this policy was not so much the loss of raw materials as the effect upon the customs revenue. English vessels taking on goods in the colonies were expected to sail directly to some home port, London in particular, and there to pay the duties levied on tobacco and other colonial commodities. In the case of Virginia and Bermuda tobacco, these duties amounted to six pence a pound impost and three pence a pound customs, and in the case of tobacco from St. Christopher and others of the Caribbee Islands, to nine pence impost and three pence customs. In 1632 some adjustments were made which lowered these amounts to two pence and three pence for all these colonies, as places "(for the present) subsisting by tobacco, although with apparent hopes of better and more useful commodities from thence shortly to be had, considering that much of that tobacco is but of meane condition."[2] All Spanish tobacco and tobacco "of the growth of any other countrie or place (being not of the plantations of his Majesty's own subjects), from henceforth to be brought into this kingdom, dominion of Wales and port and town of Berwick," should pay six pence for each pound of pudding or roll, four pence for each pound of leaf, and eighteen pence additional impost. In 1649 the duties on colonial tobacco were reduced to four pence for such as was imported in English bottoms and six pence for foreign bottoms.[3] Changes were made later, but the principle underlying these impositions remained unaltered. In the case of tobacco, as formerly of commodities imported by the great trading companies,[4] drawbacks were allowed when it was re-exported to the Continent.[5] As at this time some tobacco from Virginia was shipped to the outports and thence carried to the Continent without unlading and paying

unload his tobacco until he reached London, *Virginia Council Minutes*, I, 482 (line 61).

1. *Virginia Magazine*, II, 228; IX, 37; XI, 50, 54; *Calendar State Papers, Colonial, 1574–1660*, pp. 89–90.
2. *Acts Privy Council, Colonial*, I, §291.
3. Stock, *Debates*, I, 213–214.
4. Carr, *Select Charters of Trading Companies*, p. 35.
5. *Acts Privy Council, Colonial*, I, p. 175.

the customs, a proclamation was issued by the king in 1631, requiring that all tobacco should be brought to the port of London only, and so be under the direct supervision of the farmers, but it is very doubtful if the proclamation was consistently obeyed.[1]

5. The navy and the mercantile marine were to be enlarged. Rules and regulations of the kind stated above were bound to be of little avail as long as England had no sufficient mercantile marine of her own and as long as foreigners had command of the sea and control of the carrying trade. To meet the competition of the Hanseatic leaguers and the Venetians as well as of the merchants of the ports of northern Europe, England had early made concessions to her own seaport towns, companies, and individuals enabling them to build ships for carrying purposes. But as all such mercantile enterprises were either municipal or private, their scope was inevitably limited and their effect slight. Early statutes requiring that certain goods from the Continent should be imported into England in English ships, English owned, and for the most part English manned, fared little better, for England needed the trade of the "strangers" and wanted their ships for the carrying of her own manufactures. Later legislation forbidding outsiders to engage in the English coastwise trade was more successful. These statutory requirements became more workable when inserted in the charters of the trading companies erected by the crown. In the charter of the Fellowship of English Merchants, a provision was introduced stating that all goods, exported or imported, must be carried in English ships manned for the most part by English sailors, and the same provision appears in the charter of the Levant Company of 1592. But again the results were slight. Even at the end of the sixteenth century, England was not ready to shut out entirely all merchant strangers from trafficking with the realm, and the rule was frequently set aside by licenses.[2] It

1. *Proclamations*, January 6, 1631; *Acts Privy Council, Colonial*, I, §§269, 270, 271, 275, 276, 280, 292, 311, 312, 332. When one realizes the fact that the colonies lay outside the fiscal boundaries of the realm and would normally pay customs duties on all commodities sent to England, it is easy to understand the clauses in the charters granted to corporate companies, engaged in trade or the settlement of plantations, which allowed freedom of trade and exemption from customs for a certain number of years. This was particularly true of the Virginia, Bermuda, Massachusetts Bay, and Providence companies. A similar freedom was sometimes conceded temporarily to merchants and promoters for their relief (*Acts Privy Council, Colonial*, I, §199). But all these exemptions were exceptional and did not affect the general rule.

2. 5 Richard II, statute 1, c. 3; 6 Richard II, c. 8; 14 Richard II, c. 6; 4 Henry VII, c. 10; 1 Elizabeth, c. 13; 5 Elizabeth, c. 5, §§viii, xi; 8 Elizabeth, c. 1 (private acts); Hakluyt, *Navigations*, II, 306–314; III, 89; VII, 144.

may have had some effect under James I in keeping Dutch ships out of English harbors.

These commercial regulations of the Tudors and early Stuarts, which contain in essence most of the principles embodied in the later navigation acts, were not lost sight of during the disturbances and confusion of the period from 1640 to 1650. Whether the controlling power were king or parliament, executive or legislative, no material change was made in policy, either commercial or colonial.[1] The colonies continued to receive preferential treatment in the matter of customs dues, and to some extent from 1640 to 1650 were bound by the parliamentary requirement that all goods should be imported in English vessels manned by English seamen. This obligation was first imposed in 1645, in response to a petition of the Greenland Company, in connection with the Greenland fishery, and in 1647 was extended to the plantations, which were forbidden to allow any trade with foreign ports except in English bottoms.[2] But more important even than the conditions laid down in charters and statutes was the normal development during these years of England's own commerce and industry—a development that gave new life, accompanied though it was by commercial and industrial growing pains, to a prosperous merchant-capitalist class.

1. Beer, *Origins*, ch. XI.

2. Ordinances of 1645, 1647, and 1649; Stock, *Debates*, I, 164 (where the reasons are given), 185–186; Firth and Rait, *Acts and Ordinances*, I, 679–680, 912–913; Husband, *Collection of all the published Orders, Ordinances, and Declarations, 1642–1646*, p. 646. Mr. Harper writes me: "The reference to the Ordinance of 1647 seems a little confusing, since it suggests that the provisions of the Greenland ordinance were imposed upon colonial trade. My impression from studying the statutes concerning the fisheries and those concerning the colonies has been that the two had separate origins and that one did not lead to the other. As I read it, the Greenland statute was directed to prohibiting the importation of whale oil, whale fins, and whale bone into England unless they were 'immediately fished in Greenland by the Subjects of this Kingdome, and in ships set out from hence,' and appears to be a logical descendant of a long line of fishery statutes. The Ordinance of 1647 seemed to me to find its ancestry in the earlier royal regulations concerning the colonies, and to be a bargaining provision rather than a direct command: For the next three years no customs duties were to be charged on exports to the colonies 'provided alwaies, that none of the said Plantations' permitted goods of their growth to be carried from any of their ports 'to any foreign parts and places, except in English Bottomes' in which case 'the Plantation so offending, shall be excluded from the benefit of this Ordinance, and shall pay custome.' "

# CHAPTER II

# THE DUTCH RIVALRY

THUS by the year 1650, in one way or another, often at random and never effectively, the English executive authorities had laid down a fairly definite body of rules governing England's commercial relations with the outside world and especially her relations with her colonies in America. Circumstances were soon to bring these rules into more exact statutory form and to place them in the hands of parliament for definition. The supremacy of the Dutch had reached a point where, if England were to succeed in her effort to win mercantile preëminence on the seas, she must meet and overthrow Holland's monopoly of the carrying trade, particularly in the northern field from the Garonne in southern France to Archangel in Russia, where the Dutch flyboats were in almost complete command of the situation.[1] The rivalry had existed for many years and had found its first serious manifestation in the Far East, where the Dutch were slowly driving the English from the trade with the Spice Islands and where local Dutch officials had seized and tortured English merchants at Amboyna in 1623.[2] But as long as England was distracted by the excitements and exigencies of the constitutional and religious struggle at home little success could be won in the field of commerce and the colonies.

During the first half of the seventeenth century the Dutch forged rapidly ahead and England was powerless to stop their progress in Muscovy, Norway, the shores of the Baltic, and most of the cities and states of Germany. They controlled the commerce of Flanders, Ireland, and Scotland; were the distributing agents for the colonies in America and the West Indies; and had been the pioneers and remained the leaders in deep-sea fishing and in all the whale and her-

---

1. V. Barbour, "Dutch and English Merchant Shipping," *Economic History Review*, II, 265–266.

2. *A Remonstrance of the Directors of the Netherlands East India Company, presented to the Lords States Generall of the united Provinces, in defence of the said Companie, touching the bloudy proceedings against the English Merchants, executed at Amboyna. And The Reply of the English East India Company, to the said Remonstrance and Defence.* Published by Authority (London, 1632).

ring fisheries of the North Sea and adjoining waters.[1] They were in
actual possession of large areas of territory in the East and West
Indies, in Brazil, and on the North American continent along the
Hudson River and near-by coasts, and were soon to extend their control there by the conquest in 1655 of the Swedes on the Delaware.
They had in their hands the English cloth trade with northern
Europe and the East India spice trade,[2] particularly in pepper, and
were becoming a dangerous competitor in the production and distribution of England's staple manufacture, woolen cloth. In the relations between England and the Netherlands, herring, pepper, and
woolen cloth were pawns in the commercial and diplomatic game,
as were to be later fish, furs, and molasses in the relations between
England and France. Such unexciting and drab commodities had a
way of influencing opinion among those concerned with trade and
of shaping governmental policies in international affairs more even
than sugar and rubber do today. Englishmen in office and in mercantile circles were well aware of the humiliating position in which
the country was placed, but for the moment were powerless to do
anything about it. The Dutch were exhibiting so many points of
superiority over the English, particularly in the naval, mercantile,
and commercial fields, that there seemed little chance of English success on the basis of ability alone. In the building of ships, in the
conduct of their finances, in the handling of the carrying trade from
port to port along the northern and western European coast, and in
the dexterity, diligence, and skill of their artisans the Dutch were
superior to the English and were destined to remain so for three-
quarters of a century, and even longer.[3] It took the English mercantilists a long time to disabuse their minds of the menace of Dutch
rivalry in trade and commerce.

The success of the Dutch may be traced to many causes.[4] Their
early appearance in the East and West Indies, in Manhattan, Guiana,

1. Jenkins, *The Herring and the Herring Fisheries*. On the "Trades Lost," see
Child, *Discourse of Trade* (ed. 1695), preface and pp. 21–26.

2. On spices imported, 1662, "Report of the King from Treasurer Southampton,"
*Calendar Treasury Books*, I, 432.

3. Disputes between the Dutch West India Company and the British Company of
Merchants trading to Africa continued as late as 1767, regarding exclusive rights of
possession to certain localities on the Guinea coast. *Board of Trade Journal*, 1759–
1763, pp. 374, 392, 398; 1764–1767, pp. 362, 409. The disputes were not ended even
at that date.

4. An excellent epitome of these causes may be found in *The Case Stated between*

Curaçao, and St. Eustatius, and the preponderance of influence obtained in the years from 1605 to 1632, owing to early rights of possession, had given them a rare advantage in the race not so much for territory as for markets. By force of arms, they had ousted the Portuguese, while the latter were still under the domination of the Spanish king, from many of their territories in the East and the West, and had begun their great career in the East Indies, with their capital at Batavia, the chief city of Java, the richest and most beautiful island of the Malayan archipelago. By the beginning of the seventeenth century they had driven the English almost entirely out of the Russian interior; had frightened them away from the Muscovy trade—where in 1615, says a contemporary, the English had only two ships instead of the former seventeen;[1] and had taken over the position formerly held by the English as teachers and masters in Russian economic life.[2] They were sending 500 ships to Norway and Denmark, 2000 to Spain, 20 or 30 to Archangel, where the English had only two or three, 10 to Guinea, 3 to China, 7 to the East Indies, 700 to 800 to the Baltic, and not less than 1000 fishing busses into the North Sea. This rapid expansion was due in some measure to the early command which the Dutch had obtained of the sea, as the result of three great sea fights—that of the Slaak near Thalen at the mouth of the Scheldt in 1632; that of Tromp off the Flemish coast near Gravelines in 1639; and that of Admiral Loos at Itamarca off the nose of Brazil in 1640—which put an end to the supremacy of Spain on the ocean. These victories were the more remarkable in that the Dutch were not a fighting people nor was their system of government well adapted to the needs of naval warfare. In the years that followed, their navy suffered from want of money and from the difficulties which Tromp had with a federal system of government,

*England and the United Provinces, By a Friend of the Commonwealth* (London, 1652). There is among the Tracts relating to Trade in the British Museum (712. m. 1) a treatise called *The Advocate or a Narrative of the State and condition of things between the English and Dutch nation, in relation to Trade, and the consequences depending thereupon, to either Commonwealth, as it was presented in August, 1651,* which contains a list of the advantages the Dutch "had clearly gotten above us" and a statement of the "means whereby they have persued and upheld these Advantages." Mr. Harper, who called my attention to this pamphlet, says that no one has ever identified its author.

1. I. R., *The Trades Increase* (London, 1615), p. 4.
2. "The Struggle of the Dutch with the English for the Russian Market in the Seventeenth Century," *Transactions,* Royal Historical Society, 4th series, VII, 51.

in which five admirals had to be brought into line in support of a common plan.[1]

To the Dutch trade was a national sport and merchandising was accounted, not the enterprise of a class but a function of the state. To the English, on the other hand, it was but one of many interests and its pursuit was viewed as an inferior form of activity, in which merchants but not the gentry engaged, and its social importance was considered distinctly less than that obtained by the possession of land.[2] The efforts of the Dutch aristocracy—Oldenbarnevelde and others—to build up the mercantile life of Holland and to present a united front to the world stand in striking contrast to the position taken by the king and nobility of England who, absorbed from 1630 to 1640 in their own problems, were content to look on while Holland was striking the Spanish flag from the seas. That the Dutch policy in mercantile as in naval matters had its dangers as well as its advantages later events were to show, when the great commercial companies of Holland became almost states within a state, and their directors had almost the dignity and standing of state officials, a fact strikingly true of the Dutch West India Company, supported and subsidized by the state, in its relations with New Netherland in America.

The Dutch early obtained control of the fisheries in the North Sea and elsewhere, a control which the English resented as an encroachment upon waters which they claimed as their own. But they were helpless in their resentment. They could not drive the Dutch away

---

1. *The Journal of Maarten Harpertzoon Tromp* (ed. Boxer), with an introduction of seventy pages and a translation of a contemporary Portuguese document concerning operations in the Channel.

2. "Writers on commerce frequently urged the English government to seek the expert advice of merchants on economic questions and the English council of state was contrasted unfavourably with the Dutch States General, in which it was said all members were specialists in commerce and decided policy in terms of needs," Ashley, *Financial and Commercial Policy*, p. 6. Slingsby Bethel, in *Observations on the Letter written to Sir Thomas Osborn* (London, 1673), supporting Holland against France, refers with approval to the declaration of Louis XIV, that the exercise of commerce in a gentleman was no prejudice to his qualifications, p. 13. In Joseph Hill's *The Interest of These United Provinces, being a Defence of the Zeelanders Choice* (Amsterdam, 1673) is the following: "As to the capital, ours [the Dutch] comes to be greater in regard that as the merchants grow rich in England they buy land and breed up their sons to be country gentlemen; whereas we, especially in Holland, continue the stock and our children in the Trade. . . . That the merchants here should be richer than there is no wonder to me, who know so well the frugality of the one and the prodigality of the other" (the work is not paged).

or compete with them on even terms, for the latter had raised the art of fishing to a science and made it contributory to their shipping, their supply of seamen, their trade, and their private wealth. Though the English merchants studied the Dutch methods and tried to imitate their skill, they were able to accomplish little.[1] Their efforts were at best half-hearted, while those of the Scots were ruined by constant neglect.[2] James I might thunder in proclamations (1609, 1614) against these invaders of the "narrow seas,"[3] and Sir Julius Caesar might declare that "the trade of fishing, with busses in his Majesty's seas, doth most properlie and rightly belong to his Majestie" and might be won "if his subjects were so industrious and would take the same course as their neighbours do,"[4] but the Dutch ignored all the Stuart claims and continued for many generations to make fishing in English and other waters "the chief pillar and support of these states." Even as late as 1753 English merchants engaged in the whale fishery could say in a petition to the Treasury that unless bounties were continued they could not possibly carry on the fishery "against the superior skill and dexterity of the Dutch acquired by their long experience in and almost sole enjoyment of this valuable and important branch of commerce."[5]

In the building of their ships the Dutch had the advantage of better artisans and workmen, and though they paid higher wages— two pence in the shilling more than the English—they were able to operate at lower cost. They could also build their ships more rapidly, partly because of their control of the timber trade of the Baltic,

1. *London's Blame, if not its Shame* (London, 1651); Simon Smith, *The Herring Busse Trade* (London, 1641). Smith was an agent of the Royal Fishery and in this pamphlet gives a detailed statistical account of how fishing should be carried on.

2. Insh, *Scottish Colonial Schemes*, p. 20.

3. The "narrow seas," as described by Sir William Petty, lay "within a line beginning at the Isle of Scilly, passing thence to Cape Cleeve in Ireland, from thence by the back or west of Ireland to the northwesternmost point thereof, thence by the Hebrides westward to Shetland, thence to Cape Van Staten, thence to the Naze of Norway, thence to the next land of Jutland, thence to the Elb's mouth, thence to Holland, Zealand, and Flanders to Calais, thence to Hey Sant Is. [Isle d'Ouessant, that is, Ushant off Brest] in Brittany and thence to Scilly, where we began" (*Petty Papers*, I, 231; cf. 217, 227, 241–242). Others, more expansive in their claims, carried the English seas from Cape Finisterre to the North Cape, including the waters that washed the shores of the Low Countries and of France. Historical Manuscripts Commission. *Eighth Report*, appendix, Trinity House, p. 255. See also *Board of Trade Journal*, 1708–1715, pp. 520–521.

4. Historical Manuscripts Commission, *Exeter*, p. 86.

5. Public Record Office, Treasury 1:351.

where they had groves of woods which furnished a continuous supply of the necessary material, and partly because of the large supplies which they accumulated in Holland and assembled near their shipyards ready for immediate use.[1] They showed great skill in planning their ships for the particular purpose intended—timber ships, herring busses, and the flyboats or freighters that Sir Josiah Child praised so highly.[2] These flyboats were made to hold a great bulk of merchandise and yet to sail with fewer seamen by two-thirds, thus saving two-thirds in wages and victuals. Consequently the merchants and merchant companies of such towns as Hull, Yarmouth, Newcastle-upon-Tyne, and even London itself were accustomed to make use of Dutch ships for freighting purposes and even to purchase them for their own use, to the scandal of Trinity House and in the face of protests from English shipowners against the exporting of English goods in strangers' bottoms.[3]

The Dutch took better care of their vessels, guarding them with fair success against the worm, which wrought such havoc upon the English boats, both of the royal navy and of the merchant marine.[4] This minute animalcule did an enormous amount of damage to all the ships of the period, despite experiments with sulphur or brimstone, lead, tar, and various forms of metal sheathing, and was not successfully combatted until sheet copper was finally made effective shortly before the American Revolution.[5] In carrying on their mercantile business the Dutch not only could count on a more efficient, honest, and better qualified body of workers but they also

1. On the other hand, the Venetian ambassador had this to say in favor of English ships. "English royal ships are built of soft wood, which is grown with great secrecy, so that when a cannon ball penetrates it simply makes a clear round hole without splintering, Dutch ships are built of Norwegian oak, which is of another nature, so that when a ball enters the body of a ship the wood rends and splits" (*Venetian Papers*, 1664–1666, p. 146). Compare on this point Albion, *Forests and Sea Power*, pp. 37–38.

2. *Discourse of Trade*, p. 101; Barbour, "Dutch and English Merchant Shipping," *Economic History Review*, II, 279–280.

3. Historical Manuscripts Commission, *Eighth Report*, appendix, Trinity House, pp. 239–246. Trinity House strongly opposed the buying or making free of any foreign-built ships, *ibid.*, p. 255.

4. For the destructive work of the *teredo navalis* or sea-worm, Albion, *Forests and Sea Power*, p. 11.

5. So says Albion, but as early as 1655 General Goodson in the West Indies was demanding frigates "well sheathed and carefully coppered." *Calendar State Papers, Colonial*, 1674–1676, §239; *Venetian Papers*, 1659–1661, p. 272, where it is said that "ships going to the Indies were sheathed with plates to preserve them from the worm that riddle ships in those waters, which are not found in the Mediterranean." Brim-

stocked their vessels with a greater variety of merchandise and made better bargains with their customers, colonial and other. To the planters in Virginia and the West Indies they were more than welcome, for they sold better articles more cheaply and with longer terms of payment than did the English and French merchants. They effected more frequent turnovers of stock and were content with smaller profits. Sir William Berkeley in 1651 said to the Virginia assembly, "We can only feare the Londoners who would faine bring us to the same poverty, wherein the Dutch found and relieved us,"[1] and Sir Charles Wheler of the Leeward Islands added his testimony in 1671 when he said that English merchants traded at twice the profit the Dutch did and would give no credit, while the Dutch gave a year, and further the English would not take the poor man's tobacco or the worst sugar, as would the Dutch.[2] As late as 1750 Lewis Morris, judge of the vice-admiralty court of New York, expressed his surprise that certain merchants of Amsterdam should have shipped goods in an English vessel to the Danish and Dutch islands (St. John and St. Eustatius), "when [the Dutch] are known to be the cheapest carriers in the world."[3] The Dutch also entered into the logwood trade and supplied the wood cutters with the sort of goods they needed in their rough life on the Muskito Coast.[4] They aided even the English merchants in India, who much preferred to deal with the Dutch ships, because of the care which their captains took of their cargoes, whereas the English merchandise was frequently spoiled by salt water.[5] In fact everywhere throughout this period the business methods of the Dutch were felt to be superior to those of the English.[6]

stone was brought from Italy, copper from Barbary, saltpeter from India, and timber from the Baltic and the colonies. *Calendar Treasury Books*, IX, 485, 723, 755, 1130, 1316. On Kent Island in 1632 Claiborne had a barrel of brimstone to keep his boats from the worm. *Maryland Magazine*, XXVIII, 36. In 1685 one Henry Alured wished to patent an invention "for making and covering the planke of ships with a bitter and sulpherous matter, so as to defend the planks from being pierced and eaten with worms." Historical Manuscripts Commission, *Eighth Report*, appendix, Trinity House, p. 259.

  1. *Virginia Magazine*, I, 77; VIII, 147.
  2. *Calendar State Papers, Colonial*, 1669–1674, p. 290.
  3. Records of Admiralty, New York, II, 161; Hough, *Reports of Cases . . . in New York*, pp. 64–65.
  4. Long, *History of Jamaica*, I, 329.
  5. Foster, *English Factories in India*, 1651–1654, p. 117 note. Cf. 1642–1645, p. 142.
  6. Mims, *Colbert's West India Policy*, pp. 49–50.

This superiority in business management was manifested at home as well as abroad. The Dutch system of concentrating their mercantile activities in their chief cities, of bringing in raw materials and taking out manufactured goods—chiefly woolens, but also silk and cottons, and a great variety of arts and crafts—of storing drugs, spices, tea, coffee, chocolate, and the like in their own warehouses, and thence distributing them to various parts of Europe and elsewhere, made it possible for them to control the markets and to cut into both the French and the English trade.[1] Thus they established early the principle of the staple and applied it in a manner similar to that which England later adopted in the act of 1663. In this way they were enabled to enforce their own regulations regarding English woolens and draperies, despite the protests of those engaged in the growing English industries.[2] Behind all these activities lay better financial conditions, due to the great profits made in early ventures resulting from the opportunities brought to the merchants by the truce with Spain of 1609. Credit became easier, debt was diminished, and the state was able to borrow of England many hundreds of thousands of pounds.[3] Sir Josiah Child "attributed the prosperity of the trade of the Dutch to their fidelity in their seal, encouragement of inventors (whom they reward, while they make the invention public instead of granting a patent, as here), thrift, small ships, low duties, poor-laws, banks, mercantile law, easy admission of burghers, inland navigation, low interest, fisheries, colonies, religious liberty, education." He said that the Dutch possessed great stocks of capital invested particularly in the India trade, were able to demand easy terms in making loans, and were in a position to draw into this one vast industry a great multitude of merchants and stores of shipping.[4]

Furthermore, in England, specialization had not reached anywhere

1. This subject is discussed by Lewes Roberts in *The Treasure of Traffike* (London, 1641), pp. 58–64. The limited range of England's exports at the Restoration is well stated by Fortrey, *England's Interest and Improvement* (Cambridge, 1663), pp. 21–22. During the Commonwealth the Dutch made such advances in the manufacture of woolen goods that the English cloth trade appeared to be in jeopardy. *Petty Papers*, II, 79.

2. *Calendar State Papers, Domestic*, 1649–1650, p. 94; 1650, pp. 21–22. On the troubles of the Levant Company, *ibid.*, pp. 41–44.

3. *The Case Stated between England and the United Provinces* (London, 1652), p. 19. For the financial position of the Netherlands in the seventeenth century, see Ehrenburg, *Capital and Finance in the Age of the Renaissance*, pp. 349–352.

4. Historical Manuscripts Commission, *Eighth Report*, appendix 1, pp. 133–134; *Discourse of Trade*, preface. In his first treatise on Usury (1665), Child said, "The

near the state of perfection that it had in Holland, where detailed knowledge of the quality of the goods and the conditions of the world market had enabled an entrepôt trade to develop far more rapidly than any similar trade across the channel. Antwerp had risen to prominence much earlier than Amsterdam and had become a trading center the like of which the world had never seen before, even though its wholesale trade was largely controlled by foreigners who flocked there, much as in the eighteenth century the English merchants flocked to Lisbon and became the chief directors of its trading activities. For this reason, and because of the ruin wrought upon Antwerp during the Dutch War of Independence, Amsterdam soon forged ahead in the race and in the seventeenth century was considered the best-organized commercial city in Europe. It became the home of many Protestant merchants, attracted thither because of religious toleration, equal taxes, and a favorable geographical location.[1] Its bank was founded in 1609 to deal with foreign trade and to facilitate commerce and exchanges with other countries. Because of their excellent business conditions these and other cities of the Netherlands were able to impose lower customs dues, partly it is true because of the rivalry of Amsterdam and Rotterdam, which were constantly bidding for the trade of the merchants, offering privileges and lowering duties, each against the other. During these years England, on the other hand, was facing what to many appeared to be a trade depression, of which the Dutch were thought ready to take advantage,[2] and though she had been spared the miseries which the Continent endured during the Thirty Years' War, she had herself suffered from the disasters of the civil wars at home. Little wonder

Dutch low interest (at least three per cent lower than ours), through our own supineness, hath robbed us totally of all trade, not inseparably annexed to this kingdom by the benevolence of divine Providence, and our act of navigation."

1. Sir William Temple in his *Observations upon the United Netherlands,* chs. V, VI, calls attention to the influence of toleration in the Netherlands as over against compulsory conformity in England. In the Netherlands, he says, every man except a Roman Catholic had a right to practice what religion he pleased. The same is stated by Pieter de la Court in his *Political Maxims of the State of Holland* (1702), pt. I, chs. XIV, XVI. This work, written mainly by De la Court, contains two chapters on financial policy by Jan de Witt, and was first published in England in 1702 under the title, *The True Interest and Political Maxims of the Republic of Holland.*

2. John Battie, *The Merchants Remonstrance* (1648, revised and enlarged); and for a summary of the advantages which Holland and Zealand had over England, see "Treatise on the Trade of England" (about 1675), British Museum, Additional Manuscripts, 22781.

that the merchants looked to the Continent for models in the re-organization of their trade.[1]

Finally, in the very year which saw the death of Charles I, the Dutch were able to obtain from Denmark, by treaty of October 9, 1649, called the "redemption treaty," certain special advantages regarding the passage of Dutch vessels through the Sound, the narrow strait that separates Denmark from Sweden and forms the entrance into the Baltic. By this treaty all Dutch ships, owned by Dutch subjects, no matter what or whose goods might be in the cargo, were to pass freely, other vessels being obliged to pay a toll or duty according to the cocquets taken out at the custom houses of the exporting country. In case of war Denmark threatened to close the Sound to all English ships. As the price of this "redemption treaty" the States General of the Netherlands agreed to pay annually 350,000 gulden. To recover the Baltic market for masts and other naval stores was one of the chief objects of Charles II's negotiations after 1660, and in the main these and later efforts were successful, for in the eighteenth century all ships paid the Sound duty, Dutch as well as the others.[2]

A rupture between the two countries was contrary to all the traditions of the past, based on their common Protestantism and their mutual enmity for Spain. England and Holland had similar political and religious sympathies, which brought them into close alliance, and they had stood together in earlier days as comrades against a common enemy. England had sent her troops to serve in the Low Countries and many a soldier—Dale, Gates, Miles Standish, and others—who was afterward a leader among the colonists in America

1. As early as 1660 Francis Cradocke urged England to imitate Holland, Florence, and Genoa, particularly in matters of banking and commercial organization (*An Expedient for Taking away all Impositions and for Raising a Revenue without Taxes*, London, 1660). Sir William Petty was a great admirer of Dutch methods, having spent a year in the Netherlands in 1644–1645. *Petty Papers*, II, 185–186.

2. Hill, *The Danish Sound Dues*, p. 155; Carte, *Original Letters*, II, 161, 210; Schoolcraft, "On Relations with the Dutch," *English Historical Review*, 1904; the same, "Negotiations between Charles II and Denmark," *ibid.*, 1910; Barbour, "Dutch and English Shipping," p. 281; Albion, *Forests and Sea Power*, pp. 164–167; *The Case Stated*, p. 30. For the situation in the eighteenth century, *Board of Trade Journal*, 1708–1715, pp. 111, 116, 166, 175; 1715–1718, p. 405; 1735–1741. p. 252, and index of all these volumes under "Sound." The toll was taken at Elsinore, where in the years from 1733 to 1740 the English government had an agent or consul, Robert Tigh, who transmitted lists of all vessels passing through these waters. The right of Denmark to exact these dues was not universally recognized, but they were paid under some protest by all countries until 1857.

had had his military training and experience under Leicester, Willoughby, and Vere in the defense of Holland against Spain. English capitalists had loaned money to the Dutch, and Dutch merchants had carried on their business in London, under the favorable terms of old treaties, in exactly the same manner as the English merchants themselves.[1] In general, reciprocity had governed all understandings and concessions and the ancient ties were not easily broken. But community of feeling based on religious grounds and sentiments of political liberty were bound to give way before the powerful disruptive force of mercantile rivalry and trade distrust, engendered in part among the English merchants by the manifest Dutch superiority in craftsmanship and industrial enterprise and in part by a certain aloofness of the Dutch—"cold and heavy," as Sir William Temple later called them—which aroused dislike and even hostility. The Dutch attack on England's ally, Portugal, and the seizure of Portuguese territory in Brazil and the Far East had seemed to be acts of unfriendliness, while the rapid advance of the Dutch toward a monopoly of trade and to a supremacy on the sea was construed as ingratitude toward a country which had been largely instrumental, according to the English view of the case, in helping them to attain their independence. Speakers in parliament and writers of pamphlets and newsletters commented with some asperity on the fact that the Dutch were now turning away from their old allies and endeavoring to injure and even ruin them in the field of trade. Relations thus strained were inevitably rendered more tense by the actual clashes which took place in both the East and the West, in India and the Moluccas on one side and in New England and along the Delaware on the other. Rival merchants and captains sent home complaints to their respective governments and demanded reparations for acts of aggression. The Amboyna massacre was but the most conspicuous of many similar though less brutal encounters. To the English charges the Dutch replied in kind, asserting that the English were jealous of their success and were only waiting for the time to come when they could rob them of their hard-won advantages.

During the years from 1619 to 1649 many agreements had been reached between the two countries and many attempts had been made to reconcile conflicting interests. The leading mercantile antagonists were the English and Dutch East India companies and

1. Cheyney, *History of England, 1588–1603*, I, ch. VI; II, 256.

disputes between them regarding areas of trade, spheres of influence, and monopoly of staple products were of yearly occurrence.[1] Though compromises were reached, concessions made, and letters "of faire promises and shewes of friendship" exchanged, affronts continued to be offered on both sides. The agents of the English East India Company frequently complained of the Dutch menace on the Madras coast, "one of the best flowers in their India garden," while the Dutch resented, both in the East and the West, the aggressive methods of the English and their seizure of Dutch vessels "contrary to the law of nations and the universal practice of all the princes of Europe."[2] Outwardly, however, the peace was kept, and in 1645 the Long Parliament could speak of "the firm union and constant intercourse of friendship and real affection" that existed between the two countries. Embassies were exchanged on both sides and demands made by the merchants and shipowners for compensation and reimbursement were successfully met.[3]

On the side of England the period from 1640 to 1649 was barren of policy as far as foreign commerce was concerned. In 1643 a plantations committee was appointed by parliamentary ordinance, with the Earl of Warwick as governor and lord high admiral of the plantations in America and chief of all resident governors in the colonies. This committee continued until 1650, when it was discontinued and its functions transferred to the newly appointed Council of State. These commissioners of 1643 had received no instructions regarding trade and consequently they paid very little attention to this important matter, to the great dissatisfaction of the merchants who during these years believed that they were facing a serious business depression, and made known their grievances in petitions and pamphlets. In 1641 Lewes Roberts, citing the example of Holland, begged king and parliament to remember that England's trade was England's treasure and should receive at the hands of government privileges, protection, and encouragement.[4] The writer of the *Decay of Trade,* published in the same year, also emphasized treasure by trade,[5] and Sir Thomas Roe, the ambassador,

1. Foster, *English Factories in India, passim.*
2. *New York Colonial Documents,* I, 56.
3. Rushworth, *Historical Collections,* VI, 182, 184, 197–202.
4. *The Treasure of Traffike, or a Discourse of Forraigne Trade* (London, 1641). Roberts was a prominent merchant of London and a director of the East India Company.
5. *Decay of Trade, A Treatise* (London, 1641). See also *The Petition and Remon-*

speaking in parliament at the time, made the decay of trade his main theme, saying, "We have no treasure but by trade, for mines we have none."[1] Henry Parker, of the Merchant Adventurers of Hamburg, wrote in 1648 of the many causes "that make trade so dead amongst us" and urged England not to neglect the merchants, who had suffered ruin because of the obstructions and calamities of the civil wars.[2] Thomas Violet, of the mint, in *A True Discovery* (1650), said that "by these deceits commerce is spoiled, traffick decayeth, these things that are needful for man's preservation grow dear, the handi-crafts work ceaseth and the workmen betake themselves to other places."[3] Though conditions were not as bad as these men supposed, for the civil wars had not proved especially damaging to foreign trade, they saw, after the fashion of merchants, only a melancholy state of affairs in the commercial world, and some of them were already demanding a council or committee, made up of competent men, to study and improve the situation. As early as 1641, Henry Robinson, a merchant of London, recommended the appointment of a commission to sit weekly for the purpose of advising and consulting regarding the advantages of commerce,[4] and in 1648 Henry Parker wrote, "Let it be lawful then to propose either that a certain number of able merchants may be made privy councillors specially designed to intend matters of trade; or let some other honourable council be empowered solely to promote the commonweal of mankind."[5] Nevertheless they had no hope that the Long Parliament would take action in their behalf, and awaited impatiently for conditions to improve.

We can easily anticipate, therefore, that as soon as the civil struggle was over and the country had settled down to a state of reasonable peace and quiet the merchants would make an effort to secure from parliament or the Council of State some consideration of their needs and would demand some share in the shaping of parliamentary

strance of the Governor and Company of Merchants trading to the East Indies (1641) and *The Remonstrance of the East India Company* (London, 1641). The first petition of the company had been written by Thomas Mun, presented to parliament in 1628, and published in that year. The second, cited above, urged parliament to consider its case and if its trade was found unimportant to suppress it, otherwise to support it by a public declaration.

1. *Sir Thomas Roe, His Speech* (London, 1641).
2. *Of a Free Trade* (London, 1648), pp. 35–36.
3. *A True Discovery, to the Commons of England* (London, 1650), pp. 4, 51.
4. *England's Safety in Trade Increase* (London, 1641), p. 40.
5. *Of a Free Trade*, p. 36.

legislation. How early this happened cannot be stated with certainty. The great companies—the East India Company, the Muscovy Company, the Levant Company, and the Governor and Company trading to France—as well as the mayor and aldermen of the City of London, where lay the merchants' halls and counting houses, all, at one time or another and for various reasons, sent in petitions to parliament in behalf of the recovery and advancement of their respective trades. Parliament, in its turn, made use of the merchants on its committees and called upon them for advice, as in the case of the "committee of merchants appointed for regulating the officers of the navy and customs," of which we read in 1649.[1]

The Council of State, which was established by parliament in February, 1649, had its first meeting at Whitehall on February 16. It had already been given definite instructions to look after trade and was vested with power to appoint committees. At an early sitting it determined that the whole council or any five of its members should be a committee for trade and plantations. On May 19 the Rump Parliament made its famous declaration establishing the Commonwealth and extending its authority over "all the Dominions and territories thereunto belonging." This pronouncement brought the plantations directly under the authority of the "people of England," that is, of parliament itself and its executive committee, the Council of State, a situation that continued only as long as the Puritan control lasted and no longer, for the declaration ceased to have any validity after 1660, when the colonies came once more under the authority of the crown and its executive agents. But for the moment its effect was to commit the Commonwealth government to an interest in the dominions beyond the seas, their trade, and their welfare.

The good intentions of the Rump Parliament became manifest when, in January, 1650, a bill was brought in and finally passed on August 1, for "the advancing and regulating the trade of this Commonwealth" and for the erection of a special council of trade to look after this business. On September 27 another bill was brought in and passed October 3, which is sometimes called a "navigation act," but which had for its immediate object the punishment of four rebellious colonies, Barbados, Bermuda, Antigua, and Virginia, by forbidding them to have any manner of commerce by traffic with

1. *Commons' Journal*, VI, 381; *Calendar State Papers, Domestic*, 1649–1650, March 12, 15, 20.

strangers, prohibiting any foreign ship to trade with them except by special license, and ordering "Generals at Sea" to seize all ships endeavoring to do so.[1] The preamble to this act restated the doctrine, already laid down in the declaration of May 19, 1649, that parliament had supreme authority over the colonies, a doctrine that was certainly though slowly taking shape, anticipatory of its final legal acceptance after 1689 and its actual enforcement after 1763. The other statements of policy, touching commercial contacts with strangers, were, as we have already seen, neither novel nor unexpected,[2] having been repeatedly enunciated before 1640. Coincident with the passage of the act, special agents were sent to various foreign countries as resident ministers to transact all things that pertained *ad amicitiam et liberum ac antiquum commercium* between the English and their rivals abroad. This period of exceptional activity, in setting up the Commonwealth and furthering the interests of the merchant class, reached its climax with the passage on October 9, 1651, after long debate and discussion in parliament and the Council of State and with, as we may well believe, much pulling of wires and matching of wits, of an ordinance which has come to be known as the "first navigation act," the first parliamentary statute that in any comprehensive way defined England's commercial policy.[3]

The terms of the ordinance, which was directed frankly and openly

1. Stock, *Debates*, I, 215–218; Firth and Rait, *Acts and Ordinances*, II, 403–406, 425–429; Harlow, *Barbados*, pp. 62–63; above, Vol. II, 255.

2. The statement made in *The Cambridge History of the British Empire*, I, 216, that these doctrines were "all novel and hitherto unaccepted" can hardly be defended. The only doctrine that might be so called is the one defining the authority of parliament and that certainly was not "novel," as it had been enunciated more than a year before. Parliament's legal authority over the colonies before 1689 is a debatable matter (see Vol. III, 284–285, note). The protests of Massachusetts in 1646 (Winslow, *New England Salamander*, pp. 123, 137–138) and of Barbados in 1651 (Harlow, *Barbados*, p. 65) do not invalidate in any way my own statement, made on p. 631 of the *Cambridge History*, that "Prior to 1763 the colonies had not denied the right of the British Parliament to legislate for them," for in each of the cases noted above the circumstances were quite exceptional and the action is to be explained on other grounds.

3. G. N. Clark in *History*, January, 1923, pp. 282–286; Ashley, *Financial and Commercial Policy*, pp. 152–163; Harper, *The English Navigation Acts*, pp. 40–53. The ordinance was introduced into parliament by Lord Whitelocke on August 5, 1651 (Stock, *Debates*, I, 223–225). It has sometimes been called "Cromwell's Navigation Act," but Cromwell can have had no part in either its inception or its passage. He was away in Scotland from July, 1650, until August, 1651, fought the battle of Worcester on September 3, and did not return to London until September 12. He was not interested in trade and his mind and heart must have been full of his victory and its aftermath to the exclusion of all else.

at the Dutch carrying trade, in the hope of driving Dutch ships out of the colonial market, were very simple.[1] No goods, the growth of Asia, Africa, or America, were henceforth to be imported into England, Ireland, or other English possessions in any but ships owned by Englishmen or men of the plantations, the masters of which were to be English, and the sailors "for the most part," subjects of the Commonwealth. Except in the greater range of its application, as covering the commodities of three continents instead of one, this first clause contained nothing new in principle, for similar clauses are to be found in earlier statutes and in some of the trading companies' charters. But times were changing and never before had the carrying trade of the world been so extensive and replete with the possibilities of profit and power. Hence never before had it been necessary to issue so sweeping a prohibition.

A second regulation was more of the nature of a new experiment, the outcome of which must have seemed to its proponents a matter of considerable uncertainty. No goods or commodities of foreign growth, production, or manufacture could be imported into any territory of the Commonwealth "in ships belonging to the people thereof" (as the ordinance states), except from the place of their growth, production, or manufacture or from ports of first shipment.[2] This was aimed at indirect importations through Holland of goods from Asia, Africa, and America, as well as at indirect importations of Eastland, Mediterranean, and other European goods. It meant that neither an English nor an alien merchant could import European goods except from the place of actual production or from the port of first shipment, and that foreign-owned vessels could carry to England only the commodities of their own people. Because of this restriction the Dutch as well as other foreigners, who wished to carry European products to England, would be debarred from the Continental port-to-port trade north of the Strait of Gibraltar, a trade which had become almost a monopoly of the Dutch shippers. But

1. Firth and Rait, *Acts and Ordinances,* II, 559–562. According to Professor Johnsen ("L'Act de navigation anglaise," *Revue d'histoire moderne,* new series, III, 5–15), the act was designed not to drive the Dutch out of English ports, but to ward off a possible Dutch menace. He bases his conclusion on a study of the Port Books in the Public Record Office (Andrews, *Guide,* II, 127–130), finding as he believes that from 1640 to 1651 the Dutch trade with English ports was negligible. The evidence, however, seems insufficient and the conclusion must be considered conjectural only.

2. It is not clear whether these foreign ships were to be manned by English sailors or whether the crew might be "for the most part" natives of the place of departure.

the prohibition could work both ways. If it cut off the Dutch flyboat from the port-to-port trade, it also cut off the English ship from a free and open trade with the Continent. The latter could no longer go to the ports of Holland, Germany, and France, where goods were warehoused, awaiting delivery, or ramble about from one coast town to another picking up a cargo, unless that cargo consisted of goods grown or produced in the country from which they were taken. Except in rare cases, this meant a longer voyage, greater expense, and the danger of returning to England in ballast or light-loaded, involving sometimes serious loss. The regulation was not a wise one, for, aimed at the Dutch, it curtailed, and seriously, the commercial freedom of the English merchants themselves.

Additional clauses required that no foreign vessel, foreign owned, should engage in the English coastwise trade—a very old rule again given statutory form—and that no salted fish should be brought to England or the plantations, except such as had been caught by English vessels and the fish cured and the oil made by English subjects.[1] The latter clause had as its object the recovery of the Greenland, North Sea, and Newfoundland fisheries from the Dutch.[2] Every attempt to wrest the fishing supremacy from them had failed hitherto and this one was destined to prove as futile as those that had preceded it.

The only exceptions that were made to the rules thus laid down—and these exceptions give a clue in part to the authorship of the ordinance—were as follows: the act was not to apply to the Mediterranean trade; to East India goods taken on east of the Cape of Good Hope; to silks from Italy brought overland to the cities of Holland and Flanders; or to the colonial products of Spain and Portugal which did not have to be taken on at the place of growth but might be laden anywhere, provided they were shipped in English vessels. These exceptions, it will be noticed, concerned the region of the "rich

1. Clause 5 of the act of 1651 forbade the exportation also of salt fish in any except English bottoms, but this clause was repealed in 1657 (Firth and Rait, *Acts and Ordinances*, II, 1099–1100). Ashley, in commenting upon this clause, says that it "seems certain, however, that an effort was made to include other exports in the trades which were to be confined to British shipping," but that it was successfully opposed by the exporting interest (*Financial and Commercial Policy*, p. 20).

2. IXΘYOΘHPA *or the Royal Trade of Fishing* (London, 1662, introduction written in 1661). In this work the author says that the Hollanders had discovered Newfoundland and in the year 1629 sent twelve or fourteen ships there to buy up the fish taken by the king's subjects.

trades," as they were called, from the Bay of Biscay through the Mediterranean to the Levant, including the Wine Islands, Guinea, and the East Indies, where the exports were of small size and weight in proportion to their value.[1] In this region the competition of the Dutch was felt less than in the north, from the Garonne to Archangel, and the need of protective regulations against their carrying trade was much less imperative. It was in this region too that the largest companies operated, those that did business in the East and West Indies and in the Mediterranean beyond the Straits. They were the ones most likely to profit from that part of the ordinance which provided for freedom of trade within the Mediterranean and Levantine seas. It seems reasonable, therefore, to argue that the East India and the Levant companies had something to do with the insertion of this particular clause in the ordinance, as it must have worked greatly to their advantage.[2]

Though it is difficult to reach a satisfactory conclusion regarding the authorship of the ordinance as a whole, the suggestion made above provides an opening wedge. It is not easy to believe that any large number of intelligent merchants, acting independently, whether of London or the outports, would have agreed to so injurious a policy as to bar the English carrier from seeking in the most convenient and advantageous Continental market the necessary goods for his cargo. Though many of these men were writing pamphlets, presenting grievances, and demanding that the advancement of trade be given a more prominent place than it had hitherto had among the crying needs of the day, no one of them had ever suggested a regulation so harmful to his own interests and to the shipping of England as that which the ordinance contained.

On the contrary, what these merchants did want can be found in the instructions issued in 1650 to the council of trade set up by parliament in that year to order and regulate trade in all parts of the country for the best advantage and profit of the Commonwealth.[3] The appointment of this council was the result of addresses to the Council of State from several groups of merchants, just who they

1. Barbour, "Dutch and English Shipping," p. 265.
2. In February, 1650, the Levant Company did urge that goods from the eastern Mediterranean be imported only from the place of their growth or manufacture and not from the Netherlands, and that navigation within the Levantine seas might be free. *Calendar State Papers, Domestic,* 1650, pp. 106–108.
3. Printed in Andrews, *Committees,* pp. 115–116.

were we do not know, who presumably drafted the instructions in such form as to represent the best independent mercantile thought of the day. These instructions, by whomsoever drafted, are certainly not in accord, either in spirit or in language, with the terms laid down in the ordinance of 1651. Though both the documents went through the hands of the Council of State—the instructions a year before the draft of the ordinance—and were then debated in parliament, they cannot have come originally from the same source. The instructions are open, broad-minded, and progressive in plan, a programme for the future; the terms of the ordinance are restrictive, coercive, and monopolistic, a programme to meet a special emergency, without regard to their effect on trade as a whole. They constitute a reactionary measure, apparently drawn up by the Council of State itself and passed through parliament by a group of influential men, some perhaps lobbyists, others members, connected with or employed by the powerful incorporated merchant companies of London, at a time when the question of a free and open trade versus monopoly and a closed trade was a burning issue and the outports were challenging the supremacy of London.[1] The authors of the ordinance

1. In 1646 Thomas Johnson, merchant, wrote against the monopoly of the Eastland Company as oppressive to the poor clothier, impairing the cloth trade, leading to the decay of navigation, and obstructing returns. *A Plea for Free-mens Liberties or the Monopoly of the Eastland Merchants anatomized* (London, 1646).

The object of the following pamphlet is clear from the title, *A Discourse, consisting of Motives for the Enlargement and Freedom of Trade, especially that of Cloth and other Woolen Manufactures, ingrossed at present contrary to the Law of Nature, Nations, and this Kingdom. By a Company of private Men who style themselves Merchant Adventurers* (London, 1645). Another pamphlet by "S. E." entitled *The Toutch-Stone of Mony and Commerce* (n.d., but about 1659–1660) was addressed to the parliament of the Commonwealth in favor of making London, Bristol, Plymouth, Dover, Portsmouth, Hull, and Yarmouth free ports.

On the other hand, Henry Parker of the Merchant Adventurers, in *Of a Free Trade* (1648), queries whether freedom of trade was a proper means for the improvement of trade and discusses the subject at considerable length. Also Ralph Maddison, in his *Great Britain's Remembrancer, Looking In and Out* (1665), has a chapter against making the ports free, especially to the Dutch.

For arguments in defense of companies and their privileges, at the time of the debate on the establishment of the Canary Company in 1665, see Skeel, "The Canary Company," *English Historical Review*, XXXI, 541–543. The discussion and debate pro and con went on into the next decade. See *The Uses and Abuses of Money and the Improvements of it* (London, 1671), in which the writer declares that foreign trade is not beneficial to the kingdom, because in the hands of a few particular persons and corporations, and *The Present Interest of England Stated. By a Lover of his King and Country* (London, 1671), which wishes all companies to be laid open, upholds liberty of trade, and expresses the hope that England and Holland will work together.

were clearly in favor of such special commercial privileges for themselves as would not interfere with their plans for the overthrow of
the Dutch trade; the authors of the instructions, without thought
of the Dutch competition, were already anticipating the demands of
the nonconformists under the Restoration for a relaxing of the
state's control over industry and commerce.[1]

That there was no sympathy between the Rump Parliament and
the special council of January, 1650, appears from the fact that the
parliament neither asked for the council's advice on any matter nor
accepted such advice when offered. During 1650 and 1651 the council prepared several bills for the recovery and advancement of trade
and made seven reports to the Council of State and seven to parliament, not one of which was acted on, as far as we know.[2] That the

---

1. Though the ordinance went five times to committee we read very little of the
debate which accompanied its passage, whereas the instructions, if we may judge from
the two attempts—one successful and the other unsuccessful—that were made to
amend the tenth article, were adopted after ample discussion in the House of Commons. *Commons' Journal*, VI, 430, 451.

Mr. Harper thinks that the council of trade had more to do with the ordinance of
1651 than I have seemed to suggest in the statements made above. It may be so.
Five of the sixteen members of the council of trade were members of the parliamentary committee for the act; another member, Maurice Thompson, had some connection with the measure; and the secretary, Dr. Benjamin Worsley, claimed that he
wrote *The Advocate* (above, p. 23, note 4; below, p. 60) in favor of it. But these
facts are a little beside the point. My interest lay in the contrast between the terms of
the instructions and those of the ordinance rather than in any connections which
the council may have had with the framing of the ordinance.

Mr. Harper writes further: "The fundamental philosophy of the law of 1651 was
such, I believe, that it might well commend itself to a body of merchants. Speaking
very generally, the greatest threat to England's obtaining leadership in world commerce was the tendency for the small fry of her tradesmen to go to the nearby entre-
pôts of the Netherlands and Germany to acquire the products desired. The Dutch
could supply merchandise more cheaply because of their entrenched position. English
shipping suffered in that it was called upon only for the short haul from Holland
rather than for the long haul from Asia, Africa, or America, the Mediterranean or
within the Sound. English merchants obtained a retailer's rather than a wholesaler's
profit, and the nation as a whole suffered because of its dependence upon its principal mercantile rivals as a source of supply. I recognize that there would be considerable opposition to forcing English merchants to go to the source of supply, especially from the Merchant Adventurers and from the East Coast merchants whose
trading connections were chiefly with the Dutch. But despite outport cries against the
Navigation Act being a London monopoly, the outports thrived and even gained at
the expense of London. As far as the cries for free trade were concerned, my impression is that they were directed against the monopoly features of chartered companies
rather than against national regulations of the type of the navigation acts."

2. Robinson, *Certain Proposals* (London, 1652), p. 7; *Calendar State Papers, Domestic*, 1650, p. 399; 1651, pp. 16, 29, 38, 107, 230; 1651–1652, p. 87.

sentiment of the special council of trade was not in accord with the restrictive clauses of the ordinance is evident from its report of May 26, 1651, in which it said, "Trade being the basis and well-being of a Commonwealth, the way to obtain it is to make it a free trade and not to bind up ingenious spirits by exemptions and privileges which are granted to some particular companies." This statement shows that the special council of trade did not favor the great companies of the City of London and therefore could not have had any part in shaping the ordinance. A later writer in 1656 or 1657 says that the act seemed to have upon it only a London stamp and a contentment to subject the whole nation to that city, "for most of the outports are not capable of the foreign trade to Indies and Turkey."[1] Now it was just those who were interested in the "rich trades" to the Levant and the East Indies that were most likely to profit by the ordinance. It would look therefore as if the ordinance of 1651 was the work of the great commercial companies concerned in the "rich trades," as over against the lesser merchants of London and the outports, who had profited from the "lost trades."

The influence of the trading companies, which adhered to the old idea of the monopoly, was undoubtedly very great with parliament and the Council of State. The Commonwealth was dependent for its financial support upon London and the companies, particularly the East India Company,[2] and it is not difficult to believe that these corporations brought pressure to bear upon the Rump Parliament to legislate in their behalf as against the outports, which favored the "lost trades" (that is, the trades controlled by the Dutch) and an open commerce.[3] The writer already quoted continues, "The Londoners having the sole trade do set what price they please upon their commodities, knowing the country can have them nowhere else but by them, whereby not only the outports are undone but the country brought to the devotion of the City. But a great abuse is here, for the City are not contented with this act, but only as far as it serves their own turns, for they procure (upon some pretext or other) particular licences for many prohibited commodities contrary to that

1. Additional Manuscripts, 5138, fo. 145; Andrews, *Committees*, pp. 24–30, for an account of the special council of trade.

2. *Calendar State Papers, Domestic,* 1650, pp. 128, 129, and elsewhere.

3. In later years, about 1675, the customs receipts of Bristol were estimated at one-fifth of those for the entire kingdom and those of London at two-thirds. Thus London's receipts would be ten-fifteenths, those of Bristol three-fifteenths, and those of the rest of the kingdom two-fifteenths of the whole. *Petty Papers,* II, 229.

act, as namely French wines, and free both of customs and excise tax, and for the importation of whale oil and skins, so as either directly or indirectly they will have the whole trade to themselves." As we have seen, the special council of trade was never taken very seriously by the governmental authorities and by 1653 its activities were reported as "merely nominal." The natural conclusion is that however appointed—a matter of no little importance, as yet obscure —it was ignored by parliament because of the influence of the companies. We know that for a long time to come the outports were to continue their struggle against the dominance of London and that this situation during the next hundred years was of considerable significance in the history of colonial trade.[1] There seems, therefore, ample reason to accept the opinion of a contemporary writer that the "act was procured by some few men for their own interest" and that these men were London merchants, members of the great companies, partly engaged in the East India and Levant trades and partly elsewhere. All the evidence at hand points to this conclusion.[2]

At the same time the ordinance had very little effect upon the commerce of the colonies, except so far as it barred the Dutch from the colonial trade. It resembled in no way the later navigation acts of 1660 and 1663, save in the one matter of shipping and the requirement that vessels be English owned and manned. It contained no enumeration and staple clauses, such as later bore so heavily on the complete freedom of colonial trade. Under it colonial products might be sent to any foreign market, as the enumerated commodities could

1. For the relations between London and the outports in 1748, see the *Scots Magazine* for that year.

2. *English Historical Review*, VIII, 531. The only one of these merchants that can certainly be identified is that robust Puritan, Maurice Thompson, a member of the East India Company and a merchant widely engaged in colonial trade. Thompson's connection with the prohibitory act of October 3, 1650, is mentioned (*Commons' Journal*, VI, 474). Of him it was said later that "he was always violent against the kingly government; he was intimate with the Protector, sat in the High Court of Justice and sentenced some of the beheaded lords, so is incapable of holding any office [under the Restoration]. He was once a poor fellow in Virginia, but got a great estate out of the wars, mostly rent out of the bowels of the King's party. His brother, Major Robert Thompson, was also very great with Cromwell" (*Calendar State Papers, Colonial, 1661–1668*, §1221). On the Thompsons, see Volumes I, II, indexes, and for their life in Virginia, *Virginia Historical Index*.

Sir Josiah Child in *A Treatise wherein is Demonstrated* [various things about the East Indian trade] (London, 1681) says (p. 1) that Lord Chief Justice Oliver St. John was the "principal engineer of the first act of navigation." This statement is made by other contemporaries also, but seems to rest on nothing else than rumor.

not be sent after 1660, and English and colonial vessels might take on manufactured goods at any continental port and carry them directly, as they could not after 1663, to any port of the colonies. The ordinance was not designed to limit colonial trade, or to prevent English merchants from trading with the plantations. Though it restricted the English trade with continental Europe, it left open to English ships, manned by English sailors, the trade with the colonies in the West Indies and on the mainland. English and colonial vessels could carry the manufactured goods of Europe freely to America and the sugar and tobacco of the plantations freely to Europe or elsewhere. Thus a London merchant could send a ship, properly manned and owned, to the Continent with English commodities, there take on European goods and sail to America or the West Indies, and return to Europe—France, Holland, or Hamburg—prepared to make up a cargo of the growth of those countries and thence return to England. This profitable trade, which according to later writers cut out the sugar from Brazil and gave a great impetus to the sugar from the English West Indies, was stopped by the enumeration clause of 1660 and by the Staple Act of 1663, and was greatly injured by certain French preferential duties, which were intended to favor the French colonies and burden the foreigner.[1] The ordinance, by endeavoring to prevent the bringing of the commodities of Europe to England or the colonies in strangers' bottoms, was aimed not at all at the colonial trade but at the home industry and carrying trade of the Dutch, in the hope of encouraging instead the employment by English merchants of English shipping, particularly in the region of the "lost trades," and thus stimulating the English carrying trade so far as to exclude the Dutch from English and colonial ports. How far the ordinance accomplished its purpose, in view of the difficulties encountered in enforcing the European clauses, it is difficult to say.

Whether the ordinance offered an affront to the Dutch sufficient to serve as a *casus belli* is a question that can be discussed but not answered, except so far as the statement may be made that no act

---

1. *Calendar State Papers, Colonial*, 1669–1674, p. 215. There is a paper among the Shaftesbury Papers in the Public Record Office (no. 8, doc. 10) which was written by someone opposed to the enumeration, because he thought the latter distinctly favorable to the French and Dutch sugar planters, leading them to increase their sugar output to England's injury and loss. On the French sugar legislation, Mims, *Colbert's West India Policy*, ch. XII, and *The Tariff settled by the French King and Council, September 18, 1664* (London, 1713).

of this kind, performed by an independent and sovereign power, could constitute a pretext for war, within the meaning of the law of nations. The answer to the question must be sought rather in the spirit that provoked the war than in any legal warrant for it. Between the two countries relations had been strained for many years, but every effort had been made to avoid a breach and negotiators had passed back and forth in the attempt to maintain "a neighborly and friendly commerce."[1] The Dutch had grievances based on the losses of ships at the hands of the English and on the refusal of the English to recognize certain of their claims—such as the right to search neutral vessels and to exercise supremacy in the "narrow seas" —which not unnaturally, in view of their own superiority on the ocean and in commerce, aroused among them feelings of resentment and dislike. Contemporary writers on the English side attributed the war to two chief causes—the refusal of the Dutch to strike their flag when meeting the English fleet in these waters and the endeavor on the part of the Dutch "to take possession of our inheritance," that is, to encroach upon England's preserves in commerce and the fisheries.[2] On neither side is there mention of the ordinance of 1651 as a cause of the war.

In part at least the ordinance was an act of retaliation for the "redemption treaty" of 1649 between Holland and Denmark,[3] and it may have been drafted in a somewhat more vindictive spirit, to England's own disadvantage, because of certain incidents, which at the time aroused exceeding bitterness at Whitehall and Westminster. These were the refusal on the part of the Dutch to admit Walter Strickland, a member of parliament and later of the Council of State, who was sent as an agent to Holland and for over a year was kept waiting for an audience with the States General;[4] and the murder by Scottish loyalists of his successor, Dr. Dorislaer (Dorislaus) in April, 1649, at The Hague. But however this may be, at bottom, as the

1. *Commons' Journal*, VI, June 18; *Calendar State Papers, Domestic, 1649–1650*, p. 30, "Endeavor that a good correspondence and nearer union be preserved between the States."
2. *The Case Stated*, p. 13.
3. Gardiner, *History of the Commonwealth and the Protectorate*, I, ch. XIII; II, 81–84. "Redemption" meant the lifting of the Sound dues in favor of Holland, that is, "all ships owned by Dutch subjects, no matter what or whose might be their cargo, should pass freely through the Sound." Hill, *The Sound Dues*, p. 155.
4. *Commons' Journal*, VI, June 18; *The Case Stated*, p. 5; Thurloe, *State Papers*, I, 123, 124–125, 128, 133–134; Strickland's letters to William Frost, secretary to the Council of State, *ibid.*, pp. 112–130.

writer of *The Case Stated* says, the act was passed for "the managing of our trade to our own advantage."

The Dutch made strenuous efforts to have the ordinance withdrawn,[1] but parliament refused to consider their request, saying that "it would be for [its] dishonour to revoke an act of that nature for the pleasure of any foreigner," particularly "if it should be done out of fear." Therefore "they resolved that they would maintain it." That there were those in parliament who wanted war with the Dutch and to that end helped to give the measure its provocative character is evident from Sir George Radcliff's letter to Colonel Holles, August 23, 1652, in which he said, "I see no probability of any accorde between the two Republiques, yet there are some in both parts that indeavour it, but I believe they wilbe over voted by those that are for warre."[2] The war of 1653-1654 between England and Holland was largely a matter of psychology, due to the conflicting interests of two peoples overwrought by thirty years of commercial rivalry. It was not due to the ordinance of 1651.

That the act injured England's commerce more than it did the commerce of Holland future events were to show. Had Englishmen's minds not been clouded by animosity because of England's seeming humiliation at Dutch hands,[3] wiser counsels might have prevailed and the fact would have become apparent that in the face of losses during the civil wars English merchants could not afford the pleasure of revenge at the price of so serious a limitation upon their own freedom of trade. Trade was already seemingly depressed, the East India Company was declared to be in serious straits, and the government itself was hard up for funds. What was needed was peace and an opportunity for normal recovery. As Lord Burghley said, nearly a century before, "War is a curse and peace the blessing

1. An early petition against the ordinance of October 3, 1650, is printed in *New York Colonial Documents*, I, 436–437.

2. Historical Manuscripts Commission, *Bath*, II, 106. Roger Coke in *England's Improvement*, treatise III (1675), wrote, "But the Rump Parliament designing a War against the Dutch . . . made a thing Intituled An Act for Encouragement and Encrease of Shipping and Navigation, commonly called the Act of Navigation. . . . A War they designed and a war they had with the Dutch."

3. "Trade, Mr. Dorveil, is the subject that we are upon, in which there can be no such thing as friendship, especially whilst the beggary is on our side. You buy our commodities as cheap as you can and sell your own as dear." *A Dialogue between Mr. Smith* [an Englishman], *Monsieur Ragouse* [a Frenchman], *Menheir Dorveil* [a Dutchman] *and Mr. Manoel Texira* [a Portuguese]. *In a Walk to Newington* (London, 1701).

of God upon a nation; a realm gaineth more by one year of peace
than by ten years of war." Whether intentionally or not the ordinance
was followed not by peace but by war and the losses of ships captured or destroyed in the Channel or off the coasts of England and
Holland, where the principal actions took place, must have seriously
injured England's European trade. As Scott says, "the estimated
benefits were remote; while the losses were immediate and, in certain instances, pressing." It would seem to have been the better part
of wisdom, at least until England's trade was on a more secure footing and her navy more certain of its place on the sea, for the Commonwealth government to have accepted the Dutch advances made
in June, 1651, whereby England was granted "substantial commercial
concessions."[1] As it happened the evil effects of the ordinance appeared almost at once and in order to meet them the Council of
State was obliged to grant licenses to foreign vessels and privileges
to English vessels in order to satisfy the most pressing needs.

Upon Holland's naval and mercantile supremacy the ordinance
had but little effect, although her losses during the war were probably as heavy as those of England. It is true that the Dutch ambassadors, sent to England in 1651, sought to obtain the withdrawal of the
measure, and when that failed continued to try, during the winter of
1651 to 1652, and afterward on to 1657, and hopelessly on to 1659, to
enter into a marine treaty with England, which should recognize
the principle of free ships, free goods, yield the right of search in
the case of Dutch vessels carrying properly authenticated passports,
and limit the term "contraband" to articles directly used in waging
war;[2] but as those demands were flatly opposed to England's interests the negotiations came to nothing. Despite the ordinance and the
losses of the war that followed, the Dutch continued to trade with
the colonies, and though the English men-of-war seized a few ships
in Barbados and Virginia for trading contrary to the ordinance, the
number was not large. After the war was over in 1654, the colonists
continued to be left pretty much to themselves; they paid very little
attention to the Commonwealth law and welcomed the Dutch as
warmly as ever. In 1651 and 1652 Massachusetts, in her own estima-
tion already a commonwealth and not a colony, set up a mint, annexed sundry towns of New Hampshire and Maine, carried on a

1. Scott, *Joint-Stock Companies,* I, 251.
2. Catterall, "Anglo-Dutch Relations, 1654–1660," *Report,* American Historical Association, 1910, p. 103.

flourishing trade with France, Holland, and other parts of Europe, and allowed all nations free admission to her ports. Virginia and Barbados, believing that they had been granted an open trade by the terms of their surrender to the parliamentary fleet, trafficked when and where they liked. The English navy had no command of the sea and occupied itself chiefly with such enforcement as it could effect in European waters. The execution of the ordinance overseas was largely in the hands of the colonists themselves and they were not a very dependable body of sea-police.[1]

For more than half a century longer the Dutch continued to be England's greatest rival in commerce. In a "Treatise on the Trade of England," of date about 1675, the estimate is given that the Dutch had 900,000 tons of shipping to England's 500,000, which if true would show that the commerce of the Dutch provinces had not been seriously injured by any of the navigation acts.[2] McCulloch in his edition of Adam Smith's *Wealth of Nations* says, "It may be fairly doubted whether, in point of fact, the navigation law [of 1651] really weakened the naval power of the Dutch and increased that of this kingdom."[3] The mercantilist writers of the day testify to much the same effect in continuing to express their fears of Dutch competition on into the eighteenth century: Roger Coke (1670, 1671, 1675), William de Britaine (1672), Henry Stubbe (1672), the author of *The English Ballance* (1672), Sir Josiah Child (1668 and later editions), William Petyt (1680), Sir Francis Brewster (1695), the author of

1. Hutchinson, *History of Massachusetts Bay* (Mayo, ed.), I, 162, 166–167; *Massachusetts Colonial Records*, IV, pt. I, 120–121; *Connecticut Colonial Records*, 1636–1665, p. 261; *Rhode Island Colonial Records*, I, 261, 356, 389; Bruce, *Economic History of Virginia*, I, 351–354; *Virginia Magazine*, I, 75–81, 141–142; *William and Mary Quarterly*, I, 16, 17; Hening, *Statutes at Large*, I, 382–383; *Calendar State Papers, Colonial*, 1574–1660, pp. 418–419. A document printed in Thurloe (*State Papers*, V, 80–81) concerns the relations of the London merchant with the Virginia tobacco planter, who was beginning as early as this to complain of his injuries at the hands of his factors in London.

Among the charges brought in 1665 against Francis Lord Willoughby, governor of Barbados, was one (no. 8) that he favored the Jews, who had engrossed the greater part of the trade of the island and dealt principally "with those of their tribe in Holland, whose commodities they vend to the prejudice of the English manufacturers, and make returns in ships of their own under colour of English bottoms to the prejudice of the English navigations" (State Papers Domestic, Entry Book, 18, pp. 156–157; *Calendar State Papers, Colonial*, 1661–1668, §989, i, greatly abbreviated). On the Jews in Barbados at this time, see Samuel, *A Review of the Jewish Colonists in Barbados in the Year 1680* (1936).

2. Additional Manuscripts, 22,781, p. 11.

3. IV, 381–382. McCulloch's essay on the navigation acts in *ibid.*, note XI, is an important contribution to the general subject.

*The Naked Truth in an Essay on Trade* (1696), Defoe (1712), and on to John Withers, who in 1713, in *The Dutch better Friends than the French,* felt called upon to answer nine current objections to the Dutch as England's rivals in trade.[1]

The decline of the Dutch supremacy was due rather to internal than external causes. We know that the federal system of government had many disadvantages in administering efficiently the affairs of the navy, because of the lack of coördination among the various local bodies. Herein lay an element of weakness which contributed eventually to English success. The author of *Commerce de la Hollande* adds as a contributing cause the heavy taxation due to the enormous loans that the Dutch were obliged to make in order to meet the expenses of the wars with the Commonwealth, Charles II, and Louis XIV. Oliver Goldsmith writing a century later, in 1762, and arguing that a long period of indolence, trade, and money-making leads to deterioration, cites the Dutch of the years after 1675 as an example of what may be "the result of total inattention to war and an utter exterpation of martial ardour." "Insulted by the French [he says], threatened by the English, and almost universally despised by the rest of Europe," they lost their leadership in the field of commerce and their place of prominence among the powers of Europe.

1. Roger Coke, *A Discourse of Trade* (in four parts, part II all about the superior Dutch); William de Britaine, *The Dutch Usurpation;* Stubbe, *A Justification of the Present War against the United Netherlands;* Sir Josiah Child, *Discourse of Trade* (the earlier writings, *Brief Observations,* 1668, written in 1665, and *A Short Addition to the Observations* contain less on this point than do later editions, notably that of 1695); William Petyt, *Britannia Languens;* Sir Francis Brewster, *Essays on Trade;* Defoe, *An Enquiry into the Danger and Consequences of a War With the Dutch* (speaks of the strength of the Dutch and adds "No part of our commerce is free from them or out of their reach"). There were others, however, who had less fear of the Dutch rivalry and were eager for friendly relations between England and Holland even before the war of 1673. See *The Present Interest of England Stated* (1671) and Joseph Hill *The Interest of These United Provinces, being a Defence of the Zeelanders Choice* (1673). Withers, however, makes the strongest plea, couched in almost indignant language, against what he thinks to be the popular notion that as soon as peace is made with France then "Holland must be crushed as an inveterate Enemy to our Church and Monarchy." Also *The Dutch Barrier: Ours or Interest of England and Holland inseparable . . . to which is added an Enquiry into the Causes of the Clamour against the Dutch,* London, 1712, and *An Enquiry into the Danger and Consequences of a War with the Dutch,* London, 1712, both in the Huntington Library. John Bennett in *The National Merchant* (1738), p. 72, ascribes the decline of the Netherlands to two chief causes, neglect to plant colonies and overstraining in matters of trade.

# CHAPTER III

## ENGLAND'S COMMERCIAL SYSTEM
## DEFINED: 1660–1662

THE year 1654 is noteworthy in English annals. Cromwell had become Protector by virtue of the Instrument of Government in December, 1653. The Dutch war was brought to an end by the Anglo-Dutch treaty of April, 1654, and the English demands, as embodied in the ordinance of 1651, were tacitly, if not officially, agreed to, though the Dutch continued to call the measure "unfriendly and unneighborly." In the same year, April–July, England made commercial treaties with three powers—Sweden, Portugal, and Denmark. That with Denmark, the last to be made, contained two important provisions, one opening the Sound to all traffic, and thus granting England equality of treatment with other powers in respect of trade in the Baltic and the imposition of tolls and duties; the other permitting the subjects of each country to trade freely with the other, except in those colonies to which it was forbidden to sail or trade without special leave or license previously obtained. The second with Sweden—the outcome of the mission of Bulstrode Whitelocke to Queen Christina—enabled England to enter into friendly relations with the power that controlled Finland and the provinces to the south of the gulf of the same name, whence, as also from Norway, came the bulk of England's supply of naval stores and masts.[1] This treaty was the more important because in 1655, the year after Christina's abdication, Sweden and Holland, rival powers for commercial supremacy in the Baltic, became estranged and the Dutch seized New Sweden on the Delaware and sundry Swedish possessions in Africa. The third, with Portugal (as noted in a previous chapter), was in effect a requital upon that power for the assistance it had given the Stuarts, in that it compelled King John to grant England, in return for protection against the Dutch, preferential treatment for her merchants in Portuguese ports and valuable commercial privileges, particularly a share in the

---

1. Albion, *Forests and Sea Power*, ch. IV.

Brazil trade, which were important concessions because of England's awakening ambitions in the West Indies.[1]

More important even than these treaties in disclosing the direction of Cromwell's policy was the renewal in the same year of the old Puritan programme of abiding hostility for Spain and the despatch of the fleet under Admiral Penn and General Venables to the West Indies for the purpose of extending England's control in the Caribbean and of fastening Protestantism upon such of Spain's possessions in the West Indies as might be made available for the purpose.[2] This attempt at conquest on a large scale proved a humiliating and lamentable failure and ended with nothing more important than the taking of Jamaica in 1655. Undeterred by this failure, after careful consideration as to the wisest course to pursue, Cromwell decided to continue the enmity for Spain, as long as that power remained an obstacle in the way of England's expansion. This he accomplished by a declaration of the justness of the war against the great colossus in 1655 and by entering into a treaty with France two years later.

Though nothing commensurate with the original plan came of the expedition to the West Indies, the capture of Jamaica and the treaty with France had far-reaching results. The capture gave an immediate impetus to England's colonizing ambitions and shape to her commercial programme, while the treaty with France established friendly relations with the power that was destined to become England's greatest commercial and colonial rival in the eighteenth century. These years from 1651 to 1660 show that a great commercial struggle was taking place among the powers of western and northern Europe and that significant issues, other than those that were political and diplomatic, were at stake. Portugal was rendered harmless by the treaty of 1654; Spain, as a superior power, was dethroned by the treaty of the Pyrenees in 1659; Sweden, Denmark, and Holland were for the moment occupied with their own affairs, engaged as they were in a commercial competition for the control of the Baltic, with Russia an ominous figure in the background; while France, the real victor in the Thirty Years' War, was already preparing for her dual rôle under Louis XIV and Colbert, as the predominant European power on both the land and the sea. Facing all

1. The texts of all these treaties are given in Davenport, *European Treaties,* II, 7–47, with admirable introductions, bibliographies, and footnote references.
2. This famous expedition has already been discussed at length in Vol. III, ch. I.

these Continental rivals was England, beginning to formulate for the first time a definite naval and mercantile policy and to map out a series of measures that she confidently hoped would win for her both profit and leadership on the sea and in the colonies. In the field of expansion we are entering upon a series of noteworthy movements that usher in the modern era.

The capture of Jamaica presented a new world of opportunity for industry and colonization, with alluring openings for the merchants and capitalists of London and elsewhere, who were seeking profitable investments in the lands overseas. The various treaties, the additions of territory, and the cessation of war made for a renewal of enterprise, which had been checked and thwarted by the years of conflict through which England had passed. Commerce and the colonies were very much in the minds of men in the later part of this decade and religious and political controversies were passing into the background. Merchants, sea-captains, promoters, and others with money to invest were eager to engage in new activities. But progress was slow. The financial difficulties of the Protectorate, the depression in trade which continued despite the ordinance of 1651 (and perhaps partly because of it), the constitutional experiments and political uncertainties of both Commonwealth and Protectorate, and the prevailing discontent owing to diminishing returns, rise of prices, and widespread unemployment made the last years before the Restoration a time of discouragement and dismay. These depressing circumstances may have stirred men's energies, but they dampened their hearts and darkened their outlook. The debt of the state was estimated in 1659 at more than two million pounds. "We allotted the old Protector [Oliver Cromwell]," says a contemporary writer, "no less than a constant revenue of 1,900,000 *lbs* to support the government, yet that sum at the year's end cleared not the account—What a debt have we contracted? 'Tis judged not less than three millions."[1] Money had been wanted for so many necessary and extraordinary expenses that the Protectorate for three years before its close had been on the verge of bankruptcy. Scott says that "there could be few stronger arguments for a change of the whole government than the financial errors of the Long Parliament, the Protectorate, and the re-called Long Parliament," which had involved the country in a deficit more than double that of the largest recorded crown liability

1. *A Discourse for A King and Parliament* (London, 1660), pp. 9, 18. See Vol. III, 40–42.

before 1641.[1] In 1658 and 1659 the country was approaching insolvency and a serious industrial crisis. To continue the Puritan rule was suicidal. The only remedy that could improve the commercial situation and bring about a revival of trade and consequent prosperity was the giving over once and for all of the rule of the Puritan minority. Men wanted tranquillity, an end of war, and a reduction of taxation.

Because of trade depression and the heavy indebtedness—made up of the long overdue arrears due the men of the army and navy and the royal debts of the later days of Charles I and the period of exile of Charles II[2]—attention was centered more than ever before on the best ways and means wherewith to meet the prevailing distress. For some years a group of London merchants had been endeavoring to persuade Cromwell to adopt a broader commercial policy and to inaugurate a more comprehensive and centralized system of colonial control. But Cromwell, entangled in a web of political and religious complications, heritages of the past rather than harbingers of the future, never seems to have visioned colonial, commercial, and naval affairs as ends in themselves, but subordinated them to the exigencies of Puritan government and supremacy. With his death and the collapse of the Protectorate, both in power and in reputation, during the administration of his son, the demands of the merchants and men of affairs became increasingly insistent and after the Restoration their petitions and overtures were reworded and readdressed and sent to Charles II and his ministers. The latter, facing tremendous responsibilities, were thoroughly alive to the necessity of restoring the solvency of the kingdom and were all well aware of the fact that in the enlargement and improvement of trade lay the surest remedy for the financial ills of the time.[3] There were many groups

---

1. Scott, *Joint-Stock Companies*, I, 258–262; II, 129–130.

2. For a decade after 1660, "scarcity of money," and the "difficulty," "deadness," and "decay" of trade are the terms used to express the general situation (*Calendar Treasury Books*, I, 1660–1667, pp. 252, 315, 342, 723). Dr. Shaw, in the preface to this volume, presents the financial conditions that confronted Charles II on his return (pp. xv-xxiv). He speaks of "the severe financial trouble of the first years immediately succeeding the Restoration" and of "the extremity of the financial distress of the time," and, he adds, "in the growing financial troubles alike of the country and of the Government it was all the Commons could do, it ultimately proved more than they could do, to avert a national bankruptcy." On the financial conditions that prevailed during the period preceding the Stop of the Exchequer, see *History*, January, 1930, pp. 333–337.

3. The same sentiment prevailed in Scotland. In 1660 no subject was more often

committed to this task. The king himself, good natured and generous, but shrewd and sympathetic; many who had served him during
his fallen fortunes—the Duke of York, Sir Edward Hyde, soon to
become the Earl of Clarendon, and Lord Culpeper; royalists, who
had felt the pinch of poverty and had suffered for their allegiance—
Carteret, Berkeley, and Craven; parliamentarians, who had been
active and in office during the minority rule—Anthony Ashley
Cooper, Sir William Morice, and George Monck, soon to become
Duke of Albemarle; and merchants, such as Andrew Riccard, Martin Noell, Thomas Povey, James Drax, Maurice Thompson, and
many more—all were ready to respond vigorously to the new call
and to make the advancement of trade one of the first objects of the
government. Many of those who had remained in England during
the Puritan period and who had sat on special boards and committees dealing with trade matters were well equipped to recommend
a clear-cut and statesmanlike policy for the advancement of foreign
commerce, the increase of the revenue, and the oversight of the colonies. Of the latter there were by this time Virginia, Bermuda, Barbados, the Leeward Islands, Jamaica, Massachusetts Bay, Connecticut, Rhode Island, and Maryland—a number sufficiently large to
demand England's immediate attention.

The merchants and other capitalistic promoters, who had been
engaged in colonial trade since the acquirement of Jamaica in 1655
and who now turned to the new government with hopeful expectations, found in Sir Edward Hyde a willing listener. Hyde had been
made lord chancellor at Bruges in 1658 and immediately after the
Restoration was created Earl of Clarendon. He urged upon the king,
both in exile and after his return, "a great esteem for the plantations
and the improvement of them by all ways that could reasonably be
proposed to him" and upon parliament the "infinite importance of
the improvement of trade," and he sought whenever possible to
demonstrate to both king and parliament the desirability of enlarging the navy in order to check the "immoderate desire" of England's
neighbors and rivals "to engross the whole traffic of the universe."[1]
King Charles himself was very willing "to increase the trade of the

discussed by Scottish officials and legislators than the best way to manage the trade
of the country. The royal boroughs urged the promotion of trade upon the Scottish
parliament, which passed acts in their interest. Davidson and Gray, *The Scottish Staple
at Veere*, p. 213.

1. Andrews, *Colonial Self-Government*, pp. 14–15.

nation" and listened with approval to Clarendon's statement that the receipts from the plantation trade might repair some of the deficiencies in the exchequer.

One of the earliest demands of the merchants was for the appointment of a council or committee of trade, and one of Thomas Povey's earliest suggestions was that a body of competent persons be selected to constitute such a council, and he presented very forcible arguments to show how such a council should be composed and what should be its functions.[1] Povey's interests lay in the field of the plantations rather than in that of foreign commerce, but he was quite cognizant of mercantile as well as of plantation problems and competent to offer advice in both particulars. There had been a trade committee appointed under the Protectorate in 1655, for which Noell and Povey may have been in part responsible, but it was large and unwieldy and in no way, either in membership or function, the kind of committee that Povey wanted. It accomplished little and came to an end in 1657. During the Interregnum the control of trade was lacking in simplicity and effectiveness. It was exercised by no one familiar with its intricacies or invested with sufficient authority to act promptly or with effect. There existed an excess of machinery and a consequent waste of time and energy. After 1655, the business world, particularly of London, jealous of its privileges, became thoroughly dissatisfied with the way commerce had been neglected and the plantations ignored.[2] They had not profited by the navigation act of 1651 and though many of them hoped that the war with the Dutch would be of infinite benefit in substituting English for Dutch carrying trade, they had slowly come to realize that neither ordinance nor war had brought about the desired result.[3] They were enormously attracted by the capture of Jamaica and though they were convinced that there was nothing more to be expected from Cromwell or his successor in the matter of trade, they were not all agreed that the revival of the monarchy was the best way to take advantage of the situation. Among those who opposed the Protectorate and criticized its shortcomings were some who feared lest a restored court and a rehabilitated body of gentlemen-courtiers might look down on commerce and the merchants as beneath their dignity,

1. Andrews, *Committees*, pp. 56–57. Mr. Higham thinks that Povey got his ideas on this point from the Dutch (*Colonial Entry Books*, p. 9). It is quite possible, but equally likely that he got his ideas from the French.

2. Andrews, *Committees*, pp. 38–48.     3. Clarendon, *Life* (ed. 1827), II, 235.

and that commercial affairs might suffer further discouragement were a Stuart to come once more into his own.[1]

But there need have been no anxiety on this score for the courtiers were to prove as eager promoters as the merchants themselves.[2] In response to the many demands that were made by such experienced merchants as Riccard, Noell, Povey, Drax, and Thompson, and by such occasional pamphleteers as Francis Cradocke,[3] himself a merchant, Clarendon as lord chancellor said on August 29, 1660, "The king doth consider the infinite importance the improvement of trade must be to this kingdom, and therefore his Majesty intends forthwith to establish a council for trade, consisting of some principal merchants of the several companies, to which he will add some gentlemen of equality and experience and for their greater honour and encouragement some of my lords of his own privy council. The king," he adds, "is very solicitous for the improvement and prosperity of his plantations abroad, where there is such large room for the industry and reception of such as shall desire to go thither, and therefore his Majesty likewise intends to erect and establish a council for these plantations, in which persons well qualified shall be wholly intent upon the good and advancement of those plantations."[4] Much the same language was used in the letter which he (or others) had sent about two weeks before to the Mayor and Court of Aldermen of the City of London, asking them to obtain from the merchant companies the names of "their most knowing and active men," such as were suitable for appointment on these councils.[5] Great pains

1. *The Grand Concernments of England* (London, 1659), pp. 15–17.

2. The courtier-promoters at Whitehall turned out to be among the leading advocates of trade and the colonies during the decade after the Restoration (Vol. III, 183). While there is little in the journals of the House of Commons and the House of Lords to show the nature of the debates on the bill for the encouragement of navigation, there is ample evidence to evince the great amount of attention paid by the king and the lord chancellor to the importance of trade as helping to increase the royal revenue. One may read with profit the proceedings in both houses for the year 1664, particularly the king's message of April 29 (Stock, *Debates*, I, 325) and his narrative speech from the throne of November 24 (*ibid.*, I, 328–330), as well as other speeches and representations of those years. See Vol. III, 69.

3. Francis Cradocke, *An Expedient for taking away all Impositions* (London, 1660), p. 10. See also *The Toutch-Stone of Mony and Commerce*, by S. E., a Lover of his Country (London, 1659–1660), pp. 18, 33.

4. *Collection of His Majesties Gracious Letters, Speeches, Messages and Declarations, since April 4–14, 1660* (London, 1660), pp. 78–79; Stock, *Debates*, I, 282.

5. Andrews, *Committees*, pp. 65–66; Guildhall: Town Records of London, Remembrancia, 9, no. 5.

were taken in drawing up the lists, a business that took more than two months. Even then, after the commissions had reached the Crown Office (November 7), ready to pass the great seal, the commission erecting the council for foreign plantations was held back awaiting further revision. Therefore, one commission is dated November 7 and the other December 1, 1660. A few months before, in answer to a petition presented to the king by divers merchants and others trading to the English plantations in America, the king in council had appointed a committee of its own members to consider any petitions, proposals, memorials, or other addresses that might be sent in concerning plantation affairs and to make report to the council of its findings.[1] The Privy Council committee, thus established, continued, with changing membership, until in 1675, with broader powers than those possessed by its predecessor, it merged into a royally commissioned committee of the Privy Council, known as the Lords of Trade, 1675–1696. To this body, for twenty years was entrusted the entire charge of trade and the plantations.

The two select councils of 1660 had a checkered career.[2] They were unwieldy bodies, one containing sixty-two members and the other forty-eight, selected from all classes—lords, baronets, merchants, sea-captains, and planters—many of them familiar from personal knowledge with the needs of the colonies and of colonial trade. Among them were Noell and Povey, the London merchants who had been active under the Protectorate and whose recommendations, particularly the "overtures" of Povey, were taken over bodily and with some additions were issued by the king as the instructions for the council for foreign plantations. Probably Povey wrote also the instructions issued to the council of trade, so that he, more than any other single individual, deserves the credit of having prepared the first draft of the regulations, under which these and later bodies functioned from 1660 to 1782.

The two councils of 1660 had an active but brief term of service, coming to an end, in fact if not legally, in 1665, when the distractions of the time—the plague, the Dutch war, and the fire of London—prevented further meetings. The council for trade was abolished in 1668 and a new council commissioned. This in turn was set aside in 1672, after an inactive existence of four years, and its duties were transferred to the select council for foreign plantations, which had

1. *Acts Privy Council, Colonial,* I, §484.    2. Andrews, *Committees,* ch. IV.

been revived, August 3, 1670. The new council for trade and plantations of 1672 was under the leadership of Anthony Ashley Cooper, Lord Ashley, afterward the Earl of Shaftesbury, with John Locke, the philosopher, as his associate, both of whom were especially interested in the settlement of Carolina. The council sat from October 13, 1672, to December 22, 1674, and accomplished a great deal of important work.[1] One of its secretaries was Dr. Benjamin Worsley, who had been the secretary of the council of 1651 under Sir Harry Vane, and as a physician was attracted to the idea, as was Sir Hans Sloane later, of raising plantation products for the pharmacopeia.[2] He made a number of attempts to promote the cultivation of senna. Worsley had known the plantations since 1649 and in all probability had had some part in drafting the navigation act of 1660. He was for a number of years the expert adviser of the crown in all that concerned plantation interests and from 1670 to 1672 was regularly employed in the service of the council of those years with a salary ranging from £200 to £600 "for assistance in matters relating to the foreign plantations." His services terminated June 24, 1673, and he was succeeded in the office of secretary by John Locke.

Owing to the financial bankruptcy of the kingdom and the fall of Shaftesbury from power, the council was abolished in 1674 and its duties reverted to the committee of the Privy Council mentioned above. This committee was raised to the status of a royal commission by the issue of a patent, February, 1675, investing its members with the same duties as those performed by the Shaftesbury council. This important commission, undergoing frequent changes in personnel, notably after the Revolution of 1689, but composed always of privy councillors, men high in rank, office, and influence, sat for twenty years, performing its best work before 1689, after which it deteriorated rapidly.[3] In 1695, under the pressure of the growing mercantile interests, parliament determined to reëstablish by statute the former system of select councils, but William III, deeming this plan an encroachment on his prerogative and doubting, as we shall

1. The records of these councils, in the form partly of entry books and partly of original documents, are preserved in the Public Record Office. One volume, the "Journal," after having been lost for 200 years, has recently been recovered and is now in the Library of Congress.

2. *Calendar State Papers, Colonial,* 1669–1674, §342; *Calendar Treasury Books,* III, IV, index, s.v. "Worsley"; *Proceedings,* Massachusetts Historical Society, 1878, pp. 215–216.

3. Below, pp. 272–285.

have occasion to note later, the wisdom of such a course, interposed his authority and on May 15, 1696, appointed a select council of his own, by commission under the great seal. This body, which is usually known as the Board of Trade, lasted for eighty-six years.

The series of instructions issued to these various councils and commissions from 1660 to 1696, taken together and in their historical sequence, constitute a commercial and colonial code which for more than a century determined the policy of the executive authorities in England toward the colonies and trade in general. First given shape by the merchants Noell and Povey, and elaborated by Shaftesbury, Locke, Benjamin Worsley, and probably others, these instructions underwent only minor changes during the whole period of their enforcement. Their fundamental purpose was the supervision and regulation of domestic and foreign trade, the encouragement of home manufactures, the care of the poor, and the advancement of fishing and shipping. Of this programme the care of the plantations was an integral but subordinate part, for viewed as an important source of such raw materials and tropical products as England needed, these plantations became rather a commercial than a territorial necessity, and the various councils were strictly enjoined to discover how they could be improved and made useful to the mother state.

While king and Privy Council were thus defining rules and procedure, parliament was giving statutory form to policy and system. Except for the ordinance of 1651, which had no validity after 1660, statements of policy since 1600 had been made only in orders in council or in royal proclamations, issued during the years from 1621 to 1640. These had contained certain specific applications of widely accepted principles of colonial relationship, such as were common to all the maritime states of Europe at the time. The need of supplanting the order in council by an act of parliament was first felt by the Long Parliament and reached its fullest expression before 1660 in the ordinance of 1651. Those who recognized the importance of so doing were, doubtless, actuated by many motives. They may have wished to substitute parliament for the Privy Council as the controlling organ of government in matters of trade, navigation, and the colonies, and so, perhaps, unwittingly, to anticipate that movement, which was to go forward at such a rapid pace in the eighteenth century, whereby the authority and importance of the council were to undergo a steady decline. They may have wished to enforce, more emphatically than before and on a wider and more effective scale, the main features of the early orders and especially the shipping provisions of the ordinance of 1651, which had thus far failed to wrest the carrying trade from the Dutch and had probably injured English trade with the Continent more than it had helped it. They wanted at this time, as they had never wanted as much before, to make use of the colonies and to rectify, if possible, the unfavorable balance of trade with Europe, notably in the region of the "lost trades" and the "narrow seas," where the imports exceeded the exports. They wished to protect the interests of the English merchant and to increase the customs revenue by making the realm the center and staple through which the commodities to and from the plantations would have to pass and so to prevent a direct trade either way between continental Europe and the English plantations in America.

Who drafted the bills introduced into parliament for the carrying out of these purposes is not certainly known. Treasurer Southampton said in 1661 that he had recently been conferring with "some principal merchants and some parliament men principally employed in framing the act."[1] We shall probably not go far wrong if we name as among these men Noell, Povey, Crispe, Riccard, Drax, and Benjamin Worsley, the last named of whom said, in recounting his career to Lady Clarendon, that he was "the first sollicitour for the act for the management of trade and navigation and put the first file to it, and after writ the advocate in defence of it."[2] But behind it also were such office holders and parliamentarians as Joseph Williamson, Richard Nicolls, John Werden, Robert Southwell, and George Downing, the last named of whom was the most implacable enemy in England of the Dutch supremacy and always a leader in measures for its overthrow; also such ranking statesmen, members of the royal household, and courtier-promoters as Arlington, Carteret, Berkeley, Ashley, Coventry, and the Duke of York, all of whom were interested in the programme, whether they had a hand in framing the document or not. Among them, too, was George Monck, Duke of Albemarle, who at the outbreak of the Dutch war in 1664 remarked in his characteristically blunt fashion, "What mat-

---

1. State Papers Domestic, Charles II, 44, nos. 12 and 66; Privy Council Register, Charles II, Vol. II, 453–455. The section containing this important statement is omitted from the *Acts Privy Council, Colonial*, I, §537, but is printed in the *Calendar Treasury Books*, I, 305.

2. Bodleian, Clarendon Papers, 75, fo. 300.

ters this or that reason. What we want is more of the trade the Dutch now have."[1] Royalists and old parliamentarians were alike agreed on the need of maintaining and advancing the commercial policies of the Commonwealth and the Protectorate and on the importance of a larger marine, an increase of seamen, closer relations with the plantations, and a firmer control of the fisheries as a means of improving trade and adding to the revenue—the end and aim of it all.[2] Class lines had little place in the support of these measures, for they concerned not class leadership or influence but the safety and prosperity of the realm as well as the profits of those engaged in trade.

The first of the two chief acts of navigation and trade was passed by the Convention Parliament, September 13, 1660, and confirmed, July 27, 1661, by the regular parliament which met at Westminster on May 8 of that year. The second was passed by the latter parliament on July 27, 1663. Other and supplemental measures were added in 1662, 1670, 1671, and 1673, which contain modifications and explanations but in no way alter the main features of the policy.[3]

The opening paragraph of the act of 1660 provides that no goods or commodities whatever, no matter where from or where produced, could be imported into or exported out of any English plantation, except in English ships, of which three-fourths of the sailors should be English and the master an English subject. This simply meant that no foreign ships—Spanish, Portuguese, French, Danish, Dutch, or other—could engage in trade with the plantations, at any time or in any way, or import any of the colonial products into England.[4]

1. Jane, *Heresies of Sea Power*, p. 151.

2. In a report of the commissioners of the customs regarding the desire of the Scots to be included within the terms of the Navigation Act, October 6, 1661, the commissioners recommended that the request be not granted because the Scots traded "at large with mixture of other nations, especially the Dutch, to whom they are most contiguous and who no doubt will worke into them as well as shipping as mariners against which the act principally aims at." The lord treasurer, in his turn, added that the main end of the act was the increase of English mariners, and that no other shipping or mariners, not even Scottish, could "engorge," for this would defeat the ends of the act (State Papers Domestic, Charles II, 44, no. 12. Omitted in *Acts Privy Council, Colonial,* I, §537). It is well known that any act passed in the colonies, which affected adversely the revenue of England, was immediately disallowed.

3. The debate on these measures, as far as it is recorded in the journals, can be followed in Stock, *Debates,* I, 281–400.

4. It is probable that in this particular the act was well obeyed. Hunter said in 1718 that no foreign vessel had been to New York since he had been in office, and Keith, who had been a surveyor general of the customs in the colonies and was at the time

They could not unload and sell their cargoes in any colonial port or load there for shipment to England or the Continent any article made or produced in an English colony. The question was asked afterward, in 1720, whether Spanish ships, coming from Spanish possessions in America and laden with the products of those countries, could unload and sell their cargoes at an English plantation, in this case Barbados, and there take on a new cargo. The question was sent to Richard West, the standing counsel of the Board of Trade, and by him answered, as it had to be answered, in the negative, for the clause of the act is perfectly clear on this point and no exceptions or licenses were allowed.[1] A form of this trade had been going on for years, with Jamaica as the entrepôt, where the governors had connived at the coming of Spanish ships and the planters had welcomed them, because they bought negroes and English-manufactured goods and paid for them in silver coin and bullion. Such a trade was contrary to the navigation acts, which forbade the exportation from the English colonies of any goods or commodities in foreign vessels. Its legality was frequently questioned, but the English government allowed it, because of its monetary importance.[2]

Foreigners could not trade with the English plantations, but English and colonial ships could trade freely with the foreign plantations, provided they did not export thence certain specially enumerated colonial commodities and provided they were willing at a later time to take the not very serious risks of capture by French or Spaniards for violating the treaties of neutrality of 1670 and 1686.[3]

---

deputy governor of Pennsylvania, informed the Board of Trade that he could "never learn or discover that any trade was carried on by the French to the British settlements in violation of the Act of Navigation" (*Calendar State Papers, Colonial*, 1714–1718, §§227, 739). Nevertheless there is record of ships, chiefly Dutch and Portuguese, being seized for importing the products of the plantations into England.

1. Chalmers, *Opinions of Eminent Lawyers*, II, 269–270; *Board of Trade Journal*, 1718–1722, p. 200.

2. Beer, *The Old Colonial System*, I, pt. 1, 362–363; Nettels, *Money Supply*, ch. I. This trade raised two interesting questions: were negroes and money commodities under the navigation acts? If so the trade was clearly illegal. The English crown lawyers easily decided the first question in the affirmative; but the second, a very serious one from the point of view of the money supply of England and the colonies, seemed to be covered by clause xv of the act, "Provided that this act or anything herein contained extend not to bullion," and therefore never became an issue.

3. *Calendar State Papers, Colonial*, 1716–1717, §572; 1717–1718, p. 251, §§598, 633, 636. For the treaties of Madrid (1670) and London (1686) see Davenport, *European Treaties*, II, 187–196, 309–323. The question became of considerable importance after 1713, when traders carried the horses, asses, negroes, etc., of the British

Strictly speaking, their vessels could not be condemned or their cargoes confiscated by English officials or vice-admiralty courts, even though such trading might be forbidden by treaties of peace or royal proclamations. Though this view of the case was not always adhered to, and vessels were seized for violating the treaties, nevertheless the practice was not contrary to any English statute, and the lawyers of the day were agreed that only acts of parliament and not treaties were binding on English subjects. In the eye of the law, the latter were not obliged to obey the terms of a treaty or to submit to the orders contained in a royal proclamation, unless they wished to do so. The king could never do more than admonish his subjects to keep the law that was already in existence.[1]

This regulation regarding shipping and the regulations that follow

West Indies to the French islands and brought back French sugars. The planters objected strongly to the practice, but were unable to prevent it because it was not contrary to the navigation acts. Some of them wished parliament to pass a new law preventing it. Barbados and Nevis tried to check it by imposing duties on such foreign sugars as were imported into their ports. Antigua by local act prohibited such importation on the ground that it glutted the island market, lowered the price of sugar, aided the French islands, and led to the re-exportation of French sugars to England as a British product. The planters had much to say also about the superiority of the French and Dutch colonies as newer, fresher, richer, and more fertile than their own and consequently able to supply sugars at lower cost and so to undersell the British producer (*Calendar State Papers, Colonial,* 1717-1718, §§103, 148, 227, 317, 487, 547, 611, pp. 194, 195, 231, 236, 251, 330). In 1736 Montserrat passed an act "for the more effectual preventing all trade in those ports between his Majesty's subjects and the French," because of the seizure in that year of two Montserrat vessels at Martinique under an edict of Louis XV issued in 1727, interpreting the treaty of 1686 (printed in part in Gee, *The Trade and Navigation of Great Britain Considered,* Conclusion, pp. 6-7). According to the treaty all English or other foreign vessels were to be seized that were found within a league of any of the French island ports. This incident led to considerable diplomatic correspondence (*Board of Trade Journal,* 1735-1741, pp. 136, 142, 148, 154, 155). As to the treaty of 1670, Spain insisted that "in the course of navigation [the English] ought not to touch upon [Spanish] coasts or trade with any of her subjects." (Stock, *Debates,* IV, 791, 792). For Walpole's ideas on the subject, *ibid.,* pp. 793-794.

1. Gooch, *English Democratic Ideas in the Seventeenth Century,* p. 55. This point about the binding nature of a royal proclamation came up in connection with Endecott's seizure of Thomas Morton in 1628. Morton denied that the royal proclamation of November 6, 1622, prohibiting interloping and disorderly trading with the Indians in New England, could bind him in any respects whatever. Morton knew his law better than did Endecott. Even the commissioners of the customs in England expressed a doubt "whether an information [in a vice-admiralty court] will lie on the said proclamation; on which doubt the King has taken the advice of his learned council" (*Calendar Treasury Books,* IX, 146, 208). The most conspicuous case of this refusal to obey a royal proclamation is to be found in the colonial disregard of the Proclamation of 1704, laying down a uniform valuation for foreign coins in the colonies.

in the next sixteen paragraphs of the act are largely a confirmation of the rules laid down in the ordinance of 1651, which had to be re-enacted, because after the Restoration of the monarchy the Commonwealth ordinance ceased to be binding in law. But they differ from the ordinance in certain important particulars. Whereas in 1651 the clauses of the ordinance relating to direct shipments from Europe required that all goods brought in English or alien ships should be from the place of growth or the usual ports of first shipment, in 1660 only certain specified or enumerated goods were so designated. Furthermore by the act of 1660 the rules regarding the mastering and manning of English ships were worked out in greater detail and the requirement was made more rigorous that ships of foreign countries importing enumerated goods produced within their borders had not only to be owned but also to be built and manned there.

According to the act, no goods or commodities of Asia, Africa, or America could be imported into England or the plantations except in ships owned by the people of England, Ireland, Wales, or Berwick-upon-Tweed, or built in and belonging to the plantations.[1] Neither Newfoundland[2] nor Guinea[3] was rated as a plantation; Tangier was a borough and a port but not a plantation;[4] and oddly enough at first the three lower counties of Delaware were not so considered, for in January, 1686, Henry Guy, secretary to the Treasury Board, recommended that they be so adjudged and that the merchants trading thither be required to give security and pay duties as did those of the other colonies.[5] But a decade later the Treasury recovered its wits and in matters of trade the counties were classed with the other proprieties.

---

1. It must be remembered that the navigation act applied only to merchant vessels engaged in trade and not to vessels of the royal navy or to vessels contracted for by the Navy Board to transport supplies necessary for the navy. In the latter case navy vessels were not subject to the usual customs inspection—a matter which made some trouble with customs collectors in the colonies—while vessels contracted for by the Navy Board could be "unfree," however manned, and even be owned by foreigners.

2. *Calendar State Papers, Colonial*, 1685–1688, §1097.

3. *Ibid.*, 1699, §755.

4. 25 Charles II, c. 7, ii, "Tangier only excepted." The trade of northern Africa through Tangier was one of the advantages that England hoped to secure from the possession of this Moroccan port. For arguments in favor of such a trade, see *The Present State of Tangier* (1667?) and *A Discourse touching Tangier* (1680), both anonymous. Also, Vol. III, 32, note 1, 69.

5. *Calendar Treasury Books*, VIII, 517. In 1696 the commissioners of the customs were rating the three lower counties among the plantations, because they were under Penn's proprietary government (*House of Lords Manuscripts*, new series, II,

Of these ships the masters and three-fourths of the sailors had to be "English." In 1662, by the Statute of Frauds, which was designed to explain the Act of Navigation,[1] this word was defined to mean "only his Majesty's subjects of England, Ireland, and the plantations,"[2] thus excluding the inhabitants of the Channel Islands, the Isle of Man, and Scotland, none of whom could trade directly with the plantations, and in case any of their merchants did bring plantation goods into England he would have to pay alien customs. The Scots strongly protested against this definition as not only unjust but illegal, since a Scotsman was English under the common law.[3] But the English authorities were determined that all benefits from the act should accrue to the realm of England only. In this sense the act of 1660, as well as that of 1662, was directed as much against the Scots as against the Dutch, inasmuch as the Scots during these years were systematically making use of Dutch-built shipping.[4] Appar-

21), and in that year they appointed a separate collector for New Castle (*Calendar Treasury Books*, XI, 513; *Pennsylvania Colonial Records*, I, 534, 543). This was before the counties had a separate legislature.

There was a "sub-collector" at New Castle as early as 1677, but he had nothing to do with collecting the plantation duty, being only a subordinate under the ducal collector at New York to receive the provincial not the parliamentary duties. Lewis, *Thomas Spry*, pp. 48–52.

1. *Calendar Treasury Books*, X, 339, 558, 571–572, 698.

2. 13–14 Charles II, c. 11, §vi; *Calendar Treasury Books*, XIV, 324, 406.

3. Ridpath, *The Case of Scots-Men Residing in England and the English Plantations* (1703), pp. 3–4; Chalmers, *Opinions*, II, 392. This definition of the statute was accepted by Edward Randolph (*North Carolina Colonial Records*, I, 440; *House of Lords Manuscripts*, new series, II, 451) and by the House of Lords in committee (Stock, *Debates*, II, 143). In 1682 Randolph, who hated the Scots and would have been glad to see them entirely barred from all the advantages of the navigation acts, seized a vessel belonging to Boston, which had one "Robt Wallis a Scotchman-born to be her master and owner." The defense was that the ship was owned by Boston men, and the fact that Wallis was a Scotsman did not affect the situation. The ship was discharged. In anger Randolph wrote, "all Scotchmen are here accounted his Maties subjects in New England" (C. O. 1:49, pt. 1, no. 52; calendared only by title, *Calendar State Papers, Colonial*, 1681–1685, §690. See also *Calendar Treasury Books*, XIV, 324, 406). In 1670 a ship from Holland with commodities for Barbados was seized and condemned and the goods sold "on pretence that she was not sailed with so many English as the Act of Trade requires, though they had a number of Scotsmen who hazarded their lives in the last war against the Dutch, and take it wondrous unkind to be thus debarred the liberty of subjects" (*ibid.*, §163). For an interesting case of an alleged Scottish ship carrying passengers and household goods to the Delaware River see *Calendar Treasury Books*, VII, 1455; VIII, 212–213, 1009; *Pennsylvania Colonial Records*, I, 90–91. The vessel was seized and condemned in 1683 by the governor and council of Pennsylvania. We shall have occasion to notice this case again.

4. Barbour, "Dutch and English Merchant Shipping," p. 287.

ently a Scotsman resident in England, with fixed home and family there, could purchase and enjoy lands and liberties and trade as if he were an Englishman, without naturalization or denization. He was accounted a subject of the king of England within the meaning of the statute. It is, however, doubtful whether a Scotsman-born, who had a home only temporarily in England and paid rates there, could be accepted as an "English" sailor and be counted with the three-fourths complement.[1] But one thing is clear—a Scotsman in Scotland was an alien; and for the ensuing forty-seven years, from the point of view of the navigation acts and England's commercial policy, Scotland was reckoned as a stranger land. We shall have frequent occasion to demonstrate this situation, as we follow the relations between the two countries down to the time of the union.[2]

In the case of the Channel Islands—Guernsey, Jersey, Alderney, and Sark—an exception was made as regards their shipping, which

1. Solicitor General Powys, answering the question whether a Scotsman-born, but being an inhabitant of and having a family in England, was to be deemed his Majesty's subject within the meaning of the acts of trade, decided in the affirmative. The case came up in connection with two Scotsmen, Mowatt and Moncrief, born in Scotland, but for divers years residents and housekeepers in Wapping, who had been required by the custom house to pay alien duties. On receiving Powys' opinion that they had lived there long enough to be styled subjects of England, the Treasury ruled in their favor and ordered the excess payments to be returned (*Calendar Treasury Books*, VIII, 1501, 1525; IX, 170). On the other hand many a Scottish sailor, living in Wapping or elsewhere in England, married to an English wife, and even paying scot and lot in the parish was reckoned a "stranger" and not counted in the three-quarters group (*ibid.*, VII, 797). See below, p. 73, note 1.

2. The editor of the *Calendar of Treasury Books*, Dr. W. A. Shaw, has the following note (in the volume for 1667–1668, p. 202) on a remarkable statement made in a letter from the Treasury to the governors of the plantations: "This recital here given of the Act [of 1660] contains the following extraordinary words: 'and for the further and more peculiar appropriating the trade of these plantations to the Kingdom of England *exclusive from all other His Majesty's dominions.*' These words are not to be found in either of Charles' Navigation Acts, 12 Car. II. c. 18 and 15 Car. II, c. 7. In the former of these acts Ireland is joined with England, Wales and Berwick-on-Tweed in the enjoyment of the benefits of the Act, and this stipulation is again enacted in the Act of 14 Car. II, c. 11 for preventing frauds, etc. The words italicized reveal (what the Statute Book conceals) how far in the mind of the English Government the Navigation Act was directed against Scotland (as well as against Holland)."

Unlike Ireland, Scotland was construed as an alien kingdom, in that it did not belong to the crown of England and its laws did not have to pass the Privy Council, as was the case with Ireland under the operation of Poynings' law, before being acted on in the Irish parliament. An order in council and the great seal of England had effect in Ireland as they did in Scotland, but the great officers of England had jurisdiction in Ireland only and not in Scotland.

was construed as English built,[1] but no exception was made as regards their commerce. Although under section fourteen their inhabitants could trade directly with any of the ports of Spain or Portugal or with those of the Azores, Madeira, or the Canaries, they were not allowed by the Act of Navigation to deal directly with the English plantations,[2] to serve as mariners on board ships that had a right so to do, or to bring colonial raw materials into English ports. The last-named privilege (of bringing raw materials into English ports) remained undetermined for some time, until in 1671 it was brought up before the Privy Council for adjudication. The petitioners from the Channel Islands tried to plead the ancient privileges of the island of Jersey, but the Privy Council refused to allow any departure from the express terms of the act, believing that the Channel Islanders were in league with the French (as they probably were) in conducting their trading business. When a French ship from St. Malo returned from Virginia to Guernsey laden with tobacco (itself a breach of the law) and was seized by English customs officials, the islanders resisted, alleging "the privileges of the island for their justification." They rubbed out the king's broad arrow, obstructed the officers in the performance of their duty, and finally made it possible for both ship and cargo to get away to France.[3]

Though occasionally such colonial products as Barbados rum were brought from Guernsey to English outports and admitted there, the importation was clearly contrary to the statute. But it was not until

1. 12 Charles II, c. 18, §vii.

2. A ship was seized in 1685 in East New Jersey for so trading (C. O. 1:55, no. 169; inadequately calendared in *Calendar State Papers, Colonial*, 1685–1688, §261. The ship was the *Dolphin*. For the importance of the seizure in the history of East New Jersey see *Journal of the Courts of Common Right and Chancery of East New Jersey 1693–1702*, Edsall, ed., pp. 135–136). For a debate on the right of the inhabitants of the island of Jersey to trade with America see *Calendar Treasury Books*, III, 1011 (1672). Another ship was seized at Portsmouth, New Hampshire, because coming from Jersey with goods not landed first in England as the law required (*Calendar State Papers, Colonial*, 1701, §669. Compare, 1702–1703, §697). The nearness of the Channel Islands to the French coast and their close association with the merchants of St. Malo led the English to believe that their trade was far too often a French trade in reality. Captain Taverner of Newfoundland reported a Guernsey ship upon the fishing banks at St. Pierre in 1716, with eight boats one season and sixteen the next, its principal officers and most of its men Mallouins. Taverner was informed that several other Guernsey ships were in fact French vessels, owned, provisioned, and manned. *Calendar State Papers, Colonial*, 1716–1717, p. 15.

3. *Acts Privy Council, Colonial*, I, §§927, 932, 936, 957, 963, 1068, 1072, 1084, 1182; *Calendar State Papers, Colonial*, 1675–1676, §840; *Calendar Treasury Books*, III, 978, 1011, 1170; IX, 1297.

1744 that the rule was definitely laid down by the Treasury,[1] that no one should bring from the Channel Islands into any port of the kingdom products from the English colonies, because not first taken on at the place of their origin. The Channel Islanders were not "English" nor the islands a "plantation." Of course accidents might happen and vessels, which had not originally obtained their cargoes at the place of growth, might be driven into an English port by stress of weather, or to escape an enemy, or to take on a supply of wood, water, and provisions, things always allowed, and in such cases the customs officials were inclined to be lenient, though invariably with an eye open for possible frauds. But these happenings were exceptional and did not affect the general rule that the Channel Islands were in largest part outside the privileged area of the navigation acts. From this time forward the islands became the center of a vast amount of smuggling. Wool, East India calicoes and silks, and Virginia tobacco were frequently exported from England to the islands in far larger quantities than the islanders needed or their consumption would warrant, and the suspicion was well founded that many of these goods eventually found their way to France. This traffic was carried on in defiance partly of the acts of trade and navigation and partly of the acts passed in 1678, 1689, 1693, and 1704 prohibiting trade with France.[2]

In the case of the Isle of Man no exceptions of any kind were made. Returned to the house of Stanley on the Restoration, with the countess dowager and Charles Stanley, eighth earl of Derby, as its proprietors, the island lay wholly outside the privileges of the act of 1660 and of all the acts that followed. Its customs were not under the control of the royal officers, who apparently knew very little about them, and the island became a rendezvous for smugglers and owlers engaged in running prohibited goods, chiefly rum and tobacco, into England, Ireland, and Scotland. At times the Treasury was able to come to an agreement with the proprietors,[3] whereby a royal customs official was allowed to reside on the island, collecting

1. Treasury 27:21, p. 474.

2. *House of Lords Manuscripts,* new series, II, 194–195; VI, 210, 255, 256, 295; *The Mercator,* no. 156; *Lords' Journal,* XV, 667, 670; 3–4 Anne, c. 13, "Importation of French Goods Prohibitive Bill." Inasmuch as any foreigner endenized could qualify as the master of a ship trading to the plantations, provided there was nothing in his letter of denization forbidding it (*Calendar State Papers, Colonial,* 1701, §507), any individual inhabitant of the Channel Islands could qualify under this rule.

3. Certain privileges were accorded the Earl of Derby, such as the right to import from or export to the island "such household provisions as have been usually allowed

the customs on lease or farm from the proprietor.[1] But this was not always possible or successful and the running of goods went on for another century.[2] In 1765, parliament bought out the governmental rights of the proprietors of that date—the Duke of Atholl and others —and brought the island directly under the control of the Privy Council and the king's officers. But even this did not stop smuggling, for by the acts passed in 1765 and 1766 the colonists were forbidden to carry rum to the Isle of Man and were required to give a bond not to do so.[3] It is much to be feared that some of these same colonists were none too scrupulous in bonding themselves and often engaged in the pleasurable and profitable sport of carrying rum and tobacco to the Isle of Man for illegal running into England and Scotland in the years immediately before the American Revolution.

Let us return for a moment to the situation in Scotland, where the

to himself and his ancestors"—beer, bullocks, herrings, feathers, puffins, fish, and hawks from the island and to the island horses, geldings, plate, and other household and traveling necessaries. *Calendar Treasury Books,* IX, 1261–1262.

1. For instances of this kind see Treasury 27:10, *passim,* and for the question how far the statutes extended to the Isle of Man, Chalmers, *Opinions,* I, 203–204 (1727). It was well understood that the Channel Islands and the Isle of Man were not bound by the acts of parliament, unless expressly named in the acts. But the islanders generally denied that parliament could legislate for them at all and asserted that the navigation acts did not run in Jersey. The commissioners of the customs would not allow this claim. *Calendar Treasury Books,* XII, 300.

2. On February 16, 1683, Henry Guy, in the name of the Treasury, wrote to the commissioners of the customs as follows: "The Lords Commissioners of his Mats Treasury, having received an intimation from Ireland of some fraudulent practices of Merchants in the Isle of Man, by which meanes his Majesty is much prejudiced in his customes and imported excise in the three Kingdomes, and that the said Island (by the advantage the Merchants take there to break Bulk and run their Wines, Tobacco, and fine goods from thence in small Boats on shore in the creeks of the three Kingdoms without paying any Duty) is become a meer nusance to the King's Revenue, Their Lops desire you to consider whether there is anything fitt to be done (more than has been already) for his Majestys service" (Treasury 27:6, pp. 110 ff.; letters of March 10, 1683, *ibid.,* p. 122, and of August 21, 1683, p. 200). In the letter of August 21 mention is made of "a scandalous person there under your commission against whom if our complaints were of no creditt yet the notoriety of the Plantacon and other prohibited trade that to this day [August 21, 1683] is slipt through that place contrary to the two Acts of Parliament in force there, will evidence him a fraudulent or at least a useless officer there." On the same subject, *Calendar Treasury Books and Papers,* II, 1731–1734, §207; *Board of Trade Journal,* 1708–1715, pp. 121, 241, 243, 244, 248, 250, 254–256, 257; *Calendar State Papers, Colonial,* 1710–1711, §§40, 128, 135; report of the board, February 17, 1710, C. O. 389:21, pp. 71–74, on complaints from Whitehaven of illegal trade in colonial tobacco carried on by the Isle of Man.

3. 5 George III, cc. 26, 39, §v; 6 George III, c. 43; *Scots Magazine,* 1764, pp. 456–457 (smuggling); 1765, pp. 77–82 (case of the Duke of Athole), 165 (parliamentary debate, March, 1765), 308, 335–344 (abstract of the act, 5 George III, c. 26).

relations with England were much more intricate and much more difficult to settle. About two weeks before the ratification by parliament, on July 27, 1661, of the act of 1660, the Scottish parliament itself passed an act of trade, modeled on the law of England, that was designed to place England in exactly the same situation with regard to Scotland that the English had placed Scotland with regard to England.[1] It was undoubtedly passed as a retaliatory measure, but was not intended to be enforced should England suspend the operation of her act in Scotland's favor, which the Scots profoundly hoped would be the case. But the effect of the Scottish threat was exactly the opposite of what was expected, for the act increased the feeling of bitterness in England and probably had something to do with hastening the ratification by parliament of the act of 1660 two weeks later. On hearing of this ratification the Scots sent the earls of Glencairn and Rothes as delegates to England, who on August 30 petitioned Charles II to interpose with the English parliament that Scotland might be admitted to the privileges of the act, on the ground that by limiting the import and export of foreign goods to English, Welsh, and Irish vessels it would ruin the shipping and trade of the Scots. The first reply of the Privy Council was favorable to Scotland, for by order of August 30, 1661, the board suspended temporarily the operation of the act. But in the meantime the petition of the Scottish lords was referred to the lord high treasurer and by him to the commissioners of the customs for report. On October 30 the latter replied in a long statement, which was made up after serious debate and many conferences among the commissioners themselves.[2] This report is of great interest as presenting the arguments that must have been used in the Convention Parliament to bring about the passage of the first navigation act of 1660.

The commissioners said that if this Scottish act should stand and the English act be suspended in Scotland's favor, it would abate the royal revenues and bring infinite loss to the king and much prejudice to his English subjects. It would also "overthrow the very es-

1. Stock, *Debates*, I, 445–447; *Statutes of Scotland*, VII, 257, "Act for encouraging Shiping and Navigation." At the same time the Scots set up a council of trade, also modeled on that of England.

2. The documents in the case are in State Papers Domestic, Charles II, 44, no. 12. The entire statement is in four sections, of which only the second is printed in the *Acts Privy Council, Colonial*, I, §§536, 537. One section is given in Beer, *The Old Colonial System*, I, vol. I, 87, taken from the *Calendar Treasury Books*, I, 305–306. The entire report has never been printed.

sence and design of the act of navigation" by discouraging the building of English ships, by aiding the Dutch and other nations to England's disadvantage, and by driving the English out of the trade abroad, because the Scots would set lower rates and so undersell the English wherever the two peoples came into competition. They said that the liberties which the Scots asked for of trading from port to port "would be very prejudicial and improper to be granted, because the Scots are to us strangers and as prohibited by law." Their trade would not be covered by bond, and even if it were, as the Scots promised would be the case, "what security is good from strangers that have no real estate?" If bond were given it could not be sued for to the advantage either of the king or of the people. If the Scots were residents in England, the commissioners continued, if they had responsible estates, and if they would submit to the same laws and rates as the English themselves, then they might be admitted, for "wee know them subjects with us under one sovereign and would gladly admitt them into one brotherhood of trade, but otherwise wee conceive it destructive to the English interest, prejudicial to his Majesty in his customs and duties, and absolutely pernicious to the act of navigation, which the English seem to cherish as a child of theyr own, both for publique and private honour, safety, and advantage to the English nation."

Lord Treasurer Southampton, with Ashley, Anglesey, and George Carteret as signers of the statement, decided that the suspension of the act could be effected only by act of parliament and not by order in council, an important constitutional decision, quite apart from its bearing on the Scottish question. Such suspension in any case would be clearly contrary to the act of 1660 and could not stand in law, for by it "English shipping and mariners must necessarily be the lesse imployed the more the others are, and if the Scotch can undersayle or [under]trade them, as in the French trade we understand they can £40 in every hundred tunn, then the Losse must be greater. And if the Dutch (which is very possible) get any covert under the Scotch the ill consequence is more," and the Englishman's trade would certainly fall off.[1] "And if these pay single customs which should pay double, your Majesties Customs must needs decrease."

1. That the Dutch did profit from the Scottish trade, owing to the use made by the Scots of Dutch-built shipping, and that they stood in very close contact with the Scottish exporters in the royal boroughs is clearly brought out in Davidson and Gray, *The Scottish Staple at Veere.*

Even the proposal that the Scots be allowed to trade to the plantations in no more than five or six ships was rejected, because "your Majesty's customes might be concerned thereby nigh twenty thousand pounds by the year."

On receiving this report from the lord high treasurer, the Privy Council, November 22, 1661, reversed its decision and referred the petitioners to parliament for redress. Scotland reverted to its position as an alien country. In 1667 parliament, after long negotiations, passed an act "for settling freedom and intercourse of trade between England and Scotland,"[1] and under its terms English commissioners met Scottish commissioners in the effort to carry out the intent of the act. But the demands of the Scots were too sweeping,[2] and in the end nothing was accomplished. Conditions remained exactly as they had been before. A few dispensations were granted to individual Scotsmen, which aroused the criticisms of the commissioners of the customs and others in the opposition, because of the injury wrought upon the English customs revenue by such royal interference, but otherwise the situation underwent no change from this time to 1707, and the Scots continued to be debarred from any direct trade with the colonies during these years. An attempt at union was made, as we shall see, under William III, and another at retaliation in 1693 and 1695, but without result. Admission to the trading monopoly of England by the Union of 1707 finally reconciled the discouraged Scots to the loss of their parliamentary independence.[3]

Thus no Channel Islander, Manxman, or Scotsman resident in Scotland could trade directly with the plantations, though a Scotsman residing permanently in England or the plantations could enjoy many if not all the privileges of the act. A Scotsman in the colo-

1. 19 Charles II, c. 13.

2. Bruce, *Report on the Events and Circumstances which produced the Union of the Kingdoms of England and Scotland* (1799), I, 189–214. The Scots demanded "an absolute inclusion in the act of navigation, as Englishmen; and that in all things relating thereto, they be considered as English and enjoy equal privileges; and demaunded that as well their foreign built shipping, as those of their own built may be comprehended in this priviledge" (*ibid.,* II, cclxxxv, "An Abstract for his Majesty," May 20, 1668). For the Scottish objections and arguments, 1667–1669, *ibid.,* II, appendix, xxxi–xlv.

3. Keith, *Commercial Relations of England and Scotland 1603–1707;* Dicey and Rait, *Thoughts on the Union between England and Scotland,* pt. ii; Defoe, *History of the Union* (1709). Now that the navigation acts have been repealed and under the improved trading conditions of the twentieth century, many Scotsmen wish to recover their parliamentary independence.

nies could hold office, do business, and have all the advantages of
English subjects under the common law interpretation of his status
(at that time more binding even than an act of parliament) to the
effect that he was a king's subject born within the king's allegiance.[1]
An Irishman, at first allowed to trade under the act and always
qualified to serve as master or sailor, was later debarred, as we shall
see in discussing the Irish situation, and forbidden to have any direct commercial connections with America, except in certain specified
particulars. All aliens were likewise debarred, unless they had been
naturalized or made full denizens.[2] An endenized Frenchman or
any other foreigner could serve as the master of a vessel trading to
America and presumably could trade there, if the terms of his denization allowed.[3] A Jew born abroad, whether resident or not in England or the colonies, was never fully recognized as qualified, partly
because it was always a debatable matter whether Jews should be
admitted at all and partly because the English authorities were never
quite certain that a colonial governor had a right to endenize a foreigner in the colonies.[4] Nevertheless many a Jew did engage in busi-

1. *Calendar State Papers, Colonial,* 1700, §517; Beer, *Old Colonial System,* I, vol.
II, 88–91. How far Scotsmen forbidden to trade with the plantations, to serve as mas-
ters, or to make up the three-quarters group as sailors could enjoy these privileges in
case they should take up their residence in the colonies is a question not easy to an-
swer. Probably they would be allowed to serve on colonial but not on English vessels.
But in case any of them returned to his native land presumably his privileges ceased.
It was a debated point, as we have already seen, whether such an one returning to
England and taking up his residence there could continue to serve. Yet in 1699, John
Sansom of the Custom House in London wrote to the Board of Trade that, according
to an opinion expressed by the Privy Council, natives of Scotland inhabiting with their
families in England, Ireland, Wales, or Berwick-upon-Tweed were to be accounted
English within the meaning of the acts (*Calendar State Papers, Colonial,* 1699, §763).
Berwick men were always suspected of being in reality Scotsmen. Cf. *ibid.,* 1701, §507.

2. In the matter of naturalization, an interesting case came up in New York in 1691
as to the right of certain Dutch merchants there to trade under the act. The customs
officials demanded of them the payment of "stranger duties," on the ground that they
were not "natives of New York" but natives of Holland, had not been naturalized by
act of parliament, and had not been born within the colony since the capture by the
English. The commissioners of the customs and the Treasury decided in favor of the
merchants. *Calendar Treasury Books,* IX, 1159. For a similar Maryland case, *Maryland Archives,* XLIX, xxii, 323–324, 388, 391–393.

3. *Calendar State Papers, Colonial,* 1701, pp. 28–29, §§390, 464, 507. An act of
naturalization made a foreigner in all respects an English subject, but letters of denization from the king gave him no more privileges than were expressly mentioned in
the document.

4. Start, "Naturalization in the English Colonies of America," *Report,* American
Historical Association, 1893, pp. 323 ff. The question of denization was raised by a

ness in the plantations, either under special acts locally passed or under letters patent of denization, and in Jamaica especially Jews carried on their trade, possessed lands, and enjoyed the rights and privileges of natural-born subjects, with the approval of the secretary of state. They could not, however, vote or hold political office.[1]

The requirement that three-fourths of the sailors be "English" was more precise than the "for the more part" of the act of Henry VII or the "for the most part of them" of the ordinance of 1651, and by just so much was it impossible of enforcement, particularly as the further rule was laid down that the proportion must be maintained for the whole voyage.[2] The practice soon became common of filling up vacancies caused by desertion, sickness, death, or other causes, by taking on foreigners, notably in the Mediterranean, the Baltic, and the Caribbean, or East Indians, lascars, negroes, and others in East India and West India waters. This course was often rendered either necessary because frequently English, Irish, or colonial sailors could not be obtained, or advantageous because it was cheaper to employ foreigners and blacks who served for lower wages.[3]

number of the colonial governors in 1701. Codrington wrote to the Board of Trade, "The Acts of Trade say especially the master shall be an Englishman. I humbly conceive nothing less than naturalization can make an Englishman. One of the Acts indeed allows a denizen to be master of a ship in the creeks of England, Ireland and Guernsey, but all the acts say the master of a ship trading to the plantations shall be English. I beg you will send me the opinion of the Attorney and Solicitor General." The board endeavored to settle the question by referring it to Trevor and Hawles, who replied, "We think a Foreigner endenized is qualified to be master of a ship trading to the plantations, unless there be a provision in the Letters Patent of Denization to the contrary" (*Calendar State Papers, Colonial*, 1701, §§26, i, 82, 390, 404, 464, 472, 507, 755). The question came up again in 1736, when the board, fortified by legal opinions expressed in 1703 and 1719, agreed that "no foreigner, naturalized in the plantations, can thereby claim the priviledges of a natural born subject of this kingdom." *Board of Trade Journal*, 1735–1741, p. 92.

1. *Calendar State Papers, Colonial*, 1661–1668, §140; 1717–1718, §622. A case occurred in Connecticut, where one John Carsen, a Jew and an alien, was tried before the governor and council of the colony, on information furnished by William Dyer of New York, for landing goods at New London. Evidently Dyer charged that Carsen was a Jew and could not trade under the navigation acts. Connecticut Archives, Trade and Maritime Affairs, I, nos. 26–28.

2. By the Statute of Frauds, 13–14 Charles II, c. 11, §vi, "English" was defined as covering his Majesty's subjects of England, Ireland, and the plantations; and by the acts of 1660 and 1662 the three-fourths proportion had to be maintained for the whole voyage.

3. Chalmers, *Opinions*, II, 131. Nehemiah Grew in 1707 opposed the three-quarters rule on the ground that it prevented competition and so led to the increase of wages among British seamen. "The Meanes of a Most Ample Encrease," p. 129.

Allowances were made in the act for cases of sickness and death and for seamen taken prisoners by the enemy, but no allowance was made for runaways or deserters, who for one cause or another (brutality, rotten food, breach of agreement, or desire for change) were accustomed to clear out at every port. Desertion was the bane of every ship captain. Confronted with the necessity of continuing the voyage, the captain was compelled to take what he could get and often to return home with more "strangers" than the law allowed. During the first few years after its enactment the law was but lightly enforced, inasmuch as many vessels had gone out before the act was passed and their masters, ignorant of the regulation, would come back without the proper proportion of English seamen. Even after these cases were disposed of, the lord high treasurers, Southampton, Danby, and Rochester, were inclined to be friendly toward vessels which, having left England with the proper complement of men and having lost many by sickness, drowning, desertion, or impressment, were unable to find Englishmen in distant ports, and so had to return without the required quota. Sometimes the masters would come in with the number short by only half a man. In such cases the treasurer was willing to order the ship discharged, unless on further examination it was found that the master had sworn falsely, as was sometimes the case. Danby, who was treasurer from 1673 to 1679, "several times [gave] relief where ships having gone out regularly manned [had] by reason of some necessary [misfortune] returned wanting something to their full complement of the master and three-fourths being English."[1] It inevitably took some time for a trade, confined by so many "tyes and observances as are put upon it by the act of navigation,"[2] to accustom itself to the new channels. Though we read of many ships discharged, doubtless more were seized and condemned, for there were at the port of London a regular surveyor and assistant surveyors of the act of navigation, who were constantly on the watch to seize vessels and prosecute their owners before the court of exchequer. These men, as part of the customs personnel, were inclined to severity.

An interesting case came up in 1692, when one William Dowrich, a merchant of Plymouth, England, not being able, on account of the war, to obtain English seamen, manned his ship, which was engaged in carrying provisions to the West Indies, with French Prot-

<hr />

1. *Calendar Treasury Books,* V, 973.     2. *Ibid.,* I, 250.

estants from a place called "Stonehouse," about a mile from the town. His ship was seized as violating the act of navigation and he petitioned the Treasury for relief, on the ground that these people were inhabitants of England, had been invited over by William III after the Revocation of the Edict of Nantes, and had been promised royal protection and assistance and the immunities of natural-born subjects.[1] He claimed further that as French Protestants had been impressed to serve on English war ships they were imputed as English and therefore he was not guilty of breaking the act. His contention was upheld by the commissioners of the customs, who recommended that the ship be released.[2] Again, one Patrick Ogilvie, trading from Boston to Barbados and thence to London in a New England-built ship, having lost four men by desertion took on five Portuguese, who had been discharged from a condemned ship at Bridgetown and wanted passage back to Europe. Four of these promised to work for their passage and to pay half a moidore apiece for the fifth, who could not work because he was lame. The ship was seized at London as having five Portuguese and only eleven Englishmen making up the crew. The master sought relief because the Portuguese had served without wages. Unfortunately the report of the commissioners has not been preserved, but probably no relief was granted.[3] Two other interesting cases appear offering new reasons in mitigation. A ship was seized at Boston in 1727 and the master gave in his plea that some of the mariners deserted and he was obliged to take on foreigners because he could not wait to find Englishmen as the convoy was about to sail. Another master, his crew depleted by sickness and death, was obliged to take on four

1. Later the inhabitants of Annapolis Royal in Nova Scotia asked permission to employ the French inhabitants there on their fishing vessels "for the want of Englishmen," but the Board of Trade advised against it, because to do so would "in great measure hinder the nursery of our seamen." *Calendar State Papers, Colonial*, 1717–1718, pp. 173–174, §527.

2. Treasury 27:12, p. 211; *Calendar State Papers, Colonial*, 1701, §507; *Calendar Treasury Books*, IX, 1579–1580, where the name is given as "Nathaniel Dowrish."

3. Treasury 4:9, p. 258. The *Dolphin*, seized by William Dyer at Elizabethport, East New Jersey, June 22, 1685, comes into this category. It was owned by an Isle of Jersey man, had only one English sailor on board, one of its masters was a Frenchman and one a Bermudan, and it was bringing European goods directly to the plantations without certificate or making entry. Thus it broke the acts at four points. It was brought to trial, but a jury decided against Dyer, who was charged with the costs of the suit. On refusing to pay, he was imprisoned. C. O. 1:55, no. 169; *Calendar State Papers, Colonial*, 1685–1688, §261 (imperfectly calendared). Above, p. 67, note 2.

Frenchmen, a situation construed as an "act of God."[1] In times of war, as in 1691, 1702, 1709, 1740, and 1756, the proportion was reduced to one-half or even to one-quarter,[2] for a great many ships under the circumstances were unable to get English crews owing in part to the embargoes, and their masters frequently petitioned for relief.[3] Because of this scarcity of seamen it was further enacted in 1707 that foreigners serving two years on English ships would be considered natural-born subjects of England.[4] Ships under contract with the navy, when specifically exempted, were not obliged to conform to this rule or to any other of the shipping rules of the time as laid down by parliament.[5] Just who made up the remaining quarter, one-half, or three-quarters, as the case might be, is not material, as apparently anybody—French, Dutch, Swedes, Norwegians, Portuguese, and even Greeks—could be hired as "strangers" to complete the crew, provided the other fractional part was composed of "English" subjects.

According to section seven of the act English-built ships were defined as those of England, Ireland, Jersey and Guernsey, and the plantations. The question naturally arose as to whether foreign-built ships could be utilized and, at first, was answered in the affirmative (§§ x, xi), in case the owner took oath that such vessel was duly certificated and registered, according to the requirements of the act. Registration was always effected at some convenient local port and the certificate eventually lodged with the general registry of the exchequer at Westminster, which was kept up to date by the customs officials in London.[6] But the privilege of using foreign-built ships without restriction was soon withdrawn by the explanatory act of

1. Records of Admiralty, Massachusetts, III, 28; V, 107b (1742). In a similar case a Philadelphia-built ship (1698) was seized because two of the English sailors deserted and foreigners were taken on as Englishmen could not be obtained (*Calendar Treasury Books*, XIII, 298). In another instance a vessel sailed with 32 Englishmen: 3 died at Alexandria; 16 ran away at various places; 2 were pressed in the Downs, leaving 21 places to be filled. The master took on 7 foreigners and 3 foreign passengers, thus arriving at England with 11 Englishmen and 10 foreigners. The vessel was seized but eventually released. *Ibid.*, IX, 870–871. Compare, *ibid.*, pp. 493, 1004.

2. *Calendar State Papers, Colonial*, 1708–1709, p. 198; Stock, *Debates*, II, 34, 44–45, 46; *House of Lords Manuscripts*, new series, V, 44; 6 Anne, c. 37, §xix; 13 George II, c. 16.

3. *Calendar Treasury Books*, IX, 485, 493, 862.

4. 6 Anne, c. 37, §xx.

5. *Calendar Treasury Books*, IX, 1399, 1412.

6. The English owners of a foreign-built vessel had to take oath in the presence

1662, according to which such ships were to be treated as alien ships and held liable for all duties that alien ships were required to pay.[1] Henceforth foreign-built ships were rated as English-built, only in case as prize ships they had been legally condemned and purchased or as ships bought in the ordinary course of trade they had been naturalized or made free. At all times in peace ships were naturalized by private act of parliament or, in the special emergencies of war, by orders in council or royal warrants. Such ships were duly registered as free ships of the kingdom, privileged to enjoy all the advantages of English-built ships or such of them as were specifically named in the act or warrant.[2]

of the proper officers before receiving the certificate of registration. The master was not allowed to do this. The requirement of the oath made trouble for Edward Randolph in dealing with Quaker attestations in Pennsylvania. In 1698 he wrote to John Bewley, customs collector at Philadelphia, as follows: "If you admit him [one Puckle] or any other Quaker to register his vessel without laying his hand on the Bible and kissing it you are inexcusable. . . . I will certainly suspend your office. Take it as you please." *Calendar State Papers, Colonial,* 1697–1698, §759, ix, p. 395; *Calendar Treasury Books,* XV, 409.

1. For hardships arising out of the act of 1662, Stock, *Debates,* II, 267, 274, 297, 307, 359, 361. The greatest trouble arose in connection with the Baltic trade, where, if England were to retain any sort of control, foreign-built ships had to be bought, inasmuch as the English did not know how to build ships big enough or long enough to carry heavy timber and masts (*ibid.,* p. 306). Complaints on this score were frequent after the year 1670 and both Coke and Child express their opinions freely on the subject. The author (James Houblon?) of "The Discourse touching the Grounds of the Decay of Navigation," writing soon after 1685, urged that the government restore to the merchants the liberty of buying ships in any of the northern parts or foreign countries, in order to recover the trade in timber, masts, planks, pitch, tar, hemp, and potashes, hitherto controlled by Norway, Sweden, Denmark, and the East Country. He says: "We have hardly one ship built proper for these trades . . . so that they are almost fully in the possession of Danes, Sweeds, and Dantsickers, whose ships are built proper for such bulkie commodities, sail with few hands and are freighted by England at ½ the charge of an English ship. But let these ships so bought be manned with all English, victual'd and fitted in England and limited so as to be kept to the northeast and eastern trades and that none go below Galis [Calais] southward or to the plantations, which trades are to be kept to English-built ships, then will navigation be increased and fall into the hands of the English" (Bodleian, Rawlinson, A, fo. 283b). I owe the privilege of seeing notes on this manuscript to Miss Violet Barbour.

2. C. O. 324:4, pp. 321–324; *Acts Privy Council, Colonial,* I, §§649, 937, 1272; *Calendar Treasury Books and Papers,* IV, index under "Naturalizing." Many instances are given in Stock, *Debates,* as, for example, III, 287. In 1693 it was said that "by the common construction of the Acts of Trade and of the practice thereupon for many years past, a foreign-built ship truly owned and manned by English may import tobacco from their Majesties Plantations without forfeiture of either ship or goods, as is attested by Mr. William Waterson, one of the most ancient and experienced officers of the Port of London." *Calendar Treasury Books,* X, 181.

Owing to the ambiguity with which section six in the act was worded, differences of opinion arose as to just what would happen should a foreign-built ship be found trading with the plantations. Could such a ship be used, provided its owner paid alien duties at the English port of entry or was it liable to forfeiture as an "unfree" bottom trading contrary to law? In a document among the Treasury Papers, entitled "Suspensions and breaches of the navigation acts during war," the statement is made that foreign shipping could be employed only in trade with the kingdom of England and that no dispensations were to be permitted for trade with the plantations, Scotland, Ireland, or Tangier, but this had reference to foreign-built ships standing on terms of equality with English-built ships and paying the same duties.[1] A better case is that of a Dutch-built ship, owned and legally navigated by Englishmen, that was seized for violating the law. The board of customs commissioners, in reporting on the case, said that, "A foreign built ship, owned and manned by English, may import tobacco from their Majesties plantations as free as any English built, without forfeiture either of ship or goods, and this has been the constant practice of this port of London for many years past."[2] It would seem to have been the practice of other ports also, for we have an instance of a "foreign built vessel not made free," owned in Exeter, giving bond in 1695 to return from Virginia with colonial products to some port of the realm.[3] Up to that date, therefore, it is evident that Englishmen had been accustomed to use foreign-built ships, which if not made free were required to pay alien duties.

This privilege was, however, seemingly taken away by the act of 1696, which restrained the subjects of England from trading in English shipping, foreign built, directly to and from the plantations, a portion of the act which aroused vigorous protest at the time from petitioners, who were the owners of foreign-built ships, with which they had been accustomed to engage in the plantation trade, paying alien duties.[4] But in practice it is doubtful if any change was made. Twenty-two years later a bill was proposed by the Treasury to prevent foreign-built ships from entering the general registry at Westminster by way of Scotland, unless the vessel had been Scottish property at the time of ratifying the treaty of union and registered

---

1. Treasury 11:1, 49–51.          2. Ibid., 1:21, no. 56.
3. Maryland Archives, XX, 547–548.
4. House of Lords Manuscripts, new series, II, 233.

accordingly.[1] The question was referred to the Board of Trade, which after consideration asked Attorney General Northey for his opinion as to the meaning of the clause in the act. The attorney general replied that "foreign built ships of English property and manned by English, though purchased since the year 1662," might "make the voyages that any foreign ship made free before that time might have made" and might "lawfully trade in the enumerated goods paying alien duties."[2] As this opinion of 1718 coincided with that of the customs commissioners of 1693, we may assume as fairly certain that foreign-built ships, not made free but of English ownership and manned by Englishmen according to law, could engage in the plantation trade, without fear of forfeiture, provided their owners paid alien duties.[3]

Difficulties were always likely to arise regarding English-built ships taken by the enemy and afterward bought, owned, and manned by Englishmen, or regarding such English ships as were taken as prize and afterward rebuilt in a foreign country. In the first case the decision was reached that such ships on their return to England should not pay customs duty;[4] and in the second that though rebuilt the ships remained English if they had any part of the original vessel—even a single plank—still left in them. Ship carpenters could readily tell whether a vessel had been built or rebuilt in Sweden, Holland, or Denmark and so could detect a foreign-built ship in case an attempt was made to conceal its identity. Attorney General Northey once decided that unless rebuilt with a new keel and long employed in England, a foreign vessel remained a foreign vessel, no matter how otherwise changed.[5] One ardent mercantilist raised the ques-

1. C. O. 388:15, M, 179; *Board of Trade Journal*, 1714–1718, p. 346.

2. Chalmers, *Opinions*, II, 266–268. Northey may have been referring here to enumerated goods from the Continent not to those from the plantations.

3. It was often very difficult to determine whether a ship was "free" or not (*Maryland Archives*, XX, 589–591; XXIII, 3). There is no doubt that many a customs officer in the colonies construed the act to mean that a foreign-built ship trading to the plantations was liable to forfeiture, but there are no cases entered in existing vice-admiralty court records of that kind, although there are many of seizure for want of a register or for not being "qualified." Some of these may be cases of "unfree" ships, though not so recorded.

4. *Calendar Treasury Books*, IV, 379. This evidently refers to the duty of eleven pence for every twenty shillings of their value charged upon ships taken as prize and legally condemned. Twenty years later (1685) all foreign-built vessels employed in the coastwise trade paid at every port of delivery five shillings a ton, half for the use of the chest at Chatham and half for the use of the Trinity House hospital at Deptford (1 James II, c. 18). After 1694 the latter sum was paid to Greenwich Hospital.

5. *Calendar State Papers, Colonial*, 1714–1715, §§615, i, ii, 624. A foreign-built

tion whether "English built" did not require that the vessel be constructed of English timber, but such rendering of the term was impracticable in view of the dearness and scarcity of English oak and beech. Plantation planks and deals were sought for and obtained whenever possible throughout the eighteenth century, but plantation oak was never considered the equal of English oak or plantation pines for masts the equal of those from the eastern Baltic lands. Furthermore, plantation lumber was frequently insufficiently seasoned and liable to warp, so that however much England might look to the colonies for her naval supplies she was never, in colonial times, quite able to rid herself of the suspicion that all the plantation products were of inferior quality, as undoubtedly many of them were. Admiralty and naval officials were always strongly prejudiced against allowing ships for the royal navy to be built anywhere outside of England, but neither they nor anyone else (except perhaps the English shipwrights) seem to have objected to the use of colonial-built ships for the merchant marine. The requirement of the navigation act that merchant vessels be English or colonial built enormously increased the demand at home for English oak and cut heavily into the supply needed for the navy. Hence both the Board of Trade and

ship, taken from the French by the Dutch and never made free in England, was on one occasion obliged to take refuge in Antigua. The attorney general declared that it was a foreign vessel but not liable to seizure. A case arose in 1686, when certain merchants purchased in Sweden a foreign bottom for £65, took it to England, pulled it to pieces, and rebuilt it with English materials of a final value of £1300. It had been originally "a wracked outlandish bottom," and was rebuilt and refitted in English form. The ship was seized as a foreign bottom. The owners prayed that the vessel be naturalized or made free, but legal advice declared that it should not have been seized at all because it was already a free ship, having been "rebuilt in the King's dominions" (*Calendar Treasury Books*, VIII, 227, 1070, 1180, 1998). Another case is that of a mariner who bought a derelict flyboat, evidently built in Holland, from the serjeant of the court of vice-admiralty of the Cinque Ports. He spent £400 in refitting it and asked for its naturalization. The commissioners of the customs had no objection, so the Treasury consented, "although the case of a derelict is not expressly within the words of the Act of Frauds," 13–14 Charles II, c. 11, §v (*ibid.*, p. 2105). The *Lebanon Galley* was seized at Newfoundland by Commander Leake of the *Hampshire,* at anchor there, because foreign-built. The facts seem to have been that the vessel was colonial-built, because of the peculiar wood [cedar?] used, and had been taken to Rotterdam and changed from a brigantine into a galley (Bodleian, Rawlinson, B, 383, fos. 565–596). The evidence in the case is imperfect. A very hard instance is that of a ship seized as foreign-built, although it had been rebuilt at Wapping in keel, rigging, timber, and repairs at more than three times the original cost. The vessel was owned and manned by English subjects. In reporting on the case the customs commissioners said that "the constant construction of this Board has been that the keel gives the denomination to the superstructure." *Calendar Treasury Books,* X, 1214, 1225.

parliament refused to accede to the demand of the master ship-wrights of the River Thames in 1724 that merchant vessels be built solely in England.[1] It has been estimated that before the American Revolution nearly a third of the ships under British registry were colonial built.[2]

Simple as seemed to be the rule regarding the carrying trade, it was never very clear and involved many troublesome problems in practice. Shippers found in the act both loopholes and ambiguities. The colonists soon discovered that there was nothing in it to prevent their shipping the commodities of foreign plantations to Europe and as time went on they freighted considerable quantities of French sugar and carried them to Holland. Much of this trade must have been pursued in violation of the treaty with France of 1686 and in connivance with French colonial officials, and it must have been accompanied by a good deal of illegal trading, of which the British governors in the West Indies very frequently complained. Many difficult situations arose. Could Brazil sugars be imported from Lisbon in an alien ship, when it was well understood that any English ship, properly owned and manned, could do so, because the products of the Spanish and Portuguese plantations did not have to be brought from the place of their origin? The matter was made the subject of an extensive correspondence on the part of Sir Richard Fanshawe, ambassador at Lisbon to the king of Portugal, 1662–1664, who presented proposals for regulating the trade and suggested the erection of a Brazil company to handle it. The answer was no.[3] Was a ship trading from Norway, but built in Altona, Denmark, and carrying commodities of Norwegian growth, liable to seizure on its arrival in

1. *Board of Trade Journal,* 1722–1728, pp. 130, 131, 136, 137–138; C. O. 5:915, pp. 413–433. Samuel Wragg, a resident of Edenton, North Carolina, agent in England for the assembly of that colony in 1742, and a trader in both North and South Carolina for seventeen or eighteen years, wrote Lord Townshend regarding a bill that was introduced into parliament at this time, confining the navigation to the American plantations to British ships only. He said that "no benefit could arise from it, for, my Lord, Four Fifths of the Navigation to our Plantations is carried on in Plantation Built ships, nor is there Timber in the whole Kingdom to furnish ships for our navigation to America only . . . the consequence of restraining this Navigation . . . would be to raise the Freight possibly one Third." On Wragg, *Board of Trade Journal,* 1722–1728, p. 254; 1742–1749, pp. 15–16; and *North Carolina Colonial Records,* index. The Commissioners of the Customs were in favor of the bill, but parliament would have none of it.

2. Albion, *Forests and Sea Power,* pp. 74–75, 115.

3. Treasury 27:13, p. 385. There are five documents among Fanshawe's papers bearing on this subject.

England? According to the eighth article of the act, it was liable, but the decision is far from certain, depending on the legal question as to whether Denmark and Norway were to be considered one country for the purpose of the navigation acts.[1] Could an English ship, sailing with a cargo of logwood from Spanish Honduras to Venice, there take on commodities suitable for trade in Guinea, go to Guinea, buy negroes there and take them to any of the West Indies, thus managing an indirect trade without touching at England at all? If met with by an English man-of-war could such a ship be seized and libeled for condemnation in a court of vice-admiralty? The answer depended on whether the ship belonged to some one of the plantations and whether Guinea was reckoned a plantation. If neither was true, then the trade in all its parts was legal; if either one or the other was true, then the ship was liable to forfeiture.[2]

Other questions of a somewhat different character concerned the frequent necessity of defining the words "Goods and Commodities." Was money, that is, gold and silver coin or bullion, a commodity? If so deemed by the economists of the day, it was not so interpreted in enforcing the acts of trade. Were negroes "goods" within the meaning of the act? The decision was finally rendered in the affirmative.[3]

1. *Calendar Treasury* [*Books and*] *Papers*, 1729–1730, p. 129.

2. *Calendar State Papers, Colonial*, 1699, §§619, 755.

3. The earliest decision was rendered in 1689, when "the judges certified their opinion that negroes were merchandize" (*Calendar State Papers, Colonial*, 1708–1709, §226). This was the local ruling in the Leeward Islands (*ibid.*, 1699, p. 355). It was finally confirmed by Attorney General Eyre in 1708 (Chalmers, *Opinions*, II, 277). The claim that negroes were not merchandise was made in the case of the brigantine *Eagle*, seized in New York in 1715 and tried in the vice-admiralty court there (*Calendar State Papers, Colonial*, 1714–1715, §629, viii). The full account of this case, which is very inadequately calendared, is in C. O. 5:1051, fo. 70, "The case of the Brigantine Eagle of New York, condemned in the Court of Admiralty there the 16th August, 1715." It belongs to the period, 1697–1715, just before the extant vice-admiralty records for New York begin. In these records (II, 180) will be found an instance where salvage was allowed on negroes as goods. In 1700 negroes were sold as goods in the case of a ship condemned for illegal trading (*Calendar State Papers, Colonial*, 1700, §454). Again in a Boston case, "Two negroes, Four Casks of Brown Sugar, two Casks of Cocoa and two Pateraroes" were all lumped together as goods (*Transactions*, Colonial Society of Massachusetts, VIII, 181–182; Records of Admiralty, Massachusetts, II, 96). Negroes were always adjudged lawful prize, unless they could prove their status as freemen. In case they could so prove—a difficult matter as many negroes on prizes taken in war were from the French or Spanish islands—the judge of the vice-admiralty court released them to go where they would. Many took service on merchant ships or ships of the royal navy. In a South Carolina case (1737) three negroes, who had been found casually floating about in a canoe ten leagues off Cuba (they had escaped from the Isle of Pines), were claimed by the Admiralty as

Were live turtles to be similarly rated and could they be brought from the Danish island of St. Thomas and landed and sold at Nevis? The ship that did this was seized by the collector of customs at Charlestown, Nevis, and the matter was referred to the Treasury at home. The final decision does not appear, but if a live negro was a commodity, surely a live turtle was one also.[1] In considering the application of the act one realizes that the officials both at home and in the colonies must have been confronted with many knotty problems and must have been surprised sometimes at the manifold varieties of human ingenuity and cleverness.

a perquisite. The judge of vice-admiralty awarded them to the Admiralty, provided no owner appeared within a year and a day, but allowed the master of the vessel £12 for salvage and charges (Records of Admiralty, South Carolina, C–D, 147–167, 262). The question not unnaturally arises whether the term "dead commodities" in the Barbadian act of 1663, establishing the four and a half per cent duty, was not intentionally so expressed in order to exclude negroes from its operation.

1. C. O. 155:1, pp. 299–300.

# CHAPTER IV

## THE ENUMERATED COMMODITIES

THUS far, except in the matter of trade with the Continent, the act of 1660 differed but little from the ordinance of 1651 and did not do much more than reënact a law which had been rendered void by the return of the monarchy. But at this point, in section eighteen of the act, appears a regulation that is not to be found in the Commonwealth ordinance, though a similar rule had been enforced frequently before 1640 by orders in council and at least had been implied in the instructions to the Council of Trade of 1650.[1] This regulation said that inasmuch as the colonies were the natural sources of raw materials needed in home industries, these same materials should be monopolized by the mother country and not be allowed to go elsewhere. An early expression of this principle was, as we have already seen, the order in council of 1621, which declared that all commodities brought from Virginia should be "appropriated unto his Majesty's subjects" and that no tobacco "or any other commodities whatsoever" should "be carried into any forraine partes until the same have been first landed [in England] and his Majesties customs paid therefor."[2] The requirement of 1660 was both broader and narrower than the order of 1621. It was broader in that it included commodities of the West Indies as well as those of Virginia and Bermuda; and it was narrower in

[1]. "They are to take into their consideration the English Plantations in America or elsewhere and advise how those Plantations may be best managed, and made most useful for this Commonwealth, and how the Commodities thereof may be so multiplied and improved as (if it be possible) those Plantations alone may supply the *Commonwealth* of *England* with whatsoever it necessarily wants." Andrews, *Committees*, pp. 115–116.

[2]. *Acts Privy Council, Colonial*, I, §77. Above, p. 39. Of course England did not consume all the colonial commodities herself. A very large part of them were reexported to the Continent. The Antiguan planters once wrote, "Britain alone consumes but a smal part of the produce of these colonies, and the rise [in the price] of sugar always depends upon the encouragement there is for the [re]exportation of it." *Calendar State Papers, Colonial*, 1717–1718, p. 236.

Both the Virginia Company of London and the Council for New England strongly objected to the enumeration as stated in 1621. The latter said in 1622, "To restrayne trade to this Island (that consists on Tradeing) is hard." *Proceedings*, American Antiquarian Society, 1867, p. 68.

that at first it limited the number of the enumerated commodities to a few leading staples and said nothing about "all other commodities whatsoever."

The list as given in the act of 1660 and the subsequent act of 1663 is short but highly selective, covering certain valuable raw materials of the English plantations, for which England would otherwise have been dependent on competing European rivals—sugar, tobacco, cotton, indigo, ginger, and speckle-wood, together with the various dye-woods, such as fustic and braziletto. These commodities were "enumerated," that is, could be shipped only to England, Ireland, Wales, and Berwick-upon-Tweed, in ships English owned and manned. They could not be carried from an English plantation in any English or plantation vessel to a European port or laden on board a foreign vessel designed for a European destination.[1] No English ship could go to the plantations for the purpose of taking on enumerated commodities and thence depart for Europe with all or even a part of its cargo, for according to the act its owner was obliged to return directly to England. Furthermore no English ship could import into England any foreign plantation commodities, if navigated by people of the country from which the commodities were brought. The enumerated products of every colony, whether English or foreign, had to be brought to England in ships owned and manned according to law.[2]

1. This was decided by 22–23 Charles II, c. 26, §§x, xii. In the act of 1663 the list reads, "sugar, tobacco, cotton-wool, ginger, indigo, speckle-wood or Jamaica wood, fustick or other dyeing woods" (§ix). Speckle-wood, called "granadilo" in Jamaica, was used for cabinet work and other special purposes where a fine-grained, handsome wood was needed, as for inlaying. It was not a dye-wood. Speckle-wood is mentioned in the list given in 4 Geo. II, c. 15. It seems to have been called also "Princes Wood," *Calendar Treasury Books,* VIII, 329.

An order was issued, October 29, 1667, to seize an English ship which had arrived in Leghorn with part of her lading from Barbados, on the ground that no ship could go from England to the plantations until she had given bond "to return hither with her lading . . . and the like care is taken by the Spaniards, Dutch and Portuguese and all other countries that have colonies out of Europe" (*Calendar Treasury Books,* II, 198). Vessels, not infrequently, broke their bonds, clearing for one place and going to another, *ibid.,* IX, 1437.

2. The question arose in 1730 in connection with the products of the Spanish plantations in America. It was well understood that logwood, coconuts, spices, drugs, and other commodities of the growth of the Spanish plantations could be imported, as was frequently done, from Jamaica and that tobacco of the growth of Brazil, a Portuguese plantation, could be imported from Barbados, but could Spanish tobacco be brought likewise into England from the English plantations?

There were four parts to this question: 1. Could tobacco of the Spanish plantations be brought into England in English ships, duly manned, from any of the English

This eighteenth clause was not introduced into the bill until the third reading and it may have been an addition recommended in the report of the committee of the whole house, of which Sir George Downing was the chairman and reporter. On the other hand, the entry in the *Commons' Journal* seems to show that the clause was not in the report but was tendered at the time of the third reading and after undergoing some changes was passed with the rest of the bill.[1] The matter is not important. The clause enumerated the commodities, already mentioned, that were considered necessary for England, either in the household, the pharmacopeia, or the woolen manufacture, or that were specially important, as in the case of tobacco, for the customs revenue. As calicoes (cotton), pepper, and indigo were among the commodities brought from India by the East India Company and had to be paid for in cash, it is not unlikely that cotton, ginger (a substitute for pepper), and indigo were enumerated in part at least to offset that trade.[2] Sugar and tobacco were

plantations? The answer of Attorney General Yorke was no. 2. Could English subjects import into England directly from the Spanish plantations tobacco of the growth of these plantations in English ships duly manned? The answer was yes, if from the place of its growth or first shipment, otherwise no. 3. Could tobacco of the Spanish plantations in pudding or roll, containing less than 200 wt., be imported from either the Spanish or the English plantations, notwithstanding the act of 10–11 William III, forbidding the importation of tobacco in bulk? The answer was yes, as the act was binding only on the English plantations on the continent of America. 4. Could English subjects, as the law stood, carry tobacco of the growth of the Spanish plantations directly from those plantations to Europe, without first coming to England? The answer was yes, as there was no law to prevent it. Opinion of P. Yorke, February 1, 1730, Treasury, 1:275, no. 12.

The whole question of the Spanish trade with England and her colonies was complicated by the desire of the English mercantilists to secure as large share as possible of the Spanish silver coin and bullion, for which the demand in England always exceeded the supply. England had somehow to meet the drain on her hard money due to her trade relations with such places as the Baltic kingdoms and the East Indies, with which the balance of trade was unfavorable. This necessity led to the cultivation of the trade of the colonies with the Spanish Main, even to the point of breaking the navigation acts, tacitly, if not formally. Nettels, *Money Supply*, ch. I.

1. Stock, *Debates*, I, 278–279. Downing was one of the commissioners of the customs and after 1667 was secretary to the Treasury Board. He was a determined opponent of any relaxation of the act from this time on. In 1676, when the Barbadians protested against the enumeration of sugar, as they had often done before, Downing was adamant in his refusal to consider their request (*Calendar State Papers, Colonial*, 1675–1676, §1106, inadequately calendared). That he was the author of the clause, as is sometimes stated, cannot be proved one way or the other.

2. John Cary, *An Essay on the State of England in relation to its Trade* (Bristol, 1695), pp. 52–60. It was claimed that the use of calicoes from India was driving out the linen (silesia) that was obtained from Germany by means of an exchange of manufactures, an exchange which offered England a reasonable balance of trade.

enumerated as commodities wanted in industry as well as for revenue. Thus one of the objects of the clause was to give employment to English workmen engaged in sugar refining and the distilling of molasses, in tobacco cutting and rolling, and in woolen and cotton spinning, weaving, and dyeing. Except for tobacco, the raising of which was legally forbidden at home, England produced none of these things. She did have fish, hides, grain, and lumber, so that it was not necessary to add them to the list, and inasmuch as these were all important staples of the northern colonies the clause distinctly favored New England, New York, and Pennsylvania.

Another effect of the clause was to reverse the situation created by the ordinance of 1651, that is, to open the Continental trade to English merchants and to close it to those of the colonies that handled the enumerated staples.[1] Between 1651 and 1660 trade with Europe had been open to the colonies and closed to England; henceforth, with certain exceptions,[2] it was open to England and as far as the enumerated commodities were concerned was closed to the colonies. Of course, all the enumerated commodities could be re-exported from England by English or colonial merchants, but such re-exportation added extra hazard and increased freight rates, victual and wage charges, and time, that could ill be spared, during which the merchants would be out of their money. Joshua Gee estimated this loss at forty per cent.[3] Under these circumstances the price of the commodities would have to be high for a colonial owner or shipper to make a profit, and it may well be doubted if any merchants in the colonies ever engaged in the re-exporting business. Probably that business was largely, if not entirely, controlled by the English factors. For the colonists the test of the enumeration lay in the answer to this question—would England be able to increase her own consumption of the enumerated colonial commodities so far as to take off the entire surplus either for herself or for re-exportation? If she could and the customs rates and other importation charges were not too high the colonies would not suffer from the monopoly. In fact, however, they did suffer in one respect at least. The enumeration of sugar and tobacco led to a glutting of the English market and a consequent reduction in the selling price of these staples, because in

1. In 1689, an English ship was reported as arriving with a cargo of sugar from the West Indies at Bilbao in Spain. The English agent there was instructed to seize both vessel and cargo. Treasury 1:9, no. 34.

2. Below, p. 93, note 6.          3. C. O. 324:8, L, 24.

the case of tobacco the colonists never had an entire monopoly of the English market.[1] This situation was not relieved even by re-exportation, and England refused to lower the customs duties. On the contrary she raised them on both commodities from time to time, and she did this in the face of indignant and prolonged protests, from English merchants and colonial planters alike.

Sugar remained on the enumerated list until 1822, but in 1739, after heated debates on both sides, an act was passed allowing British West India planters to send their sugars directly to points south of Cape Finisterre in ships built in and sailing from Great Britain and navigated according to law.[2] But the act was so clogged with restrictions as to prove of slight advantage as far as Continental markets were concerned; yet it did raise the price of sugar at home and so proved helpful to the planters at the expense of the English sugar refiners. Tobacco remained enumerated to the end of the colonial period, subject to heavy duties in England. Furthermore it was restricted as to the form in which it could be shipped, for after 1699 bulk tobacco was not allowed to be imported from any of the plantations on the continent.[3] Inevitably therefore it became the object of a certain amount of smuggling not only in the British Isles, notably Scotland, but also in every country on the European continent where there were protective duties and the control of tobacco was a monopoly of the state.

1. As we have seen, tobacco raising in England was never successfully stopped even in the seventeenth century. Furthermore, England imported considerable tobacco that was not the growth of her own plantations. Charles Carkesse, inspector general of imports and exports and secretary to the board of customs commissioners, reported, November 12, 1730, that tobacco entered between Christmas, 1722, and Christmas, 1729, came from the East Indies, Holland, Ireland, Portugal, Spain, and Turkey. Treasury 1:275, no. 12b.

2. 12 George II, c. 30; Stock, *Debates,* IV, index, under "Sugar"; Pitman, *Development of the British West Indies,* ch. VIII. The passage of the Molasses Act of 1733 and of this supplemental act of 1739 were both mercantilist defeats.

3. 10–11 William III, c. 21, §xiii; 9 George I, c. 21; repeated, 2 George II, c. 9; *Maryland Archives,* XIII, 198–199; XIX, 90–91; *Calendar State Papers, Colonial,* 1685–1688, §1397; 1689–1692, §§2140, 2307. A ship was seized in 1700 for bringing a part of its tobacco in bulk, when it should have had the tobacco in casks or hogsheads (Treasury 4:7, p. 399). When the question arose in 1730 as to whether Spanish pudding or roll, which was not in hogsheads but was partly made up, could be imported from the English colonies into England, the customs commissioners wished to bar it as "manufactured goods." In his report on the matter the attorney general refused to commit himself on that difficult point and said that the issue must be decided on the basis of "fact and usage," whatever that may mean. *Calendar Treasury Papers,* 1729–1730, p. 405; 1731–1734, pp. 11–12.

Cotton and ginger were raised in Jamaica, Barbados, the Bahamas, and the Virgin Isles, though the greater part of the raw cotton that England used at this time came from the Far and Near East, that is, from India directly or from Smyrna and the region thereabout, often by way of Venice.[1] The imports from India were, however, more often of finished or piece-goods than of the raw material. It is more than likely that by means of the act the Treasury hoped to encourage cultivation of these exotics in the West Indies, where the quantity tended steadily to increase, though never reaching dimensions of more than secondary importance.[2] Cotton was used for wicks as well as for cloth; ginger was a spice ranking next to pepper as a condiment; and indigo came in considerable quantities from Jamaica, where the amount in 1701, according to Governor Beeston, reached seven-tenths of England's supply, perhaps a much exaggerated statement, for fifteen years later we are told that the British islands produced "but very small quantities";[3] fustic, a yellow dye-wood, was largely a Jamaica product, but Brazil-wood, braziletto, and logwood of the best sort grew in the Spanish and Portuguese possessions and could be brought from Spain and Portugal as well as from Brazil and Honduras, if in English ships.[4] By a legal decision of 1714 only the logwood grown in Jamaica and the Leeward Islands, hardly at that date a native product and later of a distinctly inferior variety, was construed as coming within the enumeration.

1. Treasury 11:22, nos. 502, 516; 23, p. 310. For cotton exports from India, Foster, *The English Factories in India, passim.*

2. Beer, *Old Colonial System,* I, vol. II, 30, 80; Pitman, *Development of the British West Indies,* pp. 17, 130, 208, 303; *House of Lords Manuscripts,* new series, VI, 102, 106, and elsewhere.

3. *Calendar State Papers, Colonial,* 1701, p. 128; 1689–1692, §2757; 1717–1718, p. 391. It is possible that Beeston included in his estimate indigo from Hispaniola, re-exported from Jamaica. A writer in 1714 said that the indigo from Hispaniola and Guatemala was fast undoing that from Jamaica (*ibid.,* 1714–1715, p. 60). In 1748 James Crokatt and other merchants trading to America stated that one of the most considerable branches of the French-American commerce was indigo, with which the French supplied all European markets; that in England alone the consumption was upward of 600,000 lbs. weight per annum; and that formerly great quantities of it were made in the British plantations, though of late neglected. They wished encouragement for the staple in South Carolina. *Scots Magazine,* 1748, p. 201.

4. Treasury 11:12, p. 299, where the question is asked whether Brazil sugars could be imported into England in English ships, and answered in the affirmative. Also *ibid.,* 4:7, pp. 91, 116, where it is stated that braziletto could not be imported into England from Lisbon in a Portuguese ship. The Bahamas were said to produce an excellent variety of braziletto, but one hears very little of it. *House of Lords Manuscripts,* new series, VI, 412.

Logwood was a staple of diplomatic as well as commercial importance. Nearly all the logs imported into England, either from Jamaica, the entrepôt of the English logwood trade, or from Philadelphia, New York, Newport, or Boston, came from the Spanish territory of Honduras and adjoining parts. This region was more or less uninhabited, except by the natives (Moskito Indians) and by the logwood cutters, who off and on, as temporary residents, had been frequenting these coasts for nearly a century. Before 1660, this dyeing wood had been looked upon with disfavor in England as injurious to the cloth, and its importation had been prohibited.[1] Logically, therefore, it could not have been included among the "other dyeing woods" of the act of 1660. That it was soon to be so included, however, appears from the clause of the act of 1662,[2] which legitimatized the import of the wood into England, as having "by the ingenious industry of these times" become available for dyeing purposes.[3] By the treaty of 1670 with Spain, the subjects of either king, English or Spanish, were excluded from trading with the colonial possessions of the other, except under special licenses reciprocally granted. But this agreement was very loosely observed, as far as the Caribbean was concerned, and from this time forward the logwood trade continued, carried on in largest part during the seventeenth century by way of Jamaica, to the merchants of which the industry was a vital commercial necessity, and, in lesser part at first but steadily increasing later, by way of continental colonial ports, all of which secured their supplies directly from Honduras.[4] The trade

1. *Commons' Journal*, I, 121, 124, 130, 131; 23 Elizabeth, c. 1.

2. 13–14 Charles II, c. 11, §xxvi; *Calendar State Papers, Colonial*, 1675–1676, §556. Logwood is mentioned in the act of 1673 and because of that fact is included among the enumerated commodities in Dyer's commission as collector for East New Jersey in 1682. *Courts of Common Right and Chancery*, p. 139.

3. One Richard Brett had a monopoly of logwood importation, but in 1662 that privilege was taken away and the trade placed under the control of the farmers of the customs. In compensation for his loss Brett was given a pension of £250. The farm was continued until 1676, when on September 13 of that year Charles II, by royal letters patent, granted the logwood duties to the Earl of Rochester for the use of Nell Gwyn, and she received them until her death in 1687. *Calendar Treasury Books*, I, 124, 401, 417, 505, 578; V, 88, 1184; Treasury 11:7, p. 273.

4. In 1679 the naval officer of Jamaica reported forty-seven sail that came with cargoes of provisions and other native commodities from New England, Ireland, Madeira, etc., which after discharging went on to the Bay of Campeche for logwood and other forms of trading and did not return to Jamaica (C. O. 1:43, no. 37; *Calendar State Papers, Colonial*, 1677–1680, §945, inadequately calendared). Thomas Banister wrote in 1715, "Our logwood trade in the Bay of Campeche and Honduras . . . employs a great number of New England ships and has been very profitable to our plantations

was always insecure, on account of the uncertain relations with Spain, which denied England's right to cut logwood there or to engage in the commerce at all, and the English government was very loth to give it open protection, preferring to pursue a policy of connivance.[1] Spain seized many a logwood ship and drove out the logwood cutters; and every now and then a diplomatic crisis arose, which was averted with difficulty, because England did not want war, until in 1763 a *modus operandi* was reached whereby Spain allowed England to cut and load logwood unmolested.[2]

But the question as to whether logwood as the product of a Spanish plantation could be enumerated remained to perplex both the shippers and the Treasury and customs officials until well on in the eighteenth century (1714). This perplexity arose in large part because of the carelessness with which a phrase in the act of 1671, for the regulation of the plantation trade, was worded. The act of 1660

and the British nation. To us the employ of so many ships, to the king and kingdom by the great number of sailors this trade makes and maintains . . . all which are usually brought from the plantations and left here in England for his Majesty's service. But this trade was forgot in the treaty of Utrecht, though the nation has eagerly desired it for above fifty years last past" (*A Short Essay*, London, 1715, pp. 10–12). There are papers calendared in *Calendar State Papers, Colonial*, which contain excellent accounts of the logwood trade and the clashing interests with Spain in 1714. The writer of one of them says that to part with the logwood trade "would be to part with a limb from the body in respect to our woollen and other manufactures." For the logwood situation in 1717, *ibid.*, 1717–1718, §§104, 104, i, p. 103, where mention is made of Jamaica logwood which had only recently been introduced there. The writer of *Popular Prejudices against the Convention and Treaty with Spain* (London, 1739) insists, however, that at that date very little cacao and "not a ton of logwood" from the English colonies had been imported to England (pp. 9–12). In 1699 the question came up whether an English ship could carry logwood from Honduras to Venice and the answer was that there was no law to prevent it, unless the ship were of the plantations (*Calendar State Papers, Colonial*, 1699, §§619, 755). In 1738 an English ship bound for Amsterdam put in at Charles Town, laden with logwood from Honduras, and the captain asked for a survey, as the vessel was unseaworthy. In the judge's decree nothing is said about the enumeration of logwood (Records of Admiralty, South Carolina, C–D, 247–250). By 1750 logwood was frequently included in colonial bills of lading, most of it, however, being brought directly from Honduras. After 1767 the New England merchants protested strongly against the obligation to carry foreign logwood to England before carrying it elsewhere, showing that at that time they considered foreign logwood an enumerated commodity.

1. "Meanwhile there should be no further discouragement to those engaged in the trade who may be permitted to proceed therein at their own peril." *Calendar State Papers, Colonial*, 1677–1680, §938. Cf. *ibid.*, 1716–1717, §§388, 484, ii–x, 546, p. 303; 1717–1718, 104, i, where the history of the dispute is dealt with at length; *Board of Trade Journal*, 1735–1741, pp. 57, 59.

2. Cook (Mrs. Ernest Fast), "The British Logwood Trade," an M. A. essay in the Yale University Library.

enumerates commodities "of the growth of his Majesty's plantations"; that of 1671 leaves out these words,[1] thus penalizing colonial ships carrying foreign logwood to Europe, which under the earlier act they could certainly do. As a result many colonial ships with Honduras logwood on board were seized and condemned, though the New England captains always claimed that Honduras logwood was not enumerated.[2] In 1699 the law officers of the crown upheld the interpretation of the customs officials,[3] but in 1714 Attorney General Northey reversed this decision and gave it as his opinion that Spanish logwood was not an enumerated commodity.[4] This opinion was sustained later in 1731 and 1768.[5]

As time went on this list of the enumerated commodities[6] was very considerably extended, partly for the sake of the industries in

1. 22–23 Charles II, c. 26, §xii, at the end.

2. Toppan, *Edward Randolph*, IV, 257, and elsewhere. In 1728 the commissioners of the customs were so uncertain about the enumeration that they sent a special request to the board asking for its opinion, *Calendar State Papers, Colonial*, 1728–1729, §39.

3. The question seems to have come up first in 1688, in the case of a ship carrying logwood to Holland. The Lords of Trade sent the data to the attorney and solicitor general, saying, "If [such ships] were met at sea or otherwise questioned for the certificate of bonds given according to the act of navigation, they plead that the said logwood is of the growth of Honduras or some other place within the Spanish dominions and not of the growth of the English plantations, and that therefore they are not obliged to give bond or shew any despatches, by means whereof the law is evaded and his Maj. defrauded of his duties." The law officers, Powys and Williams, replied that as such allegations might cover fraud the clearings should be demanded (C. O. 1:64, nos. 22, 23; *Calendar State Papers, Colonial*, 1685–1688, §§1633, 1634, by title only). In 1712 Archibald Cummings insisted that logwood was an enumerated commodity. For earlier instances, *ibid.*, 1685–1688, §§1066, 1221, 1238; 1699, §§594, 755, 791; 1701, §§805, i, 818. For a later opinion, Chalmers, *Opinions*, II, 265–266.

4. Hargreave Manuscripts, 141, fo. 136b.

5. *Ibid.*, 231, fos. 10–12; Additional Manuscripts, 8832, pp. 198–201. This decision was not agreeable to James Abercromby, who in 1752 would have had an act passed placing both logwood and coconuts in the enumerated list. "Examination," p. 80.

6. The enumerated commodities mentioned in this chapter must not be confused with the enumerated commodities which could be imported from the Continent only in English ships or, if alien duties were paid, in a ship of the country producing them. These commodities included all Russian goods, as well as masts, timber, boards, foreign salt, pitch, tar, rosin, hemp or flax, raisins, figs, prunes, olive oils, corn or grain, sugar, potashes, wines, vinegar, and spirits called aqua vitae or brandy wine, together with currants and Turkish goods. The enumeration of these articles marked the principal change regarding importations from Europe in the policy of 1660 as contrasted with that of 1651 (above, p. 64; Harper, *English Navigation Acts*, pp. 53–54). These articles were called enumerated, because any articles specifically mentioned in the acts were "enumerated." 12 Charles II, c. 18, §§viii, ix; 13–14 Charles II, c. 11, §xxiii; *Calendar State Papers, Colonial*, 1717–1718, §620, i; *Calendar Treasury Books*, IV, 613, 850.

England that would be benefited thereby, and partly for the sake of the customs revenue. First, cacao, though never strictly speaking enumerated, seems to have been construed as coming within the intent of the clause.[1] This interpretation was undoubtedly based on certain words in a later act, that of 1673, where "cocoanuts," though not contained in the list of enumerated commodities, are entered among the articles upon which the enumerated commodities duty had to be paid.[2] But the meaning is far from clear, as are so many other meanings in the acts of trade and navigation, and later in 1752 James Abercromby, when commenting on the instructions issued by the commissioners of the customs in England to their officers in the colonies, declared that there were still grave doubts and difficulties, which it was the business of the commissioners to remove. He cites logwood and cacao as cases in point, because if not enumerated they ought to be. "Hitherto merchants have not so construed them, as they are not so enumerated in the plantation bonds as they now stand." There would seem to have been a contradiction between the law and the practice,[3] due in part to the fact that with cacao as with logwood the chief supply came from the Spanish possessions in the

---

1. *Calendar State Papers, Colonial,* 1675–1676, §256; *Maryland Archives,* XX, 264, 352; instructions to collectors, 1697, *House of Lords Manuscripts,* new series, II, 473.

2. 25 Charles II, c. 7, §ii at the end. In 1670 Jamaica reported 46 cacao walks (*Calendar State Papers, Colonial,* 1669–1674, §271), but in 1690 Dalby Thomas said that cacao had almost ceased to be a commodity of importance from the plantations (*An Historical Account,* pp. 23–24; cf. *Calendar State Papers, Colonial,* 1710–1711, p. 260). In 1688, the Treasury, acting on a report from the commissioners of the customs, allowed one Peter Henriques, a merchant of London, to import twenty tons of cacao-seeds from Holland, on the ground that the Dutch had "by some artifice imported of late great quantities of cacao from the Spanish West Indies into Holland, which (with the scarcity of that commodity in Jamaica and the difficulty of having it from the Spanish as formerly) hath made it very scarce in this kingdom." Treasury 4:5, p. 274; 11:10, p. 161; *Calendar Treasury Books,* VIII, 1946, 1984.

3. Neither logwood nor cacao is mentioned in 3–4 Anne, c. 10, §viii, and cacao is omitted in the report of the commissioners of the customs to the House of Lords in 1695 (*House of Lords Manuscripts,* new series, II, 17). It is mentioned in combination with "sugar," etc., as if among the enumerated commodities, in 9 Anne, c. 27, §ii, but is not contained in the list given in 1731 in 4 George II, c. 15. Abercromby speaks of cacao as not enumerated in 1752, but both logwood and cacao are entered as enumerated in Baldwin's *British Customs* of 1770 (appendix, p. 211; oddly enough on p. 201 only cacao is so entered). In Antigua, December 2, 1743, a libel was filed in the court of vice-admiralty against the *Charming Molly,* Richard Pitts, master, for loading cacao without first giving bond to carry it to some other plantation or to England (Records of Admiralty, Antigua, December 2, 1743). It is definitely included in the list given in Dyer's commission. Above, p. 91, note 2. Clearly the customs officials deemed cacao an enumerated commodity.

New World and to the further fact that the customs officials, despite the opinions of the lawyers, were always inclined to give the revenue the benefit of the doubt.

The enumeration of rice came about in a curious way and its history presents quite a different story from that of either logwood or cacao. In the years from 1700 to 1704 one Michael Cole,[1] an itinerant sea-captain, accustomed to trade from England to the plantations, particularly South Carolina and the Bahamas, persuaded the lord high treasurer, Godolphin, and the commissioners of the customs to obtain the inclusion of rice in a clause of a revenue bill of the latter year, which enumerated molasses also as an incidental feature.[2] Cole insisted that the carrying to Holland and Lisbon of such an important commodity as rice, which the people of South Carolina prepared better "than any in Europe (or the world)" and which Governor John Archdale called the best rice anywhere,[3] was "to the great prejudice of the trade of the kingdom and the lessening of the correspondence and relation between the kingdom and the colonies."[4] He asserted that 340 tons had been shipped in that very year (1704) to Holland, without paying any duty to the crown, at a loss to the English exchequer of £1470. This appeal to the revenue aroused the commissioners, who recommended that "rice, molasses and rum, and all other goods of the growth and product of her Majesty's plantations be alike restrained with tobacco and other goods enumerated in the present laws." The appeal was heeded, a member of parliament was found who moved the attachment of a rider to the revenue bill, and the lucrative rice trade which South Carolina had carried on with Holland and Portugal was temporarily brought to an end. A certain amount of illicit trading inevitably followed, though on how extensive a scale it is not possible to say. Vessels from South

---

1. On Cole, *Calendar State Papers, Colonial*, 1700, §§326, 634. Cole was something of a busybody and afterward, on a voyage to South Carolina, when seven of his men deserted and he was obliged to take on foreigners, his vessel was seized as not English-manned, November 2, 1717 (Treasury 4:9, p. 355). He was one of the complainants against that somewhat irascible and contentious New England sea-captain, Elias Hasket, governor of the Bahamas, in what Hasket styled "an idle and malicious story." Both men seem to have been birds of a feather. *Calendar State Papers, Colonial*, 1702, p. 447.

2. 3–4 Anne, c. 5, xii; Stock, *Debates*, III, 96.

3. "Archdale's Account," Carroll, *Historical Collections of South Carolina*, II, 98; Original Narratives Series, *Early Carolina*, p. 289; *Calendar State Papers, Colonial*, 1716–1717, p. 132.

4. This is the stock phrase, found in most of the navigation acts.

Carolina were reported as carrying rice to Newport, Rhode Island, and there transshipping to Portugal, but the evidence is neither certain nor considerable.[1]

So manifestly disadvantageous was this enumeration of rice to the southernmost colonies and of so little benefit to England, which did not want rice except for re-export to northern Europe, that in 1721 an agitation was begun for its removal. Joseph Boone, agent of the colony, who had gone to England in 1705 and again in 1717 to plead its cause against the proprietors,[2] pictured in graphic terms the distressed condition of the people there. He took advantage of the occasion to present to the Board of Trade a paper containing arguments against the enumeration. The board in its report of 1721 agreed that the enumeration was injurious to those merchants who had formerly been accustomed to supply Portugal with rice, and gave figures to show that the obligation to bring rice to England before sending it to Portugal involved additional freight charges and other extra costs equaling a third of the value of the cargo and practically killing the trade as far as Spain, Portugal, the Straits, and other parts of Europe to the south of Cape Finisterre were concerned. In letters to the Treasury it recommended that the enumeration be retained but that shipment directly to those points be allowed.[3] The Treasury, however, was slow to act. In 1722, through Horatio Walpole, auditor general of the plantation revenues and a member of parliament, a group of English merchants, trading to Carolina, Spain, and Portugal, handed in to the board a petition which was presented to the House of Commons six weeks later, to the same effect.[4] But par-

---

1. *Calendar State Papers, Colonial,* 1708–1709, §268; *Board of Trade Journal,* 1704–1709, pp. 522, 569. Joshua Gee agreed that the enumeration of rice was one of the mistakes of parliament (*Trade and Navigation of Great Britain,* 3d ed., 1731, p. 22). A great deal of South Carolina rice was smuggled into Holland during the years following the enumeration, the ships bringing back tea, linen, brandy, and other liquors (Treasury 64:312). Rice was re-exported to the Continent from both English and Scottish ports. Important re-exporting centers were Cowes (Isle of Wight) and Kirkwall Harbour (Scotland), into which many a South Carolina ship entered before going on to Dutch and German ports.

2. Boone first arrived in England in 1705, with a petition, endorsed by sundry inhabitants of South Carolina and merchants of London, against the proprietary rule. *Calendar State Papers, Colonial,* 1706–1708, §229; *House of Lords Manuscripts,* new series, VI, 406–408. See Vol. III, 244.

3. *New York Colonial Documents,* V, 612–613; *Calendar Treasury Papers,* 1720–1728, p. 79; *Board of Trade Journal,* 1718–1722, p. 388.

4. Stock, *Debates,* III, 456; *Board of Trade Journal,* 1718–1722, pp. 330, 385.

liament as well as the Treasury procrastinated and finally dropped the matter altogether. Seven years later, the merchants presented the case directly to the Treasury[1] and, despite objections raised by that ardent mercantilist, Nicholas Toriano, who was opposed to any relaxation whatever in the enumeration of sugar, tobacco, and rice, and who would even have had the New Englanders barred from building and freighting their own ships,[2] that influential body at last gave its approval and said that it had "no objection against their applying to parliament . . . when they shall think it proper." This the merchants did and in 1730 parliament at last legislated in their favor.

By the act passed in that year and by a supplemental measure passed in 1735, the restriction on rice was so far removed as to allow South Carolina and Georgia to export rice freely and directly to any European port south of Cape Finisterre.[3] But as this privilege did not cover Holland and Germany, the region of the Caribbean, and the Spanish Main, where lay the best markets, the agitation was continued and petitions were sent in in 1744–1745, begging that the two colonies be permitted to ship to the Dutch, French, and Spanish islands and to the African continent south of the Straits, on account of the "great increase of freight and cost of unlading and relading." But the commissioners of the customs, to whom the Board of Trade referred the new appeal, replied that while to do so might be advantageous to the colonies, it "would require such great alterations in the laws relating to trade and the plantations [that] they could not take upon them to judge how far it might affect the general trade and navigation of the kingdom." Consequently nothing was done. In 1758 James Wright, agent for South Carolina, brought the matter up again, asking for permission to export rice directly to any European port,[4] a request which was definitely refused. The matter then hung fire for some years, but finally in 1764 and 1765,[5] among the new acts of revenue and trade, a series of measures was adopted that widened the area for North and South Carolina and Georgia to include all points south of these colonies, thus meeting the wishes of

1. *Calendar Treasury Books and Papers,* 1729–1730, p. 332.

2. *Board of Trade Journal,* 1722–1728, pp. 114, 121. In 1724 Toriano upheld the petition of the Thames shipwrights against shipbuilding in New England, *ibid.,* pp. 130–131, 135–138, 144; C. O. 5:915, pp. 431–433.

3. 3 George II, c. 28; 8 George II, c. 19; Stock, *Debates,* IV, index, under "Rice."

4. C. O. 5:371, pp. 79, 84.     5. Treasury 27:24, p. 286.

those who had petitioned in 1744 and 1745.[1] But the enumeration was never removed for the markets north of Cape Finisterre.

In the same brief sentence of the act of 1704 which contains the enumeration of rice appears the enumeration of molasses also. The causes of this enumeration are many and complex. While an increase of the revenue was the chief reason for the enumeration of rice, other factors must be considered in explaining the enumeration of molasses, factors that were a part of the social as well as the financial life of the nation.

Until 1688 English merchants had been accustomed to import large quantities of molasses from Holland and France, some of which came from the English plantations in America. They were not interfered with in this trade, partly because molasses was not a "foreign enumerated commodity" and so could be freely imported from Holland and France,[2] and partly because it was considered a manufactured article and therefore, according to one interpretation, did not come under the act of navigation at all, which concerned raw materials only.[3] As more and more molasses continued to come in, the commissioners of the customs and the London distillers and sugar refiners took alarm and the latter petitioned the Treasury against the practice, alleging that it was contrary to the act of 1660, as they construed the act, "fatal to the trade of the petitioners," and "immediately prejudicial to his Majestys revenue to the extent of £50,000 per annum," because the Dutch were buying up the molasses and other materials of the plantations. This reference to revenue losses excited the commissioners, as was always the case when the revenue was threatened, and in 1689 they took up the matter in earnest. After hearing several refiners and distillers and taking the opinion of the attorney general "and others of his Majestys learned council therein" they put a stop to the trade, upon what the importers called "a nice distinction wherein the lawyers themselves are doubtful that [molas-

1. 4 George III, c. 27; 5 George III, c. 45, §xx; 9 George III, c. 27, and for the later agitation, *Board of Trade Journal,* 1759–1763, pp. 420–421; 1764–1767, pp. 9, 22, 32.

2. See above p. 86, note 1. There was some doubt before 1704 as to whether molasses was or was not an enumerated commodity. A stop was put in 1689–1690 to importations from France "as supposed to be prohibited by the Act of Navigation," *Calendar Treasury Books,* IX, 483.

3. Up to 1689 molasses had been deemed a manufactured article and its importation from France had always been allowed. Then the commissioners of the customs put a stop to its admission as prohibited by the act of navigation because they said it was raw material. *Calendar Treasury Books,* IX, 482–483.

ses] is not a manufacture and therefore prohibited to be from hence by the aforesaid act of navigation."[1] Doubtless the refiners and distillers were afraid, one that the Dutch would work up a corner in molasses and the other that the demand for molasses might curtail the supply of raw sugar upon which their business depended. The commissioners of the customs feared a loss to the revenue, which in all these enumerations was always uppermost in their minds. The Board of Trade was ready to do anything that might enlarge the output from the West Indies of any and all these commodities, and believed that by proper attention the imports from Jamaica might be made to yield fivefold the revenue that had hitherto been collected on its products.[2] The time was one when the kingdom was at great expense for the war with France and the defense of the plantations and when available cash for the proper maintenance of the navy was wanting in every direction.[3] Ships, seamen, and convoys were all suffering and the Treasury was often helplessly indifferent to the demands made for upkeep, wages, enlarged complements, and increase in the number of ships. The many "states of account" of the period show the amount of figuring that was done upon these items of expenditure.

But another and equally important aspect of the case must be considered. From molasses, by a process of fermenting and distilling, came rum and the use of rum in England was increasing in the years before the act of 1704.[4] It was beginning to be employed in the army and navy; it was becoming a necessary ingredient in the concocting of "that heathenish liquor called Punch,"[5] which was already a fa-

1. Treasury 4:5, pp. 242, 255, 307; 11:10, pp. 186–187; 11:11, pp. 110, 179–180; *Calendar Treasury Books*, VIII, 1998, 2173. Giles Bigges and Peter and Pierre Henriques were the importers. On this subject, Stock, *Debates*, II, 295, 306, 307–310.

2. *House of Lords Manuscripts*, new series, VI, 103.

3. *Ibid.*, V, no. 1973. The act of 3–4 Anne, c. 3, was "for the better enabling your Majesty to carry on the present war and to defray your other necessary expenses," and it gives as the official reason for the enumeration the fact "that the production and making of rice and molasses in the plantations and the carrying of them to divers foreign markets, without first being brought into this kingdom was contrary to the intent and meaning of the aforesaid laws." (*Statutes of the Realm*, Records Commission ed., VIII, 332, 335–336.) Special instructions to enforce the enumeration of molasses were sent to the governors of the colonies in 1708. *Calendar State Papers, Colonial*, 1706–1708, §1599, ii.

4. Wood, *Survey of Trade* (1718), p. 227; Cooper, *The Complete Distiller* (London, 1757).

5. Wilson, *Distilled Spiritous Liquors, the Bane of the Nation* (2d ed. 1736), p. xx; Oldmixon, *British Empire in America*, II, 143, 155; Pitman, *British West Indies*,

vorite drink; and its manufacture was giving rise to distilleries in England and employing large numbers of people. John Cary, the well-known mercantilist pamphleteer and merchant of Bristol, complained as early as 1691[1] that great quantities of molasses were shipped off to Ireland and stills erected there, to the injury of the production of England. He said that the use of rum was increasing among the sailors, who could buy the Irish distillation at one-half to two-thirds of the price they would have to pay in England, and that great quantities were shipped to Holland, where the Dutch surpassed the English as refiners and distillers, obtaining their rum from English as well as Dutch molasses, running it into England in small parcels, and disposing of it to the damage of the English trade. Cary wanted distilling encouraged in England, that spirits might be produced at home and for plantation use, instead of allowing the molasses to be carried to Ireland and Holland for distillation there.[2]

Of even more concern to the English mercantilist was the fact that from molasses could be obtained brandy and low wines as well as rum. Though William Blathwayt was a great believer in rum as a substitute for brandy, others did not agree with him and rum never became in England a liquor that suited the taste of the well-to-do as did brandy, or of the poor as did gin. It was always foreign to the English palate. But brandy was popular among the better classes and only a few years before (1690) a lively discussion had accompanied the passage of a bill through parliament for encouraging the distilling of brandy from corn, without any admixture of molasses. Sugar merchants and planters handed in many petitions against the bill as injuring the sugar trade and emboldening "the clandestine importation of foreign [French] brandy," which had been forbidden by an act of 1689.[3]

pp. 389–390. "Arrack punch" was also known and in the colonies too, for Governor Spotswood mentions serving it at Williamsburg. "Arrack" was a general name for liquor in the Far East, and fourteen varieties of it were known. The commonest kinds were distillations of the juice of the coconut palm, of sugar, and of rice.

1. Additional Manuscripts, 5540, pp. 34–35.

2. This competition of the Dutch in distilling rum and refining sugar was a cause of frequent grumbling in England at this time. Nathaniel Grew wrote about 1709 that brown sugars were refined in Holland, Flanders, and Hamburg and sent to England to her unspeakable loss. The Dutch controlled the loaf-sugar trade, so that Italy, Spain, Turkey, the East Country, and Hamburg each had nearly as many sugar houses as all England. "The Meanes of a Most Ample Encrease," p. 81.

3. William and Mary, 1st sess., c. 34; 2 William and Mary, 2d sess., c. 9; Stock, *Debates*, II, 31, 39, 42–44, 50–52, 53, 55–56. Also for a later discussion, *ibid.*, III, 304, 312, 314. In *An Answer to the Merchants' Observations against Passing the Bill*

Leaving out of account all question of revenue, the regulations on molasses were, therefore, due to three chief causes: first, the desire to keep English plantation molasses out of the hands of the Dutch and the French, already England's successful rivals in refining and distilling; secondly, the determination to prevent the importation into England of Dutch and French molasses and so to increase the stock at home from England's own plantations; and, thirdly, the hope of meeting the home demand for brandy from England's own distilleries and thus offsetting the supply from France, the importation of which, whether clandestine or legal, was opposed by a large number of mercantilists as injuring the balance of trade and increasing luxury and profligacy. The enumeration of molasses was a distinct victory for the merchants and sugar planters over the landed gentry, who had welcomed the acts encouraging distillation from corn as making possible a profit from their own acres and increasing the value of their landed estates.[1]

*to prevent the Running of Foreign Brandies* (one page, folio, about 1710) the statement is made by the distillers that as many as sixty English boats had been seen at Calais, many carrying wool, all of which brought brandies back to England. An earlier statement, made in 1689, is to the effect that "considerable quantities of wines and brandies [were] bought in France by merchants who [lacked] opportunities to import the same into England in English built ships as the law directs." *Calendar Treasury Books,* VIII, 2146.

1. Agitation on behalf of rum as a substitute for French brandy in the navy began with the Barbados assembly as early as 1679 (*Calendar State Papers, Colonial,* 1677–1680, §969). A later writer, whose dates are often quite inaccurate but whose statements of conditions are probably reliable, says that rum was first introduced into the navy, but that it took some time for the sailors to get used to it, as it was "a spirit harsh and disagreeable, especially when new" (*The Distilleries Considered, in the Connection with Agriculture, Commerce, and Revenue of Great Britain,* Edinburgh, 1797). Others thought that rum was a "wholesome liquor" (Wilson, *Distilled Spiritous Liquors,* p. 45) and that the sailors could not get on without it, when once it had become palatable to them. It had been in use for a long time before Admiral Vernon, of the grogram cloak, made it less raw by mixing water with it in 1743, whence the name "grog." In 1689 distilling in England was declared inconsiderable (*An Impartial Inquiry into the Present State of the British Distillery,* London, 1736, p. 22), but by 1736, the date of the Gin Act, it is said that there were 300 members of the Company of Distillers engaged in the business and 1200 outside (*ibid.,* p. 8). At that time the proportion of malt spirits to rum was estimated at four to one (*A Letter from a Member of Parliament,* 1736) and the writer says that the effort to offset French brandy had been going on for forty years (p. 14). A rare and valuable contemporary work is *A Compleat Body of Distilling, explaining the Mysteries of that Science* (1749), in two parts, by George Smith of Kendall, which shows how far distilling in England had gone by the middle of the century. Similar information can be obtained from A. Cooper, *The Complete Distiller* (London, 1757), which is a sort of encyclopedia of the subject.

The early part of the eighteenth century witnessed the high-water mark of drunk-

Naval stores were enumerated in 1705 and again in 1729,[1] for the simple reason that they were required for the royal navy, which was in dire need, throughout the entire period of the Spanish War, of sufficient building material. The initial impulse came from the discovery that one William Partridge of New Hampshire was carrying on a lucrative business in lumber with Portugal and that other New Englanders, stirred by the reports of large profits, were preparing to export lumber to Europe on a considerable scale. Certain officials in America—Bellomont of New York[2] and Bridger and Furzer, the commissioners sent over to inquire into the possibilities of New England as a source of naval supplies[3]—urged that this trade be diverted to England, partly for the sake of the navy and partly for the sake of the balance of trade. The Board of Trade was at first satisfied with Partridge's explanation that the lumber was not fit for the royal navy, but later it changed its mind and in two representations to the House of Lords of December 21, 1703, and November 30, 1704, formulated recommendations for a definite naval stores policy.[4] It

enness in England and furnishes an excellent example of the evils of drinking spirits (Askwith, *British Taverns, Their History and Laws,* 1929). This situation, taken in conjunction with the other conditions of city life (Henry Fielding, *An Enquiry into the Causes of the late Increase of Robbers,* London, 1751, and Hogarth's famous picture "Gin Lane") and the horrors of the debtors' prisons, is important for colonial history. Immigration to the colonies, the successful effort to establish the settlement of Georgia and the unsuccessful attempts to found another "Georgia" in Maine similar to the organization of the southern colony, can be understood only after a thorough examination has been made of the social and industrial life of England in the first half of the eighteenth century. The Board of Trade was greatly interested in this question of settlement, for the purpose of peopling old colonies—such as Jamaica, the Bahamas, the Virgin Islands, North and South Carolina, and Georgia—and filling up empty spaces also in Nova Scotia and Maine. It wanted to relieve conditions at home and increase the population in America that the colonies might be made more profitable to England. *Board of Trade Journal,* 1734–1741, pp. 39, 99, 241, 244, 330, 332, 333.

1. 3–4 Anne, c. 10, §viii; 2 George II, c. 35, §xvi. No enumeration clause was introduced into the naval stores act of 1721, 8 George I, c. 12.

2. Bellomont wrote to Partridge, April 22, 1700, "I do not say there is an act of Parliament against such a trade, but there are reasons of State for preventing certain mischiefs that our law-givers did not imagine would ever be practiced. I have made such a representation of this presumptuous management of yours, that I dare undertake there will come an order from the King to put an effectual stop to it, and an Act of Parliament to that end" (*Calendar State Papers, Colonial,* 1700, §364, vi). Bellomont did not live to see his prophetic utterance come true. He died in 1701.

3. Lord, *Industrial Experiments, passim,* an account of the naval stores business in the colonies.

4. Stock, *Debates,* III, 35–36; *House of Lords Manuscripts,* new series, VI, 93–95, 108–109. Partridge, who had been lieutenant governor of New Hampshire from 1697

drafted a bill, which was presented by William Blathwayt, a member of the board, January 22, 1705, was passed without difficulty, and received the royal assent in March.[1] The object of the bill was to encourage the importation into England of naval stores from the plantations by granting a series of bounties on tar, pitch, rosin or turpentine, hemp, masts, yards, and bowsprits sent over, with the express proviso that all such commodities be sent to England only. For reasons not stated, while the bill was in committee, iron and copper were ordered to be left out, and later, when in 1729 the bounties were continued, rosin also was omitted.[2] The remaining commodities, thus enumerated, were such as had been previously brought in largest part from the Baltic states—Sweden, Norway, and Russia —at an overbalance of England's trade amounting in 1703 to £350,-000,[3] with the fear constantly present that these countries would place obstacles in the form of prohibitions upon exported commodities or extra duties upon foreign imports. Could naval stores be secured from the plantations it would aid greatly in improving England's general balance with the European continent, an advantage that the mercantilists were beginning to realize and appreciate.[4] The question of revenue was not involved, as by both the acts bounties or premiums were allowed to all engaged in this business enterprise.[5]

Copper was enumerated in 1721, in response to a letter from Francis Harison, surveyor and searcher of customs and former judge of vice-admiralty at New York, to the commissioners of the customs in

to 1699, went to England in 1704, and appeared before the Board of Trade to answer questions and to make proposals for the exporting of naval stores.

1. Stock, *Debates*, III, 89; 3–4 Anne, c. 10.

2. Iron was not enumerated until after 1763, though Joshua Gee thought that it ought to be as early as 1729. A case came up in the vice-admiralty court of Philadelphia regarding the violation of the naval stores enumeration by a vessel with rosin on board. The judge decided that inasmuch as rosin was not mentioned by name in the act of 2 George II, c. 35, it was not an enumerated commodity, and he dismissed the libel (Records of Admiralty, Philadelphia, I, 50–52). On the other hand, rosin was a "foreign enumerated commodity" and could not be imported from either Holland or Germany (13–14 Charles II, c. 11, §xxiii). On Dutch rosin, *Calendar Treasury Books*, IX, 1735.

3. *House of Lords Manuscripts*, new series, V, 334; *Calendar State Papers, Colonial*, 1717–1718, 819.

4. The matter was discussed at considerable length in 1735, when Sweden imposed a ten per cent duty on all foreign imports. *Board of Trade Journal*, 1735–1741, pp. 19, 29, 41, 277–278.

5. The enumeration of naval stores was opposed by Thomas Banister, who believed that its removal would be beneficial to both crown and colonies. *A Short Essay*, p. 3; Stock, *Debates*, III, 448.

England, which the latter referred to the Board of Trade. Harison wrote on October 12, 1720, that copper ore had been mined "very rich and in great plenty in a newly discovered mine of one Mr. Schuyler in New Jersey" and he feared that the ore "would soon be carried into the channel of our Trade to Holland unless prevented." He wrote again, April 17, 1721, that there was shipped "on board the snow *Unity,* Robert Leonard master, for Holland one hundred and ten casks of said Copper Oare which we have not as I can find any law to prevent."[1] The letter was read at the board on June 15 and a communication prepared for the Treasury.[2] On considering this communication, the Treasury decided that if there was no law to prevent the carrying of copper ore to foreign parts there ought to be, and that the matter was of such consequence to the revenue, the arts, and the coinage as to deserve the attention of parliament.[3] Therefore, in the following December, a clause was added to an act "to prevent the clandestine running of goods" which stated that as copper was being produced in the plantations and carried to foreign markets, without first being landed in England, it must be enumerated as were other commodities in the same class.[4]

For this act parliament had no other warrant than the unsupported word of Francis Harison, a man none too reliable in the informa-

1. C. O. 5:971, D, 104; the letter is referred to in *Calendar Treasury Papers,* 1720–1728, p. 60.

2. *Board of Trade Journal,* 1718–1722, p. 285.

3. *Calendar Treasury Papers,* 1720–1728, p. 60.

4. 8 George I, c. 18, §xxii; Stock, *Debates,* III, 448, 481. Some years before, 1712, a scheme was set on foot in England "for Improving the Mines, the Mineral and Battery Works in New England"; subscriptions were opened "for setting up Iron and Steel Works in New England and Copper Works in Connecticut"; and a company was chartered under the great seal known as the Governors, Mineral Masters General, Assistants and Society of the City of London. In origin this company claimed to go back to the time of Elizabeth. I can find nothing more about it. Its papers are in C. O. 5:865, nos. 82–85, and its leading features are given in *Calendar State Papers, Colonial,* 1711–1712, §439. For earlier companies of the kind, see Scott, *Joint-Stock Companies,* II, 430–439.

Great interest was aroused at this time and in succeeding years among men in England with money to invest—noblemen and merchants and men in office—in mines of all sorts, copper among the others, especially in Nova Scotia. The Duke of Chandos was heavily involved, but none of his schemes were successful (Chandos Letter Books, 45, 46, 47, Huntington Library). The mining of copper seems to have had a peculiar fascination for the members of parliament, who believed that rich stores of the metal could be obtained from the colonies, and that such stores should be prevented, at all costs, from going to Holland. A Copper Mines Company was in existence in 1733, which wished to supply the mint with copper for coinage. *Calendar Treasury Books and Papers,* 1731–1734, p. 427.

tion he furnished. But that there was apparently some justification for his statement regarding a mine in New Jersey a letter previously written by Governor Hunter to the Board of Trade and a later act of the New Jersey assembly in August, 1734, imposing a duty on copper ore not exported directly to Great Britain, bear witness.[1] Hunter's letter aroused no alarm because it reported only shipments to Bristol, and the New Jersey act, which was designed to help the enumeration by cutting out the coastwise trade, though disallowed because it affected the trade and shipping of the kingdom, had nothing to do with the main issue. This issue was the rumored sending of copper to Holland and on the strength of one man's statement copper was placed on the enumerated list. The act was unnecessary, for the amount of copper obtained from the British plantations in colonial times was negligible, but the reasoning was the same as that which led to the enumeration of naval stores. England with diminishing woodlands was also an England without mines, and the uses of the metal for the sheathing of ships,[2] in the arts and industries, and for the coining of money were already assuming very considerable proportions.

Beaver and other furs were enumerated in 1721, to keep them out of the hands of the French, with whom England at this time was in conflict over the fisheries and the fur trade in America. The latter reached enormous proportions. The skins (pelts, furs, hides, parchments, drillings, halves, and laps) of elk, moose, deer, wildcats, bear, raccoon, wolves, otters, minks, muskrats, martens, fishers, and beavers were used for hats, clothing, robes, and the covering of trunks and boxes.[3] Very little illicit trade in furs is recorded, though occasionally a seizure took place, as of furs brought from Gibraltar, instead of directly from America,[4] and the assumption is reasonable that as

1. *New York Colonial Documents*, V, 462; *New Jersey Archives*, V, 7–9, 267–268, 375, 376, 406–407; *Board of Trade Journal*, 1735–1741, pp. 6, 45–46, 105.

2. Above, p. 27. Hammersly, *Naval Encyclopedia* (1886). Sheathing with tar, hair, and fir-boards was tried without success; lead was used as early as 1620 but proved ineffective against the worm. In 1706 a memorial was presented to the Board of Trade recommending the employment of American tar in combination with other ingredients, but we hear nothing more of it. *Calendar State Papers, Colonial*, 1706–1708, §671.

3. On the furs shipped from South Carolina, above, Vol. III, 206, and for itemized statements of those sent down to New York from Albany for shipment to England in 1700–1701, see Weaver's Account, Custom House Report, Hall of Records, New York, "An Account of His Majesty's Revenue in the Province of New York, January 6, 1700 to March 25, 1701," in great detail.

4. *Calendar Treasury Books and Papers*, 1735–1738, p. 218.

France had an ample fur trade of her own, there was little induce-
ment for the colonists to break through the parliamentary restriction.

As early as 1726 Martin Bladen, one of the most influential members of the Board of Trade and a man greatly interested in British
mercantile policies, laid it down as a general principle that "all the
products of the colonies for which the manufacture and trade of Britain has a constant demand be enumerated among the goods which
by law must first be transported to Britain before they can be carried to any other market" and that "every valuable merchandize to
be found in the English colonies and but rarely anywhere else and
for which there is a constant demand in Europe shall also be enumerated in order to assist Great Britain in the ballance of trade with
other countries."[1] But it was not until after 1763 that this thoroughly
orthodox mercantile idea was given application.[2] Then it was that the
list of enumerated commodities was further extended by the inclusion of coffee, pimento (Jamaica pepper),[3] cacao, hides and skins,
whalefins, raw silk, pot and pearl ashes, iron, and lumber—all from
America, and gum seneca from Senegambia.[4] But the returns were
bound to be relatively trifling. In 1766 and 1767 when Great Britain
was endeavoring to strengthen her whole financial system, the rule
was laid down that even if a commodity were not enumerated it had
to be sent to England, Scotland, Wales, Berwick-upon-Tweed, to another plantation, or to some country south of Cape Finisterre, thus
making Great Britain the staple for all colonial commodities, as far
as central and northern Europe was concerned. At the same time an
earlier rule which had been for many years discontinued that consuls
and ministers in foreign countries should make reports on the character of the trade in their respective ports was revived and enforced.[5]
This was what many of the mercantilists wanted and had wanted
from the beginning, for it prohibited all direct trade in colonial products to countries north of Spain, and made England, with the exceptions noted, the magazine of all the commodities produced in the

1. *North Carolina Colonial Records*, II, 628–629.
2. 4 George III, c. 15, §§xxvi, xxvii.
3. Jamaica pepper is a kind of allspice, with an aromatic flavor, resembling a mixture of cloves, juniper berries, cinnamon, nutmegs, and pepper (Postlethwayt, *Dictionary of Commerce*, II, 467). It is an important Jamaica staple today.
4. Senegambia was a royal colony from 1763 to 1783 (Martin, *The British West
African Settlements*, p. 64; 5 George III, c. 37, §4). A seizure of gum seneca was
made in 1733. *Calendar Treasury Books and Papers*, 1731–1734, p. 463.
5. *Board of Trade Journal*, 1764–1767, p. 136. Below, pp. 148, 424.

plantations. By this sweeping restriction, the enumeration in its application to the American colonies was brought to its highest point of completeness.

At the same time it must always be remembered that what appears to have been a mercantilist victory would not have been so easily won had not the extension of the enumeration coincided with the financial needs of the kingdom. As will be noted in a later chapter parliament refused many times to follow the lead or to meet the demands of the merchant-capitalists, and many a parliamentary member considered the men engaged in business as serving rather their private ends (their "private and mean purposes," as one speaker put it) than the interests of the country at large. The period after 1763 was less than ever a time of mercantilist ascendancy.

# CHAPTER V

# THE SYSTEM COMPLETED: 1663–1673

THE act of 1660 covered two of the main objects sought to be attained by the navigation acts—the increase of shipping and the enumeration of colonial commodities, the first in the interest of England's mercantile marine, and the second looking to the enlargement of the revenue, the multiplying of raw materials, the advancement of England's domestic industry, and the comfort of her people. A third and final object was still to be considered—the making of England the staple for all European goods imported into the colonies, that is, the imposing of the requirement that all commodities from other countries which were wanted in the plantations should pass through England as the sole exporting center before shipment overseas to America. This objective, which was the counterpart of that sought in the enumeration—whereby England was made the sole receiving staple for certain colonial products— was dealt with in the Act for the Encouragement of Trade, passed July 27, 1663.[1] The act as a whole was not adopted without a protest from the House of Lords, but the protest of the upper house did not touch the feature in which we are here interested.[2] In its main purpose the act was concerned with the relief of tillage, but in two of its clauses provision was made that all commodities of the growth, production, and manufacture of Europe, destined for the plantations, should first be carried to England, Wales, or Berwick-upon-Tweed, in lawful shipping, lawfully manned, and there be put ashore before being carried to America. This meant that with a few exceptions all the European import trade of the plantations had first to pass through England as a staple and that all European manufactured goods had to be unladen in one or other of the ports of the realm and there related for export as if they were English commodities. In case of such re-export the same drawbacks were allowed—except (by later interpretation) on foreign ironware and cordage[3]—that were granted under similar circumstances to goods re-exported to foreign countries.

1. 15 Charles II, c. 7, §§v, vi.
2. The peers objected to the clauses (xii, xiii) relating to the export of money and bullion and the treatment of Ireland.
3. *Board of Trade Journal,* 1714–1718, p. 119.

Certain exceptions are mentioned in the act. First, salt for the fisheries of New England and Newfoundland, much of which came from the Isle of May (Maio) of the Cape Verde group belonging to Portugal, the sole right of exportation having been granted to England by Portugal in the treaty of 1661. Later the privilege was extended to Pennsylvania, New York, Nova Scotia, and Quebec.[1] In 1739 Virginia and in 1755 Maryland and North Carolina prayed, but without success, for a like concession, Maryland sending to England a petition signed by Lord Baltimore and "all the eminent merchants," and North Carolina a similar petition from the merchants, traders, and planters of the colony.[2] Later letters from Governor Dobbs of North Carolina outlining the needs of the province, that of salt in particular, went unheeded.[3] The southern colonies throughout the colonial period were not allowed to import salt directly either from Spain or Portugal or from England; they were obliged to take what they needed for the curing and packing of their beef and pork from their northern neighbors at double freight and an advanced price, or else to make their own salt by evaporating sea-water. They could have got salt of a kind from some of the Caribbee Islands—Tortuga or Turks Island—but they complained that the variety from that quarter was too strong, corroding and destroying the meat juices.

Secondly, servants, horses, and provisions from Scotland and Ireland and later linen from the latter country,[4] an exception that ceased to apply to Scotland after 1707 and in the case of Ireland led to some ingenious attempts at evasion, as when certain shippers listed candles and soap as "provisions" and, when brought to book, offered to prove their point by eating them.[5] Ireland took full advantage of the privilege accorded her and shipped both servants and provisions, grain in small quantities, salted beef and other meats in larger quan-

1. Pennsylvania, 1726, 13 George I, c. 5; New York, 1730, 3 George II, c. 12; Nova Scotia, 1762, 2 George III, c. 24; Quebec, 1763, 4 George III, c. 19. For the New York and Virginia petitions, *Board of Trade Journal*, 1728–1734, p. 73; 1735–1741, pp. 278–279.

2. Treasury 1:360, February 9, 1755; *Maryland Archives*, L, 266, 267–268.

3. *North Carolina Colonial Records*, V, 322; VI, 1030; IX, 269–270. References to these various petitions can be found in *Board of Trade Journal*, 1754–1758, p. 79; 1759–1763, pp. 258, 265, 267–268, 336, 399.

4. 3–4 Anne, c. 8; *House of Lords Manuscripts*, new series, V, no. 1958; VII, 233; Stock, *Debates*, III, 40–41.

5. *Some Thoughts humbly offered toward a Union between Great Britain and Ireland* (1708), p. 19; *Calendar State Papers, Colonial*, 1677–1680, §1304, "One witness swore that soap was victuals and that one might live upon it for a month, which the jury readily believed and found [for the defendant]."

tities, to Newfoundland and the West Indies, and general provisions to the French islands, a trade not forbidden by English law and so publicly tolerated that the governors of the islands were quite unable to prevent it. But Ireland could never compete with New England and the Middle Colonies as purveyors of food to the West Indies, and was never encouraged by the continental colonies as a whole to send over servants, particularly Roman Catholics, who were feared and disliked and in Maryland were discriminated against by an act imposing a duty upon them, in order "to prevent the importing of too great a number of Irish papists" into the province.[1] There is some reason to think that under cover of this privilege of sending provisions and servants the Irish exporters carried contraband goods in time of war and manufactured goods in time of peace, though the evidence is hard to get at.[2]

Thirdly, wines from Madeira and the Azores, a traffic that attained considerable proportions in the northern colonies, in which wheat, flour, and pipe-staves were exchanged for butts and pipes of wine brought directly from the islands and not from any other part of Europe.[3] The chief interest in this clause of the act lies in the dispute that arose and remained more or less unsettled till the end of our colonial period, as to whether wines from the Canaries, a Spanish not a Portuguese group, could also be imported.[4] The first recorded case occurred in 1685, when a Teneriffe merchant was charged with shipping Canary wines directly to America, without first landing them at an English port. The lord high treasurer, informed of

1. *Maryland Archives*, XXX, 328; *Calendar State Papers, Colonial*, 1714–1715, p. 249. Nevis (near Montserrat, which abounded in Roman Catholics) made a law in 1701, that no one should be obliged to buy an Irish servant. *Calendar State Papers, Colonial*, 1701, pp. 573–574.

2. Many of the governors reported their suspicions, but the evidence does not seem conclusive that any such illegal trading was extensively carried on. The seizure of the ship *Oxford* at Barbados in 1712 is a case in point. *Calendar State Papers, Colonial*, 1714–1715, index.

3. An interesting case of this kind arose in North Carolina when the master, Thomas Gardiner, ship *Betty and Peggy*, was charged by the collector at Port Brunswick with having clandestinely landed in the colony casks of Madeira wine not taken on at Madeira but from some other port of Europe. He was discharged by the vice-admiralty court on producing the proper certificate of clearance, because the collector was unable to substantiate his libel. Records of Admiralty, North Carolina, February 12, 1744 (no paging).

4. For the early history of the Canary trade see Miss Skeel's article, "The Canary Company," in the *English Historical Review*, XXXI, 529–544; *Calendar Treasury Books*, I, 733.

the fact, instructed the customs commissioners to use their utmost endeavors to have the vessel condemned.[1] Another and more important case came up in 1686, when London merchants were charged with the same offense and their vessel was seized by Captain John George in Boston harbor.[2] Trial was ordered in Massachusetts, but the court there demurred giving judgment, on the ground that the Canaries were in Africa and not in Europe, and a decree was rendered giving the ship and lading back to the consignee, John Usher, pending an appeal to England. The case was referred to the commissioners of the customs, who said that the importation of wine from the Canary Islands directly to the plantations was contrary to law, "in regard the said islands have in construction and practice been constantly understood to be in Europe, although they have been sometimes laid in the mapps of Africa." As the merchants in question promised to offend no more, the commissioners recommended that the ship be released and the transgressors discharged from further prosecution.

In 1702, Randolph, who had seized many ships in New England for this alleged breach of the law, brought the matter up again and called for a ruling.[3] As might have been expected the customs officials and later the Board of Trade[4] upheld the strict construction of the law and many of the Canary merchants themselves seem to have understood that Canary wines had first to be brought to England in English bottoms, before going to America.[5] But the legal authorities had their doubts and from the beginning were convinced that the official ruling was wrong. They insisted that the Canaries were more African than either the Azores or Madeira and so ought to be equally privileged. Attorneys General Sawyer in 1686, Northey in 1706, and the standing counsel of the board, Francis Fane, in 1737, all agreed that the Canaries were a part of Africa and that their wines could be carried legally directly to the plantations.[6] The Spanish minister and

1. *Calendar Treasury Books*, VIII, 170.
2. *Ibid.*, pp. 897, 956–957, 994–995. The facts are given on p. 995, and copies of opinions in the case are in Blathwayt's Entry Books, I, 201–204, 210–211, Treasury 60:88.
3. C. O. 388:8, E, 9, p. 13.
4. *Ibid.*, 389:28, pp. 43–45, representation of August 15, 1721, against a proposal of the Spanish minister to open a trade from the Canary Islands directly to the British plantations. Another representation was sent February 3, 1718, *Board of Trade Journal*, 1715–1718, p. 333.
5. *House of Lords Manuscripts*, new series, VI, 204.
6. *Calendar Treasury Books*, VIII, 957; Hargreave Manuscripts, 141, fos. 35b–36; Chalmers, *Opinions*, II, 275–276.

the Canary merchants in England, who wanted the liberty of a direct trade, took the same position, though they agreed that the inhabitants of the islands "would be affronted to be called Africans."[1] In 1736 the board found itself in an awkward dilemma, for with its standing counsel deciding one way and the commissioners of the customs deciding another, and Dr. Halley, the astronomer, to whom it appealed to know whether the Canaries were in Europe or Africa, apparently too preoccupied to answer at all (he was then eighty years old), it decided, perhaps wisely, to take no further steps for the moment.[2] Canary wines were imported openly in both New York and Boston and probably elsewhere and as far as the vice-admiralty courts are concerned there is but one case recorded of seizure for this reason.[3] It may be that the conflicting opinions of the authorities and

1. *Board of Trade Journal,* 1715–1718, p. 332; 1718–1722, p. 300.

2. *Ibid.,* 1735–1741, pp. 98, 111, 128, 129, 130, 155, 163.

3. Consul Crosse said in 1719 that the government of Boston freely allowed the importation of Canary wines, and we know that the Massachusetts assembly passed an act in 1734 granting rates and duties, so worded that the Board of Trade said it permitted Canary wines to be imported "contrary to the Acts of Trade" (*ibid.,* p. 98). Long before, in 1704, Governor Dudley had thought they were not included in the act (*Calendar State Papers, Colonial,* 1704–1705, p. 187). In 1719 Archibald Cummings reported the annual importation into Boston of 1800 pipes of Azores, Madeira, and Canary wines (*Calendar State Papers, Colonial,* 1716–1717, p. 267). New York must have done much the same, for in 1738 Canary wines are mentioned among the imports (*New York Colonial Documents,* VI, 127). There is a case of condemnation in the Records of Admiralty, Rhode Island, July 12, 1740, for an attempt to import Canary wine under the guise of Madeira. Among the documents in the case is an instruction from the consignor at Teneriffe (April 20, 1740), ordering the supercargo to make the attempt. *New England Quarterly,* VI, 144–154, article by Dorothy S. Towle.

The case of the *Eagle* galley, which was seized in 1704 at New York and was the subject of considerable correspondence for other reasons than that it had Canary wines on board, is deserving of attention. The facts are given by the collector, Thomas Byerley, who libeled the ship (*Calendar State Papers, Colonial,* 1704–1705, §379) and by Lord Cornbury, who opposed the seizure, in his letter to the Treasury, April 30, 1704, among the Treasury Board Papers, bundle 90, no. 62. This letter is not printed in the *New York Colonial Documents.* The ship was tried in the vice-admiralty court, Roger Mompesson, judge, the proceedings of which are in C. O. 5:1084. Neither Cornbury nor the attorney general, Weaver, opposed the admission of the wines and Weaver's opinion coincides with that of the English lawyers. Most of the documents in the case can be found in *New York Colonial Documents,* IV, V, index, under "Ships Eagle Galley," and in *Calendar State Papers, Colonial,* 1704–1705, index, under "Eagle, galley." There are additional documents in Treasury 1:95, no. 10 (cargo and report of commissioners of the customs to the lord high treasurer, July 11, 1705, with enclosure—Byerley's letter to Godolphin of June 1, 1704).

In another case, that of the *Cole and Bean* galley of South Carolina, there were Canary wines on board, but the ship was condemned in the Charles Town vice-admiralty court on other grounds. Bodleian, Rawlinson, A, 270, fos. 43–47.

the "conceived notion that Canaries are confiscable" deterred many British merchants from undertaking the trade.[1]

The idea of the staple was old but its application to the colonies, with the whole realm of England as the mart, was new.[2] The objects of the act, as stated in the stilted language of the text, were to maintain a greater correspondence between the plantations, peopled by the king's subjects, and the kingdom of England; to keep them in a firmer dependence upon it; to make them more beneficial and advantageous unto it in the further employment and increase of English shipping, vent of woolen and other manufactures and commodities; to render the navigation from the same more safe and cheap; to constitute the kingdom a staple, not only of the enumerated articles of those countries, but also of the articles of other countries and places, for the shipping of them, and to follow the usages of other nations in keeping their plantation trade to themselves.[3] In 1663 the colonies were increasing in population and importance; old settlements were being strengthened and new settlements projected. Plans for the seizure of New Amsterdam were under consideration and a general advance for the benefit of trade and colonization was receiving the careful attention of the Duke of York and those in his con-

1. Historical Manuscripts Commission, *Polwarth*, II, 14.

2. The staple in England was a fiscal device for the easier and more certain collection of the customs revenue. The Scottish staple was a device for the improvement of the foreign trade of Scotland. The latter was located at Veere (Campvere) on the island of Walcheren as early as 1541, and its object was to enhance the prosperity of the Scottish merchant class and exclude the foreigner. Until 1672 the export trade of Scotland was the exclusive right of the royal boroughs—Dundee, Perth, St. Andrews, Aberdeen, Montrose, Cowper, and others—and was conducted through a continental town, either Veere or Middleburg, at a time when security could be gained only through concentration. In England the staple was a royal affair; in Scotland it was primarily an affair of the boroughs (Davidson and Gray, *Staple at Veere*, part III, ch. I. See also Rooseboom, *Scottish Staple in the Netherlands,* and Van Brakel, "A Neglected Source for the History of the Commercial Relations between Scotland and the Netherlands during the 16th, 17th, and 18th Centuries," *Scottish Historical Review,* October, 1919). The rise of Glasgow to commercial prominence was coincident with the decay of the royal boroughs. It was due to the abolition of the archbishopric in 1688, to the royal grant of self-governing privileges in 1698, and to the Union of 1707, whereby all the Scottish ports were placed on the same footing at home and on an equality with the English ports in respect of the navigation acts. The superior location of Glasgow soon put that city in the lead. *History of Glasgow,* I (by Robert Renwick), II (by George Eyre-Todd); John Gibson, *History of Glasgow,* ch. XII, appendix, xxiii.

3. Repeated in 22–23 Charles II, c. 26, §§x, xi, and embodied in the circular letter sent, August 25, 1663, to the governors of the colonies, *Calendar State Papers, Colonial,* 1661–1668, §539. The calendaring is too brief; the full text is in C. O. 1:17, no. 72.

fidence, who as courtier-promoters were interested in the founding of new colonies—the Jerseys and the Carolinas, and later the Bahamas—and in the erection of the Royal African Company, the Royal Fishery Company, and the Hudson's Bay Company, all enterprises that were closely identified with the plans of the merchants of London and the Whitehall group.

To Englishmen colonies were slowly becoming a part of the established order of things and the proper principles according to which their relationship with the mother country was to be determined were already undergoing definition. A new era was opening and the dependence of the colonies upon England had to be made clear at the outset. To allow the colonies to buy elsewhere than in England their woolens and the finished products of other countries and to carry them from the place of purchase directly to their own ports, passing by the merchants and manufacturers of England and taking advantage of the lower French and Dutch prices, to their own profit but to the injury of English trade and customs revenue—such a policy was inconceivable.[1] It was necessary to consider not only the loss of the customs revenue, the damage to the balance of trade, and the political misfortunes that were certain to accrue, but also the possible

---

1. Note the words of the royal warrant sent to the "Governor of Roanoke" (*sic*) in 1675, which are interesting not only as being addressed to some one who did not exist (as there was no "Governor of Roanoke"), but also as containing in brief the essential reasons for the passing of the navigation acts. What the writer of the warrant had in mind in using the address "Governor of Roanoke" is beyond explanation, unless he was thinking of the governor of North Carolina. Like warrants were sent to the other governors under their proper names. *Calendar Treasury Books*, IV, 852.

The warrant reads as follows: "In spite of the Act of Trade 15 Car. II., great quantities of European goods have been imported into your colony not being laden in England, Wales or Berwick; to the great detriment of the King's Customs and of the trade and navigation of England. We have issued our royal proclamation for the prevention of such unlawful and evil practices for the future [two days before, November 24, 1675, Brigham *Proclamations*, pp. 126–128, *Calendar State Papers, Colonial*, 1675–1676, §713, *Acts Privy Council, Colonial*, I, §1046]. You are to publish same in the colony of Roanoke and punish offenders. We are informed that the subjects of some of our colonies have taken great liberty, not only in supplying themselves with European commodities from other places than England, but also bring such goods into other of our colonies to the discouragement of fair traders and the diminution of the King's Customs." The proclamation of the 24th and this warrant of the 26th disclose, even better than the act itself, the working of the English mind.

In depositions before the High Court of Admiralty, 1702–1704, two statements are made. "It was ever practicable for English merchants, thô resident in Holland or Portugall, to send their English or plantation built vessels, navigated according to the acts of navigation, with their cargoes [of European goods] to Newfoundland and other of her Majesties plantations, and soe much the deponent hath often seen prac-

frustration of the government's efforts to emerge solvent from the bankruptcy of the Puritan administration and the deficit caused by the king's debts, and to place the kingdom once more in a sound financial condition. Trade was becoming essential to the attainment of prosperity and the value of commerce and the colonies, as means whereby this result was to be attained, was recognized by all responsible men during the first years of the Restoration when the acts of navigation and trade were passed.

Immediate steps were taken to put the acts into execution. Letters were written to the governors of all the colonies, ordering them to see that all foreign trade with the plantations was strictly observed and reminding them that any neglect or connivance on their part would be followed by heavy penalties. The act of 1660 required of them, at the risk of being discharged from their employ if they failed, a solemn oath, binding them to do their utmost that the act "be punctually and *bona fide* observed," an obligation that was repeated and reinforced by letters sent from the Privy Council, June 24, 1663.[1] The governors were also ordered to keep account of all vessels trading to their particular colonies and twice a year to send to England the names of ships and masters. They were to transmit copies of all bonds, such as the act required all masters to give at the port of clearance, holding the latter to a faithful observance of the law requiring them to carry their cargoes to England or to some other plantation.[2] They were to scrutinize all foreign-built ships com-

---

ticed in Holland with freedom of the Custom House in England." And again from a merchant long resident in Portugal, "He sent severall English built ships with cargoes [of European goods] from thence to Newfoundland and brought the same back to Portugall and the same trade was practiced by several other English merchants then residing there and in Spain (such ships being navigated according to the act of Navigation) and that the deponent never met with any interruption in the said trade but looked upon the same to be lawful trade." Bodleian, Rawlinson, B, 333, fos. 565–598.

1. *New York Colonial Documents*, III, 45–46; *Massachusetts Colonial Records*, II, 86–87, where the colony promises to obey the law. Both Walter Clarke and Samuel Cranston, governors of Rhode Island, refused to take the oaths, just as they refused to allow the erection in the colony of a court of vice-admiralty. Rhode Island had her own way of doing many of these things. No wonder the colony got a bad reputation in England for contrariness as well as for illegal trading and piracy (*Calendar State Papers, Colonial*, 1697–1698, §§282, ii, 521, 901, 1071; 1699, §§101, 1002, xv; 1700, §913), though in the eyes of the Board of Trade she did not compare with Massachusetts in the days of Shute and Burnet.

2. The idea of the bond, of which much will be said later, was not new. The Privy Council issued an order in 1633, requiring all commanders of ships coming from any of the plantations to give bond to bring their vessels and lading, without

ing to the colonies to see whether or not such ships were trading legally, had the proper certificates of "freedom," and had given the required bond in England. The staple act of 1663 enacted further that all masters furnish the governors with complete information regarding their ships and cargoes, and placed the governors themselves under the additional obligation of taking oath, giving bond, and furnishing security at the exchequer in England before their departure for America. The original bond had to be deposited with the king's remembrancer and a copy was kept in the Plantation Office.[1] By a later ruling all governors appointed by the proprietors were to have their bonds approved by the attorney general, their securities accepted at the exchequer, and their certificates issued out of the remembrancer's office.[2] Bonds in the case of the corporate colonies, Connecticut and Rhode Island, the governors of which were not selected in England, were to be taken out in America, though the form of such bonds does not appear to have been drawn up even as late as 1722.[3] From time to time special trade instructions were issued to the governors of all the colonies, which in the case of the proprietary colonies were sent to the proprietors. Thus in all the colonies—royal, proprietary, and corporate—the governors were made the sole responsible agents for carrying out the acts of navigation and trade in America.[4]

During the period from 1660 to 1672, experience soon showed that an efficient administration of the acts was going to be both difficult and slow. Before two years had passed the merchants of Exeter were petitioning parliament regarding violations of the act of 1660, and on August 26, 1663, the king issued a proclamation repeating his command for a punctual and efficient execution and observance of the law and calling on the customs officers for a faithful performance of their duties. Later, in 1667, he issued another proclamation recalling

breaking bulk, into the port of London or some other port of the kingdom, there to enter and unlade their goods. *Ibid.*, 1574–1660, p. 165.

1. *Board of Trade Journal*, 1722–1728, pp. 15, 20; 1728–1734, p. 408.

2. *Ibid.*, 1709–1715, pp. 433, 437; 1715–1718, pp. 199, 200, etc.

3. *Connecticut Colonial Records*, 1717–1725, p. 364; *Rhode Island Colonial Records*, IV, 327; *Board of Trade Journal*, 1718–1722, p. 353. The form of the bond to be furnished by the governors of the royal colonies was drawn up in 1697 by the attorney general (Treasury 27:14, p. 19). Legally the election of the governors in Connecticut and Rhode Island should have received the approval of the crown as did the appointment of those in the proprietary provinces, but this was never done.

4. *New York Colonial Documents*, IV, 281–292; *Acts Privy Council, Colonial*, III, 21; *Board of Trade Journal*, 1718–1722, pp. 347–348, 353, 355.

dispensations that had been authorized by the Privy Council three years before.[1] A more effective gesture was the capture of New Amsterdam in 1664, whereby an important center of Dutch trade with the colonies was eliminated.[2] It is doubtful, however, whether this somewhat high-handed exploit had any material effect on the Dutch trade as a whole, for Roger Coke could still write in 1670 that of all the world the Dutch were "the most considerable and the richest and the most mighty by trade." The Dutch recovered their colony in July, 1673, but held it less than a year, New Amsterdam becoming New York again in 1674. From that time forward Dutch trading connections with the colonies were largely confined to interchanges, both legitimate and illegitimate, at Amsterdam and other Dutch ports in Holland and at Curaçao, Surinam, and St. Eustatius in the Caribbean. Direct trade with Holland was contrary to the acts and had to be carried on surreptitiously, but direct trade with the Caribbean, particularly with Surinam on the part of the New Englanders, was lawful and frequent, unless the returning ships brought back European commodities, which was strictly forbidden but frequently indulged in. Most of the trade in this quarter was in the hands of colonial shippers and sea-captains, for the Dutch control of colonial freighting was rapidly nearing its end, the Dutch West India Company having been ruined by England's treaty with Portugal in 1661 and the loss of New Netherland in 1664. With Scotland, after the failure of the efforts at conciliation and union in the years from 1667 to 1670, matters remained about the same until 1680, when there took place a renewal of Scotland's interest in colonial trade, owing to the decay of religious influences in government, and the merchants of the royal boroughs, acting in conjunction with the Scottish parliament, began to bestir themselves in behalf of trade in the East and colonization in the West, the consequences of which will be discussed later. With Ireland also there was no trouble until the exclusion of that kingdom from the privileges of the navigation acts created a situation so unsatisfactory as to become the subject of an acute and unneighborly controversy.

For the moment, however, the most pressing issue was not with Holland, Scotland, or Ireland, but with the colonies themselves, for

1. Stock, *Debates*, I, 317; *Calendar State Papers, Domestic,* 1663–1664, p. 256, Brigham, *Proclamations*, pp. 114–116.
2. *New York Colonial Documents*, III, 43, 44–46; *Calendar State Papers, Colonial,* 1661–1668, §357.

rumors had been coming in that despite the commands of parliament and the warnings of the crown English merchants trading with America and even colonial sea-captains also were evading the act and engaging in a direct trade with Europe. There seemed to be no way to stop this practice, as long as colonial governors failed to prevent it by refusing clearances to vessels carrying enumerated commodities to Europe, for an English captain could easily leave England without stating his destination and so avoid taking out bond to return immediately to the mother country as the law required. But if not stopped the practice would mean a heavy loss to the English customs, especially in the case of tobacco, which had been enumerated largely for revenue purposes. The captains of English ships and even perhaps a few of those of the colonies also could easily take on ladings in America and run across to a Continental port in Holland and there dispose of their cargo at a better price and at a lower customs rate than in England. As they paid no customs at the port of departure they clearly gained and the English exchequer lost by their failure to touch at an English or Irish port during the passage.[1]

This form of direct trade with Europe had many varieties, one of which was peculiar and, as far as we can see, not designedly an evasion of the enumeration clause. Under the act any captain, English or colonial, could carry enumerated commodities from one plantation to another, without paying a customs duty at either end and without going to England at all. This form of coastwise traffic in enumerated commodities was permitted in order that the colonies might be supplied with what they needed for their own consumption and thus build up a coastwise trade for their own benefit. This intercolonial exchange of staple commodities was largely in the hands of colonial merchants and ship captains, for it is doubtful if the English merchants often engaged in it. New Englanders were carrying the tobacco of Virginia, Maryland, and North Carolina to New York

---

1. "We are informed that there are divers practices for defrauding us of the said customs by ships sailing hence without giving bond for their return as by law is enjoined, and foreign vessels which by too much connivance are suffered to lade within your government . . . and by many small vessels that come from the neighboring plantations and take in goods for other parts and return neither to this kingdom nor the said plantations." Charles II to the colonial governors, December 18, 1672 (*Calendar Treasury Books,* IV, 15). In 1684 the customs commissioners were instructed to write to the consul at Rotterdam to seize certain ships arriving there from Virginia and New York with tobacco, without having touched at England or Ireland. *Ibid.,* VII, 1119.

and Boston and Marylanders and Virginians were sending theirs to Barbados and other islands in the Caribbean.[1] How far this trade had gone or whether it was of frequent occurrence there is no possibility of saying, as the evidence for it is very slight. But the English officials and members of parliament often acted on reports that were none too reliable, because containing generalizations that were insufficiently supported and often unwarranted by the facts. In one abuse of this intercolonial privilege they saw an evasion of the act and another instance of an illegal trade directly with Europe. This particular abuse was as follows. When once a shipper had carried his tobacco or sugar from one colony to another, he may have thought that the letter of the law had been obeyed and, disregarding its manifest intent that all the cargo should be set ashore for the use of the colonists themselves, he would carry a part (or perhaps all) of his lading to some European port—Hamburg, Middleburg, Flushing, Rotterdam or Amsterdam—and there dispose of it to advantage. Should an English captain do this, who had already given bond in England, he may have thought that his securities were released from the penalties imposed and that he was free to go where he pleased. But probably the offenders, the tale of whose misdeeds was brought to the attention of parliament by English merchants trading to Virginia, were mainly New Englanders, who hardly considered the law as binding on them in any case, because they lay beyond the "narrow seas."

As this direct trade to Europe, in whatever form it might appear, menaced the efficiency of the enumeration clause and threatened to affect the customs revenue, parliament took the matter in hand and in 1673, added a supplementary and explanatory clause to the act for the encouragement of the Greenland and Eastland trades, which contained a simple but ingenious remedy.[2] By this clause all vessels from England arriving at the plantations and intending to take on a lading of enumerated commodities—the captains of which could not show to the governor or, later, to the naval officer or royal collector, or both, a certificate that they had taken out bond in England—must pay a duty at the port of clearance. This payment, which came to be known as the "plantation duty," was a penny a pound on tobacco and other amounts for other enumerated commodities. The captain

1. *New York Colonial Documents*, III, 183; *Maryland Archives*, V, 289; *Calendar State Papers, Colonial*, 1669–1674, §1059.
2. 25 Charles II, c. 7, §ii; Stock, *Debates*, I, 398, 399, 400.

was also obliged to deposit a bond with the governor, naval officer, or collector to the effect that if he did not unload the goods at some port of another colony he would take them directly to England. That which the English captains had to do the colonial captains and masters had to do also. Thus bonds accumulated in every colonial port and played an important part in the commercial history of the colonies throughout our entire colonial period.

The act of 1673 did more to systematize the commercial activities of the colonists than did any other regulation of the navigation acts except the enumeration, of which it was an integral part. It affected not only the commercial relations between England and her colonies but also the relations of the colonies among themselves. Nearly all the chief ports, particularly of the mainland, did an extensive coastwise and island freighting business and re-exported constantly enumerated products to England or to some one or other of the English continental or West Indian plantations. The colonists in their own vessels carried tobacco up and down the coast and to the West Indies and brought back sugar, rum, and molasses to Boston, Newport, New York, Philadelphia, Norfolk, Brunswick, and Charles Town, either for local use or for reshipment. Hundreds of their cargoes contained not only sugar and tobacco but other enumerated commodities as well. Hence the imposition of the plantation duty and the obligation to furnish bonds became a part of a great many colonial mercantile transactions and raised many questions as to the operation of the act. The new requirement made necessary the installation in colonial ports of a large number of customs officials, for whom there had been no need before, appointed after 1696 on the English establishment by the customs commissioners under authority from the Treasury.[1] The business of these officials was to receive, retain, and if necessary prosecute, the bonds in the common law courts and collect the duties, which were supposed to be those of the English book of rates, payable in silver or its equivalent at sterling values.[2]

The object of the act was not revenue but the regulation of trade.

1. The early instructions, issued in the years from 1673 to 1675, contain excellent epitomes of the English view of what the law imposed (*Calendar Treasury Books*, IV, 424, 451–452, 521, 659, 824). For these officials and their duties, see below, ch. VII.

2. 12 Charles II, c. 4; Baldwin, *British Customs*, p. 63. In the case of tobacco the plantation duty was a penny a pound instead of the English duty at that time of two pence. Beer suggests that those who drafted the act of 1673 overlooked the additional penny. *Old Colonial System*, I, vol. I, 83.

Its chief purpose was to prevent evasion of the enumeration clause of the act of 1660, by rendering unprofitable a direct trade with Europe in enumerated commodities. Treasurer Danby said in 1675 that the duty was "to turn the course of a trade rather than to raise any considerable revenue to his Majesty," and William Blathwayt in 1692 said the same when he explained that the requirement "was imposed less for revenue than to hinder the exportation of enumerated commodities to other places than are allowed by law." In the same year the commissioners of the customs themselves defined the object of the duty as "less for revenue than to prevent exportations of goods from colony to colony and so to foreign countries, evading the English customs."[1] Of course, indirectly, the law aided the revenue by stopping a leak in the system and so making more effective the working of the enumeration clause, which had revenue as one of its main objects, but the first idea was to stop the leak and not to increase the customs returns. The scheme was not ideal from the mercantilist point of view, for the conservative English merchant did not like an arrangement which permitted any vessel, English or colonial, to carry enumerated commodities from one colony to another, and John Cary of Bristol would have had all ships going from England to America pledged to bring the commodities directly back to England.[2] In fact, however, the trade worked out much as the mercantilist desired, because, as we have seen, English ships only rarely engaged in the American coastwise trade, since doing so would have been both expensive and unprofitable, and consequently the plantation duty came more and more to be identified with colonial-built and colonial-owned vessels doing a local business.[3] In fact one complainant, in a case where his tobacco was seized, when laden for transportation to another colony, spoke of the practice as "according to the usage and custom of the plantations."[4]

1. *Calendar Treasury Books*, IV, 705; *Calendar State Papers, Colonial*, 1689–1692, §§2065, 2306. In 1692 the object of the act was defined by the commissioners of the customs as follows: ". . . not so much to raise a revenue to the Crown as to prevent an unlimited trade then in practice of carrying tobacco to another [plantation] and conveying it thence into divers parts of Europe to the great hurt and diminution of the customs and the trade and navigation of the kingdom." *Calendar Treasury Books*, IX, 1965.

2. *An Essay on the State of England* (Bristol, 1695), pp. 71–72.

3. In a letter of 1692 to the Treasury, the commissioners of the customs said that the penny a pound duty was only payable on such tobacco as was carried from one of his Majesty's plantations to another. Treasury 1:18, no. 83.

4. Records of Admiralty, North Carolina, IV, paper about 1758, without date or page.

The imposition of the plantation duty raised a number of questions difficult to answer, though answers of a kind were generally found for all of them. If a captain took out a bond in the colony and paid the duty would he still have to carry the goods to England, in case he did not unload and leave them in the colony to which he was bound? There is reason to believe that the Boston merchants, inclined at this time to follow their own bent in trade, thought that if they paid the duty they could then carry their goods to Europe, as if they were re-exporting them from England.[1] So uncertain was the phraseology of the law that in 1676 the Lords of Trade sent to the attorney general, Sir William Jones, requesting an opinion on this point. The latter replied that if bonds were taken out in England then no plantation duty was required, but if the vessel had furnished no such bond or had come from another place than England then the captain must give bond, pay the duty, and carry the goods either to another colony or to England, for, he added, "the statute of 25 Car. II does not in any sort repeal the act of the 12th, but only imposes a duty where the bond was not confined to a bringing to England."[2] This opinion itself lacks both clearness and completeness, and the obscurity was not removed until 1696, when in the great administration act of that year, the opinion of the attorney general was clarified and given statutory form: if not left in the colony the goods must be taken directly to England.

Other questions arose. Would the captain, in case he took his cargo to another colony, with the intention of unshipping there a part or the whole but for some reason or other decided to take a part or the whole to England, have to pay on arrival the English duty, even though he had already paid the plantation duty in the colony? There is reason to think that he would,[3] although it is probable that in so unusual an instance the plantation duty would be refunded.[4] The double duty could hardly have been considered either legal or just,

1. *Calendar State Papers, Colonial*, 1677–1680, pp. 488, 489; *Maryland Archives*, V, 448.

2. *Calendar State Papers, Colonial*, 1675–1676, §§798, 814; C. O. 5:903, p. 106. The calendaring is imperfect.

3. *Calendar State Papers, Colonial*, 1677–1680, p. 530, mentioning the double duty.

4. "Touching the peny per pound for tobacco carryed from Virginia to N. Yorke, the Commissioners think that if good security is given in Virginia that all the tobacco carryed thence to N. Yorke shall come streight to England and pay the Customs here then they believe it wilbe agreed (by the Commissioners of the Customes here) to quit them of the peny per pound paid in Virginia." *New York Colonial Documents*, III, 352, 393; *Documentary History*, II, 33.

particularly after 1685, when the tobacco duty at home was increased. Again, would the captain have to pay a second plantation duty at the second port of clearance in the colonies? Such a payment, though possible under a strict interpretation of the law, seems unlikely, for it would have meant giving a bond and paying a duty from colony to colony, as when a New England captain peddled tobacco from port to port in the West Indies. The case is not entirely hypothetical, though it must have been very rare.[1] Again, was tobacco taken from Maryland to Virginia or vice versa to pay the duty? Governor Nicholson raised this question in 1692,[2] saying that in his opinion "tobacco taken from one colony to another ought to pay duty according to the Act," but the Lords of Trade returned no answer, perhaps because no satisfactory answer could be returned. A more interesting case is that of the Leeward Islands, where it had been the custom for ships to go from one island to another in order to make up a cargo or to bring their sugars into one place for the purpose of convoying to England. The Treasury ruled that the Leeward Islands, being all under one government, had always been esteemed a single plantation and that consequently no duty should be collected.[3] It said further that such sloops and boats as plied among the islands were merely coasters and in no way different from vessels sailing between the ports of a single colony, as, for example, Maryland, where by special order of the Lords of Trade such vessels were exempted from entering with the collector. Oddly enough, vessels carrying tobacco in bulk, that is, not in casks or chests,[4] could go where they liked without giving bond or paying duty, for the act of 1699 which forbade bringing it to England as an enumerated commodity said noth-

1. This interpretation of the law seems to have been the reason for the seizure of the four bags of cotton by Samuel Sheafe, the deputy collector at Portsmouth, in 1699 (*American Legal Records*, III, Introduction, p. 50). The cotton had been imported into Boston from Barbados and into Portsmouth from Boston. Sheafe libeled the cotton because the Portsmouth merchants who bought it at Boston had not given bond "as the law required." See next note.

2. *Calendar State Papers, Colonial*, 1689–1692, §2075. The answer in the Sheafe case was that the acts of trade "were not intended against coasters in the plantations," and that trade between Boston and Portsmouth was a small-boat trade. The libelant denied this, saying that Boston, though a part of New England, was a distinct government from New Hampshire, as much so as was Barbados. *Calendar State Papers, Colonial*, 1702–1703, pp. 604, 606.

3. Treasury 4:9, p. 24; 27:14, pp. 135–136; *Calendar Treasury Books*, XI, 217, 227.

4. Tobacco stript from the stalk was forbidden by 9 George I, c. 21, §xvii (1722), but this clause was repealed in 1729. Stock, *Debates*, IV, xv.

ing about its exportation to another colony,[1] in consequence of which, wrote Edward Randolph, "great quantities are yearly carried from the tobacco plantations in bulk and from thence into Scotland, to the discouragement and damage of fair traders and to the great diminution of his Majesty's revenue."[2] The matter was not important, despite Randolph's fears.

The place of Scotland and Ireland in the operation of the navigation acts requires a further consideration. As we have already seen, by the acts of 1660 and 1662, Scotland was regarded as an alien country and Scotsmen were barred from the English coasting trade and from trade with the plantations. Her seamen were not classed as "English" and her shipping could not be used to carry goods to America. By the act of 1663 she could send over servants, horses, and provisions, and in the case of servants this was beneficial all around, for Scottish servants were much in demand, particularly in the West Indies. A few licenses were issued, one to Captain John Brown, who had a patent for setting up sugar refineries in Scotland and was allowed to employ four Scottish ships in the plantation trade in sugar. But these licenses, if ever actually used, were not long continued.[3] Petitions from English merchants against the Scottish navigation act of 1661 were met by recommendations, July, 1664, from the special council of trade of 1660 that the English duties on salt, coal, corn, and cattle be reduced, in order to encourage a better balance of trade with Scotland, and that every effort should be made to obtain a repeal of the Scottish act.[4] But these recommendations were merely temporizing measures that meant nothing as long as England refused to admit Scotland to the privileges of her own system. Finding that no concessions were to be obtained which in any degree would meet their wishes, the Scots made an application to Charles II to revive the plan for a treaty of union, which had once before, in 1604, been discussed without result, and the king in his speech to both

1. 10–11 William III, c. 21, §xxix. *Calendar State Papers, Colonial,* 1728–1729, §§262, i, 562. Laws forbidding the export of bulk tobacco to England were passed by both Virginia and Maryland, but these colonies seem to have taken it for granted that shipping in bulk to other colonies was permissible. Hening, *Statutes,* III, 344, 491; *Maryland Archives,* XV, 151; XIX, 90–91.

2. C. O. 388:8, E, 9, p. 3.

3. *Calendar State Papers, Colonial,* 1661–1668, §§543, 848. For the licensing of two Scottish ships to pass from Scotland to New York, see *Acts Privy Council, Colonial,* I, §§841, 848, 850; *New York Colonial Documents,* III, 180–182.

4. *Calendar State Papers, Domestic,* Charles II, Vol. III, 651. For the Scottish act, above, p. 70.

houses of parliament in 1670 recommended that the matter be taken into consideration. In appealing to the king the Scots were not acting of serious purpose; they probably brought forward the issue in order to gain time. The question was debated for a year, but the difficulties in the way of an agreement proved in the end insuperable.[1]

Then the Scots entered upon a course of illicit trading that adds immensely to the picturesqueness of this period.[2] Thinking that they had been unjustly treated they were willing to do anything, legal or illegal, whereby they might outwit the English, for feelings ran high on both sides. The presence of many a Scot in the colonies, particularly in the middle continental section and in parts of the West Indies, roused the suspicion that Scot was in league with Scot for the nullification of the acts, and this suspicion, coupled with unmistakable evidences of illicit commerce, particularly on the part of Maryland, Virginia, and Pennsylvania,[3] grew steadily stronger during the ensuing twenty-five years, until in the plantation field and in certain branches of commerce enmity of the Englishman for the Scot became almost an obsession. Many of those who were especially zealous in their efforts to enforce the acts saw in the Scot the greatest obstacle in the way of their successful execution. There can be little doubt that the exclusion of the Scots troubled the English more than it did the Scots themselves.

The Irish situation was quite different and much more complicated. At first it was intended that Ireland should be included within the privileged area to which the acts applied, as regards both ships and seamen and the carrying trade. But in 1662 the Irish parliament passed an act granting a subsidy of tonnage and poundage to the king, in which plantation products imported from England—the most important of which were sugar and tobacco—were to pay but half the customs given in the English book of rates,[4] a provision which gave pain to many an English merchant. Consequently in 1663, for this and other reasons, the trading privilege was revoked and Ireland, construed as a commercial rival, was forbidden after that date to send any exports to the plantations, except those specifi-

1. Bruce, *Report*, I, 189–214, 216–230; II, documents, xxxi–xlv; Defoe, *History of the Union, passim*; Dicey and Rait, *Thoughts on the Union*, appendices.

2. Keith, *Commercial Relations of England and Scotland*, pp. 118–128; *House of Lords Manuscripts*, new series, II, 464–466.

3. *Calendar Treasury Books*, X, 698–699.

4. *Irish Statutes at Large*, II, 419; Stock, *Debates*, I, 460–461; *Calendar State Papers, Colonial*, 1675–1676, §1193 (very meager, see C. O. 1:38, no. 96).

cally mentioned in the act, or to receive directly any of the enumerated commodities. English residents in Ireland protested vigorously against this exclusion, claiming that Ireland was "in a manner incorporated and become one body with England" and should not be barred from any of the advantages of the realm.[1] But England's fear of Irish competition was too ingrained to be removed, and the merchants replied that as Ireland lay "so much more commodious and nearer than this kingdom do's for all the southern trade, their freight is considerably less than what we pay here" and if they were allowed equal advantages "they will thereby be enabled to undersell us in all foreign markets."[2] The fear of being undersold was a veritable nightmare to the mercantile gentlemen of London and of the outports too, and determined their attitude toward not only the Irish and the Scots but the Dutch and the French as well. They seemed to have been always timorous, constantly complaining that they were being "beaten out of the trade," and whenever trade seemed to be languishing or in decay, as was perennially claimed to be the case, they found the cause in the competition of rivals, at home, abroad, and in the colonies. Henceforth, therefore, Ireland had commercial communications with the colonies only by way of England. To but a very limited extent could she engage in an independent trade of her own.[3]

1. Sir Walter Harris, *Remarks on the Affairs and Trade of England and Ireland* (1691), pp. 34–44. There is at least one exception to this statement. A Mr. Clements, in *The Interest of England as it stands with relation to the Trade of Ireland Considered* (1698), wrote many years later, "Let us always remember that this Island (or Province) is a Colony; that England is our Mother Countrey; that we are ever to expect Protection from her in the Possession of our Lands; which we are to cultivate and improve for our own Subsistence and Advantage, but not to trade to or with any other Nation without her permission and that 'tis our incumbent Duty to pay Obedience to all such Laws as she shall enact concerning us," p. 23.

2. *Board of Trade Journal*, 1708–1715, pp. 301, 353. In 1704 Mr. Justice Tracy of the Court of Common Pleas and Mr. Baron Smith of the court of exchequer, in a report to the House of Lords, gave as one reason for England's attitude toward Ireland the fear that "the [plantation] trade would be in a great measure diverted from hence and carried elsewhere" (*House of Lords Manuscripts*, new series, V, 346), that is, to grant the Irish demand would "rob this kingdom in great measure of this flourishing [plantation] trade" (*Calendar State Papers, Colonial*, 1685–1688, §613). Baseless as this fear probably was, it was ever present in the mind of the English merchant.

3. The proposal that a mint be set up in Ireland, as necessary if a linen manufacture were to be established there, was opposed by Sir Isaac Newton as placing Ireland on a parity with England. "Ireland [he said] is one of the English plantations . . . annexed to the Crown of England like other plantations and ought to be inferior to this kingdom and subservient to its interests. And therefore we are unwilling that any opinion of ours should be made use of for promoting any design

During the years 1680 to 1685, the Irish situation presented the customs officials with a problem that proved exceedingly troublesome and difficult to solve, due entirely to the carelessness of parliament. Even after the passage of the act of 1663, which barred Ireland from the plantation trade, bonds continued to be issued in the form prescribed by the navigation act of 1660, which admitted Ireland to all the privileges of the act. Thus from 1663 to 1671 the bonds read one way and the act of 1663 reads another. Ireland was allowed to trade by the bonds and forbidden to do so by the act. The resulting confusion was so great that the Treasury took the matter up in 1670 and called in the crown lawyers and the farmers of the customs to discuss the matter.[1] It first thought of a test trial before the court of exchequer, but finally decided to appeal to parliament and obtain the passage of an act removing the contradiction. Consequently in 1671 a clause was inserted in the act for preventing the planting of tobacco in England, ordering that the word "Ireland" be stricken from the bonds.[2] Legally this settled the matter until 1680, when the act expired and was not renewed, why it is difficult to say.[3] With the failure to renew the act the former conditions recurred and it became possible once more to ship enumerated commodities from the colonies to Ireland, to the great concernment of those whose business it was to collect the king's revenue.

After the passage of the act of 1671, an official was appointed to reside in Dublin and to correspond with the customs officers in the various Irish ports. From time to time he was to give an account of

which may tend to draw thither the money and trade of this nation and to make them of equal dignity and dominion with ourselves and perhaps at length desirous to separate from this Crown upon some fit opportunity of joining with its enemies." *Calendar Treasury Books*, XIV, 107 (September 2, 1698).

1. On June 20, 1670, Downing wrote to the attorney and solicitor general and the farmers of the customs: "The Lords Commissioners of the Treasury desire you to be here on Monday next at 3 in the afternoon about ships going from the plantations with sugars and tobacco into Ireland and from thence into foreign parts, in regard as they are informed there is to be a Tryall about it at the Exchequer next Tuesday" (Treasury 27:2, p. 318). The farmers said that "by the act [of 1660] they might take bonds to let such shipping go to Ireland but that by the act [of 1663] they can take no bond but to return to England." *Calendar Treasury Books*, II, 463. Also 461, 601.

2. 22–23 Charles II, c. 26, §4.

3. Why the law was not renewed must be left to conjecture. Parliament sat from October 21, 1680, to January 10, 1681. On November 23 leave was given to bring in a bill to renew, but the bill, if introduced, was not passed. Thus the matter was not forgotten but it was probably pushed aside by the press of other business. Stock, *Debates*, I, 421–422.

all such vessels as were found to be trading with the plantations and he proved himself "very useful in defeating many ships engaged in such irregular trade and probably deterred others from [engaging] in like illegal practices."[1] Though the commissioners of the revenue in Ireland said that during the years from 1671 to 1680 plantation goods were imported directly into Ireland as freely as when the trade was open, the trials of ships seized for illegal trading during that time number certainly twenty-five. Therefore, the Treasury was right in its statement that while the act of 1671 was in force the importations of tobacco from Maryland and Virginia was attended with no little risk of loss.[2] Seizures also took place in Maryland and Virginia, in the former by Christopher Rousby in 1677, in the latter by Edward Randolph in 1680.[3]

In the meantime, two years after the act of 1671 was placed on the statute book, the act of 1673 was passed imposing the plantation duty. As a consequence it became necessary, after the expiration in 1680 of the act of 1671, to determine: first, whether tobacco, sugar, and other enumerated commodities could be legally carried from the plantations to Ireland; and, secondly, whether such commodities should pay the plantation duty as if taken to another plantation or should be exempt from such payments as if trading directly with England, provided bond had been taken out before the ship left England for America. The question put before the law officers was this: were the enumerated commodities coming from the plantations, without having paid the plantation duty there, liable to seizure on their arrival in Ireland for not having done so? Without waiting for an answer, which would undoubtedly have been in the affirmative, the Privy Council on February 16, 1681, five months after par-

1. Treasury 11:13, p. 329; *Calendar Treasury Books,* III, 1084, 1093, etc., index under "Kirby, Thomas" in this volume and succeeding volumes.

2. Beer, *Old Colonial System,* I, vol. I, 96. In *Calendar Treasury Books* for these years will be found many details of the difficulties encountered and the vessels seized. In C. O. 1:25, no. 55* are orders issued by the governor and council of Antigua, May 29, 1677, stating that abuses had been committed contrary to the bonds given in England, by ships unloading in Ireland, Scotland, and other places, and if such abuses were discovered the bonds would be put in suit (this section is omitted in *Calendar State Papers, Colonial,* 1677–1680, §275).

3. C. O. 1:46, no. 72; 48, no. 10; *Calendar State Papers, Colonial,* 1677–1680, §1625 (inadequately calendared); 1681–1685, §380. In 1679, the Treasury considered the possibility of granting Edward Randolph, as "an officer designed for New England," a commission under the great seal, "such as he desires," "for the preventing the going of plantation ships into Ireland without first coming to England." Treasury 27:4, p. 71.

liament had failed to renew the act, issued an order remitting the plantation duty for those only who would agree to take out a new bond to carry the enumerated commodities to England only.[1] By this order anyone after 1681, who carried enumerated staples to Ireland under the old bond of 1660, would have to pay the plantation duty.[2] This order was posted in England and sent to the collectors in the colonies, but it evidently was not sent either to the royal governors or to the proprietors.[3]

This was the difficulty that underlay the Badcock case in Maryland and the dispute between Lord Baltimore and the commissioners of the customs in England in 1681.[4] The latter insisted that tobacco ships loading in Maryland, the bonds of which (of 1660) allowed them to carry their lading directly to Ireland, should pay the plantation duty. The masters of certain ships, who must have left England after the order in council had been issued in February, 1681, and therefore have been in the colony sometime in May of that year, refused on clearance to pay the duty and Nicholas Badcock, the customs collector, appealed to Lord Baltimore for help. The latter, upheld by his own council, declined to interfere, saying that Badcock "should not meddle with the ships." He was his own governor in the colony at the time and at the height of his powers as proprietor by divine right. The council that backed him up was his "private,

1. *Acts Privy Council, Colonial*, II, §26; *Calendar State Papers, Colonial*, 1681–1685, §19. Another order was issued in December, 1683, *Acts Privy Council, Colonial*, II, §137.

2. C. O. 324:4, pp. 96–100 (very inadequately calendared in *Calendar State Papers, Colonial*, 1681–1685, §1200). In the instructions of 1683 sent to William Dyer, the first appointed surveyor general of customs, appears the following, "Therefore where the bond given before lading shall be to carry the sayd goods to England or Ireland all such enumerated goods are lyable to the payment imposed by the sayd act of the 25 of the king. And for your better information and direction in this matter herewith will be delivered to you a copy of his Majesty's order in Councill of the 16 February 1680[1] concerning the same. And you are to give in charge to the collectors and all other his Majesty's officers in the sayd colonys that the sayd order in Council be duly observed." Connecticut Archives, Trade and Maritime Affairs, I, doc. 12, §16.

3. In 1685 the Treasury instructed the commissioners of the customs to send word of the renewal of the act of 1671 to the governors of all the plantations (*Calendar Treasury Books*, VIII, 298). Apparently this had not been done before.

4. *Maryland Archives*, V, 289, 293, 294, 304–306, 345; *Calendar State Papers, Colonial*, 1681–1685, §403; *Acts Privy Council, Colonial*, II, §64; *Calendar Treasury Books*, VII, 1454. Beer has an excellent account of the affair, *Old Colonial System*, I, vol. I, 98–100; for its aftermath see *Maryland Archives*, XVII, 451–457, Blakiston's complaint and Baltimore's answer.

secret, and continual council," upon which no one could sit who was of lower rank than lord of a manor—a family affair, the business of which was to support the divine right of proprietors even against the king, and to exact obedience from the people of the colony, by virtue of their oath of fidelity to the proprietor. These exaggerated proprietary claims undoubtedly help to explain Baltimore's attitude. At the same time we must recognize the fact, in extenuation, that Baltimore clearly did not know of the issue of the February order noted above, for he based his refusal to uphold Badcock on the honest belief that the act of 1671 had expired and the trade to Ireland was once more open.[1] The masters, therefore, got away without paying the duty, amounting, as was alleged, to £2500. The king in council, in reprimanding[2] and penalizing Baltimore, took the strictly legal ground that under the act of 1673 and the order of 1681 the plantation duty had to be paid—exactly as if the tobacco had been shipped to another plantation—and that in any case it was the duty of the proprietor of Maryland, who held his propriety under charter from the crown, to assist, not to obstruct, the king's officers in the performance of their duty. Baltimore was given the choice of paying the money or running the risk of losing his charter by writ of quo warranto. Evidently he paid.[3]

The murder of Badcock's successor, Christopher Rousby, a man well hated in Maryland, aroused considerable excitement in England and was the immediate cause of the erasure of the word "Ireland" from the bonds,[4] of its omission from the instructions to the collec-

1. *Maryland Archives*, V, 279. See Vol. II, 357–358.

2. The Treasury also wrote Baltimore a very sharp letter, charging him with misrepresenting the facts. *Calendar Treasury Books*, VII, 566.

3. William Dyer, by his instructions of 1683, was ordered to wait on Lord Baltimore and "in case you shall find that his lordship has not given order for the speedy payment of the said sum of two thousand five hundred pounds according to his Majesty's directions, you are to wait on his Lordship yourself alone and to desire that (according to his Majesty's commands) his Lordship will give order for the speedy payment of the said sum . . . and return to us his answer that we may govern ourselves accordingly," §23.

4. The wording of the bond of 1660 is, "That the same commodities shall be by the said ship or vessel brought to some port of England, Ireland, Wales, or the Town of Berwick-upon-Tweed." After 1685 the word "Ireland" was simply scratched out and the bond used as before. For an instance of such usage, Treasury 1:21, no. 56. Reginald Wilson, Blathwayt's deputy auditor in Jamaica, reported in 1682 that some of the certificates issued by the Bristol and Chester custom houses contained the word "Ireland," while others did not (*Calendar State Papers, Colonial, 1681–1685*, p. 306), and that the collectors were uncertain how to act.

tors in 1685,[1] and of the decision in the same year to revive the act of 1671. The last-named decision evoked a heated protest from the Irish revenue commissioners, who declared that the act ought not to be renewed as it brought in no revenue; but the commissioners of the customs in England, knowing that the acts of 1671 and 1673 were designed less to produce revenue than to preserve England's monopoly of the enumerated commodities, refused to listen to the protest, because to recognize the Irish claim would be to "rob this kingdom in great measure of this flourishing trade." The Treasury did nothing to redress Ireland's grievances and, with the renewal of the act in 1685,[2] confirmed eleven years later by the act of 1696, Ireland's relations with the plantations were defined for nearly a century.[3] The Maryland episode had been of no little importance in shaping England's commercial policy during this formative period.

Outside official circles, contemporary opinion, as far as it can be ascertained from existing pamphlet literature, was not unanimous in support of the acts. Sir Josiah Child, though he believed that the navigation act of 1660 was one of the most prudent that was ever made in England and had improved trade, agreed, very frankly, that there were many merchants who had suffered from its defects and that in consequence serious objections could be raised against it.[4]

1. *Maryland Archives,* V, 448, §4; *House of Lords Manuscripts,* new series, V, 346; and for a copy of the bond used in 1695, *Maryland Archives,* XX, 547–548. See Dongan's instructions, June 20, 1686, calling his attention to the fact that the word "Ireland" was to be "left out of the conditions of such Bonds," *New York Colonial Documents,* III, 383.

2. 1 James II, c. 17, §xiii; Stock, *Debates,* I, 431–432. In 1690 traders to Barbados, Jamaica, and the Leeward Islands protested vigorously against the stoppage of a direct trade with Ireland, alleging the great want in the islands of provisions, clothing, and utensils in sugar making, and the impoverishment of the islands owing to the additional duties imposed by the act of 1685, *Calendar Treasury Books,* IX, 462–463.

3. See Note at the end of this chapter.

4. Child was deputy governor of the East India Company, 1688–1689, and later a victualler of the navy. In 1665 he wrote a tract against usury that was printed in 1666 and another, during the "Sickness Summer," *Brief Observations concerning Trade and Interest of Money,* which, with the first tract and *A Short Addition,* was printed in 1668. These were preliminary to his *Discourse about Trade,* which must have been written in 1678 or 1679 (on p. 99 he speaks of the navigation act as "now of 17 or 18 years standing"), in which he praises the act, but states his objections to it (pp. 94–95). This treatise was reprinted in 1693 (a *Discourse concerning Plantations* having appeared in 1692) without alteration even of the errors, but with a different title, *A Discourse of Trade.* In the same year appeared *A New Discourse of Trade,* a third edition of which was issued in 1718. There were later editions also.

Carew Reynel, in 1674, denounced the limitation of trade to English bottoms, deeming it disadvantageous both as to merchandise and the convenience of ships. He would have foreign-built ships admitted to English registry, as likely to be cheaper than English built, and would allow foreigners to trade freely with England, as the best way to cheapen goods, both those exported and those imported, and to reduce the costs of transportation. He believed that by opening the trade to foreigners home commodities would bring a higher value and foreign goods be sold at lower prices.[1] There were others too who were convinced that to forbid the employment of foreign-built vessels was disastrous for England, owing to the rapid diminishing of the English woodlands, which made impossible the building of enough English vessels to meet the demand. Dalby Thomas, in 1690, said the same of the enumeration, that it increased the cost of carrying colonial staples, chiefly sugar, to foreign markets and so injured trade.[2] John Pollexfen, a merchant of London and a member of the Board of Trade, in 1697, believed, much as did Petty, Davenant, and Defoe, that many laws regulating trade were inconvenient if not unnecessary and that generally speaking trade should be allowed to take its own course. Though Pollexfen thought the act on the whole a good one, he was convinced that most of the trade laws passed since 1660 were calculated to advance the interests of a few tradesmen rather than to promote the welfare of the whole nation.[3]

One of the most persistent and determined opponents of the navigation act of 1660 was Roger Coke, a grandson of the great justice and law writer, Sir Edward Coke, and a kinsman of the advocate general Sir John Cooke, the latter a son of Sir John Coke, a secretary of state under James I. Roger Coke was of a distinguished family. He had been engaged in foreign trade since 1650 and was well aware of its difficulties and its needs. In three pamphlets he comments at considerable length on the mischiefs and inconveniences which had arisen and were bound to arise from the acts, hindering rather than promoting shipbuilding and navigation, foreign trade, and the fishery. The act of 1660, he says, was passed in the interest of a few merchants, "who may take what they please and have what they

1. Carew Reynel, *The True English Benefit, or an Account of the Chief National Improvement* (London, 1674), pp. 14–15.

2. Dalby Thomas, *Rise and Growth of the West Indian Colonies and of the Great Advantages they are to England in Respect of Trade* (London, 1690), pp. 32, 49. Also reprinted in *Harleian Miscellany*, II.

3. *A Discourse of Trade, Coyn and Paper Credit* (London, 1697), pp. 147–149.

please," preventing trade from being free because it debarred multitudes of merchants and traders, thus making a few men masters of the trade of England. The greater part of the trading world, he adds, "is excluded from trading with us at home and the greater part of the nation is excluded from trading with us at all." He believed that by means of the act the king's customs and a small number of particular men grew rich while the nation was impoverished and that the higher the customs the worse the trade.[1] He was in favor of the Dutch system of excise rather than the English system of customs, as equally good for revenue and far better for trade. He is exceptionally severe in his remarks about clause eight of the act and the rules requiring that timber and other "foreign enumerated commodities" be imported only in English ships or ships of the country producing them. In ten years, he says, England had not built a single ship for the Greenland, Muscovy, and Norway trades and for that reason had lost the Norway trade entirely and was in danger of losing the Turkish, Spanish, and Guinea trades and the fisheries also. He concludes that the Dutch, "except in Turkey and up the Elb," were already masters of the trading world and were likely to win out in these directions, because English-built ships cost double those of the Dutch and were sailed with near double the charge of the Dutch and other nations.[2]

Coke believed that Ireland and the plantations would be enriched by a free trade,[3] and in that belief he was only anticipating the opin-

---

1. *A Discourse of Trade* (London, 1670), pp. 24-31, 36, 40, 41. Coke's later pamphlets are little more than elaborations of the first, which was written in 1668 and published in 1670. Another pamphlet issued in 1694 (2d ed., 1696), *A Detection of the Court and State of England,* in two volumes, is mainly political, but at the end of Vol. II (appendix, pp. 50-75) is a discourse on trade, in which all the older arguments are repeated. He gives twenty-three "expedients," whereby the English nation might be secured against the growing greatness of the Dutch and French. He wrote also *Reflections upon the East Indy and Royal African Companies, with Animadversions concerning the Naturalization of Foreigners* (1695), in which he argues against monopoly of trade and in favor of naturalization.

2. *England's Improvement* (1675), part iii, pp. 34-37, 38. Ships for the mast trade had to be very large and strong and built for the special purpose. Coke's statement is borne out by the application of a London merchant to the House of Commons for permission to use a foreign-built ship to supply masts and other stores, because he was not able to purchase an English-built ship suitable for such a purpose (Stock, *Debates,* II, 297). In 1764-1767 there was patented in England "a floating machine particularly useful to bring timber and masts from America," without ships (Huntington Library, HM, 220). There is nothing to show that such a contrivance was ever made use of.

3. *Discourse of Trade,* p. 37.

ions of many writers of a later time, who had no sympathy with the parliamentary policy of Irish exclusion. Sir William Petty, an able economist and advocate of an open trade and an Irish landholder under the Cromwellian settlement, writes in this way, "I have lately perused all the acts relating to trade and manufactures which are of force in Ireland and could without tears see them all repealed as incroachments upon the law of nature. For trade will endure no other laws *nec volunt res male administrari*. To what magnitude will the statutes both of England and Ireland swell if they grow at this rate. How hard it will be for our lives, liberties, limbs and estates to be taken away which we can never remember nor understand. Oh that our book of statutes were no bigger than a church catechism."[1] Child, Brewster, Cary, and Gee, to mention some of the more conspicuous mercantilist writers who approved of the acts, all found mistakes in them, though Cary, unlike the others, thought that on the whole parliament had erred on the side of leniency. He wished that the legislative body would go on framing more effectual and exclusive measures than these were showing themselves to be and would add supplemental laws that were capable of more successful enforcement. His *Essay on Trade* is perhaps the most uncompromising defense of orthodox mercantilism in the seventeenth century.[2]

The colonists, on the other hand, were in the beginning far from satisfied with the regulations limiting their freedom of trade or with the position to which parliament assigned them of subordination to their fellow subjects of the realm. Their strongest protests were mainly, though not entirely, confined to the period immediately following the passage of the acts, when so far-reaching and unexpected an interference with their previous trading practices was bound to arouse feelings of regret and resentment. As private colonies, chiefly

1. *The Petty-Southwell Correspondence, 1676–1687*, p. 59. The Stuart kings favored the acts, for Charles II had given his approval and James II told Petty in 1686, in "a private and ample conference . . . voluntarily and expressly," that he would do nothing to break either the navigation acts or the Cromwellian settlement. *Ibid.,* p. 234.

2. *Essay on Trade* (Bristol, 1695), p. 69. Joshua Gee said in his "Memorial" to the Board of Trade in 1721 that the act of 1660, notwithstanding some mistakes in it, did not a little contribute to the increase and prosperity of the colonies (C. O. 323:8, L, 24). Gee, the son of Peter Gee, was a boatbuilder and merchant of Boston and had large tracts of land and a shipyard between Copp's Hill and the water. In his younger days he frequently held town office there. He died in 1724. The name was originally pronounced with the *G* hard. It was sometimes written Ghee, Ghy, Gey, and Gay.

under corporate or proprietary rule, they had enjoyed a very considerable measure of commercial independence, dealing with whomsoever they pleased, and they felt the more severely the pinch of constriction, which came with the narrowing of their accustomed commercial activities.

The Barbadians petitioned almost at once, asking to be released from the operation of the act and to have liberty to transport their produce in English bottoms to any port in amity with England, on the ground that free trade was the life of all colonies and that such monopoly devices would ruin them.[1] They even offered, at one time, to increase the four and a half per cent duty, which they thoroughly disliked, "if his Majesty would grant them some privileges which the act of navigation doth debar them of."[2] They declared that "whosoever he be that advised his Majesty to restrain and tie up his colonies in point of trade is more a merchant than a good subject . . . [one] who would have his Majesty's islands but nursed up to the work for him and such men." They said that the act, if continued, would in time drive the French and Dutch to extend their own colonies and raise their own sugar, to which they would give preferential customs rates. This prophecy had much truth in it, for the French had already begun to increase their sugar plantations in St. Christopher, Guadeloupe, Martinique, Marie Galante, and Grenada, and De Witt of Holland was urging the Dutch to establish more and better colonies, on the ground that "the ingenious, frugal, and industrious Hollanders are more fit than any nation in the world to erect colonies and

1. *Calendar State Papers, Colonial,* 1661–1668, §§85, 129, 578, p. 205, 1565, 1679 (inadequately calendared), 1816; C. O. 31:2, pp. 179–180 (*Calendar State Papers, Colonial,* 1675–1676, p. 208, inadequately calendared); Harlow, *Barbados,* pp. 87 ff., 168 ff.

2. *Calendar State Papers, Colonial,* 1661–1668, §561. The four and a half per cent was a duty imposed by the Barbadian assembly, September 12, 1663, on all exported dead commodities of the growth or produce of the island (Hall, *Laws of Barbadoes,* pp. 55 ff.). It was passed in order to make secure the land tenure of the inhabitants and to get rid of all proprietary claims (*Calendar State Papers, Colonial,* 1701, §220, i; above Vol. II, 268). During the 175 years when the act was in force the disposition of this duty was a constant subject of dispute between the Barbadians and the home government, the former insisting that it should be used for the benefit of the island, the latter that it was at the disposal of the Treasury in England to disburse as it pleased. There is nothing ambiguous about the law, as Beer thinks (*Old Colonial System,* I, vol. I, 182). A similar law was passed later in the Leeward Islands (Higham, *Leeward Islands,* p. 24; Harlow, *Barbados,* pp. 145 ff.). We have no sufficient reason to believe that the duty was ever used for illegitimate purposes, as Oldmixon says.

live on them."[1] The Barbadians particularly disliked the enumeration, which was no part of the commercial policy of either the French or the Dutch, and they feared lest this regulation should prove such a burden that the foreign competition would soon beat them out at home and undersell them in the Spanish and German markets.[2]

To all these protests the home government had but one reply: any concession or alteration would be contrary to the "nation's best interests at home." Sir George Downing, an uncompromising opponent of an open trade, in an argument before the Lords of Trade in 1676, upheld the integrity of the navigation acts, insisted on their maintenance for the benefit of shipping and the welfare of "Old England," and declared that the "liberty of carrying the products of our plantations to all parts" would quite destroy the trade of England and in the end that of Barbados also. As a pitiless opponent of the Dutch supremacy he was angered by the thought that before the acts were passed three-quarters of all the ships trading to Barbados were Dutch, and he sternly reasserted the absolute necessity of bringing all plantation commodities directly to England.[3] Despite further expostulations on the part of the Barbadians, English authorities refused to enter into any compromise, believing that the whole frame of trade and navigation would be destroyed if the requests of the colony were granted.[4] Toward any satisfactory settlement of the four and a half per cent issue they were equally adamant. Though the Barbadians petitioned many times, from 1668 on, for the abolition or adjustment of that duty,[5] which to them and the Leeward Islanders was probably a greater grievance than even the enumeration or the plantation duty, the English government met these complaints with an inexorable *non possumus*.[6]

Virginia and Maryland were in a position similar to that of Bar-

1. Jan de Witt, *A Treatise . . . to Erect Dutch Colonies in Foreign Countries.*
2. "The French king permits his subjects on the Caribbee Islands free trade with all nations, and of late has taken away two-thirds of the customs on Commodities imported into France from thence, and they pay no customs there" (*Calendar State Papers, Colonial,* 1661–1668, §842). For the later grievances of the Barbadians (1675), *ibid.,* 1675–1676, §§714, ii, 811, 812, p. 424. For the reply of the Lords of Trade denying their requests, §1116.
3. C. O. 391:1, pp. 240–242; *Calendar State Papers, Colonial,* 1675–1676, §1106 (inadequately calendared).
4. *Ibid.,* §§526, 707, 714, ii. For the Leeward Islands, *ibid.,* 1661–1668, §792.
5. *Calendar State Papers, Colonial,* 1661–1668, §1769; Harlow, *Barbados,* pp. 194 ff.
6. *Calendar State Papers, Colonial,* 1661–1668, §1121; 1696–1697, §§125, 272, 481; 1700, §981; 1701, §§220, 220, ii.

bados, in that they too had enjoyed freedom of trade, chiefly with the Dutch, during the civil wars and the Interregnum. Virginia tobacco, it is true, had been enumerated as early as 1621, and on several occasions after that date both colonies had been enjoined to send what they produced as surplus directly to England. In the case of Virginia a mandatory clause to that effect had been inserted in Sir William Berkeley's instructions,[1] but there is reason to believe that after the opening of civil war in England these injunctions had not been strictly enforced, if enforced at all.[2] As early as March, 1651, Berkeley, who since 1646 had his own plantation of 1090 acres at Greenspring (near Williamsburg) and had been engaged there in raising tobacco,[3] charged the Rump Parliament with tyranny and slaughter (with paper bullets) in forbidding the planters "to buy, or sell but with those they shall Authorize with a few trifles to Coszen us of all for which we toile and labour."[4] After 1660 Berkeley repeated his complaints, declaring that he was not willing to enrich some forty English merchants to the impoverishment of a whole people. The acts of 1660 and 1663, he said, with some bitterness, gave only a restricted market, kept the price of tobacco low, prevented the population from growing, and brought poverty and distress to the colony.[5] About the same time as or shortly before Berkeley's last complaint, John Bland, a merchant residing in London, who, according to his own statements, had engaged in much traffic in Virginia tobacco with the Dutch, presented in a long and forcible memorial his arguments against the acts and in behalf of an open trade with Holland.[6]

---

1. *Virginia Magazine*, II, 280; VII, 267; XVI, 124.

2. *New York Colonial Documents*, III, 43–44.

3. Hening, *Statutes*, II, 319–320; *Virginia Magazine*, V, 383–384. The first grant to Berkeley was in 1643, amounting to 984 acres. His interest in tobacco raising is set forth in a letter of July 7, 1665, to Governor Nicolls of New York, with whom he was on intimate terms. "This year we have little Tobb to spare from this place, but the next Cropp, about the beginning of October I will send you two hundred hogsheads at least, if you send me word what you think it will yield me, and I find it will be above the market here." Later, on January 22, 1667, he wrote, "I am sending great quantities to Barbadoes" (Huntington Library, Blathwayt Manuscripts, Virginia). Giles Bland, son of John and collector of the plantation duty in 1675, charged Berkeley with illicit trading. British Museum, Egerton, 2395, fos. 511, 515, 517; Beer, *Old Colonial System*, I, vol. II, 161.

4. *Virginia Magazine*, I, 76.

5. C. O. 1:20, no. 4; *Calendar State Papers, Colonial*, 1661–1668, §1123 (inadequately calendared); "A Perfect View of Virginia," Force, *Tracts*, II; Berkeley's Answers to Queries, June 20, 1671, Hening, *Statutes*, II, 511–518, especially 515–516.

6. *Virginia Magazine*, I, 141–151; Beer, *Old Colonial System*, I, vol. II, 109–115.

Both of these remonstrances were written before the passage of the act of 1673 and both represent the first recoil among the tobacco planters in Virginia and the Virginia merchants in London from the blow which the acts administered. To the planters and merchants alike such a blow was construed as an irreparable injury, working ruin and disaster, and only time and a process of adjustment could dispel the fears which the first impressions aroused. There is nothing to show that either Maryland or Virginia suffered seriously from the enumeration or the plantation duty. In the long addresses on the tobacco problem in the lower house of the Maryland assembly, which was quite capable of stating any views that it might hold on the subject, the speakers never questioned the rightness of the enumeration, of the staple, or of any fundamental part of the navigation acts. In actual practice there was a minimum of smuggling in the province. In Virginia complaints soon came to an end; the colony adapted itself to both requirements. The passage by the assembly in 1658 of the act imposing a two shillings per hogshead export duty on tobacco, which was made perpetual in 1680—a duty that was designed to meet the cost of the colony's government—would seem to show no widespread feeling of ill-will. After 1673 the only other protests of the seventeenth century that have come down to us are those of the inhabitants of Sittenbourne parish in Rappahannock county and of the inhabitants of Lower Norfolk county, who in 1676, two years after the duty was first levied in the colony, complained of it and asked for liberty to transport their tobacco to other colonies without paying any duty at all.[1] Though attempts to collect this duty in Virginia and in Albemarle county, North Carolina, may have added to the unrest which already existed in those colonies, it cannot have been in any sense a major cause of the insurrections that took place there in 1676 and 1677, under the lead of Bacon in one place and Culpeper in the other, because at that time it had hardly come into operation. Nor had it anything to do with the later uprisings in

1. *Virginia Magazine*, III, 38, §8. In these complaints, which were sent in at the request of the royal commissioners, Jeffreys, Berry, and Moryson, despatched to Virginia in 1676 after Bacon's rebellion was put down, the two shillings per hogshead appears as much more of a grievance than the plantation duty (*Calendar State Papers, Colonial,* 1677–1680, §§116–141). Throughout the long discussion in the Maryland assembly, 1666–1676, regarding the necessity of stinting tobacco there is not a word to show that the planters ascribed the glut to the navigation acts (*Maryland Archives,* II, 43–44). In fact, during these early years before 1696 the plantation duty was very loosely enforced and cannot have weighed heavily upon the planters.

Maryland, New England, and New York. There were other incitements to a rebellious spirit in the colonies in those years that are sufficient to explain these events and among them the plantation duty plays but a small and insignificant part.[1] Later, after 1700, William Byrd, II, could find "no inconvenience" in an extension of the enumeration.[2] The *Case of the Planters* in 1733 was directed against an increase of the customs duty in England, always the most serious incumbrance resting upon the tobacco industry in the colonies, and not against any provision of the acts of navigation and trade.[3] As was true of the sugar planters of Barbados, the tobacco planters of Virginia and Maryland soon learned that there was no use in further expostulation and that their best policy was to improve their output and adapt themselves to the situation.

Jamaica occupied a somewhat different position from that of Barbados, Maryland, and Virginia, because it began as a conquered colony in 1655 and so was late in reaching a settled industrial condition. In order to encourage the peopling of the island the English authorities granted the inhabitants important privileges, such as relief from all customs payments in England for five years, 1664–1669.[4] But among these privileges freedom of trade was not included, despite the many pleas which Governor Modyford made in its behalf.[5] What the island wanted was people, especially negroes and servants —the latter Christian, preferably Scottish—and it wanted them more than it did relief from the navigation acts, and even Modyford said in 1676 that if only they had more servants and slaves they would "not feel those lesser obstructions laid on them by Acts of Parliament."[6] As the prosperity of the island increased, the planters found the acts less and less of a grievance, partly, no doubt, because they were not as dependent as were Barbados and Virginia upon one com-

1. I have discussed these incitements in *Narratives of the Insurrections, 1675–1690* (Original Narratives Series), and find no reason to change the opinions there expressed.

2. *Board of Trade Journal,* 1718–1722, p. 328.

3. *The Case of the Planters in Virginia, as represented by themselves, signed by the President of the Council and Speaker of the House of Burgesses; to which is added a Vindication of the said Representation* (London, 1733); Sioussat, "Virginia and the English Commercial System," *Report,* American Historical Association, 1905, I, 73–97.

4. *Calendar State Papers, Colonial,* 1661–1668, §§664, 998, 1003.

5. *Ibid.,* §§739, 784.

6. *Ibid.,* 1669–1674, p. 304 (very inadequately calendared), §264, iii. For a letter from Governor Beeston, August 7, 1696, to the same effect, *ibid.,* 1696–1697, §130.

modity as a staple;[1] partly, because their nearness to the Spanish
Main opened up a lucrative but illicit trade with the Spaniards,[2]
which in 1703 Sir Gilbert Heathcote, agent in England for the island,
begged the government to connive at;[3] and, partly, because the commercial development of the island followed rather than preceded the
passage of the navigation acts. Governor Vaughan said in 1676 that
the acts were punctually obeyed,[4] but later Governor Beeston, who
was more of a pessimist, wrote of them as "so severe that discourages
all people. . . . We must have nothing [he adds] but from England
and they do not supply us, whereas were there liberty we could have
it from our neighbours at easy rates."[5] His later letters and those of
his successors do not repeat the complaint, and it may be that relief
was obtained by smuggling.[6]

New England, by which according to the usage of the time is
commonly meant the colony of Massachusetts Bay, had existed as an
independent Puritan commonwealth since 1652, and its people looked
upon themselves as outside the operation of the acts, because they
had not been represented in the parliament that passed them and
therefore were beyond parliament's jurisdiction.[7] The Puritans had
built up an open trade system of their own, which was in conflict at
many points with the system of the mother country. They did not
want to be drawn within the confines of the English system and tried
in every way to avoid it. They wished to trade freely with the Dutch
and to receive Dutch ships into their own harbor. They wished to
take their surplus products where they pleased.[8] They ignored the
acts as much as they could, trading directly to Europe and encouraging foreigners to trade with them, hoping to win out by persistence.[9]
Though they passed laws requiring that the acts be strictly obeyed

1. Note the wide variety of staples in 1670, *ibid.*, §271.

2. "Within the last 16 months there has been 20,000 lbs traffick with the Span-
yards, that produced hides, cocoa, indigo, jewells, pieces of eight and plate" (C. O.
1:43, no. 87). In addition, mention is made of 5396 servants, 11,816 slaves, and
3375 tons of logwood.

3. *Calendar State Papers, Colonial*, 1702–1703, §1059.

4. *Ibid.*, 1675–1676, §§800, 960.

5. *Ibid.*, 1700, p. 19.

6. *Calendar State Papers, Colonial*, 1700, p. 185, §685, p. 552; 1701, §§12, 473;
1712–1714, §326, etc.

7. *Massachusetts Colonial Records*, V, 200–201.

8. *New York Colonial Documents*, III, 46; *Plymouth Records*, XII, 198, 202; *Calendar State Papers, Colonial*, 1677–1680, §41.

9. *Calendar State Papers, Colonial*, 1661–1668, §§28, 539, 711; 1675–1676, §§787,
840, 843, pp. 407, 466 (9); *Acts Privy Council, Colonial*, I, §1068.

and insisted, when questioned, that they were doing their uttermost to obey them,[1] they took the ground that legally the acts did not apply to them, as, according to those learned in the law "the lawes of England are bounded within the fower seas, and do not reach America."[2] Though a seizure had been made by the king's agents, Deane, Kellond, and Kirke, as early as September, 1661, and though definite instructions were given to the king's commissioners in 1664 to see that all the acts were punctually observed, nevertheless England had already relaxed the operation of the acts in New England's favor.[3] But she had no intention of exempting the New Englanders permanently, and with the sending over of Randolph in 1676, and particularly after his return to New England late in 1679 the policy of enforcement was taken up in earnest. Randolph charged the Puritans with constant and direct trade to foreign countries and with exporting thither enumerated commodities, neither giving bonds nor taking oaths. He declared that they connived at illicit trade, making it impossible for the collector to get justice in the courts of common

1. *Massachusetts Colonial Records*, IV, pt. II, 31, 86–87 (years 1661, 1663, in reply to Privy Council's letter, *Acts Privy Council, Colonial*, I, §601, where promises are made to obey the navigation acts); V, 155 (1677), 200–201 (the court's reply), 202, 347–348, no. 6. According to Gershom Bulkeley—in his postscript to the *Will and Doom*, where is recorded the opinion of a juror in an admiralty trial at Hartford—Connecticut took much the same attitude as did Massachusetts, asserting that the English government could not "meddle with this case, the Act of Navigation having never been established by this General Court." Connecticut Historical Society, *Collections*, III, 263.

2. In "A Brief Relation of the Plantation of New England" (*Hutchinson Papers*, in *Collections*, Massachusetts Historical Society, 3d ser., I, 97) is contained the following: "It has indeed been objected that in New England they did many years transgress the Act of Navigation. But the transgressions of some few particular persons was not the fault of the government there, who did in 1663 make a law that the Act of Navigation should be strictly observed [*Massachusetts Colonial Records*, IV, pt. II, 87] and have been to the uttermost of their powers careful about it." In Edward Randolph's answers to queries of October 10, 1676, drawn up with the aid of Robert Mason (so stated in *Calendar State Papers, Colonial*, 1677–1680, §640) is the following remark: "As for New York there was several things in matters of Trade that occasioned a difference between the two governments, which att length rose so high that it came to a stop of Trade, the governor of New York not permitting any European goods to be imported into that colony from Boston that had not a certificate or other sufficient proof to have paid customs in England; which has ever since occasioned a misunderstanding between them." C. O. 5:903, p. 136, reduced to two lines in *Calendar State Papers, Colonial*, 1675–1676, p. 465. These two statements can hardly be reconciled.

3. *Massachusetts Colonial Records*, IV, pt. II, 35–36, 193; *New York Colonial Documents*, III, 51–54, §11; *Acts Privy Council, Colonial*, I, §§504, 990, and elsewhere.

law, where the juries always decided against the king. And, finally, he complained that the colony, insisting that it was not bound by parliamentary statute, had usurped control of its own commerce, by erecting a naval office in 1681, which practically neutralized his own authority by keeping all fines and forfeitures instead of sharing them, as the law directed, with the informer and the king. The resistance of the Puritan commonwealth was long and determined, but in the end the English system won the day, though it required the over-throw of the Massachusetts Bay charter to complete the victory.

NOTE. Sir Walter Harris, in his *Remarks* (1691), is very severe in his comments on the English commissioners of the customs, "who pretended they could increase the revenue by imposing hard things on Ireland," and he criticizes others also, who "under pretence of trade" obtained the passage of several acts very disadvantageous to Ireland (p. 33). At the same time he agrees that the Irish were improvident and lacking in enterprise, but thinks that much of the trouble was due to the prodigality and excesses of the English there.

In the same year, 1691, when Harris issued his pamphlet, an effort was made by Ireland to obtain relief, in connection with a ship which discharged tobacco from Virginia at the port of Belfast. But the commissioners in their report adhered strictly to the letter of the law, saying "that the aforesaid ship should discharge her tobacco in some port of England, Wales, or Berwick, and at no other place. And that the commissioners of Ireland may be reminded of the Acts of Parliament now in force for bringing the enumerated commodities to England, Wales, or Berwick only. And that the officers of their Majesties customs in the several parts of Ireland may be forbid to accept of entries for any of the said commodities but what shall be imported from some part of England, Wales, or Berwick." To this the Treasury agreed (Treasury 1:12, no. 12). On the other hand, in 1731, a group of English merchants, replying to inquiries before the Board of Trade, testified that they had no objection "to a liberty being granted to Ireland to import from our own plantations all such commodities as are not enumerated" (*Board of Trade Journal*, 1728–1734, pp. 184–185). The board sent in a report on the subject to the Duke of Newcastle, secretary of state, favorable to the wishes of the merchants, as of "advantage to the trade of Great Britain" and of "very little effect on the revenue." As a result an act was passed by parliament in that year allowing the importation of non-enumerated commodities into Ireland. 4 George II, c. 15; *Calendar Treasury Books and Papers*, 1731–1734, pp. 34–36, 123, 216–217.

A brief account of the effects of the navigation acts on Ireland in the eighteenth century may be found in Hutchinson, *Commercial Restraints of Ireland* (1779), pp. 181–183. He says, "Let the reason for this restrictive system at the time of its formation be examined, and let us judge impartially whether any one of the purposes then intended has been answered. The reasons respecting America were to confine the Plantation trade to England and to make that country a store-house of all commodities from its colonies. But the commercial jealousy that has prevailed among the different states of Europe has made it difficult for any nation to keep great markets to herself in exclusion of the rest of the world. It was not foreseen at those periods that the colonies, whilst they all continued dependent, should have traded with foreign nations, notwithstanding the utmost efforts of Great Britain to prevent it. It was not foreseen that those colonies would have refused to take any commodities whatever from their parent country, that they should afterward have separated. . . . Nor could it have been foreseen that Ireland, excluded from almost all direct intercourse with them, should have been nearly undone by the contest" (pp. 205–206). Immediately after its publication this pamphlet was suppressed and burnt by the common hangman.

Attention may be called also to *A Representation of the State of the Trade of Ireland* (Dublin, 1750), pp. 17–18, and to a remark by George Rawdon to Viscount Conway at Ragley in Warwickshire, dated December 7, 1672, "But the late act requiring all things to be landed in England, which come from our plantations, and to pay custome there will undoe this kingdome." State Papers Domestic, Charles II, 330, pt. ii, no. 243.

# CHAPTER VI

# STRENGTHENING THE METHODS OF
# ENFORCEMENT: 1675-1696

IT is not surprising that the attempt to put in force a new system
of commercial and colonial control and to confine plantation trade
within fewer and more restricted channels, thus inducing many
changes in existing habits and practices, should have been at first
largely a failure. Until 1675, despite the efforts of the Treasury and
the commissioners of the customs,[1] the acts were very inadequately
enforced and it was frequently necessary to ease the situation by
granting licenses, authorizing occasional suspensions, and admitting
foreign shipping, particularly during times of war. But in 1667 and
again in 1674, the king revoked all orders granting dispensations[2]

---

1. Until 1671 the English customs duties were farmed, but in September of that
year the king appointed a board of commissioners to manage the customs revenue.
The plantation duty was never farmed. The Irish customs were sometimes farmed
and sometimes not. The four and a half per cent was farmed until 1684, first at
£7000 and then at £5000 a year. For the last named see Patent Rolls, 22 Charles II,
part 5, membrane 3; *Calendar Treasury Books*, IX, 1775. On the farms, see Harper,
*The English Navigation Acts*, sect. VII to p. 85.

2. The following communication from the Treasury to the plantation governors
was signed by the newly appointed lords commissioners of the Treasury (May 24,
1667) and is dated September 12, 1667. It admirably illustrates the situation in that
year. The text is in Treasury 11:1, pp. 49–51, and is calendared only in part in
*Calendar Treasury Books*, II, 201–202.

After citing the clauses of the various acts and the content of the order in council
of March 8, 1665 (*Acts Privy Council, Colonial*, I, §649), the instruction proceeds.
"Yet his Majesty minding to have the said acts fulfilled as much as possible the
affairs of the time would permit, did extend and limit the said license and dispensa-
tion only to the kingdom of England and not to any other place whatsoever. And
his Majesty well considering of what importance it is to the wellfare of this nation
in general as well as to his Majesty's revenue in particular that these laws be duly
and strictly observed: and finding that notwithstanding all the penalties against the
transgressors thereof several ships have been permitted or taken the liberty to trade
or convey goods and merchandize between the said plantations and other parts of
his Majesty's dominions, viz, Scotland, Ireland and Tangier and also into foreign
countries contrary to the true and express meaning of the said Acts: which his
Majesty cannot but in great measure impute to the neglect of duty in his Governors
of the said Plantations, who have not been so careful as they ought in debarring all
trade with such ships as have come without certificate from England, nor in taking
bond from such as are permitted to trade from other Plantations, and returning the

and in 1675 the Privy Council made its attitude clear by asserting that his Majesty was "very tender" in all cases that encroached upon the act.[1] Breaches were numerous during these years. Secret trade with the Dutch and French in the West Indies went on without interference, direct connections with the European continent were maintained with Holland and Hamburg—the chief distributing centers for the Continental trade in colonial products—and "unfree" ships and foreign-built ships illegally made "free" were employed in the service of the colonies.[2] The colonial governors, as the reprimand of 1667 clearly shows,[3] were not living up to the obligations imposed by their oaths and their bonds, and in the West Indies were admitting the French, Dutch, and other foreigners to trade at their respective ports. Governor Wheler of the Leeward Islands wrote in 1672 that he believed he was the only one who was doing his duty.[4]

To meet the situation the Privy Council as well as the Treasury issued in 1669 peremptory orders addressed to the governors of Maryland, Virginia, Bermuda, Barbados and the Leeward Islands (then

same to the chief officers of the Customs in London as is particularly directed: the want whereof hath bin the cause that several ships have gone with their lading to Tangier, the Straights and other foreign places: and though his Majesty might justly proceed to put into execution the penalties of the law against some of the said Governors, yet being desirous rather at first to advise all of them to proceed rigorously against them, He hath thought fit to admonish and forwarn you to be more careful for the future, assuring you that he will look upon any neglect or connivance in this kind as a great disservice to his revenue and contempt to the lawes and his authority, and therefore in particular he requires you to be punctual in debarring all ships from trade in your plantations or from taking in any goods or merchandizes these which shall not bring certificate from the chief officers of the Customs in England, that bond is given to return thither according to the intent of the law, and for other English ships coming from other of our plantations that you take sufficient bond that they shall carry all the goods so laden to some other of his Majesty's plantations or directly into England before they take in any lading, and transmit the copies of all the said bonds and will every year to the chief officers of the Customs in London according to the tenor of the Act aforesaid, and that due and timely care may be taken to prosecute offenders according to law and in all matters and things wherein you are concerned by the said Acts or any or either of them to cause due execution thereof according to the trust and power committed to you."

1. Proclamation of August 23, 1667 (Brigham, *Proclamations*, pp. 114–116). For the dispensations of March 8, 1667, March 11, 1674, and November 24, 1675, see *Acts Privy Council, Colonial*, I, §§649, 982, 1047.

2. *Calendar State Papers, Colonial*, 1685–1688, §1221.

3. Above, p. 144, note 2.

4. *Calendar State Papers, Colonial*, 1669–1674, p. 328. Before Wheler's time the Leeward Islands were governed by deputies appointed from Barbados, and charges of illegal trading were common, *ibid.*, §309; *Calendar Treasury Books*, II, 439–440.

under one government), New York, and Jamaica, bidding them obey their instructions, take their oaths, look out for the proper giving and transmission of bonds, and strengthen the system generally by seeing to it that only such ships traded to the plantations as were legally entitled to do so and no others.[1] But conditions improved very slowly. Six years later, in 1675, both the commissioners and the farmers of the customs reported that no information had been received as to what the governors were doing to enforce the acts, and they added further that, with certain exceptions, no copies of bonds had been received and no lists of ships sent over.[2] It was fast becoming evident that the laws were not obeyed and that if the system was not to break down at the very beginning vigorous measures must be taken and the machinery of enforcement greatly improved. Therefore, the Lords of Trade, commissioned by the king as a special supervisory committee of the Privy Council in February, 1675, and invested with the necessary functions and authority, acting in conjunction with the Treasury, decided on a much more active policy.

On November 24 of that year, fortifying themselves afresh with such information as they could obtain from the farmers of the customs and the recently appointed commissioners of the customs[3] and instituting a searching inquiry into the conduct of the governors, they caused a proclamation to be issued, in the name of the king, requiring and commanding "all and every his subjects" that for the future they do not presume to disregard the acts, and calling on the governors to compel those under their authority to do all in their power to aid the collectors and other officers of the customs in the execution of their duties.[4] This proclamation was followed up by a letter from the custom house of December 10 transmitting copies for publication and a letter from the king himself giving the reasons for the issue of the proclamation and requiring avoidance "of all such unlawful and evill practices for the future."[5] After further inquiry the lords drafted a letter to the governors on their own account, charging them with connivance in permitting such liberty of trade as prevailed with foreign plantations and with carelessness in failing

1. *Acts Privy Council, Colonial*, I, §§827–829; *Maryland Archives*, V, 45–48.
2. *Calendar State Papers, Colonial*, 1675–1676, §§694, 695, 728.
3. *Ibid.*, §§694, 695.
4. Brigham, *Proclamations*, pp. 126–128. This was probably the proclamation read to the council in Pennsylvania in 1685. *Pennsylvania Colonial Records*, I, 148.
5. C. O. 1:37, no. 8, i, ii (not calendared).

to detect frauds and bidding them fail not in sending over lists of ships and bonds. Declaring that they were "resolved to be very strict inquisitors and to exact from them [the governors] a frequent and punctual account," they insisted again, as so often before, that the law must be obeyed.[1] They drafted a new and more rigid form of oath[2] and another of the commission for taking the oath and sent both to the Privy Council for confirmation.[3] From time to time during the next twenty years copies of these oaths and commissions were despatched to individual governors, those of the corporate as well as the royal and proprietary colonies, with warning letters reminding them that continued disobedience might be followed by loss of office.[4]

In 1681 an order in council was issued setting forth the rules about bonds and certificates and requiring that these rules be posted in all the custom houses in the kingdom and due notice be given to all the collectors in America. This order was repeated three years later, when a special instruction regarding bonds and certificates was prepared, commanding the governors "to cause diligent inquiry to be made" as to whether the condition of the bonds had been duly performed and if not to see that this was done and that no securities be accepted "but those who are sufficient and responsible inhabitants." The governors were ordered further to look out for forged certifi-

---

1. C. O. 324:4, pp. 37–39 (insufficiently calendared in *Calendar State Papers, Colonial*, 1675–1676, §§872–875).

2. The old oath reads, "You shall swear that you will to the best of your skill and power as long as you shall continue Governor of this Plantation well and truly execute and perform all matters and things which by the Statutes made in the 12th and 15th years of His now Maj. reign you are required (as Gov^r of this Plantation) to be sworn to the performance of, so help you God." *North Carolina Colonial Records*, I, 227–228.

The new oath reads, "You shall swear that you will to the best of your skill and power so long as you shall continue in the Government or Command of this Plantation well and truly execute and perform, and cause to be executed and performed, all matters and things which by the Statutes made in the 12th yeare of his now Ma^ties Reigne, Intituled An Act for the encouraging and Encreasing of Shipping and Navigation, and by the other Statute made in the 15th of His said Ma^ties Reigne, Intituled An Act for the encouragement of Trade, You are required as Governor or Commander of this Plantation to be sworne to the performance of, so help you God." C. O. 324:4, p. 53.

The order for "Passing the Commission for giving the Oaths" is dated October 24, 1677 (*Acts Privy Council, Colonial*, I, §1171; *Calendar State Papers, Colonial*, 1677–1680, §§451, 454, 466). The text of the commission is in C. O. 324:4, pp. 49–54.

3. *Acts Privy Council, Colonial*, I, §§1080, 1171.

4. Letter to Governor Stapleton, January 9, 1678, *Calendar State Papers, Colonial*, 1677–1680, §§567, 568.

cates, to prevent the landing of goods "but by warrant from the collector in the presence of an officer," and to see that all masters of ships, before taking on any of the enumerated commodities, should produce their certificates of bonds furnished in England.[1] Already, some years before, orders had been sent to the Admiralty that ships of the navy should seize all foreign vessels trading to the plantations and that additional frigates should be despatched to such waters as the Caribbean and the Chesapeake as guardships to prevent the carrying of enumerated commodities to any other place than England.[2] In 1683 the commissioners of the customs recommended that instructions be sent to the farmers of the revenue in Ireland, ordering them to transmit to England all information possible regarding ships trading between Ireland and the plantations,[3] and at one time or another letters were written to the king's agents or consuls abroad to watch in European ports for enumerated commodities illegally shipped from America.[4]

But the success of these efforts depended to no small extent upon whether or not the customs officers in the colonies could be kept up to their duty. By every contrivance of words appropriate to the occasion, the English authorities endeavored to impress upon the surveyors and collectors there the importance of their functions. In addition to such instructions as were sent to the governors for communication to the collectors, at least three additional sets, in 1673,

1. *Acts Privy Council, Colonial*, II, §162. Of the many circular letters sent out under this order, only a copy of that to Charles Lord Baltimore has been preserved. This copy was sent in 1693 by the commissioners of the customs to the Treasury, with recommendations that "the several matters [therein] contained for enforcement of the said Acts" be communicated to Governor Richier of Bermuda, who was having trouble with the customs collector there. This document is entered only by title in *Calendar State Papers, Colonial*, 1693–1696, §553, ii, with no clue there given as to its significance. The full text is in C. O. 37:1, no. 12, ii. A similar letter of May 24, 1680, to the governor of Connecticut, is printed in Hinman, *Letters of English Kings and Queens to Connecticut*, pp. 123–126. A later circular letter of April 10, 1685, is in C. O. 324:4, pp. 142–143 (very inadequately calendared in *Calendar State Papers, Colonial*, 1685–1688, §120). Others are in *ibid.*, 1693–1696, §§537, 543, 564, 2249, and in Treasury 27:13, p. 157. The purport of all these letters is the same—the acts must be obeyed.

2. *Calendar State Papers, Colonial*, 1661–1668, §1884; *Acts Privy Council, Colonial*, I, §829.

3. *Calendar State Papers, Colonial*, 1681–1685, §1200.

4. December 10, 1683, *ibid.*, §1447; *Calendar Treasury Books*, VIII, 982–983. James Kennedy was the agent in Holland; he seized many ships. There were residents or consuls in most of the leading western and central European cities and in all the maritime ports. In 1735 one was recommended for the "Pope's dominions."

1685, and 1697, and probably more, were transmitted directly to the customs officials themselves, constituting a code of customs law for their guidance.[1] A study of these documents shows that whether the results were satisfactory or not the Treasury and the commissioners of the customs, in coöperation with the Lords of Trade, were doing their best to carry into effect the laws which parliament had imposed upon them and were finding that the task of altering the channels of trade, both at home and in the colonies, was a task of enormous difficulty, requiring time, vigilance, and endless persistence, qualities notoriously not possessed by the men in office of that day.

The results, even under the pressure of the new orders and instructions, were again far from satisfactory. Reports of the continued

1. The instructions drawn up in 1673 were drafted by John Sansom, a clerk to the secretary of the customs board, to which additions were made by Treasurer Danby the next year (*Calendar Treasury Books*, IV, 285, 460, 471. They are printed, *ibid.*, pp. 451–452, 460). Those of 1685 are in *Maryland Archives*, V, 446–452; XVII, 392–398. Those for 1697 are in *House of Lords Manuscripts*, new series, II, 472–481. There were probably others, for in the instructions issued to the first surveyor general, William Dyer, in 1683, reference is made to instructions sent several times before that date to the collectors and comptrollers. "You shall herewith receive copyes of such instructions as have been from time to time transmitted by us to the collectors and comptrollers of his Majesty's customs in the respective colonyes and plantations," §18.

The general regulations, as understood by Patrick Mein, Dyer's successor, can be gathered from the orders which he sent to the collectors in Virginia, December 24, 1686. The following items (selected from among the thirty-one articles of the document) may be noted. Canary wines and brandy and any other waters from Madeira or other islands were to be imported direct; "Ireland" was to be left out of the bonds; certificates granted in the plantations were to be made out on blanks sent from the custom house, London, to be signed and sealed by the governor and the collector; certificates of English bonds were to be left with the naval officer, but cocquets and other warrants with the collector; even if the plantation duty were paid the captains had to give bond to go to some other plantation or to England; in case enumerated commodities were shipped from one plantation to another, a new bond had to be given, if any portion of the cargo were carried on to England; duties were to be collected in money and not in goods, but if that were not possible then whatever was easily salable might be accepted; money was to be remitted in good bills or in ready money to the proper officers at the custom house in London; goods not disposed of were to be sent to the royal warehouse keeper; ships giving bond in England were not to pay duties in the colonies; no security was to be used more than twice, unless former bonds had been discharged or the security was shown to be exceptionally good; local vessels were to get their permits from the collector, who himself was to watch for forged cocquets from Scotland or Ireland, to grant no "bills of store," to engage in no trade, either as agent or factor, or to be a partner in a trading ship. Collectors could appoint deputies and were from time to time to report regarding the coöperation of the governors. C. O. 1:61, no. 34; by title only in *Calendar State Papers, Colonial*, 1685–1688, §1073.

evasion of the acts and of the leniency and negligence of the governors, particularly in connection with the foreign colonies in the West Indies, came in with annoying frequency.[1] Massachusetts Bay continued to be hopelessly impenitent. The evidence of the customs commissioners, petitions from divers merchants, and the reports of the indefatigable Randolph—"undeniable testimony," the Privy Council deemed them—convinced the authorities at home that all was not well with New England, as far as obedience to the acts was concerned. Randolph wrote in 1677, the year after his arrival, that the Massachusetts people were violating "all the acts of trade and navigation, by which they have engrossed the greatest part of the West India trade, whereby his Majesty is damaged in the customs above £100,000 yearly and the kingdom much more."[2] These and other charges were influential in bringing about the annulment of the Massachusetts Bay charter in 1684 and in giving an opportunity for the first important experiment in colonial administration that England tried out in America in the seventeenth century—the erection of the Dominion of New England, which lasted from 1686 to 1689.[3] In Maryland the troubles that Lord Baltimore was having in his attempt to maintain his proprietary privileges against the rising tide of popular discontent among the inhabitants of his province, the ill-treatment of the collector Badcock, the murders of Rousby and Payne, his successors, the complaints of Blakiston, their successor, the hostility of the planters toward the royal frigate that cruised up

1. *Calendar State Papers, Colonial,* 1685–1688, §1288; 1689–1692, §2295; 1693–1696, *passim.*

2. C. O. 1:40, no. 67; 47, no. 79. In 1676, in his Answers to Queries, Randolph wrote, "There is no notice taken of the Act of Navigation, plantation, or any other laws made in England for the regulation of trade. All nations have free liberty to come into their ports and vend their commodities, without any restraint; and in this as well as in other things that government would make the world believe they are a free state and do act in all matters accordingly, and doe presume to give passports to all masters accordingly, not only belonging to that colony but also to England, without any regard to the rules prescribed by his Majesty." *Hutchinson Papers,* II, 232.

3. With the failure of that experiment the Treasury and the commissioners of the customs again faced the problem of enforcing the navigation act in New England and of finding a suitable person to take the place of Randolph, whose career of usefulness there was at an end. At first they considered one Wildgos, but he proving unacceptable they finally selected Jahleel Brenton (1690), who was appointed collector, surveyor, and searcher of customs at £100 a year and at the same time surveyor of woods and timber in the provinces of Maine and New Hampshire, with an allowance of £50 a year for expenses. *Calendar Treasury Books,* IX, 56, 58, 59, 238, 486, 687, 784, 828, 1392.

and down the Chesapeake and watched the bottle-neck opening between the Virginia Capes, the comments of Randolph—who in 1695 was in Maryland and sat on the governor's council[1]—on the derelictions of the colonists in general, were all causes of embarrassment to the authorities at home. To these perplexing events must be added the continued carrying of the enumerated products to Ireland, the forging of certificates and cocquets—chiefly, as was suspected, by the Scots and the Irish—and the controversies that were constantly arising as to the interpretation of the acts themselves.

But at this juncture no phase of the situation was more troublesome or more provocative of consternation and wrath among officials and merchants alike than the activities of the Scots.

The effort to bring about a union between the two countries, which had been broached twice before, was brought up again in 1689, shortly after William and Mary had become the sovereigns of England, but again the effort was a failure.[2] The reason for this is not difficult to discover. Illicit trade between Scotland and the colonies had been going on ever since the last negotiations had come to an end and was becoming a source of constant and painful irritation.[3] In 1684 William Penn was called upon by the Treasury to pay £53 due the king from the proceeds of the ship, *Alexander* of Inverness, Scottish-built, which had been seized in Pennsylvania for trading contrary to the acts.[4] English merchants dealing with Maryland declared that their business was in great measure destroyed and ruined by the many ships going directly from Scotland to Virginia, Maryland, and particularly Pennsylvania, the tobacco being sent overland from the Chesapeake to Delaware Bay and thence shipped directly to Scotland.[5] Randolph reported in 1693 that the New England and

1. *Maryland Archives*, XX, 236–237. Randolph, as surveyor general of customs, was engaged at this time in supervising the trade of Pennsylvania, Maryland, and Virginia. He resided in Maryland, a strategic point for his purpose. *Calendar State Papers, Colonial*, 1693–1696, §§573, 1220.

2. Bruce, *Report*, I, 233–234; II, doct. xlvi; Stock, *Debates*, II, 351.

3. On this illicit trade, of which the records of the time are full, see *Calendar State Papers, Colonial*, 1677–1680, §1017; 1693–1696, §§2303, 2304; 1696–1697, §§501, 655, 666, 684, 759, i, 769, 796, pp. 223, 231; *Calendar Treasury Papers*, 1557–1696, p. 348; Toppan, *Edward Randolph*, V, 142, 222, 232; VII (Goodrick, ed.), 354, 367, 386, 517.

4. *Calendar Treasury Books*, VII, 1455; VIII, 212–213, 1009; *Pennsylvania Colonial Records*, I, 90–91. This vessel was renamed the *Mary* or the *Recovery* of Southampton.

5. Stock, *Debates*, II, 195; *Maryland Archives*, XX, 262, 340–341; XXIII, 87. In

Scottish merchants had entered into a combination to defeat the law in just this way. Both he and Governor Nicholson sent over lists of Scottish merchants and vessels engaged in this traffic, and the latter narrated instances where the vessels seized had been unwarrantably discharged by the juries in the local common law courts.[1] To the commissioners of the customs in England the evidence must have seemed overwhelming. They received petitions and reports, not only calling attention to actual cases but even outlining the methods employed: the use of forged certificates and false cocquets which, their informants said, were made in Glasgow, bearing counterfeit seals of the custom house, not only of London but of the outports also—Newcastle, Berwick, Bristol, Bideford, Whitehaven, Liverpool, and Plymouth.[2] How far these statements are to be depended on is another question. It was easy to complain about this trade, but extraordinarily difficult to detect it, and even when it was detected it was almost impossible for Randolph and the local collectors to obtain convictions. Many seizures were made, bonds declared forfeited, and counterfeit certificates and forged cocquets discovered and reported, but more ships got away than were seized.[3] Randolph complained to Nicholson in 1695 that "by the partiality of juries and others," he could do little to stop the trade, for the colonists steeled themselves against him, obstructed his efforts, charged him with injustice and excess of zeal, and even caused him to be arrested and confined in jail along with felons and other criminals. Quary, the Philadelphia surveyor and judge of vice-admiralty, who had no easy time himself, said that the colonists treated Randolph barbarously.[4]

As early as 1678 Treasurer Danby had approved the suggestion that a "correspondent" be sent to Scotland "to give an account of

the instructions to William Dyer in 1683 the commissioners of the customs said, "We are well assured that several ships belonging to Scotland, Ireland and New England (having loaden the enumerated plantation goods in his Majesty's colonys) have carried the same to Scotland and other places contrary to law," §11. And again, "Whereas we have been informed that great quantities of European goods are carryed to his Majesty's plantations and there landed contrary to law, particularly from Scotland, Ireland and New England," etc., §15.

1. *Calendar State Papers, Colonial,* 1693–1696, §§2303, 2304.

2. Treasury 1:26, no. 53; 61, no. 9.

3. The Maryland collector, David Kenneday, complained in 1698 "that whilst he is going to a justice of the peace perhaps ten or twelve miles from the place where he has occasion for assistance, the traders may take liberty to run what goods they please," and even when he was able to inspect a ship "the narrowness and darkness" of the holds made a thorough search impossible. *Maryland Archives,* XXIII, 402.

4. *Calendar State Papers, Colonial,* 1697–1698, §811. Also pp. 408–409.

ships coming directly from his Majesty's plantations in America to Scotland and discharging their ladings without first unlading in England, Wales, or Berwick,"[1] but apparently this plan, if ever carried out, proved ineffective, for in 1694, when the facts were brought to the attention of the Privy Council, it was thought the better part of wisdom to stop the leak, if possible, at the American end, and instructions were sent to Andros in Virginia and Nicholson in Maryland to hire vessels to guard the Chesapeake waters.[2] The effect of this experiment was slight, as the waters were wide and the hiding places many, so when Randolph's unfavorable reports began to come in with vexatious regularity, the commissioners of the customs urged the Treasury to take more energetic measures, that is, to appoint "a skillful and experienced commander" to cruise along the coast, in the hope of preventing "this great evill leading to the diminution of his Majesties revenue and the trade and navigation of this kingdom." They begged the Treasury to write to the government of Scotland and called its attention to the fact that "under colour of a law lately passed in Scotland for a joint-stock to Africa and India, wherein several merchants of England" had interested themselves, the trade was to be more openly carried on than before and the mischief resulting therefrom was likely to become more troublesome than ever.[3]

This law, to which the commissioners referred, was passed in 1695, supplementing an earlier act of 1693, which the Scottish parliament had adopted for the purpose of encouraging foreign trade.[4] Despairing of an understanding with England the Scots determined to strike out for themselves and nothing that they could have done was more

1. *Calendar Treasury Books*, V, 1000.

2. *Acts Privy Council, Colonial*, II, §558.

3. On this subject, Keith, *Commercial Relations of England and Scotland, 1603–1707;* "Scottish Trade with the Plantations before 1707," *Scottish Historical Review*, January, 1909; *North Carolina Colonial Records*, I, 439–440; *House of Lords Manuscripts*, new series, II, 446.

4. Stock, *Debates*, II, 472–473, 473–479; *Acts of the Parliament of Scotland*, IX, 377–381. Commercially Scotland developed more slowly than did England, owing partly to the fact that religious and political controversy dominated Scotland longer than it did England, and partly to the monopoly of trade enjoyed by the royal burghs. But in the years from 1660 to 1689 religion and politics lost in considerable measure their control over national policy, and in 1672 trade was thrown open to the unfree burghs. It is not strange, therefore, that in 1693 and 1695 trade acts should have been passed, for both the nation and parliament were becoming commercially conscious. On the general subject see the *Records of the Convention of the Royal Burghs*, vols. I–III; Mackie and Pryde, *The Estates of the Burgesses in Parliament* (1923); Thomson, *The Parliament of Scotland*, pp. 135–137. Above, p. 53, note 3.

certain to put fear into the hearts of the English officials and trading companies than this almost reckless bid for a share of the world's commerce. King William at the time was on the Continent, but he had authorized his commissioner in Scotland, the Marquis of Tweeddale, to allow the passage of some act favoring trade. He never saw the act itself, as it was rushed through the Scottish parliament and approved by his commissioner before his return. Later, in reply to an indignant expostulation from the English parliament, he acknowledged that he had been ill-served by his commissioner and the secretary, Johnston, both of whom he immediately dismissed from their offices.

The act authorized the creation of a corporate body or joint-stock company, by the name of the Company of Scotland trading to Africa and the Indies, to which was granted power to plant colonies and build forts and factories in places not possessed by other English peoples, the consent of those inhabiting there having first been obtained. The amount of capital was not fixed by the charter, but it was stipulated that at least half the stock was to be held by Scotsmen residing in Scotland and that no stock originally so held should ever be transferred to anyone else. Complete monopoly of the trade with Asia, Africa, and America was conferred for a term of thirty-one years and all goods imported by the company during the ensuing twenty-one years should be admitted free of duty, except sugar and tobacco that were not the growth of the company's plantations. Many merchants in England—Jews, Englishmen, and London Scots—were interested in the project and subscribed heavily to the stock, a thing they had no right to do, inasmuch as the English East India Company had already received a monopoly of the trade by charter from James II, confirmed by William III, the latter of whom was thus placed in an embarrassing and equivocal position. Those of his English subjects, who were not of the English company but were threatening to trespass on its privileges by backing the Scottish undertaking, were in no less of a dilemma, for *ipso facto* they were interlopers, liable under the law. Later, threatened with impeachment by the House of Commons, the London subscribers withdrew from the Scottish company.[1]

1. In his admirable volume, *The Company of Scotland trading to Africa and the Indies,* Dr. G. P. Insh ascribes the passage of the act to three causes: the Scottish desire to find in a Scottish colony a new market overseas; the desire of the London merchants to break through the monopoly of the East India Company by establishing

Immediately the Treasury, the commissioners of the customs, the trading companies, and parliament itself became thoroughly alarmed lest the new venture destroy the trade and navigation of England and transfer trade supremacy to the people north of the Tweed. The commissioners declared that the Scottish act "must have a very fatal influence upon the trade, navigation and revenue of customs in England," and representatives of the Royal African Company also added the weight of their fears that the act was "nationally pernicious." When once the Scots had "colonized themselves in the plantations," the company declaimed, "our commerce in sugar, cotton, wool, skins, masts, etc., will be utterly lost; for their privileges are such that their nation must be the magazine for all those commodities, and the English plantations and the traffic thereby lost to us, and the exportation of our own manufacture yearly decreased; and thereby this nation will lose the benefit of supplying foreign parts with those commodities, the want of which, in order to balance our trade, by reason of our losses at sea, is too sensibly felt; and the Act of Navigation, which was designed for the benefit of this nation, will be useless to us."[1] England in that year, 1695, seemed afflicted with something approaching commercial hysteria, what with the failure on one side of the navigation acts in the colonies and the menace of Scottish trading ambitions on the other.

In reality these were two entirely separate issues, but they tended to coalesce and offered on England's part the opportunity for a single

in Scotland a base for Eastern trade; and the persistent efforts of the Edinburgh merchants to build up an African trade, for the disposal of the product of the looms of East Lothian. Behind the movement was the longing of a country, recently set free from the tyranny of theological controversy, to apply its energies to a career of industry and commerce, from which it had been hitherto excluded.

In his edition of the "Darien Shipping Papers" (Scottish History Society *Publications,* 3d ser., VI), Dr. Insh says that William Paterson was not the founder of the Scottish company, but was influential in its organization, as liaison officer between London and Edinburgh, and was the originator of the scheme for the Scots colony at Darien. The real significance of the Scottish company lies in its competition with the East India Company, and the struggle between the two companies was of greater importance than the Darien episode. After the Darien project had failed there was "an aftergame to play" and what that was is told in Dr. Insh's edition mentioned above. It is connected with Eastern not American history, except so far as London merchants trading to America were accustomed to buy Persian and East Indian goods and calicoes for shipment to the American colonies.

On the general subject see Scott, *Joint-Stock Companies,* II, 207–227; Stock, *Debates,* II, 132, note 2, and index under "Darien Company," and *House of Lords Manuscripts,* new series, II, §§955 (pp. 3–62), 1050, 1051 (pp. 238–245).

1. *House of Lords Manuscripts,* new series, II, 13, 17.

blow in rebuttal. In March, 1695, during William's second parliament, a bill was brought forward for the better securing the plantation trade, but it never got farther than the second reading.[1] In December, 1695, the Bristol representatives, Yate and Day, wrote to John Cary, author of the *Essay on Trade* and a member of the Bristol corporation, that the bill "was so unfortunate as to be cast out the last parliament, but we shall consult with the most judicious in those affairs we can meet with and endeavour it may have better success now, and if it should be put in with the act that will be brought in to secure our trade against the Scotch East India Company it will go on the better."[2] During the early months of the first session of the third parliament of 1695–1696, the opinion found voice that if the Scots were once located in the plantations they would cut into the trade of the English in tobacco and sugar and then would undersell them in home and foreign markets because of the liberty to trade customs-free which was granted by the act. On these subjects parliament and the merchants were becoming exceedingly sensitive, for the time was one in which new impulses were stirring and new views were taking shape regarding England's commercial and colonial outlook. It was no accident that the period of private colonization had come to an end and that England was ready to embark on a programme, destined to grow steadily more definite and precise, of colonial policy and administration. For these years mark a turning point in England's relations with her colonies—a transitional era not only in the organization of the government at home but in the whole idea as well of the place the colonies should occupy in the commercial scheme which had already found definition in the acts of trade and navigation. The importance of English trade had attained large proportions since the revolution of 1689, the accession of William and Mary, and the battle of La Hogue, which gave promise of England's eventual supremacy at sea, and searching inquiries by parliament and by committees appointed for the purpose were already under way into the state of the trade with France, the danger of the Scottish menace, the balance of trade at large,[3] the state of the trade in general, the condition of the revenues, and the general welfare of the nation. Men were asking in parliament and out why trade was in decay and what

1. Stock, *Debates*, II, 112.
2. Additional Manuscripts, 5540, fo. 85.
3. *House of Lords Manuscripts*, new series, II, 25, where the difficulties of determining the balance are shown.

should be done to remedy the situation,[1] and they were singularly alive to the part that Scotland was playing, both in her illicit relations with the American colonies and in her organized efforts to defy the English navigation acts and to compete with England's commercial companies on their own ground. And as the inquiry continued and widened men became somewhat aghast at the ominous outlook for the future.

Into this atmosphere, surcharged with suspicion and unrest, came the many reports from America, of which those drawn up by Edward Randolph were the most effective. Given leave of absence by Governor Nicholson and the Maryland council in the autumn of 1695,[2] he went to England and there conducted a well-directed campaign looking to the passage of a new bill by parliament for the enforcement of the acts already passed and the checking of the illegal trade which was beginning to assume, in his own eyes and the eyes of others, such alarming proportions. He convinced the commissioners of the customs of the truth of his statements and was able to bring it about that his suggestions became the basis of their recommendations to the Treasury and to parliament. At one time or another he was summoned to testify before the committee of the Privy Council, the Lords

1. In view of the controversy current at the time over free trade and monopolies and of the rivalry between London and the outports, the opinion of the Bristol merchants on the issue is full of significance. "We have seen the act of the Scotch parliament for encouragement of trade and judge it will be best to quench that nation's falling thereon in the beginning, which we apprehend cannot be done more effectually than by discouraging their dependence on English stocks to manage it, and here we think it not amiss to put you in mind that we conceive the foundation of this act to proceed from the restraint put on the merchants of England from trading to the East Indies and the coast of Africa by those two companies or monopolies, which hath made them seek protection from Scotland, that they may trade thither under the shelter of this act." The Bristol men, who were at war with the London monopolists, would throw these companies open by making them regulated companies, that none would "choose to trade thither from Edinburgh who could be permitted to do it from London." Additional Manuscripts, 5540, fo. 90.

2. *Calendar State Papers, Colonial,* 1693–1696, §1831; *Maryland Archives,* XX, 236–237. *Edward Randolph, 1676–1703,* edited, vols. I–V by R. N. Toppan; vols. VI–VII by A. T. S. Goodrick (Prince Society) is an important work but very incomplete. There are unprinted Randolph letters and papers among the Colonial Office and Treasury papers, in the Huntington Library, and elsewhere, and with them a supplemental volume could easily be made up. The memoirs or introductions by the two editors vary greatly in merit, that of Goodrick being far superior to that of Toppan, which presents the traditional New England bias against Randolph and in facts and conclusions follows Palfrey closely. Both memoirs omit many important episodes in Randolph's career and ignore almost entirely the English relationship. A new life of Randolph is greatly needed.

of Trade, the select committee of the House of Lords, and even before the committee of the whole House of Lords itself.[1] He was called
upon to answer questions, present proposals, and to comment on certain features of the act, which parliament, meeting on November 22,
1695, "assembled together with resolutions to promote trade,"[2] was
determined to pass. However unpleasant may have been his experiences up to this time in America—both in New England and the
colonies farther south—his self-esteem must have been flattered at the
influence he was able to exert at home during the critical period from
1696 to 1701. He may not have been liked even by the British officials,
for he was never in any sense popular among those with whom he
came into contact, but he was respected and inspired confidence, and
to him more than to any other single man was due the shaping of
the measures which England adopted at this time to strengthen her
colonial and commercial systems. Yet even he would have accomplished little or nothing had not the spirit of the times been attuned
to his efforts. He was indefatigable in endeavor and insensitive to
rebuffs, and his determination, often overzealous and almost fanati-
cal, to compel the enforcement of the acts and to do what he conceived to be his duty, cost what it might, served him well in England, where honesty and respect for the law, as Randolph interpreted
it, was none too common and where persistence in well-doing was
rather the exception than the rule. The English authorities found his
statements seemingly confirmed by the reports of others—merchants
in England and officials in America—and they were prepared to give
an attentive hearing to whatever he might say and to listen to whatever plans he might desire to bring forward. Randolph must have enjoyed these years in England, broken though they were by returns to
America and a renewal of his troubles there—interludes of contact
with unsympathetic and hostile colonists—for he was intimate with
Southwell and Blathwayt[3] and came into frequent and agreeable as-

1. *Acts Privy Council, Colonial,* II, §612; *Calendar State Papers, Colonial,* 1693–
1696, §2237; 1696–1697, §§93, 113; *House of Lords Manuscripts,* new series, II,
233, 234, 247, 411–414; Stock, *Debates,* II, 168, 170. He testified as to other things
than trade, such as wool in New England and the erection of a system of vice-
admiralty courts.

2. *Report,* American Historical Association, 1892, p. 36.

3. Randolph was Blathwayt's deputy auditor in Maryland and so naturally would
see his principal on his return to England (*Maryland Archives,* XX, 476). He was
commended by the Lords of Trade to the commissioners of the customs "for his
faithful service" (*Calendar State Papers, Colonial,* 1693–1696, §2275). In 1698 he
said that he had been back and forth across the water fifteen times (Randolph to

sociation with nearly all the offices of the government. For the time being he basked in the sunshine of official appreciation and approval.

Randolph arrived in England probably early in October, 1695, and immediately got in touch with the commissioners of the customs, to whom he sent papers, October 16 and December 17, containing information and advice regarding illegal trade and its suppression.[1] On December 13 he despatched a long memorial to the Lords of Trade on the same subject, with additional comments on convoys and the desertion of seamen,[2] and he spurred on the commissioners to draft a presentment based on his own recommendations and other papers, which they sent to the Privy Council, by whom these documents were referred to the Treasury.[3] The committee of the Privy Council also invited him and the commissioners of the customs to appear before them. In the meantime the latter were engaged in drafting a bill to be laid before parliament, designed to remedy "a great many things which the former acts [were] short in," as two of their members reported to the select committee of the House of Lords on January 8, 1696.[4] In the shaping of this measure, which on the 16th was said to be finished and in the attorney general's hands for proper wording and presentation to parliament, they must have had the efficient cooperation of Randolph, who not only continued on intimate terms with them but appeared personally before various of the executive bodies answering questions and proffering advice. Leave to bring in a bill was granted by the House of Commons, January 23, and the bill passed its first reading on the 27th. It was sent to committee on March 9, where it underwent considerable alteration. Passed on March 19 it immediately went to the upper house, where in committee Randolph was allowed to appear and to listen to the reading of certain of its clauses, and he was invited to prepare a provision relating to a proposed system of vice-admiralty courts for the colonies. After further amendments, in which the House of Commons finally

the Earl of Bridgewater, September 20, 1698, Huntington Library, El. 9758). The total number of his crossings was seventeen. Toppan, *Randolph*, II, 181.

1. *Calendar State Papers, Colonial*, 1693–1696, §2187; 1696–1697, §149.
2. *Ibid.*, 1693–1696, §2198.
3. *Ibid.*, §2237; *House of Lords Manuscripts*, new series, II, 445.
4. Stock, *Debates*, II, 151–152; *House of Lords Manuscripts*, new series, II, 7. James Chadwick, one of the commissioners of the customs, and Randolph are named as the authors of the bill by William Penn (Historical Manuscripts Commission, *Portland*, IV, 31). In its final, official form the bill was prepared for presentation to parliament by Chadwick and Blathwayt, both of whom were members of parliament as well as office holders. Stock, *Debates*, II, 155.

concurred, the bill was passed and received the royal assent, April 10, 1696.[1]

Except that it concerned trade instead of customs, the act of 1696, "An Act for preventing Frauds and regulating Abuses in the Plantation Trade," was similar in purpose to that of 1662, "An Act for preventing Frauds and regulating Abuses in his Majesty's Customs."[2] It accomplished for the plantations what the act of 1662 accomplished for the realm.[3] It was a comprehensive measure of administration, containing nothing that was new in principle but much that was new in the way of enforcement, derived from the experiences of the preceding twenty-five years. It was supplemental to the acts of 1660 and 1673 only, and to that part of the act of 1660 which had to do with shipping. It did not deal directly with either the enumeration or the staple, though in its application it touched the enumeration very closely. Its main purpose was to prevent "the great abuses that were daily being committed to the prejudice of English navigation and the loss of a great part of the plantation trade of this kingdom, by the artifice and cunning of ill-disposed persons [the Scots]." Therefore it enacted as follows.

That after March 28, 1698 (amended from 1697 in committee) no goods or merchandise whatsoever should be imported into or exported from any colony or plantation of his Majesty in Asia, Africa or America, or be laden or carried from any one port or place in the said colonies or plantations to any other port or place in the same (or to the kingdom of England, dominion of Wales, or town of Berwick-upon-Tweed, added in committee) in any but English-built ships or the build of Ireland or of the said colonies or plantations (including the build of Guernsey and Jersey, §xvii), all of which were to be wholly English owned. The only exceptions allowed were such ships as might be taken as prizes and condemned in one of the courts of admiralty in England, Ireland, or the plantations. All ships, prize and other, were to be navigated with the masters and three-quarters of the seamen English, Irish, or colonials. The only change here made is the exclusion of English shipping, foreign-built, from the planta-

---

1. *Ibid.*, II, 165, 166, 167, 170, 171–173; *House of Lords Manuscripts*, new series, II, 7, 17, 21, 22–23, 233–234; *Calendar State Papers, Colonial*, 1693–1696, §§2187, 2243.

2. 13–14 Charles II, c. 11; 7–8 William III, c. 22.

3. *North Carolina Colonial Records*, I, 440; *House of Lords Manuscripts*, new series, II, 447.

tion trade, even though the owners paid alien duties. As this class of shipping had been admitted under the former acts and its employment was customary both in London and the outports, the restriction aroused general complaint and frequent petitions were sent in asking for exemptions.[1] In the years immediately following the passage of the bill many such ships were made "free" by act of parliament, while others were allowed to trade, without rebuke, provided they paid alien duties.

That all the clauses of the act might "be punctually and bona fide observed according to the true intent and meaning thereof," as the phrase runs, the governors were to take a solemn oath, in addition to all the other solemn oaths required of them as office holders under the crown, before such person or persons as the king might designate, to obey the acts faithfully with the fear of God and the king in their hearts. As they were supposed to have done this under a similar oath imposed by the act of 1660 and had manifestly not been true to their trust,[2] the new occasion was made somewhat more impressive than usual. The customs board, with the advice of the attorney general, drafted the commission and, with the assistance of Randolph, made up ten groups of names, in each of which Randolph's own name appears, of those who were to administer the oaths to their respective governors. This commission was solemnly passed under the great seal, thus becoming a document of the highest authority, and the list of names reads like a roster of the leading men in each of the colonies.[3] Randolph must have been impressed with the importance and responsibility of his mission, when in 1697 he bore back to America these ten or more official documents and knew that in his hands rested the power to bring the governors to account. How far he was

1. *House of Lords Manuscripts*, new series, II, 233; Stock, *Debates*, II, 267, 272, 274, 275, 276, 290, 297, 304, 307, 344, 349, 359; *Calendar Treasury Books*, IV, 549.

2. Patent Roll 3201, membranes 22–25, contains the commission to Randolph, dated September 22, 1678, authorizing him to administer the oaths to the governors of Massachusetts, Plymouth, Rhode Island, and Connecticut. The Rhode Island governor refused to take the oath at this time, but Governor Treat of Connecticut did take it (*Connecticut Colonial Records*, 1678–1689, p. 49, May 14, 1680), and in a letter to the king of January 24, 1681, the colony promised to give all the aid and assistance to Randolph that it could (Hinman, *Letters*, pp. 120–122). This promise was made in reply to a letter from Charles II, November 12, 1680, instructing the colony to execute the act of 1673, as far as it applied to Connecticut. It is probable that before 1696 most of the governors had taken the oath, but had been unable to live up to its requirements.

3. *Calendar Treasury Books*, XI, 296–298.

able to execute the task cannot be said, for we know that he never visited some of the colonies at all,[1] but he doubtless carried it out as far as he could, for we have definite record of his administering the oath in a number of instances.[2] In later years the oath was administered by the governor's council. In default of taking the oath or in case of failure to carry out its terms, the governor was liable to be deprived of his post and to forfeit £1000, and Randolph said ironically, in a later report on his mission, that as far as he had observed the governors took the oaths "not in obedience to the acts of trade but to avoid payment of £1000."[3] Early instructions, such as those of Dongan of New York, had imposed no penalty, but those drawn up by the committee of the House of Lords in 1697 tended toward severity—a severity which became even greater as the years passed. The instructions to Cornwallis of Nova Scotia (1749–1752) and to Bernard of New Jersey (1758–1760), for example, declare that in case of dereliction the governor would lose his position, forfeit £1000, and "suffer such other fines, forfeitures, pains and penalties [as are provided in the laws], and receive the most rigorous marks of our highest displeasure and be prosecuted with the utmost severity of law" for his offense against the king. The guilty governor might also forfeit all right to further employment under the crown.[4] In 1701 some doubt arose as to whether a lieutenant governor—in this case of St. Christopher—could be removed and fined, the attorney general ruling that he could be removed but not fined.[5]

Though naval officers and their functions are clearly foreshadowed

1. Randolph visited all the colonies on the mainland and also Bermuda and the Bahamas, but he never was in Jamaica, Barbados, or the Leeward Islands.

2. *House of Lords Manuscripts*, new series, II, 422–425; *Maryland Archives*, XIX, 65; XXIII, 70–71, 309, 311–321, 344–345; *Pennsylvania Colonial Records*, I, 521; II, 116; *North Carolina Colonial Records*, I, 841–843; *Calendar State Papers, Colonial*, 1697–1698, §125. For the New Hampshire commission, *Province Papers*, II, 312. In 1699 Bellomont, governor of New York, took bonds of both Governor Fitz John Winthrop of Connecticut and Governor Cranston of Rhode Island in the amount of £3000. He says that a penalty of £5000 "was frightful to Gov. Winthrop," so he reduced the amount. *Calendar State Papers, Colonial*, 1699, pp. 532, 535.

3. *Calendar State Papers, Colonial*, 1697–1698, §769.

4. *New York Colonial Documents*, III, 383–385; V, 151 (Dongan and Hunter); Stock, *Debates*, II, 204–206 (House of Lords instructions); *New Hampshire Province Laws*, II, 650 (Benning Wentworth); C. O. 218:3, pp. 391–399 (Cornwallis); *New Jersey Archives*, 1st series, IX, 307 (Bernard). Despite the somewhat terrifying wording of the penalizing clause no governor was ever amerced or removed on this account.

5. *Calendar State Papers, Colonial*, 1701, §§390, 507. The Act for Punishing Gov-

in the act of 1663,[1] the name first appears in the act of 1696. There had been naval officers of a sort—clerks in the naval office—from the beginning, but naval officers as such do not appear before 1676. Randolph had complained that such officials as served in this capacity were very unreliable because not subject to a penalty in case of misbehavior,[2] and it is quite likely that he was responsible for that clause in the act which required all naval officers to give security to the commissioners of the customs in England or suffer the loss of their posts. Until such security had been given and accepted and the commissioners had confirmed the appointment, the governor was to be held liable for the misconduct of his subordinate.

Perhaps Randolph was also the author of another very significant change in the situation whereby the customs officials in the colonies were placed on a better footing. He had had enough experience in dealing with customs problems in New England to be ready to ask for more authority in handling these problems and in meeting the many obstacles that hostile colonists were forever putting in his path. He had been collector and surveyor general and knew whereof he was complaining. Hitherto the whole customs organization in the colonies had been loose-jointed and disattached; henceforth it was to be a part of the customs establishment of England, and those who were members of it were to be governed by the same rules that governed their fellow officials at home. What these rules were had already been determined by the Statute of Frauds of 1662, so that from this time on (but only until 1767 as it happened) the provisions of that statute were to apply to America as well as to England. All the customs officials were to be on one establishment, listed in a common register, paid from the same exchequer, and to enjoy the powers, exercise the functions, and suffer the penalties of the customs officials at home. All were to be under the commissioners of the customs in London, who, subject to the higher authority of the Treasury, administered the customs service of England, Wales, and the colonies. The distribution and salaries of those in the colonies were all determined by Treasury warrants issued November 20, 1696.[3]

ernors for Crimes Committed in the Plantations (11–12 William III, c. 12) covered governors, lieutenant or deputy governors, and commanders in chief, but had nothing to do with the observance or non-observance of the acts of trade.

1. 15 Charles II, c. 7, §viii; *Maryland Archives*, XX, 245 (for a naval officer's commission).

2. *House of Lords Manuscripts*, new series, II, 449, 450.

3. Treasury 11:13, p. 387.

The government had waited a long time before deciding to invest the colonial customs officials with such wide and almost arbitrary powers. Randolph said in 1682 that he could find no law in the book of rates for breaking open warehouses and entering by force to search for prohibited goods, and with all his desire to do so he refused to attempt it.[1] No such powers were granted to Dyer as surveyor general in 1683, and even two years later, when the English authorities were endeavoring to strengthen the system all along the line they instructed Patrick Mein, his successor, to do no more than "enter into any ship, bottom, boat, or other vessel, as alsoe into any shop, house, warehouse, hostelry, or other place whatsoever, to make diligent search into any trunk, chest, pack, case, truss, or any other parcell or packadge whatsoever, for any goods, wares, merchandizes, prohibited to be exported or imported, or whereof the customes or other dutyes have not been duely paid and the same to seize to his Majesty's use."[2] But by the act of 1696 the right of forcible entry was granted to any customs official in America, who was authorized to apply to the proper authority for a writ of assistance and to take a constable, a justice of the peace, or any other public official inhabiting near the place, and in the daytime to "enter and go into any house, shop, cellar, warehouse or room or other place, and in case of resistance to break open doors, chests, trunks and other packages, there to seize, and from thence to bring, any kind of goods or merchandize whatsoever, prohibited and uncustomed."[3] As a matter of fact, however, the use of force in the colonies was not warranted by the terms of any commissions that we have found, issued by the commissioners of the customs after 1696. As far as we know no one of the collectors in his instructions was told that he might obtain a writ of assistance and break open locked doors, chests, trunks and other packages, and it may be doubted if any of them, as far as his commission was concerned, would have felt justified in doing so.[4] In England such a writ might be obtained from the court of exchequer upon oath made before the Treasury by the person who asked for it, but in America it would have to be secured from a superior court of judicature or from a justice of the peace, on oath and probable suspicion, and such

1. C. O. 1:48, no. 111.          2. *Maryland Archives*, V, 521.
3. 13–14 Charles II, c. 11, §§iv, v; 7–8 William III, c. 22, §vi.
4. For early commissions, *Maryland Archives*, XXIII, 46, 326–327; *Pennsylvania Colonial Records*, I, 534. The only commission that I have seen of date later than 1750 is that of Benjamin Hallowell, printed in Quincy, *Reports*, p. 433, note 20. The

writs would have to be special writs or warrants issued on definite information and for the daytime only. No general writs were issued in any of the colonies, except in Massachusetts after 1750, because the courts refused to grant them, on the ground that they were not warranted by the act and hence were illegal. Such writs were issued in Massachusetts first by Governor Shirley and then by the superior court of judicature, and continued to be so issued and used until after the Stamp Act. Even these writs did not expressly authorize the use of force. This clause of the act of 1696 is very important because of the part it played in the famous trial in Boston in 1761, associated with the names of Otis, Gridley, and Oxenbridge Thacher.[1]

Inasmuch as the clauses of the act of 1673, relating to the plantation duty, had never been clearly understood, the act of 1696 declared definitely that even if the duty were paid at the colonial port of clearance, bond must still be furnished by the captain to carry the enu-

commissions were probably all alike, the later ones being printed on parchment from an engraved plate. There are no commissions of this kind to be found in the Massachusetts Archives.

Hutchinson in his *History of Massachusetts Bay* (Mayo ed.), III, 67, says distinctly that the Massachusetts collectors in their determination to enforce the Molasses Act of 1733 "merely by the authority of their commissions had forcibly entered warehouses and even dwelling houses, upon information that contraband goods were concealed in them." I have seen no commissions from the customs board granting this authority, though a collector may have felt that he was warranted by the act of parliament in exercising it. In 1696 the riding surveyor of Cecil County, Maryland, was instructed "to make search by breaking open any chest, trunk, lock, truss or pack as fully and amply as any Navall Officer within this Province (by Law) might or could do" (*Maryland Archives*, XX, 389). This commission was issued not from England, but by Governor Nicholson, who was applying literally the acts of 1662 and 1696.

From the evidence at hand it would appear that Collector Robinson of Salem and Marblehead, who in 1727 and 1728 was particularly zealous in his search for prohibited and uncustomed goods, must have come very near to exercising the right of forcible entry, if he did not actually break locks and batter down doors. Judge Menzies of the vice-admiralty court said in his decree, that Robinson was guilty of great disorders and unwarrantable proceedings and that he and his waiters "not satisfying themselves with the assistance of the governor in having a constable, went around armed with pistols, which they produced and threatened to shoot his Majesty's subjects" (Records of Admiralty, Massachusetts, III, fo. 58). I doubt if Menzies would have upheld the right of forcible entry.

1. On the subject of the writs of assistance and of the significance of the clause relating to them in the act of 1696 see Quincy, *Reports,* pp. 395–540, where Judge Horace Gray, in appendices A to D, discusses the subject at great length. Contemporary comment on the methods employed by the customs officials in Massachusetts seems somewhat hysterical, even though such instances of an abuse of power as that of Collector Robinson and his waiters did occur.

merated commodities to England, in case such commodities were not landed for actual consumption at the first colonial port of entry.[1] Efforts were also made to guard against false or forged certificates, such as Randolph and others alleged had been frequently used by Scotsmen and Irishmen trading to the plantations in violation of the law, by imposing a penalty of £500 in case of discovery. Such certificates might be of three varieties: certificates of bonds given in England for the return of enumerated commodities; of bonds given in the colonies for the same purpose; and of bonds given in England for the legal freighting of manufactured goods sent to America. In case of suspicion that the certificate was a forgery, the governor or naval officer might require of the captain a composition or temporary bond, which he would refuse to cancel until word had been received from the port of clearance in England that the certificate was authentic.

The colonists were to pass no laws contrary to the spirit or letter of the act or of any other act of parliament that related to the plantations.[2] They seem to have been careful to obey this clause, as well as all other clauses in the statutes of the realm that mentioned them by name, but they were not always successful in doing so, partly because they were not as familiar as they might have been with all parts of the acts and partly because they could not always understand them. However much individuals may have broken the laws, as they did over and over again, I doubt if any colonial assembly deliberately and with intention violated any act of parliament unless it be the coinage act of 1708. The number of such acts is not large, for parliament never attempted to interfere in the internal life or government of the colonies, and the opportunity for offense, except in matters relating to trade, commerce, and navigation, was therefore rare. A case in point may be noted. On October 23, 1705, the Virginia assembly passed a law requiring that anyone holding an office of public trust in the dominion should have been a resident in the colony for a full term of three years. Under the terms of this law, one Francis Kennedy, a collector deputed by William Keith, the surveyor general of customs for the southern district, was fined for having exercised his

1. This clause was henceforth regularly embodied in the trade instructions to the governors.

2. This clause (IX) of the act of 1696 is the only one among all the clauses of any act of parliament passed before 1765, in which the laws or government of the plantations in relation to the laws of England are so much as touched upon. Every act of parliament passed before 1765, that in any way concerned the colonies, had to do with trade or navigation and nothing else.

office contrary to the local law. The case was brought to the attention of the customs board in England, which memorialized the Treasury asking that the law be disallowed as contrary to the act of 1696, which empowered the Treasury and the board to appoint without any restriction as to residence. The case was complicated by the fact that the local law excepted such persons as were appointed by the king, but said nothing about such as were deputed by the surveyor general. The Board of Trade, to which the matter was referred, brushed aside this distinction as a quibble and recommended disallowance. The Privy Council approved the recommendation of the board, disallowed the law, August 31, 1715, and instructed Governor Spotswood to obtain the passage of a new law to the same effect, "so it be not liable to the objections therein mentioned." In so instructing the governor the council correctly assumed that the Virginia assembly had acted unwittingly.[1]

Two further clauses of the act made infinite trouble. According to section eleven, all suits touching the king's duties, arising out of this act or any other acts, were to be tried before juries composed only of "natives" of England or Ireland or of the plantations, and, according to section twelve, all places of trust in the courts of law or "what relates to the treasury of the said islands" were to be in the hands of the "native born subjects" of England. The mere wording of these clauses, let alone their meaning, must have puzzled many an official. Were "natives" the same as "native born subjects" and was the phrase "of the islands" a slip of the pen for "of the colonies"? In each case the answer must be in the affirmative,[2] but the instances show how carelessly the act was drawn. Then as to the meaning: were Scotsmen "native born subjects"; and were trials for breaches of the acts to take place before juries only? There were many Scotsmen holding office and places of trust in the plantations and after the passage of the act serious doubts arose as to whether they were doing so legally. Commissary Blair in Virginia, Patrick Mein and Alexander Skene in Barbados, Andrew Hamilton in East New Jersey, Robert Livingston in New York, and a great many lesser lights here and there all came under suspicion. Blair resigned voluntarily, Skene was dismissed, Hamilton was succeeded by Basse, and Livingston was

1. Treasury 27:20, p. 382; *Calendar State Papers, Colonial*, 1714–1715, §§483, i, ii, 504; *Acts Privy Council, Colonial*, II, 853; Hening, *Statutes*, III, 251–252.

2. That "of the islands" was synonymous with "in the English colonies" appears in *Calendar State Papers, Colonial*, 1702, p. 143, where the phrase is repeated.

charged with his Scots birth before the Board of Trade, which allowed the case, however, to lie by without decision. In 1699 the attorney general ruled that anyone born in Scotland was a natural-born subject of the king and could serve as a governor in the colonies or hold any other office there. Consequently most of the Scotsmen were restored to their positions. The decision was far from satisfactory to the colonists—Randolph would have had all Scotsmen turned out neck and crop—and the matter was not finally settled until the passage of the Act of Union in 1707.[1]

The second question was much more troublesome, for it involved a seeming contradiction in the terms of the act and led to wide difference of opinion as to how the act was to be interpreted. In section two the text reads, "and condemnation thereof made in one of the courts of admiralty in England, Ireland or the said colonies or plantations," and in section seven, that all penalties and forfeitures were "to be recovered in any of his Majesty's Courts at Westminster, or in the Kingdom of Ireland, or in the Court of Admiralty held in his Majesty's plantations respectively, where such offence shall be committed." These clauses seemingly required that trials for breaches of the acts of trade should be held in courts of vice-admiralty, which were courts of civil law without juries. But in section eleven appears the further statement that should a suit in the plantations be brought

---

1. 5 Anne, c. 8, §§iv, v, vi. The *Calendar of State Papers, Colonial*, from 1696 to 1707, contains many items relating to this subject, of which 1699, §§39, 71; 1700, §162; 1701, §401; 1702, §212; 1706–1708, §§794, 883, 889, 905, are the most important. See also *New York Colonial Documents*, IV, 253, 258.

In Virginia the question was raised by Blair himself in 1697, after a copy of the act had been received (*Executive Journals, Council*, I, 364). The local decision was that a native of Scotland in the council of Virginia came within the law (*Calendar State Papers, Colonial*, 1696–1697, p. 461). But when the case came before the Board of Trade that decision was reversed (*ibid.*, 1697–1698, §§610, 638). The Virginia opinion reads: "The councill then present severally declared that by the constitution of the country from the first settlement and by the severall lawes made here from time to time, his Majesty's governor and council have been and still are sole judges of the General Court; and all except natives of England, Ireland and the Islands being disabled by the said act from holding any place of trust in the courts of law and his Majesty's councill having ever as such and no otherwise been allowed judges of the General Court, are humbly of the opinion that a native of Scotland of his Majesty's council is also within the act" (C. O. 5:1359, pp. 47–50). Daniel Parke of the Leeward Islands throws light on the popular estimate of the act when he writes: "I will not presume to say that that Act was intended to exclude any Scotchman from sitting in any Court of Judicature or being one of the Treasury in any of the Plantations; but this I do affirm, that if that was not the design of the Act, the Act had no design at all." *Calendar State Papers, Colonial*, 1697–1698, §655.

against a "ship or goods to be forfeited by reason of any unlawful importations or exportations there shall not be any jury, but of such only as are natives of England," etc., thus implying that such trials were to take place in the common law courts with juries. Many efforts were made in the next few years to reconcile these statements. It would almost seem as if the act were in two parts, one representing an attempt, perhaps by Chadwick or some clerk in the custom house, to incorporate into it certain sections of the Statute of Frauds of 1662, inasmuch as the statement about juries is virtually a repetition of a clause in the earlier act[1] and was in conformity with the known practice in England[2] and in the colonies before 1697, where trial by jury was the rule; and the other showing the handiwork of Randolph, who two weeks before the bill was passed was invited to appear at the bar of the House of Lords in committee and present a clause, which he must have prepared beforehand, regarding vice-admiralty courts in the colonies.[3] Apparently the right hand did not know what the left hand was doing, which shows again how carelessly the act was prepared. That the discrepancy was not discovered in debate is astonishing, the more so because the House of Lords, in committee, agreed that a clause should be prepared "suitable to the Act 22–23 Car. II." (1671). The clause in this act expressly says that trials for failure to conform to the act of 1660 shall take place "in the court of the High Admiral in England, or of any of his vice-admirals, or in any court of record in England," a phrase that in itself is none too clear, but that certainly gives warrant for trial in the vice-admiralty courts in the colonies.[4]

It is little wonder then that, after vice-admiralty courts were finally set up in the colonies in 1697, this manifest contradiction in the text of the law should have led to great uncertainty as to what parliament really wanted. Penn called the clause "darkly and inconsistently worded"; Randolph in 1702 wrote to the Board of Trade of the many defects in the acts of trade "which renders them obscure and useless

1. 13–14 Charles II, c. 11, §xi.
2. Because such trials in England took place either in the local vice-admiralty courts; before a baron of the exchequer sent from Westminster to sit locally; or before the barons of the exchequer sitting at Westminster Hall, who even in the case of a local trial before an itinerant baron rendered the final judgment. Harper, *The English Navigation Acts*, sect. X.
3. *House of Lords Manuscripts*, new series, II, 234; Stock, *Debates*, II, 170.
4. 22–23 Charles II, c. 26, §xi (at end); *House of Lords Manuscripts*, new series, II, 233.

in the plantations";[1] and Robert Quary, judge of the vice-admiralty court in Philadelphia, for once agreed with Penn in the hope that parliament would "please to explain that dark contradictory act, not only in that particular, but in several other points" also.[2] But those whose business it was to enforce the acts of trade usually had no doubt in their minds as to the proper interpretation. The eleventh clause might mention juries but the second and seventh clauses mentioned vice-admiralty courts, and no reference to juries could possibly take away the right of vice-admiralty courts under the civil law to try breaches of the acts of trade in the plantations without juries. Attorney General Northey of the common law and Advocate General Cooke, a civilian, when asked for an opinion, agreed that the act was confused and ambiguous but that it did intend to establish vice-admiralty courts in the colonies, and they believed further that if a suit were first begun in a vice-admiralty court then no other court could claim jurisdiction. At the same time Cooke tried to reconcile the two statements by adding that parliament apparently wished two different kinds of courts to have cognizance of these cases and that if the common law court requiring juries should receive the case first then the jurymen must be of the peculiar brand named in the acts, though he believed that vice-admiralty courts took precedence. This decision left things about where they were before. The controversy

1. C. O. 388:8, E, 9, p. 1.

2. *Calendar State Papers, Colonial,* 1697–1698, §1700; *House of Lords Manuscripts,* new series, IV, 326. Roger Mompesson, a common law lawyer and later a judge of vice-admiralty in New York, in 1699 argued as follows: "I conceive the intent and meaning of the lawmakers was to oblige the Admiralty (in all causes that they try in the plantations upon that act or any former act relating to trade and which gives them jurisdiction in those cases) to try by juries, or else the clause is wholly void and ineffectual. For by a former clause the penalties and forfeitures are to be recovered in any of his Majesty's courts of Westminster or in the kingdom of Ireland or the courts of admiralty held in his Majesty's plantations respectively. So that by this clause it appears no suit can be brought in any court of the plantations, but in the admiralty only. Then comes this other clause that upon any actions, suits or informations that shall be brought, commenced or entered in the said plantations upon any law court there shall not be any jury, but of such as are of natives, which fully implies that the tryalls in the courts there in those cases mentioned shall be by juries, and since there is no court there that hath connisance of these causes but the admiralty that court must try by juries, or else the intent and meaning of the parliament must be wholly voyd and of none effect in the world" (C. O. 5:1262, M, 15; *Calendar State Papers, Colonial,* 1704–1705, §122, by title only). Northey, Cooke, and Mompesson all differed in their interpretations of this clause of the act.

lasted for ten years and longer, but in the end the vice-admiralty courts won the day.[1]

The wording of the bonds prescribed by the act of 1671 was now revised and the term "Ireland" finally left out. From this time forward, without equivocation, Ireland was placed beyond the pale of England's commercial privileges and her industry and trade were made subservient to the interests of the realm. To prevent any attempt to circumvent this restriction, which at this time applied to Scotland as well as to Ireland, by claims of disablement or stress of weather, a further clause was added, forbidding any ship to put into an "unlawful" port, that is, of Scotland or Ireland, unless first it had stopped at an English port and paid the duties. A slight exception was made in favor of an Irish ship, but not of a Scottish, whereby such ship, if stranded or leaking or unable to proceed on its voyage, might enter an Irish harbor and for security put its goods on shore, but only until such time as the goods, at the charge of the owner, could be laden on some other vessel for transportation to England.

Up to this time no one had known certainly whether the governors of private colonies—proprietary or corporate—could be brought under the operation of the acts of trade. The matter was debated at great length and Randolph—as was to be expected—insisted vehemently that the governors of all the colonies should be made subject to the same obligations and penalties. As Randolph's opinion was concurred in by the law officers of the crown, a clause was added, despite vigorous protest from the proprieties, enacting that all governors appointed by the proprietors and all elected by the corporate companies should receive the king's approval and should without exception take the oaths required by the acts to be sworn to by the royal governors. In point of fact, however, though the governor of Connecticut took the oath, which the governor of Rhode Island at first refused to do, the election of the governors in these colonies never received the crown's approval. In another respect also, and that a very specific one though of only temporary significance, did the act show distrust of the private colonies. Randolph had already raised the alarm in reporting to the commissioners of the customs that under the Scottish act of 1695, the Darien Company had liberty to plant colonies in places not in-

1. *Calendar State Papers, Colonial*, 1702, §§585, 596, 708, p. 481. I have discussed this phase of the subject in my Introduction to Mrs. Towle's edition of the vice-admiralty records of Rhode Island (American Legal Records, III).

habited and he presumed that the Scots meditated purchasing land for a settlement and setting up a trading center, either in West New Jersey, in the three lower counties, or on one of the islands in the rivers or off the coast, wherever they could find a place to locate. He recommended that no proprietor, planter, or other person or persons be allowed to transfer any island or plantation to any Scottish agent, factor, or other "foreigner" under penalty of high treason.[1] The act does not go as far as Randolph wanted it to, but in forbidding any proprietor or corporate colony to sell a part of its territory to other than a natural-born subject of England, Wales, Ireland, or Berwick-upon-Tweed, it embodied his recommendation in principle.

Finally, the act required that all ships, either in England or the plantations, including prize ships made "free," should be entered first in a local registry and the record thence be transferred to the general registry at the exchequer in Westminster in order to prevent evasion.[2] In this respect the requirement of the act was much more rigorous than had formerly been the case and a new form of registration was introduced that caught napping a good many of the masters who had left England before the act was passed or had neglected to change their old register for a new one.[3] Not having a register or not having

1. *House of Lords Manuscripts*, new series, II, 447, 448, 488–489; *Calendar State Papers, Colonial*, 1693–1696, §2187 (7); *North Carolina Colonial Records*, I, 441. We are told that in 1698 the Privy Council drafted a proclamation prohibiting any of his Majesty's subjects from entering the service of a foreign prince (*Record of the Governor and Council of East Jersey*, p. 200). From the entry in the *Record* it is evident that such a proclamation, which would apply to a colonial as well as to an English subject of the king, was actually issued and received by the governor of East New Jersey sometime before June 15, 1698, but I have been unable to find a copy of the proclamation or any further reference to it.

2. There was a register general and a deputy register general of trading vessels at the custom house, who, if we may judge from the information sought, kept track of entrances and clearances as well as the registration of the trading vessels of Great Britain. *Board of Trade Journal*, 1714–1718, pp. 64, 332, 335.

3. Vessels were frequently seized for failure to register. Such a case came up in 1750, when a ship, the *Snow*, owned by Benjamin Barons of London, but formerly of Lisbon, arrived in Boston without a certificate of registration. The vessel was seized and condemned, but the master, taking it for granted that Barons had registered in England, "prevailed upon the officers at Boston to permit the ship to return to Lisbon, upon his giving bond with Barons' agent in the value of the vessel and cargo that a register or an order from England equivalent to it should be produced by the 12th of March next." The commissioners of the customs declared that they could give no relief, as the vessel had violated the act of 1696, but the Treasury, because of a "certificate regarding him given by prominent merchants of London remitted the king's thirds in cargo and ship" (Treasury 11:22, pp. 579–580). An earlier instance occurred in Philadelphia, when in 1698, Quary seized a ship for failing to have a

a proper one rendered the vessel liable to condemnation as a foreign bottom. During the first few years of its enforcement the act was construed very loosely and many cases of failure to have a proper register were dismissed without penalty.[1] The registration oath was to be taken by the owner and not by the master, a feature of the law not always understood and sometimes, inadvertently, overlooked. A collector in Burlington, New Jersey, for example, allowed the master to take the oath, but when the matter was called to his attention acknowledged that he had made a mistake, alleging as his excuse that the vessel was the first ever registered there. Again in Maryland the governor's council decided, though the wording of the law seems perfectly clear on this point, that masters of ships petitioning for registration in the province might register, provided they took oath as to who the owners of the vessels were.[2] These were matters that required some time to adjust. The certificate of registration once obtained formed a very important part of the ship's papers.

The registration clause in the act of 1696 applied only to decked ocean-going and coastwise vessels and not to undecked boats doing business within plantation waters. Such boats—sloops, shallops, lighters, moses-boats, wood-boats, flatboats, periauguas, wherries, and canoes—were given permits by the naval officers of the locality and were exempt from taking out bonds. There were occasional differences of opinion as to the meaning of the law and doubts arose as to

register of the type required by the act of 1696. Quary's story of the case can be followed in *House of Lords Manuscripts*, new series, IV, 332–333.

1. This subject will be referred to again in the chapter on the courts of vice-admiralty. A few illustrations may, however, be given here. In 1701 the Board of Trade sent word to Lieutenant Governor Nanfan in the case of the ship *Elizabeth and Katherine*, condemned for not having registered, that it had "not thought fit that the utmost rigour of the law should be exerted," but had "given reasonable time for producing certificates of the registry of ships, when the equity of the case required it" (*Calendar State Papers, Colonial*, 1701, §928; Bodleian, Rawlinson, A, 272, fo. 133, where the proceedings in the case may be found). The same happened in Virginia, Jamaica, and elsewhere, and, with the exception of the *Cole and Bean* galley, the masters were allowed time in which to secure certificates. The *Cole and Bean* galley had a register, taken out in 1695, but did not have one according to the form required by the act of 1696. The court condemned the vessel on this ground (Bodleian, Rawlinson, A, 270, fos. 43–47). A case is recorded of the year 1729, when a ship captain, "ignorant of the trade to America," omitted supplying himself with a register, and had his ship seized in Philadelphia (*Calendar State Papers, Colonial*, 1728–1729, §§661, 672). The Board of Trade wrote to Governor Gordon to do what he could legally in his favor.

2. *Maryland Archives*, XXIII, 405. The owner had to swear that "no foreigner, directly or indirectly" had "any share or part or interest therein."

what constituted a decked, sea-going vessel. Coastwise navigation, sailing within the waters of Chesapeake Bay or among the islands of the Bahamas and Leeward Island groups, and fishing voyages off New England, Nova Scotia, and Newfoundland were almost as dangerous as an ocean voyage and demanded boats possessing seaworthy qualities. Yet as a rule colonial vessels employed therein were not required to register under the forms laid down by the act. Hence collectors and judges of vice-admiralty did not always know what to do in special cases and sometimes libeled and condemned with doubtful justification. But there do not appear to have been many instances of this kind.[1]

With the passage of the act of 1696, the statutory regulations governing the trade and navigation of the kingdom, as far as the plantations were concerned, were complete. In the years to come, decisions, rulings, explanations, and supplemental measures were to render the

1. *Ibid.*, V, 83–84; XX, 465; XXII, 116–117; *Massachusetts Colonial Records,* V, 337, 384; *Calendar State Papers, Colonial,* 1702–1703, p. 533; *Early Pennsylvania* (Original Narratives Series), p. 318.

In the Bahamas certain local sloops or wood-boats were condemned in the vice-admiralty court for not registering, this being done, as the owners charged, "without any orders of government or giving any notice that [the deputy governor] required the inhabitants to register their wood boats," built in the Bahamas and navigated there for cutting wood and raking salt (*Calendar State Papers, Colonial,* 1701, p. 646). These boats had local licenses and permits. There is a Virginia case, of date 1700, where a sloop, "a very small open vessel" plying on the Chesapeake, was condemned for not having a register, though the owner claimed that he had a permit from the deputy collector at Annapolis. On petition, the king, governor, and informer each remitted his third, amounting to £4. *Executive Journal,* II, 102–103.

A slightly different situation developed in Massachusetts. There the coasters of the province had not been accustomed to register or to do more than make a report at the custom house, though the judge of the vice-admiralty court thought that they should do so. In 1723 he decreed that according to his understanding of the act such vessels, passing from province to province, should comply with the law and be prepared to deliver certificates of registration with their inventories or be liable to confiscation (Records of Admiralty, Massachusetts, II, 165b). From the same records we learn that fishing boats in New England were not registered, *ibid.,* p. 115.

An interesting case arose in New Jersey in 1671, when a vessel engaged in the coasting trade was seized for not entering at Woodbridge, as the act of 1663 required. The captain claimed that there was no clause in that act or in any other act requiring him to enter his vessel at "every port, haven or harbour," to which he might go, for the navigation acts did not concern "small vessels, that trade on this coast from town to town." He said further that it had not been the custom of the province to require this of small vessels and as no law requiring it had been published it was not to be expected of him. The case was tried by jury, but the latter reported that the matter was "of too great weight for them" and desired that other jurymen might be selected. On May 8, 1671, a new jury was impaneled, but we hear no more of the case. *New Jersey Archives,* I, 65–72.

acts as a whole more intelligible and more workable and to smooth out the many difficulties that inevitably arose.[1] Five days after the bill received the royal assent, a circular letter was despatched by the Lords of Trade to the governors of all the colonies, with orders that this act and "all other laws made for the encouragement of navigation and the securing the plantation trade" be published and "strictly put in execution."[2] In Maryland and perhaps elsewhere the act was submitted to the attorney general of the province, who reported on it at length, and measures were taken at once for putting it into force. The lawyers were asked about any colonial legislation that had been passed conflicting with the act; public inquiry was set on foot as to whether there were any "Scotchmen" in places of trust; the clause about the registration of ships was ordered to be posted in every county court house; the naval officers were instructed to give security to the commissioners of the customs in England; and all the customs officers were warned to look out for forged or counterfeit certificates. Maryland sent over for two dozen copies each of the act and the book of rates for the use of the several counties and ordered that the act be read twice a year in every county court in the province.[3]

The letter of the Lords of Trade was followed the next year by a new and elaborate set of standing instructions to the governors (March 8, 15, 1697)[4] and at about the same time (April 12, 1697) the commissioners of the customs, having received one hundred copies of each of the navigation acts, wrote to the governors transmitting these copies and requesting obedience and coöperation.[5] On March 17 a committee of the House of Lords, appointed to consider the state of the trade, addressed the king asking that an additional instruction be sent to all the governors and at the same time transmitted the form that this instruction should take, designed to cover not only the

1. Governor Beeston of Jamaica had his "doubts about the sense of some of the acts of trade," and (as we have noted above) Edward Randolph enumerated a number of defects that in his opinion rendered them "obscure and useless in the plantations" (*Calendar State Papers, Colonial*, 1700, §815; C. O. 388:8, E, 9). That Randolph should have made this remark seems to show that he was disappointed in the acts. Though in time many of the difficulties disappeared, the Treasury as late as 1763 could still complain of "the defects and contradictions of the Laws of Trade," *Board of Trade Journal*, 1759–1763, pp. 389, 390; 1764–1767, p. 29.

2. C. O. 324:5, pp. 382–383; *Acts Privy Council, Colonial*, II, §626.

3. *Maryland Archives*, XX, 567–570; XXIII, 355–356.

4. *House of Lords Manuscripts*, new series, II, 472–481, 494–498.

5. Treasury 27:16, p. 79; *House of Lords Manuscripts*, new series, II, 483–488; *Maryland Archives*, XXIII, 349, 358.

royal colonies but those that were corporate and proprietary as well.[1]
This instruction the newly commissioned Board of Trade embodied
in a circular letter "to signify to the plantations the king's pleasure as
expressed in that address" and recommended that in the future it be
inserted in all instructions to the governors.[2] From this time forward
all governors who were sent from England to the plantations were
given before their departure printed copies of all the acts relating to
trade, together with books of rates and blank specimens of all certificates. Regularly thereafter, as part of their customary orders from the
king, they received trade instructions, drafted by the commissioners
of the customs and containing concise outlines of the laws for the
purpose of bringing the governor's obligations up to date. These trade
instructions, relatively brief at first, became very formidable after
1715 and particularly after 1753, when some ninety-two acts of parliament were listed for the governors' perusal and guidance.[3] A thorough knowledge of the acts was an essential part of the governors'
equipment, for the instructions themselves were often perfunctory
and of little use in enabling him to secure their enforcement.

For nearly forty years the authorities in England had been concentrating their best efforts upon trade and commerce—the most important objects engaging their attention and the attention of all who were
concerned for the welfare of their country. With the passing away
to a very considerable extent of religious controversy as a factor in
state politics and with a lessening of the importance of political and
constitutional issues, the more material problems of trade, foreign
commerce, shipping, and the colonies pressed forward for solution
and were engaging, as they had never done before, the solicitude of
the best minds in the country. No one can read the records of parliament, the Privy Council, the Lords of Trade, the Treasury, and the
commissioners of the customs or study the writings of the pamphleteers of the period without being impressed with their sense of the
seriousness and urgency of the situation. England still had religious
difficulties to face that concerned her standing as a Protestant king-

1. Stock, *Debates*, II, 204–206; *Calendar State Papers, Colonial*, 1696–1697, p. 409.
2. The trade instructions designed for the proprietary colonies were sent to the
proprietors in England, who were required "to give security that their deputy governors obey the king's commands in respect of the acts of trade." *North Carolina
Colonial Records*, I, 496–504.
3. For the trade instructions see Labaree, *Royal Instructions to British Colonial
Governors*, II, §§1035–1076; *Royal Government in America*, pp. 69–71.

dom; she had to weather, as she would always have, recurring constitutional and political crises that affected her administrative organization and the relations between crown and parliament; she was confronted with war and the struggle for naval supremacy, that brought her both debt and glory and strained to the uttermost her badly managed financial and material resources; and she had always with her the poor, the vagrant, and the criminal, whose very presence was a social enigma the hidden meaning of which during these years was beyond her power to discover. But underlying all these, as the dominant interest of the English government, was the necessity of winning commercial and colonial leadership among the maritime powers of Europe. To this end the acts of navigation and trade were passed and to this end time and energy were expended in the effort to make these acts effective both in the realm and in the colonies.

It may well be doubted if at first Englishmen in office had any true realization of the difficulties that were bound to accompany any attempt to apply to the colonies so rigorous a system of commercial restraint or anticipated the resistance that was certain to be met from those in the plantations whose previous freedom of action rendered such checks and balances unwelcome and irksome. England herself was at first poorly equipped for the performance of so stupendous a task. With an inadequate navy, slow-going ships, deficient finances, a world of great distances to police, a body of unwilling colonists to discipline, and an official personnel that was none too well informed or dependable, England's leaders faced the situation with blind courage and a sublime confidence in the rightness of their course. Not until after four decades of experimentation and failure, of many discouragements and but few successes were they able to win the day, as far as the day was ever won under the old British system of colonial and commercial control. The seventeenth century shows us that system in process of formation; only in the eighteenth century was it brought to any sort of completeness of plan or smoothness of operation.

Three agencies were set up during these early years for the carrying out of the acts and for bringing the colonies under a more direct form of control and supervision. These were the customs service, the courts of vice-admiralty, and the Lords Commissioners of Trade and Plantations, commonly known as the Board of Trade. To these we must now turn our attention.

# CHAPTER VII

# THE CUSTOMS SERVICE IN THE COLONIES

AS may be conjectured from what has already been said, the machinery in the colonies for carrying out the acts of navigation and trade was at first very rudimentary and imperfect and the efforts made for many years to render it more effective were discouragingly unsuccessful. The long and deeply indented coast line of the continent, the many large rivers, bays, and regions distant and uninhabited, where the running of goods, among an unwilling and often hostile people, could go on unimpeded; the absence of ports in Maryland and Virginia, where vessels could enter and officers reside; and the large areas of territory which the collectors and other customs officials were forced to supervise made the colonial seaboard a field within which evasion was easy, when attempted, and detection and prevention were difficult and slow.[1] The proximity of foreign possessions in the Gulf of St. Lawrence and the West Indies, with French settlements in the one and French, Dutch, Spanish, and Danish settlements in the other, led to frequent exchanges of uncustomed and prohibited goods that were beyond the law, despite the efforts of the governors and others to circumvent it. The small fees and percentages, the scarcity of hard money, the quarrels among the officials themselves, and the poverty of the colonists and their resistance to all restrictive measures made connivance and fraud a not uncommon occurrence. The unwillingness of the Treasury to increase the number of customs officials, except as imperative need and constant complaint compelled them to do so, and the inability of the Admiralty to furnish a sufficient number of frigates and scouting boats for the arrest of offenders in American and West Indian waters rendered the chance of a successful escape sufficiently good to be frequently taken. In the matter of the enumerated commodities the system in the long run worked fairly well, but in that of the manufactured goods from England and the Continent, with England as the

---

1. Governor Dobbs in 1764 stated very clearly what the difficulties were in North Carolina (*North Carolina Colonial Records*, VI, 1023). Other governors frequently sent over similar complaints. For example, *Maryland Archives*, XX, 463–464; Treasury 11:13, pp. 432–433.

staple, it was less successful, owing to the frequent opportunities which the propinquity of foreign colonies offered for smuggling. Nevertheless, taking the old colonial system as a whole and the acts which have thus far been discussed, we may safely say that while in theory and definition they were rigid and uncompromising, they were in practice elastic and adjustable and did not at any time before 1764 seriously interfere with the growth or prosperity of the colonies.

The center and mainstay of the whole colonial structure was the governor, who was the representative of the crown in the royal colonies and the chief link in the chain of connection binding mother country and colonies together. But a distant governor was a difficult man to control.[1] Even after more than thirty years of effort on the part of the home government to mold this executive official into an administrative agent for the carrying out of the acts of trade, no very certain results had been achieved. During these years letters and instructions from the king, Treasury, commissioners of the customs, and the Lords of Trade had followed, one after another, emphasizing the governor's accountability and impressing upon him the absolute necessity of an efficient and punctual performance of the duties which the acts of parliament imposed upon him. Even so, at the close of the seventeenth century, no very precise conclusions had been reached as to the extent of his powers or the nature of the responsibilities resting upon him.[2] Probably most of the governors were doing the best they could, but the acts were so obscure, interpretations so often conflicting, instructions so difficult to carry out, and obstacles in the way of effective enforcement frequently so formidable that the best of them were handicapped at the start. As the number of the acts increased and the volume of trade expanded, many perplexing questions inevitably arose and the governors were obliged to leave the answers to subordinates, over whom they had but an uncertain control.[3] When

1. On this point, Blathwayt wrote in his "Reflections on a Paper concerning America" (Blathwayt Papers, Huntington Library) that "the sending of good Governors to the Plantations is much insisted on with good reason, for where his Majesty has so few officers of his own appointment they ought to be the more careful of their Duty and at so great a distance from his Majesty's eye great Temptations happen whereby his Majestys service does often suffer."

2. In 1698 Randolph sent over a list of five queries regarding what was expected of a governor (*Calendar State Papers, Colonial,* 1697–1698, §769, i). These queries concern chiefly, but not entirely, the governors of the proprietary and corporate colonies.

3. An important additional duty was imposed by the crown in 1696 on the governors as vice-admirals: "That all commanders of his ships that are sent to any of

to the local incumbents we add the patent officers—officials appointed by the crown in England, who often held by deputy—we find ourselves confronted with an important group of functionaries in every royal colony, far removed and none too amenable to discipline, whose business was concerned, in one way or another, with the task of looking after the royal and parliamentary revenues and seeing that the acts of trade as well as many an executive command were duly carried out.

First among these officials, in point of time and importance on the commercial side, was the naval officer, who took the place of the governor as the eyes and ears of the crown in all that concerned the shipping clauses of the acts. The act of 1663 had provided that no vessel should lade or unlade any goods until the captain or master had first made known to the governor of the plantation or to such person or officer as he might appoint both the arrival of the ship and its name and the name and surname of its master or captain, and have proved to him, by showing a certificate of registration, that it was English built and that no foreigner, directly or indirectly, had any share or part therein. The captain was also to deliver to the governor or his

his plantations for the defence and service thereof be under the direction of the governors of each of these respective plantations during their continuance there. And further that when any captain or commander of any of his ships in any of his said plantations shall have occasion for seamen to serve on board his ships under their command they make their application to the governors and commanders in chief of his Majesty's plantations, to whom as vice admirals his Majesty is pleased to commit the sole power of impressing seamen in any of his plantations in America or in sight of any of them, such governors and commanders in chief being at the same time required upon such application to take care that his Majesty's ships of war be furnished with the number of seamen that may be necessary for his Majesty's service on board the said ships from time to time." *Calendar State Papers, Colonial*, 1696–1697, p. 313 (greatly abbreviated).

The ships of the royal navy were instructed always to aid the governor, whenever called upon to do so. This instruction is well illustrated by an incident which occurred in South Carolina in 1734. A case came up in the vice-admiralty court there, when a warrant was issued against one Captain Gordon of a ship lying in Rebellion Road. The marshal of the court attempting to serve it was fired on. Then the judge issued a warrant against the captain for assault and applied to the governor for assistance. The governor directed Captain Anson of H.M.S. *Squirrel* to help, and the latter sent the master of the ship to support the marshal. In the struggle that ensued Captain Gordon was killed. The master was acquitted. *South Carolina Gazette*, April 19–26, October 26–November 2, 1734.

Quarrels frequently arose between the governor and the navy officials, as between Governor Hamilton of Jamaica and Rear Admiral Hovenden Walker concerning the "inhabitants of the island being press'd on board the Queen's ships." *Calendar State Papers, Colonial*, 1712–1714, §277, xiv.

appointee a certificate of the bond taken out in England and signed by the commissioners of the customs there, and also a true and perfect inventory or invoice of the cargo. In the act of 1696 this "appointee," whose selection was definitely placed by the act in the governor's hands, is specifically called the "naval officer," a name which originated in the colonies and had been in use there for twenty years, if not longer.[1] Instructions relative to his employment were frequently sent from England and handed to him by the governor, and as frequently was the statement made that the naval officer was the governor's man.[2]

The earliest naval officers in the royal colonies were, of course, the governors themselves, and when, as in Barbados and Jamaica, the designation "naval office" appears, it undoubtedly means a clerical office under the governor's immediate control.[3] In Massachusetts the secretary of the colony was instructed to perform a naval officer's duties and in Pennsylvania as well the earliest official of that name had only local duties to perform.[4] The first recorded appointment of a naval officer, *eo nomine,* seems to have been in Jamaica in 1676, where Reginald Wilson, a man reputed at the time to be experienced in marine and mercantile matters and familiar with the acts of trade, was named overseer of the harbor and naval officer by Governor Vaughan, with authority to set up a naval office at Port Royal. Wilson was also the collector of the provincial duties, levied by the assembly for defraying the expenses of government, and was a man of influence in the island. He received from the governor a well-defined body of instructions, which are extremely interesting as covering a wider range of duties than were performed by later naval officers, and are important as disclosing his dependence on the governor and the latter's acceptance of ultimate responsibility.[5]

1. The naval officer is mentioned in the instructions of 1683 to William Dyer, as if he were already a well-known official in the colonies (§11), and we know that the name was frequently used there before 1696. See also *Calendar State Papers, Colonial,* 1677–1680, §1590; 1706–1708, p. 577; *Virginia Magazine,* XXV, 268.

2. For example, *Calendar State Papers, Colonial,* 1697–1698, §894, i.

3. *Ibid.,* 1661–1668, p. 280; C. O. 1:41, no. 113, where Thomas Speed, deputy to Charles Willoughby, clerk of the navy office, is mentioned as of date 1672–1673. Other similar clerks in Barbados are also listed (*Calendar State Papers, Colonial,* 1677–1680, §495, by title only). A history of the naval office in Barbados is given in Additional Manuscripts, 22617, fos. 141–142, February 16, 1694.

4. *Massachusetts Colonial Records,* IV, pt. II, 73; *Maryland Archives,* V, 24–25; Pennsylvania *Statutes at Large,* II, 84.

5. C. O. 138:2, pp. 78–79, 86–93, greatly abbreviated in *Calendar State Papers,*

In Virginia and Maryland, where there were many creeks and rivers and no fixed ports of entry, the early appointees had to cover more than one county, a practically impossible task as far as efficiency went.[1] But as time went on the number was increased and eventually became six for each colony. These men were often, at the same time, members of the council, collectors, and even justices of the peace, a form of pluralism common in the colonies and neither illegal nor contrary to the governors' instructions. Indeed, the combining of offices was an inevitable necessity in the early history of the colonies, where the scantiness of the population and the scarcity of competent men made it obligatory for one man to hold two and even more positions.[2] The Board of Trade frowned upon the practice as undesirable and tried to prevent it and in 1705 sent out in the name of the king an instruction forbidding councillors to serve as naval officers, but

Colonial, 1675–1676, §800; see also ibid., p. 422, §960; 1677–1680, §482; 1681–1685, §§732, 1200; 1704–1705, §1351. For Maryland, ibid., 1696–1697, p. 609; 1699, p. 312; 1700, pp. 310–311; 1702, p. 84; 1706–1708, pp. 497, 627, 737, 742; 1711–1712, §345; Maryland Archives, V, 291; XIII, 203; XX, 160–161. Governor Nicholson said in 1699 that some of the naval officers of Maryland received a variety of instructions and some none at all. Calendar State Papers, Colonial, 1699, p. 312.

1. The Patuxent district in Maryland included eight counties—St. Mary's, Calvert, Talbot, Ann Arundel, Charles, Somerset, Dorchester, and Cecil. In a presentment from London merchants trading to Virginia appears the following statement in support of an argument in favor of fixed ports for the discharge and loading of ships: "It having been found by experience that by the present practice of ships lying dispersed up and down at the election of the masters and commanders far remote from the places of the officers' abode and their fixed residence, the said officers have not been able to attend the due delivery of ships." C. O. 5:1360, p. 72 (not calendared), March 7, 1705. See below, p. 204, note 4.

2. Pluralism prevailed widely, notably in the tobacco plantations and in the West Indies. Many examples could be given, but certain selected cases must suffice. (1) Nehemiah Blakiston of Maryland (d. 1694) was collector of the provincial revenue, collector of the plantation duty, naval officer, and member of the council (Maryland Archives, XX, 120, 124–125, 131, 142, 175–176). Ralph Wormely in Virginia was collector, naval officer, and secretary at the same time (Calendar State Papers, Colonial, 1697–1698, p. 331. Cf. ibid., 1696–1697, p. 548; 1700, pp. 310–311). Miles Cary of Virginia in 1700 petitioned the council "that he being Register of the court of admiralty and since by his Excellency's favour made Navall officer of York River district and being humbly of opinion that the said offices are Inconsistent, it not being suitable that one and the same Person should be obliged to seize ships and vessels for Illegal traders and to be a Party in the tryall of them, [prays] to be Discharged from the said office of Register" (Executive Journals, II, 126). (2) Captain Kerr of the royal navy in 1706 wrote the Admiralty from Jamaica that he was surprised to learn of one Gyde being given a commission as victualling agent when he was already agent for the sick and wounded and also a prize officer, and a person "who hath not a navy education" (Admiralty 1:2005, Kerr, October 27, 1706). (3) Joseph Blenman of Barbados, who up to 1750 had served more than twenty-two years in the island, was holding at the

the Virginians loudly disapproved of the order as working a great hardship on the colony. There was less pluralism in Maryland than in Virginia though the distances were greater, the colony more thinly populated, and available men more difficult to obtain. One naval officer there in 1697 was charged with "severall irregularities"—negligence and forgetfulness among them—and was dismissed; and George Plater, who was both receiver and attorney general, was ordered to give up one of the offices or reside "in town" (Annapolis), else "his Majesty's business will be much retarded and impeded."[1] In the years from 1682 to 1684 Massachusetts, by act of assembly with the power of appointment lodged in the governor, established three naval offices, one each at Boston, Salem, and Newbury.[2] Randolph was enraged at this assumption of authority, which he considered the work of a "faction" in the general court, an insult to himself and his office and a fraud against the king.[3] He recommended that the act be disallowed, but this was not possible as the crown in granting the charter of 1629 had made no reservation of the right of disallowance, because that charter was designed only for a company resident in England. After 1691, under the new charter, the power of appointment fell into the hands of the royal governor, without nomination by the assembly, and from that time on Massachusetts, in all that concerned the naval officer, fell into line with the royal colonies. In the

same time the offices of attorney general and judge of vice-admiralty, a combination so incongruous that Governor Henry Grenville wrote his brother George in England, July 9, 1751, "The impropriety of two such important offices uniting in one cannot but strike at first sight and the truth is that no such impropriety does subsist in any other of the king's governments, as I can learn, nor did it ever [here] till of late years, when Mr. Blenman, I am told, obtained this office of the Admiralty by great sollicitations and I fear with no very commendable views. . . . [The offices] are in their nature so incompatible that I think no honest man would wish to hold both" (Grenville Correspondence, Huntington Library, Stowe). (4) William Pym Burt of St. Christopher was charged with engrossing "many considerable and lucrative posts" there, "a strange and inconsistent medley of Treasurer, Liquor Officer, Powder Officer, Governor of Brimstone Hill, and Colonel of the Forts and Fortifications of the Island." He seems also to have been judge of vice-admiralty and aspired to be chief justice of the court of king's bench and common pleas. He had married the governor's sister (*Board of Trade Journal*, 1742–1749, pp. 305, 315, 319). (5) In the years from 1764 to 1767, protests were entered from Virginia against the same person holding the offices of treasurer and speaker at the same time, *ibid.*, 1764–1767, p. 369.

1. *Maryland Archives*, XXIII, 166–167.

2. *Massachusetts Colonial Records*, V, 337–338, 383–384, 439. For the law of October 10, 1676, *ibid.*, 155.

3. C. O. 1:48, no. 111; *Calendar State Papers, Colonial*, 1681–1685, §579 (greatly abbreviated).

Carolinas there were naval officers before 1698, appointed by the governors under instructions from the proprietors, who were frequently reminded of their duty by the crown.[1] In 1682 Rhode Island, by act of assembly, set up an office at Newport, the incumbent to be appointed by the governor, who was authorized to administer the oath "according to law to any ship captain by law liable"; and twenty years later Connecticut established, also by act of assembly, naval offices at thirteen different ports to take cognizance of all vessels trading to and from the colony.[2]

The question of the appointment of the naval officer presents some difficulties, for it led to important changes in the royal policy of assignments in the colonies. A controversy arose as early as 1676 over the king's selection of one Abraham Langford, a clerk in the naval office in Barbados. In the face of the language used in the act of 1663, the king disregarded the governor's rights and appointed the naval officer himself, thus diminishing the governor's local patronage. Governor Atkins, offended at the king's action, claimed that under his commission the seal of the province was good against the king, but he was unable to maintain his position.[3] Though the intent of the

1. *North Carolina Colonial Records*, I, 492; *Calendar State Papers, Colonial*, 1702, p. 173.

2. *Rhode Island Colonial Records*, III, 110, 119; V, 58, 133–135; *Calendar State Papers, Colonial*, 1710–1711, p. 264; *Connecticut Colonial Records*, 1689–1706, pp. 374–376; *Talcott Papers*, I, 164, 229; Connecticut Archives, Trade and Maritime Affairs, I, no. 43. The position of the naval officer in Connecticut was peculiar. The right of granting clearances at any one of thirteen ports was contested by Shackmaple, royal collector at New London, who seized all vessels so clearing, because they did not have a proper certificate, signed by both collector and naval officer. Quary and later Birchfield, surveyors general, upheld Shackmaple, and collectors in other colonies refused to recognize Connecticut clearances. The Connecticut government was consequently in a quandary. First it reduced the number of ports, adding Greenwich to Stamford, Branford to New Haven, "Kennelworth" to Guilford, Lyme to Saybrook, and Groton to New London. But that did not help matters, even though one case tried at Boston was dismissed by Byfield, judge of vice-admiralty there, on the ground that for all Connecticut vessels to go to New London to clear would be a great hardship. But the New York court was not so lenient and condemned the *John and William*, October, 1716—March, 1717, and again November, 1717. Then as the New York trade was fundamentally important to the colony, the Connecticut authorities appealed to the king. Though the solicitor general reported favorably on the appeal, the suit was prolonged before the High Court for nearly ten years and probably never was finally settled. What the commissioners of the customs did about the ports is equally obscure. The documents are in the Connecticut Archives and the *Connecticut Colonial Records*. See p. 196, note 4.

3. *Calendar State Papers, Colonial*, 1675–1676, §§896, 947; 1677–1680, §482, iii, p. 535.

law seemed plain, the Treasury called on William Blathwayt to make a report on the subject, but unfortunately Blathwayt's answer has not been preserved. When the act of 1696 clearly confirmed the governor's right, the issue became once more important and the governors showed themselves inclined to renew the struggle against the royal interference. Governor Grey of Barbados in 1699 declared that as the act reasserted the right of the governor to appoint the naval officer, only his "duty and tender regards" for the royal patent prevented him from turning out the existing incumbent and taking the office under his own care and protection, adding that the people of Barbados were entirely opposed to appointments by royal patent.[1] Mitford Crowe, a little later, had no such scruples and in the case of one Samuel Cox deliberately defied the royal authority. The Board of Trade, though reminding Crowe that appointment by patent had been the rule in Barbados since 1676, reopened the case and sought a legal opinion from the solicitor general, James Montague. It asked whether the selection of a naval officer was vested in the governor exclusive of the crown and whether, as in this instance, the governor could dispossess an officer holding by royal patent. Montague replied very plainly that the acts vested the appointment in the governor and that if the crown named one man and the governor another, the latter was the one to whom the masters of ships should apply. He was quite certain that anyone authorized by letters patent from England was not the officer mentioned in the acts of parliament, but he hinted that if the governor were wise he would ease the situation by appointing, as of his own free will, the person whom the king wanted. The board did not like Crowe, who was an unamiable public servant, and probably, if it had had a chance, would have told him to take Montague's hint and not be so tactless and disobedient. But Secretary Sunderland cut the knot by ordering Crowe to mind his own business and not to question a royal patent. Crowe subsided, and when a week or two later the board had occasion to write Handasyd of Jamaica, it said that if he would consult the acts he would find that the nomination of the naval officer was in the hands of the governor only in case of a vacancy, a manifest untruth.[2]

1. Ibid., 1699, §879.

2. C. O. 29:11, pp. 230–232, 293–296; Calendar State Papers, Colonial, 1706–1708, pp. 577, 682, 714, 760, 767, 768, §§1539, 1546, 1577; Board of Trade Journal, 1704–1709, pp. 413, 460, etc. The report of Solicitor General Montague is in Calendar State Papers, Colonial, 1708–1709, §39. There was a notable quarrel in Rhode Island in

This decision, which the board afterward reversed many times, was in the interest partly of patronage and partly of a desire in England to effect a greater centralization of authority for the sake of increased efficiency. So many rumors had come to Whitehall of collusion between the governors and the naval officers, of duties unperformed or badly performed, and of extravagant fees and charges that it may have seemed best to the English authorities to make the naval officer dependent not on the governor but on the crown. Love of patronage always grows with·use and the pressure of political obligation, and the harassed department officials of England found in the colonies new opportunities to help friends and needy dependents. Though during the early part of the eighteenth century by far the greater number of the naval officers were the governors' appointees, those of Jamaica, Barbados, and the Leeward Islands and a few among the continental colonies held by virtue of his Majesty's warrant and commission.[1] Later the proportion was reversed.

1743 over the appointment by the crown of Leonard Lockman as naval officer, the colony claiming that this was an encroachment upon its chartered privileges. In the end the colony won the day (*Rhode Island Colonial Records*, V, 70, 96, 271; Kimball, *Correspondence of the Colonial Governors of Rhode Island*, I, 226–228, 242–243, 245–246). In 1741, the judge of vice-admiralty in Massachusetts spoke of the naval officer as "the officer by him [the governor] thereunto authorized and appointed" (Records of Admiralty, Massachusetts, V, 48b), and he was generally so considered.

1. In the Bahamas, Governor Woodes Rogers appointed his own naval officer (*Calendar State Papers, Colonial*, 1717–1718, p. 373), and that this had been true earlier appears from the expressions "a servant of the governor" and "a governor's man" applied to this official in 1702 (*ibid.*, 1702, pp. 82, 84). In New York and New Hampshire the naval officer was appointed by Bellomont (*New York Colonial Documents*, IV, 664); in Maryland by the governor (*Maryland Archives*, III, 19; C. O. 5:1276, Sharpe's "Answers to Queries," January 14, 1762); in Georgia by the governor; and in the Carolinas until 1729 also by the governor under the direction of the proprietors. The governor appointed the naval officer in Massachusetts, until in 1733 the king chose to override the governor's authority by choosing a man of his own, Benjamin Pemberton (State Papers Domestic, George II, 156, no. 198). In Barbados during the governorship of Henry Grenville (1746–1756), in a controversy that arose between the naval officer and the collector and comptroller of the customs, the question came up as to whom to appeal the case and the statement is clearly made that the governor appointed the naval officer (Blenman's report, March 12, 1749, "the naval officer who was appointed by your excellency." Grenville Papers, Huntington Library). In the Leeward Islands, however, Codrington the younger said that he did not name the collectors and naval officers (*Calendar State Papers, Colonial*, 1696–1697, §1405).

Despite the actual facts in the case and even after a large majority of the naval officers had become the appointees of the crown, the trade instructions to the governors continued to read, "His Majesty having been informed that the naval officers appointed by the governors in their respective plantations," etc. (C. O. 324:26, pp. 231–233). One would suppose that the commissioners of the customs, who drew up these instruc-

By 1752, however, appointments by the governor had either become very infrequent or ceased altogether, and it would appear as if in all the royal colonies, except Nova Scotia and Georgia, the governors had lost their patronage in this field. The naval officer had become a direct appointee of the crown, either under the great seal, as in Barbados, Jamaica, and the Leeward Islands, in two of the six districts of Virginia, and in a few other cases; or under the sign manual, as in all the other royal colonies.[1] Inevitably, of course, the governors, because of their instructions, continued to exercise considerable influence over the management of the office and its incumbent, greater indeed than the orthodox mercantilist deemed wise, in view of the need, as the mercantilists saw it, of the concentration of greater authority in the hands of the executive officials at home. The tendency to center colonial patronage in England is a factor of no little importance in tracing the growing centralization of the entire British system as we advance toward the climax of the Revolution.

The naval officers were not in any sense under the authority of the customs board of England; they received their appointment either from the king or from the governor[2] and their instructions from the latter, which was probably the reason why the naval officer was so

tions, would have known better than to repeat this erroneous statement year after year. That they did so repeat it was undoubtedly due to that bane of good government everywhere—bureaucratic routine, which characterized the work of all the English departments during our colonial period.

1. "List of Offices in the American Colonys the nomination to which was vested in the Board of Trade by Order in Council of the 11 of March 1752." Chatham Manuscripts, no. 95 (Public Record Office).

2. *Calendar State Papers, Colonial,* 1681–1685, §617; 1697–1698, §§894, i, 943, etc. The functions of the naval officer as understood by Charles Carkesse, secretary to the commissioners of the customs, in 1713, were as follows: "the Nature and use of the Naval Officer in the Plantations is to take an Acco.[t] of the Arrival of all ships trading thither with their Ladings and how Navigated and the like of all ships going from the Plantations or from one plantation to another and to take Security (if not given before in Great Britain) that all Enumerated Goods be carried to Great Britain or from one plantation to another, and no ship can Load or Unload without the permission of this Officer as well as the Collector."

"The Duty of the Naval Officer in the Plantations is (as I take it) to take an Account from all Masters of Ships arriving in any of the Plantations of the Name of their own Ships, their own name and Sirname with the particular marks and numbers of the Goods on board where they belong to and by whom owned and how Manned and gunned and at their Lading in the Plantations (if the Ships are bound to England, Wales or Town of Berwick) to oblige the Masters to enter into Bond in that Office for his return to England Wales or Berwick (the word Ireland being now and for some Years past ordered to be left out of all such Bonds by the 22d and 23d of King Charles the 2d for preventing the planting of Tobacco in England and regulating the Planta-

often called the "governor's man." Their commission from the king was general,[1] but their instructions from the governor were specific. As there was no corresponding official in England whose duties could be copied, the naval officers in the colonies acquired their functions slowly, but by the beginning of the eighteenth century these functions were fairly well understood. The naval officers were to give security to the commissioners of the customs[2] and to be in actual residence at the place of their appointment; to grant certificates of entrance and clearance, which would be valid only when signed by the collector also, and to take oaths of the master or boatswain of all

tion Trade) or to some of Her Majesty's Plantations and there to unlade and put the same ashore and at the going away of any of said Ships from the said Plantations they are also obliged to clear in his Office and give him an Accot of their Lading which the Naval Officer enters into a Book kept for that purpose, and to which every Master of a Ship entring in the said Office sets his name at his entring inwards and at his clearing outwards, and upon the Governour of each respective Plantations his Signing a Let pass for every Ship or Vessel (made out also and signed and Sealed by the said Naval Officer) the Naval Officer gives to the Master or Commander of the Fort (if be any where the Ships ride) a permit under his hand directed to the Gunner of such Fort to permit such Ship or Vessel to pass as having done all in that Place which the Law required, a particular Account whereof the Naval Officer is obliged to render Quarterly in a List to the Governor of each respective Plantation and to return one of the same kind at the same time hither to the Honorable Commissioners of her Majestys Customs in London . . . whose great use by the practice now used in the said Office in the several Plantations abroad is to prevent foreign Ships from Trading in our Plantations and to discourage all Clandestine Trade as much as possible they can." Additional Manuscripts, 22617, fos. 143–144, December 30, 1713.

James Abercromby in his "Examination" (1752) has an excellent statement of the duties of the naval officers, pp. 46–47, but it is too long to be inserted here and adds but little to the statement by Carkesse.

1. Bodleian, Rawlinson, A, 171, fo. 199; Patent Roll, James II, part 19, membrane 33. Most of the commissions for the naval officers may be found on the Patent Rolls; the form is always essentially the same (*Calendar State Papers, Colonial, 1681–1685*, §§295, 617; 1685–1688, §560; 1714–1715, §306; *House of Lords Manuscripts*, new series, II, 475, §11; 486, §5; *Maryland Archives*, XXIII, 254–256). Occasionally special directions seem to have been sent to the naval officers at the same time as to the collectors by the commissioners of the customs, but this was due to the fact that the naval officers did a good deal of customs business (*Calendar State Papers, Colonial, 1712–1714*, §326, i). The position of the naval officer in Maryland was peculiar, because he had to serve two masters. As a member of the provincial system he collected the hogshead and tonnage duties levied by acts of assembly, 1661 and 1704; and as a crown official he looked after entrances and clearances. His office was in the gift of the governor, but the choice was often directed either by the secretary of the colony or by the proprietor. *Maryland Archives*, XLI, 518–519; XLII, 649–651.

2. For copies of naval officers' bonds, *Wolcott Papers*, p. 214 (a Connecticut bond); *Maryland Archives*, XX, 256–257; XXIII, 229, 287, 346–347. Many copies of such bonds are in volumes V and XXIII of the *Archives*.

vessels leaving the colony;[1] to examine all certificates and cocquets and navigation bonds brought in by incoming masters and to see that they were correct and authentic; to sign and seal them—the naval officer had his own seal—and to turn them over to the collector, who would either retain them himself or lodge them with the governor; to obtain detailed information regarding every ship entering and clearing—its kind and build, when and where registered, master's name, owner's name, tonnage, guns,[2] men, and cargo —keep an accurate list of all this information, and turn the lists over to the governor, who would transmit them to England.[3] Coöperation with the collectors was a necessary part of the naval officers' duties.[4] In some colonies—the West Indies—they seem to have acted as im-

1. *Calendar State Papers, Colonial,* 1714–1715, §§306, 317; *Maryland Archives,* XX, 502.

2. In the list of thirty-three ships allowed to sail to Virginia and Maryland, January, 1690, despite the embargo, the guns carried run from 6 to 40, with an average of 16. *Calendar Treasury Books,* IX, 478–479.

3. These lists, formerly known as Naval Office Lists but now as Shipping Returns, are to be found, chiefly in the Public Record Office, for all the colonies from 1689 to 1765. A few exist of a later date. The earliest lists are missing. John Pollexfen, commenting on the early Maryland lists, said, "These accounts are very imperfect and made up in such shape and fashion that no exact computation can be made from them; some omitting dates of clearing. The officers should be directed to make up their accounts yearly, to insert the dates when ships are cleared, and to be careful in spelling the names of places and ships" (C. O. 5:749). The Maryland naval officer in 1698 was requested to transmit his lists, among copies of bonds and other papers, to the port of Annapolis in order to be kept among other shipping papers lodged in the clerk of the council's office in the new state house (*Maryland Archives,* XXIII, 406–407). For further comments on the imperfections of the earlier lists see *Calendar State Papers, Colonial,* 1699, §856; C. O. 29:6, pp. 211–212 (abbreviated in *Calendar State Papers, Colonial,* 1697–1698, §482); *ibid.,* 1702, p. 701; *Virginia Magazine,* XXI, 385.

4. *Calendar State Papers, Colonial,* 1697–1698, §§894, i, 943; Treasury 29:9, p. 4; *ibid.,* 27:5, p. 47. The instructions issued in 1698 to the governors "regarding giving security for naval officers" show well the official intent in this respect. "His Majesty having been informed that the Naval Officers being the Persons appointed by the governors in his respective plantations in America to take bonds and give certificates for clearing of ships, have generally neglected to comply with the directions of the late Act of Parliament for preventing frauds and regulating abuses in the Plantation Trade [1696], which requires their giving security to the commissioners of the customs in England for the due discharge of their trust. And it having been further represented to his Majesty that besides the security which the said naval officers are obliged by law to give, it would be very expedient that according to the constitution of the customs in England, which has provided a control upon the actions of every officer employed therein, the concurrence of the collectors appointed by the commissioners of the customs in his Majesty's respective Plantations should also be made necessary to so important an act as that of signing certificates for clearing ships . . . you do not admit

migration agents,[1] registering incoming passengers and servants, and they may have done the same in the continental colonies as well, collecting some of the statistics that the governor was accustomed to forward to the secretary of state or the Board of Trade as enclosures in his regular letters. In the West Indies also they were at times employed to furnish supplies for ships of war and even to provide the vessels themselves. But as the Admiralty did not approve of this practice, it was later given up and, after some experimenting, which did not prove successful, other expedients were adopted.[2] Though it is impossible to say how many vessels they actually seized themselves, they undoubtedly did coöperate with the customs officers in this particular and in the West Indies not infrequently seized vessels single-handed.[3] In times of war they acted with the collector in getting "the trade in readiness against the time the convoys should arrive," assisting them to round up the tobacco or sugar ships at some designated place of meeting.

Usually the naval officers were paid by fees, but sometimes by percentages. Quary once complained that Pennsylvania took away "from the naval officers 4lb per cent of their allowance for collecting and

---

or allow any certificates signed by the naval officer or officers aforesaid for the clearing of ships . . . to be valid and effectually for that end without the concurrence of the collector appointed there by the commissioners of his Majesty's customs" (C. O. 324:6, pp. 371–372, neither calendared, nor printed in *Acts Privy Council, Colonial*). A similar letter dated November 10, 1698, is in the Connecticut Archives, Foreign Correspondence, I, no. 73, and another dated January 22, 1699, in no. 76.

1. C. O. 1:43, no. 87. This was also the case in Rhode Island, under an act of 1712. *Rhode Island Colonial Records*, 1707–1740, p. 133.

2. *Calendar State Papers, Colonial*, 1697–1698, §427.

3. *Board of Trade Journal*, 1709–1715, pp. 10, 53; *Calendar State Papers, Colonial*, 1708–1709, p. 273; 1709–1715, p. 145 (Jamaica). Fauconnier, as naval officer, seized ships for illegal trading (*New York Colonial Documents*, IV, 1144). Many ships carried goods in and out of the colonies without entering or clearing, and as this form of illegal trading affected the naval officers' business, the latter could make out a good claim in support of their action.

The question as to whether the naval officer had the right to issue warrants of arrest, as a privilege accorded by his patent, was raised by Abraham Langford in 1677, who called the power to do so "one of the chiefest perquisites" of the office. The governor disputed the right, but the Lords of Trade upheld the patent and admitted the legality of Langford's claim. There is, however, nothing to show that the right was exercised by the naval officers generally (C. O. 1:41, no. 107; *Calendar State Papers, Colonial*, 1677–1680, §§482, 493, 495). Nicholson employed the naval officers to assist in the apprehension of pirates in Virginia (*ibid.*, 1700, §523, xiv. See also *ibid.*, 1702, §§428, 537, 925; *Maryland Archives*, XXIV, 141, 143). They were also used, in one case at least, to take charge of treasure obtained from wrecks. *Calendar Treasury Books*, IX, 767–768.

receiving. This looks [he adds] like the dog in the manger, since the gentlemen of the councill cannot have those places themselves [because of the order forbidding councillors to be naval officers] they would starve those who have them."[1] Bellomont said in 1700 that the general assembly of New York had made the naval officers' fees so inconsiderable that " 'tis worth no man's acceptance," and that the Massachusetts assembly had reduced them "so low that they are not sufficient for the true subsistence of an honest man."[2] As a rule both forms of payment taken together were insufficient to attract the best men, unless some other employment were available. Yet the office was much sought after and grants in reversion were not unknown. It was generally held during the king's pleasure, but sometimes for life, and was a post of dignity and influence in the colonies, particularly as the incumbent was often in the confidence of the governor. The fees that the naval officer could demand were determined first by the governor, then by the assembly, and after 1763 by the home government, which was endeavoring to methodize the whole system by drawing control more and more into its own hands.[3]

There were in the colonies collectors or receivers of the provincial revenues levied by the colonial assemblies to meet the costs of their own adminstration.[4] There were also collectors or receivers general of the king's casual revenues, sometimes called the "casual receivers," who had no principals in England, being appointed directly by the crown, and who were in no way connected with the commissioners of the customs at home. Their relations with the colonial governors, the king's representative in the colonies, as well as with the customs officials, were always a matter of some doubt and even of controversy.[5] Grenville in Barbados insisted that the casual receivers would "break through their instructions if they passed by the governor and

---

1. *Ibid.*, 1706–1708, §483.
2. *New York Colonial Documents*, IV, 602–603; *Calendar State Papers, Colonial*, 1700, §100.
3. Pennsylvania *Statutes*, II, 347; *North Carolina Colonial Records*, XXV, 196–198, 225; 5 George III, c. 45, §xlvii; 10 George III, c. 37, §ii; 19 George III, c. 22, §v; British Museum, Kings Manuscripts, p. 206; C. O. 225:5.
4. Giesecke, *American Commercial Legislation before 1789, passim.*
5. The controversy in New York in the first years of the eighteenth century became something of a scandal. The receiver general there was to collect and receive all rents, quit-rents, duties, customs, excise, escheats, fines and forfeitures, and impositions arising and becoming due to the king or his government within the province. His duties can be found stated in the commissions to Plowman, 1687–1689, who was turned out for being a Papist (*Calendar Treasury Books*, VIII, 1663–1664; IX, 718, 1620), Chid-

went immediately to the Treasury or any other board," but that is what generally happened.[1] The casual revenues came from licenses, escheats, waifs, strays, wild cattle, horses, and hogs, treasure trove, goods of suicides and felons, wrecks, shares in prize goods, fines in vice-admiralty courts,[2] the king's thirds from ships seized for illegal trading, whales, deodands,[3] and certain fines in the county courts which accrued to the king by virtue of his prerogative. All these went also to Baltimore and the Penns in their respective proprietorships, and were claimed by Lord Fairfax from his Northern Neck grant. Except perhaps in Maryland, they nowhere amounted to much and in some of the colonies were a negligible quantity. Governor Payne of the Leeward Islands said in 1774 that the casual revenue from seizures there was "too inconsiderable to deserve mention of it. It is indeed next to nothing."[4] Baltimore derived no little income from his casual revenues, though the assembly contested some of his claims, and Fairfax's agent, Robert Carter, in 1724 denied vehemently the king's right to these revenues in the Fairfax lands, specifying particularly deodands, goods of felons and suicides, and fines in the

ley Brook (*ibid.*, IX, 254, 439, 443, 543, 556, 561, 562, 576, 578, 642, 700, 852), Weaver, and Byerley, which are entered in the King's Warrant Books and on the Patent Rolls. The salary was £200 a year and the revenues were to be received in money or in goods *ad valorem*. These men were constantly quarreling both with the governor and with the assembly. Byerley was collector as well as receiver general and was finally suspended by Cornbury for alleged breach of the acts of trade, Fauconnier, naval officer and a Cornbury follower, being given his place. *New York Colonial Documents*, IV, *passim;* Osgood, *American Colonies in the Eighteenth Century*, II, 77–84.

1. A receiver of the king's casual revenues in Barbados is mentioned in *Calendar Treasury Books*, IX, 341.

2. These fines must have amounted at times to very considerable sums, for the judges in vice-admiralty imposed frequent penalties upon those who offended against the king's peace. The largest amount that I have met with is £1250, the fine imposed by Judge Morris upon Edward Burrows in 1739 for his "great crime." All that I know of the offense is that Burrows "defrauded the Moors" (Records of Admiralty, New York, I, 109–116; *New York Colonial Documents*, VI, 157–158).

3. A deodand was anything in motion, animate or inanimate, that was the cause of a death, such as a mill, a rolling log, a falling tree, a ferry boat that tipped over, an animal, or any weapon (above Vol. II, 208, note 2). A ship in fresh water (not in the main sea or in an arm of it) might become a deodand, if, careened, it unexpectedly turned over and killed a shipwright working upon it (*Executive Journals, Virginia*, II, 130–131; Mortimer's *Dictionary*, under "Ship," column 4. For the deodands in Virginia and Maryland, Karraker, *American Historical Review*, XXXVII, 712–717). A famous wreck was that off Jamaica in 1690, for which see *Calendar Treasury Books*, IX, 785, 790, 834, 1534, 1656, 1665, 1717, 1721. The king's share was one-tenth, pp. 844, 858.

4. Governor Payne, "Answers to Queries," C. O. 152:54.

county courts. "These things," he writes, "are not very considerable at present, but it may happen that in time they will be worth struggling for."[1] The king eventually won out in the matter of fines in the county courts, which according to the lawyers were "franchises of the crown," but he was obliged to recognize that most of the other revenues were the legitimate perquisites of the proprietor of the soil.

Much more important than the casual revenues was a group of royal accessions to income that were regular, not casual, such as the quit-rents and the duty of one shilling in Maryland, which were collected by the receiver general and placed at the king's disposal. They were for his Majesty's private use and were not public revenue. The quit-rents were paid out by royal warrant directed to the receiver general, and previous to delivery were entered at the office of the auditor general. They might be used in any colony and for any purpose, and constituted a fund from which the king, through the Treasury, might draw at his pleasure.[2] The £8000 from Jamaica, after 1728, was collected by its own receiver general, who accounted for it only to the governor and the assembly and not to the king or

---

1. Grenville Papers, January 5, 1749, Huntington Library; Brock Papers, *ibid.*, Carter to Cage, November 18, 1724. For Baltimore's revenues and the attitude of the assembly toward them see *Maryland Archives*, XIII, 311–314, and *Calendar Treasury Books*, IX, 1402, 1081–1085, 1214, 1326, 1344, 1442, 1458, 1836; XIV, 123, 162–163, 182–184, 187. The 2*s.* per hogshead of tobacco exported from Virginia was appropriated for the charges of the colonial government. *William and Mary Quarterly*, second series, V, 250–251; *Calendar State Papers, Colonial*, 1728–1729, §46, iii.

2. Two excellent examples of this use may be noted.

(1.) Thomas Lee, president of the council and acting governor of Virginia, during the absence of Gooch in England and before the arrival of Dinwiddie, suffered by fire in 1729 the loss of his house "Mt. Pleasant," his out-houses, and all his household goods and movables. The house was burned by a gang of transported felons in revenge for Lee's action against them as justice of the peace. Inasmuch as Lee's loss was incurred in doing his duty as a servant of the crown, Governor Gooch presented the case to the Board of Trade, suggesting a contribution from the exchequer. The board viewed the request favorably and made a recommendation to the Treasury. The Treasury concurred and issued a warrant in the king's name for the payment to Lee of £300 "as his Majesty's bounty" from the quit-rents of Virginia. The warrant was directed to the king's receiver general in that colony. *Board of Trade Journal*, 1729–1734, p. 41; *Calendar Treasury Papers*, 1729–1730, §348, p. 85, §390.

(2.) On the death of Gov. Johnston of North Carolina the British Treasury owed him £12,000 arrears of salary. As the quit-rents from North Carolina were not sufficient to meet this debt the Treasury sent a warrant to the receiver general of South Carolina to pay the entire amount from the quit-rents of that province. All but £2018 was paid before the Revolution. The remainder was not received by the heirs until 1798 and then came out of the British exchequer. Andrews, *Journal of a Lady of Quality*, pp. 294–295, 310–312.

to anyone appointed by him,[1] while the four and a half per cent from Barbados and the Leeward Islands was collected by officials, generally local, named from England, and after 1684, when the system of farming was given up, holding office under the sub-commissioners of that revenue at the custom house in London, who received there the payments sent over from the West Indies. These payments might be in cash, but more commonly they were in kind—sugar, ginger, or cotton according to the commodity exported—which when received were stored in the king's warehouse on the Thames and sold by auction in the usual way.

All the royal revenues, except the permanent revenue from Jamaica, were reviewed by the surveyor and auditor general of the plantation revenues in England, who was appointed in 1680 for the purpose of keeping a closer watch upon what was due the king from the plantations and of bringing all these monies into a more certain method of account, that misappropriation and mismanagement might be checked and prevented. The first incumbent was William Blathwayt, who served in that capacity for thirty-seven years, a hardworking and reliable official. Under him and his successors, Walpole and Cholmondeley, the extent of whose services cannot easily be ascertained because of the disappearance of most of their papers, were deputy auditors in the royal colonies, who inspected the accounts of the receiver general and every six months sent (or were supposed to have sent) a particular account of all revenues accruing to his Majesty in America.[2] This system of financial accounting was a part of the effort made by the Lords of Trade to strengthen the king's control over the plantations and to increase his revenue. While waiting for the new experiment to justify itself, the king and the Treasury sent letters to the governors of Virginia, Barbados, the Leeward Islands, and Jamaica, the only royal colonies in existence at

1. Whitson (Mrs. A. J. Butterfield), *The Constitutional Development of Jamaica,* p. 153.

2. It is curious that Blathwayt's deputy auditor in Massachusetts, the first in that colony, should have been Isaac Addington, a man who could have had but little sympathy with the extension of English administrative methods into the province. I have found nothing to show that he ever actually served in that capacity. Both the receiver general and the deputy auditor could demand of the collector all necessary information regarding the shares which were due the king from the sale of forfeited vessels and confiscated cargoes. In this way they served as a check upon the customs officials, in all that concerned the prosecution of a ship or the suing of a bond, and just so far were able to prevent concealment, collusion, and embezzlement.

the time, informing them of Blathwayt's appointment and ordering them to look after the auditing business until the deputy auditors should be appointed. Afterward they were to give every assistance possible to those entrusted with the care of the service, taking especial pains not to remit or compound any fines or forfeitures whatever, until they had received orders from England to do so, and not to suffer any law to be passed that would lessen or impair the royal revenues. This method of audit, though seriously relaxed and reduced in importance as time went on, remained a part of England's financial management of the colonies to the end of the colonial period.[1]

In addition to these men there were the customs officials, to whom reference has frequently been made in this chapter and previous chapters. Their business was simply and solely to collect the plantation duty, a parliamentary not a royal revenue and one designed primarily to regulate trade and not to increase the revenue.[2] They were appointed from England by the commissioners of the customs in London, under warrants issued by the Treasury and, as we have already seen, were in all respects identical with the customs officials at home. Until 1767 all were part of a common establishment; after that date they constituted an American establishment entirely separate from that of Great Britain.

The act of 1673, imposing the plantation duty, went into operation on September 1 of that year, but it was not until November 20 that by royal warrant the governors of Maryland, Barbados, St. Christopher, Nevis, Jamaica, Bermuda, Carolina, Montserrat, Antigua, and Virginia were instructed to swear into their places such collectors and surveyors as might be appointed and to take securities from them.[3] Not however till the 27th was a list of such appointees made out.[4] But as these men could not enter on their duties until their commissions were drawn up, it is quite certain that most if not all of those in the original list did not go to America at once, and it is

---

1. Blathwayt's commission is printed in *Massachusetts Colonial Records*, V, 521–526. The letters to the governors are calendared in *Calendar Treasury Books*, VI, 597–600; VII, 121, 125, 263. For accounts of the office, Andrews, *Guide*, II, 142–148, and Bond, *Quit-Rent System*, ch. XIV. For Blathwayt himself, Jacobsen, *William Blathwayt*, a thoroughgoing study of the man and his times.

2. See above, pp. 121–122, 149, note 1.

3. *Calendar Treasury Books*, IV, 424, also 613. That portion of the act which related to the Greenland trade was not to go into effect until April 20, 1624, *ibid.*, p. 376.

4. *Calendar Treasury Books*, XI, 312–313, 392.

likely that some of them never went to America at all. Those appointed for Virginia, Bermuda, and Maryland were apparently the first to get under way, followed by new appointees for the West Indies and one after another by those for the remaining colonies. Collections may have been made in Maryland, Virginia, Bermuda, and the West Indies in 1675 and 1676.[1] In the other colonies the business started more slowly—in South Carolina in 1676, in North Carolina in 1677, in New England as a whole under Randolph in 1678, in New York before 1682, in Pennsylvania in 1682, in the Bahamas before 1704, in Rhode Island in 1709, in Connecticut between 1707 and 1715, and in Nova Scotia in 1715.

Thus gradually along the mainland and the West Indies there came into being a series of officials, located eventually at forty-nine different ports and rivers and including more than ninety surveyors general, surveyors, riding surveyors, collectors, comptrollers, searchers, preventive officers, landwaiters, and tidewaiters. In addition there were clerks and accountants in some of the offices and watermen and boatmen with boats and canoes at the waterside.[2] The number grew, not according to any prearranged plan but as new officials were needed and pressure was brought to bear upon the Custom House and the Treasury to create new districts and to enlist new men for the purpose of preventing smuggling and the running of goods.[3] Among the customs officials themselves there was an extensive overlapping of duties and combination of offices, as when one man would be collector, surveyor, and searcher, naval officer and collector, surveyor and searcher, collector and comptroller, and comptroller and surveyor, thus often holding two and occasionally three offices at the same time.[4] This merely meant that in the smaller ports

1. Dr. Shaw tells us that the receipts in England from the plantation duty, as entered in the accounts of the customs cashiers, begin in 1676 (*Calendar Treasury Books,* VIII, xiii, note). Collections in the colonies, therefore, must have been made in that year or the year before.

2. In 1759 Thomas Chapman, appointed collector at Guadeloupe (recently taken), asked for (1) a suitable house; (2) two clerks, at least, with fixed salaries; (3) a custom house boat as usual; (4) strong iron chest for keeping the cash; (5) books, papers, and instructions. These requests may represent conditions prevailing in other ports also of intermediate size. Treasury 1: bundle 392, fo. 62.

3. The establishment of a new custom house at Falmouth (Portland) is a case in point. It took a long time for the Treasury to give its consent.

4. The situation in Connecticut is of considerable interest. As early as March 9, 1685, William Dyer, surveyor general, appointed, as one of his deputies, Daniel Wetherell at New London. Wetherell was an assistant in the colony, a pillar of the church, and

one man did all the work. There was always a certain amount of friction between the collectors and the naval officers, between the surveyors general and the collectors, and between the collectors and the governors, and charges of bribery, connivance, and negligence, engaging in trade (which the customs officials were strictly forbidden to do),[1] and handing in imperfect and erroneous accounts were not uncommon.[2] However well contrived in theory may have been the system of checks and balances and the supervision of one official by another—such as, the surveyor general of the collector, the comptroller of the collector, and the collector of the naval officer—the plan never worked well in practice. Those employed in the service were of all kinds and grades of intelligence. Some got their jobs because their fathers had served in similar capacities in England, others were transferred to the colonies from the establishment in England or Ireland, still others were recommended by friends or relatives in England or America or by agents in England, while a large number

"very fierce" for the government, of whom Gershom Bulkeley gives a vivacious account in his *Will and Doom* (Connecticut Historical Society, *Collections*, III, 262–263). Jahleel Brenton, who in 1690 succeeded Randolph as the last collector, surveyor, and searcher of all New England (*Calendar Treasury Books*, IX, 486, 687, 784, 828, 872, 1392), reappointed Wetherell, as one of his deputies for Connecticut ports, and Wetherell continued in that capacity until John Jekyll, displacing Brenton, was sent over as collector at Boston, when, as Jekyll had no authority to appoint deputies, all Brenton's deputies were dismissed. Quary, commissioned surveyor general in 1703, was given charge of the New England district and in 1707 made his well-known trip to New England, bearing a letter to the governor of Connecticut and certified copies of his commission and instructions. Finding Wetherell at New London he turned him out as "a great rogue" and issued a commission to Captain John Shackmaple, October 1, 1707, as royal collector there, with power to appoint deputies. The governor and council of Connecticut did not like Quary's interference and refused to recognize Shackmaple, because he had only a commission from the surveyor general and not one from England. Though the Treasury warrant for a royal patent was issued in 1715, Shackmaple's commission from England did not finally pass the seals until May 3, 1718. From that date forward Connecticut had a royal collector at New London. The documents in the case are in the Connecticut Archives and elsewhere.

1. This rule is frequently stated, as, for example, *Board of Trade Journal*, 1715–1718, p. 246.

2. Some instances of this will be noted later on, particularly that of Dinwiddie, surveyor general of the southern district, 1738–1751, who was sent to Barbados in 1738 to investigate conditions there, and that of Paterson, surveyor general of the Barbados district, who came into conflict with the collector and the receiver general in the island. A case is mentioned in *Calendar Treasury Papers*, 1729–1730, pp. 342–344, where the collector at one port ("the Hole," Holetown) charged the collector and comptroller at Bridgetown (both in Barbados) with "abuses, mismanagement and violations of the acts of trade."

were office seekers or hangers-on.[1] Sometimes the Treasury in its warrants showed an interest in the qualifications of those appointed, but more often it accepted without further inquiry the testimony of the customs board and issued warrants as matters of routine.

At the head of the service in America was the surveyor general, the first of whom was William Dyer, who in 1683 was sent over on a roving commission for the whole area, which was to begin with Barbados, to extend thence to Jamaica and Bermuda, and afterward to include the continent, particularly the Carolinas and New York. Dyer was to examine the books of the collectors, to see that the collectors were living up to their obligations, and, as far as possible, "to endeavour to reduce all his Majesty's officers in the colonys to one uniform method and practice in the execution of their respective dutyes." He was also to inquire into the capacity and fitness of the officials and to suspend, with the consent of the governor, such as he found defrauding the king. He was especially enjoined to look into the situation in the Carolinas, where the king's officers had "been imprisoned, molested and hindered" (the "Culpeper Rebellion"), and in New York "very narrowly," where Peter Smith, "our collector there," was reputed to have managed his accounts so as to cheat the

1. In "Letters from Jamaica," New York Public Library, is a letter regarding a vacancy among the surveyors in Jamaica. The writer says that a place there is "more easily obtained than one [in England] though it were but the eighth part of the value." He adds, "if you think proper to write a letter to my Lord Bollinbroke to remind him of his promise I will inform you of the nature of the thing, or it might be done more effectually this way if you desire the favour of Dr. Chamberlain to carry me to my Lady Massam and offer her a piece of good plate of 100 or 150 guineas it would answer the end. This is a thing not very difficult to obtain and a place of that nature that a person might make a handsome fortune in 7 or 8 years," p. 5.

Patrick Mein and George Muschamp were both related to customs officials in England, the latter being the eldest son of William Muschamp, for many years commissioner of the revenue in Ireland. For Mein, below, p. 199, note 3. We are told that a collector of customs at one time in New Hampshire was "a younger son of the Lord Bishop of London, named Reynolds, about 21 years of age and has been of late an officer in the Guards" (Essex Institute, *Historical Collections*, XLII, 219). Thomas Miller, the collector involved in the so-called "Culpeper Rebellion" in North Carolina, was an unsavory character as his later career shows. After his escape from the Albemarle, he was made collector at Poole, got into arrears to his Majesty, was arrested, and died in prison (Treasury 4:5, p. 297; above, Vol. III, 255, note 2; 256, note 1). Note also Parke's comments on the surveyor general in Barbados and the Leeward Islands, "My Lord Weymouth first coyn'd this office for his couzen Thym [Thyme?]" (*Calendar State Papers, Colonial*, 1706–1708, p. 694). President Jennings in Virginia promised William Byrd's brother-in-law, John Custis, the place of naval officer "if Major Allen should die" (Byrd's letter, February 7, 1711. Virginia Historical Society, File VII). The case of Thomson the poet, who held the office as a sinecure, will be noted later.

king of his revenues. As soon as Dyer had finished his survey, he was to take up his residence as collector of New Jersey and Pennsylvania.[1]

Either Dyer never undertook the mission entrusted to him at all, or else he was unsuccessful in his attempt to do so, for in January, 1685, he was superseded in the office by one William Carter, who was to cover Maryland and Virginia and such other colonies as the customs commissioners should see fit to include within his inspection area.[2] It is highly probable that Carter never went out, for in the following November Patrick Mein was selected to survey the whole area outside of New England, New York, and New Jersey, covering at first Virginia and Maryland and later, in 1689, the West Indies. He was in Barbados as surveyor general of customs, 1691 to 1703 at least. He held office for more than a decade, much longer than was originally intended, since in his case, as in the cases of Dyer and Carter, the mission was looked upon as only temporary.[3] Edward Randolph had been appointed surveyor, collector, and searcher for New England in 1678, but he did not receive a regular commission

1. Connecticut Archives, Trade and Maritime Affairs, I, doc. 12, "A True Copy compared with the Orriginall by me, John Allyn secretary, March 31, 1686." Captain William Dyer had been appointed in 1674 as the Duke of York's collector in New York and remained in that office until 1681, when he was charged with "establishing and imposing unlawful customs on goods, compelling people to pay them and using soldiers to maintain him therein" (*New York Colonial Documents*, III, 287. The soldiers were the men of the independent company, ordered over in 1674 to take over the town from the Dutch). He was sent home for trial, but as no one appeared against him he was released, and evidently received the new commission as a reward (*ibid.*, p. 321). He was in England at the time these instructions were issued, as they are dated only three months after he was set free of his bond, September 30, 1682, *Calendar State Papers, Colonial*, 1681–1685, §719. See above, Vol. III, 101, note 1; 110, note 2.

Dyer's commission as collector for East New Jersey was drafted January 4, 1682, but the oath required was not taken until April 1, 1685 (*Journal of Governor and Council*, p. 118; *Journal of the Courts of Common Right and Chancery*, pp. 138–139). Dyer was the son of the Quaker Mary Dyer, who was executed at Boston in 1660. The name is usually spelt Dyre in the records.

2. *Calendar Treasury Books*, VII, 1496.

3. Patrick Mein (the name may have been pronounced "Myne," *Maryland Archives*, VIII, 209, or "Meyne," *Calendar Treasury Books*, IX, 176) was the son of a loyalist who had served Charles I and Charles II (*Calendar Treasury Books*, VIII, 352–353) and as a reward had received a customs post in Ireland, as had his son also before the father went to America. This son, Charles, examiner of outport books in the custom house, London, in 1693 sent in a petition to the Privy Council in his father's behalf (*ibid.*, VIII, 1556; *Acts Privy Council, Colonial*, II, §528). Mein's commission as surveyor general was issued November 8, 1685, and is printed in *Maryland Archives*, V, 521. In 1694 the customs commissioners reported on his employment as follows (Additional Manuscripts, 22617, fo. 141): "And upon this occasion we humbly observe to

as surveyor general until 1691,[1] after Mein had been transferred to the West Indies and had taken up his post at Bridgetown in Barbados. Randolph never had anything to do with Jamaica, Barbados, or the Leeward Islands. After his death in 1703, he was succeeded by Robert Quary, who had served under the proprietors in South Carolina, and Quary in turn, 1714, by William Keith. So many reports came to the commissioners of the customs in England of frauds committed and illegal trade carried on, that they recommended, June 25, 1709, the division of the territory into two districts, the southern and the northern, one comprising Carolina, Virginia, Maryland, and Pennsylvania, together with Jamaica and the Bahamas, to be placed under Quary; the other, East and West New Jersey, New York, Connecticut, Rhode Island, Massachusetts Bay, New Hampshire, and Newfoundland to be placed under one Robert Armstrong, formerly Governor Bellomont's secretary and naval officer. But the Treasury

your Lordships that Mr. Mein's office of surveyor general of the Plantations is temporary and was intended so to be, and that his allowance of 20 sh. per day [the same as that allowed to Dyer and Carter] should cease upon the printing of his survey which has long since been done; but that the late calamity by the earthquake at Jamaica obstructed for some time and since that we thought it highly necessary for his Majesty's service to order the said Mr. Mein to abide and superintend the officers of customs in Barbados during the absence of both the commissioners of 4½ pr ct. who were obliged to come over to England for the recovery of their health, intending as soon as Mr. Canfield who is returning back shall be arrived at Barbadoes that the said Mr. Mein should hasten away to Jamaica and from thence return to England." Mein remained in Barbados and became a councillor there; he did not return to England until 1709. See also, *Calendar Treasury Books*, IX, 256, 266, 1370; XV, 278; XVIII, 492.

1. *Calendar State Papers, Colonial*, 1689–1692, §1793. Randolph was a persistent applicant for office, but a number of his applications were unsuccessful. He was a surveyor, collector, and searcher, 1678; surveyor of the woods, 1685; surveyor general, 1691; surveyor general for prizes, 1697; deputy auditor, 1680. He was commissioned deputy searcher for Maine, New Hampshire, and the Isles of Shoals, January 25, 1682 (*New Hampshire Historical Collections*, VIII, 157–161) and deputed the office the same day to Walter Barefoot, as collector, and Thomas Thurton as deputy searcher (*Calendar State Papers, Colonial*, 1681–1685, §379, full text in C. O. 1:45, no. 9). Barefoot set up a notice in Great Island, ordering vessels to make entry with him as acting collector under Randolph. The president and council of New Hampshire charged him with having done so without their permission, "in a high and presumptuous manner" and in "a high contempt to his Majesty's authority set up in this place," and they sentenced him to pay £10. Thurton likewise got into trouble "for abusive and contemptuous language against the council," and was sentenced to be confined in Hampton jail for a month and to pay £20 fine. Should he not pay this he was to be "sold," as for debt, by the treasurer of the colony (C. O. 1:54, no. 102; *Calendar State Papers, Colonial*, 1681–1685, pp. 43–44, imperfect, §430, and Index under "Barefoot" and "Thurton"). There is much about Barefoot in Libby, *Maine Province and Court Records*, I, II, indexes.

rejected Armstrong and selected Maurice Birchfield, 1709–1715, in his place.[1]

A third surveyor general, Edward Perrie (1709–1717), was created for Barbados, the Leeward Islands, and Bermuda,[2] and he was succeeded by Charles Dunbar (1717–1743), who on complaint of Robert Dinwiddie, surveyor general of the southern district—sent in 1738 to investigate conditions in Barbados—was dismissed, with the whole custom house staff, five years later, for being concerned in frauds and irregularities discovered in the collection of the four and a half per cent and plantation duties.[3] A later incumbent of the position, W. Paterson, got into a dispute with the deputy auditor and the receiver general over their respective jurisdictions, when he ordered the collector to receive the casual revenues, which properly lay within the province of the receiver general.[4] In this case the surveyor general was clearly in the wrong, for according to the instructions of the receiver the collector was to do no more than keep account of the fines and forfeitures and to make a record of the persons to whom they were paid. He had no authority to receive the money himself. Paterson is an interesting character. Governor Grenville called him "an ungrateful scoundrel, improper in all respects as an inferior officer of the crown, absolutely denying the authority of the government, though he is directed by his instructions to apply to the governor's authority in all cases of dispute and difficulties relating to the king's revenue." Again Grenville writes, "[Paterson] is a poor Scotchman, who holds his office of surveyor general in trust for Thomson the poet, whom Lyttelton procureth the place for originally, but Thomson being fat and gross of constitution could not or would

1. This seems to be the first instance in which the Treasury turned down a recommendation by the commissioners of the customs, and the latter, in dutiful language, protested against being so treated. They asked in compensation that Armstrong be made collector and surveyor at Piscataqua. On Birchfield, see Hunter's opinion in *New Jersey Archives*, 1st ser., IV, 49–50. Evidently the Treasury made a poor choice.

2. An elaborate abstract of Perrie's instructions may be found among documents relating to illicit trade with St. Thomas and Curaçao, C. O. 388:17, N, 173; Treasury 38:256. Governor Parke considered the office useless (*Calendar State Papers, Colonial, 1706–1708*, p. 694). Perrie was the son of John Perrie, Blathwayt's deputy in the Leeward Islands (1691, *Calendar Treasury Books*, XI, 309), and the father of Jonathan Perrie associated with the Duke of Chandos in the latter's effort to obtain possession of the Equivalent Lands of New York, Vol. II, 231, note.

3. *Calendar Treasury Books and Papers*, 1741–1745, pp. 269–272, 527–529.

4. Instructions to the receiver general, September 22, 1721, are among the papers relating to the customs dispute in Barbados, Treasury 1:329 (at the end).

not venture into this part of the world and therefore recommends this Paterson to fill it in his room. Whereupon Mr. Lyttelton prevails with Mr. Pelham to have Paterson's name inserted in the commission and Thomson allows him a small provision for executing the office."[1]

Following Birchfield in the northern department came Caleb Heathcote (1715-1721),[2] Thomas Lechmere (1721-1727), James Stevens (1728-1732), John Peagrum (1732-1742), Thomas Lechmere again (1742-1760), and lastly John Temple (1760-1770). Following Keith in the southern department were Richard Fitzwilliam (1725-1730),[3] George Phenney (1730-1737), Ernault Hawkins (July 5-Dec. 24, 1737), Robert Dinwiddie (March 24, 1738-1749, promoted from the collectorship of Bermuda), and Peter Randolph. It is doubtful if Hawkins ever entered on his appointment. Sometime about the middle of the century four districts were created, three for the mainland including Jamaica and the Bahamas, and one for Barbados, the Leeward Islands, and Bermuda, but their respective heads are of no particular importance in the history of the customs service. The best of these men, though often relatively inconspicuous, were indispensable to a proper maintenance of the system, for they had oversight of their respective districts, appointed collectors in the place of those who died or resigned (as many did because of the poor pay), conferred with and proffered advice to the governors, sat as councillors extraordinary, *ex officiis* after 1733,[4] in the councils of

1. Grenville Correspondence, Huntington Library, letter of April 20, 1748.

2. Fox, *Caleb Heathcote,* ch. VIII. One Devereaux Bacon was appointed for the post, but did not go out.

3. Richard Fitzwilliam, governor of the Bahamas, 1733-1740, comes into colonial history as one of the commissioners for running the dividing line between Virginia and North Carolina. In Byrd's "Secret History" of the Dividing Line (Boyd, ed. *William Byrd's Histories*) he bears the fictitious name "Meanwell." A part of the "Secret History" (February 27—March 11, 1727), an original not a copy, is to be found among the Brock Papers in the Huntington Library.

4. On July 26, 1725, Fitzwilliam memorialized the lords justices to this effect, "That Col. Quary, former surveyor general for South America [the southern district] (the better to enable him to recover some debts due the Crown and to do the Duty of the said office) was added a thirteenth to the Council in the several governments in his District. That your memorialist has at present divers law suits to carry on in behalf of the crown, and that in regard it would be of particular service to him in the prosecution of the said suits and in the execution of his said employment, he prays that your excellencies will be pleased to add him in the like manner to the council in Virginia, South Carolina, and Jamaica, they being in his district." C. O. 323:8, L, 67.

The memorial was referred to the Board of Trade, which in a representation of

the colonies within their districts and, because not residing in any one place, were more likely than the governors to see that all the acts were obeyed. They could serve as informers in the vice-admiralty courts, and often did so. They were transported from place to place either in the king's ships without charge or, if that were not possible, in hired sloops, being given an extra allowance for the purpose of conveying themselves, their servants, and their baggage. Randolph once put in a bill for £99 for such extra expenses and Dinwiddie did the same for a larger sum to cover the costs of his trip to the West Indies, including clerks, lawyers' fees, a sloop for cruising among the islands, and his passage back and forth from America. They were paid twenty shillings a day out of the public exchequer, with an additional amount for boats, boatmen, and contingencies. They were at the head of the service in the colonies and to them appeals were taken when disputes arose among the local officials. Once, when a quarrel arose between the naval officer and the collector and comptroller in Barbados, that island of many disagreements, and the question was raised regarding the one to whom the matter should be referred, Blenman, the local attorney general, was called upon for an opinion. In his report he said that the dispute should be referred to the surveyor general, "the supreme officer of the customs," who was possessed of a "plenitude of power over the inferior officers." In answering the governor's special inquiry as to his own rights in the case he said that he dared not "venture to say what power in particular your excellency may have over the officers of the customs in this government," to which the governor replied, "My power over officers of the customs in this government has never been particularly ascertained."[1] In fact, the governor had no authority to appoint, remove, or discipline customs officials of any kind, a situation of which

July 28 (C. O. 324:11, pp. 29–31) brought the matter to the attention of the Privy Council, but no action was taken. The surveyors general continued to ask for the privilege as a right of office, until in 1733, by order in council of that year, their request was made the subject of a general instruction to the governors (*Acts Privy Council, Colonial*, III, §277). By this order they were to be members extraordinary of the councils, no longer in ordinary as had been the case hitherto (*Board of Trade Journal, 1722–1728*, p. 187; *1728–1734*, pp. 352, 354, 357, 358, 366, 368). This meant that they could not sit as a member of the council acting as an upper house of assembly or exercise any legislative or judicial functions. This question was decided in 1742 (*ibid., 1742–1749*, pp. 2, 8–9, 16, 36).

1. Grenville Correspondence, Blenman's report and the governor's letter of April 28, 1750 (Huntington Library).

Governor Crowe complained as early as 1708, but without result.[1] The governor could not legally name either a clerk or a tidesman.[2]

The collector was the central figure and operating agent in the colonies for gathering in the plantation duty and no custom house could exist without him. He was the earliest of the officials to be appointed and the one upon whom fell the weightiest obligations. All others, of either superior or equal rank, were supervisory or preventive in the duties they performed. He was not allowed, except in emergency, to be served by deputy or to be absent from his post without leave, though there are exceptions to both requirements. He was not obliged to serve on juries, to bear arms in the local militia, or to be assessed for local taxes, although each of these exemptions was disputed in a number of cases and led to complaints from the collectors to the home government, by whom they were always sustained.[3] Besides receiving the plantation duties the collector was to see that all goods were properly entered in his presence and that of the naval officer and to take particular pains that no cargoes be landed at his port or cleared therefrom without his warrant, thus being made co-responsible with the naval officer for the entering and clearing of ships.[4] One of his most important duties, which he shared in common with the surveyor general, naval officer, surveyor, and searcher,

1. *Calendar State Papers, Colonial*, 1708–1709, §180.

2. Bellomont did appoint tidewaiters in New York, but his doing so was considered irregular. Lieutenant Governor Day also appointed a collector in Bermuda, but he was not upheld in England (*ibid.*, 1700, §§652, 737). At the request of the commissioners of the customs, the governors sometimes gave instructions to the collectors (*Maryland Archives*, XX, 125) and were expected to warn them "to be diligent and careful on pain of dismissal."

3. It was always a serious matter to resist or assault a collector. The captain of the *Bilboa* in 1744 threatened to shoot the collector of the port of Boston and employed other means to intimidate him, such as luring him aboard and then declaring that he would blow up the boat or set it on fire. As a consequence the judge of the vice-admiralty court mulcted him heavily. Similarly, it was a serious matter to refuse to furnish a manifest or to answer questions when asked, as Timothy Folger of Nantucket once learned to his sorrow (Records of Admiralty, Massachusetts, V, August 3, 1744; February 12, 1768).

4. For instructions issued to the collectors in 1696 and 1697 see *Maryland Archives*, XX, 351–355; XXIII, 46–48, 254–258. The instructions to George Plater are in *Calendar Treasury Books*, IX, 1443. For the importance of the collector as a check upon the naval officer, *Calendar State Papers, Colonial*, 1697–1698, §894, i (3). In Virginia and Maryland, before the establishment of the tobacco inspection houses, the running of goods in out-of-the-way places was not uncommon. Edmund Jennings, president of the council and acting governor, in 1705 sent in a memorial to the commissioners of the customs, urging the settlement of ports of entry, because under the existing system the collectors were unable to account for all the ladings without riding long distances

and other "seizing officers," was to act as informer before the vice-admiralty court and to become the libelant in the trials of breaches of the acts of trade. He was required to keep in his office books of rates and copies of all the laws and to know the rules thoroughly and in detail.[1] There is no doubt that at times he was puzzled just how to interpret the acts and at other times was none too zealous in his attempt to do so. When special instructions were sent out in 1734 some of the collectors claimed that the oaths were so phrased that no one could swear "with a safe concurrence" and, they added, "several of the articles are so worded as to be unworkable."[2] The trouble that arose in Barbados between the collector and the casual receiver, to which reference has already been made, was largely due to the ambiguity of their respective instructions. The collector received his orders from the customs board and the casual receiver his from the Treasury under the king's sign manual, and it is evident that neither of the principals in England knew exactly what the other was doing. Efficient team work was not characteristic of the administrative departments in England.

about the country. He adds that the trade from plantations to plantations was carried on clandestinely because "they load without the presence of any officer and enter at large without the examination of any officer. This lessens greatly the amount of the 2 sh. a hogshead and the plantations duties. The loading often takes from one to five months which raised duties" (C. O. 5:1361, p. 74; by title only, *Calendar State Papers, Colonial,* 1704–1705, §989, iii).

1. In 1698 in Maryland the collector had in his office, "An Account of the Acts of Parliament relating to Trade, paper books, paper and other necessaries sent in [by the commissioners of the customs in England], together with printed navigation bonds for the naval officers," etc. Full lists are given in *Maryland Archives,* XXIII, 362–364. It is not unlikely that later the collectors were given also copies of one or more of the following: Edgar, *Vectigalium Systema* (1714); Crouch, *A Complete View of the British Customs* (1725) and *A Complete Guide to the Officers, etc.* (1732) (for Crouch, see *Calendar Treasury Books and Papers,* 1731–1734, pp. 447, 507); Carkesse, *The Act of Tonnage and Poundage and Rates of Merchandize, Rules of the Book of Rates, Statutes on the Customs since this Act, Tables of Port Dues and Fees, Bounties and Premiums, etc. Also Supplement of Acts to 1738* (2 vols. in one, thick folio, 1728–1738); Manley, *A Collection of the Laws of the Customs now in Force* (London 1742); Saxby, *British Customs* (London, 1757), and Baldwin, *A Survey of the British Customs* (1770). These were written by officials in the London Custom House and were designed especially for the British service. I find, however, no mention of them as in use in the colonial custom houses, but among the books carried by a Maryland sloop in 1754 appears the Crouch volume (Records of Admiralty, South Carolina, E–F, p. 73). This particular list of books is a very remarkable one to have been carried by a Maryland sloop dealing in staves and planks. The sloop was owned by Patrick Creagh of Annapolis, and among the books are Lilly's *Astrology,* Seneca's *Morals, History of Popery,* Watts' *Essays,* and eight volumes of the *Spectator.*

2. Treasury 1:318, no. 20.

Among the other troublesome tasks of the collectors were the looking after plantation bonds, the scrutiny of certificates and cocquets of bonds taken out in England, and the detection of forgeries and erasures.[1] If the collectors had reason to suspect that the certificate of a bond, purported to have been taken out in England, had been altered or was false they were to demand of the ship captain a temporary or composition bond until word could be got from England that the certificate was authentic, or if that were refused to seize the vessel. In case the captain furnished bond—either a plantation or a composition bond—in the colony, the collector was to make certain that the sureties were good and that the terms of the bond were carried out. He and the naval officer signed and sealed[2] these bonds and examined the securities, for there was constant complaint that colonial bondsmen were not to be depended on. Nicholson once wrote of "the poor and common securities as was formerly used" (1697),[3] and the Treasury was so acutely aware of this aspect of the bonding system that it introduced the practice of requiring all masters of ships going from England to the plantations "to give such security before they depart, well knowing that the bonds taken in the plantations are generally from persons of insufficiency." Part of the collectors' duties was to sue out the bonds in the local common law courts, due notice having first been given, and the obligation to do this, under peremptory orders from England, in the face of the poverty and distress of many of those haled into court, was a constant cause of friction and of irritation toward the whole system of naviga-

1. *Board of Trade Journal,* 1708–1715, pp. 325–326. The bonds themselves were printed half in Latin and half in English on parchment (Treasury 1:21, no. 56), the bond proper being in Latin, with the blanks filled in similiter, the conditions in English. Many of the later bonds are entirely in English (*Maryland Archives,* XX, 267–268, and elsewhere). On September 2, 1746, a vessel was seized at Boston, tried in the vice-admiralty court there, and condemned, because the captain had among his papers a certificate of registration that bore marks of alteration by means of erasures, with manifest evidence of fraud. The vessel and cargo—mackerel, shingles, and staves —were declared forfeited (Records of Admiralty, Massachusetts, V, under date, no pagination).

2. The naval officer and all the chief customs officials had seals, specimens of which can be found among the Custom House Papers, volumes I to VII, in the Historical Society of Pennsylvania, as follows: Vol. I, 30 (naval officer, Bahamas); *ibid.* (collector); I, 88 (New York); III, 295 (Custom House, Philadelphia); VI, 695 (naval officer, Georgia); 718 (Barbados Custom House); 756 (Dominica, comptroller); VII, 875 (collector, comptroller, deputy naval officer, Boston Custom House). All are of date 1760 to 1768.

3. *Maryland Archives,* XXIII, 86.

tion bonds.¹ All such bonds as were not discharged according to law, that is, by return of certificate from England showing that the captain had fulfilled his obligation,² remained in the hands of the naval officer and the collector and after a stated lapse of time were put in suit. The time was fixed at eighteen months.³ Failure to discharge the bond was taken as presumptive evidence of intention to defraud, though it is perfectly possible that in some cases the certificate might have been lost by the foundering or capture of the ship at sea, in which case the conditions of the bond could not be fulfilled. If no prosecution took place within three years or if judgment was not rendered within two years after the suit had been begun, then the bond was void and the securities were released. Frequently the sureties disappeared or defaulted; at other times the masters of ships would persuade honest men to go on their bonds and then fail to fulfil the conditions, thus leaving their bondsmen in the lurch to suffer a considerable money loss.⁴ The king's share of all monies thus recovered was ordered in 1698 (and the practice probably held throughout the colonial period) to be applied to the maintenance of the customs system in the colonies. It was never included among the casual revenues.

The collector himself had to furnish a bond amounting to £500, security for which might be found in England and the bond signed at the custom house in London. In all probability, however, the bond was taken out in the colonies as often as possible, because the fees required at the exchequer, where the securities had to be approved by the king's remembrancer, were often as much as a year's salary was worth.⁵ The collector was obliged to return his accounts every half year or at best every year, duly attested by the surveyor general and the comptroller (where there was one) and sworn to before the governor or deputy governor, who received a small sum for so doing.⁶ Grenville in Barbados said that his only perquisite was "a poor 10 pistole fee for passing the custom house accounts." The collector

1. *Ibid.*, V, 117–118; VIII, 430–432; XXII, 428–429, 458–459; XXIII, 57–59, 84–86, 91, 121–123; XXIV, 363, 394.

2. *Calendar State Papers, Colonial*, 1696–1697, p. 422.

3. 7–8 William III, c. 22, §xiii; Crouch, *A Complete View of the British Customs*, pp. 7, 89; *Calendar State Papers, Colonial*, 1696–1697, §1178, iv.

4. *Ibid.*, 1712–1714, 326; *Maryland Archives*, XIX, 524, 552; Treasury 1:20, nos. 54, 226–267; 26, no. 27; 50, nos. 8, 12, 27.

5. Treasury 1:6, p. 154.

6. *Calendar Treasury Books*, V, 728–730.

transmitted the monies received, which after 1729 included also the six-penny monthly payments from all mariners toward the maintenance of Greenwich Hospital,[1] in specie or bills or, when that was not possible, in goods amounting to the value of the money according to the current rate of such commodities in the plantations.[2] When this was finally done at the end of his tenure of service, the collector's bond was discharged. In many of the colonies the collector had charge of the Mediterranean passes issued by the Admiralty under treaty arrangements with the Barbary states, though in Massachusetts Bay this was usually looked after by the secretary, in Rhode Island by the governor through the agent in London, and in Connecticut, where very few were needed, through Massachusetts Bay. He was expected to bind himself not to engage in trade, either directly or indirectly;[3] not to serve as a merchant or factor; and not to have any financial interest in vessels trading with the colony. But this requirement was very imperfectly observed, for collectors were frequently charged with being owners, partners, and sharers of and in vessels that entered or cleared from the ports of their residence. The attempt to prevent the practice was largely a failure, though by an interpretation of an old statute of Henry VI (20 Henry VI, c. 5) it was contrary to law.

Collectors were constantly charged with a great variety of misdemeanors—illegal trading, connivance at illegal trade, compounding breaches of the law, accepting bribes and excessive fees and handing in imperfect and even erroneous accounts—but accusations, true and false, and offenses, great and small, were to be expected in connection with so large a body of men, often untrained, ignorant, and mediocre, underpaid and overworked, and engaged in carrying out, within districts that were generally too large for any one man to cover, an unpopular code of commercial law, the details of which

1. Andrews, *Guide*, II, 60–63.
2. *Calendar Treasury Books*, V, 728. The statement in William Dyer's instructions reads as follows: "You shall also take care that the balance of each account (if in money) be speedily remitted to Richard Kent, Esq. receiver general and cashier of his Majesty's customs for the time being residing in London, or if the ballance thereof shall be in goods and cannot conveniently be converted into money that the same be by the first opportunity shypt and consigned to Dr. John Shaw, his Majesty's warehouse keeper or to his Majesty's warehouse keeper for the time being," §18.
3. *Maryland Archives*, XX, 505–506. In the instructions to Nicholson in 1702, the governor is warned not to entrust a collector's duties to anyone "much concerned in trade." C. O. 5:1360, p. 284; *Calendar State Papers, Colonial*, 1702, §1053, by title only.

were often a matter of dispute, even in high legal circles at home.[1] The work was troublesome and exacting and before 1763 frequent leaves of absence were sought for by petition to the Treasury, either for the recovery of health or the prosecution of private business. If the commissioners of the customs approved, the Treasury generally granted such leaves of absence without deduction of salary, provided a satisfactory substitute could be obtained, but in extreme cases, such as those of Weaver in New York and Brenton in Boston, the latter of whom "loitered in England" for two years and more, it peremptorily ordered them to return to their posts and to forfeit their salaries for the periods of their absence.[2] Many instances of service by deputy could be cited, but the Treasury frowned upon the practice in the case of any of the customs officials, and once at a later time, when William Paterson, the surveyor general of Barbados, already mentioned, asked for a twelve months' leave, it declared that "there is no precedent of such indulgence having been granted to any officers of the customs in the plantations, nor do we think it proper that it should be granted."[3] Though as a matter of fact this statement is not

1. Cases of misfeasance in office are not often recorded, but one instance appears in the records of North Carolina, when Samuel Swann, collector at Port Brunswick on the Cape Fear, was ordered by the judge of the court at Edenton (170 miles away) to answer for his seizure of a periaugua some time before. As Swann had not brought the vessel to trial before either a vice-admiralty or a common law court, the judge feared that there had been collusion between the collector and the owners of the vessel. This was a long-distance case and not easily handled. The judge fined Swann £6 proclamation money for failing to appear. Records of Admiralty, North Carolina, July 7, 1732.

The charges brought against Daniel Moore, collector at Charles Town, by the merchants there in 1767 were printed in a pamphlet, *A Representation of Facts relative to the Conduct of Daniel Moore*, March–September, 1767 (printed by Charles Crouch at his printing office in Elliott Street). Moore was charged by one hundred and eleven merchants with collecting excessive fees and other misdemeanors. Henry Laurens' quarrel with Egerton Leigh, judge of vice-admiralty, South Carolina, is well known. His *Extracts from the Proceedings of the High Court of Vice-Admiralty in Charlestown, in the years 1767 and 1768* (1769) contains "General Observations on American Custom House Officers and Courts of Vice-Admiralty," and in his correspondence may be found additional comments of a decidedly pungent character. Leigh answered the pamphlet in *The Man Unmasked* (1769). Unfortunately there are no original records of admiralty for South Carolina after 1763. For the Laurens case see Wallace, *Life of Laurens*, and *Transactions*, Colonial Society of Massachusetts, XIX, 178 note, where Laurens' characterization of the collectors as "rapacious, haughty, insolent, and overbearing men" is quoted.

2. *New York Colonial Documents*, IV, 602–608, 663–664, 778–779; Massachusetts Historical Society, *Proceedings*, 2d series, IV, 154; *Acts Privy Council, Colonial*, II, §251.

3. Treasury 11:24, p. 81.

strictly true, it does express the intention of the board at all times when officially quoted. After 1698, before receiving their salaries, the collectors and others had to furnish certificates that they were alive and in active service "at the respective times to which their salaries are allowed,"[1] a requirement imposed upon all the customs officials in England. As nearly as possible the Treasury laid down the same rules for the plantations that were already in force for the service at home.

The surveyor was a kind of supervisor, check, and policeman combined, his chief duty being to enter the vessels and search for uncustomed goods. He was an official distinct from the collector only in the larger custom houses.[2] In the smaller offices his duties and those of the comptroller, collector, and searcher were performed by the same man. Randolph and Brenton in New England were the only officials who bore three titles, but many bore two of them. William Rhett was surveyor and comptroller of South Carolina; Robert Armstrong was collector and surveyor of Piscataqua, Archibald Cummings was surveyor and searcher at Boston, Ralph Hopton was collector and searcher at Holetown, Barbados, and so on. There does not appear to have been much significance in these double or triple titles, for men so designated in one list would be called "collectors" in another.[3] The comptroller was supposed to serve as a check upon the collector, inspecting his accounts, joining with him and the others in examining vessels, and seeing that the navigation acts were enforced. He compared his account of the goods laden with the entry in the naval office and with the certificate given by the collector, and no ship could sail until these two items were found to agree. He attested all the accounts of the collector and himself made out half-

1. Audit Office, Declared Accounts, bundles 773, 818, rolls 907, 1064.

2. In 1716 at Boston the staff consisted of a collector, comptroller, and searcher and surveyor—three officials regularly to be found on the English establishment. In 1720 only a collector and a searcher and surveyor are named, with a boat and two boatmen. But in 1768, after the setting up of the American Board of Customs Commissioners the number was greatly increased, divided into three groups: (1) those on the plantation establishment—collector, comptroller, surveyor, searcher, and tide surveyor; (2) those who acted by deputation from the surveyor general—four port waiters, two of whom served as weighers and gaugers; and (3) those who were employed by the collector and comptroller—eight able-bodied men, employed as tidesmen and boatmen, when vessels with dutiable goods on board were expected to arrive. Massachusetts Historical Society, *Proceedings,* 58, p. 429.

3. There do not appear to have been instructions issued to the surveyor and comptroller separately. For an instruction to the surveyor and comptroller together see *Maryland Archives,* XX, 167–171.

yearly statements of charges and discharges, which were sworn to before the governor and then signed by the collector.[1] The searcher (*scructator*), as the name implies, inspected and explored all vessels coming in and out for anything uncustomed or illegal and searched persons of whom "sinister suspicions might be had."[2] He was especially designed to check illicit trade. The riding surveyor, a well-known officer on the coast and along the northern boundary of England, first appeared in Maryland at the head of Chesapeake Bay on the eastern side between the Bohemia and the Sassafrax rivers. Later another was appointed for the entire five counties of the Eastern Shore. His particular business was to see that no irregular trade was carried on between Maryland and Pennsylvania, that is, Delaware Bay, and to prevent the running of goods anywhere within his district.[3] This region was a particularly sensitive spot and the seat of much bad feeling between the two colonies. Bellomont wished to appoint a riding surveyor for the eastern end of Long Island, as he believed that there was a great amount of surreptitious landing of prohibited goods there, but he probably never carried out his purpose. Five or six years later a royal collector was named for Connecticut (1707), who was expected to act as a preventive officer for the eastern Long Island section. He resided at New London, which is only two or three hours' sail from the chief Long Island port, Sag Harbor. The term "preventive officer" is occasionally found attached to that of collector, where the latter was concerned with remote and isolated regions. Sometimes it is found alone, as "a preventive officer of illegal trade" in Newfoundland, though in this case it was of short duration, the incumbent, Archibald Cummings, soon being transferred to the Boston service. Others were at Plymouth and Nantucket.[4] The tide surveyor and the tidewaiter were to go and stay on board an incoming ship until it was unloaded; the landwaiter or waterman was to board the ship at the pier, notifying the collector

1. *House of Lords Manuscripts,* new series, II, 474; *Maryland Archives,* XX, 166, 170; XXIII, 360–361.

2. The surveyor or searcher appointed for Nova Scotia in 1746 was to attend the water, with a boat and one or two boatmen, and to visit the several bays and creeks and "to rummage all ships and vessels on their first arrival." Treasury 11:22, p. 85.

3. *Maryland Archives,* XX, 284–285, 303, 388–390 (instructions); XXIII, 7, 358–360 (instructions), 362; *Calendar Treasury Books,* XV, 161.

4. *Calendar State Papers, Colonial,* 1708–1709, §348, i; 1711–1712, §386, i. Jeremiah Basse was collector and preventive officer at Burlington (Andrews, *Guide,* II, 223). For those at Plymouth and Nantucket, Massachusetts Historical Society, *Proceedings,* 58, pp. 432–437.

and comptroller of the progress of unlading and assisting the searcher in supervising the actual landing and disposal of the goods.

At first most of these officials were paid by percentages. There was no uniform rule and the fraction allowed varied widely and was frequently changed. It ran from one-eighth to three-fourths of the receipts, with two-thirds of that amount allotted to the collector and one-third to the comptroller or one-half to the collector and one-fourth each to the comptroller and the surveyor. The average in the latter part of the seventeenth century was about one-half of the receipts to be divided if necessary. Occasionally other forms of renumeration were tried, as when the collector was allowed to keep what remained after all expenses had been met, an arrangement that left nothing for the exchequer. This may seem strange until it is remembered that the plantation duty was not imposed for revenue purposes, and that the government would have been more than satisfied if the duty had met the cost of collection, which it never did. The expenses increased greatly as time went on, not only because of the larger number of officials required by a growing colonial population and an expanding commerce, but also because of the substitution of salaries for percentages.[1] With the reorganization of the system after 1696, the following changes were made. All officials in the continental colonies and the Bahamas, and after 1730 those in Bermuda also, above the rank of tidesman, except the surveyor general who was paid directly from England, were placed upon the English establishment and invested with the rights and powers and subjected to all the penalties of the corresponding officials in the mother country. This meant also that henceforth until 1767 they were to be paid salaries out of the English exchequer and as far as possible to be placed under the same checks and controls as were provided for in the rules governing the customs service at home. The officials in Jamaica were paid out of the plantation duty and those in Barbados and the Leeward Islands out of the four and a half per cent. Many of the lesser servants, clerks, accountants, and boatmen in New York and New England especially, that were added one by one as the need arose, continued to be paid out of the king's casual revenues or the proceeds of the plantation duty.[2] As in England, so in America, pay-

---

1. Some salaries were paid before 1696. Santen, Plowman, and Chidley Brook of New York, each received £200 (one-half advanced before sailing) and were allowed £30 for books, papers, etc. Randolph and Brenton each received £100. *Calendar Treasury Books*, IX, 439, 443, 619, 1392.

2. In 1700–1701, the surveyor, searcher, and waiter in the New York custom house

ment was always precarious in these lower walks of official life. Salaries were frequently behind; officials might wait for two, three, or even five years and then be paid in a lump sum; advances made for extra expenses, if we may believe the statements of some of the officials themselves, were either not paid at all or were left to be recouped by the unfortunate official from the local incidents and forfeitures.

The establishment authorized in 1698 came to about £2000, but this amount increased with the growth of the service until in 1763 it was estimated at about £7000. In 1707 the commissioners recommended higher salaries for all the chief officials and the Treasury agreed, but after that date few changes were made. The surveyor general in 1716 was getting exactly the same amount that was paid him in 1683, a pound a day, with fifty pounds for a clerk and eighty pounds for a boatman, coming altogether to £495 a year. He also had allowances for transportation and other contingencies, including rewards for occasional and extra services.[1] The collectors received from £200 (Philadelphia), £100 (Boston), £80 (New Castle), to £40 (Perth Amboy), £30 (Roanoke), and £25 (Cape Charles), the surveyors and comptrollers in the larger offices receiving about the same, all of them having in addition fees that came to a considerable amount, and a part of the forfeitures, whenever any of them played the part of informers and libelants in the vice-admiralty courts. Compensations for injuries and sufferings incurred in the service were sometimes allowed.[2] The salaries were paid half-yearly by the receiver general and cashier of the customs on the order of the lord high treasurer or the Treasury Board. In the larger ports

were paid out of "his Majesty's Revenues in the Province of New York" (Weaver's Account, Custom House Report, Hall of Records, New York). In 1768 the tide surveyor at Boston was paid out of the duties imposed by the Molasses Act and the waiters out of the plantation duty, the molasses duty, or the fines and forfeitures. The supernumeraries were paid by the day or the piece and the costs were charged to the account of incidents, Massachusetts Historical Society, *Proceedings*, 58, pp. 429–432.

1. Dyer, Carter, and Mein were allowed a pound a day in 1683–1685; Heathcote in 1716 received the same (Massachusetts Historical Society, *Proceedings*, 58, p. 444. Also *Calendar Treasury Books and Papers*, 1729–1733, p. 40, §167, where it is stated that Keith had been paid in 1714 only £280, but that Birchfield received £495, the amount allowed to Quary. Keith, on petition, had the amount made up to him).

2. In 1711 William Rosett was allowed £50 for his "charges and expenses in the cure of a wound received by him in the execution of his duty as surveyor of the customs in South Carolina," and in 1709 John Dansey, "late collector of Accomack River in Maryland," received £30 "for his sufferings and service in the revenue." Audit Office, Declared Accounts, bundle 788, roll 996.

and in districts where much water service was required additional amounts were allowed for the rent of the custom houses and the outfitting and maintenance of boats and boatmen, though these extra expenses were quite as often met out of the king's thirds of fines and forfeitures. The fact that such allowances were sometimes made only in case the forfeitures came to the required amount could hardly have rendered the collector any the less eager to seize ships suspected of illegal trading. New York had a barge, a coxswain, and rowers in livery, who were paid out of the king's revenues in the province, and they must have made a fine appearance as they swept down the harbor to meet incoming vessels.

While the transfer of the customs officials in America to the English establishment in 1696 and the substitution of salaries for percentages were probably in the long run advantageous to all concerned. They involved penalties as well as benefits. All collectors in the colonies were thereafter subject to the provisions of the acts of parliament that regulated the customs service at home. The most important statute of this character was that of 20 Charles II, c. 2 (1668), "For the better payment of monies received for the use of the Crown," which applied to all receivers and collectors who drew their pay from the English exchequer. By this act "damages" were imposed on all who detained "for their private Lucre and Advantage" monies and duties thus paid in for the king's use. Such delinquents were charged interest, at the rate of twelve per cent a year, on all funds held beyond the time laid down in their instructions. That the law was not a dead letter, as far as the colonial officials were concerned, can be seen by examining the declarations of accounts made by the receivers general and cashiers of customs in England, where the amounts owed by the collectors in the colonies are computed with an additional charge of twelve pounds per hundred for "damages" on all arrearages unpaid. According to the figures given these "damages" came to very considerable sums.[1] Whether they were actually ever collected or not is another matter; the probabilities are to the contrary, though the records do show how almost invariably the collectors in the colonies were behind in their accounts. But as the planta-

---

1. Many examples of arrearages and damages could be given, but the following will suffice. "Philip Carteret, late collector at New Jersey . . . for 65 sh. 10 d., from June 25, 1677, to December 25, 1698, amounts to £8. 6. 7." "George Layfield, late collector at Maryland . . . for £44. 10. 8, from September 29, 1693 to December 25, 1698 . . . £28. 0. 5."

tion duty was not, in the first instance, imposed for purposes of revenue, the English authorities to a considerable extent ignored the financial defects of the business and during the period to 1763 sought for efficiency rather than profit. These parliamentary revenues from the colonies were never sufficient to meet the charges of collection and the accounts of both collectors and receivers general show frequent deficits that were never made up. The totals might have been increased had it been possible to stop the leaks, but this in turn would have meant more expense, for it was notorious that salaries were nowhere large enough to support a man without additional income from some other source, legitimate or illegitimate. Connivance on the part of the custom house officials was, in all likelihood, a common feature of the service and the presence in the records of the vice-admiralty courts of but a small number of trials for breaches of the acts of trade points to one of two things, either there was less smuggling in the colonies than has usually been supposed, or there was a great deal of smuggling that was never informed upon by the customs officials. The desire to turn a penny, honestly or otherwise, was inevitably deep in the heart of everyone whose business it was to watch the observance of the acts, but how far that desire was acted on is not for us here to decide.[1]

All of these conditions taken in conjunction with the prevailing practice of deputation and absenteeism, pluralism, the farming of offices, the commutation and composition of duties, and the deterioration of the personnel rendered any satisfactory administration of the system difficult, if not almost impossible. The confusion that existed as to functions and the greater confusion as to authority, resulting in overlapping jurisdictions and conflicting powers, prevented smoothness of operation and hindered despatch. With the naval officer legally an appointee of the governor but actually of the king, with the receiver general commissioned by the Treasury in the king's name, with the deputy auditor selected by the auditor general, and with the customs officials nominated by the commissioners of the customs, complications were bound to ensue. In 1763 Grenville estimated the money loss at not less than from £5000 to £6000 annu-

1. Hutchinson once wrote: "The real cause of the illicit trade in this province [Massachusetts Bay] has been the indulgence of the officers of the customs, and we are told that the cause of this indulgence has been that they are quartered upon for more than their legal fees and that without bribery and corruption they must starve." Bancroft Transcripts, II, 69, Hutchinson Correspondence.

ally.[1] After 1763 and the heavy expenses of the war with France the situation was reversed and money was more needed than the regulation of trade. Then the English Treasury officials turned away from the earlier policy and, by a thorough reorganization of the system, hoped to make the plantation duty a thing of profit to the realm.

Who first started an inquiry into the management of the customs service we do not certainly know. Probably some official in America, such as William Popple of Bermuda, in whom the board had confidence, or some agent in England, such as Bollan or Abercromby, who was at hand and able to present the matter in personal interviews.[2] We know that as early as 1748 the board had been aroused by letters from Shirley and a memorial from Bollan and had taken the issue into careful consideration, instructing Bollan to prepare a paper on illegal trade in the colonies and on the defects of the laws relating thereto. This Bollan did in a memorial of October 20, 1749, in which he called attention to the effrontery of the illicit traders in Massachusetts and endeavored to make it clear that nothing of importance could be accomplished until the navigation acts were revised and the vice-admiralty courts strengthened. With its usual pro-

---

1. Grenville Papers, II, 113–114; *Rhode Island Colonial Records,* VI, 375; *Fitch Papers,* II, 255. In the same year the Treasury said that the duties of customs arising in America produced but a small and inconsiderable revenue, which had "in no degree increased with the commerce of those countries and is not yet sufficient to defray a fourth part of the expence necessary for collecting it." *Acts Privy Council, Colonial,* IV, 509. After 1768 the returns from the customs were greatly increased.

2. Popple wrote at this time about illicit trade (*Board of Trade Journal,* 1742–1749, pp. 418, 423). Bollan was Shirley's son-in-law, advocate general in the vice-admiralty court of Massachusetts, and agent of the colony in England. He was in frequent attendance on the Board of Trade during these years and could present his case not only in writing (when too sick to attend in person) but also by word of mouth (*ibid.,* pp. 64, 283, 337). The same was true of James Abercromby, who had lived in South Carolina, had been proctor and advocate general of the vice-admiralty court there, had been one of the commissioners for running the line between North and South Carolina in 1734, and was afterward an agent for Governor Johnston of North Carolina and for the governor and council of Virginia until 1763. In his "Examination," originally written sometime before 1752 and revised several times afterward, Abercromby comments very severely on the ineffectiveness of England's methods of dealing with the colonies. He prepared the draft of a bill, which he hoped parliament would pass, as the "foundation for a legal and political system, whereby all our American colonies may be governed, as one great Family, connected with this, the Mother State." The bill contains six paragraphs and a "lastly," all designed as "an Amendment" to the acts of trade, "manifestly defective," whereby these acts and those relating to the customs might be made more consistent, workable, and better understood. He wished also to extend the jurisdiction of the vice-admiralty courts and to render them more adequate in point of execution. Pp. 36–37. See below, pp. 408–412.

crastination, the board did nothing for ten years, until, aroused again by a third memorial from Bollan in 1755, it sent a letter and a representation February 20, 1759, to the commissioners of the customs, outlining the great difficulties which were encountered in the execution of the acts of trade and giving an account of the many illegal and improper practices which had been set up to evade them, to the prejudice of the commerce of the country and the loss of revenue to the king.[1] The commissioners, deeply stirred by the board's letter, compared the evidence which it contained with the documents in their own office and became convinced of the seriousness of the situation. They wrote the Treasury on March 6, and on May 10 made a long report recounting the repeated instructions sent to the customs officials in America and calling attention in considerable detail to certain demonstrated facts. These facts concerned the illicit importation of rum and molasses from the French islands into the British northern colonies; the importation of goods from Europe, from Holland and Hamburg especially, directly into the colonies and the sending of enumerated commodities in return back to European ports; and the supplying of the French colonies with provisions from the northern British colonies and from Ireland. They offered advice, deferentially and dutifully but firmly given, hinting at the reduction of the duty on molasses and a stricter enforcement of the rules regarding clearances, though they were inclined to doubt in one case whether it was wise to tamper with the law and in the other whether much could be done to enforce the regulations.[2] They made also certain suggestions regarding the powers of the vice-admiralty courts, of which we shall say more later on. For the moment, however, the Treasury took no heed.

But as the expenses of war piled up and the national debt grew in size, the Treasury officials came more and more to realize that the returns from America ought to be increased. In 1762 and 1763, they sent a series of inquiries to the customs board, in one of which they asked for a copy of the Board of Trade's letter and representation of

1. In this representation the board took into consideration three main issues: (1) preservation of the woods, because of a letter from Benning Wentworth, surveyor of the woods, regarding abuses; (2) the Newfoundland fisheries, to which its attention had been called by Secretary Pitt, in regard to a Spanish claim of a right to fish there; (3) the laws of trade and navigation and the regulation of the plantation trade, its defects and abuses. *Board of Trade Journal,* 1754–1758, pp. 424, 433; 1759–1763, p. 5.

2. Treasury 1:392. *Board of Trade Journal,* 1759–1763, p. 389.

February 20, 1759, upon which the commissioners had based their report of May 10 of that year. On May 21, 1763, Jenkinson, secretary to the Treasury, sent another letter, asking why "the revenues arising from the duties of customs in America and the West Indies amount in no degree to the sum which might be expected from them," directing them "to find out the causes of this deficiency and report as soon as possible [their] opinion thereupon," and to take into consideration "in what manner the same revenue [might] be better collected for the future." While waiting for an answer the Treasury asked also for sundry legal opinions of the custom house solicitors and for lists of patent offices and other statistics, and demanded that the commissioners transmit the desired information with all possible despatch.[1] The haste of the Treasury at this juncture stands in striking contrast with its previous lethargy. Two months later the commissioners were ready with their reply, which they forwarded on July 21, repeating much that they had said in 1759 and adding other recommendations for reforms.[2] On the 25th the Treasury wrote again, instructing the customs board to order all customs officials, absent from their respective stations in the colonies, "to repair thither forthwith, without delay, upon pain of dismissal," and to issue special instructions "enforcing in the strongest manner the strictest attention to their duty and directing them all by a regular and constant correspondence to give an account, as well of their own proceedings as of the conduct of the officers under them."[3] In a letter of August 1, the Treasury asked further for a report on frauds in the customs and for an opinion how best they could be prevented by an act of parliament.[4] To this the commissioners replied, on September 16, transmitting a report on such checks and restraints as might be imposed by parliament and specially laying stress on the hopeless confusion that existed in regard to the jurisdiction of the vice-admi-

---

1. Treasury 11:26, p. 282. In May, 1763, the Board of Trade summoned Bollan to make a verbal report on illicit trade in America, which he did at considerable length (*Board of Trade Journal*, 1759–1763, pp. 359, 364).

The whole subject of illicit trade and smuggling in the colonies needs a thorough overhauling, not so much to discover what the actual extent of such practices was as to find out what the English authorities thought about it. There is no doubt that they honestly believed the trade laws were so far evaded as seriously to reduce the king's revenue, a matter of great concern to them, because at this juncture the colonial relationship was construed largely in terms of finance (*ibid.*, 1764–1767, pp. 367, 407, 409, 412, 415). The constitutional issue came up later.

2. Treasury 1:392, pp. 425–426.      3. Treasury 11:26, p. 304.

4. Treasury 11:26, pp. 284–285.

ralty courts and the uncertainties of trial and conviction in cases of seizures for illegal trade.[1]

With all this mass of evidence and these many recommendations before it, the Treasury proceeded to draft its own report to the king. At the head of the board was George Grenville, chancellor of the exchequer, with Charles Jenkinson as the most influential of the joint-secretaries, and it soon became evident, as Jenkinson's successor, Thomas Whately, wrote the next year to John Temple in America, "Preventing Smuggling is to be a favorite object of the present administration and nothing is to be omitted that can tend to accomplish it."[2] In an elaborate and very important paper[3]—one of the most so of this critical period in England's relations with the colonies—the Treasury presented the measures it had already adopted and outlined in unusually vigorous language those it believed should be further considered by the king, Privy Council, and parliament. "We observe [says the memorial] that through neglect, connivance, and fraud [words taken from the Board of Trade's representation], not only the revenue is impaired, but the commerce of the colonies is diverted from its natural course and the salutary provisions of many wise laws to secure it to the Mother Country are in great measure defeated." Calling attention to the need of a large revenue to support the military establishment necessary for maintaining the colonies, it emphasized the fact that the vast increase of the colonies in territory and population made the proper regulation of trade a matter of immediate necessity lest the continuance of the existing evils should render attempts to remedy them in the future "infinitely more difficult if not utterly impracticable."

The memorial then goes on to state in outline what the commissioners of the customs had already been instructed to do, in order that the efficiency of the service might be increased, and to say that the existing regulations were quite inadequate to cope with practices of such long standing as were those engaged in by the colonists. It asserted that success could be attained only with the coöperation of the other branches of the government, which should in this emergency "afford their utmost assistance in support of them," and that the king, Privy Council, and Board of Trade should unite in orders

1. Additional Manuscripts, 8133, fos. 85 et seq.
2. Whately to John Temple, June 8, 1764, Grenville Correspondence, Huntington Library.
3. *Acts Privy Council, Colonial,* IV, §520. The paper is dated October 4, 1763.

to the governors to aid in suppressing "the clandestine and prohibited trade with foreign nations," to make the improvement of the revenue "the constant and immediate objects of their care," and to give the officers of the customs all necessary protection and support. The Admiralty, the memorial adds, must assist on all proper occasions, ordering the naval commanders to make such disposition of their forces as would be most serviceable "in suppressing these dangerous practices and in protecting the customs officers from the violence of any desperate and lawless persons, who shall attempt to resist the due execution of the laws." Finally, it continued, parliament must play its part by the passage of laws that would provide a new and better method of condemning seizures made in the colonies, clarify the existing rules so that the officers of the revenue should no longer be in doubt as to the way to proceed in the condemnation of ships, and bring into a uniform system the judicature of the courts of vice-admiralty, under persons qualified for so important a trust.

Thus did the Treasury, in a paper of great significance, confess to the failure of the methods hitherto employed to administer the navigation acts in the colonies. In so doing it prepared the way for a new and more determined effort to enforce the customs regulations, to strengthen the official staffs both in the custom house in London[1] and in the custom houses in the colonies, to employ the navy as a more efficient police patrol in American waters, to reorganize the vice-admiralty system, to tighten up the whole commercial policy of control by effecting the passage of new trade acts—those of 1764, 1765, and 1766, and to obtain the passage of that one of the Townshend Acts which established the American Board of Customs Commissioners. This board was commissioned September 8, 1767, and held its first session at Boston on November 18. At the same time the Treasury separated the customs service in the colonies from that of England—just as the Scottish service had been separated forty-four years before—and removed the collectors and other customs officials from the English registry and entered them on a registry of their own. The commissioners, soon after their arrival in America, began

---

1. The old position of plantation clerk in the custom house was reëstablished and Henry Hulton, former comptroller at St. John's in Antigua and at this time on leave in England, was appointed to take charge of the business of the plantation department (Treasury 11:26, p. 359). Hulton was afterward one of the American Board of Customs Commissioners and became the principal deputy receiver of the six penny duty in America (Admiralty, Greenwich Hospital, Miscellanea, Various, 131).

to stiffen the rules of the service, to increase the number of cocquets and bonds, to refuse exemption to coasting vessels, and to enlarge the fees, as the colonists claimed, beyond the limits established by law. They added to the number of armed vessels engaged in the business of cruising and search, and employed new and ingenious devices to detect illicit and contraband trade. Few incidents of this period did more to exasperate the colonists, particularly those of Massachusetts, than did the passage of this hasty measure and the unwise policy adopted by the board itself. The experiment accomplished little, added greatly to the cost of the customs service in America, and brought on, in part at least, the non-importation movement of 1769–1770. English officials saw only their own financial difficulties. They seem to have had only the haziest notions of what was going on in the colonial mind or of what was likely to be the effect of such additional restrictive measures upon a people that were already growing more and more restive under an outside and a distant governmental control.

# CHAPTER VIII

## THE VICE-ADMIRALTY COURTS[1]

AN essential adjunct of the customs service and of all business connected with maritime affairs was the court of admiralty, which in the field of marine law served those who went down to the sea in ships just as the common law courts served those whose activities lay upon the land. Originating, as far as England was concerned, in the fourteenth century, the High Court

1. I have written a paper on the vice-admiralty courts in the colonies, as an Introduction to the third volume of the *American Legal Records* (1937), with regard to the historical rather than to the legal importance of these courts. For this reason I am able to omit from this chapter certain portions of the text there printed as well as many of the illustrations and references in the footnotes.

An account of this Introduction by Mr. Goebel of the Columbia Law School, printed in the *American Historical Review* for January, 1938, is so inadequate and misinforming that I wish to say something, not in defense, for the Introduction needs no defense, but in reply.

Mr. Goebel generalizes from what he knows of vice-admiralty in the province of New York to cover vice-admiralty in all the colonies, the material for which he cannot have examined. This material, in manuscript, is not readily accessible and has never been used before, except a small part of it by Judge Hough in his collection of decisions from the records of the vice-admiralty court of New York. This collection, which I obtained, edited, and caused to be printed in the text series of the *Yale Historical Publications,* was, with all its insufficiencies, the first work of importance to be published up to that time (1925) based on the original court proceedings, and it stands therefore as something of a landmark in the study of the subject.

In reviewing my Introduction, which occupies nearly eighty pages of print and concerns a phase of eighteenth century colonial history that as a whole has been in the past almost entirely ignored, Mr. Goebel, after sundry derogatory remarks regarding the competency of the historian to write on historical law and an extolling of the superior merits and methods of the lawyer-historian (an expression of opinion by a lawyer-historian with which not all will agree), finds five points of criticism to which he devotes most of his space. No one of these points is especially important or is satisfactorily substantiated by him either in fact or comment.

Mr. Goebel should have known (1) that probably no colonial governor, proprietary or royal, ever exercised plenary jurisdiction in vice-admiralty matters, certainly not before 1692, up to which time no governor was legally authorized to appoint a single judge, register, or marshal, or after 1697, when the new system of vice-admiralty courts was set up; (2) that no vice-admiralty court in the colonies had a legal right to take cognizance of prize cases unless authorized to do so by special commissions issued at the beginning of a war; (3) that the knowledge of maritime law possessed by vice-admiralty judges in all the colonies can hardly be determined by the general knowledge of law possessed by three common law lawyers in New York, not one of

of Admiralty[1] was raised by Henry VIII to a position of equal importance with the common law courts at Westminster Hall, and as time went on brought into existence a progeny of local or vice-admiralty courts—nineteen in number—with a vice-admiral in each district, exercising during the sixteenth and seventeenth centuries marine jurisdiction of considerable importance. The Cinque Ports had a special vice-admiral of their own, while the port of London was directly under the High Court itself, which had its hall and chambers in a group of buildings south of St. Paul's Cathedral, known as Doctors' Commons, the home of the doctors of civil law. The High Court had original jurisdiction in all marine causes, in all cases of prizes taken in time of war, and appointed special commissioners to sit as a court of oyer and terminer for the High Court of Admiralty in Justice Hall, Old Bailey, there to try with a jury all criminal cases arising on the high seas involving life and death. The local vice-admiralty courts looked chiefly after marine business and had little to do with the offenses of smugglers and owlers, who were generally tried either by a baron of the exchequer sent into the county or by the exchequer court itself, sitting in one of the towers of Westminster Hall as a common law court for the hearing of cases connected with offenses against the king's revenue.[2] Such procedure became necessary because local sympathies were generally on the side

whom was a vice-admiralty judge (below, p. 228, note 1); (4) that the word "forbade" used in connection with civil trials without juries in vice-admiralty courts need not necessarily imply a common law prohibition, but may be employed, as in my case, in the absolute sense of "to exclude"; and (5) that what I said about the court of oyer and terminer for the High Court of Admiralty in England, though from a strictly legal point of view it might have been made more technically precise, was not based on Blackstone, a wholly gratuitous assumption on Mr. Goebel's part, but on the records of the High Court itself, among which are a few of the court of oyer and terminer records that undoubtedly Mr. Goebel has never seen.

This is about all that Mr. Goebel has to say in his review, which in itself shows little familiarity with vice-admiralty problems in general. It is not such a notice as the reader, desiring, not unnaturally, to be properly informed, has the right to expect from so important a journal as the *American Historical Review.*

1. A very brief account of the High Court of Admiralty is given in my *Guide* to the Public Record Office, II, 304–307. No satisfactory history of the court or account of its functions has ever been written, as far as I know.

2. On this point see *Calendar Treasury Books,* IX, 264–265, 703, where it is stated that the Treasury, the Barons of the Exchequer, and the attorney general were allowed to make rules and regulations in the matter of customs seizures and forfeitures in England. An important statement follows showing the difficulties of making seizures in the year 1689. There was an inspector of customs prosecutions in the exchequer, *ibid.,* p. 7. Also, XI, 201.

of those engaged in illicit trade and local juries rarely seemed able to find in the evidence a sufficient warrant for conviction.

During the seventeenth century the common law courts, judges, and lawyers entered upon a persistent effort to restrict the jurisdiction of the admiralty courts and to extend that of the courts of common law. Sir Edward Coke and his common law successors demanded that admiralty jurisdiction be confined to the open sea only and that the courts be prohibited from dealing with cases arising within the waters of the realm, that is, within rivers as far as the first bridge that impeded navigation. By the use of prohibitions, issued by the judges of the superior common law courts at Westminster, the attack was largely successful, and as a result the local vice-admiralty courts, whose business was limited almost entirely to these semi-inland navigable waters, fell into disuse and in some instances ceased to function altogether. These common law prohibitions carried great weight in the seventeenth century, because the admiralty courts, as prerogative courts sitting without juries, were associated in the popular mind with the prerogative claims of the Stuarts. The time was one when the rights of Englishmen, of which trial by jury was one of the most conspicuous, were very much in the thoughts of men and the divine right of kings and other of the royal claims were among the questions at issue during a critical period in the history of the English constitution.

In the colonies, before 1697, there were no courts of vice-admiralty, properly so called, erected under commissions from the High Court in England, authorized by warrants from the Admiralty, which alone could convey full admiralty powers. After the middle of the century, in one or two of the West India islands and possibly though not certainly in one or two of the continental colonies, cases of prize, which normally should have been sent to the High Court, were locally handled, under authority from the governors in their capacity as vice-admirals as well as governors, when authorized to do so by commissions issued at the beginning of a war. In the main, however, particularly along the coast from Massachusetts to Virginia, where an expanding commerce demanded the settlement of many disputes of a marine character, ordinary admiralty business was dealt with in the existing common law courts, such as the county courts, inferior courts of common pleas, specially erected courts of oyer and terminer, the provincial court of Maryland, and the mayor's court of New York

City. In the corporate colonies marine matters were looked after by the governor and council, the court of assistants, and other civil bodies, sitting as admiralty courts always with a jury. Jury trial was almost invariably the rule. In practice it was insisted on in all the colonies and in Massachusetts, Pennsylvania, and South Carolina was required by law, though in the last-named colony the law never went into effect and in the other two colonies each of the laws passed for that purpose was disallowed by the crown. In truth, so fixed was the idea that trial by jury was fundamental to the dispensing of justice, in disputes of any character whether on land or sea, that the thought of a court in which a verdict could be reached by a judge sitting without a jury was exceedingly repugnant to the colonial mind. Up to this time the common law courts had been in control of all cases in which the rights of person and property were involved and the colonists were not inclined to favor the introduction of another and to many minds an alien form of judicial procedure. Hostility in the colonies to the civil law was greatly increased by knowledge of the struggle that had taken place in England between the two jurisdictions, which had ended in the defeat of the Admiralty, the decline in importance of the vice-admiralty courts there, and the curtailment of some of the powers of the High Court itself.

But with the passage of the act of 1696 and the decision to create regular vice-admiralty courts in the colonies for all cases having to do with illicit trade, conditions underwent an important change. Though ordinary marine causes might have been tried in such vice-admiralty courts as the governors were authorized to erect under their commissions from the crown—commissions which conferred only a limited admiralty jurisdiction—trials for breaches of the navigation acts lay beyond their range. Before 1696 the governors themselves had been in grave doubt as to how far their jurisdiction went and the authorities in England believed that the failure of the laws in the colonies had been due in no small measure to the want of properly authorized vice-admiralty courts possessing wider punitive functions. They saw colonial juries refusing to convict and were convinced that both judge and juries in the common law courts were only too ready to admit the slightest pretext for acquitting an offender. Such men as Nicholson and Randolph were expressing their opinions in no uncertain terms and were insisting that unless vice-admiralty courts with ample powers were set up in the colonies the laws would never be enforced. They considered the situation critical, for if the governors' vice-admiralty courts had no sufficient jurisdiction and juries in the common law courts would not convict, then vessels engaged in breaking the laws would escape condemnation, illicit trade would flourish, and the king's revenue would suffer serious losses. Hitherto the machinery of enforcement had been almost entirely in the hands of the colonists themselves. It was decentralized and ineffective, and the Admiralty, with naval administration disorganized and ships scarce and in poor condition, was wholly unable to undertake any adequate policing of American waters. If England's plans were not to fail at an important point, then methods must be contrived that would increase efficiency by centering supervision in Whitehall and Doctors' Commons.

Randolph had been writing letters home for nearly ten years advocating greater concentration of royal and parliamentary authority in America and a more uniform and rigid system of colonial management in the interest of trade and the revenue. In 1695 he returned to England and his personal influence and indefatigable activity, together with his reports and memorials, which confirmed suspicions already entertained by the Treasury Board and the commissioners of the customs that all was not well with the enforcement of the laws in the colonies, contributed largely to the passage of the act of 1696 and to the stringent administrative measures that followed. Among these measures the one dearest to Randolph's heart was the establishment of a series of vice-admiralty courts that might be invested with extraordinary powers for the checking of illicit trade. In 1697 he reaped the reward of his labors. In that year the Privy Council ordered that plans be drawn for the new courts, and it instructed the High Court of Admiralty to prepare, under warrants from the Admiralty Board, special commissions empowering the governors in the colonies to erect vice-admiralty courts, after the model of the High Court, and to appoint judges, advocates, registers, and marshals, subject to the approval of the Admiralty in England. These commissions were duly issued at various times during that year to selected governors, who were authorized to name court officials, according to a list that Randolph had already drawn up, for eleven vice-admiralty districts covering the entire colonial area. Thus there came into existence a series of courts, under the immediate control of the Admiralty and the High Court, commissioned to try, in addition to the usual marine causes, such other cases as were placed in their hands by the act of 1696 concerning commerce and the revenue.

The importance of this maneuver can hardly be overestimated. It represented a highly organized attempt of the English government to extend in one particular direction the authority of the crown in America. The situation thus created was a serious one for the private colonies, proprietary and corporate alike, and one may not wonder that the proprietors and their agents in England made a determined effort to prevent if possible this encroachment on their charter rights, as they construed them. Hitherto, the private colonies, protected by their charters, had hardly felt the weight of England's hand, but now they were to see the long arm of authority reaching out across the intervening waters to curtail their prized independence. The act of 1696, the establishment of the Board of Trade, the stiffening of the customs service, the erection of the vice-admiralty courts, and the peremptory orders to the governors to exercise greater vigilance in coöperation with the authorities at home—all are but early steps in that noteworthy effort which the Board of Trade was soon to make to standardize and consolidate England's colonial possessions in subordination to the sovereign power of the crown.

In the face of England's determination to include all the colonies within the confines of her customs and vice-admiralty systems the private colonies made no headway whatever and after a fruitless resistance were obliged to receive both courts and customs officials within their borders. For the first time in the history of England's relations with her colonies a network of admiralty and customs officials was spread over the entire colonial area, continental and West Indian alike. Peoples who up to this time had been comparatively free from royal interference were now confronted with a form of oversight and restraint that placed definite limitations upon their commercial comings and goings and imposed upon them certain judicial and jurisdictional agencies that were designed to take cognizance of and to punish their lapses from obedience to those acts of parliament which included within their scope the colonies as well as England herself.

But however much the colonists may have disliked this introduction of a form of civil law procedure which was unknown in their experience and foreign to what they believed were the ancient and fundamental rights of a free-born subject of the king, and however much they may have resented the presence of royal courts and officials looking into the way they were carrying on their trade, nevertheless they had no other recourse than to adjust themselves to the situation. The results were not entirely to their disadvantage. As time went on, in the years before 1763, they came to recognize the unquestioned fact that, except here and there and in individual cases, the acts of trade affected but little either their commercial activities or their financial prosperity. They came to realize also that the vice-admiralty courts, because including within their range marine causes that had nothing to do with breaches of the acts of trade, exercised an authority that was more often beneficial than it was oppressive and served colonial interests much more frequently than it opposed them. Over and over again were the colonists able to turn to these courts for relief in cases of trouble on the high seas or within the waters of harbors and estuaries, and rarely were they disappointed in failing to obtain the redress which they sought.

Another important point is to be noted. These courts by exercising a jurisdiction that in scope and influence surpassed the same jurisdiction in England, gave to the later admiralty system in America its peculiarly varied and vigorous character. It is a noteworthy fact in American history that the colonial vice-admiralty courts, because less amenable to precedent and tradition and more open to modification than were the corresponding English courts at the same time, laid the jurisdictional foundation of the admiralty courts set up by the states after the Revolution and of the federal courts that were established after the right to regulate commerce had been conferred by the constitutional convention on the congress of the United States. This exceptional position was not won all at once or by any single fiat of law. It was reached during the years when the British government was endeavoring to enforce the navigation acts and to see that the king was not defrauded of his revenues. It was reached the more readily because of the obscurity of the parliamentary statutes and the failure of parliament and the executive authorities to define categorically just what the duties of these courts were. For the judges, in dealing with old and new cases alike, had often to depend on their own common sense as well as on the smattering that some of them had of maritime law.[1] Such an opportunity had important conse-

1. Conclusions based on evidence drawn from conditions existing in the province of New York are untrustworthy when applied to other colonies, where familiarity with admiralty law and procedure was less highly developed. Yet even for New York

quences, for outside the customary causes with which all admiralty courts dealt, they had the trade cases as well. Within this special field there was always great uncertainty as to how far collectors, surveyors, and other informers might go in bringing matters before the courts and how far judges might go in rendering their decisions. Many a collector of the plantation duty and many a judge on the bench was puzzled to know just what the law was and how far he was justified in construing for or against the importer and exporter the statutes that he was called on to execute. When the law officers of the crown were not agreed as to their opinions and the higher executive officials in England were in doubt as to just what the acts meant it behooved the lesser lights to be cautious and to walk warily among the many conflicting interests. Nevertheless, though British customs officials in America frequently made mistakes and aroused discontent, it was rare for a vice-admiralty judge to render an unjust or erroneous verdict. American admiralty law gained greatly from the necessity under which the judge often stood of interpreting the law for himself.

Taking the admiralty courts as a whole certain differences of jurisdiction may be noted. The High Court, in first instance as well as on appeal, dealt with all marine causes common to admiralty courts anywhere. It dealt also with prizes, both in first instance and on appeal, which were tried in the hall for the hearing of causes in Doctors' Commons, but were never brought before the vice-admiralty courts held locally in the counties and in the Cinque Ports. Thus the vice-admiralty courts in the colonies had marine and prize causes in common with the High Court; marine causes in common with the English local courts; and in addition a further jurisdiction that neither of the others enjoyed over breaches of certain specified acts of parliament. Piracies and other felonies committed on the high seas lay outside the categories of the civil law, as they involved life and limb and required a jury. This need was met in the colonies by the governor's appointment of special commissions, sometimes construed as special courts of vice-admiralty and sometimes as special courts of oyer and terminer, in both cases with a jury, authorized under an

it may be doubted if Mompesson, a common law lawyer and vice-admiralty judge, had much knowledge of maritime law, and certainly Francis Harison, not a lawyer at all, could have had little more than a smattering. The Morrisses, who come after them, were, as we know, able men, but even they were not trained in the civil law. On the legal fraternity in general, Labaree, *Royal Government in America,* pp. 382–387.

act of 11–12 William III and entrusted with full power, whether on land or on shipboard, to hear and decide cases of robbery and piracy on the sea and to give sentence and judgment of death according to the methods and rules of the Admiralty.

The cases that came before the vice-admiralty courts in the colonies fall naturally into three classes, with a fourth that appears occasionally, but is never conspicuous. These are, first, ordinary marine causes, among which suits for wages and salvage are by far the most common; secondly, prize cases; and thirdly, cases arising out of breaches of the acts of trade. A fourth class would include trials for interloping, though as regards the Royal African Company, the corporation most involved, these would cease after 1698, when the monopoly of the company was broken by act of parliament in 1697.[1] It would include also infringement of such treaty arrangements, as that with Spain in 1670[2] and that with France in 1686. Trials of such offenses were, however, rare, because these treaty agreements did not have the binding force of statutes and violations of them, though common enough, particularly in the relations between Jamaica and the Spanish Main and between northern colonists and the French in the region of the Gulf of St. Lawrence, were not often the subject of legal processes.

In the first group may be found cases touching seamen's and masters' wages, bottomry, charter parties, contracts for building, furnishing, and freighting ships, claims for money lent or advanced, collisions, salvage, wrecks, whales and other drift fish. Wage cases were of infinite variety, the great majority covering the failure of owners or masters, for one reason or another, to pay the seamen their legitimate dues, which usually amounted to twenty or thirty shillings a month. Wages were, as a rule, higher on the merchant ships than on those of the royal navy, a fact of which the naval captains complained as encouraging desertion. On the merchant ships too the sailors were often allowed to bring back from the tropics certain perquisites—rolls of tobacco or planks and chips of mahogany—which they could never do in the navy. Seamen's wages came before the vice-admiralty courts because due for labor performed at sea, but masters' wages were contracted for on the credit of the owner and not of the ship

---

1. The well-known Billop case, 1682, concerned at first an act of trespass upon the rights of the Royal African Company. Crump, *Colonial Admiralty Jurisdiction*, p. 153; *American Legal Records*, II, 648–652.

2. Above, Vol. III, 204–205.

and failure to pay could usually be remedied only in the common law courts. At least that was the English law on the subject, but it was not always followed in the plantations.

Wages were refused for many reasons, such as laziness, drunkenness, neglect of duty, embezzlement of cargo, being mutinous or insolent, refusal to work in an emergency, as in a storm or on a wreck, thus endangering the lives of those on board, and very frequently for desertion.[1] Just what constituted desertion was not always easy for a judge to decide. Men ran away at ports, at the end of the first half of the voyage, and at other convenient opportunities—as to a ship of the navy in harbor or to a New England schooner off Newfoundland—and they alleged, when called to book, a great variety of reasons for doing so. The most common were the failure of the ship to adhere to the original agreement, an unauthorized alteration of the voyage, the brutality of their masters or the insufficiency or rottenness of their food. Captains were truculent men, much given to swearing and blasphemy, to beating, bruising, and otherwise maltreating their sailors, threatening to cut off their ears, to whip 'em raw, or to blow out their brains. They pinched them in provisions, knocked them about with impunity, and met their complaints with abuses and insults, often to the terror of the men's lives. The judges had frequently to deal with a tough variety of human nature. They had to determine how far the sailors' conduct had been provocative[2] and how far it had been justified, for sailors and masters were notoriously unreliable in their statements, and interrogatories and depositions were often contradictory and biased. The courts were always friendly to the sailors,[3] who had the privilege of presenting their libel as a group, instead of singly as was the case with the common law. On the other hand a judge, though ready to fine the master heavily, should brutality be proved, was often unwilling, on account of the scarcity of seamen, to grant the request of a sailor that he be

1. Wages were forfeited by law (11–12 William III, c. 7, §xvii) in the case of seamen deserting a merchant ship abroad in ports beyond the seas.

2. Judge Menzies of the Boston court decided in one case of this kind as follows: "I find that Capt. Henry Atkins the Defendant had lawful provocation to correct the Complainant and has not exceeded the bounds of Humanity, having regard to the aggrevation given. But on the contrary has endeavoured to discountenance profanenes and acted during the voyage the part of a good Christian." Records of Admiralty, Massachusetts, I, 25.

3. Judge Read of the Philadelphia court said very frankly in 1735 that "the law was favorable and tender to mariners." Records of Admiralty, Pennsylvania, I, 16–19.

released from his agreement, frequently ordering him back to his ship or threatening him with arrest as a deserter.[1]

Matters of contract were concerned mainly with charter parties, bottomry, partnership, and the building and equipping of ships, and were always liable to raise the question of jurisdiction, because as a rule such contracts were made on land. A charter party was, generally speaking, a covenant between merchants and seafaring men touching their merchandise and maritime relations. It usually concerned the hiring of a vessel for the carrying of freight. Bottomry was involved when the owner or master of a ship borrowed money upon the keel or bottom, thus mortgaging the ship as security for the payment of the loan.[2] Partnership was involved when two or more men agreed to share and share alike in some commercial venture, bearing charges and receiving profits according to a prearranged understanding. The building of a ship embraced all sorts of contracts with shipwrights, carpenters, chandlers, and others for the construction of the hull and the furnishing of rigging, canvas, ironwork, and supplies. Cases coming within these categories can be found in the proceedings of all the vice-admiralty courts and among those of the common law courts also, where partnership cases were more often tried than otherwise. Connecticut, always something of a law to herself, tried all marine causes either in the county courts or in the court of assistants with a jury. It even empowered the latter to sit as a court of admiralty with a jury to dispense "the law of Alleroone."[3]

Cases of collision were uncommon, for the seas were wide and sinkings from this cause were rare. They did sometimes happen in

1. Judge Byfield of the Boston court complained in 1729, "There are but few ships arrive here from Great Britain but the marriners are endeavouring to quit their employ, to the great hurt and overthrow of many voyages." Records of Admiralty, Massachusetts, III, 68.

2. Certain merchants of Philadelphia brought suit against Captain John Cunningham of the *Dreadnaught*, a private man-of-war, for £1350, an amount which, as the indenture showed, they had advanced for refitting and restoring the vessel. On Cunningham's return from a cruise against the enemy he refused to pay. The proctor proved the bill of bottomry and hypothecation and the ship was condemned and ordered to be sold for the recovery of the money. Records of Admiralty, Pennsylvania, I, 324–328.

3. Connecticut Archives, Private Controversies, *passim*. Miss Caulkins in her *History of New London,* p. 251, notes that the New London county courts took regular cognizance of admiralty business. The famous Hallam case was one of seaman's wages, tried in the county court with an appeal to the court of assistants. Arbitration was frequently resorted to in Connecticut.

channels and harbors, but because the damage was slight they did not often get into the courts. But salvage was another matter. So liable was it to occur that statutes were passed in England laying down regular rates of allowance for saving ships and goods from the menace of the seas and rewards for those aiding ships in distress or saving cargoes after the ships had been driven ashore. Many cases of this kind came before the courts and the awards and allowances of the judges varied according to the circumstances under which such aid was given.[1]

Among the many marine causes with which the vice-admiralty courts concerned themselves were the disputes that arose regarding whales and the whale fishery. These disputes were common in New England, where off the eastern coasts and islands whales abounded and whale fishing was carried on. By grant of the crown royal fishes, such as "whales, dolphins, sturgeon, porpoises, grampuses, and in general all fish whatever remarkable for their largeness and fatness," were handed over to the Admiralty as its peculiar rights or droits, together with the tenths of all train oil and whalebone. Consequently trials concerning these matters were viewed by royal officials and

1. One of the most famous colonial salvage cases was that of the Spanish ship, *St. Joseph and St. Helena,* which in 1752 attempted to put in at Narragansett Bay because of a leak but ran ashore on a reef off Niantic. The captain engaged a schooner, *Susanna,* to salvage the cargo, which included, besides commodities, a large amount of Spanish coin. This cargo was carried ashore at New London and stored, but local people broke into the warehouse and pilfered a large part of the money. A vice-admiralty court was held at New London by the New York judge, Lewis Morris, and the amount of salvage decided on. The supercargo thought the sum too large and wanted to appeal, but found the legal difficulties too great, and finally allowed the case to become the subject of a diplomatic inquiry on the part of the English secretary of state. Secretary Robinson wrote to Connecticut, demanding that the colony arrest the offenders who had stolen the money. But Connecticut never did a thing; probably could not. The case involved not only the schooner, *Susanna,* which salvaged the cargo, but also the *Nebuchadnezzar,* which was chartered to carry back to Spain what was left of it. This vessel was libeled in the court of vice-admiralty for the wages due the chief mate and sailors for their services on the voyage to Cadiz in 1753. A court was ordered to be held, November 8, 1754, but before it sat the libelants withdrew the process. The whole matter led to civil suits and a diplomatic inquiry and at one time promised to become a very complicated affair, affecting not only international relations but the politics of Connecticut as well. It gave rise to an almost interminable correspondence. *Wolcott Papers,* I, II; *Fitch Papers,* I (Connecticut Historical Society, *Collections*), indexed under "St. Joseph and St. Helena." Governor Wolcott failed of re-election, because the "freemen" of Connecticut thought he had not done his duty in this case. An excellent statement is in Hooker, *The Spanish Ship Case,* Tercentenary Publication, Connecticut, XXV, and see Groce, "Benjamin Gale," *New England Quarterly,* X, 700–701.

civil lawyers as belonging to the vice-admiralty courts. This view was not, however, always that of the colonists, among whom royal and Admiralty droits were held in less esteem than in England and where public opinion favored the jurisdiction of the common law. Cases of this kind fell into two groups: first, those concerning drift whales, which, dying, were cast up on the shore without previous contact, as far as known, with the fishing boats; and, secondly, those concerning whales which, having been wounded off shore or beyond and having escaped from the harpooners, were claimed, when found stranded, by two sets of fishermen. In the first instance, according to English law, the king or Admiralty had a clear right to the profits as a perquisite, though attempts to make this right good aroused intense dissatisfaction among the colonial coast dwellers, who looked on a stranded whale as their property and found in the bone, oil, and blubber articles of value to themselves and their families.[1] In the second instance the right was always denied in the colonies and the whale was awarded to the whaler who struck the first blow. As between rival fishermen the award was not always easy for the judge to make. He had to determine not only the question of title, but also the amount of shares and allowances, which "having regard to the custom amongst the fishermen," was normally five-eighths to the plaintiffs and three-eighths to the defendants.

In approaching the second chief group, that of prizes, we encounter a subject of considerable difficulty, too involved to admit of more than a very cursory treatment. The difficulty lies partly in the uncertainty and confusion attending prize captures and prize business before the passage of the act of 1708, which for the first time put the rules on a statutory basis; and partly in the ignorance that prevailed in England regarding prize jurisdiction, prize agents, and prize dis-

[1]. On February 1, 1706, Governor Dudley of Massachusetts wrote a long letter to the Board of Trade, which contained the following statement. "I have directed the judge of the admiralty at all times to receive and decide tryalls between the fishermen, which must often happen, because the wounded whales often break lose and there are disputes as to whom they belong. But it hath been always observed that besides the whales thus stricken, there are sometimes others that are wounded and slayn by thrashers and sword-fish, which follow them, whereby they become wrecks and, as they are called, drift-whales, to which no person can claym any right and do therefore justly become a perquisite to the Vice Admiral as other wrecks are. I have gotten two such —but the Inhabitants of those parts which is called Barnstable have affronted and injured the officers of the Admiralty." *Calendar State Papers, Colonial*, 1706–1708, pp. 29–30. Cf. *ibid.*, 1728–1729, §1036.

tribution in the colonies.[1] Prize was not a maritime cause within the accepted meaning of the term and legally all prizes taken in war should have been brought to England for trial at the High Court. But this obligation proved not only inconvenient but dangerous and at times impossible. Hence in the years after 1662 prizes were tried in courts called vice-admiralty courts erected for the purpose as occasion demanded. As this course was of doubtful legality the matter was taken in hand in 1689, with the outbreak of the war with France, and a certain recognition was given to the practice, though it is impossible to say how many such trials took place in the colonies, as no vice-admiralty records exist for so early a period.[2] As this mode of procedure was still considered illegal, the whole business remained unsettled until the outbreak of the Spanish War in 1702 brought it

1. Above, Vol. II, 258. In 1655 the commissioners appointed by Cromwell for managing the expedition to America, acting under authority from the Protector, erected a prize office at Barbados and appointed four men to officiate as prize agents (Historical Manuscripts Commission, *Portland,* II, 90). This would appear to be the first prize office established in the colonies. But there was no vice-admiralty court in Barbados at the time or vice-admiralty judge on the expedition so that whatever condemnations were obtained were in courts of common law. Probably few of the ships taken at the time were ever legally condemned (Crump, *Colonial Admiralty Jurisdiction,* pp. 95–97). Later Jamaica had one prize agent, Barbados one for a short time, and Antigua, after long delay owing to the difficulty of finding a man to accept the position, also had one. There were three on the continent: one for Massachusetts and two for Connecticut, New York, the Jerseys, Pennsylvania, and Maryland (the instructions in the last-named case are in *Maryland Archives,* XXV, 152–157, 191–199). Blathwayt commented on the difficulty which the prize commissioners met with in finding proper agents in the West Indies, saying that substantial planters and inhabitants having good estates in the plantations or dealings with merchants in England were not willing to accept of these agencies upon their being obliged to give such security as might render them liable to be sued in the exchequer, where they were unable to attend or answer the event of such prosecutions. "Nor will it quitt cost," he added, "to send agents well qualifyed from hence," p. 256.

2. The Committee for the Affairs of America recommended as early as 1656 that vice-admiralty courts be erected in Barbados, Jamaica, and even in New England and a commission was actually drafted for Major General Brayne, June 30 of that year. But there is nothing to show that such a commission was ever perfected (Egerton, 2395, ff. 148, 233–234, 396; Crown Office Docquet Books). Though D'Oyley in Jamaica had no admiral's commission, he exercised vice-admiralty powers as early as 1657 and settled, unofficially, a few marine disputes. He did not touch prize cases, which if adjudicated at all, had to be sent, to the disgust and indignation of local captors, to the High Court of Admiralty in England for trial and condemnation. The first vice-admiralty court erected by a governor under his commission was in Jamaica in 1662. Though such a court was not empowered to try cases of prize (since all vice-admiralty courts had to be specially authorized at the beginning of each war to try prizes, as was the case also with the appointment of prize commissioners), nevertheless

again into the open and rendered a solution imperative. Inquiry was begun in 1703 and a serious investigation started four years later, which ended in the passage by parliament of the act "for the Encouragement of the Trade to America," sometimes called the "American Act" (1708). By laying down rules governing prize captures, this act vastly improved the situation, though as with other acts relating to the colonies it left open and obscure many points at issue that were to make troublesome controversy in later years of naval warfare.[1]

Probably more than a third of all the cases that came before the vice-admiralty courts in America, during the wars from 1702 to 1763, were those of prize.[2] Cases of which the details are available present no specially picturesque or dramatic features and often no great diversity of incident. The most perplexing problems that confronted the courts were: first to prove that the vessel belonged to the enemy

between that date and 1689 a great many prize cases, arising from privateering, were tried in vice-admiralty and other courts in the West Indies. Rightly speaking, such trials were illegal, unless special commissions had been issued. So great, however, was the danger of sending prizes to England that in 1689 the Treasury gave legal recognition to the practice of local trial by allowing the captor "to resort to the next judicature port where a court of admiralty is or shall be erected." *Calendar Treasury Books,* IX, 293–294.

1. The commissioners for prizes wrote to the Board of Trade from the Prize Office, December 30, 1703, "We doubt the jurisdiction of the Courts of Admiralty in the plantations doth not extend to prizes, which however we shall not dispute though we are of opinion that, admitting a competency of jurisdiction there, those courts should however proceed in the same methods as the Court of Admiralty in England" (*Calendar State Papers, Colonial,* 1702–1703, p. 909). Two years later, after consultation with Blathwayt, Sir John Cooke, and several Admiralty officials, they expressed themselves still more strongly. In a report to the Treasury, July 25, 1705, they say, "We do most humbly offer to your Lordships consideration, that the pretended authority assumed by the Courts of Admiralty in the plantations of judging of prizes taken by her Majestys ships of warr in those parts is the principall occasion of the disorders committed there" (Treasury 27:17, p. 145). In the instructions issued by them in 1703 to the agent for prizes in Pennsylvania and Maryland, they speak cautiously of "a proper court for prizes if any such be established" in these colonies, and again, "in case you shall at any time find sufficient cause not to send any such prize ship to England," as if it were very doubtful whether the vice-admiralty courts had any sufficient authority for what they were doing (*Maryland Archives,* XXV, 152, 153). Blathwayt's report is entered in his Entry Books (Treasury 64:89, pp. 253–258). In it he speaks as if the vice-admiralty courts in the colonies were taking upon themselves the right "to dispose unduly of the prizes" (p. 255), but he does not commit himself as to whether or not they had the right to try prize cases at all. He seems to take it for granted that they were doing so. It would look, therefore, as if one object of the act of 1708 was to legalize a situation that had arisen without intention, as far as the English authorities were concerned, because, strictly interpreted, until the passage of the act all prize ships should have been sent to England for trial.

2. The vice-admiralty records of New York and South Carolina, among the con-

and not to a neutral power; and, secondly, to ascertain the right of assisting ships to share with the owners and men on board in the distribution of prize money. The captor or libelant had to show that ship and cargo, either or both, belonged to the enemy, because fraud, collusion, or conspiracy were often resorted to, in order to deceive the judge if the ship were brought in on suspicion. Sometimes the ship could be shown to be neutral and the cargo prize, as of a Dutch ship carrying goods belonging to French subjects. The judge was many a time and oft called upon to decide a case in the face of conflicting testimony, forged cocquets, passports, passes, "coloured" ships' papers, insufficient evidence, and misleading invoices, a situation sometimes bewildering in the extreme. The rights of an assisting vessel were determined largely by the distance, the intention of a captain to share in the attack, and his readiness or otherwise for battle. A vessel beyond supporting distance or one pursuing a different course was manifestly out of the picture and its claim was easily rejected.[1]

tinental colonies, show the largest number of seizures for prize. Those for New York are nearly all entered in Judge Hough's *Reports of Cases . . . in New York* and in Vol. II of *American Legal Records,* pp. 648–655. For South Carolina, between 1739 and 1763 there are recorded 43 cases tried in the vice-admiralty court at Charles Town, of which five are of vessels retaken, restored to the owners, and salvage allowed.

The king had one-third of the value of the prizes taken by the royal navy. This third, in the case of prizes taken by the East India Company in its war against the Great Mogul, amounted to £18,000. The king's share was generally given away: (1) to the commissioners of sick and wounded mariners and seamen; (2) for necessaries put on board the ships for the relief of the sick and wounded at sea; (3) as bounties for the widows, children, and parents of seamen slain in the service; (4) to the Chatham Chest. The king's halves (wrecks), thirds (ships condemned), fifths (French prize goods), and tenths (prize captures) were frequently given away, usually to the seamen. *Calendar Treasury Books,* X, 426, 443, 1066, 1693.

1. Many lesser points also had to be settled; some of which were determinable according to English navy rules, as that a man-of-war or a privateer could pursue under any colors but must attack under its rightful flag; others according to the judgment of the court, as when the proportions in which captors could share were held to depend on the tonnage and crew of the vessel seized. It was well understood that ships under a safe conduct or a flag of truce could not be taken, though enemy goods on board were legitimate prize; that vessels captured after the royal proclamation had been issued announcing the end of the war were to be returned to their owners; that no private vessel without a commission or a letter of marque could take a prize; that a private man-of-war might take a prize even though its captain were absent; that a gift of a prize by a captor, before condemnation, conveyed no title to the property. This list might be greatly extended, as every capture presented its own combination of incidents and the judge was often called upon to use with considerable freedom what he knew of law in general, without much regard for the traditions of the admiralty as followed in England.

The third chief group of cases, that relating to breaches of the acts of trade, has a more intimate connection with the commercial policy of England toward the colonies and was of no little importance in arousing a measure of discontent in certain quarters, notably in Massachusetts Bay. In the past the interest of historians in the vice-admiralty courts in the colonies has been largely centered upon cases of this kind. Judge Hough says rightly that students of our history have paid little attention to these courts except as far as they had to do with smuggling and the violation of parliamentary statutes and that such students "have given the lay reader the impression that what the Court habitually did was righteously snuffed out by the Revolution." In point of fact, however, smuggling cases formed but a small and relatively inconspicuous part of the business of the courts, as far as the records go to show, and the work that they "habitually" performed was in no way snuffed out by the Revolution. It has remained to constitute an important part of the admiralty law in America.

The cases in this group fall into two divisions: one concerning failures to observe the normal requirements of the acts, as in matters of entering, clearing, and registering vessels, neglecting to carry the proper certificates and cocquets, trading in ships that were not English owned or built or legally made free, and navigating without the necessary complement of "English" seamen or under a captain or master who was not "English"; the other concerning ships engaged in illegal or illicit trade, in one or other of its manifold forms, the captains or supercargoes of which generally acted under instructions from the owners of the vessels or from the consignors of their contents.

Vessels slipping into or out of colonial harbors without entering or clearing with the naval officer were exceedingly difficult to detect and, while suspicions were common that the practice was indulged in, there are not many cases of seizures of such vessels to be found recorded in the proceedings of the vice-admiralty courts. Evasion was easiest in regions of long and winding coast lines, with many creeks and rivers and few settled ports such as those bordering on Chesapeake Bay and the lower Delaware, or in localities hidden and remote and far removed from the official ports of entrance, where the customs officers labored, as from Stamford in Connecticut to the fishing and logging villages of southwestern Maine, including the shores of Long Island and New Jersey. In Albemarle Sound vessels of light weight and draft could easily run in to Currituck or Pasquotank inlets before going on to Edenton and Port Roanoke, and where a few vessels were seized many others doubtless got away in safety. In secluded coves and along unwatched river banks sloops and shallops and periauguas, either running goods on their own account or acting in collusion with larger vessels lying in deeper waters, made their way under cover of night and landed their barrels or bales in obscure places of concealment—in cellars, barns, empty buildings, or caves—awaiting convenient opportunities to transport them by land to the desired market. Vessels failing to enter their arrivals or attempting to unload without notifying collector or naval officer were more often discovered than those that failed to take out clearance papers, creeping away, generally at night, falling silently down creek or inlet, headed for the open river or sea, without cocquet or certificate, running the inevitable risk of seizure at the other end of the voyage, where their papers were certain to be asked for and inspected.[1]

Failure to possess among the ship's papers a certificate of registration or the possession of a certificate that was out of date, improper,

---

1. The reverse was also true. Many vessels arrived at colonial ports without certificates or permits. Edward Fuller, master of the sloop *Middleborough,* was libeled in the vice-admiralty courts at Edenton, North Carolina, February 3, 1735, for not having permits. He produced a letter from John Jekyll, collector, and William Lambert, comptroller, of Boston, showing that the molasses which he had on board had been properly cleared. As the ship had already been condemned and the decree fixed, before the letter was produced, it was ordered that if no cocquet arrived from Boston before September 2 the verdict should stand. Evidently the cocquet did not arrive, for the vessel was finally sold. This case is one of the earliest discovered in which a vessel was condemned for breach of the Molasses Act (Records of Admiralty, North Carolina, I, February 3, 1735, March 1, 1735, February 17, 1736). Another of February 3, 1737, involving the seizure of 43 hogsheads of rum and 5 hogsheads of molasses, may be of the same kind.

Sometimes an incoming ship would neglect to enter in the naval office books all the items of its cargo—as of twenty hogsheads when it had on board twenty-seven or of one hundred when it carried one hundred and thirty-six—and would be liable to seizure for manifestly attempting to defraud the revenue. Such a case would be one of "insufficient certificate," the fault perhaps of the master or, it may be, of careless officials at the custom house of clearance, in which case a composition bond would generally be allowed. In case a vessel cleared and later in one way or another took on an additional cargo, not as the law required in the presence of a customs officer, it was liable to confiscation if detected. There were conditions, however, under which the captains would be allowed to make a post-entry, that is, to insert the new items in his bill outward and so avoid the penalty of forfeiture. It may be doubted, however, if post-entries of this kind were favored by either law or custom in England.

Composition bonds are frequently met with. They were given by the masters on

or false was certain to lead to trouble and to involve the master in a controversy with the collector. Cases of this kind came before nearly all the vice-admiralty courts and the records disclose the nature of the charges and the difficulties which confronted the judge in his effort to render a decision, because the omission was sometimes due merely to inadvertence or sheer forgetfulness and not to any desire to evade the law. The act of 1696, as it happened, contained a new form of registration, more elaborate and binding than that which had been required before. The obligation thus imposed put many captains in a quandary, particularly those who had left England before the act was passed and who either had never heard of the new requirement and so were unaware of their remissness, or being away from England were obliged to continue under the old form. In all such cases the collectors were inclined to be lenient, and usually cleared the vessel on the master's giving security that he would obtain a new certificate or recover the old one within a given time. It was rare for a captain to neglect registration in either an English or a colonial port, and a certificate testifying that he had registered properly was among the most important of the ship's papers.

Smuggling and illicit trading, at all times exciting and adventurous devices for thwarting restrictive legislation—gambler's chances in the field of commerce, have ever had an attraction for the reader of colonial history, who is always liable to exaggerate their extent, because of the want of any very precise information about them.[1]

condition that if a missing register or certificate or a corrected register or certificate were not obtained from the proper authorities in England or elsewhere within a given time—nine to twelve months—the securities would be held liable for the amount of the bond. These bonds were of the nature of pledges, to be forfeited in case of nonperformance, and had to be given before the vessels could be properly entered. Other forms of bonding also appear. In Antigua, January 27, 1719, the collector appealed from a verdict of acquittal and delivered the goods to the owners under bond, by a certificate of delivery, that if the sentence were not reversed, the amount of the bond would be returned to him (Records of Admiralty, Antigua, under date). In a Pennsylvania case the claimants (owners of the goods libeled) bonded themselves to pay full value if the goods were condemned. Usually such bonds were given for the purpose of saving perishable commodities, but in this instance, the claimants wished time in which to procure certain opinions from the commissioners of the customs in England (Custom House Papers, Philadelphia, III, 277).

1. An admirable discussion of smuggling in the colonies is given in Harper, *The English Navigation Acts,* sect. XIX. Further information can be obtained from Harrington, *New York Merchants,* pp. 249–276. Present-day conclusions are favorable to the idea that the colonials were not the inveterate smugglers that older writers, as well as some modern ones, have thought them.

While a study of vice-admiralty proceedings offers no certain test of the situation—for evasion was often possible with the connivance of officers and many a ship escaped detection altogether—nevertheless such study does lead to the belief that our ancestors were not the inveterate law breakers that popular estimates have declared them to be. Certainly activities of this kind do not bulk large in the vice-admiralty proceedings. Even in Massachusetts, probably the chief offender among the colonies, the great majority of cases concerns wages, desertions, assault upon the high seas, and other matters that fall within the class of strictly marine causes. The number of trials for illegal trading, recorded in the proceedings of the vice-admiralty courts (as far as we have them) of Rhode Island, Pennsylvania, Maryland, South Carolina, and Antigua, is very small, amounting to less than five per cent of the whole. The percentage is rather higher in North Carolina, but on the other hand in New York the number is negligible. Even in some of these instances the libelant's plea was dismissed for insufficient evidence or because the charge was not sustained. No one of the vice-admiralty court records discloses attempts at illicit trade on any extended scale; for even the cases that are entered are comparatively petty or, relatively speaking, unimportant.[1]

Before the passage of the Molasses Act in 1733 the law most frequently broken was that of 1663, forbidding the direct importation into the colonies of goods from the continent of Europe. Evasion of this law assumed a great variety of forms and called out a great variety of explanations. The judges were fairly shrewd in their estimates of men and evidence and were not often imposed upon. Their duty under the law was to condemn a vessel importing goods of the growth and production of Europe—either directly or by way of the West Indies—which had not first been landed in England. They always obeyed the law, where there was no doubt as to its intent or to

1. The rarity of such cases in the New York records is probably due, in part at least, to the fact that many trials for evasion of the acts of trade at the port of New York came before the mayor's court there. An analysis of the thirty-one cases contained in the second volume of *American Legal Records* gives the following results: six vessels were condemned for evasion of an act of the province; twenty-four for breaches of one or other of the acts of parliament (two because the vessel was manned by foreigners, five for importing direct from Europe, seventeen for smuggling—fourteen inward, three outward), and one compounded. Two of the smuggling cases inward seem to have been against the Molasses Act. It is evident that before final conclusions can be reached on this point the records of other than the vice-admiralty courts will have to be searched. Nevertheless the failure to find many smuggling cases in the proceedings of the colonial vice-admiralty courts is difficult to understand.

the evidence, even though at times they must have been impressed by the defendant's plea that he could not afford the longer voyage, on account of the added expense and the increased dangers of the sea. The Massachusetts judges had to reckon with a local custom which had become established in Boston of allowing merchants to import directly from France, Spain, and the Wine Islands a few hogsheads of wine for their own private consumption, an indulgence said by the customs officers "to be common and as ancient as the port." Most of the judges deemed this practice no infraction of the law, as the wine was not for gain or merchandise, but Robert Auchmuty, who was much given to sermonizing in his decrees, refused to sanction the practice and lectured the officers for allowing it to continue. He said that it corrupted the service and that no matter how great its antiquity he would never recognize it as a right. The barons of the exchequer in England, he added, were opposed to all such "permissions, tolerations, and indulgencies and why should his Majesty's subjects here lay claim to cheaper gratifications of their pallets than those at home."[1] The Boston situation was still further complicated by the merchants' habit of bringing in foreign goods as gifts to friends, but the judges refused to connive at this habit as legitimate and invariably condemned and confiscated the articles when discovered.[2]

The Molasses Act of 1733 was the only one of the acts of trade that caused any very serious trouble in the colonies, and while evasion took place in all the leading ports from Boston to Charles Town,

1. Records of Admiralty, Massachusetts, III, 146–147, October 4, 1733. Bernard, in his *Select Letters on the Trade and Government of America*, pp. 2, 4, says that "There had been an indulgence time out of mind allowed—the permitting Lisbon lemons and wine in small quantities to pass as ships stores." He does not include wines for family use, but these are clearly mentioned by Auchmuty in his decree. Brandy from France was "by the common curse of consumption amongst fishermen considered as stores to the master and his company and it was the custom of all [fishermen off New England, Nova Scotia, and Newfoundland] to make such provision."

2. Several interesting and unusual cases of alleged violation of the act of 1663 arose in Pennsylvania at the time of the immigration of the German Palatines. The question concerned the admission of their household goods into the colony. Among these goods were, in one case, 596 scythes, 160 forebacks for chimneys weighing about five tons, 120 pieces of cast iron for stoves, 103 large iron instruments called "straw knives" and 14 called "draw knives," tobacco pipes with brass covers, three dozen spectacles, and nine kegs of brandy and "Geneva" (gin). The claim was made that in each case the number of new utensils was more than the list of passengers warranted, that many of the articles were new and could not be classified as household goods, and that to admit them established a dangerous precedent inasmuch as the Germans were given to

the center of excitement was in Massachusetts Bay. There, beginning about 1740, as far as the vice-admiralty records go to show, a series of seizures began, due largely to the vigorous efforts of the collectors, of whom Charles Paxton was the most insistent, which aroused a great deal of opposition and ill-will among the merchants because these efforts interfered with the long-established practice of bringing foreign sugar and molasses into the province without the payment of duty. The custom was well rooted and the Molasses Act, which Governor Bernard himself said was a mistake, was from the beginning "a perpetual stumbling block to the custom house officers." Manifestly it had not been enforced during the first few years, but after 1740 trials appear which show a grim determination on the part of the officers to demand the duties and an equally grim determination on the part of the merchants not to pay them. The latter usually instructed their captains to stand off some fairly remote coast, as at Nantasket or Barnstable, and there to send the barrels and hogsheads ashore in small sloops or other open-decked craft, in much the same way that European goods were smuggled in. As a rule when seizures of such cargoes took place and trial was held in the vice-admiralty court, no claimants appeared and the hogsheads, tierces, or casks were condemned *pro confesso* or by default. Should the smaller

traveling back and forth and carrying their possessions clandestinely into Pennsylvania as household necessities, when they were probably designed for sale. The attack was chiefly directed against the imported ironware, particularly the stoves, and George Mifflin, one of the witnesses, testified that he was part owner of an ironwork in the colony and was inclined to think that the price of cast stoveplates had fallen since the Germans began bringing over Dutch stoves from Rotterdam. The judge decreed that vessel and cargo should be released, but that some of the goods that were manifestly fresh and new should be forfeited.

One of the questions involved in these cases concerned the importations from Europe by the Germans of cards and hackles "being proper engines for the manufacturing and weaving of linen and woollen cloth." Such importation was contrary to the royal proclamations of January 15, 1666, and of October 24, 1686, which in the interest of the Society of Frame Work Knitters prohibited the transportation of frames for knitting and weaving to the colonies (Records of Admiralty, Pennsylvania, I, 1–10, 1735). That the Germans were employing such implements for other than home use seems unlikely from the statement in one of the dispositions, that the Palatines, settling westward of Philadelphia, one hundred and forty miles, were a laborious, industrious people, raising considerable quantities of hemp, flax, wheat, barley, and other grains, which they brought to Philadelphia in wagons for sale (fo. 105). Another witness adds bacon and eggs to the list and says that each family had one or two wagons of its own for the purpose of carrying its supplies to market. Note also the case of a ship carrying Palatine families to Philadelphia in 1724, seized by Collector Moore, *Calendar State Papers, Colonial*, 1726–1727, §844.

boat also be captured another libel was necessary and another trial took place. In the latter case, condemnation usually followed, on the ground that the smaller boat had landed the cargo without warrant and without the presence of the customs officers. Similar conditions prevailed in Pennsylvania and Maryland, where the lower reaches of the Delaware River and the great estuaries of the Chesapeake offered every opportunity for smuggling, though the inducements were not nearly as great as in New England, because the distilling of molasses and the drinking of rum were far less a part of the life of the people there than was the case in the northern colonies. Only a very few seizures of this kind are recorded, one for Pennsylvania and two for Maryland, though these are no sure index to the extent of the habit.

Evasions of the acts of trade under cover of a Flag of Truce are not often recorded in the proceedings of colonial vice-admiralty courts and there are scarcely more than half-a-dozen cases, chiefly for the years from 1746 to 1748, entered in the extant minutes or file papers of the courts for the continental colonies. Why there is not a larger number for the period of the Seven Years' War it is hard to say, as that was a time when an illicit trade of this character was notoriously carried on, particularly by merchants in Rhode Island and Pennsylvania, but it may be that the offending vessels were able successfully to elude the informers and seizing officers.[1] "Flag of Truce" or "Sanction of Truce" was the name given to a merchant ship that was commissioned by a governor of a colony—English, French,[2]

1. It has been suggested that seizures took place more frequently in West India than in continental waters and that offending vessels were tried more often in West India than in continental courts. The records of Jamaica and the other British islands in the West Indies do not, however, uphold this contention, as far as these records have been preserved. See below, p. 249, note 3.

2. A French Flag of Truce was seized and condemned in the vice-admiralty court of Bermuda in 1747 (*Board of Trade Journal, 1742–1749*, p. 269. Cf. pp. 356, 366). The vessel was the *Triumvir*, Captain John Baptist Tessere, on a voyage to South Carolina with sixty English prisoners, but also with a French cargo and two negro slaves. The cargo was deemed more than was necessary for carrying the prisoners and the ship was condemned. Dr. Henry Wilkinson has most kindly furnished me with this information and, in addition, with a list of the cases to be found in the Bermuda vice-admiralty and colonial records. Unfortunately this material was received too late for use in my former paper, but, except by way of illustration, it adds nothing to the conclusions there reached. From the data which Dr. Wilkinson has sent me I judge that cases of prize and of illegal trade are more frequently found there than are those that concern ordinary marine matters, a fact which is not surprising as Bermuda was a natural center of both activities. A number of vice-admiralty trials in Bermuda are entered in the colonial records, now in the office of the colonial secretary, Bermuda, as well as in the regular proceedings of the vice-admiralty court there.

Spanish, or other—to carry prisoners to an enemy country for purposes of exchange. The law expressly forbade such ship to engage in trade or to carry money or a cargo in excess of its needs. It might take on board enough coin to buy provisions, to defray such expenses as were incurred in the exchange of prisoners, or to repair the vessel if it were damaged by storm or otherwise, but no more. The amount of money thus allowed was from 300 to 400 pieces of eight and any vessel found with a larger sum on board or with valuables such as jewels or plate, or with provisions more than were needed as sea stores, or with merchandise that was manifestly designed for sale, was liable to be confiscated and to have all of its excess cargo declared lawful prize. A few of the most important cases, entries of which have survived, are as follows.

In 1729 a Spanish ship, sailing with English prisoners from St. Augustine to Charles Town, bought goods at the latter place and was seized for violating the act of 1660. The master in defense claimed that he was authorized to do this by Arthur Middleton, acting governor, who allowed him "to lay out some ready money and to buy necessaries of which the defendant and his attendants stood in need." He believed that the so doing was lawful and had been done by previous "messengers and agents." The judge thought otherwise, deemed the purchasing excessive, and decreed that the vessel be condemned, on the ground that it was not English owned, registered, or manned.[1] In the same colony, in 1746, the advocate general, James Wright, libeled Captain Morris, master of a merchant ship lying in Charles Town harbor, for sending armed men aboard a Flag of Truce for the purpose of taking by force deserters whom he suspected were on board. Wright charged that the action was contrary to the law of nations, against the statutes, and an affront to the peace and dignity of the king. Judge Graeme dismissed the charge on learning from Morris that the latter had instructed his men to board the Flag of Truce for purpose of inquiry only and under no circumstances to carry arms or use force.[2] In North Carolina, in 1747, John Mandesley, commander of the *King George,* libeled a Spanish merchant ship, the *Elizabeth and Annah,* sailing from Porto Rico to St. Kitts, for breach of the acts. The Spanish captain, Thomas Caneles, claimed that his vessel was a Flag of Truce, with English prisoners on board. But

1. Records of Admiralty, South Carolina, A–B, pp. 546–590.
2. *Ibid.,* C–D, 363–365.

when it was shown that the vessel carried 3000 Spanish dollars, 3300 pounds of cotton-wool, 440 pounds of green and bohea tea, besides rugs and jewels—all of the value of £1500 sterling—the judge decreed that the vessel had obtained its Flag of Truce merely as a "colour" and a cloak for trading. He released the ship but ordered that all coin above 300 dollars, the rugs, and the jewels be confiscated and distributed in the usual manner by thirds.[1]

While each of these cases illustrates one aspect or other of the working of the Flag of Truce system, no one of them concerns directly an English merchant ship engaged in evading the acts of trade. Better instances are as follows. The collector at Philadelphia seized an English vessel, which, having been taken by the Spaniards and ransomed, on its return voyage had brought away several English prisoners, under a Flag of Truce from Havana. It also had on board 70 hogsheads of sugar and divers other wares, which the captain had (as was charged) secretly and unlawfully unladed at Marcus Hook before coming up the Delaware River to report to the governor at Philadelphia, to whom he mentioned the prisoners but said nothing about the sugar and the other goods. The case involved the examination of a great many witnesses on both sides and offers an admirable opportunity to study methods of procedure in a colonial vice-admiralty court. The vessel was finally declared forfeited.[2] In 1748 the *Harra my Judy* was seized on the high seas by Commander George Ring of the *Anson,* libeled in North Carolina, and condemned. The respondent appealed to the commissioners of prizes in England on six grounds; insufficient evidence; proper credentials as a Flag of Truce; no contraband or prohibited goods on board; the ship duly registered and legally cleared; no breach of the acts of trade; at the time of capture, August 15, 1748, a cessation of arms. The judge had condemned the vessel because it had on board money, provisions, and merchandise more than was stated in the cartel and allowed by law, and in his decree had said that it was not lawful to carry on trade with the enemy in time of war, "especially to the distress of the king's good and loyal subjects, particularly in the northern colonies in America, of which within these two years last past his Majesty's subjects in these parts have had woefull experience." He allowed the appeal, but the issue does not appear.[3] The last case to be cited is

---

1. Records of Admiralty, North Carolina, November 14—December 12, 1747.
2. Records of Admiralty, Pennsylvania, I, 313–324.
3. Records of Admiralty, North Carolina, October 13, 1748.

that of the *Charming Polly,* a Jamaica vessel, built at Bermuda, which had gone to Santo Domingo with French prisoners under a Flag of Truce issued by Governor Haldane and was seized in 1758 by Captain Stephens of the *Stanwix,* as a "trading ship in disguise." The libelant charged that the vessel had obtained its Flag of Truce, "as was frequently the case," in order to carry on a trade with the enemy "of a very dangerous and pernicious tendency." But the judge, while fully recognizing the serious character of the charge, decided that the case lay outside the jurisdiction of the Charles Town vice-admiralty court and should be transferred either to the court of Jamaica or to the High Court of Admiralty in England.[1]

The jurisdiction of the vice-admiralty courts in New England was very considerably extended by parliament's action in making the courts responsible for the clause in the act of 1722 forbidding the cutting anywhere of white pines suitable for masts.[2] According to this clause, no one was to cut down a white pine of any dimension, growing outside a township or, by earlier interpretation,[3] outside the bounds of any private or corporate property, title to which had been obtained before October 7, 1690. In practice this came to mean that the king reserved for his own use all pines measuring twenty-four inches in diameter, three feet from the ground. Such trees within the ungranted area were to be marked by the surveyor general of the woods or his deputy with the king's broad arrow,[4] or if found already felled were to be seized and libeled in the vice-admiralty court. For more than ten years, ever since the passage of an earlier act, that of 1711, for the preservation of white and other pine trees,[5] the royal surveyors and their deputies (particularly the latter) had carried on an incessant warfare with the laborers, loggers, husbandmen, and sawmill owners of New Hampshire and Maine, with much mortification and loss of dignity on one side and jubilation on the other. With the passage of the act of 1722 the officials had at last, as they hoped, an efficient ally in the judge of vice-admiralty, and about

1. Records of Admiralty, South Carolina, E–F, pp. 360–378.
2. 8 George I, c. 12, §v.
3. *Calendar State Papers, Colonial,* 1710–1711, §234.
4. Respect for the king's broad arrow was none too conspicuous in the colonies. Sailors rubbed it out when placed on a ship's mast; the loggers with impunity cut trees so marked; and in a Pennsylvania vice-admiralty court one Anthony Peel was charged with saying that "he did not care a fig for the broad arrow" (Records of Admiralty, Pennsylvania, I, 8).
5. 9 Anne, c. 17.

the year 1730 we meet with their first attempt to make use of the new judicial arm.

The first recorded trial of this sort is on May 8, 1730, when David Dunbar, surveyor general of the woods, exhibited an information against a group of Maine men, who had cut, without royal license, eighteen white pine trees of twenty-four inches in diameter and upward, contrary to the act of 1722. The defendants did not appear and Judge Byfield imposed fines of £150 each, as the act required, to be paid within twenty days, one-half to go to the king and one-half to the informer.[1] In the next trial, the following year, the deputy surveyor, Jeremiah Dunbar, appeared before the court with his advocate, Robert Auchmuty (later to be Byfield's successor as judge), with William Bollan for the defendants, and Charles Paxton, recently commissioned, serving as marshal—all names familiar in Massachusetts history. Dunbar deposed that in February, 1731, he had seized and marked twenty logs, half of which were thirty inches and half above twenty-four inches in diameter, at a mill upon Royal River, the property of one Peter Wyre, who had cut the logs and hauled them thither. Wyre in defense claimed that he had cut them on his own land. Byfield considered the proof of Wyre's guilt insufficient and while he decreed that the logs should be forfeited to the king he released Wyre with costs.[2] Again, later in the year, when Atkinson and Slade, deputy surveyors, arraigned two men, one Hope, a merchant of Boston, and one Perkins, a farmer of Arundell in York county, for cutting logs, Byfield became quite indignant, blaming the libelants for delaying six months in bringing the case to trial—though the law allowed that extension of time—and dismissed the libel, because the logs had been cut on the 200 acre lot of Perkins, title to which could be traced back to the old Plough Patent, through a grant by Alexander Rigby in 1648.[3] Byfield's indignation must have approached dangerously near anger with the next case, when Drinkwater, a deputy, libeled five men for cutting, felling, and destroying white pines. The details are not given in the record, but the state of Byfield's mind is evident when he ordered the marshal to take Drinkwater into custody until he paid the charges of the suit, and in case

1. Records of Admiralty, Massachusetts, III, 78b. The activities of David and Jeremiah Dunbar can be followed in *Calendar State Papers, Colonial, 1728–1729.*

2. Records of Admiralty, Massachusetts, III, 79–81. On Dunbar's activities and difficulties, see Stock, *Debates,* IV, indexed under "Dunbar."

3. Records of Admiralty, Massachusetts, III, 104.

he did not pay to lodge him in jail.[1] It is clear that Byfield had little patience with the methods of some of the deputy surveyors in earning their salaries.

In a class by themselves, but of considerable importance as coming within the jurisdiction of the vice-admiralty courts, were violations of the treaties which England made with Spain in 1670 and with France in 1686, according to which the merchants, captains, masters, and seamen of either kingdom were to abstain from all trade in the colonial ports of the others. No certain instances of seizures have been discovered in violation of the treaty of 1670, which concerned chiefly the West Indies and the continent south of Port Royal and St. Helena Sound in Carolina, and in practice it remained a good deal of a dead letter.[2] In 1703 the Board of Trade in a communication to Secretary Nottingham begged him to take note of the fact that a distinction between the French and the Spanish in America had become more than ever necessary in point of trade, meaning that trade with Spain was to be connived at rather than forbidden, while that with France was to be strictly prevented. One would not expect, therefore, to find vice-admiralty cases arising out of breaches of the treaty with Spain, unless it might have been among the records of the vice-admiralty court of Jamaica, of which few remain of earlier date than before the American Revolution.[3] But there are many cases which come within the scope of the treaty of 1686, particularly in the

---

1. *Ibid.*, 108–108b.

2. There is one possible case of a seizure under the treaty of 1670, though the facts in the case are not very clear. Captain Chamberlen of H.M.S. *Monmouth*, in 1712, captured the sloop *Jacob*, in Port Royal harbor, Jamaica, for clandestine trading along the Spanish coast. The vessel may also have been guilty of breaking the acts of parliament. Dr. George Bramston, legal counsel to the Admiralty, had already decided that such persons as were authorized to try prizes in the West Indies had the right to decide whether a ship was liable for breaking a treaty or was only a plain prize (Admiralty 1:3666, February 20, 1703). A decision was not rendered in this case, as Captain Chamberlen got into trouble because he refused to obey the order of the vice-admiralty court to restore the sloop when ordered (*Calendar State Papers, Colonial*, 1714, §§167, ii, iv, 227, p. 145, and §277, xxiii; Admiralty 1:1596, Captains' Letters, under "Chamberlen," December 12, 1712).

3. Mrs. Butterfield has sent me her final report on the records of the vice-admiralty court of Jamaica. "The records range in date from 1742 to 1889. There are very few before 1776, but there are some cases of ships libeled for wages, and one case, the *Jupiter* of Rhode Island, for breach of Navigation Laws, as well as a few prize papers. I should think that the most numerous of the early papers (some fifteen in all beginning with 1742) are indictments for murder and piracy to be tried at courts of oyer and terminer for the admiralty of Jamaica, under the act of 11–12 William III. There are a good many murder cases, beginning with 1742 and there are the min-

region of New England and the lands to the northeast, adjoining the French possessions in Canada and the islands of St. Pierre and Miquelon off Newfoundland, as well as the West Indies, although doubts were always raised as to the continued validity of the treaty.[1]

A familiar and much frequented route for French ships in the North Atlantic ran from Hispaniola and other French islands in the West Indies to the French possessions around the gulf and up the river St. Lawrence. Occasionally these vessels, under stress of weather, leakage, or fear of enemy's ships, would put into Boston harbor and there be seized by the collector for violating the acts of trade, in that they were not English manned or owned or "free," or under special contract with the commissioners of the navy who in times of shortage were allowed to use foreign ships for specific purposes. There they would be libeled, and there the libel would be dismissed as soon as the French captain could show that the vessel was unseaworthy and needed to refit, or that it was a wreck and could proceed no farther, or that it was obliged to stock up with wood, water, and provisions. In any of these cases, under the terms of the treaty, the master and mariners were to be treated hospitably and with humanity, to receive aid and materials in a kind and friendly manner, and to be given letters of safe-conduct by which they might return safely and without harm each to his own country.

One of these vessels was seized in 1732 in Boston harbor because it unwittingly violated another clause of the treaty, which required

utes of the trial of one sailor for murder in 1776. The records become voluminous with the beginning of the American Revolutionary war, mostly of course prize cases. I have found a good many examples of the trial of breaches of the Navigation Laws in the records of the Supreme Court. In May, 1737, two vessels were condemned for importing goods illegally, and 'Divers French Sugars' were condemned for being imported without complying with the terms of the Molasses Act. Can you tell me why the Receiver-General should seize 15 Spanish vessels in the spring of 1762 and bring cases against them in the Supreme Court? These vessels were taken not as prize but for being illegally navigated."

1. The commissioners of the customs always doubted whether an information based on a royal proclamation following such a treaty would lie in a court of vice-admiralty (*Calendar Treasury Books*, IX, 146). In 1765 France denied that the treaty was legally binding, and consequently in that year the question was raised in England as to whether or not it was still in force (*Board of Trade Journal*, 1764–1767, pp. 142, 151). For New England vessels trading with the French at Cape Breton in 1726, *Calendar State Papers, Colonial*, 1726–1727, §90. In 1727 the French king issued an edict authorizing the seizure of foreign vessels coming within a league of the French colonies in America. There is something on the subject in *Calendar State Papers, Colonial*, 1728–1729, §§195, 230, 238; *Board of Trade Journal*, 1734–1741, pp. 136, 148, 154, 155; and see 4 George III, c. 15, §xxxv.

that whenever it was necessary for a ship of either nation—French or English—to enter a port of the other, it should give warning of its intention by breaking out its ensign and firing three salutes of its cannon, or if it had no cannon, three musket shots. In this particular instance, the schooner, *Society,* of Cap François, failed to give the required signals, but the judge on hearing the captain's explanation that he was too worried about the condition of his ship to remember the terms of the treaty, decided that no fraud was intended and that the vessel should be offered every opportunity to refit, even to the extent of selling, with the consent of the custom house, such part of its cargo as was necessary in order to pay the cost of repairs. Except in this one respect, which was carefully supervised by an auditing committee, the vessel was under no circumstances to break bulk, dispose of any part of its lading, or to take on any new merchandise whatever. If it did any of these things, it was liable to confiscation without hope of redress.

The part which the vice-admiralty court played in the history of the colonies has been overstressed on the coercive and oppressive sides, and insufficient attention has been paid to its great usefulness as the guardian of the rights of the seamen and a very ready help in time of trouble for all whose life lay upon the sea or who were dependent upon it for their maintenance and prosperity. In none of the leading ports, particularly on the continent but probably scarcely less so in the West Indies, could commerce have been carried on without the aid of these courts and in none of them did there exist agencies which pursued their humanitarian work with more regard for justice and fair dealing than did the judges of vice-admiralty. This aspect of the court's influence is more conspicuous in Massachusetts, Rhode Island, Pennsylvania, and South Carolina than in New York, where cases of this kind, with the single exception of salvage, tended to come within the scope of the common law, even though in the common law courts procedure was more prolonged and involved, costs of suit were greater, and the rules were less favorable to the sailor than was the case with the civil law. Furthermore, juries were more influenced by public sentiment than were the vice-admiralty judges and less likely to render a verdict in strict conformity with the law in the case, as can be seen in the Cradock *v*. Erving case in Massachusetts (1761), where the jury was charged by the judges to find for Cradock but flatly refused to do so. As far as the records bear witness, except in the one case of Edmond Porter of North Carolina,

I have yet to find an instance of manifest partisanship or injustice on the part of a colonial judge of vice-admiralty, and even in Porter's case the evidence is not conclusive.

The range of the judge's usefulness was a wide one. He issued letters of marque, ordered surveys, settled estates, and acted as administrator, whenever the necessity of doing so arose from any marine matter that came before him for decision. He protected the rights of the sailors against their masters, of masters against their sailors on one side and the owners of their vessels on the other. He defended the men from brutality and mistreatment in an age when threats, curses, and blows were an everyday occurrence, and when idleness, neglect of duty, and desertion were common incidents of every voyage. He rendered decisions in cases of wages, desertion, salvage, and insufficient and tainted food; liberated from their agreement those who were inhumanly treated; but sent back to their boats those who from unreasonable or inadequate causes wished to be released from their contracts. The vice-admiralty courts were responsible for the execution of more statutes of parliament than those which concerned trade and navigation and the protection of white pines. They enforced the many statutes relating to seamen in all their concerns, including shares of prizes, impressment, the six-penny duty, and assault on the high seas, even though in these statutes the vice-admiralty courts in the plantations were not mentioned, as they generally were not. No one can read through the extant proceedings of the courts held in Massachusetts, Rhode Island, Pennsylvania, North and South Carolina without being impressed with the service that these courts rendered as the friends of the men, English and colonial, who went down to the sea in ships.

But the judge of vice-admiralty in the colonies did more than carry out the statutes. He helped ships in times of trouble and played the part of a good Samaritan in cases of need. When a vessel from Rotterdam, the *Loving Unity,* bearing 142 Palatines destined for Pennsylvania, fell on such evil times that provisions failed, more than half the passengers died, and the remainder escaped only after tragic experiences, Byfield, judge at Boston, heard the case, fined the inhuman captain heavily, roundly berated the even more inhuman crew, and made the mate, whom one of the passengers libeled for assault, pay dearly for his brutal conduct.[1] Foreign ships that in a disabled condi-

---

1. Records of Admiralty, Massachusetts, II, 106–107b; *Publications,* Colonial Society of Massachusetts, I, 113–114.

tion sought the port of Boston for aid and sustenance were helped in their distress. The judge appointed a committee of experienced men, who made an examination of the vessels, determined the amount of refitting that was necessary, provided materials at reasonable rates, supplied shipwrights, carpenters, and calkers, and treated the vessels in all respects as if they were their own. Sometimes these experts were obliged to recommend that a ship be sold as unseaworthy, because too old, rotten, or infested with the worm, and in that case the cargo was either disposed of under the eye of the customs officials or warehoused until it might be reladen on another craft. Once, a ship sailing from Madeira to Boston was captured by pirates but was allowed to depart with a portion of its cargo. It was then, unfortunately, driven by wind and storm to Barbados, where it was obliged to sell some of its stock in order to refit. On its arrival at Boston the master was sued by the consignee for not delivering the full invoice. The judge dismissed the libel, but said in his decree that the proper course would have been to apply, by means of an "instrument of protest," to the vice-admiralty court at Barbados that an official survey might be made, for, as he said, though there was no positive law requiring surveys, the practice was based on the custom of all trading nations and an official survey in case of damage or decay had a standing in every vice-admiralty court.[1]

Wrecks and accidents were an inevitable accompaniment of a seaman's life and when such were brought to the attention of the judge, as in the case of the suit by the sailors against the owners for salvage, or by the master against the sailors for neglect of duty in a crisis, he gave every aid in his power. Sailors were allowed salvage if they had assisted in saving a ship that had stranded or had gone on the rocks or if they succeeded in retaking a ship that had once been captured by pirates or the enemy; and masters generally had a good case against their crews who refused to turn a hand in such an emergency.

1. Records of Admiralty, Massachusetts, II, 3–6; III, 27, 70, 84–84b, 99b. Such surveys were very common. There are thirteen entered in the records of South Carolina before 1759. It was customary when a vessel reaching port was found to have sprung a leak or had proved unseaworthy, or having run aground had suffered serious damage, for the captain to sign before a notary a public instrument of protest against the ship and to bring the case into the vice-admiralty court, asking for a warrant of survey. Should the judge, acting on the advice of experts, decide that the ship was "unfit for the sea," he would order it and its cargo sold at public vendue. Sometimes the warrant of survey preceded the instrument of protest, in case there was some doubt as to the condition of the vessel.

Judges of vice-admiralty had as little sympathy for a drunken or lazy sailor as they had for a blasphemous or inhuman captain or mate. Should a ship run ashore or ground upon a reef, the services of the court were immediately called into play and a survey resulted. On the receipt of an application or petition from the captain, the judge issued a warrant, sometimes on his own initiative, sometimes on an instruction from the governor or council, authorizing a committee to examine the boat, determine its position and the nature of its injuries, and report either to himself or to the council the extent of the damage. If the hull was too far gone to be worth saving, he might order it to be sold where it was for what it would bring. The owner, as well as the captain, might apply to the court for a survey, in order to obtain attested evidence upon which to base a claim for insurance money, or else he might ask the court to determine the exact cost of refloating and refitting in order that the necessary data might be at hand in making up an audit. In such cases the court acted in somewhat the capacity of a receiver, issuing orders, providing for surveys and examinations, approving estimates and costs, paying bills, and determining fees.[1] These functions of a vice-admiralty court were almost as conspicuous and important as were those that were strictly statutory and judicial, and there can be no doubt that throughout the colonial period the courts were looked to for redress and succor by merchants, masters, and mariners, whenever difficulties arose that could not be settled by agreement or that lay beyond the power of the individual to grapple with by himself.

It is clear that in the exercise of all these manifold duties, the vice-admiralty courts in America were shaping a jurisdictional authority that was broad in itself, and, because determined by no fixed statutory boundaries, might easily become broader. Much that it accomplished was based upon custom, tradition, and common sense as well as upon positive law, and it grew in stature because it was called

1. *Calendar State Papers, Colonial,* 1700, p. 659; 1702, §964. The instances in which the courts succored stranded vessels are legion. An excellent illustration is that of the *Thomas Walpole,* which went ashore in the Piscataqua near Portsmouth in 1765 (Collins Papers, Library of Congress, years 1765 and 1766). Vessels frequently ran aground in the Delaware River, striking on the flats or shoals near the mouth, in the neighborhood of Cape Henlopen, Indian River, or elsewhere. Consequently there are many cases of instruments of protest followed by warrants for surveys in the colonial records of vice-admiralty. In one instance when a vessel arrived with a damaged cargo, the judge appointed a committee to determine whether the damage was due to the bad condition of the vessel, poor storage, mismanagement of the sailors, or neglect. Leakage through the deck was a common cause of trouble.

upon to test its strength in many issues with which the English vice-admiralty had nothing to do. Inevitably, therefore, it came into conflict with other jurisdictions that possessed legal powers anterior to its own, and it was obliged to determine, either definitely or approximately, its relations thereto. These opposing jurisdictions were, first of all, the private or proprietary governments, and, secondly, the courts of common law.

Before the vice-admiralty court came into contact with the jurisdiction of the common law, it had to settle its relations with the proprietary governments, the charters of which contained undisputed grants of legal and judicial rights. But whether these grants conferred upon the proprietors admiralty jurisdiction was a matter of doubt that had to be referred to the law officers of the crown for decision. The answer was always emphatically in the negative. When some of the proprietors asked that special commissions under the seal of the High Court be issued to their governors, giving them the same powers with the royal governors of erecting vice-admiralty courts within their territories, this request too was refused. Thwarted in both these particulars, the proprietary and corporate colonies endeavored by one means or another to limit as far as possible the scope of vice-admiralty jurisdiction and to prevent the vice-admiralty courts from encroaching upon what they considered their charter prerogatives. Connecticut succeeded in doing this with conspicuous success for the greater part of her colonial career, but the other chartered colonies, after a struggle, submitted to the royal authority and admitted the royal courts within their borders.

The conflict that took place during the first quarter of the eighteenth century, in the Bahamas, in the Carolinas, in Rhode Island, and with great intensity of feeling in Pennsylvania, varied according to the character of the personnel and the nature of the problems. The issue in Rhode Island, which was under the vice-admiralty court at Boston, was at first chiefly concerned with the validity of an admiralty law passed by the colony in 1695 and disallowed by the crown in 1704; the right of the governor to issue letters of marque; and the competence of the marshal of the Boston court to act as water-bailiff in the colony. The main issues in Pennsylvania were over the right of the vice-admiralty court at Philadelphia to try vessels seized within the "body of the province," that is, within the boundaries of Penn's grant as laid down in the charter, and the right of Penn to appoint a water-bailiff "of this town and county of Philadelphia—to execute," for so the commission runs, "all writs attachments, summons, replevins, and all other processes whatsoever, to be directed upon any person or ship or goods, from any court of record within this county upon the river as the said county of Philadelphia, in case of pursuit so far as the county of Berks and upwards and—of Chester downwards do extend along the shores thereof." These were the bounds within which Penn wished to prevent the vice-admiralty court from exercising its jurisdiction, and to send all cases of illicit trade that might arise therein into the courts of common law. He charged the vice-admiralty officials with breaking in upon the jurisdiction of the common law and trying without a jury cases that were not of a maritime character, because not arising from seizures made upon the high seas.

But Penn's position was not tenable. Even the attorney general, Sir Edward Northey, said that Penn had no right under his charter to erect a vice-admiralty court or to exercise vice-admiralty functions and that seizures made on the land or on the water within the province in no way trespassed on his rights or on those of any other proprietor. The advocate general, Sir John Cooke, as might have been expected, went further and denied that Penn could appoint a water-bailiff, believing that such an appointment was an invasion of the rights of the admiralty, because the water-bailiff, as commissioned by Penn, was merely a marshal of admiralty under another name. This opinion he reversed later, agreeing with Northey that the officer was only a sheriff after all, a civil not a maritime appointee.

In North Carolina both before and after the surrender of the proprietorship in 1729, the situation was such as to give rise to a prolonged struggle between the two jurisdictions, during which the relations between the vice-admiralty court and the governor and chief justice became quite as strained as had been similar relations in Pennsylvania twenty-five years before. Governor Burrington declared in 1731 that on his arrival he found the admiralty court so little under restraint that it was drawing all sorts of business into its hands and proceeding in so extraordinary a manner as to occasion "a general discontent and ferment" among the people, "the gentleman that is judge of it," he added, "[boasting] of his success in putting down the supreme court." An inquiry into the situation, by special instructions from England, brought to light a refusal of the judge of vice-admiralty, Edmond Porter, commissioned by the Admiralty in 1728, to recognize the claims of the local judges appointed before 1729 by the proprietors. He ignored the orders of the common law courts to keep within his own bounds, thus depriving (as the complaint of the judges said) "the subjects of the benefits of the common law which is every Englishman's birthright." Porter not unnaturally defended the authority of the vice-admiralty court against what appeared to be encroachments of the common law, which took the form of a series of prohibitions issued by Christopher Gale, the chief justice. His reasons for so doing were two: first, he claimed that the issue of the prohibitions was not warranted by the merits of the case, as the common law had no right to meddle with matters of freight or pilotage and in these and other instances was exceeding its own jurisdiction; and secondly, that Gale was a judge appointed not by the king but by the proprietors and so could not hold a king's court or prohibit the proceedings of any of his majesty's courts of law.[1] This was the argument that one finds advanced in the disputes that arose in Pennsylvania and other proprieties, and it was this par-

---

1. *North Carolina Colonial Records*, II, 142, 757–762; III, 224–232, 513–515; Admiralty 1:3672, June 6, 1729; *Acts Privy Council, Colonial*, III, §182. The writ of prohibition in the Allen *v.* Northey case is given in Records of Admiralty, North Carolina, April 30, 1728, as follows: George Allen, "practitioner in physic," libeled the ship *Sarah and Mary*, Samuel Northey, master, for damage done to a chest of medicines imported from Virginia, June 18, 1726. On the application of the defendant Chief Justice Gale issued a writ of prohibition on the ground that the cause of the action was not shown to be *super altum mare*, but that the original agreement had been made "within the body of one of our counties" and was not therefore cognizable by the vice-admiralty court. Edmond Porter, the judge of vice-admiralty, on receiving the writ, adjourned the court for two hours and then ordered the trial to proceed, "notwithstanding the said prohibition." Northey was found guilty and sentenced to pay damages with costs. He refused to pay and "the court ordered an execution to be issued out" to the marshal to seize the ship, which was done, October, 1728 (Records of Admiralty, North Carolina, under dates). In another case the marshal, in trying to execute Porter's mandate, was opposed by the captain of the vessel, who threatened to shoot him if he came aboard (Deposition of Samuel Snowden, October 17, 1630). Porter ordered the captain seized and taken to jail. Again in the case of William Cook, master, against John Phelps, pilot, a prohibition was ignored on the ground that the case was properly cognizable in the vice-admiralty court only (1729). The reason for the prohibition was that the contract was made on the land (*North Carolina Colonial Records*, III, 227), but in this case at least the common law judge would seem to have strained the point in somewhat the manner of Sir Edward Coke in England. The feeling against Porter was, however, very strong in Edenton, so that on January 7, 1730, a mob threatened to murder him. In playing for safety, Porter "put up mock judges in the seat of justice." Only a few of the cases cited in the complaints (*North Carolina Colonial Records*, II, 757–763: III, 224–232) are to be found in the North Carolina records of vice-admiralty.

ticular claim that distinguishes the quarrel between the jurisdictions in the proprieties from that which took place in the other colonies and gives to it a more personal and dramatic character than elsewhere. There can be little doubt but that it was this controversy with the proprietors, particularly with Penn, that has had a good deal to do with the harsh and unjust treatment which the vice-admiralty courts have received in the past at the hands of American historians. Robert Quary in Pennsylvania, Edmond Porter in North Carolina, Joseph Morton in South Carolina, and Thomas Walker in the Bahamas were involved in quarrels not only with the common law courts but also with the claims of the proprietors who endeavored to limit, either through authority exercised by themselves and their governors or through courts erected under their charter rights, the jurisdiction of the vice-admiralty within their respective provinces.

The extent and novelty of the powers conferred by parliament upon the vice-admiralty courts in America made it inevitable that their jurisdiction should be challenged in other quarters than the proprieties, particularly in the field of the common law. This challenge was in part due to the fact that at no time was this jurisdiction clearly and succinctly defined. Even the Board of Trade had to ask Northey in 1702 if he would not say whether the new vice-admiralty courts really had a wider authority than "was allowed of or usually exercised in England" and what that authority was; "whether it included breaches of the acts of trade and whether trials of ships seized sailing upon a river in the plantations should be tried in courts of vice-admiralty or in the courts of the common law," referring of course to the Quary-Penn controversy, which was the first real test of the new situation. If the Board of Trade did not know the answers to these questions six years after the act of 1696 had been passed, it was hardly to be expected that anyone in the colonies should be better informed. Jury trial was already well established and not unnaturally the colonists, who were enjoying the "benefit of the common law, which is every Englishman's birthright," would resent and resist the invasion of civil law courts and procedure, where formerly the common law had reigned supreme, and question when they could the validity of the new system.

But the decisions of the crown lawyers, though not entirely clearing up the obscurities of the act of 1696, did affirm the right of the vice-admiralty courts to exist and to have concurrent jurisdiction with the courts of common law, and after 1704 it was generally recognized that breaches of the acts of trade could be tried in vice-admiralty courts without juries. At the same time concurrency of jurisdiction was more or less of a reality during the colonial period and common law courts did deal with some of these matters in first instance, though just why this was done it is not always easy to determine. Nevertheless, as far as we know, the jurisdiction of the common law courts to try cases that were cognizable also in the vice-admiralty courts was never questioned by the attorneys for the defendants in a suit.

Notwithstanding this fact the historic quarrel that had been going on for a century between the two jurisdictions in England found its counterpart in America, though the form that it took was more often one of amicable adjustment than of angry dispute. The powerful attack in England by Sir Edward Coke and later common law lawyers was actuated partly by hostility to a foreign, that is, a civil law procedure, and partly by a desire to increase the power of the common law courts, with their attendant enlargement of emoluments and fees. This deliberate attempt to break the power of a rival jurisdiction was never identically repeated in America, except possibly in Massachusetts. The combined influence of parliamentary statutes, the decisions of the crown lawyers, the authority conferred in the commissions to the judges, and the distrust of colonial juries felt by the custom house officials, who were as a rule the informers and libelants in fraud cases (no one of which factors obtained in England), strengthened the vice-admiralty jurisdiction in America and gave to it a virility and security that continued scarcely impaired throughout the period.

But this position was not won without a struggle. The common law courts had their champions and the jurisdiction of the vice-admiralty courts was very frequently called in question. Roger Mompesson, himself later a judge of vice-admiralty in New York, wrote in 1699, while still in England, a paper on admiralty jurisdiction in the colonies, which is an ardent plea for the employment of the common law jury. He believed that the intent and meaning of the lawmakers was that all cases of illegal trading, whether in the vice-admiralty or the common law courts, should be tried by juries ("else that clause [in the act of 1696] is wholly void and ineffectual"). He took the common law ground that "where a thing is done partly on the sea and partly in a river the common law shall have jurisdiction" and denied vehemently that the Admiralty, either at home or in the plantations, could meddle with anything "done or transacted Infra Corpore Comitatus either on the land or any stream or water where a man may see the land on each side or from one side to the other." He agreed that in certain specific cases the rule might be relaxed, and was in accord with Northey and Cooke that once a case was on trial in a vice-admiralty court neither the procedure nor the decree, no matter how faulty, could be inquired into or punished by the common law courts, and that a reversal of judgment could be obtained only from the court of appeal in England. Many of these and other points were so seriously disputed by the vice-admiralty officials in the colonies that in 1720, Richard West, a common law lawyer and the standing counsel for the Board of Trade, believed that the only remedy for the situation lay in the passage of an act of parliament, establishing and reducing to a certainty the exercise of the vice-admiralty jurisdiction. But this was never done and the dispute was allowed to go its own way to a final adjustment. It is significant to note how many times the government was advised by one person or another—West, Penrice, Abercromby, Bollan—to put its colonial house in order, through the intervention of parliament, in the half century before Thomas Pownall wrote his treatise on the administration of the colonies, and how regularly this advice was ignored and nothing whatever attempted in the way of betterment, until after 1763 when financial conditions drove the government to action. No one in particular was to blame. The Privy Council was losing its vigor, the departments of the Treasury and the Admiralty were inefficient and indifferent, the Board of Trade had no authority, there was a severe financial depression in the years from 1761 to 1764 and business was in a bad way, and parliament, not interested in the colonies, was notoriously unwilling in any way to strengthen the power of the prerogative, as it would have done had it passed a law invigorating the vice-admiralty jurisdiction in America. Any thoroughgoing reform was too big a problem for the executive members of the government to face, even if they had thought it necessary, which they did not. They could see defects but were powerless to discover remedies, because they did not think it wise to tamper with things as they were. They preferred that the world should stay just as it was and would not admit the need of a change even when such need was placed before their eyes. It was a true "Bourbon" attitude.

In certain classes of vice-admiralty cases, the question of jurisdiction was always raised by the defendant at the opening of the trial and as regularly overruled by the judge. We know of no instance where the latter admitted the defendant's plea to the jurisdiction, so that this step in the proceedings must have been largely a matter of form. The judge often recognized that there were offenses not properly within the cognizance of the admiralty and of his own accord turned them over to the common law courts. As, for instance, when a seaman having libeled master or mate for assault or injury was informed by the judge, who imposed a fine upon the defendants, that he (the seaman) would have to sue in the common law courts for his damages; or when a captain, whose vessel had been seized illegally as a prize and the charge dismissed, would be told that he might sue for damages in the common law court; or again when an owner given possession of his sloop, as against the master who refused to let him have it, was informed that he must sue at common law for the boat's earnings. Thus there was a more or less complete understanding in these cases and in others of a similar character as to where the line was to be drawn between the two jurisdictions.

A writ of prohibition was usually issued by the judge of a superior court in a colony, but in Rhode Island it was granted a number of times by the governor and council or by the governor alone. It was made use of whenever the judge, on application by the reclaimant, believed that the cause of the action lay outside the competence of the vice-admiralty court and was concerned with the land and not with the sea, or whenever he was convinced that the proceedings were being conducted in an unfair and unreasonable manner. Sometimes the writ would be refused, as was the case once in Boston in 1717, when an applicant was unable to obtain a prohibition, and again in Rhode Island, March 23, 1733, when the judge of the superior court of judicature, being moved for a prohibition to stay proceedings in the vice-admiralty court at Newport, declared that he did "not see cause to grant any prohibition." Sometimes it would be ignored by the vice-admiralty, should the admiralty be strong and the common law weak. But as a rule it was obeyed, for in nearly all the colonies the common law courts were the more powerful of the two and in Massachusetts were not only powerful but independent and self-assertive also.

The issue of the first writ, which might also be the last, was as a rule in answer to a petition of the reclaimant, with the libel as evidence, and usually followed the refusal by the judge of vice-admiralty to rule in favor of the defendant's plea to the jurisdiction. Should this first writ not satisfy the reclaimant, the judges of the superior court might order the advocates on both sides to appear before them and argue the case on its merits from the point of view of law, as the result of which either the writ would be sustained and made final and peremptory, stopping the proceedings in the vice-admiralty court, or a writ of consultation would be issued, which vacated the prohibition and ordered the vice-admiralty court to proceed. No writ of consultation could be issued when once the prohibition had been made permanent. The latter was couched in simple language, which "avoided the prolixity and cumbrousness of the English courts, too unwieldy in times of emergency and stress." The cases that called out a prohibition were, more commonly, those that concerned the Wool Act;[1] drift whales; masters' wages; contracts made on land; seizure of a vessel by a collector or of a prize by a captain of the royal navy "on shore," a term capable of many meanings; responsibility of owners for a master's actions at sea; an exorbitant fine; or an undue prolongation of the proceedings. Certain writs were but temporary, issued in case the judge of vice-admiralty refused to postpone proceedings, at the request of the reclaimant, in order to allow absent parties to return or until certain conditions had been fulfilled. More often, however, they were intended to be permanent, bringing proceedings to an end, and either staying the execution of the sentence or forbidding the distribution of the forfeitures received from the sale of a vessel. Atwood of New York once took a case out of the vice-admiralty court and ordered the judge, if he had pronounced his decree, to revoke it; and on one occasion a judge in West Florida issued a prohibition after sentence had been delivered and an appeal taken.[2] Prohibitions were available for a great variety of

1. *Calendar State Papers, Colonial,* 1720-1721, §153, i (1717).

2. Letter from Chief Justice William Clifton to Governor Peter Chester, August 30, 1774, defending himself from the charge that he had wrongfully issued a prohibition after sentence had been pronounced and an appeal granted, and citing authorities to show that a prohibition might issue as well after as before sentence was pronounced. Mississippi Provincial Archives, English Dominion, VI, 339-350. I am indebted to Dr. Cecil Johnson, of the University of North Carolina, for this reference. There is a North Carolina case of August, 1712, where in reply to a petition for a rehearsing of a verdict of condemnation, the common law court issued an injunction or inhibition stopping further proceedings until a review should be had before delegates appointed in the province by a court of chancery "pursuant to law," North Carolina, Early Wills, Raleigh.

uses, and a thorough analysis of the circumstances under which they were issued and of the ends which they were designed to serve would go far to elucidate one very important aspect of the history of the common law in America.

The writ was made use of probably in all the colonies at one time or another, but we have no certain evidence of its exercise in Maryland, Virginia, and Antigua. Of the other colonies illustrations are few from Bermuda and Barbados. But in Massachusetts, Rhode Island, New York, Pennsylvania, and the two Carolinas, prohibitions were frequently employed, with Pennsylvania offering almost no instances after 1727, when occurred the case of the *Sarah* seized at New Castle for illegal trading and that of the *Phoenix* in the same year. The conflict between the two jurisdictions reaches its highest point of belligerency in Massachusetts, as might have been expected, for there the enmity of the provincials for all royal officials and institutions was of long standing, and had been increased and deepened by the activities of Edward Randolph and the administration of Andros. There too the local common law courts had attained a position of great strength and assurance and, until the advent of the vice-admiralty court and its procedure under the civil law, had completely controlled the exercise of justice in the colony. Massachusetts fought long and hard for juries and the common law, and in no colony was the use of the writ so frequent or the complaints of the judges of vice-admiralty so bitter as in this old Puritan commonwealth.[1]

The conflict began as early as 1705–1706, with a sharp difference of opinion regarding the right of the vice-admiralty to entertain trials between whale fishermen and to determine the disposal of drift whales. So often had the common law judges drawn these cases to themselves that in 1710, when a drift whale was cast upon the beach at Barnstable, Byfield made a stand and ordered John Otis, the deputy judge, to deal with the matter at a session of the vice-admiralty court at Boston, February 10, 1711. He considered the question one of great importance and was prepared to make a fight of it. But equally determined was the common law. Immediately the judge of

1. In Williams and Bruce, *A Treatise on the Jurisdiction and Practice of the English Courts in Admiralty Actions,* 3d ed., 1902, p. 5, note 1, the following extract is quoted from the journal of the House of Representatives of Massachusetts: Resolved that "the extension of the powers of Court of Admiralty within this province is a most violent infraction of the right of trial by juries; a right which the House upon the principles of their British ancestry hold most dear and sacred." The date is shortly before the Revolution.

the superior court issued a writ of prohibition to the sheriff of Barnstable county, staying proceedings in the vice-admiralty court and
demanding the return of the writ at a session of the superior court
to be held at Plymouth on the last Tuesday in March. Byfield went
twice to Plymouth, a distance of fifty miles, and in person presented
his plea or answer upholding the jurisdiction of his court. In so doing he probably did more harm than good, for the judge, who might
otherwise have dropped the case, finding himself with an important
decision on his hands and feeling that he needed time to consider the
pleas on both sides, postponed the hearing for a year, and then for
another year, leaving Byfield to remark on the tediousness of common law proceedings and on the great discouragement as well as
damage this usurpation by the common law was doing to his Majesty's good subjects.

Unable to accomplish anything in the province, where the circumstances showed a marked animus against the admiralty and a determination on the part of the common law judges to maintain their
position of superiority, Byfield turned to England and on July 18,
1711, sent a letter to the Admiralty with copies of all the documents.
After delaying for a year the Admiralty in its turn, August 12, 1712,
sent the papers to Dr. Warters of Doctors' Commons, asking him to
consult with Sir Charles Hedges and to report as to the best thing to
be done. Warters first recommended that an appeal be allowed, but
later, after consultation with Hedges, he accepted the latter's opinion
that as the dispute was one between private persons regarding a matter of property, it did not fall within the jurisdiction of the vice-
admiralty and so its removal could do the court no injury or diminish
its authority. Therefore, he thought it would be best to "let the event
of the contest happen as it will" and that Byfield be instructed to go
no further. Byfield, humiliated, let the matter drop and the vice-
admiralty was worsted in its first encounter.

Another case had an interesting aftermath. Menzies, Byfield's successor, exasperated at a prohibition issued in 1725, made a complaint
to the Admiralty the next year. In this complaint he introduced certain caustic remarks regarding the difficulty of obtaining justice in
the common law courts, saying that "it is a thing impossible to get a
jury in the country that will do the king justice upon these tryalls."
These words coming to the attention of Attorney General Yorke, to
whom the complaint had been sent for an opinion, led the latter to

say in his report, "for it is not to be expected that any jury in the place will condemn vessels for breach of those acts of trade whereof the benefit redounds to Old England. . . . Neither will the officers of the customs adventure to make seizures, if they be obliged to pursue to get condemnations at common law where they are sure to be cast by the juries and condemned in cost and damages." These criticisms of the common law courts in the colony became known to the members of the House of Representatives, who, manifestly sensitive to English opinion at this juncture, resented Menzies' comment as "an unjust and scandalous reflection and a very base and injurious misrepresentation of his Maties true and faithful subjects of this province" and, resolving that anyone thus guilty was undeserving of a seat in the house, they expelled him as unworthy to continue a member of the same for the future. Penrice, when this act was called to his attention, though believing that the expressions in Menzies' memorial were well founded, did not know of any proper legal method whereby Menzies might be restored to his seat in the house, and could make no other suggestion regarding him than to recommend "an handsome gratuity in consideration of his sufferings in defence of the admiralty jurisdiction."[1] Thus was the popular body in Massachusetts able to express its resentment, without fear of interference from England, because of aspersions cast by the judge of vice-admiralty upon the common law courts of the colony.

There is nothing to show that Penrice's suggestion was ever acted upon, but that Penrice was impressed with the seriousness of the situation in the colonies at large appears from his comments. "The judges at common law take all advantages of the admiralty jurisdiction in distress [referring to the fact that the profits were so low as scarcely to keep a man 'out of gaol']. They ply it hard with prohibitions and seem resolved to sink it quite; unless their Lorships come timely in with their powerfull assistance. Their powerfull and timely

1. Admiralty 1:3672, Penrice's report, May 2, 1727; *Acts Privy Council, Colonial,* 1720–1745, §101; *Journals, House of Representatives of Massachusetts,* VII, index under "Menzies."

Menzies died September 20, 1728. That he was angry at the treatment accorded him appears in the case of Rex *v.* Norton, decided only two weeks before his death. In considering the libel and the plea to the jurisdiction and the plaintiff's answer thereto, he replied, "I repell the defence as above founded on the prohibition in a former case and also I repell the other defence against the jurisdiction," and at the close of the trial condemned the vessel. He fought to the very end. Records of Admiralty, Massachusetts, III, 48.

influence may yet keep it on float and not only repair its shattered condition, but restore this antient branch of the Office of Lord High Admiral to the authority and lustre enjoyed in former days." Though Penrice's view of the vice-admiralty state in the colonies is far too pessimistic, there is no doubt that, with Menzies as with Byfield, serving the crown was a thankless task in Massachusetts, while in England the making of recommendations based on the "powerfull and timely influence of the Admiralty" was no less thankless for those who were the crown's advisers. Penrice, convinced that the Admiralty was not likely to favor any improvements in the future, as it had so often failed to do in the past, and that parliament was not likely to consider any act granting a general jurisdiction to the vice-admiralty courts in the colonies—since it would do nothing to increase the power of the prerogative anywhere—ended his report lamely with the general advice that full instructions be sent to the governors to assist, maintain, and support the vice-admiralty jurisdiction by all lawful means. The Admiralty seizing upon this recommendation memorialized the Privy Council on the ground that "the course of justice hath been very much obstructed by the interfering of the jurisdiction of the common law and that of the admiralty." But when the Board of Trade was called upon to draft such an instruction it was obliged to inform the king in council, May 11, 1730, that the governors already had an article in their instructions which covered the ground, and in a later communication to the lords justices, July 2, declared that to take from the common law courts in the plantations the power of granting prohibitions would be giving up the jurisdiction of the common law, but should such courts encroach in any particular instance upon the just rights of the admiralty courts there, then an appeal to his Majesty in council was the only remedy. And there the matter ended.[1]

1. The indignation of the English legal authorities had been aroused already by the troubles in North Carolina and the quarrel between Edmond Porter on one side and Chief Justice Gale on the other, to which attention has already been called; and by the letters from Joseph Brown, judge of vice-admiralty of Pennsylvania, who in the case of the *Sarah* complained of Governor Gordon's interfering with the proceedings of the vice-admiralty court there (*Acts Privy Council, Colonial*, III, §217; VI, §§430, 433; *Board of Trade Journal*, 1728–1734, pp. 138, 196, 294). Shortly before, in the years from 1721 to 1725, complaints from South Carolina also had created some excitement among the authorities in England. Letters were received at the Admiralty from Smith, judge of vice-admiralty, complaining of Governor Nicholson for interfering in vice-admiralty appointments and jurisdiction and charging that the judges of the court of common pleas were the governor's "never failing tools." He gave the Admiralty many

With the passage of the Molasses Act in 1733 and the more vigorous enforcement of the trade laws after 1740, the situation in Massachusetts became still more strained and the intervention of the common law courts more provocative. Governor Shirley sat as a judge in the vice-admiralty court in succession to Byfield for two sessions in 1733, after which he became advocate general, with Auchmuty as judge. Later, after he became governor in 1742, his son-in-law, William Bollan, became advocate general and served in that capacity until in 1746 he was chosen as the colony's agent in England, where he remained, though handicapped by poor health, for sixteen years. In Boston Bollan was a member of the "Shirlean faction," a group of which Otis wrote that they were "full as high in their notions of prerogative as the churchmen," and at this juncture he took upon himself to urge in the strongest terms an extension of vice-admiralty authority. In three memorials dated February 26, 1743, October 24, 1749, and June 9, 1755, he brought the matter to the attention of the Board of Trade, in the first and third of which he made "many and critical observations upon the penning of the acts of parliament," calling attention anew to their obscurity and ill-wording, and in the second spoke of the fact that smugglers had of late "escaped with impunity by reason of the doubts and contests [that had] arisen in the plantations touching the jurisdiction of the courts of admiralty." In all three papers he suggested a wider extension and a more rigid definition of vice-admiralty powers. Acting upon these memorials and upon other letters and representations from such reliable officials as Governor William Popple of Bermuda that had accumulated in the Plantation Office since 1740—"relating to the great difficulties and doubts which have occurred in the execution of the acts of trade

details of Governor Nicholson's methods of persecution. The governor, he wrote, intercepted his letters and on the strength of his complaints to the Admiralty ordered the attorney general to indict him for treasonable conduct. "This prosecution is to be carried before the Governor and judges, who are both Judges and Parties, the Governor being always on the bench in such cases, Bulleying and Roaring and Suffering nobody to speak besides himself." "The Chief Justice [he adds] is a merchant and every Master of a ship consigned to him has ten times more authority than the judge of Admiralty" (Admiralty 1:3671, Penrice's report, August 30, 1723). The papers in the case are to be found in Admiralty 1:3671. Penrice's reports are dated August 30, 1723, and June 18, 1724. The cases were brought to the attention of the Privy Council, which sent word to the governors "That at their perills they do not themselves molest or intirrupt the judges and other officers of the respective vice-admiraltys." The period was one of prolonged agitation in vice-admiralty matters and the Board of Trade prepared reports on each of the cases mentioned above.

and to the many illegal and improper practices which have been set up to evade their force"—the board brought the matter to the attention of the commissioners of the customs, in a letter written by its secretary, John Pownall, February 20, 1759. The commissioners memorialized the Treasury on May 10 of the same year, saying that they had compared the board's data with their own and desired to present a series of "observations" on both the customs system and the vice-admiralty jurisdiction in the colonies.[1] The Treasury solicitor, to whom the papers were submitted, though favorable to Bollan's recommendation that the admiralty power be increased, disclosed the official apathy of the time, when he wrote, April 5, 1759, that he had not "experienced any inconsistency from the laws as they now stand and, considering how long they have subsisted," he was apprehensive "that any attempt to alter them may be hazardous and attended with dangerous consequences not to be forseen by us." On the whole he was inclined to doubt the wisdom of Bollan's suggestions.[2] The Treasury accepted the solicitor's report but took no action either at that time or two years later when Governor Bernard supplemented Bollan's report, in a letter of August 6, 1761, containing an account of several actions brought in the courts of common law, tending to set aside the jurisdiction of the vice-admiralty court and the officers of the crown in Massachusetts.[3]

But two years later, as an inevitable part of the reorganization of the customs service which was undertaken in 1763, the jurisdiction and powers of the vice-admiralty courts in the colonies came under inspection and on October 4 of that year the Treasury, examining anew the commissioners' report of 1759, memorialized the Privy Council advocating, among other things, a uniform plan for estab-

1. Treasury 1:392; C. O. 323:12, O, 61.

2. The solicitor added, "In obedience to your minute we have perused the enclosed papers. That marked No. 4, being Mr. Bollan's letter dated the 26th of February, 1742, represents the great inconveniences that prosecutions are liable to in the plantations by trials by juries in the courts of common law, which he proposes to be remedied by a more extensive and general power to the courts of admiralty. And as a further cheque to any illicit trade—he proposes that actions should be brought to recover the value where the goods themselves were carried off and have not been seized. The expediency of the first part of this proposal we are not proper judges of, and must therefore submit it. The latter experiment may be tried, but it is conceived such prosecution must be commenced within one year after the offence, if prosecuted by a Qui tam action, and within three years, if prosecuted by the king's advocate for the use of the crown only."

3. *Board of Trade Journal,* 1759–1763, pp. 225, 226; *Barrington-Bernard Correspondence,* pp. 30–33.

lishing the judicature of the courts of vice-admiralty in the colonies on a more certain foundation that justice in all cases might be diligently and impartially administered and such regulations as parliament thought proper to make might be duly carried into execution. The recommendation was approved, October 5, and the secretary of state, the Admiralty, and the Board of Trade were instructed to draw up a plan. The government, hitherto seemingly indifferent, had suddenly become alive to the weakness of the entire customs service procedure and vice-admiralty jurisdiction in the colonies and was determined that nothing should be left undone that would prevent smuggling in the future and increase the revenue of the crown from America.[1]

In response to the order of the Privy Council, the combined authorities prepared a plan, which was sent in the form of a memorial to the king from the Admiralty, March, 1764, recommending the appointment of a single judge of vice-admiralty for all North America, who was to have a concurrency of jurisdiction with the several judges of the vice-admiralty courts already existing in each district, but without power to hear appeals.[2] The memorial was referred to the Treasury, which on April 7 wrote a letter to the Privy Council expressing its approval. The latter, on the 16th, turned the memorial over to its committee for report. The committee also approved. In the meantime, parliament, in anticipation, included in the Sugar Act of 1764 (April 7) a clause which enacted that all penalties and forfeitures suable in any court of record or court of admiralty in the colonies might be recovered in any of these courts at the option of the prosecutor.[3] With the way thus prepared and after a further consideration regarding details, the plan was referred to the attorney gen-

1. That an increase of revenue from the colonies was very much in the mind of the authorities in England at this time appears from a report made in 1766 by the Board of Trade, replying to protests from Charles Garth, agent of South Carolina, regarding captains of the royal navy interfering with the coasting trade of that colony. The board expressed its sympathy but said that "the propriety of what is proposed as a remedy does depend upon the effect it will have upon the revenue" (*Board of Trade Journal,* 1764–1767, p. 247). Commercial legislation after 1763 had as its object the saving and increase of revenue to the crown much more than it had advancing the interests of the merchant capitalists of England. Elisha Williams noticed this as early as 1750, when he wrote Governor Law on two occasions that the chief object of the ministry was to save money, *Law Papers,* III, 362, 375.

2. *Acts Privy Council, Colonial,* IV, §546.

3. 4 George III, c. 15, §xli. This clause is repeated in the Stamp Act, 5 George III, c. 12, §lvii. Its intents were carried out in the act of George III, c. 22, one of the Townshend Acts.

eral, with the query as to whether the Admiralty had the power to erect such a court, leaving the existing vice-admiralty courts to continue exercising their functions as before.[1] The answer was in the affirmative. Letters patent were then issued, the Earl of Northumberland was appointed vice-admiral and Dr. Spry was named judge, commissary deputy, and surrogate. Spry gave up his position in England and entered upon the appointment, removing with his family to Halifax, where the new court was actually set up.[2]

But the troubles arising out of the Stamp Act brought the experiment to an end. Spry's commission was revoked and he was later given a post as governor of Barbados, where he died in office in 1772. A new plan was decided on, for there was no thought of stopping at this point. The Treasury officials were not impressed with the complaint frequently voiced in the colonies that the courts of vice-admiralty were infringing on English liberty by taking away trials by jury, a matter apparently referred to in the Declaration of Independence, for they were convinced and had been convinced for a long time that there was no safety in trusting a breach of revenue laws to a jury of the country where the offense was committed. But they were interested in the further complaint that the location of the court at Halifax was such as to take people for trial from one end of the continent almost to the other. To remedy this grievance they determined to constitute "a sufficient number of such courts of vice-admiralty at proper and convenient places within the said colonies and plantations" and recommended to the king, July 4, 1765, that the court "now established at Halifax" be removed to Boston and that two other courts be established, one at Philadelphia and the other at Charles Town, to be presided over by judges extraordinary, trained at Doctors' Commons, with a salary each of £800 a year—the amount allotted to the judge at Halifax by the arrangement of 1764—a sum reduced afterward to £600. These salaries were to be met out of the fines and forfeitures, but should those prove insufficient then out of the monies arising from the sale of "old naval stores," and the judges were to be forbidden to take any fee or gratuity whatever for judgments given or business done in their respective courts.

But for reasons that are not entirely clear, a change was made in this arrangement, as far as the removal of the court from Halifax to Boston was concerned. One of the Townshend Acts of 1767 (8

1. Treasury 7:299, p. 31.
2. *Acts Privy Council, Colonial,* IV, §546.

George III, c. 22) was passed "For the more easy and effectual Recovery of the Penalties and Forfeitures inflicted by the Acts of Parliament relating to the Trade or Revenues of the British Colonies and Plantations in America," and under that act four courts were established with complements of officials at Halifax, Boston, Philadelphia, and Charles Town, with jurisdiction, both original and appellate, within certain defined areas.[1] The older courts remained as before, but further right of appeal to England was forbidden, as the new courts were to act as courts of last resort. Thus control over all vice-admiralty causes in the colonies was finally centered in America and a new arrangement entered into similar to that which was effected for the customs service by the establishment of the American Board of Customs Commissioners sitting at Boston. Both arrangements marked for the colonies, at least in part, that setting of the colonial house in order which had been under agitation in unofficial circles for fifty years. They represented a drawing together more vigorously than ever before of the British bonds of control, in the interest particularly of the revenue, at a time when the colonies themselves were feeling the urge for greater freedom and an overmastering determination to govern themselves; and they show an equal determination on the part of the British government to enforce at any cost and by every means in its power the dependence of the colonies upon the authority of crown and parliament.

1. The reception of the new courts in America can be inferred from the following excerpt taken from a document in private hands. "To the Merchants and other Inhabitants of the City of Philadelphia—The Affair of the Tea which has of late engrossed the Attention of the Public being now settled to the satisfaction of Friends of Ameruca . . . A Cause is now depending in this City before Jared Ingersoll, Esq., sole judge of a new and unconstitutional Court of Vice Admiralty for the Middle Colonies . . . A Market-Boat plying between this City and New Castle County . . . as seisd by the Custom House Boat," etc. (Probably written by Timothy Matlack of Philadelphia, one of the shining lights of the ultra or "yellow" Whigs, or "red republicans" as they were called, who helped to draft the Pennsylvania constitution of 1776 and defended it with great acrimony.) Ingersoll was eligible for appointment because nothing is said in the Treasury representation of July 4, 1765, or in that of July 2, 1768, of the earlier requirement that the judges be from Doctors' Commons.

# CHAPTER IX

## THE ORIGIN AND WORK OF THE BOARD OF TRADE

GATHERING together once more the threads of our narrative, which in an earlier chapter we were obliged to drop for the time being in order to consider the acts of navigation and trade, the customs service, and the vice-admiralty courts, we are now able to resume our inquiry into the history and operation of the administrative agencies that England provided for the regulation of trade and the oversight of the plantations. These agencies are equally with the colonies themselves a part of colonial history, for over and over again they determined the way the colonies should be administered by those in whose hands was placed the requisite authority. In preserving English traditions, influencing the operations of government, and shaping the decisions of those high in office, many of the men who composed them, though sometimes in the background and relatively inconspicuous, played more important parts even than kings and statesmen. The secretaries of such executive boards as the Treasury and the Admiralty, the secretaries and clerks of such advisory bodies as the Lords of Trade and the Board of Trade, and the legal consultants and counsellors at law were the ones frequently responsible for the preservation of existing policies and the inception of new ones. How far the Plantation Office and its corps of secretaries and clerks operated to this end the following pages will show.

During the period from 1675 to 1696 the immediate oversight of the colonies was in the hands of a committee of the Privy Council, known as the Lords of Trade. With the characteristic fervor of a new body, the members of this committee took up their duties, during the first few years, with a high regard for the best interest, as they saw it, of England and the colonies. They were responsible for many important constitutional measures and laid down some notable definitions of colonial policy. Their scene of action was the council chamber in the Cockpit, with the Plantation Office located in that part of the palace of Whitehall known as Scotland Yard, under the efficient management of Sir Robert Southwell and William Blathwayt,[1] and there they applied themselves, with a considerable measure of success, to the problems of a growing and expanding kingdom. Though domestic conditions were distracting—what with plottings and the rumbles of revolution—they did the best they could and, certainly during the first decade, performed their work with energy and despatch.

The membership of the committee was largely political, made up for the most part of men of rank, and though the matters discussed at their meetings included home and foreign affairs as well as colonial, they were able to do much in the way of consolidating the colonies and laying the foundations upon which their successors were to build. They endeavored, as we have already seen, to strengthen the customs service in America and to bring about a more orderly and successful execution of the acts of trade. They kept in close touch with the governors of the colonies and sought, ineffectively often, to hold them and other royal officials overseas to a strict accountability for failure to observe the royal commands. They committed themselves to the principle of a more unified and centralized system of royal control and to the policy, never perfected, of reducing the private colonies to a nearer dependence on the crown. Though they were not able to prevent the erection of a new proprietary colony under Penn, they did bring about the annulment of the charters of Bermuda and Massachusetts Bay and made it abundantly clear that for the future the home government intended to decrease not increase the number of chartered colonies in America.

The Revolution of 1689 was disastrous rather than otherwise to this policy of a strong, centralized control of colonial affairs, for it tended to increase the authority of parliament at the expense of the crown. King William resisted this tendency to the end of his reign. He was not, however, interested in the colonies or in England's commercial welfare and possessing as he did a highly developed sense of his own prerogative he was not inclined to delegate authority to others or to draw about him men of independence either in thought or action. He continued to maintain a personal control over the many activities of the executive departments, and would have repudiated the idea,

1. Blathwayt at this time was a clerk of the Privy Council in attendance on the Lords of Trade.

later expressed by historians of the Revolution, that a Whig or constitutional parliament was starving the crown in order to make it dependent on the will of the representatives of the people. Such an interpretation of what happened in 1689 is, says Dr. Shaw, "simply moonshine." The situation shows that the whole governmental situation was in a state of transition, neither king nor parliament entirely in command, the king still influencing estimates and expenditures, with parliament beginning to realize the necessity of taking a hand in revising the whole matter of the revenue. Bad as conditions were in peace time, they were thrown into a worse state by the war with France which began in 1689. Confusion was bound to result from the effort of parliament to invade the domain of the royal prerogative not only in respect of the finances but of other governmental interests as well. The England of the last decade of the seventeenth century was a house divided against itself.[1]

In the effort to restore the vigor of the Privy Council as an executive and deliberative body in all that related to trade and the plantations, William's predecessor, James II, had broken in upon the organization of the Lords of Trade as a specially commissioned standing committee and had permitted other members of the council to attend its meetings and take part in its proceedings. This transformation of the Lords of Trade into what was in effect the whole council acting as committee was legalized by the issue of an order, January 27, 1688, appointing the whole council "a standing committee for Trade and Plantations." William, in the interest of his prerogative, continued the practice after 1689[2] and presented to the committee such a multiplicity of affairs to look after, connected with the domestic and foreign concerns of the kingdom, that inevitably commerce and the colonies suffered from neglect. What was anybody's business was nobody's business. During this period of seven years the committee was none too efficient nor were its members any too regular

1. *Calendar Treasury Books*, IX, lxxxv. Regarding the influence of the Revolution of 1689 on the control of estimates and budgets, see *ibid.*, cxiii–cxiv.

2. The committee appointed in 1689 was of the whole council (*Acts Privy Council, Colonial*, II, §275). Mulgrave said that the Lords of Trade in 1692 were the same (*Calendar State Papers, Domestic*, 1691–1692, p. 544). The "committee on appeals" appointed in 1696 was also a committee made up of the whole council (*Acts Privy Council, Colonial*, preface vi–x, §657). The presumption is, therefore, that after 1689 and until 1696, whatever it may have been legally, the Lords of Trade ceased to be a specially commissioned standing committee and became simply the whole council acting as committee.

in attendance. In consequence business of prime importance was either neglected or looked after with exasperating delays. After 1689 the members were largely new men, of narrower vision than their predecessors and of conflicting opinions, and their factional disputes stultified the entire administration of the day.[1] Treasury, Admiralty, and Navy Board—never too amiable in their relations with one another—seemed more than ever powerless to meet emergencies and to protect commerce and the merchants. During the war complaints of losses on the part of the great joint-stock companies and of those trading to the colonies were so frequent and the losses so disastrous as to bring about an inquiry by the House of Lords into the whole administration of naval affairs.[2]

This inquiry disclosed one important fact: the number of ships available for the protection of English commerce during a time of war was dangerously inadequate and the losses of ships in every direction were terrifying. The total estimate of destruction for the year 1694–1695 was more than two million pounds sterling, a result largely due to the inability of the Admiralty to furnish convoys and the necessity under which the merchants stood of risking a voyage without protection. "We have several times applied ourselves to the Admiralty for relief," said the Barbados merchants; "sometimes we had some, and other times [it] was answered they had no ships, which made several sit down with those heavy burdens on their shoulders, and some have sunk under, not being able to bear them. And we most humbly pray that your honours will take our miseries and losses into consideration and give us some better prospect of security for the future, that we may have some encouragement to adventure our little estates."[3] Even when convoys were provided, they

1. John Evelyn said that the members of the Privy Council after 1689 were possessed of a "republican spirit" (*Diary*, Bray ed., II, 11) and we know that in the change of membership men of inferior ability and far less conscientious motives were appointed. Evelyn's reaction to the times was one of pessimism. "How strangely negligent and remiss were we in preparing a timely and efficient fleet." He charged the Admiralty with putting gentlemen commanders over experienced seamen, characterized by "ignorance, effeminancy, and insolence," with the result that losses occurred which were due to negligence and to unskilful men governing the fleet and the Navy Board, while the relations between the Admiralty and the Navy Board were characterized by "tyranny and incompetency." *Ibid.*, II, 12, 19, 20, 28.

2. *House of Lords Manuscripts*, new series, II, 959; Stock, *Debates*, II, 136–150. Notice also the circumstances attending the sending over of Sloughter as governor of New York, above, Vol. III, 128, note 1.

3. *House of Lords Manuscripts*, new series, II, 77.

often sailed so late that the merchant fleets were delayed from three to five months beyond the proper time, and the traders either lost a good market or ran into the hurricanes with the risk of damage or shipwreck. One is not surprised that many a merchant preferred to take the chance of sailing alone at the proper time, armed with his guns[1] and a Mediterranean pass.[2]

But losses at the hands of the French and the prowling pirates of the Mediterranean and the Atlantic were not the only result of the aimless state into which departmental administration had fallen. As men read the reports from America, they saw, or thought they saw, illegal trade increasing enormously, and they were beginning to realize that the few frigates which the Admiralty was able to provide were hopelessly unequal to the task of guarding the long stretches of coast line of the American continent, to say nothing of the islands of the Caribbean. Piracy throve on the situation and the boldness and lawlessness of such freebooters as Sharp, Blackledge, Every, and the buccaneers during this decade and of Kidd, Quelch, Archer, Phillips, and Blackbeard later were to no small extent due to the inability of the English navy to patrol the seas.

How helpless the navy was when confronted with expeditions demanding promptitude and united action can be seen in the various attempts of the period to send reinforcements to America. One of these, which received the king's approval, April 26, 1689, got to sea March 8, 1690, after ten months of "preparation."[3] It accomplished nothing. Another, despatched in December, 1691, had no better success. Both were deficient in number of ships, quality of equipment, and complements of men. A third, under Sir Francis Wheler, sent to destroy the enemy threatening the Newfoundland fishery and to overwhelm the forces in the West Indies, reached Barbados three months late and returned to England in so reduced a state that there were scarcely enough men to man the ships. Most amazing of all were the expeditions sent in 1694 and 1695 to reinforce the garrison of New York and to relieve Jamaica. The first of these took from May to

1. All of the merchant ships of this period carried guns, sometimes as many as forty.

2. We read of the Mediterranean pass, guaranteeing protection against the Algerines, as early as 1663 (*Memoirs of the Duke of York*, pp. 41–43). The first treaty with Algiers was made in 1662. Other treaties continued to be made until 1765. All the colonies used these passes.

3. Neeser, "British Naval Operations in the West Indies, 1650–1700," United States Naval Institute *Proceedings*, November–December, 1914, pp. 1612–1615.

August, 1694, just to get started, and arrived in New York in June, 1695. The second, authorized August 3, 1694—and in order to have arrived in time should have started in October—got under way the following January. The commanders quarreled over prize money and though sundry operations were carried out and some successes obtained, the venture was a failure as far as its main purpose was concerned. A supplemental effort in December, 1696, added neither glory nor credit, and another at the beginning of 1697 arrived too late to be of service. Happily the peace of Ryswyck brought to an end these exhibitions of incompetence and gave to England a brief respite. During the next eight years, when piracy drew within its evil folds sailors out of employment, men of the plantations, and even officers of the navy, four expeditions were sent out, but "like their predecessors, one and all, failed signally to accomplish their purpose and after repeated disgraces, disasters, and tremendous expenditures of lives and money by England the French were as formidable as ever."[1]

Explanation of these miscarriages is partly to be found in the extraordinary mortality in the West Indies, which decimated the crews, and in the great scarcity of ships by reason of the war and the want of commodities necessary for the navy, conditions which continued to prevail throughout the entire Spanish War from 1702 to 1713. It is to be found still more in the disorganized system at Whitehall and in London and the absence of any sufficient spirit of cooperation among the many departments which were responsible for the outfitting of a fleet.[2] Other evils also wrought havoc with the system. There were heavy deficits in the exchequer and waste and corruption in the conduct of business. Masters would not provide ships for transport until all arrearages had been paid; contractors would not furnish meat for the victualing office without cash down or on delivery, and timber merchants refused to furnish the required materials until their terms had been met. The Treasury, pursuing a hand-to-mouth policy, borrowed wherever it could of almost any person or corporation that would loan money on the security of in-

---

1. *Ibid.*, p. 1662.

2. There was great confusion in the Transport Office during these wars, largely owing to the want of money. The War Office blamed the commissioners of transport, the latter blamed the Treasury, and the Treasury blamed the exchequer. The history of the situation can be followed in the *Calendar of Treasury Papers,* 1557–1696, in the War Office papers, and in Additional Manuscripts, 9729.

coming taxes, and in default of cash met its debts in tallies or promises to pay, secured on future receipts from excise, customs, tenths, and a variety of other revenues, and therefore liable, in circulation, to a heavy discount. The Duke of Marlborough once offered to advance the money to pay "the Blenheim debt," if the government would give him tin tallies, payable seven years or more later.[1] It was a time when all payments were delayed, when some of the nation's earlier creditors were not paid at all, when seamen in the navy and their wives became riotous in their poverty, and when employes in minor offices and laborers on the works received their due only after long and persistent effort.[2] Financial temptation confronted everyone in political office and governmental employment. Dishonesty in the form of bribery and corruption, embezzlement in high places and petty stealing in low, and cheating the government as a justifiable pastime widely prevailed and were more difficult of detection than were treasury deficits. Uncertain payments made wages and salaries insecure, and yet men had to live.

Though jobbery and graft in one form or another was an accepted evil of the day and served a certain purpose in easing the financial situation, they seemed to be particularly identified with the building and equipping of ships. An amazing amount of indifference and carelessness accompanied the letting of naval contracts, the inspection of ship timber, the conduct of the naval yards, and the administration of the royal forests. Opportunities for loot and plunder were to be met with in all stages of ship construction and temptation assailed every man in the business, from the shipwright and contractor to the teamster and the laborer in the yards. While it is probable that there was much exaggeration and fault-finding on the part of the

1. Historical Manuscripts Commission, *Portland*, X, 144–145. On this subject of finance and the coinage one should consult Dr. Shaw's prefaces to the *Calendar of Treasury Books*, IX, X, and examine the text also. The editor speaks of the "hopeless muddle" of the Treasury methods and can use such words as "tangled," "unguided," and "purposeless" to characterize the situation. The merchants complained bitterly of the great difficulties that lay upon trade not only because of the scarcity but also because of the "badness of the money," *ibid.*, X, 1193.

2. *Calendar State Papers, Colonial*, 1699, §585 (clerks of the Board of Trade); *Calendar Treasury Books*, IX, 209 (shipwrights at Woolwich); 278–279 (workmen and tradesmen); 359 (servants); 920 (clerks in the postoffice); 1144 (owners of hired ships, etc.). For the postmen and others, Andrews, *Guide*, I, 92, note 2. The Treasury records of the years 1689–1692 twice mention "His Majesty's pressing occasions" (IX, 403, 1546). In 1690 the commissioners for prizes certified to the Treasury that they had "no money and little prospect of any to pay debts incurred." *Ibid.*, pp. 949–950.

writers of contemporary memorials, petitions, and pamphlets, yet one cannot doubt the fact that there must have been an immense amount of thievery going on in places high and low and that manipulation in the interest of private gain must have been the rule rather than the exception.[1] Officials were quite ready to throw the blame wherever they could, upon epidemics, hurricanes, and storms at sea, upon deserting sailors and quarrelsome captains, upon piracy, smuggling and Scottish trade with the colonies, or upon anything else that offered a convenient pretext to explain the decay of trade and the loss of revenue. The fact remains, however, that behind all these secondary causes existed the deplorable state of the coinage, the great scarcity of money, the clumsy system of administration, the irresponsibility and greed of public officials, the dissensions among the departments and boards, and the failure on the part of those in office to exhibit any high sense of duty to the nation at large.

King William was frequently absent from England during these years after 1689 and the ultimate oversight of affairs rested with the lords justices and the Privy Council. The latter, in the person of the members of the Lords of Trade, had charge of trade and plantations and could issue its orders as it pleased and to whom it pleased. The inefficiency of these men was becoming something of a scandal. As early as 1692 the Earl of Mulgrave, a not impartial observer but an honest critic,[2] presented to the king a memorandum, in which he commented on the prevailing disregard of business by government officials and privy councillors and recommended the appointment of a select body of advisers as a standing committee for the plantations, of such a kind as would attend to their duties, meeting on fixed days and not intermittently at the pleasure and humor of a presiding officer.[3] It was evident to others as well, who were not making a profit out of the situation, that the Lords of Trade had ceased to perform any useful function.

1. Albion, *Forests and Sea Power*, pp. 47–55, 72–89. See also Note at the end of this chapter.

2. John Sheffield, third earl of Mulgrave, lord chamberlain and a member of the Privy Council under James II. He was a grandson of Lionel Cranfield (see Vol. I, index). There is an account of him in the *Dictionary of National Biography*.

3. Mulgrave in his "Memorandum" said to the king that "neither of the committees will signify anything unless you tell them solemnly at your going to Flanders that you expect exact attention at these committees and that you have ordered the clerks to write in a book the names of those who shall fail any day to come."

"If Mr. Povy give a constant weekly account to Mr. Blathwayt of all that passes at

What the pamphleteers of the period thought upon the subject is exceedingly important for our purpose, for the pressure of mercantilist opinion was, in part at least, responsible for the establishment of the Board of Trade. For many years a few contemporary writers had been viewing with disfavor certain provisions of the navigation acts and practically all of them were now becoming exasperated because of the incapacity and bias of the men in office. Roger Coke, writing in 1668, at the time of the reëstablishment of the earlier council of trade, criticized even that body, because it had been created by royal fiat and not by act of parliament, and he would have liked to see its duties extended to include advice and assistance to the king in all treaties with other princes and powers, wherein trade was concerned.[1] In 1673, while the Shaftesbury council was still functioning, Carew Reynel wrote, "It were well that there were a committee of trade, being mixt with the chief able merchants that understand trade and to continue always; who still should be on the discovery and study for the improvement of trade; so should we have trade brought more to a general benefit, and we may come to understand it is the best interest we have."[2] Dalby Thomas in 1690 wished that there might be "a great councill of trade to consist of members elected and deputed by every plantation, maritime city, company, constitution and trade, which would desire to send members to it. And from thence after a free and full examination [their recommendations might] be represented to both houses of parliament for their approbation or distaste."[3] Thomas wrote in the interest of the sugar plan-

the Committee of Plantations, in your absence, it may be seen by you. But, however, it will be some kind of obligation on that committee to look after their business." He makes the same recommendation for the Admiralty, suggesting fixed days of meeting for that board and for all committees.

He makes a strong plea for a standing committee of the Privy Council, such as existed before 1689, because he does not like a committee of "all the Council" such as was then in being (1692), "everybody's business [being] nobody's business." He speaks indignantly of the "indecent disorder there, inconsistent with the doing of business in so solemn a place." He also recommends that meetings be held in the morning, "as early as men can be persuaded to rise," evidently having little confidence in meetings held later in the day, and raising the query whether men would finish their business if dinner was in prospect and whether some might not come in a condition unfit for the work to be done. *Calendar State Papers, Domestic,* 1691–1692, pp. 543–544.

1. Coke, *A Discourse of Trade* (1670), p. 66. Written in 1668. For a reference to the council of 1668, above p. 57, and for a fuller account, Andrews, *Committees,* pp. 87–90.

2. *The True English Benefit, or an Account of the Chief National Improvement* (London, 1674). This work was licensed, September 5, 1673.

3. Dalby Thomas, *An Historical Account of the Rise and Growth of the West In-*

tations and against the sugar duty of 1685, at a time when the planters and merchants were hoping for relief, and he wanted that such duties should be imposed only on the advice of a body of men properly equipped with expert knowledge. He wanted an "Able, diligent, impartial and constant sitting councill," for, as he said, it was "allmost impossible for the Privy Council or committee of parliament, in the method they proceed by, even to inform themselves rightly if any one difficult matter comes before them." He considered it impossible for "noblemen and gentlemen by short debates partially managed, as they usually are before them, ever to arrive to a perfect understanding of the matter in question," and he proposed "a councill of trade by act of parliament . . . no judgment of theirs to be final but subject to review by Privy Council or Parliament."

Sir William Petty proposed a council of trade and plantations "to give his Majesty advice and information concerning husbandry, buildings, manufactures, money, navigation, foreign commerce, American colonies, and the like," two hundred in number, and to this overelaborated list of duties he later added land and water carriage, the enforcement of customs duties and excise, and the determining of the balance of trade,[1] a very impracticable suggestion from one of the shrewdest economists of his time. Sir Josiah Child in the second edition of his *Discourse* proposed a council of merchants for determining controversies relating to maritime affairs and a similar council or court of merchants to decide with a jury all disputes likely to arise in matters of trade.[2] In an earlier work he had doubted whether "trading merchants" were "the best judges of trade" and thought that a mixed assembly of noblemen, gentlemen, and merchants was better for making orders, rules, and by-laws for carrying on the business.[3] In fact, there was a general agreement that merchants actively engaged in making money were ill-suited for appointment on such a council, since business men were more concerned about themselves than about the nation, were biased because of their private affairs, and were inclined to run counter to one another as their interests tended to conflict. Nicholas Barbon, in *A Discourse of Trade* in 1690, said that such men had not a true idea of trade, be-

dia Colonies and of the Great Advantage they are to England (London, 1690), pp. 7–8, 45–46.

1. *The Petty Papers*, I, 11–13, 35.  2. *Discourse about Trade* (1690), p. 23.

3. *A Treatise wherein is Demonstrated* [various things about the East India trade] (London, 1681), pp. 1–2.

cause they applied their thoughts only to particular parts of it. A few years later (1694) Sir Francis Brewster, who had been educated a merchant and had lived in America and made observations there, recommended a council of trade, but recognizing, as Barbon had done, that merchants were not the best judges of the public welfare, wished to exclude from membership all artisans, mechanics, and merchants engaged in active business. He would have a committee of trade, upon which the outports as well as London should be represented, made up of merchants at least seven years out of trade, the whole number to be nine, three of whom were to be merchants and the rest from the ministry, the Admiralty, and the customs. He would have them paid salaries and sit three times a week, with three of the number present every day to receive, examine, and prepare the agenda for the general meeting.[1] John Cary, a merchant of Bristol, who with other outport merchants carried on a lengthy correspondence in 1695 and 1696 regarding the council to be erected by parliament, was a stanch upholder of a new council to take the place of the Lords of Trade. He would have a board upon which the outports as well as London should be represented, composed of men both honest and discreet, such as would "become the wisdom of the nation," the only business of which should be "to consider the state thereof as to its trade." After outlining the duties of such a board, he said that these places should not be filled "with courtiers who knew nothing of the business," for should that happen "this excellent con-

---

1. "This hath been the common Theam by men of all understanding, on which so much is said and writ that it looks like remonstrating against the government to print more on that subject, since there seems not a tendency toward it. For this reason I thought to have passed it by, but hearing such a thing is now under consideration and having lately seen a print presenting the *Modus* of a council of Trade, I venture to put my oar in the boat, though I cannot keep stroak with any I ever yet met in this matter, differing both in the Men and Number of a Council of Trade. . . . Some there be that would have a council of trade composed of men of all qualities in trade and manufactoryes; others that are not for such a promiscuous multitude, but yet would have a great number of merchants, as believing them the best judges of trade, and as I think them to be, yet whilst are in trade not the properest directors of it" (*Essays on Trade and Navigation, in Five Parts,* Part I, all published, pp. 37–40. This work was written in 1694). A. Vickaris, in an essay written in 1695, *An Essay for Regulating the Coyn* (preface dated September 2, 1695), urged that a committee of trade should be erected to sit every week, in order to discover why trade had so much decayed and why the import of bullion and coin had so greatly fallen off.

William Paterson said at a meeting of the "Wednesday Club," "Merchants are the worst and most dangerous advisers in matters of trade," to which Mr. May replied that this was true only of "mere buyers and sellers," but not of "merchants in an extended sense." *Writings,* I, 246–247.

stitution becomes only a matter of form and expence."[1] Cary did not want a council made up either of courtiers or of Londoners, for, as he said, if it were composed of courtiers it would be only a charge to the nation, and if of Londoners, it would endeavor so to rule as to bring all trade to that great city without regard to the other ports.[2]

Charles Davenant, one of the ablest of the economists and financial experts of his day, added the weight of his own convictions to the general demand. "The ill nature of our affairs," he wrote in 1695, "seems to have disposed the nation to desire that the Legislative power would interpose in the care of Trade; and an Act of Parliament to that purpose will probably be obtained. . . . Every part of the Constitution has a great interest that a Council of Trade should be settled on the kingdome. . . . Negligence in the protection of Trade is the worst part of ill administration, because it is depriving ourselves of strength and adding it to the enemy."[3] And John Evelyn, who had been intimately connected with the earlier councils and had himself written on trade, declared in a letter to Lord Godolphin in 1696[4] that such a council should be erected composed of "sober, industrious, dexterous men, and of consummate experience *in rebus agendis";* while the author of *Considerations requiring Greater Care*

1. "I think it would be a consideration becoming the wisdom of the nation if a standing committee of trade were appointed at the charge thereof [that is, of the nation], made up of men both honest and discreet, and I doubt not such may be found, whose only business should be to consider the state thereof as to its trade." The object of such a committee would be "to find out ways how it may be improved both in its husbandry, manufactures, and navigation; to see how the trade with foreign kingdoms grows more or less profitable to us; how and by what methods we are outdone by others in the trades we drive, or hindered from enlarging them; what is necessary to be prohibited both in imports and exports, and for how long time; to hear complaints from our factories settled in foreign kingdoms; to correspond with our ministers abroad about trade, and to represent all things rightly to the government, with their advice what courses are proper to be taken for its encouragement; and generally to study by what means and methods the trade of this nation may be improved both abroad and at home. If this was well settled, the good effects thereof would soon be seen; but then great care must be taken that these places be not filled up with courtiers" (Cary, *An Essay on the State of England in Relation to its Trade, its Poor, and its Taxes,* Bristol, 1695, pp. 139–140). These recommendations are so similar in their phraseology to one of the paragraphs in the Board of Trade's commission of 1696 as to lead the reader to believe that Cary had had access to some of the earlier commissions and instructions upon which the commission of 1696 was based. It does not necessarily mean that Cary's pamphlet was inspired, as Professor Osgood thinks, *American Colonies in the Eighteenth Century,* I, 132.

2. Additional Manuscripts, 5540, fos. 83, 84.

3. Harleian Manuscripts, 1223, no. 9.

4. *Diary,* II, 275. A further discussion is on p. 276.

*for Trade in England and Some Expedients Proposed*[1] thought that parliament was not favorably constituted to manage trade, as its numbers were too great to enable it to look after such things and its members were too little acquainted with the intricacies of the subject, being taken up with a multiplicity of other business. He hoped that the oversight of trade would be undertaken by the merchants, constituted by act of parliament a council sedentary at London and vested with powers adapted to the improvement of manufactures and foreign trade. In war such a council should aid the Admiralty in the matter of convoys, in peace it should inquire into the balance of trade with every nation, examine the due making of manufactured goods, draw up plans for the improvement of navigation and commerce, and consider studiously the welfare of these interests in all particulars. In some cases its members would reach decisions themselves, in others it would have recourse to the Privy Council or the Admiralty, in order to digest matters for the information or sanction of parliament. James Whiston also, in *England's Calamities Discovered*,[2] written in 1695, proposed a select society or committee of skilled and experienced traders elected by ballot, because, as he said, it was impossible for noblemen and gentlemen, not educated in trade, ever to arrive at a perfect understanding of the matters in question, and he outlined a very elaborate scheme of a council to sit at the Guildhall, thirty-four in all, two from each company of traders "with a country," two shipwrights, and two from each of four groups of colonies—West Indies two, Jamaica two, Virginia and Maryland two, and New York and New England two. In a later work, entitled *England's State Distempers*,[3] 1704, he says that he was personally active in making known his proposal in 1695 and that it met with "a general kind reception and approbation." He seems to have appeared twice before parliament in its behalf, only in the end to see, as he thought, the wrong thing done—unskilful gentlemen chosen "by the choice of favor" and not by virtue of knowledge and experience.

The general situation was a critical one. The war upon which England entered in 1689 found the country and the government thoroughly unprepared. The administrative system was unable to cope with the heavy demands made upon it and the Lords of Trade, in

1. Anonymous (London, 1695), p. 15.   2. Pp. 8–13.
3. Pp. 9–20.

whose hands lay the general supervision of all that related to commerce and the colonies, was indolent and apathetic. The lords may not have deserved the vituperative comment of a contemporary, "As to traffic and navigation there needs no information how wretchedly that hath been managed by F[ool]s and K[nave]s, though I cannot think any Englishman can be so monstrously ignorant in sea affairs as they seem to be in other directions,"[1] but there can be no doubt that such remarks were widely current. One can readily believe that at the Royal Exchange, in the coffee houses, and wherever else merchants congregated, the prevailing muddle-headedness of the departments and the councillors should have been the subject of common discussion, and that where a few men put their opinions in print there were hundreds who expressed them in the streets or over their cups. Brewster said that the need of a council of trade which would work harmoniously and efficaciously was the "common theam of men of all understandings," all of whom were fast coming to realize that the proper direction and management of trade and the colonies was as important as was their regulation.

Parliament was well aware of this necessity, for at the very time when it was passing the act of 1696, considering the erection of vice-admiralty courts, and debating measures for prohibiting further the trade with France,[2] it was itself planning to erect a council of trade and plantations and to take over from the king the prerogative of appointment in this one important particular. Though its members had no doubt as to the need of such a council, they were far from agreed as to how it should be composed and what should be its functions. Should the membership be large or small? Should it be made up of merchants only, or of men of many kinds—noblemen, gentlemen, merchants in trade, and merchants out of trade? And lastly, what should be its powers and functions, and what the scope and range of its duties?

All these questions were under consideration when, in December, 1695, the House of Lords went into committee to investigate the state of the nation's finances and the decay of its trade, and to listen with attentive ear to the grievances of the merchants. We know that as early as the 12th of that month the committee of the whole House

1. In a letter from "G. B.," Amsterdam, Feb. 14, 1696, in reply to a remark of John Cary, who complained bitterly of the character of the House of Commons. Additional Manuscripts, 5540, fo. 77.

2. *House of Lords Manuscripts*, new series, II, §§991, 994, 1006.

of Commons reported in favor of a council of trade, which, said John Cary, in writing two days later to the Bristol representatives, Yate and Day, "I think so necessary a constitution that I could not let it pass without writing you a few lines; the main thing will be to see it settled on good foundations, for in that council all things relating to trade should be debated before they come to be transacted in the parliament or elsewhere; no man can foresee the advantages which would come to this nation by the well moddeling thereof; I must beg your pardon if I do recommend you what I say on that head in my essay on Trade, p. 139."[1] He wrote again two days later,[2] "Having notice from different hands that the House of Commons had voted a council or committee of trade, we think it a constitution which will tend very much to the interest of England." He hoped that the new body would not be "made up of courtiers inexperienced in trade" and expressed the not unnatural wish of a Bristol man that it should contain representatives from the outports among its members. On the 19th Yate and Day replied, "We have yours of the 16th inst, wherein you take notice of some debates of the Committee of the Whole House in reference to a council of trade, which we think a business of great consequence and may be of no small advantage to the nation; and we find his Majesty hath thought of it and its said a commission is come forth accordingly and the persons nominated are some of the greatest quality and others of lesser rank; on which head the committee will be to-morrow [the 20th] and then this matter will be better understood. But we did not find that the House were inclinable to nominate any out of the House, and then the House of Lords would have joined in some of their number, so that affair is at a great uncertainty, and whether will prove advantageous to trade or not is very doubtful."

The Bristol corporation, taking up the letter writing in its turn, argued on behalf of the outports as against a London monopoly. It wrote its representatives that it did not necessarily want "a man out of parliament to be on the board, but a man in parliament who would stand up for [Bristol's] interests would be welcome." "London," it added, "would swallow up the trade of England, if the members of that society being in that interest should bend their endeavours to promote its advantages, and this they will do if [the board] is made

---

1. Additional Manuscripts, 5540, fo. 83.
2. *Ibid.*, fo. 84.

up of merchants chosen from that city." The aldermen urged Day and Yate to bestir themselves and to persuade the members from Bridgewater and "those western ports to join with you, who are on the same footing with us and equally obliged to secure themselves against the growing greatness of London." To this the members replied that the matter was to come up "in a week," that is, about January 1, 1696, but, they added, the king "hath [already] appointed ten or more commissioners, but whether the Commons would be satisfied with that Commission is not yet determined." They enclosed "a print," which contained the names of the proposed royal commissioners, but so unacceptable was the list that Cary could only say he considered the men proposed for membership "altogether improper for such an undertaking and we hope the House will be of the same opinion, for they are wholly unskilful in trade."[1]

In this correspondence we get a welcome look behind the curtain and see somewhat of the agitation of the outports against London and of parliament against the royal prerogative that accompanied the settlement of this important issue. On January 1, 1696, as the Bristol members had already said would be the case, the House of Commons went into committee to investigate the state of the nation, and in the course of the month was called upon to consider many petitions from the merchants, among which was one and probably more from Bristol, for that city drew up at least three petitions for presentation to the house.[2] Not, however, till the end of the month (January 31) was the committee ready to report. Then it presented its recommendations in the form of fourteen resolutions, the gist of which is as follows. That in the opinion of the committee a council of trade should be established by act of parliament, with ample powers for the more effectual preservation of the trade of the kingdom; that the members of this council, no one of whom ought to be of the House of Commons, should be nominated by parliament, should take oaths of allegiance to the reigning sovereigns, and should be empowered to prevent in the future all such miscarriages in the field of trade and commerce as had disgraced the administration since 1689. That these members should apply themselves to the study of the plantation trade and all other trades and manufactures and de-

1. *Ibid.*, fos. 85, 88, 90.
2. These were a general petition regarding trade; another regarding sugar, and a third regarding iron. The last is probably the one mentioned in the Commons' Journal, Stock, *Debates*, II, 152.

termine how best to improve them and secure them for England; should be given some measure of control over the convoy system; should look into the book of rates, in order to strengthen the balance of trade for the benefit of the kingdom; and should endeavor to regain, encourage, and promote the fishery. All of these resolutions, except four, were adopted by the house. The house refused (1) to deny its members a place on the council; (2) to allow the council to inspect the book of rates or to interfere in any way with the customs service; (3) to require the oath of allegiance to King William and Queen Mary and a repudiation of the right of the former king, James; and (4), most important of all, to control the sailing of merchant ships and to have any authority over fleets and convoys when used for the protection of trade.[1] On February 12 the bill, thus amended, was duly presented and read for the first time. On the 18th it was read for the second time and committed, but it got no further.

The rocks upon which the bill was shipwrecked were two. First, the feeling that must have prevailed among those who favored appointment by the king that the house was not agreed on what it wanted and that, as Cary wrote, the matter was "carried on by some warm men more in opposition to the King, as we conceive, than for the good of the nation." That the plan was arousing considerable bitterness of feeling is evident from the remark of the Bristol aldermen, who said, January 16, even before the plan had gone to committee, "We are sorry to hear what heats have arisen in the House about the Commissioners of Trade."[2] Secondly, the demand of the committee of the whole house that the powers of the council be so enlarged as to include "the dispose of all cruisers and convoys, which," said Cary, "will be at least eighty ships and the captains and seamen under the said commission we doubt the king may not think fit to grant it nor may it be safe to the kingdom to lodge such a separate power in times of war." Certainly King William was in no mood to hand over to a group of parliamentary appointees powers which encroached as boldly as did these upon his own powers and upon the executive authority of the Admiralty, even though the latter was doing its business very badly.

Davenant was one of those who advocated very strongly the lodging in the council of authority over cruisers and convoys, and he

1. Stock, *Debates*, II, 156–158.
2. Additional Manuscripts, 5540, fos. 92, 94.

urged that the proposed board "have in their direction and at their disposal such a number of the fleet as may be needful from time to time for the due guarding of the seas. . . . They to whom the care of Trade is committed should have at their disposal such a proportion of frigates as may convoy all the merchant fleets." He saw in such conveyance of power no menace to the authority of the Admiralty and thought that "forty frigates should be ordered by act of parliament to follow the directions of a council of trade in cruising and for convoys."[1] But others viewed the matter in a different light. Such an investment of power, almost equal to that of the Admiralty itself, was a dangerous encroachment upon the royal prerogative. Why, they asked, might not parliament, if it once brought such a council under its complete control, continue its assumption of powers, until through its own appointed agency it would not only concern itself with matters of trade, but would in time draw into its own hands the functions of the Admiralty and that part of the revenue or supply which was appropriated to the navy.[2] It might even encroach upon the military powers of the secretary of state. William Blathwayt, who, as a prerogative man, undoubtedly opposed the measure, wrote, perhaps semi-humorously, to Richard Hill, deputy paymaster of the forces then in the Low Countries, who wanted to give up his army connection, "We are establishing a council of trade by parliament and of parliament men. Don't you fear it should extend to the army which is the only thing can relieve you."[3] The danger of a parliamentary appointment was too serious to be risked, and though Secretary Sunderland favored the plan, perhaps because

1. Davenant elaborated his ideas in what he called "The Scheme." In this he suggested that directions be given to the merchants allowing them to name the number of seamen necessary to man the respective fleets, determine the proper seasons for sailing, and lay before the council information as to what convoys were needful to guard their respective trades and in what stations the cruising ships were to be posted to the best advantage and for their greater security. He wished that such a council consider the seamen needed for the several ships and principal fleets, what convoys were necessary, and what were the best times and stations, and deliver to the Admiralty memorials containing its matured opinions, to be signed by at least five members. In that way he hoped to prevent the delays which had happened in the past and which had been so injurious to the merchants, thus avoiding the uncertainties and false excuses which had been due to the frequency of verbal instructions (Harleian, 1223, fos. 3–6). Davenant's "Scheme" is more important as a commentary of the conditions which had prevailed after 1689 than as a practical remedy for their betterment.

2. Dickerson, *American Colonial Government*, p. 21, quoting from Cobbett's *Parliamentary History*, V, 978.

3. Jacobsen, *William Blathwayt*, p. 290.

he did not wish to aggravate the powerful Whig majority, the bill was dropped because of the king's opposition. Though on March 3, the house agreed to consider it in committee the following Monday, it disappeared from view and was never heard of again.[1] For the moment the prerogative, that is, the executive, had won, but parliament was to take its revenge later, when it defeated the plans formulated by the Board of Trade for royalizing the proprietary and corporate colonies in the years from 1701 to 1722.

But something had to be done and a remedy found for the existing state of affairs. With the withdrawal of the parliamentary proposal, another, that of the king himself, already drawn up the December before and worked out in detail, even to the names of the persons to be appointed, came to the front and was immediately put into the proper legal form. On March 30, the king issued the warrant to prepare; on May 12, he having in the meantime left England, the lords justices argued the bill; and on May 15, it passed the privy seal. A few days later the great seal was affixed. Thereby was erected the Lords Commissioners of Trade and Plantations, commonly known as the Board of Trade, a body destined from the first to have very intimate relations with the colonies and to represent in its policies and recommendations the leading principles that were to guide England's rulers in their control of colonial affairs until after the Seven Years' War.[2] Subordinate though the board was to the king and the Privy Council and possessed of no executive, financial, or penalizing powers, it was able to exercise both directly and indirectly, through its reports and recommendations to the crown and in its correspond-

---

1. Parliament's effort to control the appointment of a council of trade and in so doing to prevent the king from exercising his authority in this respect was but one phase of the struggle then taking place between the executive and the legislative, which was a legacy from parliament's victory in 1689. It represented also one aspect of the king's attempt to restore the integrity and deliberative activity of the Privy Council as over against the cabinet council, which began with the so-called Temple Council in 1679 and was renewed in 1689, when the whole council was made coincident with the Lords of Trade.

2. The failure of the parliamentary plan and the erection of the board by executive fiat caused a great deal of dissatisfaction among certain of the merchants. We have already noticed John Cary's disappointment. In Samuel Baston's *A Dialogue between a Modern Courtier and an Honest English Gentleman* (London, 1697) appears the following on p. 9:

"*Courtier.* But Sir what needs all this complaint, why most of their sores are heal'd, for here's a Council of Trade now settled, by which the merchants' grievances and several other things will be rectifyed.

"*Gentleman.* I confess the Council of Trade was excellently propos'd at first to the

ence with the colonial governors,[1] a far-reaching and often determinative influence. No part of the English executive was more consistently mercantilist in its relations to trade and the colonies or more conservative in its defense of the king's prerogative in America than was this advisory board, which though shifting in membership, as one influence after another affected the personnel, had an office, secretaries, and clerks, that remained fairly constant and functioned without much regard to the shifts of political and personal fortune that affected the members of the board itself. Nothing shows this better than the continuance by the office after 1696 of the traditions and policies of the board's predecessor, the Lords of Trade, for though the membership of the board represented a change, both in status and in the rank of the men who composed it, the Plantation Office had an unbroken history and an unchanging policy from 1675 to 1782.

The Lords of Trade were members of the Privy Council and so possessed the authority of that body to command and enforce obedience. On the other hand, the regular members of the Board of Trade were largely commoners, possessed of no authority to do more than advise the king as to what seemed the wisest course to pursue. They had no right to order, punish, or execute, except that in the pursuit of information they could summon men before them and take evidence under oath. Their range of investigation was wide, for their commission reproduced in large part the earlier commissions of the select councils since 1660. In placing in the hands of a single body the dual interests of trade and plantations, the king's advisers were but following the precedent of the council of 1672 and of the Lords of Trade. The earlier practice of appointing two councils, one for trade and the other for foreign plantations, had not proved successful, and in departing from it they shared in the prevailing opinion that trade and the plantations were indissolubly connected and that each was inseparable the one from the other. Since 1672 both inter-

Parliament. But the Interest of the Court quickly *beat out its brains,* and from this establishment I doubt little good will arise. My reasons for it are these. They do not understand Trade and they are the same that sit in Council and have heard the crimes of Admiralty and Navy and wanted no power to redress these grievances in Council."

On the other hand commendatory comments, with a distinctly ceremonial flavor, can be found in *Maryland Archives,* XIX, 513; XXIV, 227, 261, but these are exceptional. See below, p. 293, note 5.

1. One governor styled the board "the patrons of H.M. Colonies," *Calendar State Papers, Colonial,* 1712–1714, p. 108.

ests had been looked after by the same set of men and so they were to continue for eighty-six years more.

The members of the Board of Trade were sixteen in number, but of these only eight were working members, bound to attend regularly and to assume responsibility for the business of the board. They were each paid £1000 a year. The only one among the first appointees who had any intimate knowledge of the colonies was William Blathwayt. He had been auditor general of the plantation revenues for sixteen years and knew something about the conditions in America and the problems to which these conditions gave rise. He it was who, in all important particulars, directed the policies and activities of the board as long, until 1706, as he was one of its members. John Locke, another of the original appointees, was also fairly well informed, having been associated with Shaftesbury in the settlement of Carolina and having served as a secretary of the Shaftesbury select council from June 24, 1673, to November, 1674. But he was now an old man and in 1700 left the board because he was no longer able to live in London and would not, as he said, hold the place as a sinecure.[1] John Pollexfen, an ardent mercantilist, who while a member[2] wrote *A Discourse of Trade and Coyn,* in which something, but not much, is said of the plantations, had a merchant's knowledge of the subject and must have been familiar with the colonies from a commercial point of view. Abraham Hill, rather a scientist and a virtuoso than an economist, who took his duties seriously, as his extant memoranda show,[3] was fairly regular in attendance and must have entered into the debates with considerable energy and a desire to acquire some knowledge of his duties. The president, the Earl of Bridgewater, was an excellent and efficient presiding officer, high in the king's favor, but he was overburdened with many public duties and possessed no knowledge of his subject that was in any sense of the word profound. He was regular in attendance and did as well as he could, carrying on an extensive correspondence with colonial officials and endeavoring to keep up with the discussions at the board,

1. *Life of Mr. John Locke, written in French by Mr. Le Clerc and done into English by T. F. P. Gent* (London, 1706. 3d ed.), p. 19.

2. The *Dictionary of National Biography* says that Pollexfen was a member of the "committee of 1675," evidently referring to the Lords of Trade. Dickerson follows this statement (p. 29), but Osgood (more cautiously, I, 138) merely says that he "held office" under the committee. There is nothing to show that he was ever in any way connected with the earlier councils or with the Lords of Trade.

3. British Museum, Sloan, 2902.

as his notes and jottings, still preserved,[1] indicate, but he probably leaned heavily on Blathwayt for advice. The other three working members were Ford Grey, Earl of Tankerville, John Methuen, and Sir Philip Meadows, courtiers and diplomats, no one of whom had any special qualifications for his post, except on the political and diplomatic side. Of the "ornamental" members only the secretary of state attended with any sort of frequency. In the earlier years all the "great officers" were invited to be present, if their engagements permitted, and besides the secretary of state there came occasionally to the meetings the chancellor of the exchequer, the lord high treasurer, the lord privy seal, and the Bishop of London,[2] particularly when some important issue, such as the commercial treaty with France, the troubles of the Royal African Company, or a question of ecclesiastical policy in the colonies came up for debate.[3] On one occasion when "a matter of great difficulty and importance" was under consideration, the board asked permission to wait on its more distinguished colleagues instead of requesting their attendance.[4] Later, the presence of any of these "great men" became a rare occurrence and in time ceased altogether, though to the very end their names continued to appear in the commission. As Blathwayt directed the affairs of the board until his dismissal in 1706, so Colonel Martin Bladen was its leading member from 1717 until his death in 1746.[5]

1. His papers are in the Huntington Library, Ellesmere, 1683–9832.
2. The Bishop of London was made one of the "great officers" in 1702, *Calendar State Papers, Colonial*, 1702, p. 409.
3. *Ibid.*, 1700, §1029; 1701, §298; 1702, §§6, 13; 1708–1715, pp. 340, 344, 475; 1715–1718, pp. 25, 26, etc.
4. *Ibid.*, 1706–1708, §603.
5. A commentary upon the personnel of the board is contained in an anonymous essay or treatise, "Of the American Plantations," sent in 1715 to Secretary Stanhope and by him transmitted to the board. It contains the following paragraphs: "If this power had been always vested in persons of knowledge and integrity, to whom the plantation affairs were well known and unanimous in the design of promoting the public service only, it might have produced much good. But there having bin many persons att severall times put into that commission for different reasons than their ability, to discharge such a trust (as is well known) it hath not hitherto produced such effects as might be expected from it. And it was impossible that board should make a right judgment of wrong oppressions and maladministrations and of acts sent from the plantations to be passed into laws, or to be able to represent what regulations were fit to be made in the governments and administration of justice unless some at that board had a perfect and personal knowledge of the nature of the plantations and of the people, as likewise of their different laws and constitutions. . . . Many instances might be here given of many incredible things done and omitted by that board." The treatise goes on to recommend that merchants and former governors should be

He was the one who married as his second wife the daughter of John Gibbs of North Carolina[1] and was a friend of the Duke of Chandos, who called him the "oracle of the Board of Trade."[2]

Accepting the board as in the main a defender of the mercantile classes in England—that is, the capitalists of their day—a word may be said regarding its functions and authority.[3] It prepared representations to the king and on request sent reports to the House of Commons and House of Lords. It drew up the governors' instructions and from time to time introduced into them such alterations as seemed necessary, provided lists of councillors, drafted heads of inquiry, blocked out the terms of boundary commissions, and not infrequently suggested appointments to the crown. It had no power to carry out any of its recommendations or authority to make demands upon or issue orders to any other department or board. Once, in 1759, the secretary to the board of customs commissioners issued the following enunciation of policy, that "It being the constitution and practice of this board, in matters of revenue only to receive Directions from and to make Reports to the Lords Commissioners of the Treasury or his Majesty in Council," it could take no orders from the Board of Trade. The endorsement of this statement reads, "Representation from the Commissioners of the Customs as to not being obliged to obey the Board of Trade."

The board occasionally refused to consider business that did not belong to it, particularly such as concerned matters of a private nature, because not within "their lordships department" or consistent with "the rules of their proceedings." It was sufficiently burdened with the obligations that arose under its commission[4] to be careful

appointed; merchants who have been concerned in general trade, and governors "who have served the crown in superior stations in America, have done their duty and have behaved themselves with an unblamed integrity." The treatise bears date, October 18, 1714 (*North Carolina Colonial Records,* II, 154–166; *Calendar State Papers, Colonial,* 1714–1715, §236). Though the treatise contains much that is true, we may doubt if the addition of merchants and ex-governors would have helped to improve the quality of the board's work.

1. Above, Vol. III, 260, note.    2. The same, II, 231, note 1.

3. There is in the Library of the Historical Society of Pennsylvania a long paper prepared by Samuel Gellibrand of the Plantation Office, largely made up of certifications of documents in the office relating to certain claims of the Pennsylvania proprietors ("Penn *v.* Baltimore, Depositions," 1740, fos. 91–140). It contains very little information regarding the functions and procedure of the board. I am indebted to Mr. J. P. Boyd, the librarian, for calling my attention to this paper and for sending me a report upon it.

4. In 1760 there were twenty-two outlying members of the British colonial domain,

not to waste its time or the time of the clerks of the office with irrelevant distractions. On one occasion it informed the House of Commons that to furnish certain facts and figures would require so much labor that it would be better to send the books to the house and let the clerks there copy out what was wanted than to ask the staff of the Plantation Office to undertake the task. It had frequently to cope with the importunities of the colonial agents and solicitors, who were demanding access to its files and bundles, and to reprimand some of them very sharply—particularly Robert Charles, agent for New York, a conspicuous busybody—for their persistence in pushing their requests. Toward the end of the period before 1763 its activities partook more and more of a routine character. As with the Treasury and the Admiralty the board seems to have lost interest in any of the wider implications of colonial control and, averse to change and unable to see that the dominance of the mercantile classes was endangering the economic relations with the colonies, was content with the situation as it was. It continued to receive memorials, letters, papers, and the like and had many problems to solve, some of which at least might better have been left to the colonists themselves, for the board's attempt to regulate from a distance many matters that were distinctly destructive of the financial solvency of the colonies was bound to result in trouble in the end. The board, in common with the other organs of British control, seemed to have no comprehension of the dangers involved in a policy that sacrificed the colonies on the altar of England's moneyed prosperity. It saw everything from the standpoint of the constitutional power of the prerogative, of the commercial and industrial interests of the capitalist classes, and of the proper position that a colony should occupy in the English colonial world, and it considered any other attitude of mind as endangering that relationship with the mother country which every colony was expected to recognize and preserve.

The members of the board carried out with a considerable measure of success the terms of their commission. They pursued their in-

of which eighteen were colonies directly under the supervision of the board (*Board of Trade Journal*, 1759–1763, pp. 131–132). The board handed over a great deal of business to the secretary of state (as in the case of all that concerned the effects of the Stamp Act in America), the Treasury, the Admiralty, the postmasters general, the Bishop of London, and others. It refused at first to have anything to do with the affairs of the Royal African Company, but later it became involved in the troubles arising from the company's reorganization. It had no power to concern itself with any admiralty court cases.

quiries into all phases of colonial administration, but their main object was to promote trade not the colonies—trade everywhere, with Europe, Asia, Africa, and America—in order to create a favorable balance of trade for the realm and so to oversee and improve the plantations in the interest of England's wealth and the wealth of her merchants. Representative as they were of the eighteenth century ruling class, they were unchanging in their principles and policies and were strict constructionists in all that concerned the interpretation of the navigation acts, the prevention of manufacturing in the colonies, the advancement of the interests of the merchants in England, and the "careful and strikt maintenance of the just prerogative." In the hundreds of reports and representations which they sent to the Privy Council, the House of Lords, and the House of Commons, and in the letters which they wrote to the secretary of state, the Treasury, the Admiralty, and the governors and others in the colonies, they upheld the conventional point of view, with faithful regard for tradition and precedent, and insisted to the end that the colonies should remain, apparently forever, in a position of political and economic dependence and subordination, subservient to the mother country and a source of wealth to its people.[1]

In applying these principles, the members acted with minds open to everything except fundamental ideas. They always aimed, as they said, "at solid and particular information" and were ready to receive and consider any proposal relating to the public good or to the good of commerce and the interest of the nation.[2] They sought help and advice from a great variety of sources, held frequent hearings at the Plantation Office and entered into correspondence with all sorts of people, official and unofficial, both in England and America. Amongst their most influential advisers were the crown lawyers till 1718, and after that date their own standing counsel, whose rulings on colonial legislation determined in most cases the final decision of the king in council on the confirmation or disallowance of colonial laws. Francis

1. The best exposition of the point of view of the Board of Trade, as far as such point of view is stated in the form of a declaration, is to be found in Colonel Bladen's "Short Discourse on the Present State of the Colonies in America with respect to the Interest of Great Britain." This treatise, by one of the leading commissioners of the board and its most influential member during the nearly thirty years of his tenure, 1717–1746, is a shrewd and illuminating exposition of the prevailing doctrine. *North Carolina Colonial Records*, II, 626–635.

2. *Calendar State Papers, Colonial*, 1696–1697, §1225; *Board of Trade Journal*, 1734–1741, pp. 282, 359, 366.

Fane, K.C., who served as standing counsel for twenty-one years and was for a decade a member of the board itself, must always be considered as having played an important part, by means of his reports on colonial legislation, in shaping England's policy on the legal side. Although the committee of the Privy Council sometimes altered or refused to accept the recommendations of the board, either of its own will or upon appeals from others against reports of the board, its reasons for doing so were not based on any opposition to the principles involved, for the members of the Privy Council were probably as conservative as were the members of the Board of Trade. Though the latter had no executive powers, their influence in shaping executive and legislative action was very great, for the Plantation Office was a workshop in which was prepared material and even the finished product for many official decisions. Large numbers of orders in council, royal warrants—countersigned by the secretary of state, the Treasury, and the Admiralty—and even royal proclamations[1] and acts of parliament[2] found their origin and in some cases their final form in the debates around the board table and in the secretarial activities of the office.

Though the Lords of Trade had, as a rule, sat in the council chamber in the Cockpit, the place where the secretary and the clerks worked until 1696 was in Scotland Yard, among the lodgings, tenement houses, offices, storerooms, passageways, and other conveniences belonging to the royal palace that lay north of Whitehall Court and east to the river of the street leading from the Holbein Gateway to Charing Cross.[3] In 1696, the new board, unable to use the council chamber—because its members were not privy councillors, either as committee or, except in a few instances, as individuals—and refusing to sit amidst the dirt and filth, griminess and inconvenience of the Scotland Yard quarters, within a week after the issue of its commission, asked for a new office. The request was granted, and at its first meeting,[4] June 25, 1696, the secretary was ordered "to desire Sir Christopher Wren to hasten the fitting of the rooms designed for it."[5] While these rooms were being fitted up under Wren's direction, the

1. The text of the Proclamation of 1763 was prepared in the Plantation Office, *ibid.*, 1759–1763, pp. 380, 384, 385, 389.
2. Fane drafted one act of parliament and probably more, *ibid.*, 1734–1741, p. 87.
3. *Calendar State Papers, Domestic*, 1696, pp. 189, 200, 260.
4. The Lords of Trade continued to function at least until May 29, 1696.
5. *Calendar State Papers, Colonial*, 1696–1697, §§54, 64, 71, 76, 116, 126.

board had quarters near the "king's lodgings in the privy garden."[1]
The new office was ready by the end of August and was probably
designed to be permanent, for by the 21st the records and books had
all been transferred, under an order in council of July 7.[2] After the
fire of January 8, 1698, which destroyed most of the palace buildings
to the east and south of the Banqueting Hall, including the new
quarters, the board met temporarily at the house of its secretary in
Essex Street, Strand, but by February 26 rooms in a small house adjoining the Cockpit on the north were prepared as an office[3] and
thither the board moved, having, through the diligence of its officers,
saved nearly all the books, papers, and maps which temporarily were
lodged in the secretary's house. In these uncomfortable quarters the
commissioners remained until 1723, constantly complaining of the
leaks and the drains and the cramped accommodations, until in that
year it was given an office at the head of King's Street, in a building
that faced the "Great Area," looking toward the Holbein Gateway.
When this building was pulled down in 1746, the board moved again
and this time permanently into the new Treasury building, erected
in 1733, which is still standing facing the parade ground behind the
Horse Guards, and there it remained until its dissolution in 1782.

John Povey, a cousin of William Blathwayt, had been one of the
secretaries of the Lords of Trade, and there was every reason to suppose that he would be chosen as the secretary of the new board. But
for some reason this was not done. One William Popple was chosen.
Of this man, the founder of a veritable secretarial dynasty in the
Plantation Office, Povey wrote to Governor Nicholson, July 4, 1696,
"The commission of Trade is now opened and Mr. Popple appointed
by the King to be their secretary, a person who was but a merchant
and had practiced it for some time, til the world frowned upon him.
Many of the commissioners endeavored there might be two secretaries, that I might be continued in the service, without which they
did me the honor to say they should be in the dark: but the matter
is not determined, tho' it seems to be so with me."[4] Povey was not
appointed even as a joint secretary, and William Popple was succeeded after thirteen years by his son, William Popple, Jr., and he by
his son, Alured Popple, while a brother of Alured, William, was

1. *Calendar State Papers, Domestic,* 1696, p. 232.
2. *Acts Privy Council, Colonial,* II, §693; C. O. 326:1.
3. *Calendar State Papers, Colonial,* 1708–1709, §433.
4. Blathwayt Papers, 9625 (Huntington Library).

Horatio Walpole's secretary in France in 1728 and afterward for eight years was clerk of the reports, and another brother, Henry,[1] draftsman of the map of 1733 bearing his name, was employed for a short time as a writing clerk, until he resigned to become a regimental agent and at one time or another a representative in England of the governors of Bermuda and the Bahamas and of the island of Montserrat. Thus for more than forty years, 1696–1737, the Popples were in charge of the secretarial work of the board and, as was the case with Sir Robert Southwell and William Blathwayt before them and of Thomas Hill and John Pownall after them, they not only proved skilful and efficient organizers and secretaries, but maintained, as perhaps no one else did so tenaciously, the established traditions of the office. With only five men—three Popples, Hill, and John Pownall—in direct and immediate control during a period of eighty years, 1696–1776, it was inevitable that they should make a deep impress upon the standards and policies of the Plantation Office, deeper indeed than that made by any single member of the board itself. Many of the working members of the board were in office but a very short time, more were unfamiliar with colonial problems or colonial needs, while the larger number were more interested in the commercial and diplomatic aspects of their duties than in those which concerned the plantations as seats of government and centers of administration. Not one of them had ever visited America before the date of his appointment, and even the best informed, such as Blathwayt, Bladen, and Dupplin, had no real understanding of the colonial point of view, or, even if they had understood it, would have given it serious consideration, in the face of the "unalterable Maxim, that a lesser publick good must give place to a greater and that it is of more moment to maintain a greater than a lesser number of subjects well employed to the advantage of any State."[2] It is true that they frequently listened to and followed the advice of many whom they called before them—returned governors, merchants, agents, and others who had had colonial experience—and perused hundreds of letters from the colonies that often presented vigorously and accurately colonial sentiment, but their official utterances, as seen in the representations, which they drew up on important matters, adhered

1. There has always been some doubt as to the place of Henry Popple in the Popple family, but the matter has finally been set at rest by Alured's reference to him as his brother. *Board of Trade Journal*, 1728–1734, pp. 366, 416.

2. *North Carolina Colonial Records*, II, 629.

with undeviating firmness to the political and commercial principles by which they were guided. It must always be remembered that the board was primarily appointed for the consideration of trade and not for the administration of the colonies, and it is at least worthy of speculation whether if the English government had seen fit to follow Bladen's advice, offered as early as 1726,[1] and had appointed a secretary of state for plantation affairs or had raised the president of the board to the status of a cabinet officer, as was almost done in 1757, or had created a body of officials devoted to plantation business only,[2] some better understanding might not have been reached regarding the interests of the colonies on the governmental and financial sides.

In estimating the influence of the board, within the narrow circle of its own powers, as determined by its instructions, we can easily lay too much stress upon the part which the commissioners themselves took in shaping England's policy and too little upon the directing hands of the secretaries, the clerk of the reports, and the standing counsel. The secretary wrote the letters and aided the clerk of the reports in drawing up the representations of the board, and the standing counsel gave legal advice and made legal comments on all colonial laws that were transmitted to the king for confirmation or disallowance. These comments formed the basis of nearly all the reports of the board on colonial laws to the Privy Council and so became determining factors in the council's treatment of colonial legislation, a matter that finds mention in the Declaration of Independence. Rarely, if ever, did either the Board of Trade or the Privy Council reverse the opinion of the standing counsel. The secretary and the clerk of the reports wrote the first draft of the representations, as they were directed to do by the board, and for that purpose extracted from the files in the office the necessary information. The members of the board took what the secretary offered, and though without doubt they discussed these reports at their meetings, dictated many

1. *North Carolina Colonial Records,* II, 634.

2. The author of the essay "Of the American Plantations," already noticed, who may be said to represent the colonial standpoint, complained in 1714 that the board could not exercise its functions properly unless it had among its members some at least who "had a perfect and personal knowledge of the nature of the plantations and of the people" (*ibid.,* 164). The board itself at times realized the inadequacy of its own geographical knowledge and twice in 1715 made a special effort to secure what maps it could, protesting that it could find none in Whitehall that could be depended on. *Calendar State Papers, Colonial,* 1714–1715, §§518, 574.

statements and opinions to be incorporated in the text, and gave the secretary instructions as to the letters to be written, they must have accepted in the main the statements of principle as formulated by him and the facts that he supplied from the letters and papers that were bound up in volumes or lay unbound in bundles upon the shelves or within the presses of the clerks' quarters. At the same time, the commissioners, even during their years of least activity, were no mere figureheads, as were the members of the Privy Council in formal session. They listened to the reading of letters, heard matters debated at length before them by interested parties, their agents and attorneys, followed arguments and statements of fact presented to them at board meetings by all sorts and conditions of men, and debated among themselves matters of importance that arose in connection with colonial quarrels and disputes. Many among them were conversant with trade in general and the rules of diplomatic intercourse, and when it came to the drafting of a commercial treaty or the rendering of an opinion regarding tariff arrangements they were on familiar ground. Colonial affairs were, as a rule, secondary to the more conspicuous business of Continental trade, and the board, at least during the first half century of its existence, often sat for hours and even for days talking over trade relations with other countries from Muscovy to the Venetian Republic. Domestic industry and manufacture, the fishery, insurance, coinage, wool, smuggling, naval stores, local conditions of labor, unemployment, and the poor,[1]

---

1. The board concerned itself less with domestic affairs—the poor and local industries—than with foreign and colonial trade. Yet it did deal with both (*Calendar State Papers, Colonial*, 1696–1697, p. 622; *Board of Trade Journal*, 1708–1715, pp. 503–504). In its report of 1701, it said, "We have likewise taken again into consideration the proper methods of employing the poor; but having the last session represented to the House that for the making the poor usefull and not burthensome to the Publick, we had made divers proposals how we conceived that work might be best effected and having also in pursuance of an order of a committee of the House, at the end of the last session, prepared an abstract of all the laws now in force relating to the poor, together with the draft of a bill whereby they might be reduced into one law, and laid the same before the committee, we found that we could not make further progress on that subject untill this Honble House shall have proceeded thereupon" (March 12, 1701, C. O. 389:17, p. 168). The papers referred to in this statement may be found in C. O. 388:5, B, 6, 7, 10, 15; 388:7, A, 1, B, 1; 388:8, C, 25, 26; 389:14, 16, 17, but the list, though impressive as showing the activities of the board and the time given to the subject, is too long to be given here. The papers were used for the purpose of drafting a bill, which was laid before the House of Commons, March 13, 1700, but never passed.

It is worthy of note that the board, in common with many mercantilist pamphleteers of the period, was in favor of employing the poor in workhouses, the first of

as well as the management of the East India Company, the reorganized Royal African Company, the Hudson's Bay Company, and the
like all came within their purview, and upon these questions many
a member, who thought, it may be, that the town of Burlington and
the colony of Virginia were islands, that Campeche was a British
possession, that the Six Nations lived in the West Indies, and that
the town of Perth Amboy was there also,[1] was an authority with a
justifiable right to an opinion. Pollexfen, Pulteney, Arthur Moore,
Paul Docminique, Dupplin, Fane, Jenyns, Whately, and others were
all able men, and they must have brought well-informed minds to
bear upon problems, of whatever kind they might be, concerning
England's interests. But these men, as well as hundreds of others,
moved within a fixed orbit of thought and interpreted the world of
the colonies according to their notion of what a colony should be. If
they seriously thought of these distant plantations as something apart
from the mother country, with a right to an independent life of their
own, which may well be doubted, as men did not conceive of such a
possibility at that time,[2] they were probably convinced that what was
good for England was good for the colonies also. They took cognizance of facts and conditions, but not of fundamental principles or
underlying purposes, for such matters lay entirely outside their prov-

which was erected in London and Westminster in 1673. This plan gave to the workhouse somewhat the nature of a factory. The dislike which the working classes felt
for this scheme had something to do with their attitude toward the factory of later
times. They deemed a factory simply an enlarged workhouse.

1. Each of these geographical errors is recorded in the journal of the board or elsewhere. "America" was very commonly known as the "West Indies," as may be seen
in Edward Wells, *A Treatise of Antient and Present Geography together with a Sett
of Maps, Design'd for the Use of Young Students in the Universities* (Oxford, 1701),
where the title of one chapter (xviii) reads, "Of America or the West Indies."

2. John Cary in a letter to Edmund Bohun, chief justice of South Carolina, 1698–
1699, dated January 31, 1696, must have voiced the opinion of many of his day when
he wrote, "All plantations settled abroad out of our own people must needs be a loss
to this kingdom except they are employed there to serve its interests; nor do they answer the ends of their first settlement which were rather to provide materials for the
increasing our trade and keeping our people at work here than by those conduits let
it slide away. This is as opening a vein in a man's body and letting him bleed to
death, which might be of good use to his health, if no more blood were taken from
him than he could well spare. The health of the Commonwealth is to be preferred before that of any part when it sets up a distant interest alone, as the security of a government before that of a private person whom he endeavors to overthrow is, and
therefore our laws are severe against such and yet tend to promote the happiness of
our constitution by calling him to justice that opposes its first and fundamental design." Cary thinks that "the same respect is due from [the plantations] as from a ten-
ant to his landlord." Additional Manuscripts, 5540, fo. 61.

ince as defined by their commission. Nowhere in their journal or other official papers is there anything to show that they esteemed it their business to depart from a strict enforcement of those rules of reciprocal relationship which, they honestly believed, inhered in the very nature of the colonial connection. These rules were defined partly by statute, partly by the unwritten constitution of the kingdom, and partly by England's commercial and financial needs.

The board never questioned its obligation to require of the colonists obedience in certain important particulars. It expected them to obey the acts of trade and any other acts passed by parliament that applied to Englishmen in America as well as to Englishmen at home; to obey the orders of the king in whatever form such orders might be cast—instructions, mandamuses, dedimuses, and other documents under the sign manual; to recognize and accept their status as inferior corporations, similar to the boroughs and counties of England, with popular assemblies possessed of powers which were in no way comparable with or analogous to those of the House of Commons in England; to pass no laws contrary to those at home[1] or that legalized practices different from similar practices in England or from the customs of the Anglican Church there;[2] to recognize in all particulars the prerogative of the crown, an authority somewhat loosely defined by the common law and exercised through the king's agents and representatives in America by virtue of the king's commissions and instructions;[3] to abstain from manufacturing in any form,

1. As regards the plantations the doctrine of dependence and subordination was fundamental, particularly as far as it concerned the royal prerogative, the oversight of colonial legislation, and the improvement of navigation and trade. The following clause is in most, if not all, of the instructions. "It is our express will and pleasure that no law affecting the commerce and shipping of the kingdom, or relating to the rights and prerogatives of the crown or the property of our subjects, or which shall be of an unusual or extraordinary nature shall be passed [in the colonies] without the king's consent."

2. *Calendar State Papers, Colonial,* 1701, §§147, 157.

3. The royal instructions were private rules, which were not to be communicated even to the governors' councils, except on particular occasions, and never to be exposed to public view except with the king's consent. *Ibid.,* §627; *Board of Trade Journal,* 1704–1709, p. 180.

It was not always easy to determine just what were the powers of the prerogative. Once at least the board had to ask its legal adviser whether an assembly's taking on itself to confirm what his Majesty had before done by virtue of his prerogative was not "lessening his Majesty's said prerogative" (*Board of Trade Journal,* 1728–1734, p. 39). The board had frequent occasion to notice that the prerogative possessed definite limitations, in that it could not levy taxes by its own authority, could not interfere in judicial proceedings in the plantations, and could not unite two colonies under

whether the raw material were tobacco, wool, iron, furs, or sugar, and to confine their activities to the production of natural commodities for England's use only; to import no tools, implements, artisans, or craftsmen, either from England or the Continent, to such an extent as to injure England's manufacturing prosperity; to do nothing, either by the passage of laws or otherwise, to reduce the profits or lessen the opportunities of British merchants trading to America or to place their own interests before those of England and the realm as a whole; and, lastly, never, by word or action, to declare themselves independent of English control.

The board accepted this code as constituting its working creed. It never questioned its provisions or discussed them. Though it was to see them broken in upon over and over again by the colonists—until in practical application some of them had lost nearly all their force— it never assumed the right to modify these rules in any important particular or, except under very unusual circumstances, to allow the colonial governors to exercise any discretion regarding them.[1] Within the limits which these rules imposed the board was reasonable, honorable, and fair in its dealing with colonial questions. It not infrequently reprimanded those who came before it with "frivolous requests, urged with little reason or respect," or with grievances insufficiently supported, as against a colonial governor, "there being no proof of the facts set forth."[2] Several times it said to persons, making communications either in person or by letter, that the matter was one which lay beyond the powers of its commission,[3] and it was very

one government except by consent of the people of each colony. In recognizing that the colonial assembly had powers of its own, the board generally required that these powers be confined to matters "not repugnant to the authority and prerogative of the crown." On the prerogative after 1689, Maitland, *Constitutional History*, pp. 418–420.

1. The Privy Council in committee did the same. In 1739 it ordered the Board of Trade to write to the governor of South Carolina that in a certain particular he was "to adhere strictly to his instructions." *Board of Trade Journal*, 1735–1741, p. 287.

2. A noteworthy case of this kind is the reprimand which the board administered to Richard Partridge, son of William Partridge of New Hampshire, and agent for Pennsylvania and other colonies, who had surreptitiously obtained a copy of a letter from the Plantation Office. Partridge in being questioned "declared he would give no answer to any question that might tend to accuse himself," whereupon the board ordered that he "should not be admitted to transact business at this Board as agent for any of the plantations, until he shall have given satisfaction in relation to the said complaint." It then proceeded to lay down some important regulations regarding the use and inspection of its papers. *Ibid.*, pp. 375–376. See also, *ibid.*, 1715–1718, pp. 176, 303, 329; 1718–1722, pp. 21–22; *Board of Trade Journal*, 1742–1749, p. 296, and elsewhere.

3. *Ibid.*, 1704–1709, p. 458; 1709–1715, pp. 112, 195; 1742–1749, p. 33.

severe upon anyone who lost his temper, on one occasion charging a man who cast aspersions upon its secretary with behaving "in an indecent manner, very much unbecoming an Englishman."[1]

The board was always willing to hear both sides of a case and at times postponed further consideration until all the evidence could be brought together, even though part of it had to be obtained, if obtained at all, from America. The hearings held in its presence often took the form of a trial, with lawyers present. Such hearings, prolonged from day to day and from week to week, generally preceded the drafting of an important report, particularly when such report was asked for by the House of Lords, the House of Commons, the Privy Council,[2] or the king through the secretary of state, on such subjects as the sugar trade, the tobacco trade, the general state of the plantations, or the general situation as regards the balance of trade. In such cases, the board would set its staff at work upon the files of the office; would send out lists of questions to the custom house and elsewhere, replies to which were none too prompt; would call in merchants, quondam governors, proprietors, and former residents in the colonies, and obtain information from them as men "who are versed in the affairs of those parts."[3] Sometimes it asked that the information be sent in written form, and from this request came sundry fairly elaborate papers, which were afterward enlarged into printed pamphlets, such as those of Thomas Banister and Joshua Gee. The members of the board may not have known much about the colonies from personal experience, but they were always ready to learn what they could.[4] Some of their reports took days and weeks to prepare, that of 1721 being on the table for ten months.

The charge of procrastination which has so often been brought against the board should not be pressed too far. Though board meetings were not as frequent as some critics think they ought to have been and though attendance was lax and members were often lured away by other interests and diversions, the Plantation Office was in session all the time and the members of the staff were under a body

1. *Ibid.*, 1728–1734, p. 415.　　2. *Acts Privy Council, Colonial,* III, 62.

3. *Board of Trade Journal,* 1708–1715, p. 590; see also the board's own statement, *Calendar State Papers, Colonial,* 1706–1708, §1192.

4. It is quite true that in its ignorance of colonial conditions, the board was not infrequently misled by its informants as to the state of public opinion in America, particularly when these informants were unfriendly to the colonists.

of rules that did not err on the side of leniency. In 1714, the very year when, we are told, the board was entering on a period of deterioration, the rule was adopted that the clerks were to work from eight to twelve in the morning and from three to six in the afternoon, with the prospect, as we later learn, of having to work in the evening if required.[1] Their activities and numbers increased as time went on: a deputy secretary appeared, a clerk of the reports was appointed, additional writing clerks were taken on, and supernumerary help in the form of draftsmen and extra copying clerks was frequently employed. In attendance the members were probably no worse than those of other offices of the day. A quorum was sometimes wanting, as in 1708 and 1709, when Sunderland wrote the board that it must arrange always to have enough members in town to do business with despatch.[2] The situation became quite extraordinary in the summer of 1733 when two members were about all that could be mustered and when Colonel Bladen, on seven successive occasions, was the only member present, he doing business as if a quorum had been on hand.[3] But this was so exceptional that a reason may some day be found to explain it. On the whole, for the first sixty years of the board's history the attendance was fairly good.

The board has also been charged with neglecting its business, on the ground that laws were not reported on promptly and correspondence with the colonial governors was always in arrears. In view of what the board actually did accomplish in the main fields of its activity, the charge does not appear to be a serious one, and weighs but slightly on the debit side of the balance. Important business was sometimes put off until it could be considered "at a full board."[4] In other cases there were extenuating circumstances. The board had

1. *Board of Trade Journal,* 1708–1715, pp. 575–576; 1722–1728, pp. 121, 347; 1734–1741, pp. 19, 74, 75, 390; 1742–1749, p. 296.

2. *Ibid.,* 1704–1709, p. 455; *Calendar State Papers, Colonial,* 1708–1709, §§759, 782.

3. *Board of Trade Journal,* 1728–1734, pp. 352–357, 412. On one occasion in 1737 no business seems to have been done because, in the opinion of the editor of the *Journal,* only two members were present when three constituted a quorum. Some doubt, however, is thrown upon this view of the case, by the fact that later we find plenty of business done with only two present, *ibid.,* pp. 258, 265, 304, 306, 335, 341, 378. In 1741 when the draft of a commission was wanted in a hurry, the document was prepared in the office, the covering letter taken to Lord Munson, the only commissioner in town, to be signed, and then sent by messenger to be signed by three others in the country, pp. 381–382.

4. *Ibid.,* 1709–1715, p. 432.

great difficulty at times in getting from the crown lawyers their opinions on colonial laws and was constantly calling on the attorney and solicitor general to hurry up, finding on one occasion that the delay was due to some difficulty in regard to fees.[1] These lawyers were busy men, often members of parliament,[2] and it was a knowledge of this fact that led the board in 1718 to ask for a counsellor of its own, who might deal with the less important matters, while the crown lawyers handled those of greater moment. This experiment ended, however, in the special counsellor's doing nearly all the board's legal work and delays were almost as frequent as before. Then the board had a deal of trouble in persuading other boards and offices[3] to answer questions and to draw up statistical returns. Regarding letters to the governors it must always be remembered that correspondence with America was not the first duty of the board,[4] particularly on matters of colonial administration; that the postal service in times of war was very unreliable; that the cost of transmitting packets to and from America was very great and the board, which until 1746 paid all charges on packets of letters and papers,[5] had very little money on hand for contingent expenses; and that prompt replies to every letter received from a dozen governors, writing at length and often, called for more time than the overworked secretary had to spare. When in 1700 Governor Bellomont of New York wrote "in the anguish of [his] soul" that he was "quite dispirited from want of orders" from England, the board replied that his letters were so long and confused as to make them difficult to answer, and advised him to send letters dealing with only one matter at a time.[6] Bellomont's diffuse and involved letters must have been very trying to the English officials, for at one time or another he wrote to nearly all of them, and his prolix style must have discouraged them from attempting to answer, frequently or even at all, the many troublesome points raised. In the matter of procrastination the fault was not all on the side of the board.[7]

1. *Calendar State Papers, Colonial*, 1701, §620; *Board of Trade Journal*, 1704–1709, p. 13; 1708–1715, p. 340.

2. *Ibid.*, 1704–1709, p. 449.　　　　3. *Ibid.*, 1708–1715, pp. 16, 17.

4. In 1739 the board ordered that all letters from the governors "which have not yet been answered, be looked out and taken into consideration, as soon as conveniently may be, in order to prepare proper answers to them," *ibid.*, 1735–1741, p. 288.

5. *Ibid.*, 1754–1758, pp. 435–436; 1764–1767, p. 47.

6. *Calendar State Papers, Colonial*, 1700, §622; 1701, p. 78.

7. The writing of but one letter a year to a governor or the failure to write at all

The relations of the board with parliament and the various executive and administrative departments were regular and simple and have been adequately dealt with elsewhere,[1] but those with the Privy Council and the secretary of state need a brief consideration, because there has been, on the part of those who have written on the subject, some misunderstanding on this point.

The secretary of state was the intermediary between the king and the other parts of the British government and between the king and all foreign governments and representatives. He received the king's direction "to signify his pleasure" and he communicated the king's wishes and commands in a great variety of official papers either directly or "by his Majesty's command." As time went on and the secretariat increased in importance its functions widened and received better definition, and the two men occupying the positions of principal secretaries of state divided their duties, one taking the northern department and concerning himself with the affairs of northern Europe; the other the southern department and southern Europe, the line of separation running roughly from Paris to Constantinople, both of which cities were in the southern sphere. In theory either secretary could perform the duties of the other, though in practice such interchange took place only in cases of emergency, the other secretary generally thinking that he had quite enough work to do of his own. Early in the eighteenth century the secretary for the southern department was entrusted with the oversight of plantation affairs and the governors by their instructions were required to correspond with him whenever events occurred within their governments that demanded the immediate direction of the crown or whenever special letters requiring answers were sent to them by the secretary. The latter was therefore the only secretary of state for the colonies that existed before 1768, and was the only official in the government who had a legitimate, and indeed a prior right to exercise an executive control over colonial business. The right of the secretary to look after administration and government in the colonies was superior to that of the Board of Trade, even though in fact the board was generally

---

for two or three years can certainly be classed as a neglect of duty. On one occasion fourteen letters from Governor Mathew of the Leeward Islands were read at two successive meetings (*Board of Trade Journal*, 1735–1741, p. 132). On the other hand the governors themselves were often the culprits. In 1746 the board complained that it had received no letters or other public papers from Governor Johnston of North Carolina since 1742. *Board of Trade Journal*, 1742–1749, pp. 121, 208.

1. Dickerson, *American Colonial Government, passim.*

in closer touch with the colonies than was the secretary of state. The governors stood not a little in awe of this important official—"my noble lord" as Blakiston called Sunderland—and though their letters to him concerning policy and matters of military defense were among their most important contributions, they were always unwilling "to trouble one in such high station," as Drysdale of Virginia expressed it. They were, however, not averse to having "a good stake in the Hedge[s]," whenever patronage was involved, and some of them— Shirley, for instance—owed their appointments to their influence, or the influence of someone else, with the secretary. As a Privy Council was the highest executive body in England that possessed plenary powers over the colonies, it was inevitable that the distribution of colonial business among the council, the secretary of state for the southern department, and the Board of Trade was bound to involve considerable uncertainty and confusion.

Inasmuch as the secretary shared with the Privy Council the right of approach to the sovereign, it is not surprising that at times doubt arose in the minds of those who wished to present petitions, addresses, or reports to the king, regarding the proper procedure to follow. Nevertheless, despite this fact, it is quite clear that during the first fifty years of the board's career the method of doing the king's business was well worked out and carefully followed, with a few not very significant exceptions. The relations of the Board of Trade with the Privy Council and the secretary of state were well understood and uniformly respected, the board fulfilling its duties with efficiency, according to the standards of the day, which in official circles were none too high. The board's intercourse with the secretariat was always amicable and friendly, for each confined itself to its own particular province and rarely cut across the other's boundaries.

The secretary of state sent to the board all sorts of papers relating to the plantations that came into his hands—addresses, petitions, and complaints that were addressed to the king[1]—whenever they represented the business of trade and commerce that legitimately belonged to the board by virtue of its commission. He requested the board to draft the commercial clauses in treaties and instructions to ambassadors, to consider matters of manufactures and domestic trade that came to his attention through addresses to the crown, and to furnish

---

1. *Board of Trade Journal*, 1704–1709, pp. 216–217; 1708–1715, pp. 88, 92, 97, 107; 1715–1718, pp. 112, 114, etc.

information, render opinions, and recommend remedies in case the problems lay within its competence. In fact, whenever anything came into the secretary's office that had to do with trade and commerce and with the plantations on the commercial side, it was handed over to the board, sometimes with the request that the latter prepare a representation upon it for the king's use. Ordinarily such a representation would be sent to the Privy Council, in which case a copy would be transmitted to the secretary for his information.

In its turn the board very frequently forwarded to the secretary documents or extracts from documents that had to do with diplomacy, war, piracy, or international relations of any kind.[1] A matter of commercial interest which involved a possible diplomatic complication, such as the cutting of logwood, would be handed over to the secretary, and the two would coöperate in the settlement of the dispute, the board furnishing the secretary with all kinds of information drawn from its own files. Though the board had dealings with both secretaries, the most frequent contacts were of course with the secretary for the southern department.[2] With him there was a more or less constant exchange of papers and queries, the secretary asking the board to make inquiries, consider treaty arrangements, take certain matters into consideration, and in other ways assist him in the carrying out of his plans.

In his office during these years the secretary carried on a very considerable amount of plantation business and there are today among the papers that represent the secretary's activities a large number of bundles of original correspondence, entry books of letters written, and enclosures of one kind or another that show the secretary's connection with the colonies.[3] Both in bulk and content they are fewer and briefer than are those that accumulated in the Plantation Office, and while there is inevitably a certain amount of duplication of subject matter, the two series are at bottom quite different in the fields which they cover. It may be doubted if at any time the secretary deliberately took to himself anything that, properly speaking, fell within the province of the board. He confined his attention to matters that

1. For example, *ibid.*, 1715–1718, p. 100. On one occasion the board was directed to do this by order of the Privy Council (*ibid.*, 1704–1709, p. 84). The board sent extracts also to the Admiralty and the secretary at war, *ibid.*, 1735–1741, p. 137.

2. *Ibid.*, 1715–1718, p. 100; 1728–1734, pp. 297, 299, 306, 311, 331–332, 337, 347.

3. The whereabouts of these papers can be discovered by consulting the key to the America and West Indies series in Andrews, *Guide*, I, 280–287. See also *Calendar State Papers, Colonial*, 1714–1715, §160.

were largely diplomatic and military and left to the board those that were mercantile and commercial. This line of demarcation seems always to have been well preserved.

Much stress has been laid upon the board's want of patronage by those who believe in the secretary's encroachment on its functions and its consequent deterioration after 1714.[1] The statement is sometimes made that the secretaries, particularly Newcastle, took from the board the selection of the governors and deputy governors in the colonies and in so doing seriously impaired the influence of the board. In answer to that statement it is enough to say that before 1752 the board never selected a governor or even expected to do so, and that it is very doubtful if by the terms of its commission it would have had a right to play so important a part in directing colonial appointments. In 1702 it replied to one Jory, who had sent in a memorial in behalf of a candidate for the lieutenant governorship of Nevis, that the memorialist should make his first application to the queen, "it not being usual for this Board to represent their opinion upon matters of that kind, unless they be referred to them by H.M."[2] That the secretaries occasionally consulted the board in the matter of such appointments is clear and there is at least one instance in which the board made a recommendation on its own account, but generally speaking the selection of governors and other officials, notably those holding what were commonly known as "patent offices," was entirely

1. Neither in the commission nor in the board's own statement of its powers and duties is anything said about patronage. "We are directed to examine and take an account of the state of the trade, and to do what in us lies for the incouragement thereof, in giving the merchants and others concern'd all the satisfaction and dispatch we can in their business from time to time, as also to make constant enquiries into the condition of his Majesty's plantations in America, as well with regard to the administration of government as in relation to commerce, and how those colonies may be kept in good order and rendered most beneficial to this kingdom; to prepare commissions and instructions to governours and to examine the journals and proceedings of the several councils and assemblies and all acts and laws made by them in order to the amendment, approbation, or disallowance thereof; to correspond with all the said governours and other officers in the publick administration, and to make representations to his Majesty or the Privy Council of what may occur to us upon the heads and matters aforesaid." C. O. 387:17, p. 160; *ibid.*, 36, pp. 340–348, November 12, 1707.

2. *Calendar State Papers, Colonial*, 1702, p. 707. On May 28, 1709, Blakiston wrote to Philip Ludwell, "You seem to lay some stress upon the prevalency of the Lords of Trade and that those interests would be of great use [in the matter of colonial appointments]. I doe not know of any examples that they have ever cared to recommend anything of this nature to the Queen, but only what relates to the management of their affairs. . . . If the Lords of Trade might be of use to you I have some interest with most of them." *Virginia Magazine*, V, 45–46.

in the secretary's hands and had never been anywhere else.[1] Regarding the selection of members of colonial councils the case is otherwise. The board selected these councillors as part of its routine business and usually protested if the secretary tried to intervene. In 1702 Nottingham sent in a list of names to be inserted in Cornbury's instructions and a little later named a councillor for Barbados. The members of the board received these nominations under protest, for though in 1706 they conceded the queen's right to give directions they did not take kindly to the secretary's interference, and in the end were able to make good their claim. This right of the board became so firmly fixed that when in 1726 Newcastle, without consulting the board, appointed a councillor for Barbados on his own account, the board notified him "that it has ever been esteemed the right of this Board to recommend persons to supply vacancies in the several councils in the plantations."[2] For the first fifty-six years of its existence this was all the patronage that the board ever enjoyed or expected to enjoy.

As the board had only advisory and recommendatory powers and was neither a committee of the Privy Council nor a division of the secretary of state's office, it always experienced some difficulty in determining which channel to use in forwarding to the king in council its reports and representations. Generally it sent directly to the council, with a copy to the secretary of state, such reports as it prepared in response to a reference from the council's committee, and to the secretary of state those ordered by him in the name of the king.[3] It

1. *Calendar State Papers, Colonial*, 1700, §§87, 410; *Board of Trade Journal*, 1715–1718, pp. 209, 325, 336. In 1717 on the occasion of Secretary Methuen's coming to the board, the latter suggested that a new governor be sent to Jamaica, but it did not venture to say who the appointee should be (*Board of Trade Journal*, 1715–1718, p. 209). Blakiston sensed the situation when he wrote Ludwell, "If a person were recommended to the Queen for that office and she sent to the Lords of Trade to know the character of any person in America, then I am well assured I could be able to serve you and her" (*Virginia Magazine*, V, 46). The board did ask to be kept informed regarding the secretary's appointments, as necessary to the proper performance of its regular business (*Board of Trade Journal*, 1715–1718, pp. 15, 19, 25; *Calendar State Papers, Colonial*, 1714–1715, §352). It had some part in the revocation of Governor Nicholson's patent. *Board of Trade Journal*, 1704–1709, pp. 124, 125, 129.

In 1708 the board protested against the practice of allowing patent officers to be served by deputy, but apparently without any effect, as it had nothing to do with such appointments. *Board of Trade Journal*, 1704–1709, pp. 520, 522.

2. *Calendar State Papers, Colonial*, 1702, §§357, 358, 794, 806, 836, p. 514; 1702–1703, p. 75; 1706–1708, §1057; *Board of Trade Journal*, 1704–1709, pp. 290, 542–543; 1709–1715, p. 306; 1722–1728, p. 287.

3. *Ibid.*, 1704–1709, p. 208; *Calendar State Papers, Colonial*, 1706–1708, §§45, 974.

may have sent directly to the House of Lords and House of Commons—the matter is uncertain—such as were asked for by those legislative bodies, even though, as was usually the case, the request had come originally from the secretary of state.[1] Up to this point the procedure was simple and easily followed, but after a few years Secretary Sunderland, noticing that the board was neglecting to send the promised copy to the secretary's office and realizing that reports regarding plantation affairs had been made to the Privy Council of which he knew nothing, entered his protest. He wrote to the board that he was surprised to learn of a recommendation which he had neither seen nor even heard of before. "I thought it had been usual," he said, "to acquaint the secretary of state with all business that relates immediately to his province before it be brought to the council. I am sure it is so reasonable that I may very well expect it. Therefore I desire that it may be so from you in the future."[2] The board interpreted this to mean that in the future Sunderland wished all representations sent to him, before they were despatched to the queen in council, and it wrote in reply that it would comply with his request.[3]

For a number of years this practice was maintained, the board sending to the secretary all representations that were to be laid before the Privy Council. It was justified in so doing on the not unreasonable ground that the secretary of state and the Board of Trade, having in largest measure responsibility for colonial affairs, should each know what the other was doing. What the secretary asked, the board in its turn asked also. In January, 1709, it wrote Sunderland that having sent him several representations it had not been informed as to what had been done with regard to them and wished that the secretary would let it know.[4] Probably the secretary complied, for Dartmouth, Sunderland's successor, took pains to notify the board of the king's decision in a certain case and requested it to attend the Privy

1. Whenever the House of Lords or House of Commons wanted information from the Board of Trade, they addressed the king, asking him to direct the board (through the secretary of state) to prepare a representation on a given subject and to lay it before the house. It may be that this was considered the proper procedure. *Board of Trade Journal*, 1704–1709, p. 427.

2. *Calendar State Papers, Colonial*, 1706–1708, §§703, 1067. In 1706 Secretary Hedges directed the board to send its draft of Crowe's instructions directly to the council office, and this would seem to have been the customary procedure at that time. *Ibid.*, §610; *Board of Trade Journal*, 1704–1709, p. 293.

3. *Calendar State Papers, Colonial*, 1704–1709, pp. 307, 323, 575; 1709–1715, p. 79; 1706–1708, §718.

4. *Ibid.*, 1708–1709, §294; *Board of Trade Journal*, 1715–1718, p. 69.

Council and explain the points raised.[1] But there was bound to be some confusion between the two offices in the matter of an interchange of information and the board several times afterward had to remind the secretary that it wanted to know what was passing through his office relating to the plantations, as it had obligations to parliament that could not be met until it was notified of the king's pleasure therein.[2] This practice of sending representations to the Privy Council through the secretary of state was, however, carried so far in the next few years as to rouse the council to a realization that something irregular was taking place and brought from it a protest. On August 12, 1724, James Vernon, one of the clerks in extraordinary, wrote to the board, very peremptorily, that in the future, by order of the council, all representations transmitted "to his Majesty at this Board" must be sent directly to the clerk of the council in waiting and not to the secretary of state; and that the particular representation which had been sent to the king in council through the Duke of Newcastle would be returned to the board "to be transmitted in due form." To this demand the board agreed, stating that what the council asked was "as usual."[3] Probably from this time forward, during the period under consideration, such of the board's reports and representations as were designed for the king in his council were sent directly to the council office and it would look as if the "interference" of the secretary of state was really more "pernicious" from 1708 to 1724 than from 1724 to 1744, the first twenty years of Newcastle's administration.

As time went on the procedure became regular, the Privy Council referring business to its committee, the committee handing on queries regarding matters of fact, but never matters of law, to the Board of Trade (or elsewhere), and the latter sending back its reply to the council, with a copy to the secretary of state.[4] Before 1704 the Privy Council itself seems to have sent its queries directly to the Board of Trade, but after that date it resigned its deliberative functions more and more to itself sitting as committee and as council became merely a ratifying body. This committee of the whole council, which had

1. *Calendar State Papers, Colonial,* 1710–1711, §386.

2. *Board of Trade Journal,* 1715–1718, p. 69; 1722–1728, p. 349; 1728–1734, p. 154.

3. *Acts Privy Council, Colonial,* III, 67; *Board of Trade Journal,* 1722–1728, p. 117. Orders in council were always sent directly to the Board of Trade, never through the secretary of state. For example, *Board of Trade Journal,* 1704–1709, p. 68.

4. *Board of Trade Journal,* 1704–1709, pp. 15, 221; 1728–1734, p. 77.

been functioning since 1689, bore various names according to the business entrusted to it, and was known as the "Lords of the Committee of Council for hearing appeals and complaints from the plantations," or, later, simply "the Lords of the Committee," "Committee of Council," or "Committee." On one occasion, at least, Queen Anne was present at its meeting,[1] but later sovereigns never attended. At times the members of the Board of Trade or their secretary were called upon to attend, and once the latter reported that he had been present at a cabinet council, meeting at the house of the Earl of Nottingham.[2]

In reaching a general estimate as to the usefulness of the Board of Trade and in endeavoring to determine the extent of its accomplishments, one must emphasize less than is usually done the importance of politics, personnel, and patronage in affecting its activities. These factors played their part, but that part was not a significant one, or one that seriously interfered with the board's performance of its duties as defined by its commission. With colonial administration, on either the political or the constitutional side, it had to do only as far as it was obliged to draft the governors' instructions, to correspond with the governors on all matters connected with the well-being of the plantations, and to obtain information for the files of its office. It had to see that the royal orders were carried out, not so much for the sake of keeping colonial administration in the right path as for seeing that the colonies were doing what England expected them to do. Its main interest and that for which it was originally created was not to act as a board of colonial administration or government but to advance the trade and commerce of the realm, the very keystone of the structure, "upon which the strength and riches thereof depend." To promote trade and commerce in England's interest and the interests of her merchants is the chief injunction in the text of the commission and this was the outstanding business with which the board concerned itself during the greater part of its existence.

---

NOTE: English writers on the history of the British navy have as a rule avoided this subject of corruption. There is ample material for a study of it. In 1694 one Robert Crossfield issued two pamphlets, *England's Glory Revived* and *Truth brought to Light or the Corrupt Practices of some Persons at Court laid open,* in which with commend-

1. *Calendar State Papers, Colonial,* 1702-1703, §802.
2. *Board of Trade Journal,* 1704-1709, pp. 12, 237. For attendance by the secretary of the board at a cabinet council, *ibid.,* p. 4.

able but not always well-directed zeal he bombarded the Privy Council and the Treasury with proposals for the improvement of the service. The pamphlets, though biassed, do throw light on the general situation. In 1695 Crossfield issued *An Account of Robert Crossfield's Proceedings, House of Lords, and of the Miserable State and Condition of the Nation*, and *Justice Perverted and Innocence and Loyalty Oppressed, or Detection of the corruption of some Persons in Places of Great Trust*, in which he presented the case of the shipwright, George Everet, who brought charges against the Admiralty and the Navy Board. In the same pamphlet is printed Everet's "Memorial" and the "Petition of R.C.," the latter of which was issued separately in a folio of eight pages. For the Baston case, which concerned corruption in the Board of Sick and Wounded, see *Baston's case vindicated, or a Brief Account of some evil practices of the present Commissioners for Sick and Wounded, as they were proved*, (1) *Before the Lords of the Admiralty*, (2 ly) *Before the Lords of the Council, and* (3 ly) *Before the Commissioners for stating the Accounts*, 1695, and Samuel Baston, *A Dialogue between a Modern Courtier and an Honest English Gentleman, to which is added the Author's Dedication to both Houses of Parliament, to whom he appeals for Justice*, March 16, 1697. The scandals in the Navy Office and the yards at Portsmouth and elsewhere are treated in *Justice the Best Support to Government or a Brief Account of some Public Transactions during the Late War*, 1697. This pamphlet refers to frauds and embezzlements in 1694–1695, and contains an elaborate discussion of the whole matter, covering corruption in the Post Office and the Apothecaries' Department. It refers to both the Everet and the Baston cases, and speaks of "the griping avarice of public ministers." On the same subject see James Whiston, *England's Calamities Discovered with the Proper Remedy*, 1696, but written in 1695, in which mention is made of "The Multitude of Petitions that now lye in the Council Office (which are kept from his Majesty's knowledge) and have not been read, gives a sufficient demonstration of the inhumanity of some persons at this time in the Government" (p. 24 note). The work treats of the debauching of justice, excessive fees, buying of places, treatment of debtors, multiplication of offices, corruption of office holders, and the like, as characteristic of the general situation throughout the kingdom. In *The State of the Navy consider'd, in relation to Victualling, particularly in the Straits and the West Indies, with some Thoughts on the Mismanagement of the Admiralty for some years past*, is an indictment of the management of the navy since the Revolution of 1689, with "sailors poisoned by bad provisions or starved for want of food." In this connection one should examine *Matters of Fact relating to the Navy truly stated*, 6 pages, folio, 1705, and the *Report from the Commissioners appointed to examine and state the Public Accompts of the Kingdom*, 1703 (first paper) and *The Debts due to the Army*, 1703 (second paper). There are remarks by "an old Carpenter" in the *Petty-Southwell Correspondence*, pp. 266–267, along the same line for the year 1687. Everet's name appears in *Calendar State Papers, Colonial*, 1693–1696, §§1674, 1713. He was called before the Lords of Trade, March 12, 1696, but nothing further seems to have been done about his complaints. For charges of fraud on a large scale in 1712 in the Victualling Office and elsewhere see Boyer, *Political State*, III, 136 and *passim*; for humorous but biting comments, Ned Ward, *Wooden World Dissected*. Charges of embezzlement were brought at this time against those who were the contractors and workmen engaged in rebuilding St. Paul's cathedral. Historical Manuscripts Commission, *Portland*, X, 103–109.

That bribery, corruption, and political jobbery were not confined to the early period but were equally rampant later, during the Seven Years' War and the American Revolution, appears from various sources. Perhaps the most telling indictment of conditions in the years 1757 to 1763 is to be found in Charles Johnstone's *Chrysal, or the Adventures of a Guinea* (ed. E. A. Baker), which shows systematic corruption in high places, the levying of blackmail, and an iniquitous division of the spoils. After the capture of Havana in 1762, we are told, Henry Fox, in the paymaster general's office, and the heads of the army and the navy pocketed large sums, while the men got less than £4 apiece. When the war broke out with France in 1778 the number of ships in the navy was insufficient, naval storehouses were empty, and ships sent to America were badly rigged. Complaints by Captain Thomas Baillie regarding conditions in Greenwich Hospital were voiced in two pamphlets printed in 1779, *State of Facts relative to Greenwich Hospital* and *Another State of Facts relative to Greenwich Hospital,* which led to Baillie's trial, acquittal, and eventual ejection from the navy. An investigation by the House of Lords whitewashed Sandwich, first lord of the Admiralty, but an *Address to the Lords Commissioners of the Admiralty upon the Degenerated Dissatisfied State of the British Navy* led to a more exact inquiry in 1783, which disclosed wholesale robbery in bread, beef, pork, and other provisions. It is well known that Richard Rigby, paymaster of the forces, 1768–1784, made of his office, as others had done before him, a "paradise of jobbery." The same charge brought against Lord Ranelagh, 1689–1703, is refuted by Dr. Shaw in *Calendar of Treasury Books,* XIX, lxviii, who declares that the characterization of Ranelagh as a "rascally Army Paymaster General" is "wholly untrue and most unmerited."

# CHAPTER X

## MERCANTILISM AND THE COLONIES: HISTORICALLY CONSIDERED

HAVING examined thus far the circumstances leading to the adoption of the acts of navigation and trade, the essential features of the acts themselves, and the machinery set in motion for their execution and for the control of trade in general, we must now consider the ideas that actuated Englishmen of the period in shaping their commercial policy and in defining their relations with the plantations in America. The history of our colonies is bound up with these ideas and no successful attempt to estimate the course of colonial development is possible unless an understanding be reached regarding the motives that determined the commercial relationship with the mother country. We must know at this point the mind of the merchant-capitalist just as in previous volumes we have endeavored to know the minds of the Puritan, the Quaker, and the landed proprietor.

To comprehend what was going on in the mercantile mind of the seventeenth and eighteenth centuries and to trace to their origins the convictions and aims on the commercial side of those in the secretariat, the Privy Council, and the Board of Trade who had to do with colonial affairs is a task of considerable complexity. Men of today, living under radically different social, intellectual, and material conditions, to whom the views and practices of a bygone generation, now largely but not entirely abandoned,[1] are unfamiliar and difficult to grasp, have condemned the old British system of commercial management as injurious to the colonies and therefore fundamentally wrong. Whether injurious to the colonies or not, it was not fundamentally wrong but fundamentally right to the Englishmen of

1. Mercantilism may represent the ideas of a bygone age, but remnants of it are still to be found. A high protective tariff is one of these remnants and slogans not infrequently heard, such as "Keep the money in the country," "A favorable balance of trade," and "Foreign trade is the key to riches or ruin" (a mercantile war-cry revived as late as 1937, in relation to cotton, as in older days a similar war-cry was familiar to England in relation to wool) are others. The confusion of the seventeenth and eighteenth centuries between money as a measuring piece of wealth and real wealth in the form of consumable goods flourishes in some quarters today as actively as ever.

the eighteenth century. It is easy for anyone, without knowledge of the circumstances out of which the system arose and of the conditions that it was designed to meet, to carry back into an age of beginnings judgments based on the matured experiences of a later age. Beer speaks of the dangerous and well-nigh incurable tendency of many a modern writer to infer subjectively that because he and his fellows would find a certain arrangement insufferably restrictive today, their predecessors two hundred years ago must also have found it so.

What then were the conditions that confronted Englishmen during our colonial period? Under the Tudors England had risen from being an inferior European power to the position of one of the most important among the maritime states of the west. Some of these states were monarchies, such as Portugal, Spain, and France; one was a republic, Holland; while others were cities, Hamburg, Bremen, and Brussels. A little more in the background, as England saw them, were the three crowns of Denmark, Norway, and Sweden—the Northern Crowns, as they were often called—and still farther away were Russia, the cities of the Baltic, and the city-states of the Mediterranean. These were all potential rivals in the commercial field. The relations existing among them were charged with the spirit of commercial enmity and competition. Even in the sixteenth century trade had been gradually working its way through the crust of political and religious controversy and acquiring a preponderant influence over the international activities of all northern and western Europe. By the end of the seventeenth and the beginning of the eighteenth centuries the balance of trade had become, in the eyes of the growing body of merchants, the very *raison d'être* of the balance of power, and behind every diplomatic, military, and naval operation a trade motive could generally be found. To statesmen, merchants, and planters trade leadership had become a mainspring of policy and one of the necessary accompaniments of national prosperity, wealth, and power.[1] As the agricultural economy of the Middle Ages gave rise to a feudal order of society, so the commercial economy of

---

1. "Trade is so interwoven with the interest of princes that no nation can be truly powerful without a share of the riches that are thereby obtained. For this reason the improvement of trade is become a principal affair of the state. Since therefore trade is not only necessary to the well-being of a state it is also a game whereat nations must play." *Considerations on Two Papers* (1728), pp. 4–5. Compare also *The Interest of Great Britain considered . . . proving . . . that the Balance of Power in Christendom is the Balance of Trade* (1707). Written by J. B. and dedicated to Robert Harley. It bears the motto, *Nec Natura aut Lex operantur per Saltum.*

the seventeenth and eighteenth centuries gave rise to a mercantilist state of mind; and just as feudal ideas continued to dominate the social conditions and the land law of these later centuries, so mercantilist ideas prevailed in incipient form back in the days when feudalism was still in the ascendant.[1] It was bound to inhere in any phase or period of history when trade and commerce were essential factors in the struggle of a state to attain national security and solvency.

England in the seventeenth century, though enjoying an improved financial position after her treaty with Spain in 1604, entered after 1640 upon a period of financial depression, due in part to economic causes—rising prices following an increase in the amount of accumulated silver bullion—and in part to constitutional crises, civil war, and the financial insecurity of the victorious Puritan minority. England was still an isolated state—completely so after the loss of Calais in 1557—and was underpopulated and underdeveloped. It had a shifting and unstable population with a large part of its land still under marsh, fen, and forest, conditions that made the problem of its poor and unemployed increasingly serious as the century wore on. It had come late into competition with other European powers and its success was uncertain and its situation far from impregnable. We are not surprised that in those years—our seventeenth century of colonization—English statesmen should have deemed the welfare of the kingdom, its improvement and stability, their first obligation, and should have been convinced of the necessity of subordinating the interests of individuals, both those within the kingdom and those in the outlying parts of the English world, to the imperative needs of the realm—England, Wales, and Berwick-upon-Tweed. Monopoly for the realm was the first consideration, and this was to be maintained by preventing all others from prospering at England's expense. Such a monopoly was self-protective and in a sense selfish, but it was a monopoly deemed necessary for England's very existence.

In the maritime struggle that began early in the seventeenth century no weakling could long survive. Many interests had to be considered, for whatever would aid in the winning of the victory was of paramount importance. Agriculture, an old-time activity and in the seventeenth century still one of England's leading concerns—

1. Horrocks, *A Short History of Mercantilism* (1925), with a bibliography up to that date, and Heckscher, *Mercantilism,* two vols. (1935), deal with the larger aspects of the subject. Neither of the writers pays any particular attention to mercantilism in its relation to the colonies.

because outside the principal towns England was still an agricultural state—could no longer be depended on as a source of surplus wealth or of national strength in an emergency. Though improvements were continuing steadily, by enclosing, manuring, taking in of the waste, bettering of lands that were poor and thin, and draining swamps, marshes, and fens, yet the available arable area was insufficient in itself to sustain a growing population. But the possession of landed property was the pride of the country gentleman, the symbol of social preëminence, and ownership of the soil was the ambition of all who were making money in other than agricultural pursuits. It played a very important part in the life of the state, for membership in parliament and appointment to high official positions were still controlled by the propertied class. Industrialism was in its infancy. Manufacturing was in the domestic stage. Technical skill in the arts had yet to be developed and mechanical improvements, such as were later set in motion by the industrial advance, were very slow in getting under way. The manufacturers were everywhere subordinate to the merchants and capital and invention were largely devoted to the interests of commerce. Feudalism, mercantilism, and industrialism are stages in the organization of English society, and the century from 1660 to 1760 was the era of mercantile domination, when the manufacturers of the midlands and the south were dependent on the great mercantile houses of London and the outports for the handling of their goods. Between agriculture, the economic importance of which was declining, though the population of England was still less than twenty-five per cent urban, and manufacturing, the economic importance of which was yet to come, stood trade and commerce, the cardinal factors at that period in the life of the nation. They were England's main non-military sources of strength in the conflict with its earliest commercial rival Holland and with Holland's successor and England's inveterate eighteenth century rival, France.

During this period of a hundred years, in the minds of the influential men of England, the safety of the kingdom was more closely tied up with trade than it was with either politics or diplomacy. Most, though by no means all,[1] of the mercantilists—merchants,

---

1. There were during the early eighteenth century, a group of those who favored war with Spain, on account of the opportunity it gave to obtain bullion by the seizure of Spanish plate fleets. This group was a survival of the past, when the amassing of bullion was a cardinal object of the seventeenth century mercantilist, rather than of the

tradesmen, and manufacturers as well as pamphleteers—hated war and the diplomacy that led to war, as interfering with the prosperity of the nation, and they resented the influence of party politics in determining any governmental programme that affected trade. "What has trade to do with your political quarrels," wrote Defoe, "and what business have party men with the commerce of the nation? Trade is neither Whig nor Tory, Church or Dissenter, High Church or Low Church. If parties come to govern our trade, all our commerce will be at an end." Said another, "Peace is anticipated Heaven, war is a transient Hell." To the peaceable merchant war was like a law suit, leaving the recoverer loser. He wanted a universal calm, no apprehension of violence, no war, no thieves, no pirates, no Algerines, no Sallee-men, no Tuniziens or Tripolitans—in a word no enemy to be feared. To the mercantilist all preparations for war were a great hindrance to trade; for peace and trade, like the plowman and a kindly season, were close confederates for the nation's prosperity.[1] From such comments as this, which probably represented the opinions of a majority of England's merchants, Napoleon may well have inferred that England was a nation of shopkeepers.

Throughout mercantilist literature, from the beginning of the seventeenth century to the close of the Seven Years' War, runs the same paean of praise regarding the value of trade to England. Though the religious, political, and constitutional conflict that absorbed the attention of Englishmen from 1603 to 1660 gave birth to an enormous amount of pamphlet literature, for nothing conduces more to pamphleteering than religious and political controversy, the mercantilists of that period were not without voice and Wheeler, Mun, Malynes, Misselden, Parker, Battie, Cradocke, Roberts, Robinson, Digges, Maddison, and others, some of whom are anonymous, gave vent to their opinions regarding the importance of foreign trade and its neglect by the government. They urged its encouragement as the very touchstone of prosperity, and laid great stress on the necessity of obtaining an excess of exports over imports that a profit might be returned to the kingdom in the form of coin or bullion. They were not all agreed as between a regulated or controlled trade and a monopoly and were constantly harassed by the difficulty of discovering

eighteenth century exporter and importer, with whom the idea of bullion as wealth had lost much of its force.

1. Thomas Merchant, *Peace and Trade, War and Taxes or the Irreparable Damage of New Trade in Case of War. In a Letter to the Craftsman* (1729).

why trade was good at some times and bad at others. They studied the mercantile methods of Holland and finding them superior to their own begged the government to copy these methods so far as to accord the merchants greater privileges, more protection, and an intelligent enlargement of opportunities. They stated the remedies, as they saw them—lower customs, lower interest, increase of manufacturing, recovery of the fisheries, improved transportation, and an efficient employment of the poor.[1] By the middle of the century they were emphasizing the sovereignty of the seas, the enlarging of the area of plantations, and the making of England the emporium or warehouse, whence other nations might be furnished with foreign commodities. They were already beginning to give shape to a programme, based on the idea of the balance of trade, wherein England might receive wealth rather than pay it out, and they were willing to commit the nation to the employment of every advantage—by bargain, treaty, or force of arms—whereby success might be obtained over foreign rivals.

To the mercantilist of this period an even exchange of goods was not profitable, for only by a balance in England's favor could that be obtained which England needed—an accumulated body of treasure in the form of gold and silver coin or bullion, as the true and only embodiment of national wealth. Treasure, they said, that remains enriches, profiting king, commonwealth, and merchant alike. Money was the visible expression of wealth, wealth was the symbol of solvency, and solvency was the necessary condition accompanying all successful relations with the outside world. In a country where there existed no gold and very little silver of England's own production money could be obtained only by a favorable exchange of goods with foreign countries, of such a kind as to cause a flow of gold and silver to England. Even as late as 1712 a writer could say that the Spanish West Indies were "the happy region where gold and silver do most abound, and consequently the trade that we drive thither, bringing back most of those species, must be allowed to be the most valuable branch of commerce."[2] It was indispensable that the goods exported be manufactured goods, for it was deemed the ruin of a nation to export native products and import foreign manufactures. Though a

---

1. Andrew Yarranton in *England's Improvement* (1677) suggested a "school of industry," founded on the Dutch model.

2. *A Letter from a West Indian Merchant to a Gentleman at Tunbridge* (London, 1712), pp. 15–18.

profit might be made in that way, such a profit was at the expense of the nation's health.

When after 1660 trade and commerce became, as they never had been before, leading objects of governmental concern, the voice of the mercantilist gained emphasis and his paean of praise was more in tune with the growing importance of the subject. Several score of apt quotations could be given but only a few of the more striking ones will suffice. William de Britaine,[1] "Trade and commerce are the pillars of prosperity and safety to England." Reynel,[2] "Riches are the convenience of the nation, people are the strength, pleasure and glory of the nation, but trade preserves both." Bethel,[3] "Trade is the true and intrinsick interest of England, without which it cannot subsist. From trade there doth not only arise riches to the subjects, rendering a nation considerable, but also increases of revenue and therein power and strength to the sovereign." George Phillips,[4] "Trade is the glory, strength and security of the English Nation, the fountain and source of the Riches, Wealth and Plenty, which render it the envy and astonishment of all the neighbouring Kingdoms, and without which it were impossible to provide sustenance for the innumerable company of inhabitants wherewith the country is sufficiently furnished and the cities and towns are absolutely crowded. It is trade that preserves the body politick in health . . . trade is the blood that circulates in the veins and arteries of the Commonwealth and disperseth the animal spirits to all limits and extreme parts of the body." Whiston,[5] "All the happiness and glory of England depend upon the encouragement and good management of trade and navigation, so its neglect will be England's ruin and confusion." Anonymous, "Englishmen live by trade, their commerce has raised them from what they were to what they are, and may if cultivated raise them yet farther to what they never were. . . . Can a nation be safe without strength and is power to be compassed and secured but by

1. William de Britaine, *The Interest of England in the Present War with Holland* (London, 1672), p. 1.

2. Carew Reynel, *The True English Benefit or an Account of the Chief National Improvements* (London, 1674), pp. 1–2.

3. [Slingsby Bethel?], *An Account of the French Usurpation upon the Trade of England* (London, 1679), p. 4.

4. George Phillips, *The Interest of England in the Preservation of Ireland, humbly presented to the Parliament of England* (London, 1689), p. 16.

5. James Whiston, *The Mismanagements in Trade Discover'd, And Adapt Methods to Preserve and Exceedingly Improve It* (London, 1704), p. 8.

riches? And can a country become rich anyway but by the help of a well-managed and extended traffick?" And listen to Defoe, a little later, "England is a trading nation, the wealth and opulence of the nation is owing to trade, the influence of trade is felt in every branch of the government, in the value of its land, and the blood of trade is mixed and blended with the blood of gallantry, so that trade is the life of the nation, the soul of its felicity, the spring of its wealth, the support of its greatness, and the staff on which both king and parliament must lean, and which (if it should sink) the whole fabric must fall, the body politic would sicken and languish, its power decline, and the figure it makes in the world grow by degrees contemptibly mean." And, finally, Bolingbroke wrote in *The Second Craftsman Extraordinary* (1729), "Our trade is the sole and principal support of our Land; it is to our commerce that we owe our wealth, our grandeur and our prosperity; it is the mainspring to which the machine of our government moves and which has cost our industrious ancestors much pains and labour to cultivate and improve."[1] In fact, to all these and to others, trade was "the fairest mistress in the world."

To the mercantile mind, and to other minds as well, England's whole security and hope of success lay in the development of her trade—her foreign trade. But it was no longer treasure of gold and silver bullion that was wanted, to hoard as a miser hoards wealth. The money metals were losing something of their old-time significance. Charles Davenant said that not gold and silver were England's treasure, but any returns that were profitable to the state. And others said the same.[2] What the mercantilists of this period wanted was what all states and nations wanted and still want—and individuals no less—a wide margin of profit, a surplus laid by for emergencies, and they wanted it the more because they saw themselves surrounded by rivals and enemies, whose success meant England's failure and

1. Page 13.
2. William Wood has many pertinent remarks on this point in *A Survey of Trade* (London, 1718, 2d edition 1719). To him wealth was a "national stock," including not only gold and silver coin, bullion, wrought plate, rings and jewels, but also furniture, apparel, stock for trade and consumption, cattle, new manufactures, stores of native goods and foreign commodities. Merchant fleets and powerful navies he deemed not only the signs of a "thriving people" but "themselves real and effectual wealth" (pp. 37, 54–55). All these things were to be accounted "national stock," just as much as were coined money of England, foreign coins, and bullion (p. 74). So were all goods bought of other countries for export (p. 84) because their sale brought in a profit. He considers gold and silver of no "intrinsic value" in themselves, "except as

whose victory on land and sea meant the loss to England of influence, prestige, and power. The Dutch, French, Italians, Danes, Hamburgers, and others were competing with her and with each other for custom and trade, and were threatening at all times to cut into England's sphere and to undersell her in the markets of Europe. The pamphleteers were constantly filled with forebodings; they saw trade in decay, with others than themselves successful, and they were forever seeking to find out the causes.[1] They saw parliament lacking in interest, the country gentlemen antagonistic, statesmen indifferent, the rates of exchange high, laborers indolent and slow to work, manufacturing costs increasing, the building of ships more costly, and luxury and extravagance widespread. The mercantile mind seemed always in a state of depression.

In their consideration of these conditions the mercantilists were far from agreed as to causes and remedies. There never did exist anything that may be called an accepted mercantile system, in the sense of an established body of mercantile doctrines upon which all the mercantilists could unite, for mercantilism never had any substruc-

---

they are a settled and constant exchange for commodities of all kinds" (p. 334). He declares that people after all are the strength and riches of the nation (p. 306), and that "industry and skill to improve trade and the apt situation of a country for it are more real riches to a people than even the possession of gold and silver mines" (p. 332).

This change in the prevailing point of view regarding "treasure" can be found in Richard Gouldsmith's *Some considerations on Trade and Manufactures, address'd to the Inhabitants of the Town of Ipswich* (London, 1725), "No sum that can be dug out of mines bears any proportion with what may be made to rise from the whole labour of a trading and industrious people."

1. The subject even got into the pulpit. In a sermon preached in the chapel of the Guildhall, September 12, 1669, the Rev. David Barton of St. Margarets said, "For is it not the general complaint, and out-cry of the City, that there is a universal decay of Trade? Do not the Merchants complain? *we looke for much*, and that upon good ground; for we have sent forth our Ships richly laden and ventured them on long and dangerous Voyages; *but loe it comes to little,* our Ships return not, or if they do, the income doth not answer the expence, our Commodities hardly yeeld what they cost. Doth not the Shop-keeper complain? *we look for much*, having taken Houses at great Prices and Furnished our shops with rich wares, *but loe it comes to little,* there are few Buyers, and but small gaines, we can scarce pay our rents. Doth not the Handicrafts man complain *we look for much*, for we labour hard and work good and sufficient wares; *but loe it comes to little;* the Shop-keeper will not buy but at his own rates; so that we have little more than our labour for our Paines. And that which adds to the unhappiness of all this is, that every one of these is apt to impute this Calamity to any thing rather than the right cause and so hinder themselves of the true remedy, because they will not understand the true cause of the distemper: Either a Forreigne Nations ingrossing Trade abroad, or the Magistrates neglect of Trade at home must bear the blame." *Mercy in the midst of Judgement, By a gracious discovery of a certain Remedy for London's Languishing Trade* (London, 1670), pp. 45–46.

ture of sound principles to support it. Opinion was constantly shaping and reshaping itself, as external circumstances changed and as remedial measures were brought forward for examination. These men were in complete agreement on only a few main features, the most conspicuous of which were the importance of trade and the necessity of securing a general balance in England's favor; on all others they were in no common accord. One is frequently more impressed with the disagreements among them than with the agreements. On practically every important issue that arose in the diplomatic and political field, the differences were marked and the debates heated. And as the mercantilists were not agreed as to the effect of England's foreign and domestic policy on the trade and manufactures of England, so the members of parliament itself were often widely at variance as to how far it was desirable to go in meeting the mercantile demands. In common with the country generally they were divided into parties, the lines of which were, however, none too well defined. Social interests were quite as influential as were party sympathies in determining men's attitudes toward issues that were largely economic in character and the party predilections of that day are easily resolvable into preferences that were not political at all— church, landed proprietorship, family connections, commerce in all its manifestations, freedom, and liberty. These things were often deciding factors in the casting of a vote on such questions as open and free trade versus monopoly, East India exchanges, and the traffic with France.[1] The mercantilist pamphleteers at times bitterly reproached parliament for its neglect of the merchants' welfare and for its willingness to let factional and group loyalty, class selfishness, and landed interests control the decisions of its members.[2] At the same

1. The late Professor Ashley, in his essay on "Tory Free Trade" (*Surveys, Historic and Economic*, pp. 268–307) endeavors to show that belief in an open trade, or as it was then called a "free trade," was the special prerogative of the Tories and that on such a question as the balance of trade with France the mercantilists divided along strictly party lines. While individual mercantilists may have followed party predilections (though I doubt if it can be certainly proved in the case of any one of them, for outside of parliament party grouping at the time of the treaty of Utrecht was very nebulous) it is certainly not true of the mercantilists as a whole. Defoe in the *Mercator* is not arguing as a free trader or as a Tory. If we are to take his statements at their face value he is agitating in favor of a reciprocal trade with France, because he believes that thereby England would gain more than she would lose. The same was true of others also. Neither Child nor Barbon in the late seventeenth century was writing as a party man.

2. R. Badcour in *Considerations offered to all the Corporations in England* (London, 1722), says that the first cause of the decay of trade is the want of parliamentary

time it must be remembered that the mercantilists were business men, merchants and manufacturers, shrewd, capable, energetic, and amazingly active as promoters and organizers, but often unscrupulous, unemotional, worldly, resentful of methods that threatened their profits, generally devoid of public spirit, and as a rule unconcerned with aims and objects that lay beyond the range of a self-interested and routine existence. In view of their importance in the world of monetary and industrial affairs it is significant that though each age of the past has had its ideal no age has ever idealized the business man, and that very few of the type have handed on their names to posterity or have won a place among the great men of all time.[1]

Among those chiefly concerned in the activities of the time—the administration, parliament, the gentry, and the merchants—there existed, particularly after the treaty of Utrecht and the accession of the house of Hanover, such vital differences of opinion as to show that an orthodox mercantilism did not exist as a creed held consistently by any considerable group of men. The executive branch of the government was in the main mercantilist in its sympathies, though the secretary of state, laboring with the intricate problems of diplomacy and war, found himself constantly involved in contradictory situations, from which he was unable to extricate himself to the merchants' satisfaction. Newcastle once said that he tried to please the mercantilists as much as he could, but that he was often unable to meet their wishes. Parliament as well, in which the landed classes were supreme, often refused to coöperate with the merchants and not infrequently resisted or checkmated them.[2] John Bennett wrote, "We are indeed very happy in the constitution of our legislature,

encouragement. Of late years, he adds, the House of Commons has been filled with gentlemen, whose ignorance of trade and indifference to it has brought it to its present low estate. He claims that parliament has always been opposed to the interests of the trading classes, because composed of those who were more concerned for their landed properties than for trade, and he urges "the corporations of England" to send to parliament men interested in mercantile affairs. Defoe, in *Some Thoughts on the Subject of Commerce* (London, 1713), pp. 27–28, and *An Humble Proposal to the People of England* (London, 1729), pp. 55–57, pokes fun at parliament for many of its decisions as petty business for the "greatest trading nation in the world to be engaged in."

1. The subject has been treated by Miss Beard in *A History of the Business Man*, a work which as far as it deals with the mercantilists and the causes of the American Revolution is, unfortunately, an unsafe guide.

2. Contemporary mercantilist writers, however much they might be dissatisfied with

who have made many excellent laws for securing our liberties and our properties, but we fear our parliaments have sometimes been misled, when matters relating to trade have been brought under their consideration; for as the two houses consist of so great a number of noblemen and gentlemen, whose education have been quite different from the study of such improvements as might be made by manufactures and commerce, it is not to be expected that they should form a right judgment therein, without having matters of trade explained to them."[1] The attitude of the government was apt to be influenced by a desire either to secure the support of the landed gentry, both in parliament and in the country, to maintain itself in power, or to manipulate successfully the foreign policies on which it was embarked, during the many tortuous negotiations of the eighteenth century.

Thus even in the period of mercantile ascendancy the merchants were not having things all their own way. Among them, we are told, were the ablest, the most intelligent, and the most resourceful of all classes in the kingdom,[2] but even they could not agree as to the best way to handle trade itself. They wanted at the same time private profit and public benefit and they did not know how to attain them. Barbon said that there was nothing more unknown or about which men differed more in their sentiments than the true causes that raised and promoted trade, for the arguments advanced by the traders were biassed with private interests and ran counter each to the other as their individual advantages were uppermost. Brewster knew of no subject more writ upon or worse handled. Cary agreed with Barbon that trade in the best sense was that which was useful to the public and not that which was managed for private profit. Patrick Lindsay said, "Many are the mysteries of trade," and a retired merchant in 1733 believed that upon matters relating to commerce the ideas and activities of the traders themselves were repugnant and contradictory. "When the private interests of particular

the way the constitution worked, had no doubt as to its perfection. "Of all the governments in the world," wrote one in the *Moderator* (Sept. 25–29, 1710, no. 38), "none is more happily constituted than that of our own nation, in which Dominion and Liberty are so well reconciled that it gives to the sovereign the glorious power and pleasure of commanding freemen and to the subject the grateful satisfaction of seeing that power so lodged as that these liberties are secure."

1. *The National Merchant*, pp. 3–4, 36.

2. Addison once wrote of the merchants, "There are not more useful members in the commonwealth than merchants. They knit mankind together in a mutual intercourse of good offices, distribute the gifts of nature, find work for the poor and wealth for the rich, and magnificence to the great."

merchants clash," he added, "whose voice is to be regarded? Who is to direct the council of the nation: Hamburg, Irish, Spanish or West Indian merchant? 'Tis not the cause of the landed men, the money'd man, or the trader that is to govern, it is the general interest of the whole." Davenant argued at length that a country could not increase in wealth and power but by private men doing their duty to the public.

But what was the general interest of the whole? The merchants as well as the men in political office debated much about this thing, and they differed widely in their attempts to find an answer. They wrote about interest, coinage, credit, exchange, and banks;[1] about smuggling and the running of wines and wool; about naturalization laws and religious freedom; and about the admission of aliens and the problem of the poor and of population—all of which, they realized, had a close connection with the advancement of trade. They differed more or less on every one of these questions, just as men differ on public questions today, but they disagreed fundamentally on some major issues: such as the admission of the luxuries of France and other countries, which the fashions of the day did so much to encourage; the importation of the painted and printed calicoes of the East, in which Queen Mary loved to appear; and the bringing of silks from China, Persia, and India, a traffic which was beginning to assume considerable proportions.[2] Those opposed to these things

1. "Credit is a profitable plant that yields more fruit to our trade than the whole specie of the kingdom." *A Letter to a Member of the present Honourable House of Commons relating to the Credit of our Government and of the Nation in General* (London, 1705). Many pamphlets were written before 1694 on the establishment of credit banks, and a very large number from 1695 to 1697 on the subjects of silver, silver coins, and clipt money. John Pollexfen tells us in his *Discourse of Trade and Coyn* (London, 1697) that silver was the standard, gold taking its computation from silver at the ratio of about 15 to 1 (p. 34). After the Spanish War and its resulting heavy expenses men continued to write about coinage, usury, and credit, and also about the incidence of taxation and the distribution of fiscal burdens and their effect on land, food, labor, and trade.

2. Reynel, in *The True English Benefit* (1674), declared that England was as capable of living within herself as any nation, and should reject "French toyes, Indy and Japan trifles, stain'd callicoes, silks and such pleasant things, which fetch away our money and solid wealth" (pp. 12–13). Cary said much the same in his *Discourse of Trade* (1695), pp. 52–60. *The Ancient Trades Decayed, Repaired again, Wherein are declared the Several Abuses that have bitterly impaired all the Ancient Trades of the Kingdom, written by a country Trades-man* (London, 1678) marks an early stage in the anti-French movement. The writer urges Englishmen to drink more cider and other English drinks and to wear flannel instead of linen. As the poor wear their shirts and shifts a month without washing trade would thus be unspeakably advanced (pp. 16–

would have preferred that England live on her own or within herself and eschew all foreign manufactured importations, as she had
tried to do when parliament passed the act requiring that the dead
be buried in English wool[1] and when others, with a lamentable want
of a sense of humor, suggested that all indentured servants going to
America be required to wear felt hats, and that all servants and
slaves in the plantations, tropical and otherwise, be clothed in wool.[2]
There were others also who would have had only British-made canvas used on all British ships, in order to save the outflow of money
to northern Europe.

17). *A Proposal for Remedding our Excessive Luxury* (Edinburgh, 1700) says that England is the poorer for consuming luxuries and superfluities and other goods which are
no use (pp. 1–2). The agitation against silks and calicoes was carried on by such writers as Elking, *The Interest of England considered* (London, 1720); Anonymous, *A
Brief State of the Question* (2d ed. London, 1720), and others for many years. "People
of England unhappily and foolishly embraced the silks and callicoes of India to the
great neglect and contempt of their own manufactures and to the injury of their own
interest" (anonymous, pp. 10–11). "Ladies dressed more like the Merry Andrews of
Bartholomey Fair than like our ladies and the wives of a trading people" (p. 11). Cary
had already written in 1695, "A poor labouring man that works at the cloathing trade
brings more profit to the nation at the year's end than he that sells ten thousand pounds
worth of Indian silks and callicoes to be worn in England," and he wrote another
pamphlet to the same purpose, *A Discourse concerning the East India Trade*, 1699.
This "calicoe controversy" went on unabated for twenty-five years longer. In 1720
Henry Elking wrote *The Interest of England considered with respect to its Manufactures and East India Callicoes imported, printed, painted and stained and consumed
therein* (London, 1720) and was answered by Asgill, *A Brief Answer* (London, 1720).
Another pamphlet appeared, *The Trade to India, prov'd to be destructive to the General Trade of Great Britain* (London, 1720), and other pamphlets might be cited to
show that the opinion prevailed among merchants, tradesmen, and manufacturers that
the decay of trade was due to the consumption of chintz, which injured the marketing
of the great staples wool and silk and carried away coin. Child, Davenant, and Sir Dudley North (in *The Advantages of the East India Trade*, 1720) upheld the trade, but
others opposed it on the general principle which Janssen laid down as a maxim for
all the states of Europe that "the less they consume of foreign commodities, the better
it is for them," *General Maxims in Trade* (1713). This same principle may be found
stated in *The British Merchant*, I, 1. See also Bennett, *The National Merchant*, pp. 18–
21; *The Guardian*, Sept. 25, 1713; *Considerations on the Present State of the Nation*
(London, 1720), pp. 26–28, and on the evils of fashion and extravagance, Tim. Nourse,
*Campania Felix* (London, 1700), pp. 239–240.

1. On burial in wool, see *Orlebar Chronicles*, pp. 98, 304.

2. 18 Charles II, c. 4; *Calendar State Papers, Colonial, 1706–1708*, §§365, ii, 641;
*Board of Trade Journal*, 1704–1709, p. 271; Stock, *Debates*, II, 296. Wood had little
use for the English law requiring burying in wool and wondered why it was ever
passed. He said that gentry generally buried their dead in linen despite the act and
that it would be better for the poor to be buried "in an old sheet fit for nothing else
than in so much new wool which is thereby utterly lost" (p. 250). Dean Swift would
have laws passed by the Irish parliament prohibiting the wearing of cloths or stuffs not

The mercantilists were constantly studying the conditions at home and often complained of the many distractions that prevented a proper promotion of trade. They declared that political manipulation, commercial speculation, factional and party quarreling, and maneuvering for office all injured business. They disapproved of stock-jobbing, which, they said, throve even in times of war, rebellion, and public calamity. They cried out against promoters and bewailed the fact that legitimate trade could get no hearing in the face of the schemes of the politicians and of those whose aim was the advancement of personal and party interests. They complained of the great lack of public spirit, the prevalence of vice and extravagance, and the want of consideration for the finer things of life—art, architecture, painting, and sculpture. They wrote of the folly and corruption of the age and of the private ambitions of cunning men taking the place of regard for the public welfare of the nation.[1] "No nation under Heaven," cried Thomas Baston, "starves so many ingenious men as England."[2] In 1707 Nehemiah Grew, in an appeal to the king that never saw the light of print,[3] argued for an improvement in the quality and efficiency of the English workingman and a wider extension of manufacturing at home, claiming that Englishmen lacked both the diligence, dexterity, and skill possessed by other peoples and

of the make of the Irish nation and would exclude entirely silks, velvets, calicoes, and "the whole Lexicon of Female Fopperies." He would make burying in woolen a fashion as England had made it a law and would have the ladies content with Irish stuffs for the furnishing of their houses and for gowns and petticoats. *A Proposal for the Universal Use of Irish Manufactures* (Dublin, 1720). In *An Essay to the Restoring our Deranged Trade* (London, 1675), among verses printed at the end, appears this encomium to wool.

> "The Indians in America do wear
> The Dussels which with us prepared are,
> And in exchange do give us their skins
> Which to the Natives good Riches brings.
> Unto Peru and unto Mexico
> Much of our Woollen Manufactures go,
> The Portugal (Brazil Inhabitings)
> For clothing doth delight in no such thing
> As English and Stuffes which they do wear
> Which unto them by Sea transported are."

1. Berkeley, *An Essay toward preventing the Ruine of Great Britain* (London, 1721). Bishop Berkeley was not a mercantilist, but he expressed the thoughts of many of his age.

2. *Thoughts on Trade* (London, 1728), p. 52.

3. "The Meanes of a Most Ample Encrease of the Wealth and Strength of England" (British Museum, Lansdowne Manuscripts, 691). There is also a copy in the Huntington Library. For comments very similar to those of Grew and made in the same year

the sagacity to use to the best advantage their own opportunities and materials. The mercantilists were concerned at all times about unemployment and the condition of the working-classes, not often from motives of philanthropy—for they believed that the poor were foreordained to be poor, just as slaves were to be slaves and the sick to be sick, and should be neither educated nor raised out of their natural state as hewers of wood and drawers of water—but largely from economic motives in order that they might be more efficient factors in production.

Into the minds of men thus filled with anxiety and foreboding regarding England's future came the acutely important problem of the relationship of the realm to the outlying and dependent parts of the British world—Ireland, Scotland, and the plantations. All agreed that Scotland should be construed as an alien country, and it was not until 1707 and the Act of Union that the Scots were admitted to the privileges of the navigation acts and recognized as part of the realm. All likewise agreed, though with many differences of opinion regarding details, that Ireland and the plantations were lesser dependencies, the interests of which were subordinate to the prosperity and welfare of the superior partner. The policy may have been unwise, as we see it in the light of later events, but it represented the height of wisdom as viewed by the mercantilists of the eighteenth century; and when we take into account the mercantilist outlook and the insecurity of England's position as a nation among competing nations, it is impossible to say that they were wrong.

Ireland was nearest to England and in some quarters was deemed her most dangerous rival. Consequently from the days of the navigation acts throughout the period of trade ascendancy her commercial independence was clogged and restrained, partly by the English parliament and partly by her own, under the lash of Poynings' law. In a manner, as Sir Walter Harris said, Ireland was "incorporated and become one body with England."[1] Her people could obtain no for-

see Alexander Justice, *A General Treatise of Monies and Exchanges* (London, 1707), Part III. Also Davenant, *An Essay on the Probable Methods of making a People gainers in the Balance of Trade* (London, 1699, 2d ed. 1700); and (anonymous) *An Enquiry into the causes of the Encrease and Miseries of the Poor of England* (London, 1738). Beginning with the decade 1690 to 1700 the necessity of finding employment for the poor was becoming an important part of the mercantilist programme, above, chapter IX, p. 301, note 1. As Bolingbroke wrote later, "When poverty becomes epidemical farewell glory, farewell empire."

1. Sir Walter Harris, *Remarks on the Affairs and Trade of England and Ireland*

eign goods whatever except through English ports or ship anything except horses, servants, and provisions, and, later, linen, directly to the plantations. An independent linen industry was conceded in 1704, in order to support the Protestant interests in the north, where the growing of flax and the weaving of linen had become a major activity and where ordinarily exports to the plantations, according to a contemporary statement, attained no great proportions—only from £5000 to £9000 a year—and so affected but little the royal revenue.[1] After 1668 the Irish could send no cattle to England and were wholly barred from competing with England's chief staple, wool, either by cultivating the raw material or by making it up into manufactured goods. This monopolistic policy aroused intense opposition among the Irish and the English in Ireland, and Dean Swift, who despised the merchants and was always caustic in charging England with greedy selfishness, would have had the Irish retaliate by cutting themselves off from England entirely and using only goods of their own manufacture.[2]

(London, 1691), p. 34. Harris charged both parliaments with being imposed upon partly by the commissioners of the customs in England and partly by English merchants dealing with the plantations, both of whom believed that they could greatly increase the customs revenue by imposing hard things on Ireland. The main instigators were those interested in farming the revenues in both kingdoms (pp. 33–38). Harris outlines briefly but skillfully the Irish objections to the restraining acts.

1. 3–4 Anne, c. 8. The figures given above are from *A Letter from a Gentleman of Essex to a Member of Parliament* (1715), in which the linen manufacture of Ireland is defended against the objections of the Hamburg merchants, who opposed the concession. In 1703, the year before the act was passed, John Cary, in *Some Considerations relative to the Linen Manufacture in Ireland,* discusses the state of that kingdom with respect to its foreign trade and, believing that "the ballance whereof I take to be against them and must therefore be supplied by carrying out their coyn, which is already grown so scarce that 'tis feared in a short time there will be little left," urges that measures be taken to restore this balance, by starting industries that would in no way interfere with the manufactures of England, and recommends the raising of hemp and flax and the encouragement of the linen industry so as to enable Ireland to become a manufacturing state.

2. On Irish cattle, 18 Charles II, c. 2; 20 Charles II, c. 7; 32 Charles II, c. 2. Child, *Discourse of Trade,* pp. 95–96; Coke, *A Discourse of Trade* (1670), pp. 6, 10, 31–35, a vigorous opponent of the law as greatly injuring England; Coke's objections are repeated in *A Treatise,* pt. I, pp. 57–67; *A Letter from a Gentleman in Ireland to his Brother in England relating to the concerns of Ireland in matters of Trade* (1677), which contains the following: "More allowable to plant poyson than to manufacture with us. . . . To import our cattle to you is a nuisance ["nuisance" is the word used in the act], and to export our wool is a felony; so by gradation to erect here a manufacture ought to be no less than treason. And yet there is more cry than wool in all this matter" (p. 12); John Collins, *A Plea for the Bringing in of Irish Cattle* (1680), of considerable interest, because Collins was accomptant to the Royal Fishery Com-

The American colonies, lying three thousand miles away, beyond the sight and almost the knowledge of the average Englishman, fared better than Ireland, though in principle the treatment accorded both was the same. The plantations were not thought of as political entities or as communities with needs and interests of their own, but rather as agricultural areas or tenancies, chiefly of importance to England as farming lands, outposts of trade, and sources of wealth. At first, as private undertakings, they took on somewhat the character of private estates—proprietorships: feudal or corporate—the heads of which were endowed with wide powers and privileges conferred upon them by royal charters. But as time went on more and more of these private colonies were disestablished or royalized, that is, were taken into the hands of the crown and placed under the king's direct control, until only four of the thirty remained in private possession. The others—the royal colonies—were those in which the mercantilists were directly interested, as colonies for profit and not for empire, the whole trade of which should be restricted to the mother kingdom, else, as one writer puts it, "there could be no reason for their establishment."[1] Thus these royal colonies in America became, in a sense, pawns in the mercantilist game, living pawns, it is true, the welfare and producing powers of which were to be carefully nurtured, but pawns nevertheless, regarding which but two alternatives were possible: either to keep them in a state of dependence and to monopolize their trade; or else (to use the words of a contemporary writer, himself afterward a colonial governor), "to desert them and give them up to some neighbour [France] to England's great

pany and "formerly chief clerk in his Majesty's late Council of Plantations [1672–1674]." From 1642 to 1649 Collins was at sea, the greater part of the time with the Venetian fleet against the Turks (see his *Salt and Fishery*, London, 1682).

On the general situation, Harris and *A Letter* as above. Also *An Answer to a letter from a Gentleman in the Country to a Member of the House of Commons, On the Votes of the 14th Instant, relating to the Trade of Ireland* (1698), in which an attempt is made to answer England's contention that Ireland was England's most dangerous rival. The "Votes of the 14th" refers to the bill for prohibiting the exportation of woolen manufactures of Ireland to foreign parts (Stock, *Debates*, II, 262, note 3); *Some Thoughts* [on this bill] (1698), pp. 5, 8–9; Tolland, *Reasons—offered to the House of Commons why the bill sent down from the House of Lords entitled An Act for the better securing of the Dependency of the Kingdom of Ireland upon the Crown of Great Britain should not pass into a Law* (London, 1720); Swift, *The Present Miserable State of Ireland . . . Wherein is briefly stated the Causes and Heads of all our Woes* (Dublin, 1735), a brief survey.

1. *Some Thoughts on the Bill for Prohibiting the Exportation of the Woolen Manufactures of Ireland* (1698), pp. 8–9.

loss and injury."[1] No third possibility ever seriously entered the English mind.

Men fashion policies in the hard school of necessity and experience and not in anticipation of what later generations are likely to think about them. One cannot read the utterances of the time—either public or private—without realizing that for Englishmen to have given the colonies full commercial liberty would have been viewed contemporaneously as the surest folly, akin to national suicide. "It's far from me to grudge the advantages of any, especially English Men, in what part of the world soever they be," wrote a contemporary in 1696, "but that Old England, shall be made to depend upon the New, or any of its Colonies or Plantations, or that they should be Inriched, to the exhausting the kingdom of its People, which are its Riches and Strength; or Navigation, which are its Walls and Defence; or that the Lesser should be preferred to the prejudice of the Greater, cannot be the desire of any Honest Man."[2] As Charles Davenant, one of the wisest and best-informed men of his day, wrote, expressing the prevailing idea among thinking Englishmen, "The Plantations work for us, their treasure centers all here, and the laws have ty'd them fast enough to us, so that it must be through our own fault and misgovernment if they become independent of England. . . . Colonies are the strength of the kingdom, while they are under good discipline, while they are made to observe the fundamental laws of this original country, and while they are kept dependent upon it. But otherwise they are worse than members lopp'd from the body politic, being indeed like offensive arms wrested from a nation to be turned against it as occasion shall serve." And again, "That our subjects in the American colonies are children of the state and to be treated as such no one denies; but it can't reasonably be admitted that the mother country should impoverish herself to enrich the children, nor that Great Britain should weaken herself to strengthen America, least such procedure should in time furnish us with a subject for a melancholy reflection."[3] In view of the circumstances of the time one can hardly say that such opinions were either ill-judged or unwise.

Early in the seventeenth century, English authorities committed

---

1. Arthur Dobbs, *Some Thoughts concerning Government in general and our Present circumstances in Great-Britain and Ireland* (Dublin, 1728).

2. "The Irregular and Disorderly State of the Plantations," *Report*, American Historical Association, 1892, p. 39.

3. Davenant, *Discourse on the Public Revenues and on the Trade of England*, in two parts, part II, discourse III, "On the Plantation Trade," pp. 204, 207. Also Wood, *Survey of Trade*, pp. 135-136.

themselves to the principle, common to all maritime states of the period, that a nation should keep its plantation trade to itself, and the plantations as national assets are early mentioned in mercantilist literature. But neither the government nor the merchants appear to have taken the plantations or their trade seriously at this early time. England's improvement was their first thought and the colonies were but distant settlements of doubtful value, hardly yet recognized as worth having or keeping and by the mercantilists depreciated and at first largely ignored. The first object even of the navigation acts was navigation not trade; and the building of ships, the breeding and increase of seamen, and the preservation and defense of the kingdom preceded trade, just as trade preceded plantations in the general scheme of things.[1] Men were much more concerned during the first seventy-five years of the seventeenth century with the East India trade and the trade with France,[2] regarding each of which wide differences of opinion prevailed, as to whether they were beneficial or injurious to England because of the loss of gold and silver which they entailed. These issues were hotly fought out on each side and the plantations were hardly in the picture at all. Englishmen laid stress on Tangier, the fishery, naturalization, the rivalry with Holland, poverty, and the decay of trade, but in only a few of the leading works did the plantations have important place and then only in connection with the tobacco and sugar imports from Virginia and the West Indies. Between Josiah Child and Dalby Thomas, that is, between 1678 and 1690, perhaps the most conspicuous defender of the plantations, the opponent of "the vulgar opinion" that the possession of plantations depopulated and consequently weakened England, was William Penn, who in 1680 put forth a tract, called *The Benefit of Plantations or Colonies*,[3] which was printed but never sold, in

1. The best work to study from this point of view is Andrew Yarranton, *England's Improvement, by Sea and Land* (London, 1677). It deals with every subject of current interest but omits all mention of the plantations. A second part was issued in 1681.

2. *The East India Trade, a most Profitable Trade to the Kingdom* (1677) contains arguments opposing the bullionists' line of attack. A similar work is John Houghton's *England's Happiness or a Dialogue between Content and Complaint* (London, 1677), pp. 3–4. Also *The Ancient Trades Decay'd, Repaired again* (London, 1678). In section vii we have an expression of the feeling that underlay the act of 1678, prohibiting certain French imports. In *An Account of the French Usurpation upon the Trade of England* (London, 1679) by "J. B.," possibly Slingsby Bethel, the estimate is made that the trade with France "is a clear 1,600,000 lbs. loss to England a year, all because of *Madame la Mode*" (p. 6).

3. William Penn, *The Benefit of Plantations or Colonies* (1680). The four reasons are: 1. Colonists enriched the mother country by their staples; 2. They exported Eng-

which he gave four reasons to show that the colonists "inriched and strengthened" England, and six reasons why England's apparent loss of population was due to other causes than colonization. But the majority of the mercantilists had no very definite idea regarding the place of the colonies in England's commercial programme and were quite as likely to look on them as an injury as to consider them a benefit.

But with the debate that took place in 1685 on the increase of the sugar and tobacco duties, which a few years later called forth Dalby Thomas' remarkable essay on the West India plantations, we begin to see gradually filtering into the mercantile mind the idea that the plantations might be a valuable asset in the commercial balance sheet. Dalby Thomas estimated with considerable accuracy the relative importance to England of the West India and the continental colonies and was perhaps the first one, though Sir Josiah Child had hinted at the fact, to point out that New England was less valuable than the others, standing in the light of a competitor rather than a contributor.[1] Petty in his *Political Arithmetic*[2] dwelt at some length on the

land's surplus to other countries in Europe, which brought in money or the growth of those countries; 3. They married and multiplied and so offered a growing market for both apparel and household stuffs from England to the latter's advantage; 4. They employed shipping and seamen, which benefited dependent trades. The six reasons for England's apparent loss of population are: 1. Englishmen neglected husbandry; 2. They were too proud and the rich among them employed too many servants; 3. Great men going to London drew men from the country to attend them; 4. The country was neglected and no proper balance was obtained between trade and husbandry; 5. The decay of country manufactures caused the industrious to go abroad and beggars to increase; 6. The great debauching and corruption of manners everywhere to be seen. John Houghton in *A Collection of Letters for the Improvement of Husbandry and Trade* (London, 1681) also argued to show that "the Plantations do not depopulate but rather increase and improve our people" (pp. 35, 49).

*A History of Barbadoes, St. Christophers, Nevis, St. Vincent, Antego, Martinico, Montserrat and the Rest of the Caribby Islands, in all 28,* appeared about this time, and in 1685 R. B. wrote his volume entitled *The English Empire in America.* These books show an increasing interest in the West Indies only. Edward Wells, *A Treatise of Antient and Present Geography* (Oxford, 1701), which bears the authorization of the vice-chancellor, dated September 28, 1700, devotes less than one page out of 183 pages to the North American colonies and about the same number to the island colonies (pp. 149, 150–151). A few curious notes accompany the text. Oldmixon's work was not issued until 1708.

1. Thomas discusses the plantation system in Barbados (pp. 14–25), and in chapter III furnishes a general treatise on the colonies as a whole. His account of New England is on pages 35 and 36. See also an anonymous work of 1691, *The Interest of the Nation as it respects all the Sugar Plantations abroad and the Refining of Sugar at home* (London, 1691).

2. *Political Arithmetic* (London, 1691), pp. 75–84, 94 ff.

West India colonies, computing in his customary speculative fashion the areas of land necessary for their well-being and recommending the limitation of settlement and habitation to such ascertained areas, having regard to size and quality. He too sensed the lesser worth of New England and wished that its people might be transported into Old England or into Ireland.

But with the agitation of the year 1696 a new and wider interest was awakened. In that year a writer petitioning parliament could recommend as deserving attention another branch of the trade of the kingdom quite as important as that to the East Indies, namely, "the trade to the plantations," which he characterized as in an "irregular and disorderly state."[1] Others were saying the same thing. Cary in 1696 called the plantations "our golden mines";[2] the author of *The Free State of Noland* said that "The colonies do now increase more than ever and are like to become a fourth great member of the commonwealth";[3] Davenant, two years later, wrote of them as "a spring of wealth to the nation";[4] and John Pollexfen, discovering that they were becoming a factor in maintaining the balance of trade, deemed their staples of importance for either consumption, exportation, or manufacturing.[5] During the Spanish War, from 1702 to 1713, which some feared might result in the loss to England of all her plantations in America,[6] a new factor forced itself on the attention of the mercantilists. Naval stores—pitch, tar, turpentine, and hemp, for the upkeep of the English navy—were added to tobacco and sugar as colonial staples of profit to England, and so timely and advantageous did these plantation commodities promise to be that not only were they enumerated in 1705, but bounties were granted to encourage their production in three successive acts of parliament, from 1705 to 1729. In the year of the enumeration James Whiston could call the colonies "the most valuable jewel in England's diadem,"[7] because of their importance in aiding the general balance, a subject which during this

---

1. *Report,* American Historical Association, 1892, p. 36.
2. *An Essay on the Coyn and Credit of England* (Bristol, 1696), p. 37.
3. *The Free State of Noland, A Utopia situated beyond the Line, being part of the Great Southern Continent* (London, 1696), p. 14.
4. *Discourse on Trade* (London, 1698), II, 204.
5. *Discourse of Trade* (London, 1697), pp. 9, 87.
6. *The Dangers of Europe from the Growing Power of France* (London, 1702), p. 15. "What Englishman is able to command his passion who considers the present state of his country," p. 18. Cf. p. 50.
7. *The Mismanagements in Trade Discover'd* (London, 1704), p. 25.

period was very much in men's minds and upon which the mercantilists were much more agreed than they were upon the balances in particular cases. Then it was that Thomas Banister of Boston appeared before the Board of Trade and at the board's request drew up his *Short Essay on the Principal Branches of the Trade of New England* (1715), urging the promotion of naval stores,[1] and in general so successful was the new interest thus aroused that ten years after the publication of Banister's pamphlet, during which time the making of naval stores had gone steadily on, Erasmus Philips could say that by re-exporting the plantation commodities England was enabled to obtain a favorable balance of trade with France, Flanders, Hamburg, Holland and the East Countries of more than £600,000 a year, and that the plantations had become a constant source of wealth and might be improved to advantage.[2] While this statement need not be taken as an accurate presentation of the facts, it does show the remarkable change that was taking place in the mercantilist mind regarding the value of the colonies to the mother country. This change was undoubtedly due in part to the growing population in the colonies themselves, because of the rapid influx of Huguenots, Scots-Irish, and Germans, which accelerated in a marked degree the expansion of commerce, staples and shipping.[3]

Since the close of the Spanish War, which had raised the national debt from £10,500,000 in 1695 to upwards of £55,000,000 in 1713,

1. *A Letter to the Right Hon^ble the Lords Commissioners of Trade and Plantations or A Short Essay on the Principal Branches of the Trade of New England with the Difficulties they labour under and Some Methods of Improvement. Dedicated to William Cadogan.* Signed T[homas] B[anister] (London, 1715). The first draft is in C. O. 5:866, no. 67; *Calendar State Papers, Colonial,* 1714–1715, §508. It is dated July 7, 1715. I know of no copy of the pamphlet in this country.

2. Erasmus Philips, *The State of the Nation in respect to her Commerce, Debts, and Money* (London, 1725), p. 10. The plantation commodities referred to are tobacco, cotton, ginger, sugar, indigo, rice, and naval stores. The first chapter gives a very interesting summary of the mercantilist point of view in the year 1725.

3. Report of the Board of Trade to the House of Commons, Feb. 15, 1732, C. O. 324:11, pp. 253–302; *The Importance of the British Plantations in America to this Kingdom, with the State of their Trade and Methods for Improving it, as also a Description of the Several Colonies there.* London, 1731. This pamphlet of 114 pages was written by Fayrer Hall, who tells us that he had lived and traded in those parts above fourteen years and had seen Principio in Maryland and the Iron Works there (pp. 23, 76–77). The Records of Admiralty, South Carolina, A–B, pp. 276–360, contains a case, 1718, in which Hall was one of the libelants. At the time he was commander of the sloop, *Sea Nimph,* which with others, as private men-of-war, captured the *Revenge,* Steed Bonnet, captain. The fight lasted six hours and 16 of the captors were killed before the pirate surrendered.

men had been advancing a great variety of suggestions looking to the reduction of the debt and were speculating more than ever before on such subjects as coinage and usury, banks, credit, the distribution of taxes, and the employment of the poor. The mercantilists in particular were seeking ways wherewith to extricate themselves from "the difficulties and incumbrances [which] the late great expence have laid us under."[1] They wanted no change in the constitution of the government, but they did want to find a way to ease England's financial burdens, which were heavier than had ever been the case in the history of the realm. They thought they had found the way in the advancement of foreign trade by the extension of credit, the lightening of the high duties, the more equable distribution of the responsibilities of government, and the transfer to landed estates of a larger share of the current taxation. This controversy between the merchants and the landed gentry, that is, between the customs revenue on one side and the land tax and excise on the other, had taken on something of a political aspect in the days before 1714, but at bottom it was an economic and class issue between the merchants and the landowners, trade versus quality. It was not to reach its climax until 1733 and the Excise Bill, but even as early as 1717 the mercantilists were advancing the claim that the land should bear more of the burdens and incidence of taxation, since it profited from the advance in trade, and if trade should be doubled, as it ought to be for the good of the nation, then the value of land would be commensurably advanced. But however much they might differ on the question of taxation, all agreed, merchants and landed gentry alike, that for a nation plunged in great debts, which required large additional payments from the people, foreign trade was the true panacea in such a crisis. In the past it had enabled England to rise above her troubles and to support expensive wars and discharge war obligations. It might do so again.

The chief exponent of the mercantilist attitude of the period was William Wood, afterward secretary to the commissioners of the customs, who in his *Survey of Trade,* issued in 1718,[2] extolled foreign trade as "the strength and riches of the kingdom," and through more than three hundred pages of his book argued vigorously in its

---

1. *Essays on the National Constitution, Bank, Credit and Trade* (London, 1717), pp. 73, 88–89.

2. Wood, *Survey of Trade* (1718), pp. 132–133, 154. Banister in presenting New England's case, both before the Board of Trade and in his pamphlet, said, "I shall of-

behalf. His treatise presents a truer picture of mercantilism in its relation to the colonies than is to be found in the pamphlets of Mun, Fortrey, Child, Reynel, Haynes, Coke, Barbon, and others, who wrote before the plantations had attained their great importance in mercantilist eyes. Though Child and Davenant in their writings had devoted chapters to the plantations, Wood was the first one to treat elaborately of the subject and to give a well-articulated analysis of the situation in which England found herself after the treaty of Utrecht. He was a thoroughgoing mercantilist, accepting all the fundamental mercantilist ideas, upholding the navigation acts, opposing the commercial agreements with France in the treaty of Utrecht, which parliament finally rejected, objecting to the monopoly of such chartered organizations as the East India and the Royal African companies and to the Asiento contract, and demanding that the trade of the colonies be subordinated, as a preordained necessity, to the trade and navigation of the realm. The colonies, he wrote, "are of the utmost concern for us to preserve and encourage, and if we take care to preserve them from foreign insults and invasions they will, as they increase in people, probably consume much more of our manufactures than at present they do. They now give employment to many thousands of artificers here at home and take off great quantities, especially of our inferior manufactures, the returns of which are made chiefly in tobacco, sugar, indico, ginger, cotton, dying woods, etc, by which we are not only supplied for our own consumption, but with a considerable surplus, which is annually re-exported to Holland, Hamborough, Flanders, the East Country, Streights, etc., which amounts annually to a very great sum, and is of vast advantage to us in the general balance." And, he added, these same colonies, with industry and conduct, can "be made an inexhaustible mine of treasure to their mother country—while they are strictly made to observe the laws of it—and nothing but our arbitrary treatment of them and our misgovernment can make them otherwise than beneficial and advantageous to us."[1] This discovery of the value of the

fer to your Lordships but one argument, which I think will appear equally forcible in all ages and all countries. We take off several hundred thousand pounds worth of British manufactures yearly, and pay in such commodities as serve your necessities, and not one Article that increases your luxury or unnecessary expense," p. 2.

1. See also [Anonymous], *Directions to Judge whether a Nation be in a thriving Condition and how to advance the Wealth and Power of Great Britain* (London, 1729), pp. 28–29. In this work the writer recommends that only those persons be sent to represent his Majesty in the plantations "whose whole Conduct of Life may give the

colonies in improving the general balance is the outstanding fact of this period, as it led to a reconsideration of the place occupied by the middle and northern colonies—colonies which Child and Thomas had deemed injurious rather than beneficial to England—as useful and contributory members of the commercial and colonial group. These colonies Wood placed in their true position as copartners with the others in adding to England's wealth and prosperity, not only because they were becoming an important market for England's manufactures but even more because they were furnishing supplies to the southern and West India colonies, whose trade "enlarged [England's] stock, increased [her] navigation, and set the general balance for many years on [her] side."[1]

Having thus become convinced of the value of all the colonies to the mother country, Wood proceeds to discuss how best they can be improved and made profitable. He advocates a greater increase of white people, a wider cultivation of the soil, an avoidance of large unoccupied tracts of land, the training of servants and negroes for planting rather than trade, a general encouragement of tillage, adequate defense against invasion and insurrection to be provided by the planters themselves, better administration on the part of those "sent to reside and govern them by the king's authority," and a just recognition of the right of the colonists to enjoy "all the rights and liberties of Britons." For this purpose he would have a declaratory law passed stating that "Britons have the right to all the laws of Great Britain, for the security of the subject, while they remain in the countries under the dominion of this kingdom." He then passes on to write of the African trade as "of the greatest value" to both England and the sugar and tobacco plantations, and he extols the throwing open of the trade in 1698 as bringing about a fourfold increase in the supply of negroes. At the close of this section he deals with the Newfoundland fishery as of the greatest concern to Eng-

strongest assurances that they will not oppress the people they are sent to govern." He wishes that an entire stop be put to colonial duties on shipping, negroes, and British goods; that paper money be forbidden; that foreign coins be allowed to pass only at proclamation rates; that manufacturing be prohibited; and that only such commodities be produced as the soil in the colonies is fitted to bear. It represents mercantilism well advanced in its attitude toward the colonies.

1. P. 154. In 1689–1692 England and Ireland were supplying the West Indies with provisions, both the inhabitants and the troops there, twenty years before the northern colonies were looked upon as available for this purpose. *Calendar Treasury Books*, IX, 475, 480, 503, 505, 890, 1579, 1750–1751, 1825, 1870, 1871, especially 462–463.

land, and in the next dilates on the mischiefs attending the fishery from the intrusion of the French and the necessity of England's complete control of the fishing waters. He closes his volume with a specific enumeration of the disadvantages under which trade in general subsists and of the best means for recovering and enlarging it.[1] He would lighten it of the great duties and impositions laid upon it, would persuade the landed men to lay aside their prejudices and work in common with the merchants, would prevent the importation of mere luxuries and encourage greater frugality, would strengthen England's home manufactures by prohibiting as much as possible the admission of foreign commodities, would relieve the manufacturer of all duties on exports, thus anticipating Walpole's reforms and the nineteenth century reforms of Huskisson, would consume at home what is cheap and comes cheaply and carry abroad what was rich and would yield most money, and, in general, would give every Briton an equal right to trade in all parts of the known world.[2]

This interesting and comprehensive treatise shows us that during the first part of the eighteenth century, particularly during the years immediately following the treaty of Utrecht, there were taking shape in the mercantilist mind certain ideas that were relatively new regarding a larger British commercial world in which the plantations were already occupying a preponderant place. At the time of the navigation acts shipping, trade, and the general good of the kingdom were the main concern, later the sugar and tobacco colonies loomed large as leading colonial assets, at the turn of the century naval stores and other enumerated commodities entered in to swell the list of profitable staples, but after 1713 all the colonial resources were brought together and pooled in such a way as to give rise to the notion of a self-sufficing or self-contained empire, in which each part coöperated with each other part to form one complete and mutually sustaining whole. This aggregate of widely scattered groups, thus united for a common purpose, would, so the mercantilists profoundly believed, be capable of holding its own not only against the competing and aggressive opposition of rival powers seeking its disruption or overthrow, but also against the necessity of depending upon other nations for its material wants, at least to the extent that the general balance of trade should not be unfavorable to the English realm.[3]

1. Pp. 154, 176–177, 179, 189, 194, 211–213, 319, part IV.
2. Pp. 229, 259.
3. An excellent exposition of this self-sustaining idea may be found in *The Trade*

According to this idea of the self-sufficing empire—implicit rather than explicit in the writings of the eighteenth century mercantilists —the mother country, the sugar and tobacco colonies, the provision or bread colonies, the fisheries, and Africa formed a single economic and commercial whole, made up of widely scattered but coöperative members, each of which contributed something to the strength and profit of the whole. The ultimate advantage, however, went by design to the mother state, the kingdom or realm of England. This mother state, the elder and monopolizing partner, to whom all the others were subordinate, consisted of England, Wales, and the town of Berwick-upon-Tweed, and after 1707 of Scotland, with Ireland in large part barred from the direct plantation trade and the Channel Islands and the Isle of Man negligible parts of the system, if they can legally be considered parts at all. The sugar and tobacco colonies were Barbados, Jamaica, and the Leeward Islands (with Bermuda and the Bahamas of little importance, except as strategic outposts), where were produced sugar, molasses, rum, ginger, pepper, cotton, and dyewoods; and Maryland, Virginia, and the Carolinas, which contributed tobacco, rice, indigo, naval stores, and furs. The provision or bread colonies were Pennsylvania, New York, and New England, the leading staples of which were wheat, flour, bread, and livestock. The fisheries centered upon the waters of Newfoundland and Nova Scotia, where fishing as a source of wealth was encouraged to the almost complete neglect of the land as a place of settlement, and where the mercantile interest in fish as a colonial staple enabled the "West Country men" of Devonshire and elsewhere, in their century-long struggle, to prevent the erection of Newfoundland into a colony. The fisheries were looked upon as nurseries of seamen, encouragers of navigation and among the chief supports of the nation, because they helped to increase England's favorable balance of trade with Portugal and the Straits, where the exports exceeded the imports, by furnishing a commodity which could be bartered for wines, oil, oranges, and the like, which England wanted.[1] This was important

*and Navigation of Great Britain considered: shewing that the surest way for a nation to increase in riches is to prevent the importation of such foreign commodities as may be raised at home; That this kingdom is capable of raising within itself and its colonies materials for employing all our poor in those manufactures, which we now import from such of our neighbours who refuse the admission of ours* (London, 1730).

1. "The wines and gold of Portugal have been wholly purchased by our manufactures, fish and other products." *Letter to the Honourable A[rthur] M[oore]* (London, 1714), p. 12.

because France by practically prohibitive duties barred English fish from the French markets. By Africa, the fifth part, was meant the western coast from Senegambia to Angola, which after 1715 furnished a yearly quota of more than 27,000 negroes, who cultivated the sugar cane, tobacco, and rice fields of the tropical and semi-tropical colonies, where white labor proved wholly inadequate to meet the hard conditions that plantation life imposed. So pressing was the need of an adequate and continuous supply of negroes that the putting of the African trade "upon a right establishment" was a matter of great parliamentary concern.[1] No phases of the whole situation fill a larger place in the executive records or parliamentary annals of the period or were regulated with more difficulty or less satisfaction than the Newfoundland fishery and the African slave trade.

The mercantilists valued the northern or bread colonies partly for their value as a market for English manufactures but still more because they could supply the sugar, tobacco, and rice plantations with bread, flour, meats, fruits, vegetables, houses, horses, sheep, pigs, pipe-staves, headings, and lumber that the planters could not sufficiently produce for themselves. The southern colonies achieved some of these things and the West Indies raised, to a larger extent than is commonly supposed, what were locally known as "ground provi-

---

1. *A True State of the Present Difference between the Royal African Company and the Separate Traders* (London, 1710). The writer advocates an open trade, calling the company's former monopoly dangerous to the plantations. He gives the following yearly figures: Barbados, 4000, Jamaica, 10,000, Leeward Islands, 6000, the continent, 600, making altogether 20,600, as over against an average supply from 1681 to 1688 of only 5155. The average for Jamaica from 1685 to 1691 was 1800. An answer to this pamphlet appeared in 1711, *An Answer to the Reasons against an African Company,* which takes up the objections one by one and answers them by enumerating the advantages, pp. 28–31.

In addition to the large amount of information on this subject contained in the Public Record Office, only a small part of which is reproduced in the *Calendar of State Papers, Colonial,* and in the reports of the Board of Trade, attention may be called to a very useful volume in the Huntington Library (Stowe Collections), which belonged to the first Duke of Chandos, Vol. I, "Papers relating to African Affairs" (25 in all). The most important paper of general interest is no. 4, "A State of the Trade," which gives a history of the company from the reorganization in 1671 to 1720, a very instructive and helpful outline. See also no. 20, "On the Usefulness and Importance of the African Trade," pp. 92–95. The Duke of Chandos was a member of the court of the company and a large holder of its stock. The London and outport merchants were at one with the planters of South Carolina and the West Indies in demanding that the trade remain open. All of them petitioned parliament to that effect against the company, in the years from 1708 to 1720, when the reorganization of the company was under debate. Stock, *Debates,* III, 190, 195, 203–207, 222–226, 247–248, 276, 278, 284, 287, 298, 315, 337.

sions," chiefly for the use of the negroes, thereby lessening somewhat, but not in an appreciable degree as far as the planters themselves were concerned, the demand for outside subsistence. At a later time gluts in the West India market often drove the captains and super-cargoes from the bread colonies to seek markets elsewhere, particu-larly among the French, Dutch, and Spanish islands, but during the early eighteenth century the West India planters never were able to supply all that was needed even for the sustenance of their negroes, much less for the upkeep of their own tables, houses, and cane pieces. Inevitably, therefore, the northern colonies for many years found in the British islands of the Caribbean their most lucrative market. "There is no island the Brittish possess in the West Indies," wrote Samuel Vetch in 1708, "that is capable of subsisting without the as-sistance of the Continent, for to them we transport their bread, drink and all the necessaryes of humane life, their cattle and horses for cul-tivating their plantations, lumber and staves of all sorts to make casks of for their rumm, sugar and molasses, without which they could have none, ships to transport their goods to the European mar-kets, nay, in short, the very houses they inhabitt are carried over in frames, together with the shingles that cover them, in so much that their being, much more their well being, depends almost entirely upon the Continent."[1] He argued that inasmuch as New England had ten times the trade of all the other colonies she was therefore de-serving of the utmost consideration from the mother country. The Board of Trade recognized the importance of this trade in its reports to the secretary of state[2] and the king in council, and the idea was taken up by the pamphleteers, among the earliest of whom was De-foe, who now for almost the first time were beginning to realize that the sugar colonies could hardly subsist without the assistance of those on the American continent and that all were bound together, de-pendent on each other as "belly and members."[3] This was a notion that had not entered the heads of the older mercantilists, to whom New England and the Middle Colonies, if thought of at all, were considered rather a detriment than a benefit to the mother country. Their usefulness as purveyors of supplies to the West India colonies was not appreciated in the seventeenth century, when England and Ireland furnished the greater part of the provisions needed and when

---

1. *Calendar State Papers, Colonial*, 1708–1709, p. 47.
2. *Ibid.*, §779.
3. This simile was used by Defoe in 1704, *Review*, I, 133–135.

colonial competition was unwelcome because cutting into the business of the English middlemen.

Thus it was that for the first time, more than a hundred years after the settlement of Virginia, the value of all the colonies taken together was becoming evident to statesman and merchant alike.[1] Earlier ideas of what the colonies might signify to England had been limited in range and casual in application, but now at last a definite picture was conceived in the mercantilist mind of a colonial world, surrounded as it were by a ring-fence, the members of which were to work in coöperation with each other and in combination with England, the partner that reaped the eventual commercial advantage. This view of the place of the colonies in England's commercial system, destined to become better defined as time went on, was to give form to a body of regulative principles that were comprehensive and in a manner complete. These principles were to govern England's attitude toward her colonies from this time forward to the American Revolution.

Once having attained to a more or less precise understanding of what the colonies actually meant to England, the mercantilists readily worked into the general scheme certain other contributory factors that concerned more particularly the internal organization of the kingdom. They wanted that the government should do everything in its power to encourage home manufactures, to increase the productivity of the English working man, and to make the poor and the vagrant assets rather than liabilities to the nation, on the ground that no state could ever be rich and powerful without being populous, or ever be successfully populous without a high average of remunerative employment. The criminal, the incorrigible, and the hopelessly indolent they would ship off to America, in vague expectation that another and a rougher country would transform these people into useful laborers and artisans and so make them profitable members of society. The transportation of "wicked and evil-dis-

1. The petitions sent in to parliament, 1738–1739, during the debate on the modification of the sugar act, disclose the opinions held at that time regarding the plantation trade. The lord mayor, aldermen, and common council of the City of London said that the trade to the American colonies, particularly to the West Indies, was "of the utmost importance and almost the only profitable trade this nation now enjoys unrival'd by others" (Stock, *Debates,* IV, 663–664). Merchants and planters interested in the sugar trade spoke bitterly of the menace of the French colonies, calling attention to their flourishing conditions as contrasted with the low state of the British sugar plantations in the West Indies, *ibid.,* pp. 797–798.

posed" persons, guilty of offenses against the law, was ordered by act of parliament in 1717,[1] in order that England might be relieved of a dangerous class and the colonies benefit by an increase in their supply of labor. As to manufacturing, the encouragement of it at home had its inevitable corollary in the forbidding of it in the colonies, and hence arose those restrictive measures, beginning with the Wool Act of 1699,[2] which barred the colonies from certain forms of industry. As the years went by the making of hats and the working up of raw iron were added to the list and the refining of sugar was discouraged though never forbidden by law.[3] In their fear of competition the mercantilists sought to prevent even the transfer of artisans and the tools and implements of their trade across the seas to America, an effort that continued unabated to the end of our colonial period.[4]

Except to critics of England's policy, these measures are not im-

1. 4 George I, c. 11.

2. 10–11 William III, c. 10. Woolen manufactures were deemed "the greatest and most profitable commodities of this kingdom, on which the value of lands and the trade of the kingdom" rested.

3. *The Case of the Refiners of Sugar in England stated and the Case between the English Sugar Planters and the Refiners by some of the Planters stated, and by the Refiners answered.* A broadside printed for presentation to members of parliament at the time of levying an additional duty on sugar, c. 1695–1697.

4. On January 15, 1666, and again on October 24, 1686, the king issued proclamations prohibiting the transportation of frames for knitting and making silk stockings and other wearing necessaries to the colonies, at the urgent request of the Society of Frame Work Knitters. The policy underlying these proclamations remained unchanged for a century.

The injurious effects of the Wool Act of 1699, the Hat Act of 1732, the Iron Act of 1750, and the Paper Money Acts of 1751 and 1764 have in the past been greatly overstated. It is doubtful if any of these measures materially hampered the progress of colonial industry, which on the manufacturing side attained at best no great proportions until after 1750. The Iron Act is customarily cited as the most harmful of these measures, but Dr. Arthur C. Bining, who in his *British Regulation of the Colonial Iron Industry* (1933) has given us the first convincing treatment of the subject, reaches a different conclusion. He says that the attempt to encourage the production of pig and bar iron in the colonies for use in the manufactures of the mother country was "a decided failure," and that the clauses of the act prohibiting the erection of rolling, slitting, and plating mills and of steel furnaces for the making of secondary iron products were almost "entirely disregarded." He says further that the successful enforcement of such mercantilist measures as these was practically impossible, owing to the distance, the increasing needs and determination of the colonists, and the helplessness and indifference of the royal governors, and that the chief importance of the Iron Act lies, not in any injury it wrought upon manufacturing in the colonies but in the place it occupies among the grievances voiced by the colonists after 1763. It is worthy of notice that England imposed no restraints upon shipbuilding in the colonies or upon the manufacture of shoes, paper, glass, and other similar objects of colonial industry.

portant in colonial history, as agriculture and commerce were the leading colonial activities and the want of capital and skill and the high price of labor hindered, though it did not by any means prevent, manufacturing ventures in the central and northern colonies, but they are interesting as illustrating the general mercantilist idea of discouraging the production of anything in the colonies that would compete with the manufactures of the home country. Only in this way, the mercantilists argued, could the different parts of the British world be made mutually helpful.[1] Toward the building of ships their attitude was quite otherwise. England needed ships, the more the better, for the promoting of an adequate system of distribution, and was willing to grant to Ireland, the Channel Islands, and the plantations the right to build as many ships as they could. For this reason the colonists were allowed by the navigation act equal privileges with the English shipbuilders, and the master shipwrights of the Thames got short shrift when in 1724 they tried to persuade the Board of Trade that shipbuilding in New England should be restricted on the ground "that this New England trade had drawn over so many working shipwrights" that there were not enough left in England to carry on the work there.[2]

The one problem that neither the government nor the mercantilists were ever able to solve was how to meet the need of hard money in the colonies or to provide an adequate medium of exchange for the doing of business. Though the Board of Trade well knew that the money situation in America was serious—and it knew this at least as early as 1707—it seemed quite incapable of finding an ade-

1. The same policy finds advocates in the United States today. Not long ago American mercantilists urged that the Philippines be placed on the same tariff footing as foreign nations in such products as were in competition with domestic products. The hat makers, the sugar refiners, and the shipwrights of England were asking for the protection of their own industries exactly as were the Milk Producers Association and the Farm Bureau Federation of the United States asking for the protection of theirs a few years ago. But the English industrials were not threatening, if they did not get what they wanted, to support colonial independence, as the American farmers threatened to demand Philippine independence if their wishes were not granted. On this point see Burns, *Controversies*, p. 26, note 34.

The mercantilists of England could not see the situation otherwise, any more than could Defoe, in his *Six Distinguishing Characteristics of a Parliament-Man* (1700), understand why anyone should be elected to parliament who was disaffected to King William, was opposed to the existing settlement, was against the established church, or was out of sympathy with the prevailing interests of the party in control. Mercantilism was as deeply rooted as was Whiggism.

2. *Board of Trade Journal*, 1723–1728, p. 138.

quate solution. It did not oppose on principle the issue of bills of credit or the establishment of land banks—such as were proposed in Massachusetts and Barbados—for it was no part of the mercantilist plan to hinder the use of credit for the advancement of trade.[1] But it did look on all forms of credit as only a temporary expedient, bound in the long run to be injurious to the creditor, prejudicial to the revenue, and an unnecessary burden on the people at large. As it was always the mercantilist's ambition to make England the creditor nation, the board could but recommend the disallowance of any colonial act that threatened depreciation and so brought loss to the merchants and traders, who were as a rule the creditors in the case. This is what happened with the land bank act of Barbados, known as the act "to supply the want of cash," which was disallowed in 1706. The board wished rather to see the deficiency met by a quicker and larger importation of silver in the ordinary course of trading relations with Spain and the Spanish colonies, which it considered the only proper remedy for the situation.

It may be that England's unwillingness to provide any sort of coinage for the colonies was due to this mercantilist idea that money should come in rather than go out of the realm. To mint a special series of coins for America would have been not only an expensive and difficult task in itself but also a heavy drain upon England's own supply of gold, silver, and copper.[2] Because the mercantilists wanted the balance of trade always to be in England's favor and the drift of money always in one direction, and that toward England, they

1. Report of 1707, *House of Lords Manuscripts*, new series, VII, 255. In 1715 the board wrote Secretary Stanhope, "we find that there is a great want of money in New England for the carrying on of their trade, and other necessary occasions. . . . We think it absolutely necessary that something of the kind [the issue of bills of credit or the setting up of a private bank] be set on foot as soon as possible, to furnish a sufficient medium for carrying on of trade in those parts, the want of which is found to be a great obstruction to navigation and the improvement of naval stores" (*Calendar State Papers, Colonial*, 1714–1715, §582). The board does not appear to have objected to land banks on principle, but opposed them in the two instances mentioned because the method provided by the acts was improper and not likely to attain the end proposed.

2. Dean Swift in the *Intelligencer*, no. XIX, 1729, discusses the want of silver in Ireland and presents a situation not unlike that in the colonies. Why, he asks, should not Ireland have a mint of her own, unless it were not for the interest of England to suffer silver to remain there? He speaks of having been told that among the poorer American colonies the people cut the "little money among them" into halves and quarters for the "convenience of small traffick," and he considers the similar condition in Ireland as one of the causes of migration elsewhere, pp. 210–214.

saw in the colonies not a separate commercial group with interests of its own, but a channel through which an additional supply of Spanish and other foreign gold and silver might eventually reach England. For this reason, apparently, from the beginning to the end, England refused to deal adequately with the money problem in the colonies, even refusing to meet the many requests that were sent in for a small copper coinage for daily use. She did no more than attempt to regulate by proclamation and statute the value of foreign coins in terms of sterling. In fact, during our colonial period the financial system in America was haphazard and on a very insecure foundation, and it may be doubted if the mercantilists themselves had more than the vaguest notions regarding its operation from the monetary or bullionist point of view or regarding the actual state of the balance of trade with America. Their monetary policy was very simple: to prevent the drift of gold or silver from England to America, which would result from an unfavorable trading balance or from the sending of coin or bullion overseas; and to encourage, either by connivance or by treaty arrangements, the Spanish colonial trade which promised to furnish England with the desired supply of the precious metals.[1]

1. The desire to promote trade with Spanish America came into conflict with the treaty of Madrid of 1670 and with the navigation acts as well. The early aspects of the subject have been treated by Nettels in *Money Supply*, ch. I, and the later aspects by Miss L. M. Penson in the *Cambridge History of the British Empire*, I, ch. xi, "The West Indies and the Spanish American Trade, 1713–1748." Neither writer specially stresses the significance of the trade from the standpoint of mercantilist doctrine, though each notes its disaccord with other phases of British policy. Miss Penson brings out the important point that the decline of the trade after 1750 cut off the flow of Spanish coin into the colonies, and consequently into Great Britain, and thus added its quota to the commercial and financial stringency that followed. She thinks rightly that the mercantilists exaggerated the possibilities of the trade and in their "greed" overreached themselves. It seems to me that in this instance, as in so many others, the merchants and their spokesmen, the pamphleteers, were caught in the toils of their own unworkable notions of commercial economy and were attempting to make both the trade and the colonies fit into their more or less academic scheme of the balance of trade and the drift of money. They took no account of the instability and impermanence of trade conditions in the colonial world.

There are many pamphlets that deal with this problem, for it was a matter of considerable controversy among the mercantilists and of discussion at the meetings of the Board of Trade, references to which will be found in the *Calendar of State Papers, Colonial* and the *Board of Trade Journal,* and among the documents in C. O. 5:388. There is also an excellent exposition of the subject in *The Evident Advantages to Great Britain and its Allies from the approaching War, especially in Matters of Trade* (London, 1727). In the *Medley* (1710–1712), no. 5, and in the *Mercator* (1713–1714), nos. 85, 86, 87, 88–90, will be found opinions and estimates bearing on the topic, and

England and the mercantilists expected the colonists to be self-supporting and not to involve the mother country in any expense for maintenance. The government was willing, within certain limits, to provide for protection and defense, though the obligation to supply ordnance and other stores required for the service of the various islands and plantations abroad proved an irksome burden to a Treasury that was having trouble to meet the mounting expenses of administration and war. It was compelled also to pay the cost of all measures taken for preventing smuggling and breaches of the acts of trade, and these measures concerned not only the plantations but Ireland, the Channel Islands, and the Isle of Man, and to no inconsiderable extent Scotland where the illicit landing of both Virginia tobacco and French brandy was an ever-present irritation and where the frauds in the custom houses, particularly of Port Glasgow, led in 1723 to the establishment of a separate board of customs commissioners at Edinburgh.[1] Some of the expenses involved were so heavy as to give the Treasury pause, as when the question of fortifying Crookhaven in Ireland came up in 1704 and the secretary of state invited the merchants to contribute, which they positively refused to do, to the proper defense of the harbor.[2] But in all that concerned the administration of the plantations the colonists themselves were expected to support the charge of their own government. Only in the cases of

in no. 97 of the latter is given the amount of bullion brought into Great Britain by the Spanish trade since the peace, in exchange for English woolens.

In its later phases the trade got badly mixed up with the terms of the treaties of Utrecht and Seville, with the Asiento, with the activities of the South Sea Company, and with the influence of the French and Spanish trade in the back country of the southern continental colonies extending to the lower Mississippi. Its importance as one of the causes of the war with Spain in 1739–1740 is, of course, well understood. It has a very important place in the history of Jamaica, which was the entrepôt of the trade. The use in the eighteenth century after 1763 of Spanish vessels in trade between Louisiana and Pensacola and other parts of the British colony of West Florida—which was contrary to the navigation acts—was allowed because British goods were thereby exchanged for gold and silver and certain desired raw materials. In the case of Jamaica such trade was legalized by the act of 1765. For Spanish ships at Pensacola, Carter, *Gage Correspondence*, I, 169.

On the importance of Spanish gold and silver in determining governmental policy under William and Anne, see W. T. Morgan, "The South Sea Company and the Canadian Expedition in the Reign of Queen Anne," in the *Hispanic American Historical Review*, May, 1928, and "The Origins of the South Sea Company," *Political Science Quarterly*, March, 1929.

1. Historical Manuscripts Commission, *Polwarth*, III, 249.

2. Treasury 27:19, p. 431; *Calendar State Papers, Colonial, 1712–1714*, §349; *Board of Trade Journal*, 1704–1709, p. 74; 1709–1715, p. 432.

Nova Scotia and Georgia were appropriations ever made, before 1763, from the English exchequer for the upkeep of a colony. In the eyes of the mercantilists and the governmental authorities as well, the colonies were to remain a source of profit and not an object of expense.

Thus the interests of the colonists were inescapably tied up with the international aspects of a self-contained commercial world of which they were an integral and necessary part. Many a mercantilist of the uncompromising type would have involved them still more deeply and have preferred that the government place in the enumerated list all surplus colonial staples and so keep colonial trade entirely within the circle of Great Britain's own possessions, but this neither the administration nor parliament, to whom the interests of the merchant-capitalists were only one among many concerns, would consent to do, so that before 1764 the colonists could and did trade in various unenumerated staples with the European continent. In so doing they were hampered by certain treaty restrictions for, as we have already seen, both Spain and France were pursuing a policy similar to that of England. By the treaty of Madrid of 1670 between England and Spain an agreement was reached that the subjects of neither country should enter the colonial ports of the other for purposes of trade, which meant that legally no colonist could carry on trade with any of the ports of the Spanish West Indies on pain of confiscation of ship and goods. Despite this treaty the Jamaican merchants and others as well carried on a clandestine commerce with the Spanish islands and continent in America, and both governors and sea-captains connived at the trade.[1] On the same general principle of keeping one's plantation trade to oneself—that is, of permitting no other nation to run away with it—was based the equally important agreement reached at London in November, 1686, between England and France, for the maintenance of the *status quo* in America. By this treaty of "Peace, Correspondence and Neutrality" the subjects of the one were not to frequent the ports of, or to trade with the

1. The trade always involved a certain amount of risk. One ship master was questioned by the Spanish authorities "Whether he did not know it to be a crime to go into the West Indies: answered he thought he was as free to sail from one of his Majesty's islands to another as they were to their ports; at which they said it was contrary to their articles for any English dog to go into their ports, and condemned him a slave for four years to the quicksilver mines and on pain of death never to go into the [Spanish] West Indies." *Calendar State Papers, Colonial*, 1669–1674, p. 539. The text of the treaty is in Davenport, *European Treaties*, II, 194–195.

other, or in any way to interfere with the commerce belonging to the subjects of the other.[1]

Each of these treaties seemed to curtail the freedom of colonial trade, by agreement though not by law, and to bar the colonists from all intercourse with the Spanish and French possessions in the New World. Needless to say, however, neither treaty was observed, despite the efforts of the home authorities to maintain it, as was done in the case of England when King William abandoned the Scots at Darien. Jamaica captains unblushingly frequented the Spanish coast, taking large cargoes of English goods into Havana, Porto Bello, Cartagena, and other places along the Gulf of Mexico. There coming within view of the shores by night only, having kept out of sight during the day, they would traffic with Spanish merchants stealing out in canoes and periauguas, generally for cash. This prohibiting of a lucrative foreign trade not only limited the commercial opportunities of the colonists, but also affected materially the monetary situation. For the influx of silver by contact with the Spanish sources of supply, which the Board of Trade deemed the only remedy for an adequate money medium in America, was thereby checked and the board's remedy failed of its effect.

Of less consequence to the colonists, though a matter of very great importance in England's commercial history and so affecting the colonies indirectly, was the state of the trade between England and France. The situation was determined partly by politics, partly by national antipathies, and partly by the characteristic and deep-seated mercantilist dislike of French products and the mercantilist belief that the French trade was a pernicious trade and disadvantageous to England.[2] The orthodox mercantilists were generally agreed that the importation of "luxuries" of any kind into England, not only from

1. *Ibid.,* pp. 320–321. Later an edict of 1727 was issued supplemental to the treaty.

2. The French trade was a bad trade, first, because, as many thought, the balance was against England; secondly, because imports from France added nothing to the riches of England; thirdly, because France offered nothing that could be re-exported to foreign markets to England's profit, as was the case with re-exports to other countries; and, fourthly, because imports from France were injurious to England's morals, as cultivating a taste for extravagance and luxury. Arguments along these lines may be found in the writings of most of the anti-French pamphleteers, as far back as 1679 (see *An Account of the French Usurpation upon the Trade of England and what great damage the English do yearly sustain by their Commerce,* 1679), but are especially well stated in [John Egleton], *A Vindication of the House of Commons, in rejecting a Bill confirming the eighth and ninth Articles of the Treaty of Navigation and Commerce between England and France* (London, 1741).

France but from other countries also, was an injury not a benefit. There were two good and sufficient reasons for this belief: first, because laces, wines, linens, silks, tea, coffee, Indian cottons and French brandies, and "an infinite number of other curiosities"[1] were extravagances that did not befit a sober people; and secondly, because such commodities had to be paid for in money or raw wool, neither of which a self-respecting mercantilist would allow, if he could help it, to go out of the kingdom.[2]

For reasons that need not be discussed here—the official reason is given in the preamble of the act—parliament in 1678 absolutely prohibited the importation of a large number of French products, on the ground that "the wealth and treasure of the nation hath been much exhausted by the importation and consumption of the French commodities."[3] The man responsible for the introduction of this measure, William Sacheverell—called the ablest parliament man of Charles II's reign—was an early representative of that group which saw in France the coming rival of England and advocated the resumption of friendly relations with the Dutch.[4] Conviction on this

1. The list of objectionable French products is given in *A Letter to A[rthur] M[oore]*, pp. 111–116. See also *Considerations on the Present State of the Nation* (London, 1720), pp. 26–29. "If every gentleman that guzzles his two flasks of *Hermitage, Burgundy* or *Champaign* every day (of which the number is very considerable) would but reflect that the natural consequence of pleasing his palate to this degree may be the loss of a week's wages to a whole family of industrious labouring people, I should think it would spoil the gaiety of their cups." Mercantilist literature is full of these charges of indulgence and gratification due to the buying of French goods. Mandeville, in his *Fable of the Bees* (1714), is almost the only one to defend prodigality and lavishness (pp. 81–83). Even Defoe, who supported the articles, said in *The Mercator* (no. 142), "If there were no wines drunk in England at all, it would be no loss to the public stock. All our consumption of foreign production is a loss to the national wealth," and in *The Complete English Tradesman* (2d ed., London, 1724) he devotes a chapter to "The Luxury and Extravagancies of the Age" (II, Pt. II, ch. IV). It is interesting to note that charges similar to those against the French trade were brought against the trade with Venice and Florence two centuries before. Wright, *Political Poems and Songs*, II, 172–173.

2. All the mercantilists were agreed on the unwisdom of allowing unwrought wool to be exported. Defoe was opposed to it and declared that it should be England's policy to consume raw wool and not to export it. *The Mercator*, nos. 23, 35, 48, 137, 138. From early times vessels had been seized for exporting raw wool and in 1690 and 1692 special officers were appointed on the coast of Kent to prevent the transportation of wool (*Calendar Treasury Books*, IX, 946, 948, 1622–1623). The subject is briefly but well discussed by Lipson, *The Economic History of England*, III, 22–34.

3. 29–30 Charles II, c. 1, §xx.

4. *Dictionary of National Biography*. Sacheverell is named in *The British Merchant* (1713) as having been the father of the measure (no. 37). Defoe, enlightened as he was in many particulars, did not foresee the French menace and in *The Mercator* ar-

point was spreading and was not confined to the merchants of London, for many pamphlets were written against the French in the years following the treaty, and in 1713 John Withers issued *The Dutch better Friends than the French,* which went through four editions in a single year. This work contains the sentence, "If these Froglands were once crushed the trade of the world would be our own."[1]

Until 1713 the trade relations with France passed through a number of vicissitudes. The act of 1678 was repealed in 1685[2] and trade was once again made free, just one year before the conclusion of the treaty with Louis XIV, closing the colonial ports of each nation against the subjects of the other. But after the Revolution of 1689 the act was renewed for the same reasons as in 1678, with a further renewal in 1693 for three years "if the war with France lasts that long," and a proclamation was issued on May 18, 1689, prohibiting the importation or retailing of any commodities of the growth or manufacture of France.[3] The act expired in 1696 and an effort in that year to continue it was prevented by the prorogation of parliament. It was clear to all that up to this time the acts had not been obeyed and that illicit trade, at the hands of French privateers and the inhabitants of the Channel Islands, had been flourishing almost without limit.[4] During the War of the Spanish Succession efforts were made to put an entire stop to the trade, by statute and by orders in council, but the smuggling continued unabated. Not until the end of the war and the signing of the treaty of Utrecht did the question again become an issue. Then under the leadership of Bolingbroke and through the activities of Arthur Moore, a member of the Board of Trade and of parliament for Great Grimsby and a delegate to the congress at

gued against the Dutch as "none of our best friends in trade." He considered them still England's greatest rivals in the tobacco, woolen, and African trades and in the fishery (nos. 127, 129, 131, 132).

1. P. 33.                                    2. 1 James II, c. 6.

3. 1 William and Mary, c. 34; 2 William and Mary, c. 14; 4–5 William and Mary, c. 25; *House of Lords Manuscripts,* new series, II, 145; *Calendar Treasury Books,* IX, 146, 208.

4. The Treasury papers are full of references to preventing this trade with France, but the draft of 1696 states that despite the prohibitory measures the trade "is still continued and carried on, chiefly by the conveniency of a speedy passage by the French privateers bringing over their manufactures and returning with wool to France, which tends to the impoverishing of thousands employed in the manufactures of wool and silks in this nation, thereby lowering the rents of land and decreasing the revenues of the Crown" (*House of Lords Manuscripts,* new series, II, 194–195). Additional details are given in this draft. The attempt to prevent smuggling cost the government a great deal of money and any amount of trouble.

Utrecht, himself a "stickler" for the high church party in London, two clauses—the eighth and the ninth—were introduced into the treaty. These clauses "provided that all subjects of the sovereigns of Great Britain and France should enjoy the same commercial privileges in all matters relating to duties, impositions, customs, immunities and tribunals as the most favoured foreign nation; that within two months the English parliament should pass a law repealing all prohibitions of French goods which had been imposed since 1664, and enacting that no French goods imported into England should pay higher duties than similar goods imported from another European country; while in their turn the French promised to repeal all prohibitions of English goods enacted since 1664 and to restore the tariff of that year."[1]

The presentation of these clauses to parliament for ratification precipitated one of the bitterest battles in English commercial history, fought in the exchange, in the writings of the pamphleteers, and at the bar and on the floor of the House of Commons. Halifax, Stanhope, and the young Robert Walpole threw their weight against the ratification. The orthodox mercantilists became hysterical and abusive and condemned the clauses as ruinous for England. On the other side Bolingbroke, Arthur Moore, Davenant, Defoe, Richard Steele, and others endeavored to point out the advantages of the treaty and the desirability of a reciprocal commercial agreement with France. The measure was lost and ratification defeated by the narrow margin of nine votes, 187 to 196. Of the latter number but 118 are known to have been Whigs, showing that 78 must have opposed the measure on other than party grounds.[2] The vote was that of the

1. Lecky, *England in the XVIIIth Century*, I, 154–155.
2. The names of the members voting for and against the bill are given in a contemporary broadside list of the voters, which is reproduced in an appendix to *A Letter to a West Country Clothier and Freeholder concerning the French Treaty of Commerce by Way of Advice in the Ensuing Elections, with Cautions to those who are to Chuse Members to serve in Parliament* (London, 1713). The London members voted three to one against the bill; those from Scotland sixteen to fifteen in its favor. Of the members of the Board of Trade who were in parliament Arthur Moore voted for the bill and Paul Docminique against it. Lecky gives the vote as 185 to 194, but the broadside's list gives it as stated. Among the strict mercantilists who opposed the opening of the trade with France were Erasmus Philips, Henry Martin, Sir Charles Cooke, Sir Theodore Janssen, James Milner, Nathaniel Toriano, Joshua Gee, Christopher Haynes, David Martin, John Withers, John Egleton, and, in general, a majority of the other pamphleteers. On the whole the conclusion is reasonable that the merchants were against the bill and the landed gentry for it. This fact probably accounts for the closeness of the vote, since we are told that at the time more landed estates were repre-

country party against the moneyed interest rather than that of the Tories against the Whigs.

This famous incident in English commercial history has been the subject of much extended and misleading comment. Such older writers as McCulloch, Craik, and Lecky viewed it as a contest between an outworn theory of protection and the modern idea of free trade and they condemned vigorously the action of the House of Commons in rejecting the bill as reactionary and detrimental to England's best interests. Others, such as Ashley in his "Tory Origin of Free Trade," take a similar position, but give to the contest a highly political coloring, as if it were only a struggle between the Whigs and the Tories for party supremacy, and they are inclined to make it a party matter with lessons for the present day. Neither of these estimates is sound. The main issue was not a matter of party politics, though doubtless many approached it from a party point of view and tried to make political capital out of it.[1] It was simply the moot question as to whether trade with France was desirable or undesirable, and because the answer to that question involved a great many intricate factors, including the making up of a balance sheet which would show where lay that mysterious balance of trade with France about which men differed so widely, a large number voted yea or nay without regard to party, as the vote on the bill clearly shows.

Defoe started *The Mercator* which, with the backing of Bolingbroke, he issued thrice weekly in 1713, and argued moderately and

sented in parliament than since the Reformation (*Essays on the National Constitution, Bank, Credit and Trade.* London, 1717, pp. 23–24). Antagonism to France and the wide-spread conviction that the prevailing extravagance and luxuriousness of the time was due to the French trade carried the day, but only by nine votes in a total of 383. When, however, at a later date parliament was asked to lighten the customs duties and increase the land tax the shoe was on the other foot and the vote went the other way.

1. Richard Steele in *An Essay upon Trade and Public Credit* (London, 1714) speaks of the "Modern Whigs" as eager to persuade the world that they are the only patriots and conservators of trade and credit. That they were the only ones who opposed the eighth and ninth articles of the treaty with France and in so doing seemed to prefer no trade at all to one which was free and open. Steele adds that the Whigs had also opposed the East India trade, on account of the cheapness of Indian manufactures, and calicoes, and were making a party issue out of what was not a party issue at all. He wrote in reply to a pamphlet *Torism and Trade* (1713), in which the writer charged the Tories with being churchmen and landed gentry, and caring nothing for trade. One of his axioms is, "Trade is the great supporter of liberty and liberty is as inconsistent with Torism as moderation is with popery and virtue with vice" (p. 1). Defoe also charged the Whigs with making party use of what was not a political but a commercial matter (*The Mercator*, no. 115).

with force that the balance was in England's favor and would continue to be so in increasing measure if the bill should pass. He denied having any concern in party disputes (no. 59), wishing only "to open up the channels of our exportation, by getting all the prohibitions, high duties, and other obstructions of our trade to France taken away, that we may have as full and free a trade and as open a market for manufactures in France as possible, and this is done by the treaty" (nos. 45, 78).[1] He further adds that the passage of the bill was the only way to check smuggling and clandestine trade. Those who opposed the bill started *The British Merchant,* with the support of Halifax and Stanhope and under the editorship of Henry Martin, afterward a prominent official in the custom house, which ran to 103 numbers, issued twice weekly, during 1713 and 1714. This paper, a single sheet as was *The Mercator,* seems to one reader of today less constructive and more vituperative than the other, harking back for its arguments to Fortrey, who in 1663 strongly opposed the trade with France and furnished convenient material for use fifty years later.[2] Its contributors laid great stress upon a "Scheme of Trade" of 1674[3] and upon a Board of Trade representation of December 23, 1697,

1. Davenant and Defoe, writing not as Tories but as shrewd observers, strike a very modern note when the one says, "Trade is in its nature free, finds its own channel and best directeth its own course, and all laws to give it rules and directions and to limit it and circumspect it may serve the particular ends of private men, but are seldom advantageous to the public" ("Essay on the East India Trade," *Works,* I, 98); and the other, "We ought to trade with every nation we can get money by" (*Some Thoughts on the Subject of Commerce with France,* 1713, pp. 27–28). Defoe in his youth had been bred to the French trade, probably had as good a knowledge of it as had his opponents, and was certainly able to take a broader and more disinterested point of view. His modernness appears in his attitude toward some of the mercantilists' pet ideas, such as those regarding silks and printed calicoes. He wrote a dozen pamphlets on trade, some at considerable length, in which he handles the subject with fairness and good judgment. It would be difficult to class either Davenant or Defoe as Tories; each was a mercantilist of the unconventional type, with views of his own regarding the balance of trade and the proper management of commercial relations with foreign countries.

2. *The Mercator,* nos. 1–181, May 26, 1713, to July 20, 1714; *The British Merchant,* nos. 1–103, ending July 30, 1714. I have had access only to nos. 16 to 103 of the latter, beginning September 29, 1713. One should be careful to use the original issues of *The British Merchant,* as the reprint of 1721, in three volumes, contains a great deal of matter that was added afterward, in no way connected with the controversy. The original issues of both series have all the desultoriness and miscellaneous character of papers brought out under such pressure of circumstance.

3. This "Scheme of Trade" was issued by fourteen London merchants engaged in the French trade and it placed the balance, based on the customs books of 1668–1669, at £1,000,000 against England. The merchants were Patience Ward, Thomas Pap-

which furnished proof satisfactory to themselves of the fact that the balance of trade with France had always been unfavorable to England and was likely to remain so. Therefore they defended with vehemence the preambles to the prohibitory acts of 1678 and 1689 as stating the case correctly and justifying in all respects England's policy and the rejection of the bill.

The rejection of the French treaty determined England's policy toward the French trade for more than seventy years. Though later writers, such as Sir Matthew Decker, in his *Essay on the Causes of the Decline of Foreign Trade* (1744, written in 1739), ridiculed the prohibitory duties against France,[1] the growing menace of French rivalry and the continued warnings of the pamphleteers kept alive this mercantilist doctrine till after the American Revolution.[2] How far England's commercial policy toward France affected colonial trade is a matter of interesting speculation. It did not, of course, interfere with the direct trade of the colonies with France, in such commodities as were allowed to be exported to the European continent under the navigation acts, for we know that trade with such French ports as Bordeaux and La Rochelle attained very considerable pro-

pilon, James Houblon, William Bellamy, Michael Godfrey, George Toriano, John Houblon, John Houghe, John Merwin, Peter Paravicine, John Dubois, Benjamin Godfrey, Edmund Harrison, and Benjamin Delawne. These names show at once that Professor Ashley is quite wrong in ascribing the "Scheme" to the Shaftesbury council of 1672–1674. It has been printed several different times (Ashley, *Surveys*, p. 275, note 1) and for the purpose of the debate in 1713, in sheet form, when it was given out at the door of the House of Commons (*The Mercator*, no. 2), and inserted as a folder in *A Letter to A[rthur] M[oore]*. On this print see *The Mercator*, nos. 2, 11, 12, 28, 35, 60, 61, 93, 94–97, 98; *The British Merchant*, nos. 34, 37, 38, 46, 82. The general summing up in the former is in numbers 155 and 159; in the latter in no. 84. The evidence furnished by Fortrey and the "Scheme" is made use of in a *Letter to Sir R–. H–. wherein is considered what effect the repeal of those laws which now regulate our Commerce with France are likely to have on the Trade and Manufactures of England* (London, 1713).

1. Decker was a firm believer in the navigation acts, which he considered to be the "most glorious bulwark of our trade . . . the best acts that ever passed for the benefit of trade," p. 22. Thus he was a forerunner of Lord Sheffield.

2. *The Present State of the British and French Trade to Africa and America, consider'd and compar'd, with some propositions in Favour of the Trade of G[reat] B[ritain]* (London, 1745); G. Coade, *A Letter to the Honourable the Lords Commissioners of Trade and Plantations* (London, 1747), an essay of great moment as containing a statement of the mercantilist position in the middle of the eighteenth century; *State of the Nation considered* (3d ed. 1747) based on the desire to do anything to destroy the French trade; Otis Little, *The State of the Trade in the Northern Colonies considered* (London, 1748), pp. 15–16; *A Short State of the Progress of the French Trade and Navigation* (London, 1750). The last two pamphlets are against the French trade.

portions in colonial times and that agents were sent there by firms in America to look after their interests. But whether it ever actually interfered with the re-exportation of colonial staples from Great Britain to France, as Defoe greatly feared would be the case,[1] may well be doubted. All the enumerated staples—sugar, tobacco, indigo, cotton, ginger, rice, and dye-woods, particularly logwood in chips or planks—were in quantities large and small re-exported to France and other countries, a business in which British merchants trading to America and special firms in the ports from Glasgow to London were heavily engaged. There were French agents in Great Britain, who bought up these commodities at English or Scottish ports and there were importers in France who sent these agents to London, Cowes, or Glasgow and, after buying up what they could generally of the cheaper varieties, had to reckon with the very complicated process of getting their cargoes into France under the eye of the farmers of the customs there. These re-exportations increased rapidly in the eighteenth century and it is possible that as the Virginia and Maryland trade was suffering from overproduction and from the heavy duties imposed at English ports anything that affected or curtailed the foreign market may have been felt in the colonies. But no evidence to prove this fact has been forthcoming.[2]

More capable of demonstration is the effect of the prohibition upon the use of French goods in America. Inasmuch as the colonials could legally obtain their Continental merchandise, fabrics, and wines only through England, the rejection of the treaty clauses and the imposition and extension of the prohibitory duties on French commodities meant that French silks, linens and other desirable articles of better quality, which were coming into use in the colonies in the eighteenth century could not be obtained at all or only through illicit trading with the French and Dutch West Indies. We know that stuffs and wares of one kind or another were worn or utilized from nearly all the western and northern European from the Baltic to the Mediterranean, yet it is very rare to find in the inventories, invoices, and newspaper advertisements of the period any articles mentioned specifically as of French make. We meet with Holland lawn, linen, duck, wool, and paper; with German serge, Osnaburg linen, and Mecklenburg silk, with Barcelona silk handkerchiefs, Flemish thread, and

1. *The Mercator,* nos. 69, 78, 90.
2. The whole subject of the re-exportation of colonial staples from Great Britain is in need of a thorough investigation.

Spanish poplin; with Russian lawn, sheeting, and canvas; with Hungarian stuff, Romal or Bombay kerchiefs, Scottish tartans and cloths, and Irish linen, but almost never with the manufactures and merchandise of France. Some such commodities—silks, embroideries, gloves, and other millinery—must have come in from St. Eustatius and elsewhere in the West Indies and it is curious how record is rarely found of their presence in the colonies.[1] The omission may be due to the fact that they were smuggled articles. That the highly protective policy which England employed against France increased smuggling in America and enormously increased it in England and Scotland, Ireland, and the Channel Islands there cannot be the slightest doubt. Furthermore, in considering the historical significance of England's policy we must not forget that the rejection of the treaty provisions was intimately bound up with the assistance which France gave the revolting colonies in the years from 1778 to 1783.

There is another aspect of the case that is worthy of attention and further study. By their victory in the House of Commons the mercantilists deliberately cut themselves off from a trade which, had it been reciprocally pursued, would have proved exceedingly profitable to both countries. France was separated from England by only a few miles of water and trade with her ports permitted a turnover of business capital three or four times a year with a security of credit that was fairly normal; whereas the colonies, three thousand miles away in a primitive environment where trading conditions were always precarious and industrial development in its infancy, could assure returns from invested capital not oftener than once in from one to four years. Colonial credit was long, running usually for nine months without interest and sometimes for twelve, and ending not infrequently in bad or, as they were contemporaneously called, "desperate" debts. These disadvantages were only partly compensated for by profits that sometimes reached two hundred per cent. From a business point of view, therefore, the trade with France would appear to have been far and away the more desirable proposition. But the mercantilists did not see it in that light, for their business shrewdness was befogged by their fear of France and dislike of her products and by their conviction that the advantages of the traffic were all on

1. Both French silk and French brandy are mentioned, but not often by the name of the place of their origin.

the French side. They figured out the debit and credit entries of the balance and with no real understanding of the elements involved in the calculation created artificial barriers to protect themselves against loss. The situation inevitably gave more articulate form to the idea of the self-sufficing empire, for the mercantilists now began to look on the colonial trade, which formerly they had rated as but of incidental importance, in the light of a providential substitute for that of France and with extraordinary miscalculation overestimated the part that the colonies could play as commercial assets. Wood published his *Survey of Trade* in 1718, with new editions in 1719 and 1722, and the enlargement of *The British Merchant* appeared in 1721. This work, the *vade mecum* of the orthodox mercantilists— edited by the merchant, Charles King, "digested by the ingenious Henry Martin and dictated by Sir Theodore Janssen"[1]—was swollen to three volumes by the inclusion bodily of Janssen's *General Maxims in Trade* (1713) and of contributions from some of the most eminent of the London merchants. It made enmity for France its guiding principle.

From this time forward the colonies, in constantly accelerating measure, became a necessary asset in mercantilist eyes. The government and parliament, by the adoption of a protective policy and a system of bounties, helped to cultivate this trade, and the merchants extolled its possibilities. "We have," wrote a pamphleteer in 1720 or 1721, "within ourselves and in our colonies in America an inexhaustible fund to supply ourselves, and perhaps Europe, with what we are now beholden to foreigners for, and that at the expence of our silver and gold; and yet either our negligence or private views make us sit still, and not improve what God and Nature have laid open to us. . . . Is it not time for every honest Briton to rouse out of the lethargy we seem to be in, and attend the real good of his country, by encouraging its trades, and those trades that may bring in such a balance in our favour?"[2] To the argument that cultivating the colonial trade would be dangerous as making the colonies too rich and therefore too independent, the same writer replies that such argu-

---

1. So stated in *The State-Anatomy of Great Britain, being a Memorial sent by an Intimate Friend to a Foreign Minister* (4th ed. 1717). This pamphlet contains one chapter (III) on Whigs and Tories and another (IV) on Trade. The writer says that "Trade is the Soul of the British World, nor is it understood better in any part of the greater World" (p. 43). In view of the fact that he opposes the treaty articles with France, this statement is open to/some question.

2. *Some Considerations on the Late Mismanagement of the South Sea Stock* (Lon-

ments "are only mists raised to hide the true reason, which is party opposition; for if our colonies could arrive to such greatness as to supply us with what is above recited, there would not a man in England want imploy in our manufactures, for its evident the gains and product of our colonies center here in England," and "their dependence will be their interest."

This was the mercantilist outlook upon the colonies at the end of the first half of the eighteenth century. As agricultural areas of supply the colonies were furnishing England with sugar, tobacco, naval stores, fish, and other commodities, which partly by direct shipment as in the case of fish and partly by re-exportation as in the case of the enumerated commodities were aiding England's general balance and relieving her of dependence on other countries with which the balance was adverse. Even the northern colonies were lending their aid as purveyors to the West Indies and were no longer construed as a drag upon England's progress. And now with the barring of the trade with France, colonial commerce took on a new meaning and even the bursting of the South Sea bubble did not destroy the faith of the English merchant in the essential soundness of the idea of the self-sufficing empire.[1]

At the same time there is ample evidence to show that even if mercantilism was in the ascendant during the years before 1763, it was never in complete command of the situation. The evidence demonstrates the futility of the mercantilist ideal as applied to the

don, n.d., but about 1720–21), pp. 19–22. This treatise is characteristic of the new attitude toward the colonies. The following passage could not possibly have been written twenty-five years before, "I believe hitherto every man is convinced, that as the colonies in America grow rich, their demands are the greater for our manufactures; and wherever a colony does not flourish there the trade with us declines. So that really all the Encouragement we can give them centers in England; their sons and daughters are sent hither, and estates are bought with their improvements abroad, and consequently as they increase in riches, so land will be the more valuable here; for few fix their station there out of choice; the first reason was necessity, when that is once got over, the love either in themselves or children returns for their native land." Some of these statements are reminiscent of Dalby Thomas, but Thomas was writing only of the West Indies, while the anonymous author of this pamphlet is interested in all the colonies, continental and West Indian alike.

1. The petitions which were presented to parliament from the manufacturing towns of England in 1738–1739, during the debate on the alteration of the Molasses Act (12 George II, c. 30, June 14, 1739); in 1749–1750, during the discussion regarding the iron bill; and in 1764, when raw iron was made an enumerated commodity, show the working of the mercantilist mind. Stock, *Debates*, IV, 805–817, especially the speech of Micajah Perry, the younger; *Commons' Journal*, XXV, 1018–1063; and Bining, as above, pp. 77–80.

colonies and the frequency with which the merchant and planter-capitalists suffered defeat at the hands of parliament on one side and of the colonists on the other. This defeat was due partly to the human impossibility of maintaining intact a self-contained trading world, made up of mother country and colonies, in the face of the inevitable growth of the latter in wealth, needs, and population, and partly to the fact that the merchants, manufacturers, and planter-capitalists, each group seeking its own ends, were frequently as divided among themselves as they were out of accord with the views of many of the members of parliament. They were of course united on some things. They agreed on the "ill consequences" likely to arise from certain parliamentary proposals to break in upon the navigation acts, and declared that it would be "madness" to give up any of the advantages accruing to trade and the kingdom from the strictest enforcement of these and other legislative measures. They believed that the system once encroached upon by concessions and relaxations would eventually break down entirely to England's unspeakable loss and the foreigners' gain. They were opposed to anything that seemed to obstruct, or at least did nothing to promote, foreign trade, such, for example, as the four and a half per cent ("a monstrous tax" they called it), subsidies to the Royal African Company, Georgia, and Nova Scotia, and other forms of public expenditure that in no way profited their interests. They wanted bounties and a reduction of duties on raw materials imported into England from the colonies, but, as in the case of raw iron, they were not always able to get them, while the one outstanding system of bounties, that on naval stores, was rather a public advantage than an aid to private profit. The failure of the sugar bill of 1731, which was defeated, the modified bill of 1733 (the Molasses Act), which was passed, the fishing by New Englanders off the banks of New-foundland, the opening of markets south of Cape Finisterre to sugar and rice, the shipping to foreign countries of many colonial staples, that until 1764 were outside the enumeration, and the colonial coastwise privilege of carrying enumerated commodities from colony to colony were, at one time or another, in one form or another, by one person or another, considered inimical to the principle of a centralized and self-sustaining commercial system such as the mercantilists wanted to maintain. Generally speaking, the mercantilists, though not often saying so openly and publicly, disliked changes that were distinctly in the interest not of their own trade but of the colonies, and, in their desire for a greater concentration of authority at Whitehall, they never seem to have considered that the colonists might be, consciously and unconsciously, creating an independent life of their own, antagonistic to the mercantilist plan and apart from their usefulness to the mother country. They believed in the efficacy of legislation, but they failed to realize that in the absence of any adequate machinery for the enforcement of parliamentary laws in America the colonists were bound eventually to succeed in neutralizing and bringing to naught the mercantilist policy. That policy, as far as it applied to trade and manufacturing, was at variance with the development of a separate colonial existence, but except in narrowing the channels of trade, which, to some extent certainly, did impose hardship upon colonial shippers, its application was incomplete and imperfect, and attempts to carry it out hampered but slightly colonial freedom of action. Over and over again the colonists were able, in the interest of their own self-governing powers and industrial prosperity, to evade the orders issued and the laws passed.

# CHAPTER XI

## ENGLAND'S ATTEMPT TO ENFORCE
## HER COLONIAL POLICY

THE essential features of England's colonial policy as distinct from her commercial policy were determined at the very outset of her career as the mother of overseas possessions.[1] The basic idea of this policy, which remained unchanged throughout our colonial period, was the dependence of the colonies upon the parent state and the subordination of their interests to those of the country from which their people came. Only in this way, Englishmen believed, could the requirements be met that constituted the true design and intention of colonies and only in this way could the welfare be preserved of the senior member, particularly in matters of governmental control, trade, and the revenue. Thus they identified the colonial relationship with the commercial and financial needs of the kingdom and up to a certain point, but never completely, defined it from the standpoint of mercantilism and the balance of foreign trade. They construed all matters of defense, finance, manufacturing, local administration, and the passage of laws in the interest of the king's prerogative, of their own merchants, and of their own exchequer, and frowned on or forbade whatever they deemed disadvantageous in either connection. Simple and explicit as these objectives seem to have been in the planning they were far from simple when the question arose of enforcement, and though easy to define were to prove exceedingly difficult and in the long run impossible to apply. How to hold a group of colonies, increasing in number and growing in strength, wealth, and population, in a state of political dependence and financial subordination for an indefinite length of time was a problem that the authorities in England were always attempting to solve but they never succeeded effectively in doing so.

As we followed line by line the story of the settlements, particularly after 1660, we became increasingly aware of the demands which the maritime and commercial classes were making upon the government to set up a satisfactory and efficient organization that would

1. See Chapter I.

bring the colonies within the range of their capitalistic ambitions. These demands arose from their desire to utilize the colonies as assets of profit to both England and themselves. Before 1655 such desires had hardly come into existence, for the colonies were few in number and the times were not auspicious for either colonial or commercial expansion. During the first period of settlement private persons, not the state, were the agencies concerned. The state lent its aid but took no initiative and assumed no responsibility, and no singleness of purpose regarding the oversight and management of colonies can anywhere be found. It is true that once, in 1625, the year after Virginia had been taken into the king's hands, the Privy Council, at that time the only executive body concerned for the plantations overseas, did insert in a royal proclamation a phrase suggestive of a colonial policy, when it wrote that there should be but "one uniforme course of Government in and through the whole Monarchie."[1] But this phrase was merely an obiter dictum that was disregarded four years later when a charter was issued to the Massachusetts Bay Company and when other charters followed to various petitioners from 1628 to 1632.[2] Neither the Laud Commission of 1634 nor the Warwick Commission of 1643 was granted powers which properly speaking defined a policy of colonial administration, for the functions of each were almost entirely inquisitorial and disciplinary. The language of the act that established the Commonwealth, May 19, 1649, however much it may appear to have predicated the future power of parliament over "the dominions and territories belonging to the people of England," was unproductive of results.[3]

But as the second period of settlement approached, with its expanding interest in material prosperity, the notion that trade could be advanced by the acquisition of new markets and sources of supply began to filter in, almost imperceptibly, to the English mind. The merchants of London and the outports, seeking additional opportunities for profit, became convinced that their needs could best be supplied if the colonies were placed under a more certain, civil, and

1. Brigham, *Royal Proclamations*, p. 53.    2. Above, Vol. II, 190, note 2.

3. I am quite unable to follow Professor McIlwain in his belief that this act marked the true beginning of the constitutional issue which led to the Declaration of Independence (*The American Revolution: A Constitutional Interpretation*). The assertion that parliament had authority over all the dominions and territories beyond the seas remained meaningless during the Interregnum and the act itself had no validity after 1660. The words quoted are merely a bit of Commonwealth bombast and in no way foreshadowed a consistent governmental programme.

uniform way of government and if all the islands, plantations, and dominions of England in America were drawn together under a single executive control. Recommendations to that effect were introduced into the instructions issued to the special councils of 1660, and one of the first reports made to the king by the council for foreign plantations contained the following suggestions: (1) that he come to an understanding with the private governments in America; (2) that he promise to prevent the erection of any more colonies of that type; and (3) that he take all the colonies under his own immediate protection.[1]

These recommendations, remarkable for the time, had no other effect than to draw from the Privy Council a refusal to recognize the claims of those who had received grants from the Council for New England in 1635 and who at this juncture were petitioning for a recognition of what they considered their rights. The council declared that these claimants had no higher aim than their own personal profit and were not likely to promote either trade or colonization. It also went so far as to declare that private colonies were not to England's advantage and ought not to be increased in number, a remark that was to prove bootless in view of the fact that from 1662 to 1681 corporate charters were issued to Connecticut and Rhode Island and personal charters to the proprietors of Carolina, New York, and Pennsylvania, thus legalizing two private settlements already existing and erecting three others that were new. The futility at this time of the plans which the merchants had so carefully formulated can be seen further in the entire omission, from the instructions issued to the special councils of 1668, 1670, and 1672, of any reference to a plan of administration for the colonies, any expression of interest in them apart from their value to trade, and any evidence of a desire to set up a system of control over them under the king's immediate direction.[2] During these years the court at Whitehall was still more powerful than the counting houses in the City of London.

With the dissolution in 1674 of the council of 1672 and the concentration of authority over the colonies in the hands of the Privy Council—where it properly belonged and whence it had been delegated only temporarily to the special councils—the government found itself face to face with two unforeseen and very perplexing problems, demanding decision and action much more immediate and specific

1. *Calendar State Papers, Colonial*, 1661–1668, §3.
2. These instructions are printed in Andrews, *British Committees*, pp. 117–132.

than had ever been required in the past. These problems were: (1) how to enforce the acts of trade passed between 1660 and 1673 and (2) how to meet the danger arising from the rivalry with France, which was beginning to take ominous form after 1675. Believing that the private colonies were a menace in both particulars, the Lords of Trade—the royally commissioned committee of the council instructed to look after trade and the plantations—for the first time gave official expression to the rule that it proposed to follow. Though unable to prevent the grant of Pennsylvania to William Penn, because the personal wishes of the crown were more insistent than the convictions of the king's advisers, it did reject the petition of the Earl of Doncaster, August 31, 1682, for a propriety south of Carolina.[1] After some weeks of deliberation, the lords replied to the earl that it was inadvisable for the king to institute any new propriety or to grant away such powers as might render the plantations less dependent on the crown. Two years later they followed up this declaration with an utterance of a wider and more general character, to the effect that it was "to the great and growing prejudice of the plantations that such governments be maintained without a nearer dependence on your Majesty."[2] In reaching a conclusion so ominous to the corporate and proprietary settlements, the lords had two ends in view. In the first place they wanted to bring to an end the erection of private colonies,[3]

---

1. C. O. 1:49, no. 30 (fo. 116). The petition asked for "a grant of the Tract or Region called fflorida, bounded on the North east with the province of Carolina, on the East with the Maine Ocean, on the South with the Gulph of fflorida and Mexico; as also the Tract or Region of Guiana on the same Continent of America, lying between the River Oronoque and the River of Amazons," with all mines and quarries of gold, silver, and precious stones, power to coin money of all metals, toleration in religion to all protestant Dissenters and native Indians, freedom from customs for nineteen years, and full propriety of the soil. The proprietor was to be endowed with all other rights, privileges, and immunities to be found in the grants of any other colonies or plantations whatsoever. The very extravagance of this request by an earl, who at the time was in his minority, undoubtedly helped the lords in reaching a decision.

2. *Calendar State Papers, Colonial*, 1685–1688, §283; *Maryland Archives*, V, 445.

3. *Calendar State Papers, Colonial*, 1681–1685, §82. The determination to prevent the erection of any more private colonies is to be seen not only in the refusal of the Lords of Trade to accede to Doncaster's request, but also in the letter which Blathwayt, the secretary, wrote the Plymouth general court in 1683. In that letter he told the court that nothing could be done about granting the colony a charter until it was known what the lords proposed to do about Massachusetts Bay. He said further that the lords had made up their minds to regulate the Bay colony and if this were done and Massachusetts were brought into direct dependence on the crown then Plymouth would be brought in also and have no need of a charter. Barnes, *Dominion of New England*, p. 28.

and in the years that followed this rule was rigidly adhered to. No new proprieties were ever created after that of Pennsylvania, with the single exception of Georgia, which though for twenty years a trusteeship—neither proprietary, corporate, nor royal—was required at the end of that time to enter the royal group. In the second place, they wanted, as opportunity offered, so to transform or regulate the private colonies as to make them part of a centralized system directly under royal control.

Tendencies in the direction of greater centralization had already appeared. The seizure of Jamaica and New Netherland, the sending over of the royal commission of 1664, and the setting up of the royal colony of New Hampshire were all anticipatory of later attempts at consolidation. In the annulment also of the charters of Bermuda and Massachusetts Bay we see the same tendencies at work, hastened in these instances by charter violations that made revocation possible by due process of law.[1] But the most outstanding experiment of the kind in the seventeenth century was the erection of the Dominion of New England in 1686. As early as 1681 the Lords of Trade had come to the conclusion that New England could not be brought to a satisfactory settlement unless a general governor were sent over and maintained at the king's charge. This belief was given practical form five years later, when the lords, having become convinced that the Puritan governments were in no sense answering the purpose of colonies subservient and useful to the mother country, consolidated the three New England colonies under a single executive head. This meddling on a grand scale with self-governing and self-willed communities, of whose affairs the lords knew little that was dependable and with whose political and religious aims they could have had no sympathy, proved a disastrous failure. Begun in the interest of trade, defense, and a closer dependence of the colonies on England, it came to naught because of the strength attained by Massachusetts Bay during the preceding fifty years and of the determination of Connecticut and Rhode Island to retain the privileges secured to them by their charters. The Lords of Trade, who were responsible for the

---

1. Board of Trade Journal (Ms), IV, 57–58, very inadequately calendared in *Calendar State Papers, Colonial*, 1681–1685, §684. The instructions given its agents by the Massachusetts general court covered a wide range of concessions (*Massachusetts Colonial Records*, V, 346–349), but were silent on the one subject of the regulation of the government of the colony. It was on this ground that the Lords of Trade recommended the issue of a new quo warranto against the charter (*Calendar State Papers, Colonial*, 1681–1685, §397). The one thing Massachusetts dreaded was regulation.

experiment, with their minds fixed on England's needs and desirous of producing something analogous to the French Dominion of Canada, could not see the utter futility of attempting to bring together under a single royal governor settlements already steeped in the practice and tradition of looking after themselves. The structure fell, never to be restored, even though many suggestions to that end were made later in England, where those in authority learned their lessons slowly if, as was too often the case, they learned them at all. In its fall the Dominion left a wreckage of sorts behind and in the events that followed each of the colonies concerned showed in some measure the effects of the experiment. To a greater extent than is commonly realized party factions arose for and against England's policy, and in after times historians were to characterize the erection of the Dominion as an act of usurpation and of tyranny and those concerned in it as malicious in spirit and despotic in execution.[1]

During the remaining years of their tenure the Lords of Trade made no further effort to bring about a readjustment of the colonial relationship. Connecticut and Rhode Island resumed their charters. Unlike Massachusetts Bay, whose charter had been legally annulled in 1684, these two corporate colonies were still in full possession of the powers conferred upon them by the crown. They had submitted to the authority of Andros but had performed no act of surrender under the public seal of the colony, with a subsequent legal enrollment in England, nor had they ever had judgment entered against them in legal form. Connecticut's involuntary submission to Andros, November 1, 1687, had not made its charter void in law. Therefore, when the emergency had passed, these two colonies went on as before, the authorities in England agreeing that they were fully warranted in so doing.[2] But from this time forward we can trace the presence in all the private colonies of men who sympathized with what England was trying to do and desired, as a matter of trading profit and political privilege, the more intimate connection with the

1. Arnold, though in his *History of Rhode Island* he calls Andros a "tyrant," is almost the only one of the older historians who has a good word for him. One suspects, however, that Arnold's effort at impartiality is partly due to his satisfaction at Andros' treatment of Massachusetts Bay and his friendly attitude toward Rhode Island (I, 514–517).

2. For the legal question: in the case of Connecticut, Hutchinson, *History* (Mayo ed.), I, 344, note; Connecticut Archives, Foreign Correspondence, Agents in England, nos. 25–27, opinion of Sir George Treby, August 2, 1690; in the case of Rhode Island, *Rhode Island Colonial Records*, III, 293–294.

mother country which a royalizing of the private colonies would have brought about.

The lethargy into which the Lords of Trade had fallen during the years from 1689 to 1696 accounts in largest part for the laissez-faire attitude assumed by the English authorities of the time toward all that concerned the colonial relationship. These authorities were, however, not wholly inactive. For the moment they thought of continuing the grouping of New England, New York, and the Jerseys under a new governor to take the place of Andros, but this scheme was shown to be so preposterous that they did no more than urge the colonists to unite among themselves against the French.[1] The failure of the Dominion and the impossibility of its revival seem to have destroyed all desire to make further experiments of any kind. The Lords of Trade formulated no statement of opinion or expression of policy that discloses any interest whatever in constitutional reorganization overseas. They, as well as others in office at Whitehall, lapsed into a state of inertia which left the colonies, outwardly at least, free to return, without fear of interference, to their former condition, except for the changes wrought in Massachusetts by the charter of 1691.

But this situation could not last. The war with France, known in the colonies as King William's War or the Gallic Peril, was the more menacing because after 1689 the colonists seemed less united than ever and less inclined to coöperate for mutual protection. They were living, as they had always lived, in groups far removed the one from the other, poor and insufficiently stocked with the materials for war, absorbed each in its own problems of government, maintenance, and defense. They were jealous, suspicious, and wanting in intercolonial confidence, disinclined to make sacrifices in a common cause, and ready "by pretence or various pretences" to evade responsibility and ignore, if they could, the commands of the government at home. They found combination in action and harmonious participation in military movements impeded by an exasperating slowness of communication and transport, which over and over again thwarted the best-laid plans of offense against the enemy. As was said at the time, they were "so crumbled into little governments and so disunited in their distinct interests that they have hitherto afforded but little assistance to each other and seem as they now are but of an ill posture and a worse disposition to do it in the future." True as this was of

1. *Calendar State Papers, Colonial,* 1693-1696, §§1015, 1176.

the continental colonies, it was equally true of England's possessions in the West Indies, where the danger of attacks by sea was always present and the sufferings of the islanders were even greater than those which distressed the inhabitants of the mainland. The increase of piracy at this period, due to the inability of the Admiralty to furnish ships for the patrolling of the seas; the belief, widely prevalent, that the colonists were not only aiding the pirates but were also engaged in a wholesale effort to prevent the enforcement of the acts of trade; the growing conviction that the proprietary governments were unable to cope with the new conditions that war and trade were creating—all these circumstances were demanding the inauguration of a more drastic and efficient colonial programme.

What the principal parts of this programme were we have already seen in earlier chapters. They were the passage of the act of 1696, the appointment of the Board of Trade, the strengthening of the customs service, the erection of the vice-admiralty courts, and the issue to the colonial governors and others of orders reminding them of their duty and enjoining them at their peril to adhere rigidly to their instructions.[1] To these various measures may be added the increased powers given to Edward Randolph, the despatch of a surveyor of the woods to look after the king's forestry rights, and the sending of roving commissioners, of one kind or another and with varying instructions, to spy out the land and to report as to how the colonists were conducting their affairs.

Thus at a time when new impulses were astir and new views regarding the colonies were taking shape in the minds of those who were concerned for England's maritime and commercial future, a deliberate effort was being made to exact a stricter obedience from the colonies and to centralize, as had never been done successfully before, authority in the hands of the crown. Interference with their liberties many a colonist thought it; consolidation Englishmen in

1. The last circular letter of this kind, which was issued by the Lords of Trade, April 15, 1696 (the Board of Trade was commissioned May 15), is very mild in its terms, merely reminding the governors "to take care that the said Act and all other Laws . . . be duly Published within your Government and strictly put in execution by all Persons whom it may concern, according to the Purport thereof" (C. O. 324:5, pp. 382–383). The Board of Trade on the other hand, in its letters of the next few years to the royal governors, to the proprietors of Pennsylvania, East and West New Jersey, and the Bahamas, and to the governors and magistrates of Connecticut and Rhode Island, employed much sterner language, in order to put into the hearts of these men the wrath of the government at home. These letters distinctly made an impression in the colonies.

office called it, a necessary concentration of administrative control in order that the colonists might meet the ends for which all colonists existed—the benefit and advantage of the parent state. In this divergence of interest lies the history of the colonial relationship from this time on. Relatively inconspicuous and unobserved as this divergence often was and subtle in its manifestations, it was to widen as the years passed and to proceed at an accelerated pace down to the American Revolution. Few contemporaries in England realized the danger lurking in a persistent attempt to enforce such a policy as the one to which her authorities were committed, or imagined that the methods of interference adopted after 1763 would be so far resented in the colonies as to bring about an eventual breach. One man, however, had forebodings at a very early date. In 1707 Nehemiah Grew wrote, "The time may come when the plantation trade—the best we have—may be lost or greatly diminished, when the colonies may become populous and with the increase of arts and sciences strong and politike, forgetting their relation to the mother countreys, will then confederate and consider nothing further than the means to support their ambition of standing on their legs."[1] That this prophetic utterance found no fulfilment until after 1763 was in largest part due to

1. "Meanes of a Most Ample Encrease," pp. 205–206. Grew's foreboding is almost the earliest of the opinions expressed regarding a possible eventual striving for independence on the part of the colonists. But after his time such expressions were not uncommon. Continued disregard, particularly on the part of New York and Massachusetts, of the instructions issued to the royal governors, seemed to show that these colonies were "aiming at independency" or at least were trying to weaken, if not to cast off entirely "the obedience they owe to the crown and the dependence which all colonies ought to have on their mother country." As Governor Shute put it, they were "endeavouring to wrest the sword out of the royal hand" (Hutchinson, History, Mayo ed., II, 269, note 282; Calendar State Papers, Colonial, 1728–1729, §§5, 648. For several such citations see Burns, Controversies between Royal Governors and their Assemblies (1923), pp. 8–11, but the situation in Massachusetts and New York must not be taken as typical of the colonies in general, where opposition was much less outspoken and vehement). Mr. Pargellis has called my attention to the following paragraph in Cato's Letters (Trenchard ed.), IV, 6–7, dated 1722, letter no. 106: "I would not suggest so distant a thought as that any of our Colonies, when they grow stronger, should ever attempt to wean themselves from us. . . . [But] No Creatures suck the teats of their Dams longer than can draw Milk from thence or can provide themselves with better food: Nor will any Country continue their Subjection to another, only because their Great Grandmothers were acquainted." This figure of speech is the same as that used by James Harrington in his Oceana more than sixty years before, when he wrote that the colonies "are yet babes that cannot live without sucking the breasts of their mother cities, but such as I mistake if, when they come of age, they do not wean themselves: which causeth me to wonder at princes that delight to be exhausted in that way" (p. 9).

the fact that all attempts to centralize control in the king's hand and to carry to their extreme and logical conclusion the demands of the mercantilists either failed entirely or were so imperfectly executed as to constitute but a slight check upon the prosperity and unimpeded development of the colonists themselves. Whenever the situation became troublesome and the exercise of the power of the prerogative or the enforcement of an act of parliament threatened to curb the freedom of colonial action, the popular assemblies and private individuals concerned were generally able by one means or another to obstruct or contravene the royal will or the parliamentary statute.

Scarcely was the Board of Trade in the saddle in the autumn of 1696 when it made known the leading features of its policy. There was to be no continuance of the former inactivity. In a report of September 30 and in a second report of the following February, it inveighed against the supineness of its predecessor, the Lords of Trade, and demanded that a consistent effort be made to effect some sort of unity among the colonies under the king's immediate governance. At first it advocated the plan of putting the colonies "under one Governor," "one Military Head or Captain General," appointed temporarily by the crown as in an emergency, a single commander in chief to organize the colonies on a military basis.[1] "The importance and advantage of an Union [the board said] were by all sides agreed on, even though the methods proposed for putting it in execution were various, according to the different interests of those by whom they are made." It found its first opportunity in the appointment of a successor to Phips in Massachusetts and suggested that whoever such appointee might be he should become the civil head of all New England and New York and general of all the forces from New Hampshire to the Jerseys. But so many objections were raised to this plan, chiefly by Connecticut in asserting her right to elect her own governor,[2] that the idea of a governor general of the Andros type was given up and a different expedient adopted. When

1. The plan had been in the minds of the Lords of Trade when the question of what to do with Maryland in 1691 and Pennsylvania in 1692 came up for consideration. At that time the attorney and solicitor general reported that "upon an extraordinary exigency the crown might appoint a governor general for the civil as for the military part of the colonial governments." This opinion is cited in the Board of Trade's report of December 10, 1703, printed in the *Bulletin,* New York Public Library, XI, 469–497. See also *Calendar State Papers, Colonial,* 1693–1696, §999, and for the legal decision upon which the restoration to Penn was based, *ibid.,* §1138, i.

2. Connecticut Archives, Foreign Correspondence, II, Agents in England, no. 87.

Bellomont was sent over in 1697 he was commissioned governor of Massachusetts, New Hampshire, and New York only, and commander in chief of the militia of Connecticut, Rhode Island, and the Jerseys. The board hoped in this way to bring about a more unified state of things among the northern colonies, for the purpose of strengthening defense, checking piracy, and preventing illegal trade. The experiment lasted but a few years and was a complete failure except so far as it left Massachusetts and New Hampshire tied together under the same man as governor, but with separate commissions, for more than forty years. With the coming of peace with France in 1713 even this attenuated attempt to create a military union among the colonies was discarded, until it was revived in more elaborate form by Secretary Robinson in 1754.

While the board was willing to give the Bellomont experiment a test, it had no intention of stopping at that point should the experiment not succeed. It was determined to go much farther and to press for the adoption of a plan which, if executed, should settle once and for all the question of the status of the private colonies in their relation to the crown. There were two parts to its programme. In the first place, the board was in hearty accord with the principle laid down by its predecessor, when it declared in a report to the lords justices, August 10, 1697, that the revival of dormant titles under the grants of the Council for New England would lead to "unspeakable disturbance and confusion."[1] In the second and much more important place, it had in mind another and more constructive proposal. On February 26, 1698, nine years after parliament had won its "great and glorious" victory over the Stuarts and less than two years after the board's own appointment as a special advisory council to the crown, the board said, "If the Proprieties and Charter Governments do not speedily comply with what is required of them, we see no means to prevent a continuance of this mischief without calling in the further assistance of parliament."[2] This idea of regulating in some manner the private colonies was not new, for it had been hinted at in the resolution of the Lords of Trade in 1685, but the thought of calling upon parliament for aid was new, since in 1685 the legislative branch had not yet won its victory over the executive and the lords at that time would hardly have called in parliament to support the crown in a matter that was executive only. But in 1698 the situation

1. *Calendar State Papers, Colonial*, 1696–1697, p. 579.
2. *Ibid.*, 1697–1698, §265.

had changed and in certain matters of importance a legislative act was becoming recognized as likely to be obeyed more willingly than an order in council. Therefore, the Board of Trade decided to ask parliament to pass such an act, giving body to a well-articulated and aggressive colonial policy.

The board was in a fighting mood. It had become exasperated as report after report came in from its correspondents in the colonies of alleged misfeasances committed by governments and individuals, particularly of the private colonies, to the injury of the kingdom and its merchants. In these reports Massachusetts was charged with exercising "pretended privileges," tying up the royal appointee there and interfering with his legitimate functions; Rhode Island with opposing the king's authority in vice-admiralty matters; Connecticut with denying the right of appeal to the crown, neglecting (as had Rhode Island also) to obtain the royal confirmation of her governor, to send over her laws for the crown's inspection, and to take the oath required by the acts of trade. The proprietors of the Jerseys were charged with drifting along under what the board declared were only "pretended rights of government," and those of the Carolinas and the Bahamas with inability to protect their possessions against attacks of Spaniards and buccaneers. All the colonies were believed to be countenancing illicit trade, harboring pirates, neglecting adequate means of defense, and, in general, with going their own way despite the king's prerogative and the requirements of English law. New Englanders especially were "promoting and propagating woolen and other manufactures proper to England, instead of applying their thoughts and endeavours to the production of such commodities as are fit to be encouraged in those parts, according to the true design and intention of those settlements."[1]

Whether the charges were true or false, partly true or wholly false, reasonable or unreasonable from any point of view, is not the question. The board believed them, accepted them, and acted upon them. Sensitive as it was to anything that seemed to interfere with the enforcement of the royal prerogative or with the trade and revenue of the kingdom, it could not see that the colonies were justified in doing any of these things. It was living up to its own obligations as an adviser to the executive authorities, but it was tired of preparing letters and instructions for the king to send to the governors—mis-

1. C. O. 389:17, p. 173.

sives that were merely executive orders containing directions that were often but lamely obeyed—and now that parliament was showing itself able to maintain a steady, though half-unconscious encroachment into the domain of the prerogative, it was prepared to turn to that body for aid. As the board viewed the situation, the private colonies had become indurated against executive commands and only parliament could bring them to a proper recognition of their duty to the crown.

The time for action had come. In a representation to the king of March 26, 1701, the board, after reciting all the complaints thus far presented, continued as follows: "We humbly conceive it may be expedient that the charters of the several Proprieties and others, intitling them to absolute government, be resumed to the Crown and these Colonies put into the same State and Dependency as those of your Majesties other Plantations without prejudice to any man's particular property and freehold, which being no otherwise we conceive cannot be so well to be effected as by the Legislative power of this kingdom."[1] Answering a request of the House of Lords, to which the board sent a similar statement, it laid before that body a list of the complaints and accusations which from time to time had been accumulating in the Plantation Office, and in all probability included among them the draft of a bill such as it hoped parliament would pass. It was convinced that if such a bill were passed, as it expected would be the case, the new law would set the plantations "upon a more equal foot."[2]

Sympathy with the object of the measure was to be expected from such men as Randolph who had it in charge and later sent in a bill of £96 for his services;[3] from Basse and others in the Jerseys who opposed the pretensions of the proprietors there; from Nicholson in Virginia, Blakiston in Maryland, and Quary in Pennsylvania who believed, as did other prerogative men in the colonies, that the private colonies ought to be disciplined and that a more centralized administration ought to be set up. There were colonists too, not pre-

---

1. *Calendar State Papers, Colonial,* 1701, §§286, 420, 422. The version sent to the House of Lords, May 8 (C. O. 389:17, p. 173; *Calendar State Papers, Colonial,* 1701, §360, by title only), contains slight changes of wording. In this version the preliminary statement reads, "To cure these and other great Mischiefs in these Colonies and to introduce such an Administration of Government and fit Regulation of Trade, as may make them duly subservient and usefull to England, we have humbly offered our opinion That the Charters of several Proprieties and others," etc.

2. *Ibid.,* 1701, §473.     3. *Ibid.,* 1702, §§121, 128, 135, 137.

rogative men, who desired a closer dependence on England, partly for commercial reasons and partly to obtain the full rights of Englishmen, denied them under the Puritan and proprietary jurisdictions. All of these men felt the need of greater coöperation and mutual accord in order to meet the dangers from France and they were convinced that the maintenance of peace within and safety without could be obtained only by strengthening the English connection. In that quarter alone, they believed, lay the hope of united action.

The men who held these views were neither malcontents nor reactionaries, obstinate adherents of a wrong-headed system. They were law-abiding according to their lights, convinced that the continued existence of so many discordant communities, each seeking its own advantage, could end only in ruin. They preferred to accept their status as obedient subjects of the king and as Englishmen to obey the acts of parliament, rather than lose the protection of their mother country. Though many of them were guided by selfish and ambitious motives, more of them were honestly persuaded that the decentralizing tendencies hitherto prevailing were a liability not an asset. At the same time, it is equally easy to understand the attitude of those in the colonies who would sacrifice the larger unity for the acquirement of the power to govern themselves. Viewed from the standpoint of today, looking back over the past, we can see, as contemporary observers could not, that those who placed self-government first were American in mood, preparing the way for the Revolution and the great republic of the future; and that those who preferred the unity and uniformity of the monarchy in all its parts—at home and beyond the seas—were Englishmen, thinking, unconsciously, of the British empire that was to come. Before 1763, with mercantilism still in the ascendant, there could be no reconciliation between these opposing ideas, no compromise between these two types of political thought. Only in the nineteenth century, with mercantilism fallen from its high estate and pecuniary profit and loss no longer the leading motives, was it found possible to nurture self-governing communities within the confines of an imperial system.

The bill prepared by the Board of Trade for reuniting the proprietary and corporate colonies to the crown opened with the following statements of opinion: that severing from the crown such authority and privileges as these colonies possessed and placing them in the hands of subjects had been found to be both prejudicial and repugnant to the trade of the kingdom and to the welfare of the king's other plantations in America; and, secondly, that such independence had been found injurious to the king's revenue, by reason of the many irregularities committed by the governors and those in authority under them, countenancing pirates, illicit traders, and other offenders against the law.[1]

The House of Lords was sufficiently impressed by these arguments to grant a hearing on the bill during the months of April and May, 1701. This was the hearing that brought Penn back posthaste across the water in that year, but not in time to take part in it. Members of his family appeared for Pennsylvania against the bill; the Earl of Bath pleaded for the Carolinas; and Sir Henry Ashurst defended the cause of Connecticut. Massachusetts, Rhode Island, and the Bahamas do not appear to have been represented by either agent or solicitor. New Hampshire was already royal and Maryland was temporarily in the hands of the crown. The points on both sides were well and forcibly taken. The proponents of the bill upheld their charges with affidavits and depositions drawn from the files of the Plantation Office; the defendants countered with rebuttals based on the rights of property, the inviolability of contracts, and the heavy financial losses that parliamentary confiscation would entail. The Board of Trade had prepared its case well, but its solicitors at the hearing were deficient in influence as compared with Bath and Ashurst,[2] and the cards were stacked against them from the begin-

1. *House of Lords Manuscripts*, new series, IV, 315. The proceedings at the hearing before the committee can be found in *ibid.*, §1634. Additional information can be obtained from *Calendar State Papers, Colonial*, 1701. The subject has been treated, with something of a pro-American bias, by Louise P. Kellogg in "The American Colonial Charter" (*Report*, American Historical Association, 1903, I, 185–341).

2. Ashurst's influence with the peers was undoubtedly considerable, though that it was as great as he thought it was is less certain. In 1701 he wrote to Fitz John Winthrop, "I am soliciting the Lords day and night that, if the Bill must pass, to leave out your Colony; you have this Reputation none of the Colonys hath, a person of my quality to appear for them." In July he informed Winthrop that he had just put in a petition to the lords and was heard by his counsel "against the Bill at the Lords barr and by an Interest I made in the Lords House it was stopped." Again he wrote, "If I had not engaged in [your business] with extraordinary vigor your enemies had had their will with you. . . . I have the vanity to say that if you had not employed me you would have been in a sad condition this day" (*Collections*, Massachusetts Historical Society, 6th ser., III, 69, 75, 324, 376–377. Some of these letters are in the Connecticut Archives, Foreign Correspondence, II, Agents in England, nos. 66 and following). Doubtless Ashurst had reason for his complacency, for he was an able man and of a distinguished Puritan ancestry, but he was asking for money and it was necessary that he rate his services as high as he could.

ning. The peers were landowners and property owners and believers in the sacredness of vested interests, and they were undoubtedly moved by the injustice of destroying tangible utilities without either warrant or compensation.[1] They were probably influenced also by what Penn called "the unspeakable mallice of some people against proprietary governments without rhime or reason," evidently referring to the hostility of Randolph and Quary. They were influenced too by Ashurst's defense of Connecticut, as a colony the inhabitants of which dutifully acknowledged the king of England "as their lawful sovereign and were his good and loyal subjects, denying all the evil reports to their dishonour." It is not likely that the constitutional issue was raised at this time, as to whether or not parliament could so far trespass on the powers of the prerogative as to wipe out all at once the charters that the king had granted. The issue seems to have turned on the rights of property only.

Though the peers gave the measure a place on the calendar they were not ready to enter it as a bill that ought to be passed. Hence delays ensued, owing to the pressure of more important business, until finally when, at the recommendation of the committee before whom the hearing was held, a motion was made to refer the bill to the committee of the whole house the motion was defeated and the bill was dropped. Nothing further was done at that session which ended on June 24, 1701, when parliament was prorogued. Randolph had informed the board in June that there was no chance of success at that time but he hoped that the bill would come up again. The board instructed him to strengthen his affidavits and depositions by taking his witnesses before a master in chancery and to have all things in readiness for a new attempt. The board itself wrote to the governors and others in the plantations for additional data, which it received in full measure, much to its own satisfaction, for it was determined not to let the matter rest where it was.[2]

The second effort, made in 1702, proved no more successful than the first. The new bill was prepared by Secretary Manchester in the form of a "secretary's bill," a draft of which was submitted to the board for its opinion and observations. The board thought the terms

1. Sir William Windham speaking in 1739 said that the people of the colonies (he is referring to Carolina and Georgia) "have a property in the lands they possess, founded upon what ought to be held one of the most sacred rights in the world, the King's grant and their own industry." Stock, *Debates*, IV, 675.
2. *Calendar State Papers, Colonial*, 1701, §§279, 661, 1054.

insufficiently forcible, as not meeting the purpose which the "king" (that is, the board) had in mind, and it told the secretary very definitely that it wanted a duplicate of the bill of 1701. After some maneuvering it got what it wanted, but too late to be of service. Though the House of Commons was ready to receive the bill, the fates were working against the board, for King William died on March 8 and parliament automatically came to an end. A renewal was planned at the first session of Queen Anne's reign (October 24, 1702—February 27, 1703), but for reasons unknown a bill was never introduced. Thus the attempt which the board had made, with so much care and preparation, to obtain from parliament an act for reducing the private colonies to a common type, all together without distinction or discrimination, came to an untimely end.

Accompanying and following the failure of 1702, events took place of considerable importance. Penn, convinced that the Board of Trade would deprive him of his propriety if it could and wishing to be indemnified for so great a loss, began negotiations for the sale of his province.[1] The proprietors of the Jerseys finally yielded to pressure and surrendered their rights of government; while the proprietors of the Bahamas—islands which up to this time had been a very insecure and troublesome possession—acknowledged that their property was of no value to them, controlled as it was by pirates and buccaneers, and for the moment at least gave it up for lost.[2] The number of the private colonies requiring attention was thus reduced by three, and for the board the problem was correspondingly simplified. Whatever the members of that body may have thought was the cause of past failures they must have come to realize that their former policy was too drastic and would never receive the approval of parliament. They must have realized also that their desire for so comprehensive a parliamentary measure, which took no account of differences among the colonies themselves, was manifestly unfair, and was likely to appear to many an act of executive harshness, an abuse of executive power. Furthermore, all could see that the subject was too complicated for hasty and unconsidered decision, involving, as it did, too many interests to be rushed to a conclusion within the time at parliament's disposal. When, therefore, the board made its third trial

---

1. Stock, *Debates*, III, 16–17; *Calendar State Papers, Colonial*, 1702–1703, §§677, 837, 860. Below, pp. 395–396.
2. Below, pp. 397–399.

it modified its demands, on the general principle that half a loaf is better than no bread.

In 1706 the board brought the matter once more to the attention of parliament. In doing so it substituted "regulating" for "reuniting." The new bill, drafted by Secretary Hedges, was worded as follows, "For the better Regulation of the Charter and Proprietary Governments in America and for the encouragement of the Trade of the Kingdome and of her Majesty's Plantations."[1] Containing in its preamble a reference to the objections which the board had for a long time entertained regarding the continued possession of "such large and unlimited powers by private persons, who pretended to assume absolute Government and authority over her Majesty's subjects," it demanded that henceforth the queen should have "sole power and authority of governing the said plantations." The bill said nothing about taking away the charters. Had it been passed into law it would have had the effect of a general explanatory charter, altering the relations of the private colonies toward the crown and reducing very materially their powers of self-government, but not changing their constitutional status. The bill, however, was not passed. Presented to the House of Commons, February 6, 1706, by William Blathwayt, a member of the board and of parliament, it was defeated on the second reading by a vote of fifty to thirty-four.[2] So serious a rebuff to the board and to the secretary of state calls for an explanation, which is probably to be found in the seemingly excessive powers that the bill proposed to confer upon the executive branch of the government. By its terms the queen was to have the sole power and authority to govern the plantations, and to appoint governors, councillors, judges, justices of the peace, and all other officers for the administration and execution of the law—"the said power and authority to be forever united to the imperial crown of the realm." While in a sense similar powers were already possessed by one or other of the executive parts of the government, nevertheless, in view of the "place bill" agitation at the time which led to the passage of the Place Bill of 1707,[3] confirmation of them by statute was probably more than a parliament could stand that was engaged in weakening not strengthening the

---

1. *Calendar State Papers, Colonial*, 1706–1708, §121; in full, C. O. 5:3, no. 27. This draft of the bill contains many interpolations and erasures, showing the difficulties met in deciding on just the right wording for the measure.

2. Stock, *Debates*, III, 114, 118.     3. 6 Anne, c. 7, §§xxv, xxvi.

prerogative of the crown. How far party influences—Whig and Tory —are to be taken into account it is difficult to say. One may easily believe that the bill of 1706 was a Tory measure, supported by Queen Anne and the Anglican Church and thrown out by Whig votes. But this is too simple an explanation. It is more than likely that parliament, endeavoring to minify the powers of the executive at home, was unwilling to increase them in the colonies, and for two reasons. First, it had no confidence in those employed by the government, charging them with unskilfulness, unfaithfulness, and corruption, for ministerial government at this time was not responsible to the House of Commons; and, secondly, engaged as it was in acting as a check upon the crown in the field of administration at home, it had no intention of reversing its attitude in the field of administration abroad.[1] If weight is to be given to this second reason, it must be presumptive only, based on the conviction that parliament would act consistently, not doing in one quarter what it was refusing to do in another. It was really interested in the kingdom, not in the colonies as such, for it had never passed an act, and until 1765 was never to pass an act, that dealt with colonial government or administration or with the constitutional relations that existed between the colonies and the mother country. These matters it left entirely to the executive. It is quite possible, therefore, that the refusal to pass the bill may have been due in part to parliament's unwillingness to enter a field in which it had no direct interest.[2]

During the remaining years of the War of the Spanish Succession, the Board of Trade, though never losing sight of its main objective, made no further effort to obtain the assistance of parliament in regulating the affairs of the private colonies. But with the war over and victory won it renewed the attempt. On August 1, 1713, Jeremiah Dummer, Connecticut's agent in England, sent word to his colony that "a design was on foot for a new modelling of the plantations and making alterations in their civill governments."[3] In order to be prepared for the situation when it arose, he sat down and wrote the first draft of his famous pamphlet, *Defence of the Charters,* in the

1. *House of Lords Manuscripts,* new series, VI, 294–296, report of November 22, 1707. A copy of this report is in the New York Public Library.
2. Jeremiah Dummer reported in 1720 that parliament was so taken up with affairs at home and abroad "it is almost impossible to get 'em to think of the Plantations," Connecticut Archives, Foreign Correspondence, Agents in England, no. 111.
3. *Connecticut Colonial Records,* V, 410–411, 414.

expectation that the plan of 1706 would be revived. In this pamphlet he emphasized the value of the plantations to England in staples and trade, insisted that the corporate governments had never misbehaved and had no desire to throw off their dependence upon the land of their allegiance, and argued with telling effect that it was an act of great injustice to disfranchise any corporation by act of parliament, without giving it previous notice and a fair trial. This pamphlet was written in 1712–1713 and added to afterward, but it was not printed until 1721 and Connecticut first heard of it the next year. Therefore, it can have played no part in the agitation of this period, though doubtless Dummer repeated some of its arguments when he drew up petitions to the House of Commons in the effort to ward off the new attack.

This attack came in 1715, when the board, aroused by a series of complaints from the merchants and others regarding banks, local currency, and naval stores, and disturbed by reports of the Yamassee War and the helplessness of the Carolina proprietors, made an appeal to the secretary of state. The secretary, stirred by the facts as presented by the board, requested the latter to draft a bill. This bill, which may have been similar to that of 1706 (or possibly to that of 1701),[1] was introduced into the House of Commons, August 13, 1715, was read a second time on the 15th, and then sent to committee. There it was met by a barrage of objections from the agents of Connecticut and Rhode Island, Dummer and Partridge; from the proprietors of the Carolinas, Skipwith, Granville, and Trott; and from Lord Guildford acting for the young Baltimore, to whom the province of Maryland had recently been restored. The defense was spirited and in the end successful, for the remonstrances against the bill so impressed the members that it never emerged from committee.[2] Again the Board of Trade had suffered a signal defeat.

But as before the defeat was rated as only temporary. The board was changing its tactics but not its purpose. Instead of sending over agents such as Randolph, Larkin, and Nicholson on roving com-

1. Mrs. Dorothy S. Towle has allowed me to see the account, still in manuscript, of Partridge's expenses from 1715 to 1735. In the account appears this item, "1715, 7 mo, 27. To sundry charges about opposing a bill in Parliament for resuming the Charter Government as per accounts sent, 21–5–11; 1716, To Ditto, 42–1." As no copy of the bill of 1715 is known to exist it is possible that it resembled the earlier bill of 1701. Partridge's entry points in that direction, as does the determined resistance set up by the proprietors and the agents of the corporate governments.

2. Stock, *Debates*, III, 361–365.

missions, and depending for its information on the reports, frequently inaccurate and always exaggerated, of prerogative men in the colonies such as Quary, Basse, Dudley, and Cornbury, it began after 1713 to make more use of the royal governors. It demanded of them fuller and more detailed accounts, accompanied by corroborative documents, of happenings in their respective communities, and it sent them regularly, as it had formerly done only occasionally, long lists of queries on almost every conceivable subject. In order to deal more expeditiously with colonial laws, it requested of the king the appointment of a special legal adviser, where before it had used solicitors working with the crown lawyers. In 1718 this request was granted and Richard West became the first of a series of men, largely unknown to fame, who for nearly sixty years supervised colonial legislation and played their part in arousing dissatisfaction in the colonies with the English way of doing things.

This altered mode of procedure, coming as it did soon after the close of the war, coincided with the opening of a forty-year period of peace within the colonial borders. The colonists, relieved of the burden of defense and the cost of military preparations and entering on a time of confidence and prosperity, settled down more and more into a life of orderly and normal development, inevitably concerned for their own welfare rather than for that of England. Instinctively, if often unwittingly, they came into conflict with the merchants of England, with the acts of trade and navigation, with the claims of the prerogative, and with the financial needs of the exchequer, for the position of dependence which England made a cardinal feature of her policy could not always be squared with the self-interest of growing communities. New England, New York, and Virginia, not to mention Jamaica and Barbados, were at times, consciously and unconsciously, evading the king's instructions to his governors, passing laws that were disallowed in England, levying duties discriminating against non-residents, and in general favoring their own people, at the expense, as the Board of Trade profoundly believed, of the Englishmen at home "for whose benefit and advantage the plantations were first settled and have been and still are maintained and protected at a vast expence from this kingdom."[1]

With their attention centered upon the kingdom's balance sheet, the members of the board were angered by what seemed to them a

1. *Calendar State Papers, Colonial*, 1719–1720, p. 73.

spirit of contumacy prevailing in the colonies. Seemingly they were unable to understand that such a spirit was certain to arise as the colonies acquired a knowledge of their own financial needs and a familiarity with the habit of governing themselves. They failed utterly to comprehend the significance of such a letter as that of Wentworth of New Hampshire, who in commenting on a bill prohibiting the manufacture of iron, which did not pass,[1] said that its adoption "would have so crampt the plantations and N. England in particular that it would have been morrally impossible for [them] to subsist" and that the very idea of such a law put "all thinking men at a stand what to doe or say."[2] The board deemed anything done in the colonies that discouraged the trade, shipping, or manufactures of England, reduced the customs revenue, or encroached on the prerogative "a pernicious practice," and from this view of the case it would not swerve a hair's breadth. In a report to the lords justices of July 9, 1719, it repeated the opinion (which by this time had become a settled formula) that "owing to the ill effects of the proprietary governments," the plantations would "never be upon a right foot till the dominion of all the proprietary colonies" had been resumed by the crown and until the government of England had laid hold of every fair opportunity to accomplish that end.[3] The board in 1719 was as firm in its belief that the private colonies should go as it had been twenty years before. The Plantation Office was true to its traditions.

The lords justices, taking their cue from the recommendation of the board and deeply stirred by a petition from John Lord Carteret asking for aid in repressing the insurgent movement in South Carolina, instructed the board to prepare "several heads of a representation on the state of the government and the trade of the plantations." The Plantation Office bent itself to the task. Hardly had it completed a first draft than it was further ordered by Secretary Townshend to lay before the king "a representation of the state and condition of his Majesty's colonies on the continent of America, with their opinion [as to] what methods may be taken for the better government and

1. There is an interesting paragraph in one of Dummer's letters to Connecticut (1719–1720), giving information about this iron bill in the House of Commons, 1718. Connecticut Archives, Foreign Correspondence, II, Agents in England, nos. 110, 111. See also Bining, *British Regulation of the Colonial Iron Industry*, pp. 41–45.

2. *Calendar State Papers, Colonial*, 1719–1720, p. 163.

3. *Ibid.*, §319.

security of the said colonies."[1] This was the largest order that the board had ever received and its execution cost its secretary and clerks the labor of more than a year, from August, 1720, to September, 1721. The result is one of the most complete and illuminating of all the reports prepared by the office.[2] It was fashioned very largely out of the governors' letters and the answers to queries and out of the data and opinions furnished by such men as Thomas Banister and Joshua Gee, whose views, written out at the request of the board, were printed later and widely circulated. Among the "Considerations" of the report appears a section devoted to the question as to how best "to secure, improve, and enlarge his Majesty's dominions in America, by putting the governments on a better foot" and rendering the proprietary and corporate governments more obedient to the king's commands. To this question the board could only reply, as so often before, that the private colonies should be resumed by the crown, because some of them had shown too great an inclination to act independently of their mother country and could be restrained from doing so only if they were, all of them, "under your Majesty's immediate government." This recommendation merely repeated the familiar formula of the Plantation Office. But in addition the board made another, and for the first time, a new and very important suggestion, that the colonies be resumed not by act of parliament but "either by purchase, agreement or otherwise," thus introducing us to a new phase of our story.

1. *Ibid.*, 1720–1721, §620. The Board of Trade said that "by reason of the multiplicity of books and papers the same is drawn from it will necessarily take some time" to prepare the report (*ibid.*, §620). For material it called on the other departments of government in England, on the agents there of nearly all the colonies, and on private persons who had had experience, either personally or by way of trade, with the colonies. Instances of encroachment on the royal prerogative were reported from New York and Massachusetts. Serious boundary disputes were making trouble for Massachusetts, Connecticut, and Rhode Island. There was disorder in South Carolina and disorder in the Bahamas. The remark of Jekyll, a customs official in Massachusetts, must have come to the ears of the board and cannot have increased its confidence in the dependency of that colony. "This is a charter government and, except for the governor, every man of the council (who are elected by the people) are New England men and as far as I can guess have their dear Idol the Charter much at heart and a great love for independency in general" (*ibid.*, §190). The occasion of this remark was the quarrel of the Massachusetts assembly with Governor Shute, which led ultimately to the further regulation of the colony by the explanatory charter of 1725. On the situation in Massachusetts, Burns, *Controversies*, part I.

2. The report covers nearly forty-six pages of the *New York Colonial Documents*, V, 593–630.

It is worthy of note that while throwing blame on the colonies for injuries committed to the trade and manufactures of Great Britain, the board doubted whether all the trouble lay in America. It hinted that the existing administrative system at home, with its loose and cumbersome ways of conducting official business, had much to do with the growth of an independent spirit among the colonists. To demonstrate its point it mentioned the confusion caused by three different avenues of approach to the crown—by application to the secretary of state, by petition to the Privy Council, and by representation from itself—and it said with shrewd insight that some of the difficulties could be avoided if it itself could be made an executive department, with power to carry out the royal orders, as fully as was done by the Treasury and the Admiralty. There were times when from one point of view the board was wiser than its masters, the king and the Privy Council, but the wisdom of its remarks found no response in the minds of those high in executive command. Such machinery as Great Britain contrived for handling colonial questions was utterly unfit for carrying out such a policy as that to which the Plantation Office was committed but which it could not carry out on its own account. The colonies profited by Whitehall's ineptitude.

The report of 1721 led to the passage of the Naval Stores Bill of 1722,[1] designed to divert the colonists from manufacturing and to encourage them, by a system of bounties, to engage in the production of pitch, tar, and turpentine, and other naval necessities, but it contained no further recommendations regarding the private colonies as the subject of another bill in parliament. Instead it offered the suggestion that in the future these colonies be brought into closer relations to the crown "by purchase, agreement or otherwise," and this suggestion determined the rule of the office from this time forward. It in no way affected the board's general policy, but it did open to the board a new way of accomplishing the end it had in view.

The failures of the past had not weakened the confidence of the board in its policy or altered the convictions of the mercantilists in general that it were better to have no colonies at all than such as were not subservient to the mother country,[2] however that subservience might be obtained. The board was still of the same opinion which it had held from the beginning that the private colonies had

1. 8 George I, c. 12.
2. *Calendar State Papers, Colonial,* 1724–1726, §§193, 214.

in no way "answered the chief design for which such large grants and such privileges and immunities were granted by the crown and had not conformed themselves to the several acts of parliament regarding trade and navigation, to which they ought to pay the same obedience and submit to the same restrictions as the other plantations subject to his Majesty's immediate government." If parliament would not coöperate then other means must be tried. Though the new expedients were to be in the executive not the parliamentary field, the board had no other recourse than to experiment with them even though there was a doubt in many minds as to whether an executive instrument, such as a royal instruction or an order in council, was likely to accomplish what could be done much more effectively by an act of parliament.

"By purchase, agreement or otherwise," these were the keynotes of the new policy, and the second of these was the first to be tried. In a representation of March 22, 1723,[1] the board recommended to the Privy Council that Connecticut and Rhode Island be approached tactfully with a view to the surrender of their charters, much as had been done in the case of the Jersey proprietors twenty years before. The Privy Council, though indignant because of the prolonged quarrel between the two colonies over their boundary line, doubted whether such a surrender could be effected, but was willing that the board should make the attempt.[2] The latter immediately called in Dummer and Partridge and asked them what they thought about the matter. The agents said they had no power to act but were willing to refer the question to their principals. In reply Connecticut refused firmly but politely even to consider such a surrender. Rhode Island did likewise, but in not quite so dexterous or statesmanlike a manner, saying, as Partridge put it to the board, that the colony would by no means part with any of its privileges, unless they were wrenched from its people against their will. Partridge showed how wholly impracticable was the board's further suggestion that the two colonies, having given up their charters, should be joined to New Hampshire, and the next year, in order to ward off the danger of forfeiture, which the colony greatly feared because of certain charges originating with the vice-admiralty court of Boston, made a spirited denial of Rhode Island's connection with piracy.[3] Connecticut, greatly

1. C. O. 5:1293, pp. 280–296; *Rhode Island Colonial Records*, IV, 303–308.
2. *Board of Trade Journal, 1722–1728*, p. 213.
3. *Rhode Island Colonial Records*, IV, 333–334. The replies are reprinted by Miss

disturbed at the crisis confronting her and thoroughly frightened by the issue of an explanatory charter to Massachusetts only a year or two before, yielded on the boundary issue and said that despite the priority of her charter she would leave to the king the final decision as to where the line between the two colonies should be drawn.[1] The board accepted the situation, probably recognizing the fact, as the Privy Council had done, that there was not sufficient evidence against the colonies to justify an attempt to vacate their charters by process of law. In its representation of January 25, 1726, it recommended that the king in his executive capacity determine where the boundary line should run and it said nothing more about the surrender of the charters.[2] Though Connecticut was for the time being relieved of anxiety, her situation was not yet entirely free from peril. Four years later, after her intestacy law had been disallowed in 1728, the Board of Trade raised the question as to whether or not the colony, in passing laws affecting property, had not gone beyond the limits of its charter and rendered itself liable either to the loss of that palladium

Kellogg in "The American Colonial Charter," pp. 322–334. In Partridge's account (above, p. 387, note 1) there are several references to expenses incurred, including, "To paid for copies of Cont [Connecticut] answers to the Board of Trade about surrendering their charter, £2.2." There is an earlier item, "To 2½ guinys paid Jno Sharp he pd at L. Carterets office for copys of papers relating to Menzies and the Admiralty office." For "Menzies and the Admiralty office," see *Calendar State Papers, Colonial*, 1724–1726, §§3, 48.

1. *Rhode Island Colonial Records*, IV, 373; *Acts Privy Council, Colonial*, III, p. 15; *Calendar State Papers, Colonial*, 1722–1723, §§477, 647, 735–736. That the English authorities were predisposed in favor of Rhode Island appears from the statement made at the time (as it had been made earlier and was a tradition of the office) "we do not find any reason to alter our opinion as to King Charles having been deceived in his grant to Connecticut." This unfavorable view of Connecticut's case was held by the Privy Council, the Board of Trade, and the secretary of state. Connecticut knew that this was so, for Dummer in his letter of July 22, 1723, had informed the colony of the Board of Trade's opinion regarding the king's being surprised in his grant of the charter of 1662, and it is therefore probable that the leaders were in consequence afraid to press their claims further. Board of Trade representation of January 25, 1726, C. O. 5:1293, pp. 346–351; *Acts Privy Council*, III, p. 14; *Calendar State Papers, Colonial*, 1726–1727, §18; Connecticut Archives, Foreign Correspondence, II, Agents in England, nos. 121–127. Also, above, Vol. II, 140–141.

2. *Calendar State Papers, Colonial*, 1726–1727, §18. This important representation was drawn up after arguments by both Dummer and Partridge had been heard by the board, December, 1725—January, 1726 (*Board of Trade Journal*, 1722–1728, pp. 207–208, 209–210). Each agent was given a copy of the other's brief and the case went up to the Privy Council for final decision. After the committee of the council had agreed to report in favor of Rhode Island, Dummer, at his own request, was given another chance to be heard. But he did not appear. Did he realize that Connecticut's case was already lost?

of its liberties or to the issue of an explanatory charter modifying the colony's privileges.[1] But nothing was ever done about it. There were rumors, 1749–1764, that proceedings were to be instituted against her. These rumors arose at first from Archbishop Secker's desire to set up bishops in the colonies; later from Bishop Sherlock's refusal, as bishop of London, to assume a diocesan oversight of them and his proposal that an Anglican episcopate be established in America; and in 1764 from a certain suggestion made by Governor Bernard to Halifax.[2] But Connecticut remained unscathed to the end.

Up to the year 1702 eight of the private colonies had been royalized: Virginia, Barbados, the Leeward Islands, New Hampshire, Massachusetts, Bermuda, and East and West New Jersey. During the ensuing half century three more of the private grantees were to surrender their charters, those of the Bahamas, the Carolinas, and Georgia, each under peculiar conditions of its own. Thus the whole British colonial area of the west was brought nearer, by just so much, to a uniform system of government under the crown. By an odd inconsistency of purpose at the very time, 1715, that the Board of Trade was pushing its plans for parliamentary intervention, Maryland, which had been in the king's hands for nearly twenty years, was re-

1. *Calendar State Papers, Colonial*, 1728–1729, §§828, 1057.

2. *Law Papers*, III, 298, 324, 325, 341, 429–430; *Wolcott Papers*, p. 504; *Board of Trade Journal*, 1754–1763, pp. 19, 20, 263; 1764–1767, pp. 18, 22, 31; Cross, *Anglican Episcopate*, ch. V and elsewhere; Carpenter, *Thomas Sherlock* (1936). There would appear to have been two different threats after 1750 to the integrity of Connecticut and Rhode Island. One of these came from the proposed appointment of bishops, Bancroft Transcripts, II, New York Public Library: Johnson Letters, Samuel Johnson to Archbishop Secker (1758, hopes that the archbishop will aid in the procuring of bishops for America and replies to the possible objection at court that bishops might provoke independency by saying that on the contrary the establishment would have the opposite effect); William Samuel Johnson to the same (April 10, 1762, favoring the appointment of bishops and the reorganization of New England); Mayhew-Hollis Correspondence, J. Mayhew to T. Hollis (Boston, April 16, 1762, "We are apprehensive that there is a scheme forming for sending a Bishop into these parts"; Hollis replied, October 16, 1762, "You are in no real danger at present"). The other came from a suggestion which Governor Bernard made to Halifax, secretary of state for the southern department, November 9, 1764, that the colonial governments be reorganized and particularly that "the two republics of Connecticut and Rhode Island be dissolved" (*Collections*, Maine Historical Society, 3d ser., I, 339–343; Bernard, *Select Letters*, pp. 67–68, 81–83). The rumors of these proposals coming to the ears of the Connecticut and Rhode Island authorities occasioned undisguised, but as it happened needless, dismay. Francis Alison wrote to Dr. Stiles, "You greatly alarm me by saying that there are attempts making at home to resume the New England provincial charters," and Samuel Whittelsey, May 10, 1764, wrote much the same (Stiles Papers, Yale University Library). For Rhode Island, Kimball, *Governors' Correspondence*, II, 438.

turned to its proprietor and remained a private colony until the American Revolution. Likewise Pennsylvania under a royal governor for two years, 1692 to 1694, was restored to Penn in the latter year. But Penn, convinced that the board was determined to bring about a parliamentary regulation of the proprieties, would gladly have sold out had he (and his family after him) been able to come to terms with the British government.

Even at the risk of slowing down somewhat the tempo of our narrative we must here deal as concisely as we can with the story of the bargaining that went on, in one case unsuccessfully and in the other two cases successfully, in the effort to obtain the surrender of the three proprieties, Pennsylvania, the Bahamas, and the Carolinas.

Briefly stated, the circumstances attending the Pennsylvania negotiations were these. Declaring, May 11, 1703, that he was ready to resign his government, with a reservation of all his proprietary rights in the soil,[1] Penn entered into a correspondence with the Board of Trade, the Privy Council, the secretary of state, and the Treasury, for the purpose of reaching a friendly settlement. In 1708, saying that he had never reaped any reward for his labors, he answered the Treasury's request for what he considered "a reasonable compensation" by placing his price at £20,000, to be paid in seven-year installments. This amount was reduced in 1710 to £12,000, to be paid in part down and the rest at stated times, the agreement to be confirmed by act of parliament, because it was a money transaction. In 1714 the attorney general prepared a draft of the surrender and also a further instrument for the queen's acceptance. An advance payment was made (afterward returned) of £1000, but the settlement was delayed by differences which arose between Penn and his creditors, six in number, of whom Joshua Gee was one, to whom Penn had mortgaged his province for £6600. Before the surrender was executed or any more money paid, Penn "was seized with a distemper in his head" (elsewhere called an "apoplectic fit") which disabled him and prevented him from perfecting the sale. Though the Privy Council

---

1. *Calendar State Papers, Colonial*, 1703, §837; *Calendar Treasury Books*, XVIII, 354. Penn's own statement is as follows. "As some think that the proprietary governments are inconvenient to trade and inconsistent with the dignity of the crown, [I am] no longer willing to contend but will surrender powers of government and deliver them into the hands of the Queen, provided [I] can receive such a reasonable consideration as may be due to [my] merits and some particular mark of respect to be continued to [my] family, for distinguishing them above the rank of those who have planted under [me]." July, 1710, *Calendar State Papers, Colonial*, 1710–1711, §326.

ordered that the arrangement be authorized by act of parliament, the death of Queen Anne terminated the proceedings.

The situation was complicated by the fact that in his will Penn, who died in 1718, vested the province in two trustees, Earl of Oxford and Earl Poulett, who were instructed to complete the treaty of surrender on terms specially favorable "to the people called Quakers." This instruction, added to the difficulties already encountered, gave rise to a controversy in which the trustees, the mortgagees, the executrix (Hannah Penn), and the heir-at-law (William, Penn's dissolute son, and in 1727 Springett, his grandson) were involved, the last two of whom carried their case into chancery[1] to settle amicably their respective claims to the government and their right to appoint a governor. This uncertainty as to who was the legal proprietor disturbed the colony for a number of years and Deputy Governor Sir William Keith never was quite sure of the regularity of his commission.[2] Applications in anticipation of surrender were made by the family in 1724 but without result. Again in 1727 the children renewed the attempt.[3] Just why they failed is largely conjectural. The Board of Trade urged that the terms be accepted, according to its established policy that "all occasions should be laid hold on to recover at least the dominion of the proprietary colonies."[4] But as parliament had already thwarted that policy by refusing to pass acts enforcing it; as Connecticut and Rhode Island had defied it by declining to surrender their charters; as the crown itself had disregarded it by restoring Maryland to its legitimate possessor; so now, in all probability, the Treasury, facing at this very time the prospect of having to buy out the proprietors of both the Bahamas and the Carolinas, added the weight of its hand against the proposal by demurring at the price. No further effort of surrender was ever made and Pennsylvania never entered the royal group.

The Board of Trade was more successful in dealing with the proprietors of the Bahamas and the Carolinas and in carrying out its plan of effecting its object "by purchase."

The Bahama Islands had been granted in 1670 to a group of pro-

---

1. *Calendar Treasury Papers*, 1708–1714, pp. 128 (21), 428 (30), 573–574; 1720–1728, pp. 55–56, 393 (10).

2. *Calendar State Papers, Colonial*, 1719–1720, §285, i, ii.

3. *Acts Privy Council, Colonial*, III, §121; VI, §382.

4. *Calendar State Papers, Colonial*, 1719–1720, §319; *Pennsylvania Colonial Records*, III, 73–74.

prietors, almost identical but not quite, with those who had received Carolina. The acquisition of the islands had been in largest part the work of Ashley, who hoped to use them in connection with his Carolina interests as a center of trade and the source of other forms of commercial profit.[1] Inevitably he had reckoned without any adequate understanding of colonial conditions in general or any knowledge of this particular region as available for his purpose. The islands, first settled from Bermuda, had become the seat of a lawless and piratical life, the resort of those who, unrestrained by the Admiralty in England, kept the colonies intimidated by plundering raids from New England to Jamaica. The Bahama proprietors, though interested in the islands and anxious to organize some sort of government there, were hampered by the inhabitants, a wild and undisciplined people, who refused to obey not only their legitimate heads but even the acts of parliament on the ground that these acts "did not reach so far as to encompass them."[2] One of the earliest governors sent out was Elias Hasket, a thick-ribbed sea-captain from Salem, who at his capital, Nassau on the island of New Providence, with others of his own kidney, was soon charged with high-handed proceedings, resistance to the authority of the proprietors, hindering the royal officials in executing their duty, and open dealings with pirates. He was soon deposed and sent back to England to meet accusations of oppressive and riotous conduct. The Board of Trade, as early as 1701, complained to the proprietors of the ill state of affairs in the islands but, getting no satisfactory response, recommended that the Bahamas be resumed by the crown.[3]

Attacked during the war by the combined fleets of France and Spain, the latter of whom claimed sovereignty over the islands, the Bahamas were devastated in 1703 and in three onslaughts between 1704 and 1709 were practically depopulated. The board repeated its demands that the charter of the proprietors be forfeited by law, or if that proved impossible (as was sure to be the case because suits against them were estopped by the privilege of peers) then that a governor be appointed, as in an emergency, by the crown, until ne-

1. Above, Vol. III, 200, note.
2. *Calendar State Papers, Colonial,* 1700, §451.
3. *Ibid.,* §§308, 308, i; 1702, §§265, 547, 549, 702; 1702–1703, §§79–81. Hasket papers are printed in the *Historical Collections,* Essex Institute, Vols. 51, 71, and there are many papers relating to the Bahama situation in *Calendar State Papers, Colonial,* 1728–1729, §§292, 352, 384, 660, 701, 737, 920, 937, 965.

gotiations might be completed for buying out the proprietors. Governors were appointed who either never took office or fled from the island soon after arrival.[1] Until 1714 no adequate form of control existed, every man doing as he wanted, welcoming pirates and encouraging illegal trade. During these years the proprietors practically abandoned the islands as derelict and the Board of Trade became exceedingly wrothy, because the proprietors were neglecting islands that were strategically important, lying as they did in the Florida gulf in the way of all ships from Havana and the Gulf of Mexico. They urged resumption in the interest of trade, particularly since the French had become the masters of Hispaniola.

At this juncture there appeared on the scene one of the most picturesque and energetic men of his time, Woodes Rogers, mariner of London and Bristol,[2] who approached the proprietors with two proposals: either that they assign their claims to him and others of London and Bristol, or else that they lease land and royalties to them for twenty-one years. The proprietors chose the second of these proposals, and having settled the lease completed their submission to the demands of the Board of Trade by executing, October 28, 1717, a surrender of their rights of government, military and civil, to the crown. In the deed of surrender they declared they had done this in order that the king might constitute a governor of his own, but they reserved, because of their lease to Rogers, all lands, quit-rents, issues, and profits, and laid down certain other conditions touching liberty of religion, customs and harbor dues, fishing for whales, sea-royalties, and mines. In their lease they gave as their reasons for the surrender the fact that the islands had become of little or no advantage to them, because harboring pirates and robbers to the great detriment of themselves, the inhabitants, and the many English merchants who were

1. *Calendar State Papers, Colonial,* 1706–1708, §§449, 993, 1424, 1535; 1708–1709, §340. On Holden, who was appointed governor but never went out, Vol. III, 256, note.

2. For Woodes Rogers see the article in the *Dictionary of National Biography* and *A Cruizing Voyage Round the World* (1712, reprinted in the Seafarers Library, 1928, with an introduction supplementing the account in the *Dictionary*). The book contains the story of an epochal voyage, during which Rogers rescued Alexander Selkirk from the island of Juan Fernandez, thus giving Defoe material for his *Robinson Crusoe.* The success of the voyage removed the terror of the French in the South Seas and opened the waters to English enterprise. After his return Rogers remained inactive in Bristol for five years, at the end of which time he undertook an expedition against the pirates who were battening on the Bahamas. This expedition led to the proposal mentioned in the text and to Rogers' career as a colonial governor. Rogers died July 15, 1732.

engaged in the Bahama trade. They said that Rogers had promised to defend the islands, would accept an appointment as governor, and would pay for twenty-one years at the Royal Exchange in London a total of £2400.[1]

As might have been expected the arrangement with Rogers worked badly and in the long run probably hampered rather than promoted the development of the islands. As the lease was due to terminate in 1738, the Board of Trade offered to purchase the soil ahead of time and in 1729 approached the proprietors with that intent.[2] But the latter placed the price too high, one thousand guineas apiece or six thousand guineas in all. The negotiations were prolonged, partly because of the largeness of the sum asked and partly because the lease had yet to run a number of years and the lessees claimed compensation for relinquishing their rights before the lease was due to expire. Rogers died in 1732, but his associates carried on the bargaining under circumstances the details of which are none too clear. After the lease expired the title to the soil reverted to the proprietors and their heirs, but the purchase, deferred from year to year, was not completed until 1787, when the British government was compelled to acquire possession in order to settle there loyalists fleeing from the continent during the American Revolution.[3]

The circumstances attending the surrender of the Carolina charter have already been briefly noted.[4] In the year 1719 South Carolina,

1. *Calendar State Papers, Colonial,* 1717–1718, §§166, 183, 184; C. O. 5:1293, pp. 114–115. The letter of acceptance (in two large sheets of parchment) is followed by the text of the surrender (pp. 115–126), not calendared. The surrender, being of government only and calling for no payment of money, required no confirmation by parliament, as did that of Carolina (2 George II, c. 34) and as would that of Pennsylvania had the terms offered by the Penn family in 1727 been accepted by the Treasury.

The proprietors who made the surrender of the Bahamas in 1717 seem to be identical with those of Carolina at the same time. They are Fulwar Skipwith for William Lord Craven, John Lord Carteret, John Danson, Maurice Ashley, Sir John Colleton, James Bertie and Dodrington Greville, guardians and trustees of Henry, Duke of Beaufort (for the proprietors of Carolina in 1723, *Calendar State Papers, Colonial,* 1728–1729, §§95, 115). The text of the lease is in C. O. 23:3, pp. 1–21 (fos. 36–46). It is interesting to note that Lord Carteret (later Earl Granville), when the question of the purchase of the soil came up, held out for certain reservations of his own, just as he was to do in the Carolinas in 1729. But he finally yielded the point.

2. *Acts Privy Council,* III, pp. 196–197.

3. An outline of events after 1733 is given in *Acts Privy Council, Colonial,* V, pp. 538–539. After the expiration of the lease the islands legally reverted to the proprietors and those who inherited their shares. It was therefore of the latter that the purchase was made in 1787, on the payment of £2000 to each of them.

4. See Vol. III, 245–246.

possessing a population of about 9000 souls, was suffering from poverty and heavy taxation, due in part to the great scarcity of hard money and the large issues of paper currency required by the Indian wars and partly to the constant obligation under which they stood to arm for defense against the Spaniards.[1] Aroused by the "confused, negligent, and helpless government" of the proprietors, who even in their complete failure to meet the needs of the colony were asserting their prerogatives as firmly as ever, the leaders in Charles Town rose in revolt, threw off the proprietary rule, called a convention of their own, and invited the king to take over the colony. This the king did, as he had done thirty years before in Maryland, appointing a provisional governor until a final decision should be reached. Though for the next ten years South Carolina was to all intents and purposes a province, it was not so legally for the charter was still in force. This uncertainty of status proved very disturbing to the inhabitants, who feared lest at any time the government might be restored to the proprietors, as had been done in the cases of both Pennsylvania and Maryland. Indeed, at one time in the year 1726, it looked as if such a restoration might take place. The proprietors, complaining that they were in danger of losing their lands, quit-rents, and profits from trade, petitioned for the return of their right to name their own governor, declaring that they had a very suitable man for the place, one Colonel Horsey.[2] The council and assembly in the colony counterpetitioned, asking to remain as they were, in the hope of becoming permanently a royal colony. Supported by Nicholson, the provisional governor at the time, who objected to Horsey, the assembly through its agent in London, presented so strong a case against the proprietors that the latter finally gave up the struggle. On May 27, 1727, they sent proposals to the crown offering to surrender, if satisfactory terms

1. *Calendar State Papers, Colonial*, 1719–1720, §§493, 497, i, 525, iv, 531, i, 541.
2. *Ibid.*, 1728–1729, §702, i. There is a great deal about Horsey in the Chandos Letter Books, 1723–1730. He appears to have been an energetic but unsuccessful promoter of various enterprises for the making of dyes, potashes, and particularly soap (perfumed soap for toilet use and wash balls for shaving), the last named of which he tried to market in the West Indies, but found that it was too high-priced to compete with Castile. Chandos at first took shares in Horsey's companies but later refused to coöperate. He felt sorry for Horsey and when the latter was appointed governor of South Carolina congratulated him on his appointment and expressed the hope that the new office would "make amends for all the vexations and disappointments [he had] hitherto met with." In addition to the governorship, Horsey was to receive a grant of 48,000 acres on the upper Savannah River, but he died in 1727, and the proprietors apparently made no further recommendation.

could be arranged. After considerable bargaining back and forth, the crown agreed to pay each of the proprietors £2500.[1] This sum the proprietors accepted, Carteret alone holding out, refusing to give up his rights in the soil. The patent of agreement, because representing a private transaction, was duly entered on the close rolls, while the agreement itself, because calling for a money payment, was ratified by parliament in 1729.[2] Thus another private colony came to its end.

The last of the British colonies in America to enter the ranks of the royal or public provinces was Georgia, which by the terms of its charter of 1732 was to be transferred automatically, twenty years later, from a trusteeship to a royal possession, requiring no other formality than the drafting of a document of surrender for the king's acceptance.[3]

Only four private colonies remained intact. Of these Pennsylvania, though in status proprietary, was under charter restrictions that bent her proprietor to the royal will in many important particulars, and her governor, as was also the case with Maryland, had to receive the approbation of the crown before taking office and to furnish security at the exchequer as certified by the king's remembrancer. Connecticut and Rhode Island were self-governing colonies and, with the exception of a few royal officials connected with the customs and the vice-admiralty courts and of their obligations to obey the acts of trade, were free from the crown's interference.[4] Massachusetts was in a class by herself, dually constituted, with a restless, dissatisfied, protesting Puritan soul encased within a royal body, subject far more than a majority of her people liked to rules and regulations that limited their full freedom of action and hemmed them in against their will. This peculiar situation, unlike that of any of the other

1. At first the proprietors stood out for £25,000 and £5000 additional for arrears of quit-rents.

2. The surrenders of the Jerseys, the Bahamas, and the Carolinas are entered on the close rolls not the patent rolls. That of Georgia, 1752, is entered on the patent rolls (26 George II, June 20; *Acts Privy Council, Colonial,* IV, p. 127) probably because it was considered a public, not a private, transaction; that is, an "open," not a "closed," affair.

3. "Which his Majesty was pleased to accept." These words are to be found in the "Abstract of Surrender." Index to the Patent Rolls, 26 George II, June 20, 1752.

4. It must be remembered always that there was nothing in the efforts which these colonies made to retain their charters that militated against their full recognition of the supreme power of the crown or the obligation of their people to render due obedience and allegiance as subjects of the king. The inhabitants of Connecticut and Rhode Island considered themselves Englishmen, owing obedience to the royal commands and the laws of parliament.

colonies, goes far to explain many of the incidents of Massachusetts history in the eighteenth century before the Revolution.

The Board of Trade had not done badly. To the seven colonies already royal it had added "by purchase and agreement" four more, counting the Jerseys as one, bringing the whole number to eleven, or even fourteen, if we reckon the Leeward Islands as four. With Georgia committed to an eventual royal status, this made a total of fifteen royal colonies, with four still in the private group.[1]

But the third part of the board's programme, the "or otherwise" of the report of 1721, was yet to be carried out.[2] Having done all that it could by purchase and agreement to alter the status of the private colonies and having been obliged at last to give up all further efforts in that direction, it now turned its attention to the problem of how best to regulate the entire colonial relationship in the interest of its established policy. If it could not obtain complete uniformity, it could at least do something to bring the remaining private colonies into line with the purposes of the mother country and to centralize in the hands of the authorities at Whitehall a more effective control over the whole colonial area. In the furtherance of these objects parliament was ready to coöperate up to a certain point. The legislative body was not concerned with the constitutional status of the colonies or with their internal organization on the administrative side, but it was interested in all that had to do with their attitude toward the trade, navigation, and manufactures of Great Britain and with their usefulness as contributors to British ascendancy among the powers of Europe. To this end the House of Commons, first on May 5, 1731, and again on January 15 and May 25, 1732, addressed the king, requesting information regarding "the laws made, manufactures set up and trade carried on" in America that "might in any way be disadvantageous to the prosperity, laws and general interests of the kingdom." These requests were turned over to the Board of Trade,

1. Nova Scotia was added by capture from France in 1710, but it was not constitutionally organized with a popular assembly until 1729.

2. The "otherwise" of the report was defined in the following terms: "By the uniformity and more due regulation of trade; by the good correspondency that may be established thereby between his Majesty's several plantations; and by the common and mutual defence of all, as well by preventing the great and frequent oppositions that are made to his Majesty's laws and government. By which means his Majesty's empire in America, which is of so great an extent, would be better secured from the attempts of an enemy and become, in all respects, of greater advantage to this kingdom and to his Majesty's revenue arising from these parts."

which replied in two important and enlightening representations of February 15, 1732, and February 1, 1733,[1] in which it outlined at considerable length the defects which it found in the working of the colonial system. After commenting on the neglect of the colonial governors to transmit within the allotted time "authentic copies of the several acts by them pass'd," it referred to an earlier representation of December 5, 1728—made pursuant to an order from the Privy Council—wherein it gave such information as it could obtain from the governors and others "well acquainted with the circumstances" regarding the manufacture of woolen and linen cloth. Concluding that "the height of wages and the great price of labour" would make it impracticable for the colonists to manufacture for sale, it nevertheless went to the extreme limits of the mercantilist doctrine in stating that even the small quantities the colonists produced for their own use would certainly lead to a diminution of the exports from Great Britain, and "that some expedient [ought to] be fallen upon to divert their thoughts from undertakings of this nature." It recommended that the "making, raising and manufacture of naval stores" be encouraged, in order that these staples might be exchanged for British goods and so save money in the trade with the Northern Crowns, "where these materials are chiefly paid for in specie."[2]

Thus the "or otherwise" clause was beginning to find application as early as 1732. The board with only the most rudimentary understanding of colonial human nature was proposing to force the colonies to conduct their lives according to the formulae of the mercantilists and to enter upon a phase of industrial activity that was narrow in scope, limited in its sphere of employment, and impossible of long-continued enforcement. It seems never to have occurred to the members of the board, with their fixed ideas of the place the colonies

1. C. O. 324:11, pp. 253–302, 313–370; *Board of Trade Journal,* 1728–1734, pp. 271–273, 275, 277, 278.

2. The representation goes on to say: "From the foregoing state it is observable that there are more trades carried on and manufactures set up in the provinces on the Continent of America to the northward of Virginia, prejudicial to the trade and manufactures of Great Britain, particularly in New England, than in any other part of the British colonies, which is not to be wondered at for their soil, climate and produce, being pretty near the same as ours they have no staple commodities of their own growth to exchange for our manufactures, which puts them under greater necessity as well as under greater temptation of providing for themselves at home. To which may be added in the charter governments the little dependence they have upon their mother country and consequently the small restraints they are under in any matter detrimental to her interest."

should occupy in the British colonial scheme, that the colonists would find it beyond their power to live within the confinements which the mercantilists sought to impose upon them and would inevitably break through so arbitrary and artificial an arrangement. Nowhere in the reports issuing from the Plantation Office is there any fear expressed lest the colonists might want to lead a normal political·and economic life of their own or, as a growing and resourceful people, should be allowed some measure of freedom to take advantage of their own opportunities. Even if the board had dreamed of such a possibility it is to be doubted whether, in the presence of the closed and self-centered British mind, it could have done anything to alter the situation. Its instructions admitted no departure from an orthodox routine.

The House of Commons took no action on the board's recommendation, but the next year the House of Lords addressed the king, June 13, 1733, asking for another report on pretty much the same subject, with stress laid especially on trade. Laws were being passed in the colonies discriminating against the merchants in favor of the colonists themselves. The former had been complaining for some time of the difficulties they were having in collecting their debts, partly because of the prevalence of a depreciating paper currency and partly because colonial law left them without adequate remedy against the debtors.[1] On the manufacturing side the Hatters Company, demanding that means be found to prevent the making of hats in the colonies, was adding its grievance to that of the woolen companies, which had obtained the passage of the Wool Act thirty years before, and to the charges of the shipwrights, who in 1724 had endeavored, but unsuccessfully, to put a stop to the colonial building of ships. Because of these and other "mischiefs," as the House of Lords called them, the latter obtained another report from the board, that of January 23, 1734. Acting on the information contained in this report the committee of the whole house adopted a resolution on April 5 of the same year to the following effect.[2]

Each and every colony without exception was to send over a complete collection of its laws and any law found detrimental to the king's prerogative or to the trade of Great Britain—any privilege or

1. On this point, see the reports of Fitzwilliam, surveyor general of the customs in the southern district of America, December 26, 1727, *Calendar State Papers, Colonial,* 1726–1727, §844.

2. *Lords Journal,* XXIV, 411–412. The board's report of January 23, 1734, attracted

limitation by charter to the contrary notwithstanding—that had not already been confirmed, was to be disallowed by the king in council.[1] All laws thereafter to be passed were to be sent over within twelve months, despite precedent or charter provisions. The Connecticut and Rhode Island governors were to take the oaths of allegiance and fidelity and to enter into the same security to observe the acts of trade that the other governors had to furnish. The king was to instruct the Board of Trade to revise and codify the various proposals already made, and to offer such assistance as might be necessary to encourage the colonists in applying their efforts to the production of naval stores and other commodities useful to Great Britain.[2] The committee further recommended that the judges prepare and bring in the heads of a bill, to be passed by parliament at its next session, based upon these resolutions. The resolutions were read twice and agreed to, but no bill of the kind was ever introduced.[3]

wide attention. It appeared contemporaneously as a printed pamphlet (British Museum, 8223 2/15) and parts of it were reprinted in Bennett, *The National Merchant,* pp. 109–112, and in *Caribbeana,* II, 62–64. See also *Board of Trade Journal,* 1728–1734, p. 366.

The order to the board reads: "An account of the laws made, manufactures set up and trade carried on, in any of the colonies, which may have affected the trade, navigation and manufactures of this kingdom; distinguishing when any such manufactures were first set up, what progress has been made therein and what orders or instructions have been given to discourage the same; and when any such trade was first carried on and what directions have been given or methods taken to put a stop thereto." In its reply, the board answered at great length, contenting itself, however, with information not recommendations, giving lists of laws against which objections had been laid and offering no more novel remedy than a renewal of instructions to the governors.

1. Partly in consequence of this resolution the Board of Trade continued to have printed in England collections of the laws of a number of the colonies, a series which had been begun with the issue of the laws of New York (1719) and Maryland (1723). Those of the Leeward Islands (1734), Jamaica (1738), Montserrat, Nevis, and St. Christopher (1740) now appeared from the printing office of John Baskett, printer to the king's most excellent Majesty. They are all fine specimens of eighteenth century typography.

2. Parliament had already passed laws encouraging the production and export of naval stores from the plantations, the maintenance of the quality of pitch and tar, and the preservation of mast trees.

3. The adoption of these resolutions was reported at once to Connecticut and caused a great deal of concern there (*Talcott Papers,* I, 294–298; II, 445–462). The assembly ordered that a full set of the colony's laws be sent over immediately. This set, as fast as its parts arrived, was turned over to the board's legal adviser, Francis Fane, whose report on the laws is printed with an introduction in *Publications* of the Acorn Club (1915). Connecticut was the more concerned because two appeals from her courts had recently been made and two of her laws had been disallowed, one, entitled Heretics, in 1705 and the other, the Intestacy Law, in 1728. I have written on both these subjects, once in the introduction mentioned above and again in "The Connecticut In-

The bill failed of acceptance, probably because of the constitutional issue involved. The committee which adopted the resolution was proposing that parliament override the prerogative so far as to modify in two important particulars the terms of charters which the king had already granted. It was proposing further that parliament pass an act compelling the king in council to disallow laws adopted in the colonies detrimental to England's interests, without regard to anything that the royal charters might contain to the contrary; and with the same disrespect of charter provisions it was insisting that all the private colonies send over their laws within twelve months of their enactment. There was nothing in the charters of Maryland, Connecticut, and Rhode Island obliging these colonies to send over their laws at all, because these charters had been granted before such a review of colonial legislation was even thought of. In the case of Pennsylvania the time limit was five years not one year, with a six months' allowance during which time the king in council had to reach a decision, an arrangement the board thought manifestly unfair, as it was.

Parliament had refused to pass the bill of 1701, though on other than constitutional grounds. Now in 1734, more than thirty years later, it refused to pass a much less drastic bill, even though the committee of the whole house thought it amply qualified to do so. We may believe that it was not ready to take a step so serious as openly to defy the prerogative, or we may equally well believe that parliament was unwilling to take action against only two of the private colonies, Connecticut and Rhode Island, which were manifestly the objects of the resolution. The stars in their courses were working in favor of these two self-governing communities. For years the Board of Trade had been insisting that all the colonies should be placed "on a common foot" in their relations with England. It had persistently demanded that Connecticut and Rhode Island be required to allow appeals, to send over their laws, to present their governors for the king's approval, and despite their charters to behave as did the royal colonies, contributing at least something to Great Britain's commercial and industrial prosperity. In this endeavor the board in the past had completely failed and now again the efforts of thirty years were to go for naught. Neither parliament nor the crown had been able to

testacy Law," originally printed in *The Yale Review,* 1894, reprinted with corrections in *Essays in Anglo-American Legal History,* II, and again with additions but without the notes in *Connecticut Tercentenary Publications,* no. 2.

shake the self-governing foundations of these colonies and their charters remained intact until long after the American Revolution. Connecticut continued to be predominantly an agricultural Puritan colony; Rhode Island, with an insufficient landed area, found its sources of subsistence and wealth in its commerce, with Newport its emporium of trade, one of the leading seaports of the colonial coast.

By its refusal to tamper with the colonial charters, parliament made abundantly clear that it was disposed to leave matters strictly colonial to the executive authorities. These authorities thus given possession of the colonial field were able to do very little, however, during the next few years, to uphold the Board of Trade in the enforcement of its policy.[1] Thus left unsupported by the executive and legislative alike and according to the terms of its commission devoid of all executive power, the board was practically helpless. From this time forward it limited its activities strictly to its own business and made no further effort to influence policy, otherwise than by frequently restating its convictions. With some twenty colonies to look after, commercial treaties to arrange with the states of Europe, occasional bills and proclamations to prepare, and representations and reports to compose, it fell back into a laissez-faire attitude and let well enough alone. From 1734 to the end of its career it confined itself to the ordinary concerns that came before it day by day and never went beyond the established routine of the Plantation Office. It was content to clean up accumulations rather than to originate ideas. It tried to do no more than hold the colonies as they were to a proper obedience as subordinate and dependent communities and, as far as it could. to check encroachments on the prerogative, to prevent illegal

1. Ten years later, in 1744, the weakness of the executive authorities in the colonies became so apparent that parliament was asked to come to the aid of the prerogative and pass a rider attached to a bill forbidding the issue of paper money there. This rider provided that all governors, councils, and assemblies should "pay strict obedience to such orders and instructions as shall from time to time be transmitted to them or any of them by his Majesty or his successors or by or under his or their authority." This bold attempt to bolster up the prerogative in the colonies by act of parliament, which had it succeeded would have given executive orders the force of law, failed because of the prorogation of the legislative body and was never tried again. Labaree, *Royal Government in America*, pp. 33–34, 439–440.

It is really an extraordinary fact that before 1765 parliament, though often in the mind of the Board of Trade, and even of some of the colonial governors, as a help to the executive in times of trouble with the colonies, should have been unwilling always to take any action that would strengthen the executive in enforcing its colonial policy (*ibid.*, pp. 347, 359, 360, 362, 363, 364, 439, 443–444). The colonies profited greatly thereby.

trade, and to obtain the disallowance of such colonial laws as placed restrictions on the trade of the kingdom, interfered with the free play of English manufacturing, or restrained the royal officials in the colonies in the exercise of the powers delegated to them by the crown.

This period also was one of great relaxation and inertia at Whitehall. It was a time when the executive departments, notably the Treasury and the Admiralty, were seemingly blind to the need of constructive action, whereby to strengthen the hands of those in the colonies engaged in executing the acts of parliament or in carrying out the king's instructions or the orders in council. The apathy of the British authorities was accompanied in the colonies by a steady encroachment on the part of the popular assemblies upon the powers of the royal governors there. The British crown was in a difficult position. Parliament, whose law was becoming increasingly weighty, refused to coöperate, and its own executive weapons—proclamations, instructions, commissions, and orders—were proving often without effect because they were not construed as mandatory and were not pleadable in courts of law. The impasse thus reached between the executive and the legislative branches of the government explains much of the neglect that seemed to characterize Great Britain's management of the colonies during these years and the rapid advance of the popular assemblies before 1763.

There were men both in England and the colonies who recognized the dangers of the situation and protested against the seemingly wilful indifference of those who were content with the world as it was and had no desire to change it. We have already noticed the remonstrances of such critics as West, Penrice, Popple, and Bollan, and must now deal at greater length with the writing of James Abercromby, whose indictment of the entire British colonial system is exceedingly severe and far more penetrating even than that of the better-known Thomas Pownall, whose *Administration of the Colonies* was first issued in 1764, after the French and Indian War was over. Though Pownall knew the colonies at first hand, Abercromby knew them just as well and probably had greater familiarity than Pownall with the history of the colonial system from the beginning.

James Abercromby had resided in South Carolina for at least fifteen years and had played an important part in its affairs. On returning to England in 1749 he became the agent for Governor Johnston of North Carolina and for the governor and council of Virginia until 1763. As he himself wrote, he was "more generally instructed as to the government, trade and strength of the colonies than any one else either in a public or private character who ever went to that part of the world." His work, "An Examination of the Acts of Parliament," must have been the labor of many years. It was finished in first draft in 1752 and presented to Secretary Holderness in that year.[1] It was later rewritten. Of the essay at least four copies are now extant. The treatise contains the most searching commentary that we have on the acts of trade and the British executive organization and the most downright condemnation of the system as it existed, its weaknesses and imperfections. At the same time it is so confused that one may well doubt whether any of the "ministers of state," for whom it was meant, ever read it or if by chance they did so ever took it seriously. To have put its recommendations into effect by act of parliament would have required almost a revolution in Great Britain's methods of enforcement and have led to endless difficulties and complications. One can hardly imagine any parliament as passing the bill that Abercromby drew up and included in his essay, and even had such a bill conceivably been passed its provisions could never have been carried out under the conditions existing in America at that time.

Abercromby was a mercantilist in that he was in entire sympathy with the colonial policy of the mother country, as we have thus far defined it.[2] He believed that the colonies should be made subservient

1. The full title is "An Examination of the Acts of Parliament Relative to the Trade and the Government of our American Colonies: Also the Different Constitutions of Government in those Colonies considered with Remarks by way of a Bill for Amendment of the Laws of this Kingdom in Relation to the Government and Trade of those Colonies: Which Bill is humbly submitted to the Consideration of his Majesty's Ministers of State, more particularly those in Office, before whom the Several Matters herein Treated are properly Cognizable: And for whose Use this Performance is Intended." The Huntington Library copy is a corrected draft; the copies in the Clements Library and the State Archives at Harrisburg are apparently later revisions in fair hand. The treatise itself is as verbose as its title.

A thoroughgoing study of this work, which with all its excrescences is an illuminating presentation of the mercantilist view as held at that time, will give the reader, better than any printed pamphlet of which I know, an insight into the working of the British system, with all its defects and deficiencies. It is a remarkable document to have been written by a man who had actually lived for fifteen years in America and who must have obtained at first hand a considerable knowledge of colonial sentiment. The very fact that he records no colonial opinions of any kind would seem to indicate that before 1752 no marked hostility to British policy had become manifest in America.

2. Abercromby's essay raises the question, which I have never seen satisfactorily an-

to their parent state in order to maintain the latter's independence "amidst contests in Europe for universal dominion," because, as he says, "wherever and whenever such contests happen it will be found that the auxilliary powers of the American colonies (as the sources of maritime power), in some shape or other, will contribute to the support or overthrow of European nations." He discusses in great detail the methods that ought to have been employed by the legislative body to strengthen the royal prerogative in America and he shows a remarkable understanding of the reasons why the British system had failed up to that time in accomplishing its purpose. His remedies are very specific and represent what the most ardent mercantilist would like to have applied, but which no sovereign government in its senses, much less the spiritless British government of that day, would ever have attempted to apply.

Abercromby's faith in the efficacy of an act of parliament is symptomatic of the growing conviction in England and the colonies that in parliament rather than in the crown lay the future success of the colonial policy. Abercromby believed that an executive order was certain to be obeyed only when buttressed by statute. He was convinced, and his conviction is the reason why he wrote his essay, that the earlier acts of trade, because passed at a time prior to England's great interest in her colonies and when the latter "were only commencing and taking birth," were inadequate, contradictory, and obscure. Now that the colonies had reached maturity, he wanted passed a single comprehensive statute, brought up to date and made consistent in all its parts, in order that the subservience of the colonies might be reaffirmed and their "reverence, respect and obedience" clarified and determined.

One of the most discerning of Abercromby's criticisms is his indictment of parliament for its failure to take a hand in administering the colonies. He expresses surprise that it had not hitherto "at-

swerea and which perhaps never can be answered, as to how many of the colonists were mercantilists. Professor Osgood ventures to say none (*Colonies in the Eighteenth Century*, I, 155) but I think on the contrary that there were many, and that not all of them were officials or persons identified with the local governments. Certainly many of the colonies were in sympathy with the idea of a closer connection with Great Britain and accepted the position of dependency as one that was both natural and necessary. Such a position did not necessarily imply that they were in accord with the extreme views of the orthodox mercantilists. Nevertheless many colonial merchants, such as Joshua Gee and Thomas Banister, trading with England and frequently in residence there, were mercantilist both in opinion and practice.

tended to the internal government of the colonies by taking under consideration the different powers exercised by the colonies in making of laws, and how far such powers at this time of day are, or are not, consistent with the policy and interests of the mother country." He condemns in very forcible language parliament's failure in the past to enact the laws which the Board of Trade wanted for the purpose of reducing or regulating the colonial charters and speaks feelingly of the miscarriage of the House of Lord's resolution of 1734. He thinks that Connecticut and Rhode Island should have been placed long ago in the category of the royal colonies, not by deliberate annulment of their charters but by a statutory limitation of their powers and a stricter definition of their obligations toward their mother country. He knew, as others knew, that the colonies "had of late years greatly increased in population and were daily becoming more and more powerful in strength as well as in wealth," but in common with other mercantilists he construed this growth not as a colonial but as a British asset. All the mercantilists, including Abercromby and the Board of Trade, were certain that because of their greater numbers and affluence the colonies needed the more to be rendered firm and permanent in their subservience to Great Britain and their prosperity utilized as "conducive to the general and particular state of the British people."

That Abercromby had some inklings of doubt as to whether or not this could be done at so late a date appears from his final paragraph. Though quite sure that the colonists "in this age" were so divided among themselves as to be "in no way disposed to throw off their dependency and to assume to themselves sole monarchical or a confederate sovereignty," he nevertheless feared "from the fact that they were subjects under peculiar constitutions, formed into separate societies" they might in time, unless measures were taken to prevent, "feel their own strength" and settle in their own way the crucial question as to "whether they are to remain subjects or become confederates." This apprehension, though circumstances were to prove it groundless for many years, was not without warrant. Two years after Abercromby's essay was finished and sent in first draft to the secretary of state, Benjamin Franklin presented at the Albany Conference of 1754 his plan for a union of the colonies. The question, therefore, naturally arises as to how far the Albany plan represented any deep-seated desire for civil unity on the part of the colonists themselves, how far tendencies in that direction had progressed in America up to this time, and how far Abercromby and others of the same mind were justified in their fears.

The first attempt at union of any kind in America was that of the New England Confederation, a loose grouping of four Puritan colonies, a remarkable experiment, but one that played no part in the history of the colonies outside New England and even there had no lasting influence. Except as a military factor at the time of King Philip's War, its usefulness ended with the absorption of New Haven by Connecticut in 1665. Generally speaking, it is chiefly instructive as disclosing the subtleties of the Puritan mind under various forms of storm and stress and as revealing the difficulties which confronted men of like religious views, who were trying to work in combination and coöperation. Its activities affected the history of the four Puritan colonies and Rhode Island at many points, as we have already seen,[1] but institutionally, taken apart and studied by itself, the confederation has importance only as a local Puritan device for protection and mutual harmony, in neither of which particulars was it conspicuously successful.[2]

Toward the end of the seventeenth century, under the stimulus provided by the appointment of the Board of Trade and the inaugu-

1. Above, Vol. II, index. After the last meeting in 1684 of the commissioners of Massachusetts, Plymouth, and Connecticut (the only remaining members of the New England Confederation) conferences continued to be held of representatives from New England and New York, such as that called by Leisler in 1690 (above, Vol. III, 130–131), but they were merely temporary expedients designed to meet the emergency of defense.

2. That the articles of the New England Confederation became the model of the Articles of Confederation one hundred years later is as unlikely as that the Fundamental Orders of Connecticut were the ultimate source of the so-called "Connecticut Compromise" in the Constitutional Convention of 1787. Of the Articles of Confederation Dr. Jameson says, "The seven Dutch provinces in 1620 were a confederation and that confederation had a written constitution. But surely there is a natural history of federal governments, wherein we see the operation of similar causes producing similar results, without the need of resorting to the hypothesis of imitation" (*The Arrival of the Pilgrims*, p. 16). As to the agreement reached in the constitutional convention of 1787 on the composition of the two houses, Dr. Max Farrand tells us there is no warrant for the assumption that it was of Connecticut origin or for the statement that the term "Connecticut Compromise" was used at the time by any of the members of the convention (*Report*, American Historical Association, 1903, I, 75 note). In any case the compromise by whomsoever introduced, had it been of Connecticut origin, would need to have been based on the system of town representation established by the Connecticut charter of 1662, not on that established by the Fundamental Orders, which according to the language used provided for eventual representation according to population.

ration of a firmer colonial policy, suggestions of one kind or another were made, looking to the creation of some sort of union among all or a part of the colonies. But these suggestions were little more than armchair proposals, which never reached the state of definite and precise formulation.[1] The difficulties in the way of an union of any kind were insuperable, even of union under the British crown. The military experiment under Bellomont accomplished nothing, and with his death in 1701 colonial union as a practical issue was probably more moribund than it had been in Leisler's day. A certain measure of intercolonial coöperation existed during the war from 1702 to 1713, but it was always short lived and never of much vitality. Its one important accomplishment was the taking of Port Royal in 1710 which brought Nova Scotia, neglected for forty years, into the royal fold. But after the treaty of Utrecht was signed and the colonists were relieved of the French menace and the pressure of war, the tendencies toward separatism increased as each colony centered its attention upon its own affairs.

During the ensuing forty years of peace these tendencies in no way diminished. The colonies pursued each its own way without much regard to the others, and the only chance of frequent intercourse was through coastwise commerce. Contact by land was infrequent and was always accompanied by great difficulties, discomforts, and dangers, and except for sea-captains, supercargoes, sailors, and occasional travellers, few took long voyages by sea. Probably more men went to England, the European continent, and the West Indies than to the colonies along their own American seaboard. Traffic up and down the rivers was common but was generally limited to the confines of a single colony. As population increased and spread out

1. With the appointment of the Board of Trade in 1696, a number of schemes were put on paper for the board's consideration. Such schemes were drafted by John Nelson (*New York Colonial Documents*, IV, 209–210; *Calendar State Papers, Colonial*, 1696– 1697, §250; 1701, p. 180); Stephen Sewall (*ibid.*, §358); Edmund Harrison (*ibid.*, §§620, 651); "Thirty-one Inhabitants and Proprietors in the Northern Parts of America" (*ibid.*, §653); "New England Traders" (*ibid.*, §894. The original texts of all these schemes are greatly abbreviated in the *Calendar*). In 1697, Penn produced his plan of union, an idealistic and somewhat heroic intellectual tour de force, the essential features of which he advocated personally before the board (*Pennsylvania Magazine*, XI, 495–496; Stock, *Debates*, II, 200, 202, 414). Others in England and America advanced further suggestions, none of which had any practical value (*History of the Celebration of the Anniversary of the Constitution of the United States*, Carson, ed., II, appendix prepared by F. D. Stone; "Plans of Union, 1696–1780," *American History Leaflets*, no. 14).

toward the borders, boundary disputes arose and as trade grew in volume tariff wars engendered mutual dislikes and discriminations. As each colony concentrated time and attention upon government within rather than defense without, local trials of strength took place between the popular assemblies and the royal governors, problems of finance, administration, and patronage disturbed the serenity of political life, and a mounting greed for land in all the colonies was accompanied by a considerable amount of manipulation and corruption. Poverty made large military undertakings practically impossible except when subsidized by the British government, and quarrels over quotas of men and shares of expenses kept alive feelings of jealousy and estrangement. As early as the first quarter of the century Dummer had said in his *Defence* that the colonies were "so distinct from one another in their forms of Government, in their Religious Rites, in their Emulations of Trade, and consequently in their Affections that they can never be supposed to unite in so dangerous an enterprise as seeking independence." Forty years later and only a few months before the opening of the Albany Conference, Governor Glen of South Carolina in a letter to Governor Dinwiddie of Virginia, March 14, 1754, wrote: "The French are no ways Strangers to the Superior Strength of the English Colonies on the Continent but I am afraid they have too good Reason to consider us a Rope of Sand, loose and inconnected, and indeed it is to be lamented that we have hitherto been so."[1] As late as March 4, 1765, Thomas Hutchinson wrote to Richard Jackson, "When I consider the state of the colonies, I cannot help thinking of the fable of the bundle of sticks which the father gave to his children. I know no two colonies which think alike. There is certainly no uniformity of measures."[2]

The colonies were as far apart mentally as they were geographically. Personal intercourse was rare, except occasionally among the leaders, and familiarity with the conditions of life and environment

---

1. C. O. 5:14, enclosure no. 5 in Glen's letter to Holderness; a Dinwiddie letter to Sir Thomas Robinson, June 18, 1754, is in C. O. 5:14. On August 1, 1755, Governor Hopkins of Rhode Island wrote to Phips of Massachusetts, "The present situation of affairs in N. A. may show how little dependence can be had, even in times of greatest necessity, on voluntary union and quotas of men and expenses, and this might serve to convince some who seem to love and understand liberty better than public good and affairs of state how necessary a solid union of all his Majesty's northern colonies is and how vain that expectation is which supposes the same good ends may be attained by any partial one or such an one as every colony may make and break as they please" (Bancroft Transcripts, II, 63).

2. *Ibid.,* II, 131, Hutchinson Correspondence.

of other colonies than a colonist's own was common only to a very few, chiefly men on business journeying on horseback or by water up and down the coast. The inhabitants of one colony were "strangers" (actually so called) to those of another, and the lands beyond a colonist's own borders were sometimes spoken of as "foreign" and a trip thither as going "abroad," a hazardous venture. Time was aiding but very slowly in breaking down the barriers, few of which had actually been removed before the Revolution. Trade and commerce were doing their part, wealth was accumulating in the seaport towns, and the merchant was becoming the representative of a capitalist class, to which revolution was anathema. While an unprogressive agriculture continued to be the main interest of a majority of the colonists and younger sons were moving out from the settled centers to find land and homes elsewhere, the larger towns along the coast were acquiring a fluctuating and often undesirable rank and file, as navigation opened up new routes and markets and craftsmanship demanded more varied supplies and a better grade of artisan labor. There was no "proletariat" in colonial times, if by that infelicitous word one means working classes eking out miserable lives under capitalistic oppression. But racial and religious antipathies, conflicting habits of life and conduct, and enmities arising from quarrels regarding mutual help in undertakings chiefly against the Indians (often urged but meeting with but little response), created dislikes, misunderstandings, and false impressions that bit deeply into individual souls. Recrimination and detraction were all too common and continued to be all too common for many years to come. The spirit of the time was separatist and provincial and the need for coöperation, though frequently urged by men in civil and military office, was rarely felt and less often acted on by the mass of the colonists themselves or by their representatives in assembly. Little wonder that the Board of Trade and its advisers saw no danger accruing from united action in America to the enforcement of their own policy.[1]

1. The Board of Trade frequently called attention to this spirit of separatism and the unlikelihood of union ever being effected among the colonies. Abercromby noted the same in 1752, Pownall in 1764. It became pronounced during the years 1768–1770, when the non-consumption and non-importation measures were being tried out ("Boston Merchants and the Non-Importation Movement," *Publications*, Massachusetts Colonial Society, XVII), and even after the war and the attaining of independence, it made the maintenance of united action a matter of the greatest difficulty. Nevins, *The American States During and After the Revolution, 1775–1789*, chs. X, XII.

The most powerful force overcoming these centrifugal tendencies was fear of the French and the Indians. As early as 1748 Governor Clinton of New York and Governor Shirley of Massachusetts commented on the melancholy situation that existed along the frontiers of New York and New Hampshire, and on July 8 of that year they held a conference with representatives of the Six Nations and their allies. On August 8 they wrote a joint letter to the Board of Trade[1] and Clinton followed this up with further communications, complaining of the Indian menace and outlining in general and particular terms the distresses of his province. In 1751 he informed the board that he proposed to meet delegates from the Six Nations at Albany and had invited all the other governors to be present, personally if possible, if not by commissioners, to concert measures for the future management by the colonies of Indian affairs. Only Massachusetts, Connecticut, and South Carolina responded. The conference was held July 17, 1751. The Board of Trade, aroused by Clinton's letters, submitted the evidence to the secretary of state, as it always did in matters of this kind, and discussed the issue with Sir Danvers Osborn, who was going over in Clinton's place, with Thomas Pownall as his private secretary. The board gave Osborn special instructions to inquire into the Indian trade, and on August 16 wrote the secretary (Holderness), enclosing a representation it had drawn up for submission to the king. This representation stressed the dangers from the French and called attention to the fact that the latter were greatly encouraged by the apparent unwillingness of the colonies to coöperate for the common defense. Holderness, on August 28, 1753, wrote the governors bidding them join in concordant action against the Indians and resist to the utmost of their power encroachments by the French upon the territory of the king's dominions. He declared it to be the king's will and pleasure that they keep up an exact correspondence with each other in all that concerned their mutual defense. Shirley, replying to this circular letter, suggested that an union among all the colonies was necessary, if quotas of men and money were to be made effective, the want of which, he said, would be a serious obstacle to the carrying out of "any general plan for cementing an union among his Majesty's territories."[2]

1. *New York Colonial Documents,* VI, 687.

2. *Ibid.,* VI, 452, 703; *Acts Privy Council, Colonial,* IV, 233. Glen's letter of March 14, 1754, urged that the seven larger colonies enter into an agreement for their mutual defense, ignoring the smaller colonies as negligible. But he had no thought of a

Because of these letters from the colonies Secretary Robinson, Holderness' successor, sent word to the Board of Trade, June 14, 1754, that the king thought it highly expedient that "a plan for a General concert be entered into by the Colonies, for their mutual and common defence," and ordered the board to prepare such a plan. The latter, on July 5, wrote to James DeLancey of New York, "It seems to be the opinion and is the language of almost every colony that a general union of strength and interest is become absolutely necessary," and that nothing could have facilitated such a measure more than a general congress of commissioners from each colony at Albany.[1] That many of the colonial governors were in favor of a friendly correspondence and realized the necessity of a conjoint conference with the Indians is clear,[2] but that they anticipated the formation of a civil as well as a military union or that public opinion, such as it was, favored a union of this kind is most unlikely. No one in America communicated such an idea to the authorities at Whitehall and no one there had any thought of suggesting such a thing. When the Board of Trade, having approved the plan of assembling commissioners at Albany and, as ordered by the secretary of state, started to prepare its own scheme it went no farther than to follow literally the king's instructions. Its representation, put together "with all the dispatch that the nature and importance of it would admit of," was not completed until August 9, 1754, after the Albany Conference was over.[3] Anything of a civil or political nature would have required an act of parliament to give it validity. In view of the board's settled policy of keeping the colonies dependent on the mother coun-

civil union. For the information possessed by the Plantation Office regarding the New York situation since 1743 see *New York Colonial Documents*, VI, 639–703, and on the whole subject Beer, *British Colonial Policy, 1754–1765*, ch. II.

An article in the *American Political Science Review*, VIII, 393–412, by Miss Matthews (Mrs. Rosenberry), states (p. 397) that Holderness' letter contained the phrase "to enter into articles of union and confederation with each other for the mutual defence of his Majesty's subjects and interests in North America, as well in time of peace as of war." This statement is in error. The words are not to be found in Holderness' letter (*Maryland Archives*, VI, 3–4; L, 432–433; *New Hampshire Provincial Papers*, VI, 234). They are to be found only in Shirley's letter to Holderness and in his instructions to the Massachusetts commissioners (*Collections*, Massachusetts Historical Society, 3d ser., V, 9–10; *New York Colonial Documents*, VI, 822). This fact is important as showing that the idea of a civil union of the colonies did not originate in England, where it was not even dreamed of.

1. *New York Colonial Documents*, VI, 844, 846.
2. Glen's attitude is a case in point, see note above.
3. *Ibid.*, VI, 844; *Board of Trade Journal*, 1754–1758, pp. 49, 50, 55.

try, any plan of this kind could hardly have been conceived otherwise than in terms of earlier experiments and to call on parliament to support such a plan would undoubtedly have failed again as it had failed before. The draft fashioned by the board was for military purposes only and, except so far as it was designed to guard Great Britain against the loss of her colonies, has no place in a study of colonial policy as such. Though formulated by the Board of Trade its application and execution were to be the business of the secretary for the southern department, in whose hands lay all operations connected with war anywhere. How far the board's recommendations were officially adopted cannot be said, but that they underlay the programme mapped out for the Braddock campaign and were in the main reproduced in the instructions given to Loudoun, Abercrombie, Amherst, and Gage cannot be doubted.[1]

The shaping of the military plan altered in no way the board's convictions regarding the colonial policy that Great Britain should continue to follow. That policy was what James Abercromby said it was. In principle it had existed from the beginning and it remained, though of constantly diminishing importance, hardly changed despite the loss of the American colonies for half a century longer.[2]

1. It is no part of the plan of this chapter, which has to do solely with the Englishman's outlook upon the colonies, to present the colonial aspects of the Albany Conference or to examine the scheme of union prepared by Franklin and others. The idea of such a union was first suggested by Shirley, but that Franklin had the thought of it in mind as early as 1750 seems to be shown by his letter to James Parker of Boston, in which he outlined a scheme very similar to that proposed at Albany (*Works*, Smyth ed., III, 42–43). In the various instructions issued to members of the conference by their respective governors, only those of Shirley mention a political federation. As is well known, the colonial assemblies either ignored the Albany plan or rejected it altogether. It was never officially received or acted on in England, as of course it could not be.

2. One of the last of the board's direct statements of policy, though by no means the last reference to the subject in the board's representations, is to be found in a report of April 2, 1751, when the board wrote, "There is nothing so essentially necessary to the preservation of his Majesty's government in American provinces as a careful and strict maintenance of the just prerogative, which is the only means by which the colonies can be kept dependent on the mother country" (*New York Colonial Documents*, VI, 614–639). The board by that time had given up all thought of altering the status of the private colonies, so that Bernard's suggestion to Halifax in 1764 (above, p. 394, note 2) that New England be reconstructed must have fallen on barren soil. Pownall, Bernard's predecessor in Massachusetts, had no such illusion. He was wholly opposed to any method of reorganization that involved the taking away of charters, though probably he placed his opposition to such reorganization on sounder reasoning than that which induced Bernard, as an after thought, to say that any such reconstruction would probably be wrecked on "the humor of the people."

The Albany plan of civil union had no effect upon it. That plan was never brought formally to the attention of the board—for there is no hint of it in the board's proceedings—but it is impossible not to believe that its members knew something of it, inasmuch as they received constant and abundant information of what was happening in America.[1] The rejection of the plan by the colonial assemblies would have seemed to the members, if they knew of it, a sufficient demonstration of the futility of the approval of Franklin's scheme by the conference and enough to strengthen their own faith in their own policy. The colonies could be kept dependent, they were sure of it. Thomas Pownall, severe critic though he was, had no doubt on this point. "Some say [he wrote] the colonies will revolt some day. No, their hearts are in England and England is their home, they would not risk losing the rights of Englishmen." He believed that England could and should keep them dependent, apart and separate, revising their governments but leaving them alone, with full legislative power, on the ground, which at the time found no favor with those in executive office, that subordination and self-government were not incompatible and that a measure of freedom for the colonists to consider their own interests would not destroy their usefulness to England.[2]

After the treaty of peace in 1763 and the addition of the province of Canada and the Floridas and the islands of Grenada, Tobago, Dominica, and St. Vincent to British territory, the Whitehall policy continued to take more and more the form of a centralization of control. This meant an increase of the authority directly exercised by the crown and, in general, a tightening of the bonds that held together the king's great colonial and commercial domain, now passing into empire. This centralizing process had been going on, more or less unobserved and without definite plan, for many years. From the days of the establishment of the Board of Trade, the erection of the vice-admiralty courts, the strengthening of the customs service, and the throwing of greater responsibility on the royal and other governors without any corresponding increase of authority, the disposition had been to concentrate the right of appointment to office in the hands of the authorities at Whitehall. This disposition is to be seen in the increase of the number of patent offices—one of the banes of the Brit-

---

1. Pargellis, *Lord Loudoun in North America*, p. 28, note 25.
2. *Administration of the Colonies* (ed. 1766), pp. 24, 28, 30–31, 33, 35, 38, 42, appendix iii, pp. 1–2.

ish system—filled by men, frequently served by deputy, who drew their salaries as the holders of sinecures and paid but meager amounts to those who performed the actual work.[1] It is to be seen in the crown's control of the naval officer, who properly speaking was an appointee of the governor, but whose assignment, in an increasing number of cases, was determined under the great seal in England not the provincial seal in the province. It is to be seen in the fact that of the officials engaged locally in administering affairs in America more than ninety-five per cent in five-sixths of the colonies were appointed under the great seal or under the royal sign manual which was a royal command to the governor to prepare a commission under the provincial seal.[2] It is to be seen in the mandamuses issued on the nomination of the Board of Trade to members of the governors' councils, whose selection by the governors was sometimes disregarded at the behest of friends at home or in the colony. It is to be seen in the famous quarrel that took place over the tenure of the judges in New York, as to whether they should hold during the king's pleasure or their own good behavior. This particular quarrel ended in the victory of the crown, on the general contention that an appointment during good behavior was "subversive of the interests of the crown and people and tended to lessen that just dependence which the colonies ought to have upon the government of the mother country."[3] It is to be seen in the attitude of the board toward colonial legislation on the principle that "the fewer the acts confirmed the greater the dependence";[4] in the board's defense of the governors, often half-hearted and ineffective as it was, when the latter were at odds with the popular assemblies over matters that concerned the maintenance of the true prerogative; and in the refusal of the board to approve of the enlargement of these assemblies, lest an increase in the number of the people's representatives should overset the balance of control in the colonies to the king's disadvantage.

1. A patent office was one created by royal letters patent under the great seal, and therefore conferred on the recipient a property right for life. Such recipient could not be removed except by legal process.

2. *Board of Trade Journal*, 1759–1763, pp. 177, 179; Andrews, *Guide*, I, 234–235; Basye, *Board of Trade, 1748–1782*, appendix B.

3. C. O. 391:68, November 5, 1761; *Board of Trade Journal*, 1759–1763, pp. 219–220, 229, 230, 233–234, 255, 263, 289, 320–321; Dickerson, *American Colonial Government*, pp. 195–205; Basye, *Board of Trade*, pp. 112–114.

4. Board of Trade to Newcastle, July 1, 1724, *Calendar State Papers, Colonial*, 1724–1725, §231.

This process might have been more successful had there been greater coördination among the officials and departments at Whitehall and greater certainty at large as to just where authority lay. There can be no doubt that this concentration of authority in England, accompanied as it was by a steady encroachment upon the governor's control of patronage in the colonies, without compensating increase of influence in any other direction, carried with it responsibilities that the executive authorities of Whitehall were unable to meet and problems that they were unable to solve.[1] Teamwork was not characteristic of the British administrative system at this time either at Whitehall or in the colonies. However assured the board may have been of the rightness of its policy, from the standpoint of the circumstances confronting the kingdom, it was powerless to enforce that policy as long as such leading departments as the Treasury and the Admiralty remained indifferent and inert. The failure of these executive branches to act upon suggestions and complaints cannot adequately be explained by the exigencies of war. The board was further handicapped by the weakness of its own weapons, executive only—royal instructions, orders in council, and letters to the governors—which were not infrequently flouted and successfully evaded by the colonists. When to these defects of the royal system there be added the prevalence of deputation and absenteeism, the reversion and sale of political offices, the commutation and composition of duties and customs, and the far too common practice of employing an inferior and underpaid personnel in the colonies—whether sent from England or selected from amongst the colonists themselves—we can understand why it was these centralizing tendencies, however much they were feared in America, were circumvented there without great difficulty. Distance and the exasperating slowness of communication, which made rapid action and effective coöperation practically impossible, rendered orders from England old before they were received in the colonies and left the royal governors and the popular assemblies free to fight out their quarrels very largely by themselves. Probably during these years there were few of the more irritating of the royal commands, originating with the board and given validity by the crown, that were not vigorously opposed in one or another of the colonies and in some of them deliberately disobeyed by the assemblies in their struggle for

1. Labaree, *Royal Government in America*, pp. 102–107.

self-control. These same assemblies were destined to become the agencies that eventually broke down the king's prerogative in America and undermined the system of administration which the executive authorities at Whitehall had so carefully contrived for the government of the royal colonies.

But the political and constitutional aspects of this centralizing *modus operandi* formed only one phase of the executive programme for the enforcement of the kingdom's colonial and commercial policies. The Seven Years' War had been enormously costly and its results had aroused an imperial interest where hitherto only mercantilist ideas had prevailed. These consequences centered Great Britain's attention anew upon her colonies and made it inevitable that the latter should be regarded, in an increasing measure, as assets in meeting the kingdom's obligations. After 1763 the colonial relationship began to be construed in terms of direct financial contributions as well as of indirect profits through trade and the customs. Policy underwent no change, but its enforcement was broadened out to meet the new conditions. A shift of authority also took place. The Board of Trade, which by the order in council of March 11, 1752,[1] had acquired added dignity and weight and had "attained a greater power and commanded a deeper respect than at any time in its history,"[2] now lost influence and entered upon its final decline. The executive departments awoke from their lethargy; the secretary of state began to play a more important part than he had done even in the days of Newcastle, and parliament proceeded not only to strengthen the mercantilist machinery but to declare its right also to tax the colonies, a thing it had never attempted to do before. Executive and legislative joined in the new attempt to carry out an old policy. Acting in com-

1. Basye, as above, ch. II. By the order of March 11, 1752, the board was, first of all, instructed to carry out without limitation the full terms of its commission, the text of which in 1754, stated in brief, was "for promoting the trade of this kingdom and inspecting and improving the plantations in America and elsewhere" (*Board of Trade Journal,* 1754–1758, pp. 34–35. Variant wordings are given, 1759–1763, pp. 181, 338). Secondly, it was granted the right to nominate for the acceptance of the Privy Council all colonial officials outside the jurisdiction of the Treasury and the Admiralty. Thirdly, and most important of all, it was made the sole channel of correspondence with the governors and other officials in the colonies, who were told to send all letters and reports relating to civil matters directly to the board, instead of to the board and the secretary of state, as formerly. This order was rescinded in 1761, except for that part which related to correspondence, which was retained, in principle at least, until 1766 (Basye, pp. 173–175).

2. *Ibid.,* p. 104.

bination more effectively than ever before, they sought to increase the dependency of the colonies upon the mother country in a three-fold manner: first, by extending the laws relating to trade; secondly, by perfecting the methods of enforcement so that these laws might be more strictly executed; and, thirdly, by placing upon the shoulders of the colonists themselves a part of the debt which Great Britain had incurred during the seven long years of warfare, with the distinct understanding that all money raised in the colonies should be spent there to meet British charges incurred. Thus at the very time when the popular assemblies were winning their victory over the prerogative and the spirit of self-government was abroad in the land; when those engaged in commerce were successfully adjusting themselves to the trade laws already in existence but wanted no more of them; and when the colonies were facing something of a financial crisis of their own, in the widespread prevalence of poverty and debt among the mass of the people and the heavy liabilities incurred by their planters and merchants in their dealings with Great Britain, then it was that the authorities at Whitehall sought to apply anew and in a dangerously forcible manner their time-honored policy.[1]

1. Self-government during our colonial period was not incompatible with dependence and in no sense implied "democracy," if by that evasive and much misunderstood term is meant something akin to political equality, universal suffrage, the right of the majority to rule, and popular sovereignty or government by consent of the governed. There was no struggle for "democracy," in that sense of the word, in colonial times, even though there were taking place divergences and adaptations in many directions — in law, in education, and in the principles governing the relations between church and state. There among the colonies were appearing new ideas of the ownership of the soil, of representation, of office holding and of the office held, of the franchise, of social relations, of sovereignty, and of the idea of a colony as a self-governing dominion. But many of these ideas in practical form are difficult to discover and to demonstrate as at work during the colonial period, and for this reason their state of advancement can be easily overestimated, particularly by those who desire to carry back as far as possible the origins of American ideas and practices of a later period.

But if the meaning of "democracy" be broadened out to include "freedom," a word even more vague in its connotations and always needing careful definition—in this case referring to a free man and his efforts to obtain release from alien restraints—then something quite different is brought into the discussion. There was a continuous struggle on the part of the colonists, outside of Connecticut and Rhode Island, to get rid of restrictions that were external in their origin, restrictions that were seignorial, proprietary, royal, and parliamentary. Such a struggle against government from across the seas was a part of the Americanizing process, but its results and the completeness of its success must not be exaggerated. Many of these alien restrictions remained intact down to the period of the Revolutionary War, during which time they were swept entirely away. The political and social democracy of our national era was in fact the

This is not the place to enter upon a detailed account of the methods employed to attain these ends. Owing to the large number of reports received regarding the colonists' trading with the enemy during the war and their persistence in carrying on illicit trade,[1] parliament renewed the Molasses Act of 1733 in the Sugar Act of 1764 and passed a series of new laws extending the list of enumerated commodities until, to the great satisfaction of the mercantilists, practically every important colonial staple was included. The Board of Trade recommended extensive changes in the governors' instructions to conform to the new requirements; the secretary of state ordered the consuls and ministers in foreign seaports to report on trade conditions in order to detect evasions of the acts; and the Admiralty gave directions to the commanders of his Majesty's ships to seize all colonial vessels engaged in illegal trade. At the same time, the Board of Trade called on the governors for further and better answers to queries in all that concerned trade; bade them enforce all previous regulations regarding the transmission of laws; and requested them to report as to whether or not certain acts of parliament, hitherto considered inapplicable to the colonies, might not be put in operation there.

In some respects most remarkable of all these manifestations of an increased centralization of authority was the transfer to American soil of all control over matters relating to customs and vice-admiralty. We have already discussed these transfers in previous chapters. As early as 1764 the Admiralty began a series of experiments looking to a more effective enlargement of vice-admiralty jurisdiction in the colonies, which ended in the erection under an act of parliament of 1767 of four vice-admiralty courts, at Halifax, Boston, Philadelphia, and Charles Town, designed to hear all colonial cases in first instance and on appeal. This action rendered unnecessary any further appeal to the Privy Council or the High Court of Admiralty in colonial

product of the Revolution and of the years that followed and only to a small extent, except in various matters of elimination and simplification, the outcome of efforts begun during colonial times. On the larger question of status, I doubt if before 1763 the colonists ever seriously objected to the position of dependence and subordination in which England placed them. As for political rights their vision never looked higher than the rights of their fellow subjects in England, and there was nothing democratic about an Englishman's rights in the eighteenth century.

1. Treasury 1, bundle 392, pp. 34–39. Documents in this bundle contain the information possessed by the commissioners of the customs on the subject of illicit trade. Among them are twenty-six papers retailing the facts as far back as 1739. Upon the information thus furnished the commissioners based their comments and complaints.

suits that came within the vice-admiralty jurisdiction. These courts were prerogative courts seated on colonial soil, empowered to hear cases on the spot and to obviate the delays that had always accompanied an appeal to England. Likewise the Treasury, under the authorization of the same act of parliament, removed the American roster of customs officials from the British register and in 1767 established the American Board of Customs Commissioners sitting at Boston, as a separate customs service, designed to do for the collection of the plantation duty what the new vice-admiralty courts were to do for marine causes and breaches of the acts of trade.

England's determination to centralize authority at Whitehall and Westminster; to maintain her colonies in a permanent state of subordination, politically as well as commercially; to deny them the status of self-governing communities, refusing privileges asked for and denying many that were already enjoyed; to consider her own prosperity and security before the welfare of her outlying dependencies, whose "rights," as we call them today, she neither recognized nor understood; and to belittle protests from America as the work only of agitators and radicals—all these things must be taken into consideration by anyone who wishes to understand the circumstances that brought on the American Revolution.

NOTE: Writers of the economic determinist school, who of late years have been reviving a faith in the economic interpretation of history and seeking a place in the historical sunshine, believe that the Revolution was either an attempt of "the American merchant and planter-capitalism" to obtain "release from the fetters of the English Mercantile System" (Hacker, *The First American Revolution* and *A Graphic History*) or a movement "to free [America] from the colonial ban upon her industries" (Beard, *A History of the Business Man*).

These and other similar theses can be maintained only by a system of clever, ingenious, and seemingly plausible but really superficial manipulations of fact and logic in the interest of a preconceived theory; by generalizations based on the grouping of occasional and widely scattered data; and by dependence on the statements of secondary authorities—statements frequently unfortified by proof and sometimes demonstrably untrue. Even Dr. Lipson, a writer not averse to an economic interpretation of history and one whose opinions the economic determinists are inclined to respect, is unable to accept these explanations and sums up the situation as follows.

"The extent to which economic factors were responsible for the American Revolution cannot easily be measured. At first sight it is natural to attribute the disruption of England's first empire to a policy avowedly designed to make the oversea settlements 'duly subservient and useful.' Yet contemporary English opinion held that the colonies 'felt the benefit more than the burden' of the Acts of Trade, and the view appears on the whole well-founded. Irksome as their disabilities may seem on paper, the working of the system was not unduly onerous in practice. It was modified by concessions such as those which enabled the colonies to carry on trade direct with southern Europe in certain 'enumerated commodities,' or it was evaded with the open connivance of the American authorities. This lax administration of the system helped to bring the authority and prestige of the mother country into disrepute; and habitual disregard for the laws of the parent state fostered a spirit of independence, which made any attempt at enforcement of the laws appear a gross act of tyranny. The efforts to suppress smuggling and administer the Acts of Trade with greater rigour, by substituting vice-admiralty courts for juries and employing the navy, were the more deeply resented because the colonies had grown accustomed to the latitude which alone made the Acts tolerable. Against their disabilities, real or nominal, must be set the reciprocal advantages which the colonies enjoyed in the shape of the protection, the credit and the market of the mother country. The old colonial system, as the ruthless destruction of tobacco-growing in England demonstrated, was far from one-sided. Nor were even their disabilities unattended by compensating features. Behind the shelter of the Navigation Laws which protected her from alien competition, New England built up an important shipbuilding industry. These considerations may fairly lead us to conclude that, though individuals chafed against the restraints laid upon them, the colonies would not have cut themselves adrift from the mother country on the ground of economic grievances alone: and this conclusion is fortified by the absence, in the Declaration of Independence, of all reference to the Acts of Trade beyond an allusion of doubtful significance" (*Economic History of England,* 2d ed., III, 194–196).

This is not the place to discuss the conclusions reached, but something may be said, very briefly. In the first place, there never was a hard and fast "Mercantile System" and British governmental policy, which in the long run was responsible for the Revolution, was never identical with the mercantilist programme, even before 1763 when mercantilism was in the ascendant. The government had to consider the needs of the state and the exchequer, the constitutional rights of the prerogative, and the legislative authority of parliament as well as the wishes and prosperity of the merchant-capitalists. After 1763, British colonial policy, though still favoring the merchants, was in many of its most important parts distinctly at odds with them. The Proclamation of 1763, the Stamp Act, the Declaratory Act, the Quebec Act of 1774, and the Carleton commission and instructions of 1775, were none of them mercantilist in their objectives. With equal truth may it be said that the Sugar Act, the trade acts of 1764–1766, and the Townshend Acts were designed much more in the interest of the revenue which the exchequer greatly needed than of the business prosperity of the capitalists. In 1766, the Board of Trade itself, often construed as under the thumb of the mercantilists, in defining British policy, added to "The Commerce and Manufactures of this Country" two other ends to be sought, "Your Majestys Royal Prerogative and the Authority of the British Legislature." At the same time the board made it abundantly clear that its own members, as well as the executive departments of government, were interpreting colonial policy, not in terms of the merchants' profits, but of the financial solvency of the British Exchequer, for the war debt after 1763 amounted to £140,000,000. The British government had other interests at stake than those of the merchants and always found it difficult to satisfy the merchants as much as the merchants wished to be satisfied, a situation of which the latter frequently complained. It is sheer assumption to assert that in England at this time the acts of the executive and the legislation of parliament were necessarily determined by business pressure, for the one thing the mercantilists did not want was parliamentary taxation of the colonies.

In the second place, the colonists must have known where the shoe pinched most painfully. Those of New England did protest against the measures of the years 1764–1766 and the Townshend Acts of 1767 and nearly all the colonists tried without success to neutralize them by non-consumption and non-importation devices, but in these ventures they were not preparing for revolution nor were they doing anything more than attempting to obtain a redress of trade grievances and to bring the British parliament to terms. The non-importation movement was at first a protest against commercial restraints and financial impositions and was initiated chiefly by the merchants. But as time went on it passed out of the control of the merchants into the hands of those to whom trade was a secondary consideration and who, as individualists and political agitators, were concerned for what they called "human rights and liberties." These men gave prominence, not to trade grievances which, had no other grievances intervened, would probably have been eventually redressed, but to a constitutional claim that parliament would not recognize as a claim deserving of any consideration. Behind this claim, which at bottom represented simply the determination of each of the colonies to manage its own affairs, lay a great variety of local grievances—financial, territorial, governmental, and religious—grievances that actuated each colony to uphold the larger claim, as one which all could support. It is untrue to fact to say that there was any one grievance common to all, and that grievance solely commercial or industrial.

The constitutional issue appears as early as 1765 and, as the commercial and financial complaints dwindled in importance with the failure of the non-importation movement, it became the leading issue after 1770. From this time forward, though economic grievances still occasionally appear and the retention of the tea tax made trouble, the constitutional claim dominates the scene and freedom from outside control, in many ways at that time much more a grievance than were matters that concerned trade and manufacturing, became the real objective. In very few, if any, of the resolutions of towns and local assemblies, the memorials and other official papers of the First Continental Congress, and the Declaration of Independence (which contains only one item out of twenty-seven constituting an economic grievance) is there anything suggesting a "release from the fetters of the English Mercantile System" or a desire to be freed from any ban on colonial industries. On the contrary the Declaration and Resolves of the First Continental Congress expressly state, "we cheerfully consent to the operation of such acts of the British parliament, as are bona fide restrained to the regulation of our external commerce, for the purpose of securing the commercial advantages of the whole Empire to the mother country, and the commercial benefits of its respective members." Over and over again the protestants in America ask for nothing more than to return to the "state of harmony and unity" that prevailed before 1763—a state which they considered "beneficial to the whole empire and as ardently desired by all America." They wanted so to return despite the fact that before 1763 the aims of the British authorities were much more nearly identified with the wishes of the mercantilists than they were afterward, though even during this earlier period the government hedged a good deal in meeting mercantilist demands. It is a gross historical blunder to start with the premises that British colonial policy and mercantilism were at any time convertible terms or that the colonists were ever seriously hampered by the restrictions placed upon their desire to manufacture (above, p. 349, note 4).

One may not doubt that behind the effort to obtain self-government and freedom from the restraints of British control there lay factors that were commercial, financial, legal, social, and industrial. But no one of these by itself would have brought on the Revolution. It is too great a simplification of history to regard the events of the past as nothing but a struggle of classes, a clash of economic interests, for such an oversimplification of the problem leads inevitably to an oversimplified solution. No amount of study of the social side of colonial life—much vaunted today as if it were something new—will explain the events of 1775 and 1776. It is never very difficult, by methods of grouping and omission, to phrase things in such a way as to lead to misrepresentation. To emphasize the economic aspects to the exclusion of all else is to interpret human affairs in terms of material things only, to say nothing of the spiritual power necessary to use these material resources for human welfare, to ignore the influence of sentiment and morality, and to underrate the rich and varied stuff of human nature, the distractions of statesmen, and the waywardness and uncertainty of events. The historian, if he is to keep both his levels and his proportions true, cannot fail to stress, first of all, the institutional and structural aspects of colonial life, which, despite certain present-day opinions to the contrary, are fundamental to any right understanding of the colonial past. At the same time if he is honest to himself and his evidence he cannot neglect the imponderable forces (always most difficult to identify and trace), as well as the driving influence of emotional and mass psychology. These factors are essential, however much those who can see in society, present and past, only things that are "real" and "practical"—business success and class warfare—and consider irrelevant whatever cannot be pinned down as a social or economic activity. No one should deal with the past whose ambition it is to find a single cause for all that has happened or who is unwilling to admit the existence of many causes acting simultaneously. Mr. J. A. Spender, sympathetic liberal and newspaper editor, can say, "There is as little probability of discovering one key to the problems of human society as there is of finding one remedy for the ills of the human body," and Mr. J. M. Keynes, the eminent economist, can add even more emphatically, "The view that the economic ideal is the sole respectable purpose of the community as a whole is the most dreadful heresy which has ever gained the ear of a civilized people."

Modern industrialism would seem to be responsible for these latter-day attempts to interpret the past in the light of the present and to apply the Marxian doctrine that social progress is the outcome of class conflict and of nothing else.

# INDEX

ABERCROMBIE (Abercromby), James (1706–81), British general, 418

Abercromby, James (fl. 1734–63), 418; on logwood and cacao, 93n, 94, 94n; on naval officers, 187n; his experience in colonial affairs, 216, 216n, 408–409, 409n; his "An Examination of the Acts of Parliament," 216n, 409–411, 409n; desires parliamentary bill unifying colonial administration, 216n, 260, 410; on separatist tendencies in colonies, 415n

Absenteeism and deputation, 149n, 180, 201–202, 209–210, 215, 218, 312n, 420, 421

Accomack River, Maryland, 213n

Addington, Isaac, deputy auditor in Massachusetts, 194n

Addison, Joseph, on merchants, 329n

*Address to the Lords Commissioners of the Admiralty upon the . . . State of the British Navy,* 315n

Admiralty, 83n, 279n, 284; believes in English-built ships for navy, 81; and enforcement of navigation acts, 148, 178, 220, 226, 424 (*see also* Navy); disapproves of naval officers' furnishing supplies for ships of war, 190; Mediterranean passes issued by, 208; and colonial vice-admiralty courts, 224, 230, 264, 266, 266n, 269, 270, 424 (*see also* Vice-admiralty courts [colonial]); droits of, in royal fishes, 233–234; inefficiency and indifference of, before 1763, 260, 295, 408, 421; secretaries of, their influence on colonial policy, 272; its incompetence and corruption at end of seventeenth century, 275, 275n, 276, 288, 290n, 315n, 375, 397; authority of, in relation to control of convoys by council of trade, 288, 289, 289n; and Board of Trade, 294n, 296, 310n, 422n

See also Admiralty, courts of; Admiralty, High Court of; Navy; Vice-admiralty courts

Admiralty, courts of, 160, 168, 222; attempt to restrict jurisdiction of, 224;

differences in jurisdiction of, 229–230
See also Admiralty, High Court of; Vice-admiralty courts

Admiralty, High Court of, 1, 114n, 169, 222–223, 223n, 224, 225, 226, 229, 235, 235n, 247, 255, 424; court of oyer and terminer for, 222n, 223

*Advocate, The* (1651), 23n, 41n

Africa, importations from, through Holland, 37, 41n, under act of 1660, 64; Swedish possessions in, seized by Dutch, 50; and colonial rice, 97; question whether Canaries belonged to, 111, 112; Scottish trade to, 153, 154, 154n; and slave trade, in mercantilist theory, 343, 345, 346, 346n, 356n
See also Algiers; Guinea; Royal African Company; Senegambia; Tangier

Agriculture, in colonies, 12, 345, 346–348, 350, 365, 415 (*see also* Rice; Sugar; Tobacco); status of, in England in seventeenth century, 320–321

Albany, furs sent from, 105n; colonial conference with Six Nations at (1751), 416
See also Albany Conference

Albany Conference and plan of union, 411–412, 414, 417, 418n, 419

Albemarle, George Monck, 1st Duke of, his interest in advancement of trade, 54; and act of 1660, 60–61

Albemarle Sound, 238–239

Alderney, 66

*Alexander,* ship, 151, 151n

Algiers, treaties with, 276n

Alison, Francis, 394n

Allen, George, 257n

Alured, Henry, 27n

Ambassadors, instructions to, drafted by Board of Trade, 309

Amboyna massacre, 22, 22n, 32

American Board of Customs Commissioners, 210n, 220–221, 220n, 271, 425

American Revolution, 399; corruption in England during, 315n; causes of, 375–376, 425, 425n; democracy a product of, 423n

lem discussed in assembly of, 138, 138n; uprisings in, 138–139; order to governor of, on enforcement of navigation acts, 145–146; Randolph in, 151, 151n, 157, 158n; riding surveyor in, 164n, 211; governor's council in, decision on ship registration, 173; measures taken in, to enforce act of 1696, 175; topography of, makes enforcement of navigation acts difficult, 178, 182, 182n, 204n, 244; naval officers in, 181n, 182, 182n, 183, 186n, 188n, 189n; casual revenues in, 192; 1s. duty in, 193; customs officials in, 195, 196, 199, 200, 205n, 213n, 214n (*see also* riding surveyor in); provincial court of, handles admiralty business, 224; prize agent for, 235n, 236n; vice-admiralty courts of, 241, 244, 263; products of, 345; effect on, of curtailment of French trade, 362; in hands of crown, 382, 400; restored to proprietor, 387, 394–395, 396, 400; restrictions on its proprietary status, 401; laws of, printed, 405n; not required by its charter to send laws to England, 406

Mason, Robert, 141n

Massachusetts, 54, 161n, 216n, 234n, 248, 394, 418n; protest of (1646), 36n; sets up mint, 47; annexes New Hampshire and Maine towns, 47; illegal trade in, 47–48, 140, 141–142, 141n, 150, 150n, 215n, 216, 241, 242–244; and Canary wines, 111, 112n; opinion of Board of Trade of, 115, 379; position of, on navigation acts, 140–142, 141n, 150, 150n (*see also above* illegal trade in); king's commissioners of 1664 in, 141; annulment of her charter (1684), 142, 150, 273, 372, 372n, 373, under consideration by Lords of Trade, 371n; naval offices in, 142, 181, 183, 185n, 186n, 191; West India trade of, 150; violence in customs collection in, 164n, 165n; writs of assistance in, 165; registration of coasting vessels in, 174n; new charter of (1691), 183, 374; deputy auditor in, 194n; customs officials in, 200, 215n, 243; Mediterranean passes for, 208; exasperated by American customs commissioners, 221; trial by jury in, 225,

251, 263, 263n; prize agent in, 235n; vice-admiralty courts in, 238, 241, 242, 243, 251, 252, their conflict with common law courts, 259, 261, 263–268, 263n, 265n; land banks proposed for, 351, 351n; and Dominion of New England, 372, 373n; her disregard of instructions to royal governors, 376n; governorship of, efforts of Board of Trade to combine with that of other colonies, 377, 378; and Board of Trade's attempt to royalize private colonies, 382; difficulties in, reported in 1721, 390n; explanatory charter of 1725 for, 390n, 393; restlessness of, as royal colony, 401–402; and New England Confederation, 412n; represented at conference with Six Nations (1751), 416; Shirley's instructions to commissioners of, for Albany Conference, 416n
*See also* Dominion of New England; Massachusetts Bay Company

Massachusetts Bay Company, 20n, 369

Masts, Baltic trade in, 31, 78n, 81; ships for carrying, 78n, 133n; a foreign enumerated commodity, 93n; from colonies, bounty on, 103; English fear Scottish competition in, 155; white pine for, regulations and trials concerning, 247–249, 247n, 405n

Mathew, Gov. William, 307n

Matlack, Timothy, 271n

*Matters of Fact relating to the Navy* (1705), 315n

Meadows, Sir Philip, 293

Medicines. *See* Drugs

Mediterranean, trade, 37, 38, 39, 39n, 41n, 74, 319; passes, 208, 276, 276n; pirates in, 276

Mein, Charles, 199n

Mein, Patrick, 198n; surveyor general of customs, 149n, 164, 199, 199n, 200, 213n; in Barbados, 167, 199, 199n

Menzies, Judge John, 164n, 231n; his defense of vice-admiralty jurisdiction, 264, 265, 265n, 266

Mercantilism, a natural concomitant of expanding trade, 2–3, 320, 321; and Molasses Act and act of 1739, 89n, 366; and enumeration of molasses, 101; and acts of 1766 and 1767, 106–107, 424; and plantation duty, 121;

Swedes, on Delaware, Dutch conquest of, 23, 50

Swift, Jonathan, 331n, 334, 351n

T., C., his *An Advice how to plant Tobacco in England,* 14, 14n

Tangier, 6, 64, 64n, 79, 144n, 337

Tankerville, Earl of. *See* Grey, Ford

Tar, 11, 78n, 93n, 103, 105n, 339, 391, 405n

Tariff. *See* Customs

Taverner, Capt., Newfoundland, 67n

Taxation, a subject of mercantilist discussion, 10, 330n, 341; and parliament, 358n; of the colonies, 422, 423, 425n

Tea, 96n, 356; tax, 425n

Temple, John, surveyor general of customs in northern district, 202, 219

Temple, Sir William, 30n, 32

Temple Council, 290n

Teneriffe, 110, 112n

Tessere, Capt. John Baptist, 244n

Thacher, Oxenbridge, 165

Thames, master shipwrights of, 82, 350, 350n, 404

Thirty Years' War, 30, 51

Thomas, Dalby, 337, 364n; on cacao, 94n; on the enumeration, 132; his recommendations for a council of trade, 280–281; on West Indies and New England, 338, 338n, 343

*Thomas Walpole,* ship, 254n

Thompson, Maurice, 41n, 43n; his interest in advancement of trade, 54, 56

Thompson, Maj. Robert, 43n

Thomson, James, surveyor general for the Barbados district, 198n, 201–202

Thurton, Thomas, deputy searcher, 200n

Tidesmen. *See* Customs officials (colonial)

Tide surveyors. *See* Customs officials (colonial)

Tidewaiters. *See* Customs officials (colonial)

Tigh, Robert, 31n

Timber (lumber), Baltic trade in, 26, 78n; ships for carrying, 27, 78n, 133, 133n; for English ships, source of, 27n, 81, 82n; not a colonial enumerated product in 1660 and 1663, 88; a foreign enumerated commodity, 93n;

exported to Europe from New England, 102; made a colonial enumerated commodity, 102, 102n, 106; supplied by northern colonies to southern colonies and West Indies, 346, 347

*See also* Masts; Naval stores

Tobacco, 18n, 28, 154, 305; opposition to, 12, 12n; increasing production of, 12–13; duty on, 12n, 14, 16, 17, 19–20, 85, increased, 89, 123, 139, 338 (*see also below* plantation duty on); Spanish, and English trade, 13, 14, 19, 86n, 89n; extent of colonial monopoly of English market for, 14–15, 88–89, 89n; Brazilian, 14, 86n; raising of, in England, 14–15, 14n, 15n, 88, 89n, 127, 425n; English monopoly of, between 1621 and 1651, 15–17, 19–20, 85, 85n, 137; trade in, with Holland, 17, 137; export of, to Europe, under ordinance of 1651, 44; smuggling and illegal trading in, 67, 68, 69, 69n, 89, 118, 118n, 119, 121n, 151, 204n, 353; imported into England in foreign-built ships, English owned and manned, 78n, 79n; an enumerated commodity, under acts of 1660 and 1663, 86, 86n, 87–88, 88–89, 95, 97, 137, re-exported to the Continent, 19, 340n, 342, 362, 365; in bulk, importation into England forbidden, 86n, 89, 89n, 123–124, 123n, 124n, exportable to another colony without duty or bond, 123–124, 124n, carried into Scotland, 124; cutting and rolling of, in England, 88; price of, kept down by navigation acts, 88–89, 137; intercolonial trade in, 118–119, 120, 121, 121n, 123, 204n; plantation duty on, 119, 120, 120n, 121n, 122n, 123, 129–130, 138, 138n, 204n; duties on, in Ireland, 125; trade in, with Ireland, 127n, 128, 129–130, 142n; Sir William Berkeley's plantation of, 137, 137n; discussed in Maryland assembly, 138, 138n; Virginia export duty on, 138, 138n, 193n, 204n; English fear of Scottish competition in, 156; ships and convoys, 190; manufacturing, forbidden to colonies, 303–304; place of, in mercantilist theory, 337, 339, 340n, 342,

| DATE | | | |
|---|---|---|---|
| | | | |
| | | | |
| | | | |
| | | | |
| | | | |
| | | | |
| | | | |
| | | | |
| | | | |
| | | | |
| | | | |
| | | | |
| | | | |